2000

lonely planet

Philippines

Russ Kerr
Joe Bindloss
Virginia Jealous
Caroline Liou
Mic Looby

LONELY PLANET PUBLICATIONS
Melbourne • Oakland • London • Paris

THE PHILIPPINES

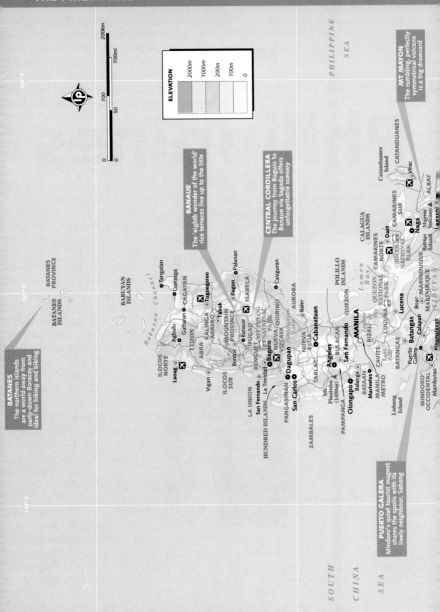

ELEVATION

2000m
1000m
200m
100m
0

BATANES
The northern islands are a world away from party-down Boracay and ideal for hiking and biking

BANAUE
The 'eighth wonder of the world' rice terraces live up to the title

CENTRAL CORDILLERA
The journey from Baguio to Banaue via Sagada offers unforgettable scenery

MT MAYON
The rumbling, perfectly symmetrical volcano is a big drawcard

PUERTO GALERA
Mindoro's quiet tourist magnet shares the spoils with its lively neighbour, Sabang

SOUTH

CHINA

SEA

PHILIPPINE

SEA

BATANES PROVINCE

BATANES ISLANDS

BABUYAN ISLANDS

Babuyan Channel

Tangatan
Gonzaga
Agbulu
Gattaran
CAGAYAN
Tuguegarao
Tabuk
KALINGA
APAYAO
MOUNTAIN
PROVINCE
ISABELA
Ilagan
Palanan
ABRA
LUZON
Bontoc
Banaue
IFUGAO
Casiguran
Vigan
ILOCOS
SUR
BENGUET
MT PULOG
NATIONAL
PARK
NUEVA
VIZCAYA
QUIRINO
AURORA
Laoag
ILOCOS
NORTE
Baguio
La Trinidad
Baler
HUNDRED ISLANDS
LA UNION
San Fernando
NUEVA
ECIJA
Cabanatuan
PANGASINAN
Dagupan
San Carlos
TARLAC
Angeles
BULACAN
San Fernando
PAMPANGA
ZAMBALES
Mt
Pinatubo
(1450m)
Olongapo
Balanga
BATAAN
Mariveles
CAVITE
MANILA
METRO
MANILA
RIZAL
Laguna
LAGUNA
Bay
QUEZON
POLILLO
ISLANDS
Lucena
CALAGUA
ISLANDS
CAMARINES
NORTE
Daet
Lamon
Bay
QUEZON
NATIONAL
PARK
CAMARINES
SUR
Naga
Mayon
Volcano
ALBAY
Legazpi
BICOL
NATIONAL
PARK
Iriga
Burias
Island
CATANDUANES
Catanduanes
Island
Virac
Lubang
Island
BATANGAS
Batangas
Puerto
Galera
Calapan
MARINDUQUE
Boac
MARINDUQUE
MINDORO
OCCIDENTAL
Mamburao
Pinamalayan
SIBUYAN
SEA

THE PHILIPPINES

Philippine Trench

INDONESIA

Palau Island

PALAWAN
Palawan boasts the St Paul Subterranean National Park and Underground River, but El Nido's setting is unbeatable

SIQUIJOR
That old black magic is alive and well courtesy of the island's traditional healers

BOHOL
Bohol's Chocolate Hills are a series of surreal, unearthly hillocks

KALIBO
Kalibo comes alive for the Ati-Atihan festival, the Philippines' biggest and wildest

Despite all those tourist footprints in the sand it still has some magic of its own

MALAYSIA (SABAH)

Philippines
7th edition – October 2000
First published – February 1981

Published by
Lonely Planet Publications Pty Ltd A.C.N. 005 607 983
192 Burwood Rd, Hawthorn, Victoria 3122, Australia

Lonely Planet Offices
Australia PO Box 617, Hawthorn, Victoria 3122
USA 150 Linden St, Oakland, CA 94607
UK 10a Spring Place, London NW5 3BH
France 1 rue du Dahomey, 75011 Paris

Photographs
All of the images in this guide are available for licensing from
Lonely Planet Images.
email: lpi@lonelyplanet.com.au

Front cover photograph
T'boli woman, Lake Sebu, Mindanao (Eric L Wheater)

ISBN 0 86442 711 5

**Although the authors
and Lonely Planet try
to make the informa-
tion as accurate as
possible, we accept
no responsibility for
any loss, injury or
inconvenience sus-
tained by anyone
using this book.**

Contents – Text

NORTH LUZON
180

SOUTH-EAST LUZON
237

MINDORO
256

THE VISAYAS
280

MINDANAO & SULU

PALAWAN

Contents – Maps

PHILIPPINES MAP INDEX

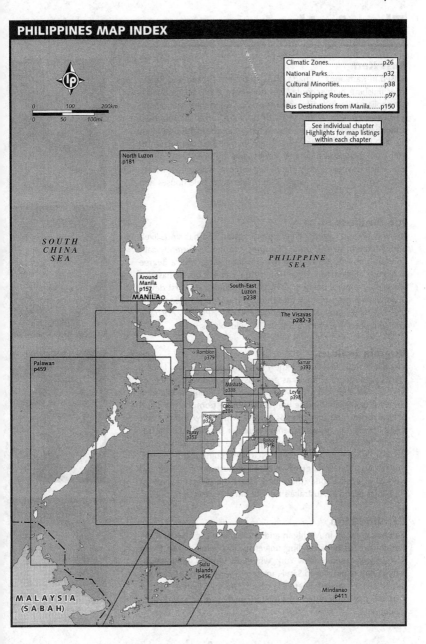

See individual chapter
Highlights for map listings
within each chapter

0   100   200km
0   50   100mi

*SOUTH
CHINA
SEA*

*PHILIPPINE
SEA*

North Luzon
p181

Around
Manila
p157
MANILA

South-East
Luzon
p238

The Visayas
p282-3

Palawan
p459

Romblon
p379

Samar
p393

Masbate
p388

Leyte
p398

Cebu
p284

Negros
p328

Panay
p353

Bohol
p316

Sulu
Islands
p456

Mindanao
p411

MALAYSIA
(SABAH)

The Authors

Russ Kerr

Raised in Kamloops, Canada, Russ studied in Finland and Russia after finishing high school. After university, a trip on the Trans-Mongolian railway led to seven years of wandering around the north-east of Asia. A few years of teaching convinced him he'd rather be a student, so Russ moved to Melbourne in 1995 to finish his PhD in political philosophy. There he met Sam, an encounter that soon produced their son, James, and the need for a steady job, which is where Lonely Planet first came in. Russ is now a freelance writer and editor, while Sam builds straw-bale houses and James runs a railway.

Joe Bindloss

Joe was born in Cyprus, grew up in England and has since lived and worked in several other countries, though he currently calls London home. Joe gravitated towards journalism after a degree in Biology eliminated science from future careers, but he has also worked as a mural painter, surveyor and sculptor. He first developed wanderlust on family trips through the Mediterranean in the old VW combi. Joe has also worked on Lonely Planet's *Australia* and *Mauritius, Réunion & Seychelles* guidebooks.

Virginia Jealous

Virginia Jealous first visited the Philippines in 1982. No Lonely Planet guide then! She was as green as grass and was completely unaware that from her destination of Camiguin Island a constant background noise would be gunfire from the mainland between pro- and anti-Marcos forces. With a few more – and mostly peaceful – travel experiences under her belt, she has returned to the Philippines regularly since 1997, working on small-scale tourism projects with NGOs throughout the country. Virginia was born in England, is based in Australia, has lived and worked in West Papua (then Irian Jaya), and presently lives on Christmas Island in Australia's remote Indian Ocean Territories.

Caroline Liou

Caroline grew up in Michigan and Louisiana in the USA and the Netherlands. After attending university in Louisiana and Hong Kong, she escaped to New York, where she worked in book publishing, before moving to San Francisco to work as the guidebook publisher for Lonely Planet's US office. She now lives in Beijing. Caroline has contributed to Lonely Planet's *China* and *Beijing* guidebooks.

Mic Looby

Mic Looby likes travelling, loves coming home, writes a bit and has a pet crayfish called Eric. His hobbies include illustrating children's books, making animated films and interactive cartoons for the Internet, and feeding Eric. He's currently working on a novel about the adventures of being a Lonely Planet author, tentatively titled *My Life as a Cog*. Mic has also updated the Philippines chapter of *South-East Asia on a shoestring*.

FROM THE AUTHORS

Russ Kerr Russ would like to thank his fellow authors for their kind and considerable assistance, and for their dedication to the project. Joe in particular provided several sections for the Facts for the Visitor chapter, Virginia tracked down plenty of details, and Mic was an unfailing source of information and encouragement. Many thanks to Sam and James for not tossing the computer (and me) out of the house during the long nights and weekends.

Joe Bindloss Thanks firstly to Karen May, for helping me put Manila through its paces. My thanks to all those in the industry who helped along the way; the Department of Tourism (DOT) in Manila, Joemar Angelo at Classica Christina, and Gabi and Josie at Pension Natividad deserve a special mention. Thanks also to all the travellers who provided top tips.

Virginia Jealous Thanks to: Virginia Borges from DOT in Calbayog for the unexpected post-fiesta lunch; Susan Tan in Guiuan for the impromptu tour and, above all, for good company; Bet Bet Pichon in Davao for possibly the best breakfast in the universe (and for everything else); Warren Manilay and all at DOT in General Santos, especially Jing and Winston; Robert at DOT in Cotabato; and Lonely Planet reader Gail Cockburn for Cagayan de Oro and surrounds information.

Caroline Liou Many thanks to all the gracious people who helped me during the research of this book: Bong Bong of Manila's DOT; in the Hundred Islands National Park Tourism Authority, Virgilio S Guitierrez and Paul, divemaster extraordinaire; in Baguio, Peter Gowe; in Kabayan, Juliet A Igloso and Bruna Todiano; in Sagada, Jessie Deguy; in Bontoc, Rita Bagwan; in Kalinga, special thanks to Victor Baculi, Anita Baculi and their family for their extraordinary generosity; Jay Bringas; Kenny O'Clair for his descriptions of hikes through Pula (Banaue) and Malegcong (Bontoc); in idyllic Batanes, Dely and Shane Millan,

Luzviminda and Bernado Cartano, and Tina Bernasconi and Amelou Juinio, who made my extended stay there seem like a vacation; in Vigan, Marjo Gasser and Louis Acosta, whose valiant efforts will hopefully save one of the Philippines' most extraordinary towns; in Bangued, Marilou Gaza and Joji Guillen-Crisologo; in Naga, Jonathan D Manaog; Ping Arcilla of Legaspi's DOT; and Alan Velasco and Henry Haylar for guiding me up and down Mt Mayon, and through the flash flood. Extra special thanks to Amelou Juinio and Jay Bringas for their warm friendship and generosity. Thank you to Nicko Goncharoff, for being with me throughout this project; Josephy Gaisano and family for their generosity in Cebu. And finally, my relatives – the Canoys of San Fernando, Cebu – who inspired me throughout this project.

Mic Looby Extra special thanks to Daisy Yanson and her Panay Adventures team, El Nido's Judith and Tani, Terry and Emily at Casa de la Playa, Nadine and her real coffee, Maggie Jewell, Peter and Clara Van Velthuijsen, Dik and Cora, John Pyle, Christophe and Claire, FD Fuzz, the Quantum Conversation group and everyone else who helped me along the way.

This Book

The first six editions of Lonely Planet's *Philippines* guidebook were written by Jens Peters. For this 7th edition, a team of writers thoroughly rewrote the text and redrew the maps. Russ Kerr wrote the introductory chapters and glossary. The Manila and Around Manila chapters were written by Joe Bindloss. North Luzon was written by Caroline Liou. South-East Luzon was written by Caroline and Virginia Jealous. Mindoro was written by Mic Looby. The Visayas was written by Mic and Virginia. Mindanao & Sulu was written by Virginia, and Palawan was written by Mic.

FROM THE PUBLISHER

This 7th edition of *Philippines* was produced in Lonely Planet's Melbourne office by coordinators Jakov Gavran (mapping and design) and Sally O'Brien (editorial). Jakov was assisted with mapping by Chris Love, Meredith Mail and Neb Milic. Sally was assisted by Miriam Cannell, Hilary Ericksen, Bruce Evans, Kristin Odijk and Jane Thompson. Layout checks and assistance were provided by Glenn Beanland and Kristin Odijk. Special thanks to Quentin Frayne for the Language chapter, Valerie Tellini from LPI for the colour images, Matt King for coordinating the illustrations of Martin Harris, Kate Nolan and Tamsin Wilson, Maria Vallianos for the cover, Leonie Mugavin for travel information, Cathy Viero for readers' letters, Kusnander for the climate charts, the Outdoor Activities unit for action images, Lara Morcombe for the index, Tim Uden for Quark assistance, Chris Thomas for the freelance mercy dash, the Ferre family for providing illustrative material and the very kind Pablo Gastar for patience with various queries. Jakov also thanks Rachel Jones and Sonja Krstevski for trips to the library. And finally, thanks to Russ, Joe, Virginia, Caroline and Mic for their diligence and dedication.

THANKS

Many thanks to the travellers who used the last edition and wrote to us with helpful hints, advice and interesting anecdotes. Your names appear in the back of this book.

Foreword

ABOUT LONELY PLANET GUIDEBOOKS

The story begins with a classic travel adventure: Tony and Maureen Wheeler's 1972 journey across Europe and Asia to Australia. Useful information about the overland trail did not exist at that time, so Tony and Maureen published the first Lonely Planet guidebook to meet a growing need.

From a kitchen table, then from a tiny office in Melbourne (Australia), Lonely Planet has become the largest independent travel publisher in the world, an international company with offices in Melbourne, Oakland (USA), London (UK) and Paris (France).

Today Lonely Planet guidebooks cover the globe. There is an ever-growing list of books and there's information in a variety of forms and media. Some things haven't changed. The main aim is still to help make it possible for adventurous travellers to get out there – to explore and better understand the world.

At Lonely Planet we believe travellers can make a positive contribution to the countries they visit – if they respect their host communities and spend their money wisely. Since 1986 a percentage of the income from each book has been donated to aid projects and human rights campaigns.

Updates Lonely Planet thoroughly updates each guidebook as often as possible. This usually means there are around two years between editions, although for more unusual or more stable destinations the gap can be longer. Check the imprint page (following the colour map at the beginning of the book) for publication dates.

Between editions up-to-date information is available in two free newsletters – the paper *Planet Talk* and email *Comet* (to subscribe, contact any Lonely Planet office) – and on our Web site at www.lonelyplanet.com. The *Upgrades* section of the Web site covers a number of important and volatile destinations and is regularly updated by Lonely Planet authors. *Scoop* covers news and current affairs relevant to travellers. And, lastly, the *Thorn Tree* bulletin board and *Postcards* section of the site carry unverified, but fascinating, reports from travellers.

Correspondence The process of creating new editions begins with the letters, postcards and emails received from travellers. This correspondence often includes suggestions, criticisms and comments about the current editions. Interesting excerpts are immediately passed on via newsletters and the Web site, and everything goes to our authors to be verified when they're researching on the road. We're keen to get more feedback from organisations or individuals who represent communities visited by travellers.

> Lonely Planet gathers information for everyone who's curious about the planet – and especially for those who explore it first-hand. Through guidebooks, phrasebooks, activity guides, maps, literature, newsletters, image library, TV series and Web site we act as an information exchange for a worldwide community of travellers.

Research Authors aim to gather sufficient practical information to enable travellers to make informed choices and to make the mechanics of a journey run smoothly. They also research historical and cultural background to help enrich the travel experience and allow travellers to understand and respond appropriately to cultural and environmental issues.

Authors don't stay in every hotel because that would mean spending a couple of months in each medium-sized city and, no, they don't eat at every restaurant because that would mean stretching belts beyond capacity. They do visit hotels and restaurants to check standards and prices, but feedback based on readers' direct experiences can be very helpful.

Many of our authors work undercover, others aren't so secretive. None of them accept freebies in exchange for positive write-ups. And none of our guidebooks contain any advertising.

Production Authors submit their raw manuscripts and maps to offices in Australia, USA, UK or France. Editors and cartographers – all experienced travellers themselves – then begin the process of assembling the pieces. When the book finally hits the shops, some things are already out of date, we start getting feedback from readers and the process begins again ...

WARNING & REQUEST

Things change – prices go up, schedules change, good places go bad and bad places go bankrupt – nothing stays the same. So, if you find things better or worse, recently opened or long since closed, please tell us and help make the next edition even more accurate and useful. We genuinely value all the feedback we receive. Julie Young coordinates a well travelled team that reads and acknowledges every letter, postcard and email and ensures that every morsel of information finds its way to the appropriate authors, editors and cartographers for verification.

Everyone who writes to us will find their name in the next edition of the appropriate guidebook. They will also receive the latest issue of *Planet Talk*, our quarterly printed newsletter, or *Comet*, our monthly email newsletter. Subscriptions to both newsletters are free. The very best contributions will be rewarded with a free guidebook.

Excerpts from your correspondence may appear in new editions of Lonely Planet guidebooks, the Lonely Planet Web site, *Planet Talk* or *Comet*, so please let us know if you *don't* want your letter published or your name acknowledged.

Send all correspondence to the Lonely Planet office closest to you:

Australia: PO Box 617, Hawthorn, Victoria 3122
USA: 150 Linden St, Oakland, CA 94607
UK: 10A Spring Place, London NW5 3BH
France: 1 rue du Dahomey, 75011 Paris

Or email us at: talk2us@lonelyplanet.com.au

For news, views and updates see our Web site: www.lonelyplanet.com

HOW TO USE A LONELY PLANET GUIDEBOOK

The best way to use a Lonely Planet guidebook is any way you choose. At Lonely Planet we believe the most memorable travel experiences are often those that are unexpected, and the finest discoveries are those you make yourself. Guidebooks are not intended to be used as if they provide a detailed set of infallible instructions!

Contents All Lonely Planet guidebooks follow roughly the same format. The Facts about the Destination chapters or sections give background information ranging from history to weather. Facts for the Visitor gives practical information on issues like visas and health. Getting There & Away gives a brief starting point for researching travel to and from the destination. Getting Around gives an overview of the transport options when you arrive.

The peculiar demands of each destination determine how subsequent chapters are broken up, but some things remain constant. We always start with background, then proceed to sights, places to stay, places to eat, entertainment, getting there and away, and getting around information – in that order.

Heading Hierarchy Lonely Planet headings are used in a strict hierarchical structure that can be visualised as a set of Russian dolls. Each heading (and its following text) is encompassed by any preceding heading that is higher on the hierarchical ladder.

Entry Points We do not assume guidebooks will be read from beginning to end, but that people will dip into them. The traditional entry points are the list of contents and the index. In addition, however, some books have a complete list of maps and an index map illustrating map coverage.

There may also be a colour map that shows highlights. These highlights are dealt with in greater detail in the Facts for the Visitor chapter, along with planning questions and suggested itineraries. Each chapter covering a geographical region usually begins with a locator map and another list of highlights. Once you find something of interest in a list of highlights, turn to the index.

Maps Maps play a crucial role in Lonely Planet guidebooks and include a huge amount of information. A legend is printed on the back page. We seek to have complete consistency between maps and text, and to have every important place in the text captured on a map. Map key numbers usually start in the top left corner.

Although inclusion in a guidebook usually implies a recommendation we cannot list every good place. Exclusion does not necessarily imply criticism. In fact there are a number of reasons why we might exclude a place – sometimes it is simply inappropriate to encourage an influx of travellers.

Introduction

On the fringes of the region's tourist routes, the Philippines is a well-kept secret among travellers. The country is quietly home to spectacular coral-fringed islands, populated by an amazing variety of wildlife and cultures – from independent hilltribes and hip intellectuals to wild fiestas and weird folk healers. The setting is no less varied, and includes extraordinary rice terraces, active volcanoes, tropical rainforest, islets like a lost Eden, underground rivers, and startling caves and hills.

Governed for so long by foreign interests and imagery, this ancient and civilised land is much more than a colourful mirror of colonial tastes. Old cliches of 'friendly natives' resigned to endemic corruption are still common coin, but travellers who get farther than Boracay's beaches are inevitably touched by the power of gracious dignity that more convincingly rules the islands.

Time also sways to another beat in the archipelago, and it is a rhythm worth picking up on the road. Filipinos tell the tale of a man who was travelling with his horse, which was heavily laden with coconuts. Along the way he asked a boy how long it might take to reach his home. The boy looked at the load on the horse and said, 'You will get there very soon if you go slowly, but if you go quickly, it will take a long time.'

This made no sense to the man, and he hurried his horse along. But the coconuts soon fell off and he had to stop to pick them up. Now he rushed his horse even faster to make up for lost time. Again he had to stop as the coconuts fell off the horse. This happened again and again until finally, exhausted, the man arrived home in the dark.

THE PHILIPPINES

PACIFIC OCEAN

CHINA

HONG KONG

MACAU

TAIWAN

LAOS VIETNAM

PHILIPPINES MANILA

CAMBODIA

SOUTH CHINA SEA

MALAYSIA BRUNEI

SINGAPORE

INDONESIA

EAST TIMOR

0 750 1500km
0 400 800mi

INDIAN OCEAN

AUSTRALIA

Happily, the message is as true in the new age of fast ferries and cybertravel as it was in the old days.

Facts about the Philippines

HISTORY
Way, Way Back

Thanks to 'Tabon Man', who left a bit of his (or her, according to some) skull in a cave in Palawan at least 22,000 years ago, a sliver of light shines into the deep, dark prehistory of the Philippines. The oldest known human relic of the islands, this bone suggests the Tabon Caves helped early Homo sapiens survive the last ice age. Later generations lived here too, leaving behind tools and terracotta jars, including the 3000-year-old Manunggul burial jar. Hailed as a masterpiece of ancient pottery, the jar depicts two people paddling a boat into the afterlife. To this day, the ocean, the boat, and other worlds, remain powerful symbols of the Philippines. Even the word *barangay*, meaning a division of the Filipino social unit, is derived from the ancient *balangay*, or sailboat (see the boxed text 'Of Boats & Belonging' later in this section).

The longest-held theory on the origins of Tabon Man is based on distinct waves of migration. Assuming that much of modern-day Asia was linked by land bridges, this theory posits that around 250,000 years ago our earliest human ancestors simply walked over to what is now the Philippines, in pursuit of their Pleistocene prey.

Then, about 200,000 years later, in strode the nomadic Negrito groups from the Malay Peninsula, Borneo and perhaps even Australia. At the same time the sea was thought to be swallowing up low-lying land, forcing the nonocean-going Negrito groups to settle permanently in this new frontier. Today, their descendants include indigenous tribes such as the Bukidnon, Karolano and Ata on the islands of Panay, Guimaras, Negros and Masbate.

After another interval of roughly 2000 years, the Neolithic Age arrived in the form of the seafaring, tool-wielding Indonesians. The Indonesian groups brought with them formal farming and building skills. It's fair to assume that this bunch was busily carving out the spectacular rice terraces of North Luzon at around the time Jesus Christ was making a name for himself in the Middle East. Modern-day descendants of these Indonesian master builders are thought to include tribes such as: Luzon's Ifugao and Kalinga; Mindoro's Mangyan; Palawan's Tagbanua; and Mindanao's Bagobo, Manobo and Mandaya.

With the Iron Age came the Malays. Skilful sailors, potters and weavers, they built the first permanent settlements and prospered from around AD 1 until the 16th century, when the Spanish arrived. The wave migration theory expounds that the Malays arrived in at least three king tides of ethnic diversity. The first wave provided the basis for the modern-day Bontoc and other tribes of North Luzon. The second laid the foundations for the most dominant of modern-day indigenous groups – the Bicolano, Bisayan and Tagalog. The third wave is thought to have established the fiercely proud Muslim Malays.

If this version of early Philippine history seems too tidy to be true, that's because it is – at least according to those who see wave migration as a Western, colonialist fantasy. After all, there's no evidence to support *any* migration pattern before Tabon Man's existence, let alone a neat order of events based on a hierarchy of ethnic one-upmanship. Even terms such as 'Indonesian', 'Negrito' and 'Malayan' are relatively recent European inventions. In short, Asia has long been more complex and subtle than its colonial masters have needed it to be, and Western theories on Eastern prehistory reflect this.

And so modern Philippine scholars have come up with a theory to try to plug the historical holes left by their predecessors. Their 'core population' theory has taken the wave migration concept and turned it into a less rigid model of prehistoric settlement. It suggests that the early inhabitants of South-East Asia were of the same racial group (the Pithecanthropus group, to be exact), with

Of Boats & Belonging

The *balangay*, which leant its name to the *barangay* (social unit), still common today, was an ocean-going vessel thought to have been used for both trade and migration. In the mid-1970s, a fleet of well-preserved balangay was unearthed in Butuan (see the Butuan section in the Mindanao & Sulu chapter). Dating back to the 4th century, some of the boats were loaded with Tang Dynasty pottery and crews of skeletons who long ago sailed off into the afterlife.

Mic Looby

more or less the same traditions and beliefs. Over time, divisions formed not from some innate desire to dominate one another, but from the demands of the environment – an environment which may well have inspired Tabon Man to settle into a cave in Palawan all those years ago.

Trade

Defying their Confucian traditions, the Chinese became the first foreigners to do business in the islands they called Ma-I, as early as the 2nd century AD. Of course, the islands' tribal communities were trading among themselves long before then. Ancient gold coins have been found in several parts of the Philippines. Engraved with local dialect characters, these strange, conical coins are thought to have been formed by pouring molten metal into the folds of palm leaves.

The first recorded Chinese expedition to the present day Philippines was in 982. Within a few decades, Chinese traders were regular visitors to towns along the coast of Luzon, Mindoro and Sulu, and by around 1100 travellers from India, Borneo, Sumatra, Java, Siam (Thailand) and Japan were also including the islands on their trade runs. Gold was big business in Butuan (on the north coast of Mindanao), Chinese settlements had sprung up in Manila and Jolo Island, and Japanese merchants were buying shop space in Manila and North Luzon.

For several centuries, this peaceful trade arrangement thrived. Despite their well-known riches, the islands were never directly threatened by their powerful Asian trading partners. The key, particularly in the case of China, was diplomacy. Throughout the 14th and 15th centuries, the tribal leaders of the present-day Philippines would make regular visits to Peking (Beijing) to honour the Chinese emperor.

By the late 15th century, a far less benign giant was awakening. Europe's aristocrats were rich and restless. The thrill of feudal tyranny had faded and they wanted more. One man who wanted more than most was Jakob Fugger, a phenomenally rich German banker with a sideline in Europe's newest obsession – spices. With a Muslim monopoly controlling the spice trade overland, Fugger longed to find an alternative spice route. Owed money by none other than King Charles I of Spain, Fugger had little trouble convincing the Spanish that sending a few ships into the unknown made good business sense. Ferdinand Magellan, denied funds to sail westward by his native

Magellan's Landing

The date of Ferdinand Magellan's landing has been the subject of a hair-splitting controversy in recent years. Recorded as 16 March 1521 in Magellan's journal, it has now been officially edged forward one day to 17 March by the Philippine Historic Institute, the main historic authority for school textbooks. This was done to conform to the introduction in 1884 of the International Date Line, that arbitrary imaginary line that Magellan unwittingly crossed more than 350 years earlier.

Until Magellan's historic circumnavigation, nobody realised that if you travel westward around the globe you effectively lose a day, according to everyone's calendar but your own. Conversely, heading eastward around the globe means you arrive home a day early – as Phileas Fogg discovered in Jules Verne's 1873 classic *Around the World in Eighty Days*.

Mic Looby

Portugal, leapt at the chance to lead this Spanish fleet. See the boxed text 'Magellan's Landing' in this section.

Spanish Era

A triumphant Magellan set foot on Samar at dawn on 16 March 1521. Magellan claimed the islands for Spain and named them the Islas del Poniente (Western Islands). Soon after, the Portuguese arrived from the east and declared them to be the Islas del Oriente (Eastern Islands). Undaunted, Magellan set about giving the islanders a crash course in Catholicism and winning over various tribal chiefs before fatally taking things one step too far on Mactan Island (see Mactan Island in the Visayas chapter).

Determined to press its claim, Spain renamed the islands after Charles I's son Philip who, as King Philip II, sent a fresh fleet (led by Miguel Lopez de Legazpi) to the islands in the mid-15th century with strict orders to colonise and Catholicise. In 1565 an agreement was signed by Legazpi and Tupas, the defeated chief of Cebu, which made every Filipino answerable to Spanish law. The Filipinos' long and bitter fight for independence had begun.

Legazpi, his soldiers, and a band of Augustinian monks wasted no time establishing a settlement where Cebu City now

Written Language

From the outset, Spanish colonisation removed more than the Filipinos' freedom – it systematically stripped much of their culture. There's little doubt that the Spanish caused the swift decline in written, indigenous languages. Only fragments remain of the precolonial bamboo tubes and tablets once written on throughout the islands. Of the dozen or so distinct systems of writing (based on a 17-letter alphabet known as *baybayin*), only two remain – Tagbanua on Palawan and Hanunuo Mangyan on Mindoro. Both defied extinction because Palawan and Mindoro were too rugged and remote for Spanish domination.

Mic Looby

stands. First called San Miguel, then Santisimo Nombre de Jesus, this fortified town hosted the earliest Filipino-Spanish Christian weddings and – critically – the baptisms of various Cebuano leaders. Panay Island's people were beaten into submission soon after, with Legazpi establishing a vital stronghold there (near present-day Roxas) in 1569. The Spanish soon discovered that in their mission to divide and conquer, half their work was done for them. The Philippines was already divided: first by nature, and second by a mosaic of barangays.

With the indigenous islanders no match for the Spanish and their firearms, the greatest threat to Spain was to come from an old enemy – Islam. To Spain's horror, the Muslims had a big head start on them, Islamic missionaries from Malacca having established towns in Mindoro and Luzon almost a century before the Spanish arrived. Legazpi finally succeeded in taking the strategic Muslim settlement of Maynilad (now known as Manila) in 1571, hastily proclaiming it the capital of the Philippines.

So began a 300-year-long religious war that still smoulders in Mindanao, the spiritual home of Islam in the Philippines. The Spanish recruited newly Christianised Filipinos to help fight the Moros (as Muslim Filipinos were dubbed – see the 'More About Moors & Moros' boxed text in the Mindanao & Sulu chapter), many of whom earned a violent living as pirates. Spanish forts were built during this period, paid for with taxes imposed on the Philippines' colonial subjects. Such forts can be seen today on islands including Palawan, Romblon, Cebu and Mindanao.

Spain's strategic colonisation meant it could woo the Filipinos' best trading partner, China. Throughout the 16th and 17th centuries, Spain's galleons – many of them built in Cavite near Manila – also specialised in taking spices, silk, porcelain and gold to the New World, and returning with Mexican silver. Moro pirates, who outsailed and outsmarted the Spanish right up until the advent of the steamship in the mid-1800s, dodged many a cannon ball to claim a share of these riches. The Moros also conducted bloody raids to make off with prisoners who were later sold on the East Indies slave market.

By the 18th century, Spain's grasp on the Orient was slipping. It was sharing its traditional trade routes with colonial rivals, was at war with England and fast running out of friends and funds. Before long, with a big shove from the powerful East India Company, Britain invaded Manila in 1762. Unaware that Spain was even at war, the authorities in Manila at first thought that the 10,000 invaders cruising into the bay were Chinese traders.

The British won few fans by violently ransacking the surrendered city, and under their freshly installed government a passionate, Filipino-led resistance movement immediately began plotting. Less than two years later, the British were chased out of Manila Bay by this homegrown force.

From the earliest years of colonisation, revolts against the Spanish had come and gone, sparked by wholesale land grabs, cruel taxes, corrupt officials and religious thuggery, but by the 19th century, this rage was becoming more focused. With the Spanish humbled by the British and the British in turn humbled by the Filipinos, a united, nationalist spirit was forming. Anticolonial sentiment was reaching new heights as friars, acting as quasigovernors, became tyrants of the most un-Christian order. Filipinos who failed to grovel at the feet of a friar risked being branded *filibusteros* ('traitors' or 'rebels', depending on your point of view), which meant being arrested, imprisoned, exiled or worse. Meanwhile, terms such as Indios, used by Spanish officials to identify 'inferior' dark-skinned Filipinos, were cutting to the core.

From these 'Indios' emerged a powerful group of nationalist heroes. The most famous of these was Dr José Rizal, multilingual medical doctor, poet, novelist, sculptor, painter, naturalist and fencing enthusiast. Executed by the Spanish in 1896, Rizal epitomised the Filipino dignified struggle for personal and national freedom. By killing such figures, the Spanish were creating martyrs. Biblical history was repeating itself and the irony – at least to the

Philippine National Hero, José Rizal

Filipinos – was as heart-rending as it was enervating.

Just before facing the Spanish firing squad, Rizal penned a characteristically calm message of both caution and inspiration to his people: 'I am most anxious for liberties for our country, but I place as a prior condition the education of the people so that our country may have an individuality of its own and make itself worthy of liberties.'

In the simmering build up to Rizal's death, the Suez Canal opened, effectively bringing an enlightened Europe and the USA closer to the Philippines. It was in this heady atmosphere that a failed 1872 uprising by Filipino patriots in Cavite became an excuse for the nervous Spanish authorities to round up scores of Filipino patriots, including priests. A mockery of a trial saw three prominent and much-loved priests publicly garrotted.

This inspired Rizal's Propaganda Movement, a peaceful barrage of literature condemning the Spanish and calling for social reform. Silenced by Rizal's arrest and exile to Dapitan in Mindanao, the propagandists were superseded by a far more aggressive movement led by Andres Bonifacio. The

Kataastaasan Kagalanggalangang Katipunan ng mga Anak ng Bayan (Highest and Most Respected Society of the Sons of the People) – better known as the Katipunan or KKK – secretly built a revolutionary government in Manila, with a network of equally clandestine provincial councils. Complete with passwords, masks and coloured sashes denoting rank, the Katipunan's members – both men and women – peaked at an estimated 20,000 in mid-1896. In August, the Spanish got wind of the coming revolution and the Katipunan leaders were forced to flee the capital.

Depleted, frustrated and poorly armed, the Katipuneros took stock in nearby Balintawak, a *barrio* (Spanish: meaning district or neighbourhood) of Caloocan, and voted to launch the revolution regardless. With the cry 'Long live the Philippines', now known as the Cry of Balintawak, the Philippine Revolution lurched into life.

The shortage of weapons among the Filipinos throughout this battle meant that many fighters were forced to pluck their first gun from the hands of their enemies. So acute was the shortage of ammunition for these weapons that Filipinos, many of them children, were given the job of scouring battle

The Flag

Exiled Filipino revolutionary Emilio Aguinaldo kept himself busy in Hong Kong by designing what is today the national flag of the Philippines. Made of silk, the flag was sewn by expat Filipina Dona Marcela de Agoncillo and her daughter. The striking design includes a sun with eight sword-like rays, representing the first eight provinces placed under martial law by Spain. The three gold stars represent the three major island groups – Luzon, the Visayas and Mindanao. The background triangles symbolise equality and unity (white), peace and justice (blue), and valour (red).

Mic Looby

Lucky Streaks

The odds may have been stacked against them, but the Philippine revolutionaries of the late 19th century managed some surprise victories, both on and off the battlefield. In 1892, while in exile in Mindanao, Dr José Rizal picked up first prize in the newly established Philippine lottery. The proceeds went towards new farming and fishing equipment in his adopted home of Dapitan. Three years later, a pair of Visayan Katipuneros (see the History section of this chapter, under The Spanish Era), Candido Iban and Francisco del Castillo, each won P1000 in the lottery. This money went towards a small printing press, which became a vital propaganda tool in the revolutionary movement.

Mic Looby

sites for empty cartridges. These cartridges would then be painstakingly repacked using homemade gunpowder made of *salitre* (the main ingredient for pork *tocino*; see the Language chapter for details) sulphur and charcoal. Needless to say, shooting practice was not encouraged.

After three years of bloodshed, most of it Filipino, a Spanish-Filipino peace pact was signed and the then revolutionary leader Emilio Aguinaldo agreed to go into exile in Hong Kong in 1897. Predictably, the pact's demands satisfied nobody. Promises for reform by the Spanish were broken, as were promises by the Filipinos to stop plotting revolution. The Filipino cause was attracting huge support from the Japanese, who tried unsuccessfully to send two boatloads of money and weapons to the exiled revolutionaries in Hong Kong.

American Era

Meanwhile, another of Spain's colonial troublespots – Cuba – was playing host to an ominous dispute over sugar between Spain and the USA. To save face, Spain declared war on the USA and the conflict soon spread to the Philippines, with the obliteration of the Spanish fleet in Manila Bay by US Commodore George Dewey. Keen to gain Filipino support, Dewey welcomed the return of exiled revolutionary General

Aguinaldo and oversaw the Philippine Revolution mark II, which installed Aguinaldo as president of the first Philippine republic. The Philippine flag was flown in Manila for the first time during the proclamation of Philippine Independence on 12 June 1898.

After a bitter struggle, Spanish troops in Manila and outlying towns were crushed by allied American and Filipino forces and Spain's 400-year occupation was over. With the signing of the Treaty of Paris in 1898, the Spanish-American War ended and the USA effectively bought the Philippines, Guam and Puerto Rico for US$20,000. Filipino representatives in Paris weren't even allowed to witness this monumental, internationally approved betrayal.

Back in US-occupied Manila, tempers were rising. Filipino revolutionaries were openly defying the Americans, and the Americans were doing likewise. Any dreams of impending Filipino independence were shattered in 1899 when Malolos, the makeshift capital of President Aguinaldo's Philippine Republic, was captured by American troops – led by General Arthur MacArthur.

The US decision to take the Philippines was not made lightly, if the confessions of President McKinley to a group of clergymen are anything to go by:

The truth is, I didn't want the Philippines, and when they came to us, as a gift from the gods, I did not know what to do with them. When the Spanish war broke out, Dewey was in Hong Kong, and I ordered him to go to Manila, and he had to; because, if defeated, he had no place to refit on that side of the globe, and if the Dons (the Spanish) were victorious they would likely cross the Pacific and ravage Oregon and California coasts. And so he had to destroy the Spanish fleet, and he did it! But that was as far as I thought then. When next I realised that the Philippines had dropped into our lap, I confess I did not know what to do with them. I sought counsel from all sides – Democrats as well as Republicans – but got little help. I thought first we would take only Manila; then Luzon; then the other islands, perhaps, also. I am not ashamed to tell you, gentlemen, that I went down on my knees and prayed to almighty God for light and guidance more than one night. And one night it came to me this way – I don't know how it was but it came: (1) That

we could not give them back to Spain. That would be cowardly and dishonourable; (2) That we could not turn them over to France or Germany – our commercial rivals in the Orient – that would be bad business and discreditable; (3) That we could not leave them to themselves – they were unfit for self-government – and they would soon have anarchy and mis-rule over there worse than Spain's was; and (4) That there was nothing left for us to do but to take them all, and to educate the Filipinos; and uplift and civilise and Christianise them, and, by God's grace, do the very best we could by them, as our fellowmen for whom Christ also died. And then I went to bed, and went to sleep, and slept soundly, and the next morning I sent for the chief engineer of the War Department (our map maker) and told him to put the Philippines on the map of the United States; and there they are, and there they will stay while I am president!

By 1902 the first Philippine Republic was dead and buried and a succession of American neocolonial governors-general ensured it stayed that way. Like the Spanish, the USA's No 1 intention was to serve their own economic needs, and by 1930 they had engineered an industrial and social revolution, with two of the biggest booms coming from mining and prostitution.

Not until 1935, once it had firmly lassoed the country's resources, did the USA endorse the Commonwealth of the Philippines, along with the drawing up of a US-style constitution and the first national election. On paper at least, democracy and freedom had come to the Philippines, but as WWII was about to prove, they came at a terrible price.

When Japan bombed Hawaii's Pearl Harbour in 1941, US troops attacked the advancing Japanese airforce. The man who gave these orders was General Douglas MacArthur, whose father had led the American charge into the Philippines 42 years earlier. Within two days, Japanese troops landed at Vigan in North Luzon, eventually driving the allied Filipino and US troops onto the Bataan Peninsula, opposite newly occupied Manila. From here, soldiers and civilians alike faced not only relentless bombardment but also hunger, disease and disillusionment. MacArthur, holed up on nearby Corregidor Island, made his now famous

Mark Twain

The US government's role in the Philippines was condemned by many of its own people – including none other than the author Samuel Langhorne Clemens, better known as Mark Twain. Twain and his fellow anti-imperialists were convinced that Americans, if they knew all the facts, would have demanded an instant withdrawal from the Philippines. In 1902 Twain described the situation thus:

> We (the US) have bought some islands from a party who did not own them; with real smartness and a good counterfeit of disinterested friendliness we coaxed a confiding, weak nation into a trap and closed it upon them; we went back on an honoured guest of the Stars and Stripes when we had no further use for him and chased him to the mountains; we are as indisputably in possession of a wide-spreading archipelago as if it were our property; we have pacified some thousands of the islanders and buried them; destroyed their fields; burned their villages, and turned their widows and orphans out of doors; furnished heartbreak by exile to some dozens of disagreeable patriots, subjugated the remaining ten millions by Benevolent Assimilation, which is the pious new name of the musket; we have acquired property in the three hundred concubines and other slaves of our business partner, the Sultan of Sulu, and hoisted our protecting flag over that swag.

Mic Looby

promise to return, and fled to Australia (see the boxed text 'I Shall Return' in the Around Manila chapter).

Japanese Era

Ordered to maintain a 'holding action', MacArthur's abandoned troops soon fell to the Japanese with the unconditional surrender of around 76,000 people – 66,000 of them Filipinos. Those still able to walk began a 120km 'death march' from Bataan to San Fernando, and on to prison camps in Capas, Tarlac. As many as 20,000 people died along the way and another 25,000 died while imprisoned. This event is honoured with the annual Araw ng Kagitingan (Day of Valor) public holiday on 9 April.

From 1942 to 1945, the Philippines endured a Japanese military regime more ferocious than anything the Spanish or Americans could have dreamed up. But unlike the previous colonial forces, the Japanese actively encouraged Filipino languages as part of their grand plan to keep Asia Asian.

In 1944 MacArthur landed at Leyte, determined to dislodge the Japanese. The main battleground in this onslaught was Manila, whose defenceless residents suffered horrifically in the ensuing crossfire. By the time MacArthur marched into the city, at least 100,000 civilian Filipinos lay dead or dying. In total, over 1.1 million Filipinos were killed during WWII.

In early 1946 Japan's General Tomoyuki Yamashita (see the boxed text 'Gold-Diggers' in the Facts for the Visitor chapter) was tried as a war criminal and hanged by order of MacArthur. In July of the same year, Manuel Roxas was installed as president of the Republic of the Philippines under the auspices of the USA, and the immense task of rebuilding a shell-shocked nation began. Far from free, the Philippines faced crippling high-interest loans in the form of US 'aid', and society (like more than three-quarters of its schools and universities) lay in ruins.

Marcos Era

First elected in 1965 under the seductive slogan 'This nation can be great again', the charismatic former lawyer Ferdinand Marcos became the first president to win two terms in office. By 1970 widespread poverty, rising inflation, pitiful public funding and blatant corruption triggered a wave of protests in Manila. When several demonstrators were killed by police outside the presidential Malacañang Palace, Marcos' image as a political saviour died with them.

Citing the rise of leftist student groups and the New People's Army (NPA), Marcos declared martial law on the entire country in 1972. A constitutional last resort designed to protect the masses, this particular declaration was designed solely to protect Marcos and his foreign business buddies. By this time, their formidable enemies included the anti-imperialist National Democratic Front (NDF) and the Islamic Moro National Liberation Front (MNLF) in Mindanao.

With martial law imposed, the Philippines was plunged into a darkness reminiscent of the Japanese occupation – only this time it was at the hands of a fellow Filipino. Curfews were imposed, all media were silenced or taken over by the military, international travel was banned and thousands of antigovernment suspects were rounded up. A painful form of peace was achieved under the Marcos dictatorship, with an estimated 50,000 of his opponents jailed, exiled or killed. Marcos then set about raising revenue by handing over great tracts of prime land to foreign investors and imposing heavy taxes on those who could least afford them.

When martial law was tentatively lifted in 1981, Marcos remodelled himself and the constitution to form a sham of a democracy. Under this 'New Republic', Marcos won a mid-year election conveniently devoid of a free press or any real opposition.

However, in 1983, when Marcos thugs gunned down political foe Benigno 'Ninoy' Aquino Jr within minutes of his return from exile, a new Filipino martyr was created. The two million mourners who paid their respects to Ninoy Aquino in Manila had begun a steady march towards a new era.

By 1986 Marcos's long-time supporters were publicly questioning their loyalty, as were many embarrassed foreign powers. Another rigged election saw Marcos beat Ninoy Aquino's widow Corazon 'Cory' Aquino, but this time 'people power' stormed the presidential palace. Within days, virtually all members of the nation's armed forces had sided with the masses, the Marcoses were airlifted out of the country by the

Marcos Record

Under the category of 'Biggest Robbery', Ferdinand and Imelda Marcos are officially recognised by the *Guinness Book of Records*, which estimates the total amount stolen by the couple to have been between US\$5 and US\$10 billion. This, according to the 1998 edition of the book, ranks the Marcos theft above the 1945 Reichsbank robbery and below the theft of the Mona Lisa in 1913.

Mic Looby

US Airforce, and Aquino was enshrined as president and national heroine. A close-up account of this tumultuous time can be found in James Fenton's *The Snap Revolution*.

Ferdinand Marcos died in exile in 1989 and Imelda Marcos soon returned to the Philippines, where she somehow wriggled out of an 18-year jail sentence on graft charges. New evidence teased from Swiss bank accounts now has her facing charges of stealing US\$13.2 billion from the Filipino people. She may also escape this monumental charge, as President Joseph Estrada continues to go soft on Imelda because of his own dubious debts to the Marcos clan.

New Era

With the cataclysmic eruption in June 1991 of Mt Pinatubo, north-west of Manila, another long chapter in Philippine history ended. Showered in volcanic ash and refused a new lease agreement, the US military bases in Clark and Subic Bay were closed down and US troops headed home. Economically, this left a sizeable hole in the Philippine treasury. One of the biggest benefits of the US presence had been the money paid by the US government to occupy bases in the Philippines. Regarded as 'aid' by the US and 'rent' by the Philippines, this much-needed cash was first paid in 1979 during Jimmy Carter's presidency, at a rate of US\$500 million over five years. When this deal expired in 1983, a US\$900 million five-year deal was struck. By 1988 a two-year pledge of US\$962 million was made, falling way short of the Philippines' new asking price of US$2.4 billion over five years.

In the official centennial year of 1998, the Philippines celebrated in typically festive fashion. But for many Filipinos, it wasn't until the US bases were closed – almost 500 years after Magellan landed at Samar – that the fight for independence was won.

Or was it? In March 1999 the Philippine senate approved a deal with the USA known as the Visiting Forces Agreement (VFA). A victory for the USA and a swift kick in the teeth for Philippine independence, the VFA – along with the Acquisition and Cross-Service Agreement (ACSA) and the Status of Forces Agreement (SOFA) – restores the presence of US armed forces in the Philippines.

As far as the VFA's extremely vocal critics are concerned, this allows for far more than war games. Under the VFA, US military personnel are exempt from all Philippine passport, visa and driving licence regulations. They also pay no taxes and are effectively unanswerable to Philippine law, as the USA can impose an 'automatic waiver of jurisdiction' or issue an 'official duty certificate' excusing US staff of any wrongdoing. The USA cannot be held responsible for any damages under the VFA, nor can it be denied access to any part of the Philippines. Needless to say, none of these privileges will apply to Philippine forces 'visiting' the USA.

Critics of the VFA range from women's and human rights groups to church elders and the Philippine Armed Forces vice-chief of staff – all of whom have presented strong, varied arguments against the VFA. Arguments *for* the VFA amount to vague hopes of economic and military benefits – none of which come close to being guaranteed in the agreement. Nor is there any mention of the Philippine ban on nuclear weapons and no provision is made for the inspection of US vessels. All of these rulings directly or indirectly violate the Philippine constitution. As one exasperated Filipino newspaper columnist said: 'So *this* is independence.'

Toxic Bases

When the US military left the Philippines in 1991, they left more than just a thriving prostitution industry. Luzon's abandoned military and naval bases at Clark, Subic and Camp John Hay turned up more than 30 toxic waste sites. Chemicals dumped here included solvents, lead and mercury, and unexploded ordnances were commonplace. Environmental groups drolly noted that the clean up of this mess was finished just in time for the US military's controversial return (under the Visiting Forces Agreement; VFA) in 1999.

Mic Looby

GEOGRAPHY

From north to south, the Philippine national boundary extends 1900km. From east to west it stretches 1110km. Mindanao, the main southern island, is the home of the highest mountain, Mt Apo. Three main islands or island groups – Luzon, the Visayas and Mindanao – divide the country into north, central and southern regions respectively.

The 11 largest islands making up the Philippines are as follows: Luzon (105,000 sq km); Mindanao (95,000 sq km); Samar (13,100 sq km); Negros (12,700 sq km); Palawan (11,800 sq km); Panay (11,500 sq km); Mindoro (9700 sq km); Leyte (7214 sq km); Cebu (4400 sq km); Bohol (3900 sq km); and Masbate (3300 sq km).

The most heavily forested island is Palawan, deforestation and agricultural activities having denuded vast areas of other islands, in particular Leyte and Samar. Most islands feature volcanic mountains, several of which have been increasingly active since the 1980s. Strong earthquakes also regularly occur. At around 10,000m deep, the Philippine Trench north-east of Mindanao is one of the world's greatest abysses.

Among the nation's 7107 islands, the three major island groups of the Philippines have mostly inland mountains, with peaks ranging from around 1000m to almost 3000m, and a total land area of 30 million hectares. While Mt Apo (2954m) in

Mindanao is the country's highest summit, the country's most commanding mountains are volcanic – namely Mt Pinatubo in central Luzon and Mt Mayon in South Luzon.

In 1991 the long-dormant Mt Pinatubo awoke violently with a series of eruptions that left more than 800 people dead and thousands more homeless. Volcanic ash blanketed crops, shut down towns and eventually forced the US military to abandon its Clark Air Base.

There are almost as many theories about the origins of the Philippines as there are islands making up the modern-day nation. Some are scientific, some are mythical. One legend has it that the islands were created when a tiring giant let a bare rocky ball of earth fall from his shoulders, causing it to shatter and form this fragmented land. Some geologists believe the islands rose from the sea in a massive volcanic eruption, which echoes through the ages in the form of the Pacific Ocean's 'Ring of Fire' volcanic region. The majority of scientists, however, prefer the idea that the islands are the tips of a long-submerged land bridge that allowed for one hell of a hike from China to Australia via Borneo, Indonesia and New Guinea.

All the main islands of the Philippines have large rivers, many of which provide vital transport routes. The mightiest river on Luzon is the Cagayan, followed by the Abra, Bicol, Chico, Pampanga and Bicol rivers. Many rivers flowing through or near urban centres have been partly or wholly degraded by industrial and domestic waste. Limestone caves can be found on many of the islands, with the best known being the St Paul Subterranean National Park's Underground River in Sabang, Palawan, and those around Sagada in mountainous North Luzon.

CLIMATE

The Philippines doesn't have four seasons. It has two: dry and wet. Generally, the dry season is from November to May and the wet season is from June to October. By far the hottest month in lowland regions is May, when temperatures hover as high as 38°C. The cooler months are December and Janu-

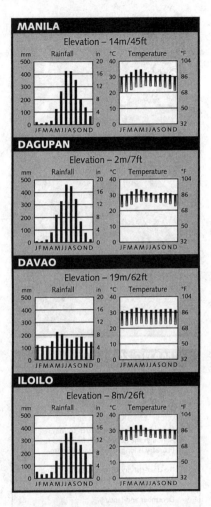

ary, but unless you're high in the mountains, 70% to 85% humidity levels tend to cancel out these 25°C low-end temperatures.

With the country's typically sudden, heavy rains, flash flooding is now more common than it should be, due to widespread deforestation and soil erosion. One of the worst flash floods in recent times struck in November 1991 in Ormoc, Leyte. Fed by rains on newly bared mountainsides,

CLIMATIC ZONES

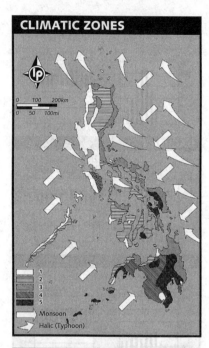

1
2
3
4
5

Monsoon
Halic (Typhoon)

CLIMATIC ZONES

1   Typical South-East Asian monsoon climate.
     Long dry season from November
     to May and intense rainy period from
     June to October.

2   Short dry season from March to May.
     Although the rainy season from June to
     February is long, it is not very intense.

3   No clear-cut dry season, with rain falling
     during most of the year. The heaviest
     showers are in the months of November,
     December and January.

4   No clear defined dry season.
     The heaviest rainfall is in the months
     of April to September.

5   No clear defined wet or dry season.

Leyte's normally tame rivers burst their
banks, killing approximately 8000 people
and leaving 50,000 homeless.

An average of 20 typhoons, known as
bagyos, whip across the Philippines each
year. Striking mainly in Luzon and the
Visayas, they generally bring heavy rains
and wind from around April to January,
with a peak season from August to November. Although typhoons can occur at anytime, their peak periods tend to coincide
with the rainy season.

Like much of Asia and northern Australia, the Philippines suffered the parching
effects of the El Niño weather phenomenon
and is now playing host to La Niña, which
has brought unseasonal rainstorms and
more flash floods. In 1999 the combined
impact of these weather patterns was
blamed for a P7.5 billion loss in the vital
Philippine fishing industry.

Recent research suggests this freakish
brother-and-sister combination may become an increasingly frequent phenomenon
thanks to global warming. For a country so
dependent on crops and fishing for survival,
this is a truly disastrous prospect. In future,
it could mean more and more roads washing away without warning, telephone lines
failing, drinking water becoming contaminated, and increased incidences of cholera
and other diseases.

ECOLOGY & ENVIRONMENT
Land

Before 1900 most of the land in the Philippines was densely forested. A mere century
later, half of this forest is gone – and of the
remaining forest, around 33% (five million
hectares) has genuine forest cover (ie, primary tropical forest). To put a rather grim
global perspective on such figures, North
America today has only 3% of its original
old-growth forest intact.

If it's any consolation, the deforestation
of the Philippines has shown signs of re-
lenting. According to Philippine forestry
statistics, from 1950 to 1978 deforestation
claimed 204,000 hectares per year. From
1978 to 1988 it dipped to 199,000 hectares
per year. From 1989 to 1995 'only' 116,322
hectares were vanishing annually.

Environmentalists have noted bitterly that
much of what's left of Philippine forests is

too high up for loggers to be bothered with, or it's scrappy secondary forest yet to be eaten up by the ravenous Integrated Forest Management Agreements (IFMA, formerly the Timber License Agreements) that have allowed most of the damage.

Obviously, this can't be blamed on the age-old communities of upland hunters, gatherers and farmers. It's a 20th century disaster and it's been caused by unregulated logging, massive farming expansion and a migrating lowland population. Throughout the 20th century, indigenous people's claims on upland regions were ignored and rich resources were plundered by a powerful elite. Poor lowland communities headed for the hills, often to jobs clearing land, and the long-time indigenous residents were pushed onto less and less fertile land.

In Mindanao in 1998, 100,000 families faced eviction from their small-scale farms to give way to the palm oil industry of Malaysia. Around the same time, families from the indigenous Manobo groups were forced to evacuate their traditional homeland and flee to Davao City due to regular military operations in the area. Despite having an officially recognised ancestral domain claim on the area, the Manobo people found themselves at the centre of a bitter land dispute with the timber company Alcantara & Sons (Alsons). The government had allowed the company to log commercially there through the notorious IFMA.

The battle to save what's left of the upland forests has begun, through indigenous land rights claims and new conservation policies, but there's still enormous pressure on the government from both domestic and foreign land interests. The Department of Environment & Natural Resources (DENR), the main environmental arm of the government, is charged with wrenching the country's resources out of corporate hands and into community-based projects. Respect of ancestral domain rights and forest boundaries is seen as integral in this fight to retain what's left of Philippine forests.

Various attempts to rejuvenate degraded forests have been plagued by unchecked introduced species and poor management, and in some cases degraded forests have simply been degraded further. New strategies for these areas include localised sustainable management programs, natural resource mapping and – at long last – taking the advice of indigenous experts.

Of course, the Philippines isn't alone in its tendency to talk rather than act when it comes to halting such degradation. Nor is it the only nation with a long history of exploitation from outside forces. Rich in mineral, timber and marine resources, the Philippines has been beaten, raped and robbed as brutally as any developing nation on earth. As recently as 1995, a mining act was amended to effectively encourage the destruction of rich wildlife and tribal areas such as those around Sipalay and Hinoba-an (Negros Province). It's a testament to the land and its people that there's so much pristine natural beauty still intact.

Sea

With a coastal ecosystem stretching almost 20,000km, the Philippines is likely to become one of the earliest global victims of rising ocean temperatures and levels. Centuries-old coral is dying almost overnight and it's no longer only divers in

Oil Spill

In March 1999 a local merchant oil tanker sprang a leak and sank near the narrow mouth of Manila Bay, creating the worst oil spill ever in a bay already heavily poisoned by sewage and garbage. The tanker's hull was torn open by a submerged object, which authorities sheepishly admitted was probably a sunken oil barge. The spill spread over about 35 hectares of the bay and proved messier and costlier than another spill a few kilometres away barely eight months earlier. Little was done to identify or punish the culprits in either case, and the media put the lack of public outrage down to a forlorn sense of collective guilt over what was once one of the world's most beautiful bays.

Mic Looby

remote spots who are witnessing this poorly understood phenomenon. Snorkellers in the long-time tourist haunts around Puerto Galera (Mindoro) and Boracay (Panay) can now see for themselves what a coral reef graveyard looks like.

In mid-1999 regional marine science studies grimly reported that increased sea temperatures were causing 'mass coral bleaching events' in the world's best coral reefs. Unless something is done to reduce global warming caused by the burning of oil, coal and gas, they estimate that the Philippines' magnificent underwater world would be gone by around 2100 – along with Australia's Great Barrier Reef.

But not everyone is blaming global warming. A climate model created by Australian scientists in 1999 suggests that mighty big climatic changes happen even without the help of rising carbon dioxide levels. The model showed that even with carbon dioxide levels kept stable, countries such as the Philippines are prone to extreme drought or flooding rains, typically in 30-year spells. By tracing such erratic wind and rainfall patterns back to shifting ocean surface temperatures, this model may help predict disastrous weather extremes and at least give people a chance to prepare for the worst.

In the meantime, increasingly desperate fishing communities are robbing waters of even staple fish species. In many areas, healthy coral reefs are being destroyed by dynamite, cyanide and chlorine fishing methods. Cyanide, by the way, stuns fish so they can be caught live and sold for a higher price, but at the same time kills the coral. Disastrously underestimated as a marine nursery, the mangrove ecosystem that once supported protected ocean life throughout the Philippine coast has more than halved since first monitored in 1918. Around 450,000 hectares of old-growth mangrove forest had dwindled to 140,000 hectares by the late 1980s. Of these, around 65% were in Palawan. An estimated 95% of the country's commercial saltwater fishponds are converted mangrove forest.

Equally underestimated is seagrass, which once sustained huge numbers of vegetarian marine creatures such as turtles, sea urchins and dugongs. Seagrass also shielded smaller organisms from predators, produced life-giving oxygen, regulated salinity levels, filtered impurities and stabilised the sea bed. Vast swathes of this stuff have gone the same way as the old-growth mangrove.

Since the Philippines (like so many nations) is still shovelling its research funds into the oil, gas and coal industry, it's up to the local coastal communities to save their own skins. Thankfully, there are some very good people doing some very good work in this area (see contact information in the following entry), and government projects such as the Coastal Environment Program (CEP).

Solutions

It's certainly not all bad news on the Philippine environment front. The country's many environmental groups are passionate and vocal, and many local governments have put their weight behind the establishment of marine and wildlife reserves and actively campaigned against destructive mining, development and energy projects.

One good news story is the little island of Danjugan (pronounced 'dan-**hoo**-gan'), off the coast of Negros. A former victim of dynamite fishing, this coral wonderland is recovering nicely, thanks to the miracle-working Negros Forests & Ecological Foundation (NFEF) and the Danjugan Island Support Fund (DISF, under the auspices of the UK-based World Land Trust). One of the few small islands in the region that's managed to hold on to its rainforest, Danjugan came up for sale a few years ago and was bought by the environmental protection group World Land Trust, using donations. Check out its Web site: www.worldlandtrust.org.

Another hopeful movement is the annual antipollution bike ride through Manila (see the boxed text 'Antipollution Ride' in the Manila chapter).

Highly recommended Philippine environmental groups include:

Negros Forests & Ecological Foundation
  (☎/fax 034-433 9234, ✉ nfefi@moscom.com)

Coral Cay Conservation (✆ ccc@coralcay
.demon.co.uk)
Web site: www.coralcay.demon.co.uk/phil/
culture.html

For excellent general information on Philippine environmental concerns, try the following Web sites:

Worldwide Fund for Nature (WWF)
www.livingplanet.org/resources/inthefield/
country/philippines/page1.htm
International Marinelife Alliance
www.imamarinelife.org
Overseas The online magazine for sustainable
seas.
www.oneocean.org
Silent Sentinels Australian ABC Science forum
about coral and global warming.
www.abc.net.au/science/coral

FLORA & FAUNA

The Philippines once supported an estimated two million species of plants and animals, many of which are – or were – endemic to the islands. Pollution of various kinds and aggressive commercial exploitation have stripped these species back dramatically within 100 years. Luckily, far more powerful than this destructive madness has been nature's ability to keep alive such unimaginably diverse examples of wildlife.

Flora

The pretty yellow flowering *narra* is the national tree of the Philippines. The unofficial national tree must surely be the *nipa* palm, which lends its name and timber to the traditional nipa hut found in villages and tourist resorts all over the country.

The orchid could also stake a claim as the country's national flower, with almost 1000 stunning endemic species, including the *waling waling* (Vanda sanderiana) of Mindanao.

Apart from crop species such as tobacco and corn that have been introduced to the Philippines, one crop unique to the Philippines is that of the *pili* nut, which is used in the production of chocolate, ice cream and even soap. It's harvested from May to October, mostly around Sorsogon in South Luzon. Abaca, a native hemp plant used to make rope, is harvested in huge quantities in Mindanao. This island is also famous for its huge durians, a fruit as smelly as it is popular. On the lovely little island of Guimaras, near Panay, rich red soil has produced what many swear are the sweetest mangoes in the world.

Fauna

The best known Philippine member of the bird family is the *haribon* (Philippine eagle), of which only about 100 are left in their natural habitat of Mindanao (for details on seeing these magnificent birds, see the Eagle Camp entry in the Mindanao & Sulu chapter). Even further south, the Sulu hornbill of Sulu, Jolo and Tawi-Tawi is another amazing and elusive mountain-dwelling bird. The Palawan peacock pheasant is also a remarkable bird, the males of this species having a metallic blue crest, long white eyebrows and large metallic blue or purple 'eyes' on the tail. Nearing endangered levels, the ground-dwelling peacock pheasant is found only in the deepest forests of Palawan.

Of the reptile family, South-East Asia travellers will be most familiar with the little, gravity-defying, mosquito-chomping gecko and its raspy 'tap tap tap' mating call. More elusive scaled beasts include the sailfin dragon and the flying lizard – discovered by national hero José Rizal while he was exiled in Dapitan on Mindanao – and a wide variety of venomous and nonvenomous snakes, including pythons and sea snakes.

The Philippines is said to still be home to the sea cow, or dugong (known locally as the *duyong*), once found in great numbers in Philippine waters but now rare. You're more likely to spot dolphins, whales and, if your timing's just right, *butanding* (whale sharks)

**The dugong is said to still inhabit the waters
of the Philippines.**

Ferrets

The government went so far as to warn of an 'ecological disaster' in April 1999, when it was discovered that European ferrets were running wild in the Philippines. According to the Department of Environment & Natural Resources (DENR), these notoriously fast-breeding creatures have been smuggled into the country and illegally sold as pets. Be warned: many of these ferocious little hunters have since escaped and may be heading for a trouser leg near you.

Mic Looby

near Sorsogon in South Luzon. The local tourism industry there is desperately hoping these plankton-feeding gentle giants will continue their present habit of surfacing from around November to May each year.

The most popular beast of burden in the Philippines is the *carabao*, a native water buffalo highly prized for its vast patience as a plough-puller.

Endangered Species

The nation's list of endangered species isn't getting any shorter – nor is it as thorough as it should be. Filipino seahorses, despite a 70% population plunge, aren't on the list because there's too much money to be made exporting them live or selling them dead and dried as souvenirs or aphrodisiacs. Travellers are likely to see them on sale in markets around the country and, most recently, at the Puerto Princesa airport in Palawan. Environmental groups recently warned that at this rate the seahorse may be wiped out within 10 years. At the other end of the biological spectrum is the equally endangered *tamaraw* (see the boxed text 'The Tamaraw' in the Mindoro chapter).

Apart from air and water pollution, many species of Philippine flora and fauna have been threatened by biological pollution – the introduction of alien species. Along with feral cats and other vermin, introduced aquatic species have proven particularly damaging. These include the giant catfish,

black bass, white goby, marine toad, American bullfrog, leopard frog, golden apple snail, water hyacinth and water fern. According to the DENR, of all these pests, only the white goby was accidentally introduced. Whether well meaning, accidental or downright barbaric, the reasons for introducing such vermin are now irrelevant as one by one native species fall victim to the invasion.

The giant catfish looks likely to kill off the native *hito*, the black bass has decimated the indigenous fish population of Luzon's Caliraya Reservoir and the white goby has become the dominant species in Mindanao's Lake Lanao by outbreeding more than 10 native species of fish. Among the introduced amphibians, the dual domination of the American bullfrog and leopard frog is expected to eventually displace many native species throughout the Philippines, and the marine toad is busy wiping out a number of native frogs in southern Negros. The golden apple snail, meanwhile, is slowly displacing the native *kuhol* snail.

One of the more humble Philippine creatures quietly facing extinction is a shellfish known locally as a *diwal* (literally, angel wings). Up to about five years ago, the diwal

Something Fishy

An incredible 80% of tropical marine fish sold worldwide come from the Philippines. A massive diversity of fish, combined with cheap labour and export-friendly air freight costs, means a veritable rainbow of species pours out of Philippine waters and into aquariums around the world each year.

Apart from the obvious damage to local fish populations and ecosystems, many of these fish die from severe liver damage within days of being transported. Such damage is common in marine creatures poisoned by sodium cyanide – a chemical first introduced in the Philippines in the 1960s to stun fish and now widely used as an easy (and seemingly harmless) way to catch large numbers of fish for both domestic and foreign markets.

Mic Looby

was a popular menu item in many Philippine restaurants. But the shellfish has proven to be too tender and juicy for its own good and even seasoned veterans of oceanic study at the University of the Philippines have been shocked to discover how seemingly fast diwal numbers have declined. Once widespread throughout Visayan waters, the diwal is now found only in pockets of the Western Visayas. While overfishing and trawling have contributed enormously to the decline, it's thought that – like many marine species – the diwal has been poisoned by chemicals from large-scale prawn farming. Sanctuaries are currently being sought to save the diwal before it's too late.

On Bohol Island, beyond the town of Corella, near the village of Sikatuna, is a Tarsier Visitors Centre built in 1999 (until its phone is connected, contact the Philippine Tarsier Foundation on ☎ 0912 411 5928). Although as yet unproven, this centre gives some hope to this poor little saucer-eyed primate.

Elsewhere, a recent project organised by the Cebu Biodiversity Conservation Foundation (CBCF) revealed that the flowerpecker, a bird previously thought extinct, is still with us in a remote forest of Cebu.

For more information on Filipino creatures clinging to existence, contact the Haribon Foundation (☎/fax 02-712 2601, ✉ emc010@wtouch.com.ph), 3rd floor, AM Bldg, 28 Quezon Ave, Quezon City, Manila. It also has a Web site at www.aenet.org/treks/haribon.htm.

National Parks

Despite rabid opposition from various land developers, energy companies and sectors of the government, a large-scale project to protect the best of the Philippines' natural resources got underway in 1992. The aim of this project is to establish protected areas – some existing national parks, some not – based on eight distinct ecological regions of the Philippines. The project is known as the National Integrated Protected Areas Program (NIPAP) and it's funded by the European Union (EU). A priority of this program is to involve the indigenous people living in or around the protected areas in the management of the resources. Some of the areas include:

Palanan Wilderness Area (North Luzon) At 200,000 hectares, this is the Philippine's largest protected area, making up 10% of the country's remaining primary forest.

Mt Isarog National Park, Camarines Sur (Bicol) Mt Isarog (1966m) is Bicol's second-highest volcano, now dormant. The park and the volcano are one and the same, as Mt Isarog stands on its own. Malabsay Falls, near the park's entrance, is a popular spot for migrating city-dwellers to picnic.

Mt Iglit-Baco National Park, Mindoro Occidental (Mindoro) One of the last remaining grazing patches left for the critically endangered tamaraw, Mt Iglit-Baco National Park is a vital – if seemingly unremarkable – expanse of steep grasslands comprising Mt Iglit and Mt Baco in central Mindoro. The problem for the tamaraw, and the indigenous Mangyan people, is that farmers encroaching into the area have caused a steady reduction in grasslands.

Mt Guiting-Guiting Natural Park, Sibuyan Island (Romblon) This 16,000-hectare mountainous forest is a rare slice of living history in the Romblon group of islands and one of the finest natural wonders on offer in Asia. For thousands of years, the spectacular slopes of 2050m Mt Guiting-Guiting have nurtured and protected a world that would have long ago been destroyed by human activities if not for its isolation. Geologically and biologically, Sibuyan Island is a relic from the ice age. Among the ancient teak trees of the park can be found several quite bizarre species of fruit bats, more than 100 known bird species and large macaque monkeys. The extremely well-organised ranger and visitor facilities here don't make the climb up Mt Guiting-Guiting any easier, but if it's biodiversity you crave, it's well worth the effort.

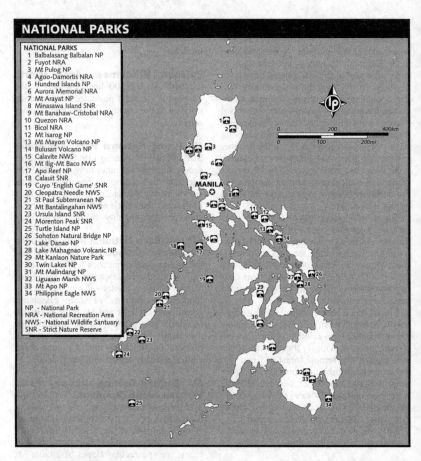

NATIONAL PARKS

NATIONAL PARKS
1 Balbalasang Balbalan NP
2 Fuyot NRA
3 Mt Pulog NP
4 Agoo-Damortis NRA
5 Hundred Islands NP
6 Aurora Memorial NRA
7 Mt Arayat NP
8 Minasawa Island SNR
9 Mt Banahaw-Cristobal NRA
10 Quezon NRA
11 Bicol NRA
12 Mt Isarog NP
13 Mt Mayon Volcano NP
14 Bulusan Volcano NP
15 Calavite NWS
16 Mt Ilig-Mt Baco NWS
17 Apo Reef NP
18 Calauit SNR
19 Cuyo 'English Game' SNR
20 Cleopatra Needle NWS
21 St Paul Subterranean NP
22 Mt Bantalingahan NWS
23 Ursula Island SNR
24 Morenton Peak SNR
25 Turtle Island NP
26 Sohoton Natural Bridge NP
27 Lake Danao NP
28 Lake Mahagnao Volcanic NP
29 Mt Kanlaon Nature Park
30 Twin Lakes NP
31 Mt Malindang NP
32 Liguasan Marsh NWS
33 Mt Apo NP
34 Philippine Eagle NWS

NP - National Park
NRA - National Recreation Area
NWS - National Wildlife Sanctuary
SNR - Strict Nature Reserve

Coron Island (Palawan) A prized diving area, and now more accessible, Coron Island's beauty lies in the fact that it was left alone for so long. Managed properly, the island's virgin forests and stunning cliffs should stay just as they are. Managed badly, the rightful owners of Coron – the Tagbanua people – could witness the destruction of their officially classified 22,000-hectare home.

El Nido Marine Reserve (Palawan)
The El Nido Marine Reserve is 430km from Manila but, like nearby Coron Island, it seems to be drifting a little closer every year, as transport routes increase. A wonderland of jagged cliffs (above and below sea level) and secret beaches, the reserve is in the Bacuit Bay area of El Nido and is home to several upmarket – and relatively low-impact – resorts. The town of El Nido is the unofficial caretaker of the reserve.

Malampaya Sound (Palawan) The Malampaya Sound, on the north coast of Palawan, is remarkable not so much for its fading reputation as the fishbowl of the Philippines but for the fact that Shell

Philippines operates a US$2 billion off-shore natural gas project on its doorstep. Around the corner, a similar project is expected to become the second major natural gas find after the Camago-Malampaya gas field. Shell also plans to run a 500km-long submarine pipeline from the Camago-Malampaya gas field to Luzon.

GOVERNMENT & POLITICS
The Political System

The Philippines' national government is based on a relatively young, constitutional, US-style model, headed by a president and vice-president elected by the people for six-year terms. The political engine room is Congress, made up of a Senate (or Upper House) with 24 members and a House of Representatives (or Lower House) with 250 members. Like the president, senators are elected by the masses, while the nation's various legislative districts hold elections to appoint a total of 200 representatives (with three-year terms). Fifty representatives are handpicked by the political parties, in theory to ensure fair representation of minority groups, women and/or the poor.

The nation's 77 provinces are grouped into 16 local government regions (including the national capital region of Metro Manila), with each region administered by a council. Each province is headed by a governor, a vice-governor and usually two board members. All are elected on four-year terms. Each province is made up of municipalities or towns, which in turn are divided into social units or village communities known as barangays. The barangay is the common political and social denominator of the Philippines. The term *barrio*, a Spanish word, is used to denote a neighbourhood.

The Philippine legal system, a Spanish and US hybrid, is headed by the Supreme Court, the highest legal forum in the land. This is comprised of a chief justice and 14 associate judges – all of whom are appointed by the president. The Court of Appeals acts as an intermediary between the Supreme Court and the municipal courts. Every city has a municipal court.

Recent Politics

When democracy was 'restored' in 1987, Philippine elections once again became part religious festival, part circus. In 1987 the new president was Cory Aquino – the nation's first woman leader. Amid impossibly high hopes, the Aquino government drew up a new constitution, ratified by national referendum, and attempted to turn the country's fortunes around. In doing so, she incurred the wrath of influential Marcos supporters. Several military coups to overthrow her came close to succeeding, and cost several hundred lives in the process. A reputedly shaken Aquino handed over the party leadership to Fidel Ramos, her defence secretary, and a former deputy chief of staff of the armed forces during the Marcos regime.

Despite his shaky credentials – including being a second cousin to the disgraced Marcos *and* a Protestant – Ramos won comfortably, supported by the powerful Lakas ng Edsa and the National Union of Christian Democrats (NUCD) political parties.

By 1998 Ramos had become something of a lame-duck president and his increasingly outspoken critics were baying for blood. With all the same old economic problems pretty much unchanged, Ramos' sober presidential term ended and a massive election win swept the populist politician and former vice-president Joseph Estrada into power. An ageing B-grade movie idol, Estrada (usually called Erap, his nickname, which is *pare* – or friendship – spelled backwards) immediately promised to redirect government funding to help the poor and

Name Game

Joseph Estrada's presidency may well mark the first time in history that the leader of a nation has operated under a stage name. Joseph Estrada is the *nom de film* of Joseph Ejercito, who changed his name in the early days of his acting career – because his embarrassed father thought the movie industry was a dirty business...

Mic Looby

fight for the rights of the long-neglected average Filipino. Sound like an over-the-top movie script? Welcome to the Philippines...

The landslide election victory that catapulted Estrada into the presidential throne in 1998 did so with such force that even the party faithful were surprised. The country's shell-shocked intellectual elite were left to reflect sourly that Estrada was a dopey latter-day Ferdinand Marcos bent on plunging the nation back into the darkest days of cronyism and shady deals. But the *masa* (masses) were convinced Estrada's trademark 'Robin Hood' screen persona would translate just fine to the theatre of politics.

Alas, after more than a year on the presidential throne, 'The People's President' hasn't really done much for the people. But who *really* thought he would? Many a voter will admit that they only supported him because they were offered badly needed money to do so. It was no secret that Estrada's cronies were buying votes among the poorer areas of the Philippine. A lot of fat cats who supplied this ready cash are now owed a lot of favours – and 'the people' are at the bottom of the government's IOU list.

One of the most significant opponents of the Estrada government, and several previous governments, has been the Bagong Alyansang Makabayan (Bayan) party. Established in 1985, the Bayan is an alliance of more than 1000 grassroots sociopolitical organisations, with a total membership of more than one million. It claims to represent the struggle for 'national freedom' by various social classes and was considered instrumental in helping to oust Ferdinand Marcos.

One of the most effective products of mid-1980s 'people power', Bayan traces its roots back to the emergence of the national democratic movement in the mid-1960s. Forced underground by the declaration of Marcos' martial law in 1972, this movement later found voice through a series of nationwide land reform campaigns and civil liberties demonstrations.

In 1999 Bayan was loudly decrying what it calls the 'oilygopoly' – a consortium of petroleum giants including Shell, Petron-Aramco and Caltex. According to Bayan,

Political Change

Keeping stocked up on P100 banknotes is tricky at the best of times, but this handy denomination was almost impossible to find during Joseph Estrada's successful election campaign in 1998. Taxi drivers, shopkeepers and even banks were all refusing to dish out their few remaining P100 notes. The reason for the scarcity was obvious to anyone familiar with Philippine politics – party officials had cleaned the banks out of P100 notes to buy votes. In less poor areas, it was P500 notes that went missing.

During the last elections, P20 and P50 notes became scarce at banks. It seems the price of votes has skyrocketed! Accusations of vote rigging during elections are commonplace and usually greeted with a buck-passing shrug by authorities. This recently prompted one provincial leader to ask of his country: 'Where else can you see registered names of voters belonging to newborn babies, every child in the family, maybe even the dogs and chickens?'

Mic Looby

the Estrada government's moves to deregulate the oil industry will open the way to massive price hikes by a powerful oil cartel. In the meantime, Bayan claims Estrada is introducing 'anti-Filipino' constitutional amendments that give politicians the legal power to inhibit freedom of speech and intimidate the media.

Human Rights

The Marcos regime, and the colonial regimes before that, have had a profound effect on the collective Philippine psyche. By setting appalling precedents in human suffering, public opinion now has it that all is well on the humanitarian front. This is compounded by the incredible Filipino capacity to forgive, if not entirely forget. This attitude of *bahala na* (a fatalistic confidence despite misfortune – considered a shameful national trait by some) hides the fact that human rights in the Philippines continue to be trampled.

According to an Amnesty International report on the Philippines, more than 145 political prisoners were being held against their will by forces within the government and militant opposition groups in 1999. Although cases of human rights violations are possibly declining, this year saw at least four people reportedly 'vanish' while being detained by the Philippine National Police (PNP), and at least nine people were allegedly killed during sieges by Muslim militia groups from the Moro Islamic Liberation Front (MILF), Abu Sayyaf and the MNLF.

Attempts by the government and leaders of opposition groups, including the New People's Army (NPA, the military arm of the Communist Party of the Philippines), were continually stalled by failed cease-fire agreements in Mindanao, where much of the violence occurred.

In many Philippine regions, farmers have long been the targets of attack during land disputes, and the culprits are usually unidentified. Suspects tend to include private security guards or figures connected with corrupt local officials, although the victims' families know better than to name names.

Also, with the re-establishment of the death penalty in 1993, the Philippines has, according to opposition leaders in 1999, moved into third place globally behind the USA and China as a government-sanctioned killer. Great concerns have been aired regarding the ways in which evidence and confessions have been obtained from Filipino death-row prisoners, who numbered 850 as of 1999. Despite local and international pleas to abolish the death penalty, or at least hold an independent inquiry into police procedures, President Estrada has refused to budge.

Meanwhile, nonprofit independent groups, such as the Children's Rehabilitation Center (CRC), are fighting what they call 'state violence' against the most vulnerable members of Filipino society. According to the CRC, the government too often turns a blind eye to human rights abuses against children and/or poor communities by military agencies, police, paramilitary forces, security guards, hired criminals, private individuals and even religious cults. The CRC says most of these violations are committed in the name of land development and industrialisation, and that opponents of such activities are inevitably branded as communists, liars or both.

According to the CRC, 600,000 urban-dwelling families lose their homes to shopping malls, golf courses and subdivisions annually. In rural areas, with the influx of imported agricultural products and massive land conversion for foreign investment, peasant families and communities are the often silent victims.

The CRC (☎/fax 02-439 4589) headquarters is at 90J Bugallon St, Project 4, Quezon City, Manila.

Political Troublespots

Both the Philippine and foreign media dutifully report on 'Muslim' violence in Mindanao, but the background for the fighting is rarely discussed. Government moves to weaken and displace the Muslim majority, crush all resistance without question and

---

Spratly Tourism

In 1999 Philippine defence secretary Orlando Mercado boldly announced plans by the Philippines to throw open Pag-Asa Island, in the hotly disputed Spratly Island group, to foreign and domestic tourism. It's a cheeky suggestion considering rival claims on the islands by the likes of China. But Philippine authorities are crossing their fingers that tourism may somehow fool rival nations into believing that the Spratlys are as Filipino as chicken *adobo* (stewed chicken, marinated in vinegar and garlic).

The navy has even helpfully proposed to ferry tourists back and forth in its own boats and planes. Like all islands making up the Spratlys, Pag-Asa Island has no indigenous presence. It does have several cottages, though these may well be booked up by some heavily armed tourists from China, Taiwan, Malaysia, Brunei or Vietnam by the time the first ripple of tourism arrives from the Philippines.

Mic Looby

offer what many see as token autonomy only serves to fuel the fire. With the island's rich resources long exploited by outsiders, it's hardly surprising that Muslim terrorist groups have evolved. These are desperate, endangered people, and kidnappings are a common form of political expression. Before straying too far from Mindanao's main cities, travellers should check thoroughly with tourist offices, bus companies and locals to make sure their destination – and the roads in between – are safe.

Another headache for the Philippine government is the Spratly Islands, one of South-East Asia's most ominous flashpoints, barely 900km from Manila in the South China Sea. As just one of the claimants to the rich fishing grounds, strategic shipping lanes and potentially huge oil reserves making up this scattering of islands and reefs, the Philippines is in a precarious position. Its rivals in this battle of nerves – China, Taiwan, Malaysia, Brunei and Vietnam – are all better equipped for battle should it come to an out-and-out land grab. The USA is certainly under no obligation to provide political or military support to the Philippines under the 1999 VFA, and it will be even more reluctant if China decides to flex its muscle over the Spratlys.

ECONOMY

Along with a complicated bureaucratic system, the Spanish colonial authorities introduced forced labour, taxes and government-backed monopolies aimed at the world market. At the same time, they replaced the ancient bartering and coin-based currency and insisted that one fifth of every gold nugget unearthed be donated to Spain. While plenty of Filipino landowners and merchants grew rich under this system, the majority of the population grew poorer than ever before.

Little has changed since, according to the findings of the first ever Philippine Annual Poverty Indicator Survey in 1999. Around 10% of the population receive 40% of the national income, while 60% must make do with 24% of the income. Around 90% of families included at least one gainfully employed family member.

A 1.7% Gross Domestic Product (GDP) growth rate was trumpeted as great news in 1999 because, well, it could have been worse. In reality, the GDP growth rate was cancelled out by a 2.3% annual population growth rate. Only a politician could twist that into something worth cheering about. Likewise, only political hype and economic sorcery could have spawned the impossibly low one-year inflation rate of 7.3% in 1998. Even self-confessed economic dunce President Estrada could work out that such a figure doesn't add up when rental prices rise on average by around 30%, water rates by as much as 100%, transport costs by 40%, food prices by 30% and labour costs by 15% annually.

Despite all the talk of economic reform under the former Ramos administration, and the billions of dollars repaid to creditors, the nation's foreign debt is bigger than it's ever been – far bigger than it was even during Ferdinand Marcos' dictatorship and economic butchery. In 1999 the country's foreign debt was US$48.6 billion and rising. Add to this the combined climatic forces of El Niño and La Niña to what is principally an agrarian economy, and President Estrada looks to be the proud owner of a bankrupt government.

Learning from Spain

Many of the harsh taxes imposed during the Spanish era backfired as the Filipinos rose in revolt against them. One such uprising was sparked by the *bandala* (meaning 'to take with force'), which required Filipinos to sell their produce to the colonial government in return for worthless promissory notes. Another doozey was the *real situado* – money sent from Mexico (also a Spanish colony at the time) to replenish a mysteriously leaky treasury in Manila. In a masterstroke of colonial accounting, this was actually Filipino money to begin with, having come from export duties imposed on Philippine goods arriving in Mexico.

Mic Looby

Military Spending

According to military analysts, the Philippines needs at least US$20 billion to match the might of its South-East Asian neighbours in the 21st century. They blame the country's steadily declining defence capabilities on successive governments that have relied too heavily on the USA for support. Until 1991 the Mutual Defence Treaty (MDT) meant that the USA could sell its ageing and near-obsolete weapons to the Philippine military. Under the rules of this treaty, the Philippines wasn't allowed to buy military hardware from any other nation. Amid an all-too-familiar cry of official corruption, P7 billion supposedly set aside for the modernisation of the Philippine Armed Forces mysteriously disappeared some time in 1999.

Mic Looby

It doesn't have to be this way. There's apparently US$13.2 billion in 'Marcos money' sitting in Swiss banks, but President Estrada seems reluctant to upset the still-powerful Marcos clan by chasing this up. Then there's an estimated P50 billion in uncollected tax, owed by the nation's wealthiest business tycoons, such as Lucio Tan, some of whom helped finance President Estrada's election campaign.

POPULATION & PEOPLE

The Philippines greeted the 21st century with a population estimated at more than 77 million people. It's also estimated that less than half of all families have access to family-planning services.

Around 60% of the populace live in rural areas, although this figure is steadily falling as rural residents head for urban centres, such as Manila and Cebu City, or urban sprawl eats up formerly rural areas. Metro Manila's population is thought to be growing at a rate of around 4% per year, while the standard of living appears to be steadily declining. A National Housing Authority report in the 1980s estimated that 25% of Metro Manila's residents were squatters.

Mainstream Culture

Ethnologically, the vast majority of Filipinos are related to Malaysians and Indonesians. Culturally, they represent both the East and the West, having long associations with migrants from China, Vietnam, Japan, the USA, Europe and India. Just as profound has been the migration of Filipinos to all corners of the globe. In the late 1980s and early 1990s, more than half a million temporary migrants were working away from home, stereotypically as domestic helpers and medical staff. Those who decide to take up permanent residency in their adopted countries are known as *balikbayans*.

Muslim communities are thought to make up about 5% of the Philippine population and the vast majority live in Mindanao and the Sulu Islands. Outside the mainstream Muslim population, five indigenous groups in this region are Islamic (see the entry on the Manobo under Cultural Minorities in this section).

Since the earliest days of sea traders, Chinese migrants have been settling in the Philippines. Today, around 1% of the total Philippine population is made up of ethnic Chinese, with a disproportionate number of influential Filipinos claiming Chinese ancestry. These include José Rizal, Cory Aquino and Cardinal Jaime Sin.

Cultural Minorities

There are more than 100 cultural minority groups in the Philippines, as defined by their language. Of these, about half have been identified as unique linguistic cultures. The other half represent a blurred grouping of distinct cultures with common linguistic traits. Ideally, each group's migration history, genetic make-up, relationship with other peoples and various other defining features should be taken into account, but many of these aspects remain at best anecdotal. For this reason, definitive groupings and areas inhabited will always be open to interpretation.

Historically, colonial invaders and the steady encroachment of mainstream cultures has weakened or destroyed traditional indigenous cultures. Today, many anthropologists remain pessimistic about the

CULTURAL MINORITIES

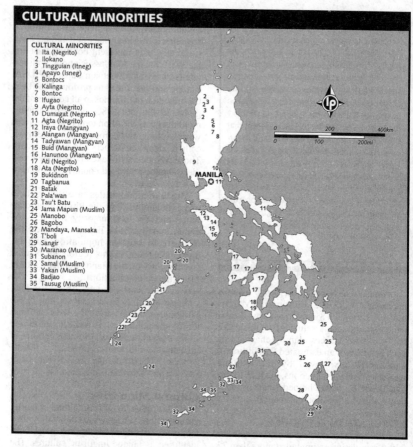

CULTURAL MINORITIES
1 Ita (Negrito)
2 Ilokano
3 Tingguian (Itneg)
4 Apayo (Isneg)
5 Bontocs
6 Kalinga
7 Bontoc
8 Ifugao
9 Ayta (Negrito)
10 Dumagat (Negrito)
11 Agta (Negrito)
12 Iraya (Mangyan)
13 Alangan (Mangyan)
14 Tadyawan (Mangyan)
15 Buid (Mangyan)
16 Hanunoo (Mangyan)
17 Ati (Negrito)
18 Ata (Negrito)
19 Bukidnon
20 Tagbanua
21 Batak
22 Pala'wan
23 Tau't Batu
24 Jama Mapun (Muslim)
25 Manobo
26 Bagobo
27 Mandaya, Mansaka
28 T'boli
29 Sangir
30 Maranao (Muslim)
31 Subanon
32 Samal (Muslim)
33 Yakan (Muslim)
34 Badjao
35 Tausug (Muslim)

government-backed programs aimed at preserving cultural minorities. There's even a view that ancestral domain rights, which recognise ancient links to the land, are often the first step towards abandonment of traditional agricultural methods in favour of cash-crop farming and other modern agricultural techniques. In the same way, tourism is regarded by some as another form of 'cultural pollution'.

For a glimpse of how readily 'cultural identity' can serve the state, see the boxed text on the (nonexistent) Tasaday people in the Mindanao & Sulu chapter. See also the boxed texts in the relevant chapters for the following (actual) groups: the Kalinga (North Luzon), the Mangyan (Mindoro) and the Tagbanua (Palawan).

The Negrito Often referred to as the aborigines of the Philippines, the Negrito are represented by the Aeta, Ati, Eta, Ita and Dumagat people. Now thought to number as few as around 20,000, the Negrito are generally the shortest, darkest and most racially victimised of the Filipino people. Spread throughout many islands, the Negrito principally inhabit the coastal fringes of North

Negrito Royals

Although neglected and dismissed by successive colonial powers, there is a long history of 'royalty' among the Negrito people of Luzon and other islands. Until the 1970s, King Alfonso and Queen Mary were two such Negrito figureheads. Far from enjoying the red-carpet treatment, this couple and their people lived in houses made of scrap materials and survived off *basura* (garbage) from the nearby US military's Clark Air Base. Despite earning the honorary rank of US Air Force brigadier general, King Alfonso and his queen vanished some time after a low-land Christian group began competing for the Americans' garbage.

Mic Looby

Luzon and the highlands of Negros, Samar and Leyte. The famously festive Ati, who live in Panay, are said to have initiated the present day Ati-Atihan festivals of Kalibo and surrounding towns.

Traditionally nomadic, the Negritos' links with the sea remain through the roaming, seafaring Dumagat people. In 1904 hundreds of Negrito tribespeople were 'exhibited' at the St Louis World's Fair in the USA. With other Philippine cultural groups as comparisons, the Negrito were charmingly used as examples of 'the lowest-type humans in the Islands'. The lighter skinned Igorots were presented as far more refined, and *mestizos* (Filipinos of Spanish or Chinese descent) were held up as the evolutionary pinnacle to which the Negrito should aspire.

The Igorot The Cordillera region of Luzon is home to the Igorot (mountain-dwelling groups), including the Apayo, Benguet, Bontoc, Ifugao, Kalinga and Tingguian. The name Igorot is derived from the Pilipino (Tagalog) word for mountaineer and was once used by mainstream society as a derogatory term for the native people of the Cordilleras. More recently, it has lost its negative connotations.

While generally considered unbowed by outside pressures, many Igorot traditions were erased or suppressed during the rise of American culture around 1900. However, most Igorot traditions remain deeply ingrained and their farming skills – as epitomised by the Ifugao-built rice terraces – are incredibly well developed.

The Apayo, or Isneg, are traditionally slash-and-burn agriculturists, who range across the highlands of provinces such as Abra, Ilocos Norte and Kalinga-Apayo. Fierce warriors, the Apayo were the last of the Igorot communities to succumb to the military might of American colonists in the 1920s. Apayao tribes are often characterised by their strong spirituality and ceremonial feasts, known as *say-am*.

The Kalinga are one of the former 'head-hunting' tribes of the Cordilleras, but their traditional penchant for finely woven textiles and age-old songs has proved a more enduring trait. Songs of the Kalinga include the *ading*, *wasani* and *dandanag*, all of which are likely to accompany the well-known *bodong* (peace rite) that is practised by various Kalinga subgroups, including the Tabuks, Tinglayans and Pinukpuks. The Kalinga are also known for their bead culture, an ancient form of currency using precious stones as 'coins'. The most precious bead among the Kalinga is the colourful *ad-jongan*, thought to be a type of agate brought by traders to the Philippines around 1000 years ago. The tribe also takes its custodianship of the land very seriously (see the boxed text 'The Kalinga & The Outside' in the North Luzon chapter).

The Ifugao, whose name comes from a word meaning 'people of the earth', are perhaps the best known of all Philippine cultural minorities. Numbering around 130,000 and inhabiting Ifugao Province, they are the original rice terrace carvers. As the creators of this 'eighth wonder of the world' – representing thousands of lifetimes of labour – it's not surprising the Ifugao are pretty handy woodcarvers as well (see the 'Bulol Carving' boxed text in the North Luzon chapter).

The Benguet people of the south-west Cordilleras (Benguet Province in particular) are particularly skilled farmers and miners. Benguet feasts are renowned for their lavishness, particularly the Pesshet, which can last for days on end. Equally spectacular is the Benguet's colourful Bendiyan Dance, often involving around 100 dancers.

The term Benguet covers two major cultural subgroups – the Ibalois and the Kankana-eys. The Ibalois hold ancestral domain rights over the southern part of Benguet, and they share linguistic traits with the tribes of Pangasinan Province to the south. The Kankana-eys, with linguistic links to the tribes of Bontoc, inhabit the north and north-west regions of Benguet Province. Cultural subgroups of the Kankana-eys include the Ibaloys and Kalanguyas. Despite having separate dialects, the Kankana-eys, Ibaloys and Kalanguyas all believe that a spirit or god known as *adikalia* created the earth and humankind.

The Bontoc are famed for their rich social traditions and reputation as former 'headhunters'. Inhabiting Mountain Province, the Bontocs are generally divided into the subgroups Aplais (to the west) and I-lagod (to the east). The languages of these groups differ substantially and they have their own dance traditions. The I-lagod's most important dance is the Pattong (or Ballangbang), while the wedding dance known as the Takik characterises the Aplais.

Bontoc groups share a formal system of social division and courtship centred around segregated 'dormitories' known as *olong* or *egban*. Inhabiting the border of Ilocos Sur and Benguet provinces, the Bagos may be considered a subgroup of the Bontocs by dint of their language, which is similar to that of the Aplai. Religiously, the Bagos – or bagong Kristiano (new Christians) – are in a group all their own.

With the north-west Luzon province of Abra as their ancestral domain, the Tinguians are Igorots only in that they inhabit the Cordilleras. Collectively, the Tinguians call themselves Itnegs. Similarly, the groups inhabiting the Cordillera mountain provinces of Nueva Ecija, Nueva Vizcaya and Quirino call themselves Ikalahan; those of Cagayan Province's mountain region in the north-east corner of Luzon are known as Gaddangs.

The Manobo The general term Manobo includes the major indigenous groups of Mindanao. Of these groups, five regard themselves as Muslim – the Badjao, Maguindanao, Maranao (or Maranaw), Tausag (or Tausug) and Samal. For details on the Yakan people, see the Basilan section in the Mindanao & Sulu chapter.

The Badjao are the 'sea gypsies' of the Sulu seas. Regarded as the least-Islamic of the Muslim groups, the animist Badjao are more sedentary than they once were, although their livelihood and traditions remain firmly linked to the sea.

The Maguindanao are famed musicians who inhabit the flood plains of Cotabato Province. The largest of all Muslim groups, they are also known for their brilliant weaving skills.

The Maranao are the traditional owners of Lake Lanao, and among the Philippines' most ingenious craftspeople. Traditional Maranao homes or ancestral houses (known as *torogans*) are decorated with detailed carvings, forming large-scale bas-relief sculptures in their own right. The beams of the torogan are guarded by swirling *naga* (mythic figures).

The Tausag were the earliest Philippine Islamic converts back in the 15th century

Minority Cultures

The Kalipunan ng Katutubong Mamamayan ng Pilipinas (KAMP) is the main mouthpiece of the indigenous people of the Philippines. Established as a federation in 1987, KAMP works to unite the various indigenous peoples' organisations throughout the Philippines and help articulate their struggles. Professional assistance or help of any other kind is always greatly appreciated. For more information contact: KAMP Secretariat (☎/fax 02-921 1058), 70-B Matahimik St, UP Teachers Village, Quezon City, Metro Manila.

Mic Looby

and as such were the ruling class of the ancient Jolo Sultanate. The Samal are the poorest of the Muslim groups, having long been the loyal subjects of the Tausag dynasties.

Of the non-Muslim indigenous groups of Mindanao, the Bukidnons (of Bukidnon Province) are well known for their ancient tradition of storytelling, passed down through the ages and performed as epic poetry.

The non-Muslim Bagobos, Mandayas, and Mansakas are regarded as masters of weaving and dyeing, as well herbal medicine. Their music, involving great orchestras of percussion players, is often used to accompany the grinding of herbs to be used as dyes or medicines.

For more information, see the 'Crafts of the Indigenous Peoples of Mindanao' boxed text in the Mindanao & Sulu chapter.

EDUCATION

From around 1900 onwards, American colonialists did a thorough job of transplanting the US education system into Philippines society. Today, children from ages seven to 12 attend elementary school, with classes usually taught in both the national language Pilipino (Tagalog) and English. Before independence was won in 1946, classes were taught in English and one or more of the 87 local languages of the Philippines. It wasn't until 1974 that Tagalog was declared the national language and a consistent bilingual Tagalog and English system was put in place. Even so, the original colonial language, Spanish, was taught in many schools until the 1980s. While the Philippines is said to have an adult literacy rate of around 90%, only 10% of children from families in the low-income bracket complete high school.

ARTS
Dance

Filipinos speak the language of dance fluently, passionately and regularly, making dance the most famous and far-reaching of Philippine cultural exports.

From mainstream, urban society to small town fiestas to remote tribal barangays, dance is as rich and varied as the islands themselves. Historically, traditional dances began by mimicking the flight of birds, particularly in mountainous regions such as the Cordillera in Luzon. Among coastal communities, dance movements often have a strong marine theme. Later, external influences drifted in from China, Indonesia, Spain or the Americas, without ever making the dances any less Filipino.

The Philippines' national folk dance is the *tinikling*. Evolving in the Visayas, it traditionally involves two boys and two girls hopping between bamboo poles, held just above the ground and struck together in time to music or hand-clapping. And yes, you can pick the novice tinikling dancer by their bruised ankles. Some say this dance was inspired by the flitting of birds between grass stems, while others suggest it was adapted from a punishment used by the colonial Spanish to discipline workers. A version of the tinikling involving four bamboo poles and large, paper fans is the *singkil*. The mountain people of North Luzon are famed for vigorous hunting dances such as the *tag-gam* and victory dances such as *balangbang*. Down south, an old favourite is the stunningly graceful *pangalay*, a courtship dance from the Sulu Islands in which women in flowing robes vie for a man's affection.

One of the best known and most successful of Philippine folk dance troupes is the Bayanihan Dance Company, which first wowed the world in 1958 at the Brussels Universal Exposition. An inspiration for dancers and dance lovers ever since, Bayanihan (from *bayani*, meaning 'group work') is based at Manila's Women's University. The Ramon Obusan Folkloric Dance Troupe is another legendary outfit, renowned for its meticulous interpretations of ethnic styles from all over the Philippines.

Ballet, particularly among the urban sophisticates of Manila, is another passion. Ballet Philippines, with its knack for blending modern elements with ancient Philippine folk tales and music, has produced such talents as Maniya Barredo, former prima ballerina of the Atlanta Ballet, and Lisa Macuja, who made the role of Giselle her own during her time with the Kirov Ballet in Russia. Filipinos pioneering modern dance include Angel Abcede, founder of the influential Chicago-based Sex Police group which promotes awareness of AIDS through hip-hop dance and music. For information on the Philippine dance scene, visit the Tanikalang Ginto Web site's dance page at www.filipinolinks.com/arts/sayaw.html.

Music

The *kundiman*, a bittersweet combination of words and music, is one of the best-loved traditional modes of musical expression in the Philippines. The modern composers Nicanor Abelardo and Francisco Santiago have taken this tradition to new heights by combining modern musical forms with ancient folklore and music.

Traditional instruments include the *kulintang* gong or chime found in North Luzon and the *kutyapi*, an extremely demanding but haunting melodic two-stringed plucked lute, commonly found in Maguindanao Province in Mindanao. Among Mindanao's Muslim communities, many dance repertoires effortlessly merge ancient rhythms with the relatively recent Islamic faith. The kulintang, a row of eight gongs mounted on a *langkungan*, or resonating platform, is often used in these performances, which have been compared to Indonesian traditional orchestrations.

Filipino classical performers of note have included composers and conductors such as Rodolfo Cornejo, Antonino Buenaventura and Antonio J Molina. Many of the Philippines' operatic performers are internationally renowned. Among them is the tenor Otoniel Gonzaga and diva Andion Fernandez.

Among the avant-garde crowd, the biggest names have been José Maceda and Lucresia Kasilig, who have both been inspired by indigenous music traditions.

Popular music has been dominated of late by the queen of stage musicals, Lea Salonga (see the later Theatre entry). Her most recent album, *In Love*, went double platinum in the Philippines and features love songs written by Filipino female composers. Another international star claimed by the Philippines is the pop music crooner Julio Iglesias Jr, whose mother is Filipino.

The father of homegrown popular folk music remains Freddy Aguilar, whose Tagalog classic 'Bayan Ko' ('My Country') has been an unofficial national anthem since inspiring the anti-Marcos movements in the mid-1980s.

Manila, and many smaller cities and towns, have also spawned lively rock music scenes, with the power ballad and heavy metal among some of the favourites of young music fans.

Literature

Philippine 'literature' prior to the Spanish era existed in the form of oral folk tales, epic poems or marathon chants. To this day, these are passed on through generations in the dialects of indigenous groups such as the Bukidnon of Negros.

Like most art made under Spanish rule, literature was primarily a religious tool, and it remained so until the introduction of American-style novels, short stories and drama. Other influences, from France in particular, were imported by the likes of novelist and essayist José Rizal, poet Francisco Balagtas and short-story master José

In the Bag

Over in Hollywood, the likes of Cameron Diaz, Elizabeth Hurley and Sandra Bullock have been seen clutching bags by expat Filipino designer Rafe Totengco. In a classic rags-to-riches tale, Rafe has become *the* name in the accessories trade and the beautiful people don't leave home without their Rafe purse or messenger bag. According to the Rafe philosophy, such bags mean you're fashion conscious, not a fashion victim.

At the lip-pursingly swanky Council of Fashion Designers' awards night in New York in 1999, the young designer shone among the dinner jackets and evening dresses by wearing a *barong Tagalog*, the Philippine national dress-shirt.

Mic Looby

Garcia Villa. Another enormously influential modern writer has been the journalist, poet, novelist and playwright Nick Joaquin.

José Rizal's works, including *Noli Me Tangere* and the masterpiece of Spanish verse *Mi Ultimo Adios* (My Last Farewell), were unsuccessfully banned by Spanish authorities for their ground-breaking criticism of colonial rule.

Painting

A unified Philippine art style began to emerge in the late 16th century under the watchful eye of the Spanish, but it was only the artists who depicted Christian themes that flourished. Thus, the earliest extant paintings depict saints and biblical scenes.

It wasn't until the late 18th century that Philippine art began to haul itself off the cross. Secular art, in the form of well-funded portraiture, became the new dominant form.

One of the first individuals to make an impact on the Philippine art scene in the early 19th century was Damian Domingo, who used single-bristle sable brushes imported from China to produce stunning miniatures. Domingo was later dubbed the father of Filipino painting.

Other secular painters to have won acclaim have been Juan Luna and Felix Resurreccion Hidalgo. Luna's vast *Spolarium* and Hidalgo's *Antigone* were regarded as masterpieces in Europe, where Luna picked up first prize at the 1884 Madrid Exposition.

Neorealism emerged after WWII, with masters such as Vicente Manansala, Victor Edades and Arturo Rogerio Luz. The vibrant, pioneering work of abstract expressionist José Joya, who died in 1995, is regarded by many as some of the best in modern Philippine art.

Contemporary Philippine painting continues to be strong and often confronting, and the lively Manila art scene was honoured in 1998 by hosting the highly regarded ASEAN Art Awards.

The British-based conceptual artist David Cortez Medalla is one the Philippines' best-known artists overseas.

Sculpture

Among the non-Christian minorities, particularly the Muslims of Mindanao and the Ifugao in North Luzon, there is a long tradition of sculpture. Mostly woodcarvings and metalwork with strong religious motifs, such work has influenced contemporary Filipino sculptors including Veloso Abueva and José Alcantara. Contemporary Philippine pottery can also trace its roots back to ancient times, with pottery recently excavated in the Ayub Cave in Mindanao, dating from between 500 BC to AD 500.

The *bulol*, the most sacred of figures carved by the Ifugao, are used to guard food supplies. Some bulol have been imbued with such life that they are believed to have killed vermin, thieves and even Japanese soldiers. During fires, some bulol are thought to have leapt up and fled to safety. Traditionally, the names of the sculptors responsible for these powerful creations were rarely recorded (one outstanding exception to the rule was an Ifugao sculptor known as Tagiling, who is thought to have lived and worked in the village of Kababuyan until his death in the 1930s). While this suggests such work was never considered art by the ancient Ifugao, it has nonetheless had an enormous influence on artists of today.

In modern times, classical Philippine sculpture has been epitomised by Guillermo Tolentino's neoclassical masterpiece, *Bonifacio Monument*, based on the revolutionary hero Andres Bonifacio. Napoleon Abueva, a Tolentino protégé known for his mixed-media abstract works, has been selected at

Cartoons

It's a well-kept secret, but many international animation giants such as Disney, Marvel and Hanna Barbera produce substantial portions of their animation in Manila. Filipino cartoonists are renowned for their competitive rates, speed and adaptability. Filipinos also excel at original comic artwork, and many have earned cult followings in the superhero genre at home and in the USA.

Mic Looby

several Association of Southeast Asian Nations (ASEAN) sculpture exhibitions.

Cinema

The Philippines is easily South-East Asia's most prolific and diverse film maker, but the industry has certainly had its ups and downs. Launched by foreigners around the beginning of the 20th century, it peaked during the 1950s and troughed in the 1970s under the Marcos regime. Swashbuckling good guy/bad guy movies remain a firm favourite and it's no coincidence that the nation's latest president made his name exclusively playing a gun-toting good guy. More recent Filipino films to make an international impact include Kidlat Tahimik's 'postcolonial' masterpiece *The Perfumed Nightmare*, about a Filipino boy taken to Paris by an American.

If you're staying at a hotel in the Philippines that has cable TV, look for the Pinoy Blockbuster channel for hours of Filipino schlock classics.

One of the healthiest centres for cinema and visual arts outside Manila can be found in Baguio, where many former Manila-based filmmakers and artists work with the traditional artists of North Luzon.

Theatre

Older, wiser brother to the local movie industry, Philippine theatre has provided a powerful artistic and political voice for countless generations. It's also, of course, lots of fun. The country's specialist in mainstream musical productions, Repertory Philippines, gave the world Lea Salonga, who starred in the Broadway productions of *Miss Saigon* and *Les Miserables*, and more recently the London production of *Hey Mr Producer!* Inevitably referred to as the Philippines' first truly international artist, Salonga has also lent her famously sweet vocals to Disney films including *Aladdin* and *Mulan*. Other big-name local stars of stage include director Behn Cervantes, and the late Rolando Tinio, whose Teatro Pilipino company successfully adapted English-language classics into Tagalog.

One of the most admired sources of fresh material is Bulwagang Gantimpala (Gantimpala Theater Foundation), based at the Manila Metropolitan Theater. Founded in 1977, this chronically underfunded independent group has consistently created politically charged, instant classics, including a stage version of *Noli Me Tangere* by national hero Dr José Rizal.

SOCIETY & CONDUCT
Traditional Conduct

The art of enjoying life despite hardships is a national pastime. A disarming laugh, accompanied by an easy shrug of the shoulders could almost be classified as an official dance movement. Whether praying, singing, drinking, dancing or discussing, the professionally social Filipino tends to be living for the moment and accepting that fate will takes its course for better or worse. This notion is best summed up by the homespun philosophy behind the simple term *bahala na*. Once interpreted as 'without god', bahala na has come to represent a kind of confidence despite everything. Essentially fatalistic, it expresses the idea that all things shall pass and that in the meantime life is to be lived – preferably in the company of one's friends and – most importantly – one's family.

Dos & Don'ts

The golden rule when travelling in the Philippines is to treat problems with the same graciousness as the average Filipino. A smile and a joke goes a long, long way, while anger or sullenness just makes things worse.

Prostitution

While prostitution certainly existed before the coming of the Spanish and Americans, it wasn't a major social problem. Prostitution became big, illegal business in 1900, when the then US president McKinley effectively condoned 'R&R' under US regulations. Since then, entire girlie-bar towns have grown around US naval and military bases in Luzon, and the Philippines has earned a reputation as one of the cheapest destinations in the world for buying women, men and children.

But a boom of an entirely different kind struck the trade in 1991 when Mt Pinatubo erupted, forcing the evacuation of prostitution central – Angeles City – and, more than a little coincidentally, all US military personnel. The sudden loss of the industry's main client base inspired a wholesale clean-up, spearheaded by the then Manila mayor, Alfredo Lim. Under new laws, Ermita's girlie bars and strip joints were boarded up and thousands of sex-trade workers were forced onto the street, or back to their hometowns.

But poverty, corruption and a tourism-led recovery saw the sex industry revive, and even prosper, by the late 1990s. Lim and his band of crusaders proved no match for the crooked police, politicians and bar owners who made a living from exploiting sex workers. An unofficial 1999 estimate put the number of adult sex workers in the Philippines at 500,000.

Now the industry is set to boom again with 'R&R' facilities to be provided under the 1999 VFA between the USA and Philippines. A familiar euphemism for the sex trade in the Philippines, 'R&R' was one of the reasons why so many Filipinos were glad to see the US military depart in 1991. Similarly, the Philippine government's boast of an increase in 'tourism jobs' thanks to the renewed US presence is seen as just another cry of 'company girls!'.

In 1998 the United Nation's International Labour Organisation (ILO) suggested that the only way to combat the worst elements of prostitution in countries such as the Philippines is to officially recognise the sex industry. ILO figures showed that the industry has grown so rapidly in South-East Asia that it is now worth between 2% and 14% of GDP in regional economies.

In a society as deeply religious as the Philippines, recognising – let alone legalising – prostitution is unthinkable. From a solely humanitarian point of view, however, official recognition could help enforce labour regulations and a degree of protection for sex workers.

For more information, contact the Manila-based Bukluran ng Kababaihan sa Lansangan (BUKAL, Association of Women in the Street). Its Web site is at www.avoca.vicnet.net.au/~win/bukal.html. Or contact the Women's International Network (✉ maltzahn@vicnet.net.au) via its Web site at www.avoca.vicnet.net.au/~win/welcome.html.

For an incredible insight into the lives of Philippine sex workers, see *Let the Good Times Roll: Prostitution and the US Military in Asia* by Saundra Pollock Sturdevant & Brenda Stoltzfus.

Child Prostitution

The Philippines has the fourth largest number of child prostitutes in the world, with an estimated 70,000, after the USA (300,000), India (400,000) and Thailand (800,000). Driven by poverty, these children are preyed on predominantly by men from virtually every Western nation on earth.

A dreadful culture of silence surrounds child sex abuse in the Philippines. While shame plays a big role in this silence, for the most part it's bought. There's big money to be made in paedophilia – not by the children themselves, of course, but by those who arrange meetings between paedophiles and children and those who threaten to report these paedophiles. There's also big bucks to be made by corrupt police on the

Child Prostitution

Child sex tourism is a criminal offence in many countries around the world. Extraterritorial laws in Australia, New Zealand, the USA and many European Union (EU) countries mean that prosecution and punishment can occur in the offender's country of residence, even when the crime took place overseas. In addition to these laws, tougher action (including imprisonment) is now being taken in countries that have been documented as centres for child sexual exploitation.

Responsible travellers can help in the campaign to end the sexual exploitation of children by reporting suspected activity to police (or social workers), firstly in the country they are in and then in their home country.

odd occasion that these paedophiles are actually reported.

While child sex abuse cases reported to social workers throughout the Philippines have been rising since 1993, it's likely this indicates an increase in abuse, rather than an increase in social responsibility. In 1993, 720 cases were reported. Within a year, the figure had more than doubled and is estimated to be increasing still. These cases included rape, sexual assault and child prostitution involving children aged from one to 18 years of age. Despite strict laws, the number of foreigners charged and convicted over such sex crimes in the Philippines is so low as to be *encouraging* foreign paedophiles.

Apart from Manila, the most notorious child prostitution haunts tend to be within easy reach of the capital. These include Pagsanjan, Olongapo, Subic Bay and – most infamously – Angeles City.

For more information, contact the Manila office of End Child Prostitution in Asian Tourism (ECPAT; ☎ 02-433 5527 or ☎ 925 2804, fax 433 1150, @ ecpat@phil.gn. apc.org), 123 V Luna Road Extension, Sikatuna Village, 1101, Quezon City, Manila. Its Web site is at www.ecpat. net/ecpat1/network.htm.

Treatment of Animals

While not worshipped in a Western sense except among the urban elite, domestic pets are common in the Philippines. Cats and dogs, usually strays, are tolerated in large numbers, although stray dogs are regularly rounded up and shot to keep rabies at bay. While most animals eventually end up as dinner – fish, pigs and chickens being the most popular – the rooster, as fighting cock, spends much of its life being pampered like a royal prince. Cockfighting is an extremely popular and lucrative pastime, and woe betide the grumpy traveller who suggests strangling a rooster that crows nonstop on an all-night bus trip! These magnificently groomed and fussed-over birds travel far and wide to cockfights and their owners often buy a separate bus seat for their prize fighters (see the boxed text 'Foul Play' in the Facts for the Visitor chapter).

RELIGION

While visitors could be forgiven for thinking basketball is the dominant religion, Catholicism is still No 1 – and has been since the Spanish took hold in the 16th century. The Philippines is the only predominantly Christian country in Asia – almost 90% of the population claims to be Christian and over 80% are Roman Catholic. Filipinos account for 60% of Asia's Christians, and their numbers are rising. In 1986 there were 50 million and, by the late 1990s, this figure had ballooned to over 65 million. There are approximately 11 million non-Catholic Christians practising in more than 350 organisations, many of which operate under the banner of the National Council of Churches in the Philippines. The largest denominations in this group include the full-blown gospel-style Philippines for Jesus movement, and the Protestant Iglesia ni Cristo, which believes Jesus Christ was just another prophet.

The largest religious minority group are the Muslims, with Islam actually an older presence than Christianity. Mindanao Muslims include the Ilanon, Maguindanaw, Maranaw, Tausag and Samal.

The country's passionate Catholic population has made Easter the most revered religious festival in the Philippines. Every April, thousands of devotees take part in the *pabasa* (an all-night discussion about all things biblical), pilgrims flock to churches and shrines throughout the islands as part of the Visita Iglesia (altar observances and processions) and Christ's death is re-enacted in great de-

Travel & Religion

Religion is a familiar travelling companion in the Philippines. Jeepneys and tricycles are usually dripping with Catholic good-luck charms, many 'fastcraft' ferry companies screen a video prayer before heading off, bus drivers and passengers often cross themselves as the journey begins, and traffic is regularly brought to a standstill by gloriously long, slow funeral processions.

Mic Looby

tail several times over as part of the Cenaculo, with many enthusiastic participants, despite the disapproval of the Catholc church.

Philippine religious faith can be found in its rawest form in the ancient animist beliefs of the upland tribes of North Luzon, Palawan, Mindoro and Mindanao. Echoes of these exist even in mainstream religion – often to the horror of institutionalised Philippine faiths. But whatever beliefs are observed, Filipinos are an inherently spiritual people.

Examples of the Philippine talent for combining faiths are most notably found on the island of Siquijor, which is home to healers renowned for their spiritual and medicinal skills. In spite of a stigma created by mainstream Christians, these healers attract big crowds every year at their Lenten Festival of Herbal Preparation. Based in the town of San Antonio, the festival kicks off on Black Saturday and centres on a ritual known as Tang-Alap, a gloriously fun-loving gathering of herbs and roots to be used in a pagan form of holy communion and dawn prayers.

Villagers throughout the Philippines long ago wove Christian rituals, such as Lent, into coinciding traditional harvest festivals. The best known of these is the marathon verse

spectacular known as the *moro-moro* and the Moriones, a passionate interpretation of the stabbing of Christ by a Roman soldier. A distinct mix of animism and Christianity is the week-long recital of Christ's passion, known in Tagalog as *pasyon*.

Another peculiarly Philippine Catholic practice is the passionate veneration of the Virgin Mary, something of an institution every Wednesday in churches throughout the land. Prayers to the Mother of Perpetual Help are held all day, often on Tuesday night and Thursday morning as well.

Even President Estrada, not known for his piety, regularly consults a spiritual adviser from the 'born-again' evangelical Catholic offshoot known as the El Shaddai. He's also not afraid to display a little old-fashioned superstition. During his inauguration, Estrada refused to accept the historical suggestion that he was to be the 13th president of the country. Instead, he dismissed the terms of three presidents who had ruled during the American and Japanese regimes on the grounds that they didn't qualify as presidents of the Republic. Thus, he became – in his own mind at least – either the eighth or 12th president and all was right with the world. Of course, eventually, some poor sap will have to be the 13th president.

Facts for the Visitor

BEST & WORST

The siren songs of the Philippines are many and varied, played by an impressive range of people and places. The most familiar hits with travellers are doubtless Boracay and Banaue but, if you have the time, the Philippines offers visitors a tropical symphony of attractions.

While the larger islands such as Luzon, Cebu and Mindanao make the most music, the little islands often have the biggest surprises. Delights in a minor key include Camiguin, for its rainforest and reef; Bantayan's beaches; and Malapascula, 'the thinking person's Boracay'. Then there are activities: biking on Guimaras, hiking on Sibuyan, and diving and snorkelling off Moalboal, North Pandan and southern Leyte.

Other highlights include sunset over Lake Sebu, in the heartland of Mindanao's T'boli people; Silay (on Negros) and Vigan (on Luzon) are beautifully preserved historic towns. The Mayon volcano's perfectly symmetrical cone and the weird *lahar* (rain-induced landslide of volcanic debris) formations of Mt Pinatubo are just two of the many volcanic sights on the islands.

And the lowlights? It hurts, but the awe-inspiring rice terraces at Banaue are showing signs of deterioration. An easy inclusion is Angeles, the prostitution and sex tour capital of the country – at least nearby Mt Pinatubo gives you something else to look at if you have to pass through. Despite efforts to clean up San Fernando (La Union) after the US military left, a dearth of decent beaches and a swag of tourists in search of prostitutes remain.

Manila would probably make most travellers' lists of 'Cities You'd Hate to Lose Your Passport In'. It's one of those places resident expats learn to appreciate, if not exactly adore, but first-time visitors often can't wait to escape the grime, crime and eye-popping chasm between rich and poor. Fair enough – though beyond the nightlife, the capital does have enough attractions to pass a few lively days.

More than a few towns would charitably fall into the 'Nice Place to Live but I Wouldn't Want to Visit' category. Danao and Subic Bay outside Manila and Mactan near Cebu City are particularly devoid of charm; Taglibaran's air pollution is sobering, and Kalibo saves all its colour and energy for its big festival.

SUGGESTED ITINERARIES

No matter what your itinerary, it will probably take up more time than you might imagine. Whether you're gazing at the surf or groping for a seat on the next bus, plane or boat, you'll be surprised at how quickly time passes. If you plan a long list of sights, it's best to plan carefully but stay loose – your itinerary is also in the hands of the transportation network, and the weather may have plans of its own (for better or worse).

Bahala na, as the Filipinos say. Be realistic and go with the flow – for example, unless you have your own helicopter, you're not going to land in Manila and hike in Banaue on the same day. Consider how you're going to get from A to B, too. A lot of travellers make a beeline for Boracay, but getting there can be less than half the fun – it's often quicker and easier to go by boat to Caticlan on Panay than trying to fly. In fact, if you're doing any serious island-hopping, getting around the Visayas is generally quicker by boat than by plane.

If time is limited, one way to conserve energy yet pack a fair bit in is to base yourself in a pleasant centre with plenty of nearby attractions for one- or two-day side trips. Sagada on Luzon and Davao on Mindanao suit this purpose well. Alternatively, head for 'doable' islands such as Samar, Leyte, Camiguin or the Romblon group, where distances are relatively short but there's a great variety of things to see and do. You could also ease into the country (or

48

take a break along the way) on a cosy little island like Biliran, off Leyte.

PLANNING
When to Go
Giving due allowance to island microclimates and the tempestuous twins (El Niño and El Niña), the best time to visit is in the typhoon off-season, from mid-December to mid-May. The catch is, Christmas and Easter fall at the beginning and end of this period. It's a good idea to plant yourself in one pleasant spot during these holidays – with the entire population gathering with families, getting accommodation and transport can be tricky.

The most lively festivals fall in January and May, and an awful lot of rain falls on the Pacific coast provinces between November and January. The dry season should arrive by about mid-February, and the rice terraces of North Luzon are magnificent in March and April. The weather is at its most travel-friendly in these months; by May, the warm weather turns hot and you'll ache for a sea breeze or the cool shade of the mountains. See also the Climate section in the Facts about the Philippines chapter for further details.

Maps
To get your bearings among the islands, you need a good map. The Philippine Department of Tourism (DOT) supplies country maps, but they aren't very detailed. The Nelles Verlag 1:1,500,000 scale *Philippines* map is a very good alternative. See also Maps under Orientation in the Manila chapter.

What to Bring
You can travel light to the Philippines, but among the essential items is a torch (flashlight) – power failures are common, and some parts of the country manage without electricity at all. A towel or sarong can double as makeshift bedding on the bare boards or plastic sheets that cover the beds on many overnight ferries. You'll also want a range of clothing, from lightweight for tropical beaches to warm (a sweater or light jacket) for the mountains or volcano summits. A sweater will also stave off pneumonia when the air-conditioning cranks up on fastcraft boats in particular.

A garbage bag will help protect your gear from water. It can also keep out the dust on long, dry bus trips. And ear plugs will keep out everything from crowing roosters to ship engines or the karaoke machine downstairs.

Tampons have become far more widely available than they used to be (the average price is P150 for a box of eight), but it's still a good idea to stock up before visiting smaller towns or bring a stash of your own from home.

There are also a few things you don't need to lug along. Mosquito nets are a bulky inconvenience – and places that have mosquitos *do* tend to have mosquito nets. Umbrellas and raincoats can be bought cheaply along the way when the need arises.

RESPONSIBLE TOURISM
Being the perfectly responsible tourist is quite a job. Battles fought over equal rights, cultural representation, the environment – you name it – have become everyday news and harder to ignore than they once were. At the same time, solutions are often less than obvious and the travel road can seem to run through a minefield of unexploded issues just waiting to blow up in your face.

Taking thoughtful steps is not a bad thing – it certainly beats blindly carrying the jockstrap of nationalism or cultural chauvinism. On the other hand, it's no fun spending your vacation walking on eggshells – and it's not fun for anyone if you're stomping on everyone's toes to take the next 'correct' step.

Tread lightly but take it easy – you're not alone in trying to put your best foot forward, and the gracious humanity Filipinos can muster in the most trying circumstances is a reliable roadmap along the way.

To get you started on the right foot, have a look at the Prostitution and Child Prostitution entries in the Facts about the Philippines chapter, the 'Sea Changes' boxed text in this chapter and the 'Breaking Down Barriers' boxed text in the Mindanao & Sulu chapter.

TOURIST OFFICES

The Philippine Department of Tourism (DOT) is the official organ of Philippine tourism. The main DOT centre in Manila has helpful staff, but you don't need to load up with brochures and computer printouts – regional outlets usually have anything the head office has and the information may be more up to date.

Regional offices can be found in Bacolod, Baguio, Boracay, Butuan, Cagayan de Oro, Cebu City, Cotabato, Davao, Iloilo City, Laoag, Legaspi City, San Fernando (La Union), San Fernando (Pampanga), Tacloban, Tuguegarao and Zamboanga. For more details, see specific destination entries later in this book.

Tourist Offices Abroad

DOT offices and contacts abroad include:

Australia
(☎ 02-9299 6815, fax 9283 1862, ✆ ptsydney@ozemail.com.au) Suite 703, Wynyard House, Level 7, 301 George St, Sydney 2000

China
(☎ 02-2866 6471, hotline 2866 7665, fax 2866 6521, ✆ pdothk@asiaonline.net) c/o Philippine Consulate General, Room 602, United Center, 95 Queensway, Central

France
(☎ 01 42 65 02 34, fax 42 65 02 35, ✆ dotpar@club-internet.fr) c/o Philippines Embassy, 3 Faubourg Saint Honoré, 75008 Paris

Germany
(☎ 069-20893, fax 285127, ✆ phildo-fra@t-online.de) Kaiserhofstrasse 7, 60313 Frankfurt am Main

Japan
(☎ 03-5562 1583/1584, fax 5562 1593, ✆ dotjapan@aol.com) c/o Philippines Embassy, 5-15-5 Roppongi, Minato-ku, Tokyo

Singapore
(☎ 065-738 7165, fax 738 2604, ✆ philtours_sin@pacific.net.sg) 06-24 Orchard Towers, 400 Orchard Rd, Singapore 238875

Taiwan
(☎ 02-741 5994, fax 773 5724) c/o Manila Economic & Cultural Office, 4th floor, Metrobank Plaza, 107 Chung Hsiao E Rd, Section 4, Taipei

UK
(☎ 028-7626 7491, fax 7626 3459, ✆ tourism@pdot.co.uk) 103 Cannon St, London EC4N5 AD

USA
New York: (☎ 212-575 7915, fax 302 6759, ✆ erydotny@aol.com) 556 5th Ave, New York, NY 10036
San Francisco: (☎ 415-956 4060, fax 956 2093, ✆ pdotsf@aol.com) Suite 507, 447 Sutter St, San Francisco, CA 94108

VISAS & DOCUMENTS
Visas

Citizens of nearly all countries (Hong Kong SAR and Taiwan passport holders are two exceptions) do not need a visa to enter the Philippines for stays of less than 21 days. However, you may well be asked for proof of an onward ticket to enter the country.

Before you arrive, you can apply for a visa to grant you a longer stay (up to 59 days). A single-entry 59-day visa currently costs anything from free of charge to US$35, depending on where you apply. You can pay a lot more and apply for multiple-entry visas (valid for up to a year), although they're still only good for a 59-day stay.

Some Philippine embassies are happy to issue a visa without actually seeing a return ticket, eg, if you have proof of sufficient funds for an onward ticket. A few embassies don't seem interested in onward tickets – you pay your money, you get your stamp. Others would first like to see 'proof' of an onward ticket; interestingly, you can just get a printout of your itinerary from an airline or travel agent showing your planned arrival and departure dates and flights. See also Buying Tickets under Air in the Getting There & Away section.

Under the Balikbayan Program, former Filipino citizens and their family members travelling together can stay visa-free in the Philippines for up to one year. The 'balikbayan stamp' required in your current passport is handled by Philippine embassies and consulates, and is free of charge.

Visa Extensions If you want to stay beyond the 21 or 59 days you've been given on arrival, you'll have to deal with a local immigration office. Fortunately, you can now buy your way past a lot of the red tape with a P500 'express fee', which may be pricey but it ensures that your application is processed in only four or five hours, rather than the usual five to seven days.

Currently, 21-day visas can be extended to 59 days for P800 (P1300 express); 59-day visas can be extended for up to six months for P800, plus a P500 'head tax' per month (plus P500 for the express service). You'll need a photocopy of the identity page and Philippines entry stamp from your passport (you can get these outside the Manila office), and you may need to show your onward plane ticket.

Manila's massive Bureau of Immigration (☎ 02-527 3265), on Magallanes Dr, squats between the Pasig River and the Intramuros city walls. A visit to this imposing edifice is a formal occasion: casual clothes like shorts and singlets are prohibited – flip-flops (thongs) are also a bad fashion statement – and you'll need proof of identity to enter the building. The doors are open from 8 am to 5 pm (closed from noon to 1 pm) Monday to Friday.

Visa extensions from 21 days to 59 days can often be handled faster by the regional immigration offices in San Fernando (La Union) and Cebu City, but remember to dress for success.

Beware: as many travellers have discovered as they were ready to board the plane out of the country, there is now an additional charge if you stay more than 59 days, on top of the visa extension fees. This is officially your Emigration Clearance Certificate (ECC) – which is effectively just another tax on tourists. In practice, visitors pay a fine equivalent to the price of the ECC as you clear emigration at the airport, which saves the hassle and paperwork of applying for the certificate itself. The cost is a steep P1000, plus a P10 processing fee. If you don't have the money to pay, you will not be allowed out of the Philippines.

The only way around this is to go to the Bureau of Immigration in Intramuros and request that you be 'blacklisted for nonpayment', which will get you off the charge but seriously affects your chances of ever getting back into the country.

The Intramuros office seems to prefer that you just pay your ECC fine at the airport rather than at the office for stays under a year, so make sure you've got the money ready when you leave.

Onward Tickets

An onward ticket for the Philippines is a good idea. First and foremost, unless you're content with a brief taste of Philippine tarmac, you're likely to need proof of an onward ticket to enter the country. The onward ticket can be for a ship (see the Sea entry later in the Getting There & Away chapter), though getting the paperwork for one-way boat passage out of the country before you arrive isn't assured.

Some travellers hellbent on leaving by boat from Mindanao to Malaysia or Indonesia get around this by biting the bullet and buying the cheapest return air ticket they can find (say, Hong Kong-Manila-Hong Kong), then not using the return portion of it.

In any case, you won't save money on a return fare by picking up a cheap air ticket in Manila. Fares from the Philippines are generally expensive, and local travel agents aren't in the business of tracking down bargains for overseas travel (they usually only quote the advertised fares given by the airlines).

Travel Insurance

A travel insurance policy to cover theft, loss and medical problems is a good idea. Some policies offer lower and higher medical-expense options. There is a wide variety of policies available, so check the small print. Some policies specifically exclude 'dangerous activities', which can include scuba diving, motorcycling and even trekking.

You may prefer a policy that pays doctors or hospitals directly rather than you having to pay on the spot and claim later. If you have to claim later, make sure you keep all documentation. Some policies ask you to call back (reverse charges) to a centre in your home country where an immediate assessment of your problem is made.

Check that the policy covers ambulances or an emergency flight home.

Driving Licence & Permits
Your home country's driving licence is legally valid for 90 days in the Philippines. Technically, you are supposed to have an International Driving Permit afterwards.

Hostel Cards
Having a Hostelling International (HI) card will save about P20 per night at a hostel, though there are only a few you are likely to stay at (see Accommodation in this chapter for more details).

Student & Youth Cards
An International Student Identity Card (ISIC) usually has a nicer picture than your driving licence, so although it won't get you many discounts in the Philippines, it's worth taking along.

Students under 24 years of age from 'recognised institutions' are theoretically eligible for 20% discounts on Philippine Airlines (PAL) domestic flights; ask the airline about its Flying Student's card (P50). Some bus and shipping companies may offer 20% discounts to foreign students.

Seniors Cards
PAL offers a 20% discount on domestic flights for passengers who are at least 60 years old. Your passport will suffice as proof of age, though you could also apply for a Golden Years card (P50) from the airline for this purpose.

Vaccination Certificates
You must have proof of vaccination for yellow fever if arriving in the Philippines from an infected area.

Copies
All important documents (passport data page and visa page, credit cards, travel insurance policy, air/bus/train tickets, driving licence etc) should be photocopied before you leave home. Leave one copy with someone at home and keep another with you, separate from the originals.

EMBASSIES & CONSULATES
You should be aware that the embassy of which you are a citizen won't be much help in emergencies if the trouble you're in is remotely your own fault. Your embassy will not be sympathetic if you end up in jail after committing a crime locally, even if such actions are legal in your own country.

In genuine emergencies you might get some assistance, but only if other channels have been exhausted. For example, if you need to get home urgently, a free air ticket is exceedingly unlikely – the embassy would expect you to have insurance. If you have all your money and documents stolen, it might assist with getting a new passport, but a loan for onward travel is out of the question.

Philippines Embassies & Consulates
Diplomatic representation abroad includes:

Australia
Embassy: (☎ 02-6273 2535, fax 6273 3984, @ embaphil@iaccess.com.au) 1 Moonah Place, Yarralumla, ACT 2600
Consulate: (☎ 02-9299 6633, fax 9262 1339, @ phsydpc@ozemail.com.au) Level 7, Wynyard House, 301 George St, Sydney, NSW 2000

Canada
Embassy: (☎ 613-233 1121, fax 233 4165, @ ottawape@istar.com) Suite 606, 130 Albert St, Ottawa, Ont K1P564

China
Embassy: (☎ 010-6532 1872, fax 6532 3761) 23 Xiushui Beijie, Jianguomenwai, Beijing 100600
Consulate: (☎ 852-2823 8500) Room 602, United Centre, 95 Queensway, Central, Hong Kong

France
Embassy: (☎ 01 44 14 57 00, fax 46 47 56 00) 4 Hameau de Boulainvilliers, Paris 75116

Germany
Consulate: (☎ 040-442 952/953) Jungfrauental 13, 2000 Hamburg

Indonesia
Embassy: (☎ 021-310 0345) Jalan Imam Bonjol 6-8, Jakarta

Japan
Embassy: (☎ 03-5562 1584) 5-15-5 Roppongi, Minato-ku, Tokyo 106-8537

Malaysia
  Embassy: (☎ 03-248 4233) 1 Changkat Kai,
  Deng 50450, Kuala Lumpur
Thailand
  Embassy: (☎ 02-259 0139/0140, fax 258
  5385) 760 Thanon Sukhumvit, Bangkok 10110
UK
  Embassy: (☎ 020-7937 1600, fax 7937 2125)
  9a Palace Green, London W8 4QE
USA
  Embassy: (☎ 202-467 9300, fax 467 9417)
  1600 Massachusetts Ave NW, Washington, DC
  20036
Vietnam
  Embassy: (☎ 04-825 7948, fax 826 5760) 27B
  Pho Tran Hung Dao, Hanoi

Embassies & Consulates in the Philippines

Manila is a good place to pick up visas for other parts of Asia, as well as further afield. The governments of most European and Asian countries are represented; many Latin-American nations also maintain a diplomatic presence. Manila's Makati district is the main area for embassies and foreign consulates.

Australia (☎ 02-750 2850) Ground floor, Doña
  Salustiana Ty Tower, 104 Paseo de Roxas,
  Legaspi Village, Makati
Canada (☎ 02-810 8749/8861) 9th floor, Allied
  Bank Bldg, Ayala Ave, Makati
China (☎ 02-879 8020) 149 Roxas Blvd, corner
  of Airport Rd, Parañaque
France (☎ 02-810 1981) 16th floor, Pacific Star
  Bldg, Gil Puyat Ave, corner of Makati Ave,
  Makati
Germany (☎ 02-892 4906) 6th floor, Solid
  Bank Bldg, 777 Paseo de Roxas, Salcedo
  Village, Makati
Indonesia *Embassy:* (☎ 02-892 5061) 185
  Salcedo St, Salcedo Village, Makati
  Consulate in Davao: (☎ 082-229 2930,
  fax 297 0139) Ecoland Dr
Japan (☎ 02-551 5710) 2627 Roxas Blvd, next
  to the Hyatt Regency Hotel, Pasay City
Malaysia (☎ 02-817 4581)107 Tordesillas St,
  Salcedo Village, Makati
New Zealand (☎ 02-891 5358) 23rd floor, Far
  East Bank Center, Gil Puyat Ave, Salcedo
  Village, Makati
Singapore (☎ 02-816 1764) 6th floor, ODC
  International Plaza, 219 Salcedo St, Salcedo
  Village, Makati

Spain (☎ 02-818 5526) 5th floor, ACT Tower,
  Gil Puyat Ave, Salcedo Village, Makati
Thailand (☎ 02-894 0404) Marie Cristine Bldg,
  107 Rada St, Legaspi Village, Makati
USA (☎ 02-523 1001) 1201 Roxas Blvd, Ermita
UK (☎ 02-816 7116) 18th floor, LV Locsin
  Bldg, Makati Ave, corner of Ayala Ave, Makati
Vietnam (☎ 02-524 0364) 554 Vito Cruz St,
  corner of Harrison St, Malate

CUSTOMS

You are permitted to bring in personal effects, and a certain amount of clothing, jewellery and perfume duty free. In addition, 200 cigarettes or two tins of tobacco and 2L of alcohol are allowed duty free.

Illegal drugs, firearms and pornographic material are absolutely prohibited. It is forbidden to export coral and mussels, certain types of orchid, or parts of animals such as python skins or turtle shells.

There is no longer any restriction on the amount of foreign currency that can be brought in; however, foreign currency taken out must not exceed the amount brought in. Visitors must also declare Philippine currency in excess of P10,000 upon entering or leaving the country.

MONEY
Currency

The unit of currency is the peso (P, also spelled piso), which is divided into 100 centavos (c). Banknotes come in denominations of 5, 10, 20, 50, 100, 500 and 1000 pesos. Coins are most common in 10c and 25c pieces, and P1 and P5.

Exchange Rates

Exchange rates are as follows:

country	unit		peso
Australia	A$1	=	P25
Canada	C$1	=	P28
euro	€1	=	P40
France	10FF	=	P60
Germany	DM1	=	P20
Hong Kong	HK$1	=	P5
Japan	¥100	=	P38
New Zealand	NZ$1	=	P20
UK	UK£1	=	P65
USA	US$1	=	P41

Exchanging Money

Most towns have some provisions for changing money, from banks and moneychangers to resorts and travel offices. In some cases (eg, Banaue), the exchange rate is quite low, and you're best to arrive with enough pesos for your stay. All in all, it's wise to plan ahead so you don't get caught short of cash – or find yourself pushing around a wheelbarrow full of pesos 'just in case'.

In Manila, you should have no trouble changing US dollars cash, British pounds sterling or Deutschmarks; Canadian and Australian dollars are also widely accepted. Moneychangers usually offer the best rates, but you should be sceptical of unrealistically high offers. Moneychangers are operated legally in the Philippines and there's no need to look for a black market.

In principle, changing travellers cheques is quite simple; you only need to remember to bring along your passport and the original purchase receipts. In practice, banks and moneychangers can be reluctant to accept travellers cheques, so to minimise hassles it's wise to plan your money conversions in towns with a couple of exchange options.

Even in Manila, only a handful of banks and moneychangers can exchange travellers cheques in currencies other than US dollars. Outside the capital, US dollars are generally the only currency accepted, either for cash or travellers cheques. The rate is generally slightly lower for travellers cheques than for cash.

There are no particular hassles with exchanging pesos, though you'll need your original purchase receipts to reconvert them upon departure, so hang on to those bits of paper.

Cash With the usual precautions, carrying cash (US dollars is the currency of choice) is no particular problem; it's actually a good idea to have a US$50 and/or US$100 note stashed somewhere secure and accessible in case credit cards or travellers cheques aren't an option in a particular situation.

As for pesos, 'Sorry, no change' becomes a familiar line – stock up on notes smaller than P100 at every opportunity.

Travellers Cheques US dollar travellers cheques are the most secure and reliable way to carry most of your funds (see the earlier Exchanging Money entry), and the major brands – American Express (AmEx), Thomas Cook, Citibank and Bank of America – are recognised in the Philippines. An instant replacement policy on lost or stolen cheques is highly desirable, so check that the company will honour this policy in the Philippines before you buy.

ATMs Credit cards can be used to get cash advances from hundreds of Automated Teller Machines (ATMs) in Manila; banks can be found in towns around the country, usually with an ATM or two as well. In the capital, AmEx and MasterCard are the most widely accepted cards, but Visa, Cirrus and Plus are also prevalent. Nationwide, Visa and MasterCard are probably the most commonly accepted cards, but it can be hit and miss – in some more remote towns you'll find provisions for cards like Global Access and Eurocard, but none for Visa.

Many ATMs in the capital (and a few elsewhere) are protected by an armed guard, and the bank will a display an 'online' sign in the window if the ATM is working. Most ATMs have a P4000 or P5000 daily withdrawal limit. Many banks cannot provide over-the-counter advances – this can be inconvenient if the ATM is down, very slow or out of money, so it's best to try ATMs during banking hours.

While there are numerous smaller regional banks that accept a range of cards, credit-card policies for the three biggest banks are as follows: Philippine National Bank (PNB) operates a Philippines-based MasterCard and does not give cash advances against any international cards.

Two of the Philippines' largest banks merged in 2000, with Equitable Bank buying out Philippines Commercial & Industrial Bank (PCI). The new entity is called the Equitable PCI Bank. Formerly, travellers could obtain cash advances on Visa cards at the Equitable and on MasterCard at PCI.

Eventually all Equitable PCI Bank branches will offer cash advance facilities for both cards, but at the time of writing this was only possible at the main branches in big cities. In the meantime, to avoid confusion and delay at the counter, ask locally and use whichever branch was formerly linked with the appropriate card.

Card holders are advised that at the time of writing the former Equitable Bank branches are most likely to offer both services. The changeover at former PCI branches is taking longer.

Credit Cards Many businesses, restaurants, hotels and resorts accept payment by plastic, and credit-card cash advances are possible in larger towns and cities; in small towns and on the less travelled islands (eg, Samar) there are often no provisions for credit cards.

Note that big-name cards are also issued in the Philippines, and a shop-front sign that reads 'Visa accepted' may well refer only to the Philippines-issued version (see the previous ATMs entry). You can get unlimited cash advances on international credit cards from Swagman Travel offices in Manila, Angeles, Apuao Grande Island, Baguio, Bauang, Boracay, Coron, Olongapo, Puerto Galera, Sabang and San Fernando (La Union) – but unlike the banks, Swagman charges a killer 8% commission.

If your MasterCard is lost, stolen or eaten by an ungrateful ATM, the tollfree number to call in the Philippines is ☎ 1 800 1111 0061. For Visa card holders, the number is ☎ 1 800 1111 9015.

International Transfers If you are travelling around Asia, Hong Kong and Singapore are more efficient places than Manila to have money sent to you. International transfers to the Philippines can be slow, though the process is much quicker and simpler if you use the right bank connections. Philippine banks have a working relationship with many overseas institutions, so before you leave, ask your home bank for the name of their 'correspondent' bank in the Philippines.

Also write down your home bank's telex number and your account details; you can then ask your bank to wire or telex funds to you (along with confirmation of the authenticity of the transfer), preferably at the Philippine correspondence bank's head office. Your money should arrive in a few days, but don't expect US dollars cash; banks normally pay out in pesos or travellers cheques.

Bank Accounts If you're in the country for a while, you might consider opening a bank account to ease money transfers, earn a bit of interest and perhaps pick up a locally issued credit card. To open an account, the requirements are similar at PNB and Equitable PCI Bank: one to three pieces of identification, such as passport, driving licence and/or credit card (PNB also requires two passport photos); plus a minimum first deposit, depending on the type of account, of P2000 to P30,000.

Costs

The Philippines is a bit more expensive than Thailand or Indonesia, but still quite affordable by Western standards. First impressions of prices in Manila or Cebu City aren't necessarily indicative of expenses for the rest of your trip. In particular, Manila's accommodation (especially mid-range) tends to be pricey compared with the provinces, where you'll find central Luzon to be among the best value for money. Isolated Batanes asks more from your wallet but, with wonderful lodges and excellent home-cooked food, you'll often get more in return.

Heavily developed tourist centres such as Boracay offer few bargains to travellers, though low-season rates in places that depend on the tourist trade are considerably lower. Nonetheless, you can get by even on Boracay for P500 a day. In any case, basic necessities are amazingly cheap year-round. Air fares within the Philippines are also good value.

The following are average prices for a few sample items:

Beer (one bottle)	P16
Bus (ordinary/100km)	P50
Bus (air-con/100km)	P60
Email (per hour)	P35
Film (36 exposure)	P175

Jeepney (in town)	P3
Hotel room (budget)	P200
Hotel room (mid-range)	P600
Laundry (1kg)	P30
Meal (basic)	P60
Petrol (1L)	P14
Shampoo	P28

Tipping & Bargaining

Tipping (about 5% to 10%) is expected, especially in restaurants, where it's a component of the staff's wages. Round up taxi fares (eg, from P64 to P70), assuming the meter is correct. Try bargaining in shops and markets, as Filipinos do. After all, foreigners are usually quoted higher prices. Fixed price stores are just that.

POST & COMMUNICATIONS
Postal Rates

Domestic airmail letters cost P5 ('ordinary' takes up to three weeks), P10 ('special' takes one week) or P15 ('speed' takes 24 hours).

Rates for international airmail letters of up to 20g are P11 (to South-East Asia), P13 (Middle East and Australia), P15 (Europe, Canada and the USA) and P18 (Africa and South America). Aerograms and postcards cost P8 to any country.

There is a 20kg weight limit for air and sea parcels. The post office needs to sight the contents, so go armed with packing materials but leave everything unwrapped.

The following are air and surface parcel rates:

Australia & New Zealand
  Air: 1st kg P457, then P236 per kg
  Surface: P364, then P145
UK
  Air: 1st kg P615, then P315 per kg
  Surface: P426, then P166
USA
  Air: 1st kg P476, then P376 per kg
  Surface: P285, then P184

Sending Mail

The postal system is generally quite efficient – even from provincial towns, mail tends to get to where it is intended to go. If you're nervous about stamps falling off mail or being removed, have the items franked instead.

Receiving Mail

Post offices in larger towns have poste restante services, where you can have mail sent to you. As elsewhere in the region, have mail addressed to you with your surname in block letters and/or underlined to help ensure that it's filed in the right place.

Courier Services

A reliable company that has branches across the Philippines is LBC. LBC only couriers documents up to 500g and delivers worldwide within four working days.

LBC rates are P440 to Australia, P770 to the UK and P550 to the USA; add P60 to P90 for the express bags.

Telephone

In much of the Philippines, phones are about as common as Velcro dentures – and about as dependable. The phone system has good intentions, but it asks a lot in return. First, you have to find a phone, which on many islands will involve a long jeepney ride or a knock on the mayor's door to borrow his daughter's cell phone. Once you've got your hands on a phone, you're at the mercy of switchboard operators and dodgy lines that make you wish they'd just strung together a big network of tin cans and taut wires instead.

OK, we're exaggerating, but not by much. Making long-distance and international telephone calls from Manila should have gotten much easier with the introduction of International Direct Dial (IDD), National Direct Dial (NDD) and Country Direct calling (international operator-assisted calls), but there are still plenty of bugs in the system.

Within Luzon you should be able to reach most numbers directly, but calls to provincial areas like Samar or Leyte can often only be placed through the operator (this depends on you being able to reach the operator in the first place!). The number for the domestic operator is ☎ 109. For directory inquiries in Manila, call ☎ 114 (☎ 112 for regional calls).

Mid-range hotels often have IDD/NDD phones in their rooms, but if you're staying in one of the cheaper places, you'll have to find a public phone. To call the Philippines from abroad using IDD, you need to first dial the appropriate IDD access number, then the country code (063). The two main local phone companies are Philippine Long Distance Telephone (PLDT) and Philcom; the numbers to dial are Philcom (☎ 0090+631) and PLDT (☎ 0090+630).

In the provinces there are few private or public phones and you can only make or receive calls from regional telephone offices for the main phone companies. At these offices, an assistant places your call through the operator and transfers it to a booth if your number's been reached. However, the national network is pretty shaky, and calls can literally take hours to get through. It's also common to be cut off or interrupted by the operator mid-call.

The telecom offices can send and receive local and international calls, but charge a deposit for international and domestic collect calls, even if you don't get through. The staff are usually very busy so if you have an important call, it's best to try and persuade the assistant to let you dial the number yourself so you can keep trying until you get through. If facilities are functioning and the operator is in the mood, offices may take messages that incoming callers leave for you.

Also, the phone companies have different arrangements for the codes they can access – few places can (or will) call 1 800 numbers, for example, and connections to cell phones vary (see Cell Phones later in this section for details).

Many places (eg, the popular destinations of Puerto Galera and Sagada) are not yet linked by land lines, which means that cell phones are the only connection to the outside world; if you're in a touristed area, many of the resorts will offer international phone services. Typical resort rates are P400 to P500 for the first three minutes and P100 to P150 per subsequent minute.

IDD calls are cheaper than operator-assisted calls, but all international calls are prohibitively expensive; direct-dial calls to America, Europe or South-East Asia cost

Telephone Codes

The country code for the Philippines is ☎ 63. The international dialling code is ☎ 00. Following are area codes for some cities. You must dial the first zero when calling from within the Philippines.

Angeles	☎ 0455
Bacolod	☎ 034
Baguio	☎ 074
Batangas	☎ 043
Bauang	☎ 072
Banaue	☎ 073
Borocay	☎ 036
Butuan	☎ 08521,
	☎ 08522
Cagayan de Oro	☎ 08822
Cebu City	☎ 032
Cotabato	☎ 064
Davao City	☎ 082
Dipolog	☎ 065
Dumaguete	☎ 035
General Santos	☎ 083
Iloilo City	☎ 033
Kalibo	☎ 036
Laoag	☎ 077
La Union	☎ 072
Legaspi City	☎ 05221
Lucena	☎ 042
Mambajao	☎ 088
Manila	☎ 02
Naga	☎ 054
Olongapo	☎ 047
Ormoc	☎ 05351
Puerto Princesa	☎ 048
San Fernando (La Union)	☎ 072
San Fernando (Pampanga)	☎ 045
San Jose	☎ 046
Sorsogon	☎ 056
Surigao	☎ 08681
Tacloban	☎ 053
Tagaytay	☎ 096
Tagbilaran	☎ 038,
	☎ 03823
Tuguegarao	☎ 078
Vigan	☎ 077
Virac	☎ 052
Zamboanga	☎ 062

around P80 a minute, but it can cost as much as P180 a minute to reach Africa or the Middle East. It may be best to get people to call you at your hotel. For operator-assisted calls to most nations in Europe, the USA, South-East Asia and Australia, Philippines Telecom offers the following system, which puts you through to an operator in the country you are calling, who will then place your call for you. You dial ☎ 105 to enter the system, followed by a specific country code (the most commonly used codes are listed in phone boxes). To be put through directly by a Philippines international operator, you just dial ☎ 108 and hope that someone picks up – all the standard operator numbers in the Philippines are almost permanently engaged.

For local calls or domestic long-distance calls, many businesses offer operator-assisted calls from their private phone (once you hang up, the operator calls back with the cost of the call). The price of domestic long-distance calls depends on the destination; local calls start at P2 per minute.

Phonecards Coin-operated phones are rare, even in Manila, but phonecard-operated phones can be found in many hotel lobbies and shopping malls. Cards are widely available and come in P100, P200 and P500 denominations.

There's a wide range of international phonecards. Lonely Planet's eKno Communication Card is aimed specifically at travellers and provides cheap international calls, a range of messaging services and free email – for local calls, you're usually better off with a local card. You can join online at www.ekno.lonelyplanet.com, or by phone from the Philippines by dialling ☎ 1 800 1 119 0015. Once you have joined, to use eKno from the Philippines, dial ☎ 1 800 1 119 0014.

Cell Phones A cell phone is handy in the Philippines, and quite a few small operators use them to run their business. Calls *to* cell phones aren't always straightforward, however, as they often have to be placed through the local operator where the phone

Useful Phone Numbers

Directory assistance	
for Manila	☎ 114
for regional calls	☎ 112
Domestic operator	☎ 109
International access code	☎ 00
International operator	☎ 108
Philippines' country code	☎ 63
Police emergency (Manila)	☎ 166
Tourist assistance hotline, Manila (24 hours)	☎ 02-523 8411

is being used (this is particularly true for 0918 code cell phone numbers; 0912 calls can usually be placed directly).

If your phone company offers international roaming for the Philippines, you should be able to use your cell phone (provided it's a relatively new model) and home SIM card in the Philippines. Cell phone calls are relatively cheap in the Philippines, but check the roaming rates charged by your company – some charge many times higher than Philippine companies.

PLDT is the major cell phone subscriber, running partnerships (not always smoothly)

Phoney Excuses

If it takes you ages just to get a crackling connection on a local phone, relax: it could be worse.

The Philippines has taken to the return of the death penalty with a vengeance, but in late 1999 President Estrada attempted to put a human face on the policy by granting a last-second stay of execution. According to press reports, when he tried to put a call through to the prison where the execution was about to take place, the line just rang busy.

We're not sure if this says more about the state of the communications system or Erap's grasp of it, but you know things are bad when Heaven puts you on hold...

Russ Kerr

with smaller outfits like Globe Telecom. Published per minute rates appear cheap, but have a look at the running costs built in to the sign-up plan. If you don't subscribe to a plan, prepaid cards work, but last only two months (and you'll have to keep a minimum amount on the card for functions like text).

In the big cities you can pick up a cell phone with text for about P5000, including a SIM card and a call card, though the newest features will cost a lot more.

Fax

In the big cities, shops offering fax services are abundant and there is a huge range of charges for essentially the same service: from P80 to P422 for one page. Small private companies can have good promotional rates – but if you need to fax from a province with only one calling agency (ie, there are no private or general phones), it's very expensive.

Sample rates from Manila (with PLDT) are: to Australia, P146 for the first page, then P67 per page; to the UK, P148 for the first page, then P72; and to the USA, it's P137, then P62.

Email & Internet Access

Email and Internet services have taken off in a big way in the Philippines, and plenty of hotels, resorts and cybercafes will allow you to keep in touch with the virtual outside world. Even many of the smallest towns and islands have email facilities. In fact, email is generally a more reliable means of overseas communication than telephones.

Rates for email/Internet access average between P30 and P40 per hour; in Cebu City, the charge is as low as P20 per hour. Heavily touristed Boracay is pricey – from P90 to P150 per hour – but the steep rate does let you log on early and late (from 7.30 am to 11.30 pm), which is a big plus.

If you've got a portable computer for this purpose, note the voltage used (see the Electricity entry later in this chapter). US-style RJ-11 telephone adaptors are commonly used in the Philippines, so ensure that you at least have a US RJ-11 adaptor that works with your modem. For more information on travelling with a portable computer, check out the Web sites at www.teleadapt.com or www.warrior.com.

Two big Internet Service Providers (ISPs) currently have dial-in nodes to the Philippines. America Online (AOL), which has a Web site at www.aol.com, has a node in Manila (US$8 per hour) and another in Cebu (US$6 per hour). CompuServe's Web site is at www.compuserve.com and it currently has two dial-in nodes in Manila – the World-Connect (INW) line is a steep US$25 per hour, while on EQUANT (EQT) the rate is US$10 per hour. If you go with either of these, it's best to download a list of the dial-in numbers before you leave home.

One option to collect email through cybercafes is to open a free eKno Web-based email account online at www.ekno.lonely planet.com. You can then access your mail from anywhere in the world from any net-connected machine running a standard Web browser.

INTERNET RESOURCES

The Lonely Planet Web site at www.lonely planet.com is a good place to start your cyber research. Here you'll find succinct summaries on travelling to most places on earth, postcards from other travellers and the Thorn Tree bulletin board, where you can ask questions before you go, or dispense advice when you get back. You can also find travel news and updates to many of our most popular guidebooks, and the subWWWay section links you to the most useful travel resources elsewhere on the Web.

Philippines-related sites pop up and vanish faster than you can say 'Page Not Found', but in addition to the many sites listed through this book, here are a few Web resources worth a look.

Tanikalang Ginto The vast Tanikalang Ginto Web directory is very catholic (with a small 'c') in its orientation – it offers useful links to nearly every topic under the Philippine sun. www.filipinolinks.com
Dive Buddies Philippines Useful info on scuba diving. www.divephil.com

Bundok Philippines Devoted to conscientious hiking and climbing on the islands.
www.geocities.com/Yosemite/3712

World Wildlife Fund (Philippines) A great resource on endangered species, and outlines the many WWF conservation projects in the country.
www.islesite.com/wwf-phil/main.htm

US State Department Mildly paranoid but useful travel information and advisories are available from the US State Department.
travel.state.gov/philippines.html

Foul Mouth: Filipino Dirty Words If you want to spice up your bland Tagalog phrases, this Web site is happy to help.
pubweb.acns.nwu.edu/~flip/dirty.html

BOOKS

Most books are published in different editions by different publishers in different countries. As a result, a book might be a hardcover rarity in one country and readily available in paperback in another. Fortunately, bookshops and libraries search by title or author, so your local bookshop or library is best placed to advise you on the availability of the following recommendations.

Lonely Planet

Lonely Planet also publishes the *Pilipino (Tagalog) phrasebook*, which includes everything from jeepney jargon to gay and lesbian lingo.

Guidebooks

Dive Sites of the Philippines by Jack Jackson is a detailed guide with good photos and reliable basics.

Travel

Culture Shock! Philippines by Alfredo & Grace Roces offers some helpful illustrations of Filipino culture, though the points made are often simplistic and too general to take to heart.

Ants for Breakfast – Archaeological Adventures among the Kalinga by James M Skibo is a healthy supplement to the Culture Shock series. The book is a travelogue of asides and insights gleaned from fieldwork among the Kalinga people of the Cordilleras.

History & Politics

In an effort to get to the bottom of a very deep pit of patronage and corruption in the Philippines, James Hamilton-Paterson penned the sordid tale of *America's Boy – A Century of Colonialism in the Philippines*. It's a great read, if a bit light on as a history. The conclusion – basically, that Philippine politics is a bottomless pit – perhaps says as much about the way new writing on 'the Third World' has come full circle to old Western notions of 'national character' as it does about the eternal return of patrons and clients in the islands.

Stanley Karnow's *In Our Image – America's Empire in the Philippines* is a straight-up analysis, another in his series of indictments of US foreign policy in Asia.

Granta 18 – The Snap Revolution by James Fenton is the full-length version of the journalist-poet's entrance into Philippine politics as he rushed to Manila to cover Marcos' 'snap election' – a call that led to the People Power movement, or EDSA (for Epifanio de los Santos) Revolution, of 1986.

Looking at life after the US military shipped out in the early 1990s, *Looted – The Philippines after the Bases* by journalist Donald Kirk gives another rendition of the familiar refrain, 'the more things change...'.

Brilliantly researched, *Power from the Forest – The Politics of Logging* by Marites Dañguilan-Vitug tells of timber plundered in the fragile archipelago.

General

Ghosts of Manila by James Hamilton-Paterson is a chilling yet entertaining 'docufiction' of life, death and the corrupt chains binding Filipinos in the city's slums. The ubiquitous author also wrote *Playing with Water – Passion and Solitude on a Philippine Island* while hanging out on an islet near Marinduque.

William Boyd's *The Blue Afternoon* skillfully weaves US-Philippine military relations into a love story/detective drama partly set in Manila in 1902.

Philippine Wildlife by José Ma & Lorenzo P Tan isn't a field guide, but it does provide an overview of the archipelago's nonhuman inhabitants, including those most endangered by humans.

Burning Heart – A Portrait of the Philippines, by Jessica Hagedorn and photographs by Marissa Roth, is a coffee-table book with a conscience. A week spent in the country by 35 international photojournalists is recorded in *Philippines – A Journey Through the Archipelago* by James Hamilton-Paterson *et al*.

FILMS

If you're a fan of seriously B-grade action or horror flicks, you've probably seen a film set in the Philippines. The islands have been the unheralded setting for about 200 internationally released films, nearly all of them belonging to the 'more blood for less' genre. The award for best (or worst) title goes to *Women of Transplant Island* (1973).

Hollywood has also been busy recreating the Vietnam War on Philippine soil. Aside from *Hamburger Hill* (1987) and *Born on the Fourth of July* (1989), the Philippines has famously been host to Francis Ford Coppola's *Apocalypse Now*. The film was shot in Baler and Pagsanjan on Luzon in 1976 and 1977. Marcos was happy to rent his aircraft for the film, though production was sometimes delayed when the dictator borrowed them back to do a bit of shooting of his own – at Muslim rebels then fighting the government. Surfers might note that there were no waves the day the renowned surf scene was filmed; instead, the crew resorted to detonating explosives in the water. Less than a decade later, *Platoon*, Oliver Stone's passion play on the Vietnam War (the US military called the script 'totally unrealistic' and refused to assist), was filmed in the Philippines while Marcos was being overthrown.

Don't blame Manila, but scenes from *An Officer and a Gentleman* (1982) were shot there. In the same year, the capital became 1965-era Jakarta in Peter Weir's *The Year of Living Dangerously*. The Philippines also did its best to act like Thailand for director Jonathan Kaplan in his teenage fantasy flick, *Brokedown Palace* (1999).

NEWSPAPERS & MAGAZINES

Anyone who misses the hoary old days of a truly free press will feel right at home in the Philippines. After 20 years of severe censorship under Marcos, the EDSA Revolution ushered in a new era for the press, as independent national and local newspapers and magazines mushroomed overnight.

A journalistic free-for-all of generally very high standards has resulted, with English-language dailies running the gamut from the sycophantic *Manila Bulletin* to the highly critical *Manila Times* (which has recently been subject to considerable pressure by a nostalgic Estrada administration). The *Philippine Daily Inquirer* is a well-written broadsheet, while the *Philippine Star* is a cheerful tabloid-style paper. Along with Cebu's *Sun Star Daily*, Dumaguete's *Visayan Daily Star* and several others, these newspapers all have good Web sites. So far, the radical *Philippine National Enquirer* is not on the Net, but look for it in Manila. Well-stocked newsstands can be found in towns and cities all over the country. The papers are peppered with Tagalog, which can be a great way to pick up some of the local lingo.

The *International Herald-Tribune*, a compendium of articles from major world newspapers (plus the *New York Times* crossword puzzle), can be found at newsstands in Manila's major hotels.

International news and bathroom reading is supplied by *Time*, *Newsweek*, *Asiaweek* and the *Far Eastern Economic Review*, available in the big hotels and in bookshops in larger cities.

For scuba divers, *The Philippine Diver* is a glossy magazine that is more environmentally conscious than most. It prints three issues a year, and has a Web site at www.diver.com.ph that's worth checking out. A local production, the popular gay-oriented *Coverboy Magazine* is widely available in the big city.

RADIO & TV

As with newspapers, there's a lot on offer over the airwaves – Manila alone has nearly 60 radio stations. If your mornings aren't complete without a chatty radio drive show, try RX 93.1 FM Monster Radio, a Manila-based music/variety station. Jazz 83.3 FM and WRR 101.9 FM are also popular. Voice of America and Deutsche Welle are available on shortwave, as is BBC World Service Singapore (3915.0kHz, 75m band).

Some 22 commercial TV stations vie for your attention span, seven of them originating in Manila. Manila stations offer both English-language and Tagalog programs, plus some US camera fodder such as *Saved by the Bell*. Satellite TV also beams CNN, ESPN, BBC World and other cable networks into many homes and hotels.

VIDEO SYSTEMS

If you want to record or buy video tapes to play back home, you won't get a picture unless the 'image registration' system is the same. Three systems are used in the world and each one is completely incompatible with the others – though many video machines can play more than one. The three formats are NTSC, used in North America and Japan; PAL, used in Australia, New Zealand and most of Europe; and SECAM, used in metropolitan France. The Philippines uses the PAL format, though NTSC videos are also available.

PHOTOGRAPHY & VIDEO
Film & Equipment

It's a good idea to bring your own slide film, as it's probably 'fresher' than the film available in the Philippines. Print film spends less time on shop shelves so it should be more reliable, but it's better to stock up where you can. Kodak Ektachrome 100 ASA costs about P175, 200 ASA is P220 and 400 ASA costs around P250.

Fast and reliable film processing is available in Manila at P30 for one-hour processing, plus P3 per print for a 36-exposure film; cheaper processing takes longer.

Technical Tips

Video cameras have very sensitive microphones, which can be a problem if there is a lot of ambient noise – filming by the side

of a busy road might seem OK at the time, but back home you'll find a cacophony of traffic noise.

Try to film in long takes, and don't move the camera around too much. If your camera has a stabiliser, you can use it to obtain good footage while travelling on bumpy roads. Make sure you keep the batteries charged and have the appropriate charger, plugs and transformer (see Electricity in this section). You should be able to get video cartridges easily in big towns, but make sure you buy the correct format (see the earlier Video Systems entry). It may be worth buying at least a few cartridges duty-free to start off your trip.

Photographing People

Some tribespeople in particular may be superstitious about your camera or suspicious of your motives. Always respect the wishes of the locals. Ask permission to photograph, and don't insist or snap a picture anyway if permission is denied.

Do *not* take pictures of soldiers and military installations, unless you enjoy explaining this sort of thing to angry authorities.

Airport Security

X-ray equipment is supposed to be safe for film, but it's not worth putting that claim to the test with your precious rolls. You can always ask to have your film inspected separately if you're passing through numerous airports, especially the smaller ones.

TIME

The Philippines is eight hours ahead of Greenwich Mean Time (GMT), also known as Universal Time Coordinated (UTC). Thus, when it's noon in Manila, it's 8 pm the previous day in Los Angeles and 11 pm the previous evening in New York; 4 am the same day in London; 1 pm the same day in Tokyo; and 2 pm the same day in Sydney.

Official time in Davao, Mindanao's capital, is curiously about 10 minutes ahead of the rest of the country. No-one's quite sure how or why it happened, but no-one seems too troubled about it.

ELECTRICITY
Voltages & Cycles
In most places in the Philippines, electricity is 220V, 50Hz to 60Hz; exceptions are in Baguio (wired once-upon-a-time by US occupation forces), where voltage is 110V; and in some top-end hotels, which have both 220V and 110V outlets.

Brownouts are common, as are low-power generators in smaller towns – and no electricity at all in others. Power cuts are generally only a minor inconvenience to travellers (unless you're big on sending long emails) – besides, the absence of electricity in far-flung corners offers a rare respite from certain modern conveniences such as videoke.

Plugs & Sockets
Plugs are the US-style flat two-pin variety, so you may need to bring a plug adaptor with you.

WEIGHTS & MEASURES
The metric system is used in the Philippines. Weights are normally quoted in kilograms (eg, in markets) and distances in kilometres, though feet and yards are still often used to describe short lengths.

LAUNDRY
Coin-operated laundrettes are nonexistent, and only a few public laundries have modern machinery. Your hotel or guesthouse can arrange laundry service, and you'll get clean undies back in one or two days. It costs P15 to P20 to have a shirt or blouse washed and ironed, or from P20 to P50 per kg.

In the big cities, you can contact one of the fast and efficient laundry services directly; they'll pick up and deliver to hotels for about P30 per kg of washing (usually with a 2kg minimum).

TOILETS
A toilet is referred to as a 'comfort room' (or CR). In Tagalog, men are *lalake* and women are *babae*. There are no public toilets, and Filipino men will often avail themselves of the nearest outdoor wall – hence the signs scrawled in many places: 'Bawal Ang Umihi Dito!' ('No Pissing Here!'). If you need a toilet, try the nearest fast-food restaurant.

When camping or hiking in the great outdoors, where there is a toilet, you should use it. Where there is none, bury your waste (at least 100m from any watercourse) and cover it with soil and a rock. If anyone lives nearby, ask if they have any concerns about your chosen toilet site.

HEALTH
Travel health depends on your predeparture preparations, your daily health care while travelling and how you handle any medical problem that does develop. While the potential dangers can seem quite frightening, in reality few travellers experience anything more than an upset stomach.

The following information covers the basics of travel health in the Philippines; for more details, Lonely Planet's *Healthy Travel Asia & India* by Dr Isabelle Young is a thorough, user-friendly guide full of valuable tips. An excellent online resource is PhilDoctors at www.phildoctors.com.

Predeparture planning
Immunisations Plan ahead for getting your vaccinations: some of them require more than one injection, while some vaccinations should not be given together. Note

---

Everyday Health

Normal body temperature is up to 37°C (98.6°F); more than 2°C (4°F) higher indicates a high fever. The normal adult pulse rate is 60 to 100 per minute (children 80 to 100, babies 100 to 140). As a general rule the pulse increases about 20 beats per minute for each 1°C (2°F) rise in fever.

Respiration (breathing) rate is also an indicator of illness. Count the number of breaths per minute: Between 12 and 20 is normal for adults and older children (up to 30 for younger children, 40 for babies). People with a high fever or serious respiratory illness breathe more quickly than normal. More than 40 shallow breaths a minute may indicate pneumonia.

that some vaccinations should not be given during pregnancy or to people with allergies – discuss this with your doctor.

It is recommended that you seek medical advice at least six weeks before travel. Be aware that there is often a greater risk of disease with children and during pregnancy.

Discuss your requirements with your doctor, but vaccinations you should consider for this trip include the following (disease descriptions are given later in this section). Carry proof of your vaccinations, especially for yellow fever.

Cholera The current injectable vaccine against cholera is poorly protective and has many side effects, so it is not generally recommended for travellers.

Diphtheria & Tetanus Vaccinations for these two diseases are usually combined and are recommended for everyone (diphtheria is common in the Philippines). After an initial course of three injections (usually given in childhood), boosters are necessary every 10 years.

Hepatitis A Hepatitis A vaccine (eg, Avaxim, Havrix 1440 or VAQTA) provides long-term immunity (possibly more than 10 years) after an initial injection and a booster at six to 12 months. Alternatively, an injection of gamma globulin can provide short-term protection against hepatitis A – two to six months, depending on the dose given. It is not a vaccine, but is ready-made antibody collected from blood donations. It is reasonably effective and, unlike the vaccine, it is protective immediately, but because it is a blood product, there are current concerns about its long-term safety. Hepatitis A vaccine is also available in a combined form, Twinrix, with hepatitis B vaccine. Three injections over a six month period are required, the first two providing substantial protection against hepatitis A.

Hepatitis B Travellers who should consider vaccination against hepatitis B include those on a long trip; visiting countries where there are high levels of hepatitis B infection, including the Philippines; where blood transfusions may not be adequately screened; or where sexual contact or needle sharing is a possibility. Vaccination involves three injections, with a booster at 12 months. More rapid courses are available if necessary.

Japanese B Encephalitis Consider vaccination if spending a month or longer in rural areas of the Philippines, making repeated trips to a risk area or visiting during an epidemic. It involves three injections over 30 days.

Medical Kit Check List

Following is a list of items you should consider including in your medical kit – consult your pharmacist for brands available in your country.

- ☐ **Aspirin or paracetamol (acetaminophen in the USA)** – for pain or fever
- ☐ **Antihistamine** – for allergies, eg, hay fever; to ease the itch from insect bites or stings; and to prevent motion sickness
- ☐ **Cold and flu tablets, throat lozenges and nasal decongestant**
- ☐ **Multivitamins** – consider for long trips, when dietary vitamin intake may be inadequate
- ☐ **Antibiotics** – consider including these if you're travelling well off the beaten track; see your doctor, as they must be prescribed, and carry the prescription with you
- ☐ **Loperamide or diphenoxylate** –'blockers' for diarrhoea
- ☐ **Prochlorperazine or metaclopramide** – for nausea and vomiting
- ☐ **Rehydration mixture** – to prevent dehydration, which may occur, for example, during bouts of diarrhoea; particularly important when travelling with children
- ☐ **Insect repellent, sunscreen, lip balm and eye drops**
- ☐ **Calamine lotion, sting relief spray or aloe vera** – to ease irritation from sunburn and insect bites or stings
- ☐ **Antifungal cream or powder** – for fungal skin infections and thrush
- ☐ **Antiseptic (such as povidone-iodine)** – for cuts and grazes
- ☐ **Bandages, Band-Aids (plasters) and other wound dressings**
- ☐ **Water purification tablets or iodine**
- ☐ **Scissors, tweezers and a thermometer** – note that mercury thermometers are prohibited by airlines
- ☐ **Sterile kit** – in case you need injections in a country with medical hygiene problems; discuss with your doctor

Polio Everyone should keep up to date with this vaccination, which is normally given in childhood. A booster every 10 years maintains immunity. Polio cases are still regularly reported in the Philippines.

Rabies Vaccination should be considered by those who will spend a month or longer in the Philippines, especially if they are cycling, handling animals, caving or travelling to remote areas, and for children (who may not report a bite). Pre-travel rabies vaccination involves having three injections over 21 to 28 days. If someone who has been vaccinated is bitten or scratched by an animal, they will require two booster injections of vaccine; those not vaccinated require more.

Tuberculosis The risk of TB to travellers is usually very low, unless you will be living with or closely associated with local people in high-risk areas. Vaccination against TB (BCG) is recommended for children and young adults living in these areas for three months or more.

Typhoid Vaccination against typhoid should be considered if you are travelling for more than three weeks in the Philippines. Vaccination increases in importance as you travel farther from modern medical facilities. It is now available either as an injection or as capsules to be taken orally.

Yellow Fever This is the only vaccine that is a legal requirement for entry into the Philippines if you are arriving from an infected area (eg, parts of Africa and South America).

Malaria Medication Antimalarial drugs do not prevent you from being infected but kill the malaria parasites during a stage in their development and significantly reduce the risk of becoming very ill or dying. Expert advice on medication should be sought, as there are many factors to consider, including the area to be visited, the risk of exposure to malaria-carrying mosquitoes, the side effects of medication, your medical history and whether you are a child or an adult or pregnant. Travellers to isolated areas may like to carry a treatment dose of medication for use if symptoms occur.

Health Insurance Make sure that you have adequate health insurance. See Travel Insurance under Visas & Documents in this chapter for details.

Other Preparations Make sure you're healthy *before* you start travelling. If you are going on a long trip, make sure your teeth are OK. If you wear glasses, take a spare pair and your prescription.

If you require a particular medication, take an adequate supply, as it may not be available locally. Take part of the packaging showing the generic name rather than the brand, which will make getting replacements easier. It's a good idea to have a legible prescription or letter from your doctor to show that you legally use the medication to avoid any problems.

Basic Rules

Food Vegetables and fruit should be washed with purified water or peeled where possible. Beware of ice cream that is sold in the street or anywhere it might have been melted and refrozen; if there's any doubt (eg, a power cut in the last day or two), steer well clear. Shellfish such as mussels, oysters and clams are a big gamble (steaming does not make shellfish safe for eating). Avoid undercooked meat, particularly in the form of mince.

If a place looks clean and well run and the vendor also looks clean and healthy, the food is probably safe. In general, places packed with travellers or locals will be fine, while empty restaurants are questionable.

Drinks Water in most areas of Philippines' cities should be safe to drink, but if you're unsure, assume it isn't. Commercially made bags of ice should be fine, as are reputable brands of bottled water or soft drinks, although in some places bottles may be refilled with tap water. Only use water from containers with a serrated seal – not tops or corks. Take care with fruit juice, particularly if water may have been added. Milk should be treated with suspicion, as it is often unpasteurised, though boiled milk is fine if it is hygienically kept. Tea or coffee is usually OK, since the water should have been boiled.

Water Purification The simplest way to purify water is to boil it thoroughly (ie, at least 10 minutes), though a vigorous boil should suffice. You could go for a water filter – total filters take out all parasites, bacteria and viruses. They are often expensive, but can be cheaper in the long run than buying bottled water. Alternatively, chlorine tablets will kill many pathogens, but not some parasites like *Giardia* and amoebic cysts. Iodine is an effective water purifier

Nutrition

If your diet is poor or limited in variety, if you're travelling hard and fast and therefore missing meals or if you simply lose your appetite, you can soon start to lose weight and place your health at risk.

Make sure your diet is well balanced. Cooked eggs, tofu, beans, lentils (dhal in India) and nuts are all safe ways to get protein. Fruit you can peel (bananas, oranges or mandarins, for example) is usually safe and a good source of vitamins. Melons can harbour bacteria in their flesh and are best avoided. Try to eat plenty of grains (including rice) and bread. Remember that although food is generally safer if it is cooked well, overcooked food loses much of its nutritional value. If your diet isn't well balanced or if your food intake is insufficient, it's a good idea to take vitamin and iron pills.

In hot climates make sure you drink enough – don't rely on feeling thirsty to indicate when you should drink. Not needing to urinate or voiding small amounts of very dark yellow urine is a danger sign. Always carry a water bottle with you on long trips. Excessive sweating can lead to loss of salt and therefore muscle cramping. Salt tablets are not a good idea as a preventative, but in places where salt is not used much, adding salt to food can help.

and is available in tablet form. Follow the directions carefully and remember that too much iodine can be harmful.

Medical Problems & Treatment

Self-diagnosis and treatment can be risky, so you should always seek medical help. An embassy, consulate or major hotel can usually recommend a local doctor or clinic. Although we do give drug dosages in this section, they are for emergency use only. Correct diagnosis is vital. In this section we have used the generic names for medications – check with a pharmacist for brands available locally.

Note that antibiotics should ideally be administered only under medical supervision. Take only the recommended dose at the prescribed intervals and use the whole course, even if the illness seems to be cured earlier. Stop immediately if there are any serious reactions and don't use the antibiotic at all if you are unsure that you have the correct one. Some people are allergic to commonly prescribed antibiotics such as penicillin; carry this information (eg, on a bracelet) when travelling.

Hospitals & Clinics

International health organisations are cautious by nature (it goes with the territory), and advise travellers to the Philippines to seek medical care for serious problems outside the country where possible. Concerns over blood-supply screening and the avail-

ability of single-use, disposable needles and syringes are frequently cited reasons.

Health care is limited in smaller centres, and generally confined to home remedies in remote areas. State-owned hospitals and private practices are often poorly equipped, so in an emergency, try to reach the nearest town and check in to a private hospital.

The local pharmaceutical racket has been under fire in the country for some time: pharmacies dispense brand-name drugs like candy, and at extortionate prices compared to neighbouring countries. Not only does this produce drug-resistant strains of bugs; it's also a strain on the budget of the average Filipino – to say nothing of the poor. Note also that doctors often demand cash on the spot for services.

The Americans did leave a number of very good hospitals – Manila's private hospitals are excellent, if expensive, and you'll get treated quickly; see Medical Services under Information in the Manila chapter for more details.

Specialised emergency treatment is in short supply outside Manila: ambulances from the capital regularly attend road wrecks three hours away. In fact, it's fair to say that emergency services are a mess, not least because of the long odds of making good time in traffic in the event of an emergency.

Dental treatment is adequate, at least in cities and towns (look for the quaint 'Lady Dentist' signs).

Environmental Hazards

Prickly Heat Prickly heat is an itchy rash caused by excessive perspiration trapped under the skin. It usually strikes people who have just arrived in a hot climate. Keeping cool, bathing often, drying the skin and using a mild talcum or prickly heat powder or resorting to air-conditioning may help.

Heat Exhaustion Dehydration and salt deficiency can cause heat exhaustion. Take time to acclimatise to high temperatures, drink sufficient liquids and do not do anything too physically demanding.

Salt deficiency is characterised by fatigue, lethargy, headaches, giddiness and muscle cramps; salt tablets may help, but adding extra salt to your food is better.

Anhydrotic heat exhaustion (caused by an inability to sweat) is rare and tends to affect people who have been in a hot climate for some time, rather than newcomers.

Heatstroke This serious, occasionally fatal, condition can occur if the body's heat-regulating mechanism breaks down and the body temperature rises to dangerous levels. Long, continuous periods of exposure to high temperatures and insufficient fluids can leave you vulnerable to heatstroke.

The symptoms are feeling unwell, not sweating very much (or at all) and a high body temperature (39°C to 41°C, or 102°F to 106°F). Where sweating has ceased, the skin becomes flushed and red. Severe, throbbing headaches and lack of coordination will also occur, and casualties may be confused or aggressive. Eventually they will become delirious or convulse. Hospitalisation is essential, but in the interim get casualties out of the sun, remove their clothing, cover them with a wet sheet or towel and then fan continually. Give fluids if they are conscious.

Infectious Diseases

Diarrhoea Simple things like a change of water, food or climate can all cause a mild bout of diarrhoea, but a few rushed toilet trips with no other symptoms is not indicative of a major problem.

Dehydration is the main danger with any diarrhoea, particularly in children or the elderly, as dehydration can occur quite quickly. Under all circumstances *fluid replacement* (at least as much as you've lost) is the most important thing to remember. Weak black tea with a little sugar, soda water, or soft drinks allowed to go flat and diluted 50% with clean water are all good. With severe diarrhoea, a rehydrating solution is preferable to replace minerals and salts lost. Commercially available oral rehydration salts (ORS) are very useful; add them to boiled or bottled water. In an emergency you can make up a solution of six teaspoons of sugar and half a teaspoon of salt to 1L of boiled or bottled water. You need to drink at least the same volume of fluid that you are losing in bowel movements and vomiting. Urine is the best guide to the adequacy of replacement – if you have small amounts of concentrated urine, you need to drink more. Keep drinking small amounts often. Stick to a bland diet as you recover.

Gut-paralysing drugs such as loperamide or diphenoxylate can be used for relief from the symptoms, although they don't actually cure the problem. Only use these drugs if you do not have access to toilets, eg, if you *must* travel. Note that these drugs are not recommended for children under 12 years of age.

In certain situations antibiotics may be required: **dysentery** (diarrhoea with blood or mucus), any diarrhoea with fever, profuse watery diarrhoea, persistent diarrhoea not improving after 48 hours and severe diarrhoea. These suggest a more serious cause of diarrhoea, and in these situations gut-paralysing drugs should be avoided.

In these situations, a stool test may be necessary to diagnose the cause of the diarrhoea, so seek medical help urgently. Where this is not possible, the recommended drugs for bacterial diarrhoea (the most likely cause of severe diarrhoea in travellers) are norfloxacin 400mg twice daily for three days or ciprofloxacin 500mg twice daily for five days. These are not recommended for children or pregnant women. The drug of choice for children would be co-trimoxazole with dosage dependent on weight. A five-day course is given. Ampicillin or amoxycillin may be given in pregnancy, but medical care is necessary.

Two other causes of persistent diarrhoea in travellers are giardiasis and amoebic dysentery. **Giardiasis** is caused by a common parasite, *Giardia lamblia*. Symptoms include stomach cramps, nausea, a bloated stomach, watery, foul-smelling diarrhoea and frequent gas. Giardiasis can appear several weeks after you have been exposed to the parasite. The symptoms may disappear for a few days and then return; this can go on for several weeks. **Amoebic dysentery** (caused by the protozoan *Entamoeba histolytica*) is characterised by a gradual onset of low-grade diarrhoea, often with blood and mucus. Cramping abdominal pain and vomiting are less likely than in other types of diarrhoea, and fever may not be present. It will persist until treated, and can recur and cause other health problems.

You should seek medical advice if you think you have giardiasis or amoebic dysentery, but where this is not possible, tinidazole or metronidazole are the recommended drugs. Treatment is a 2g single dose of tinidazole or 250mg of metronidazole three times daily for five to 10 days.

Fungal Infections Fungal infections occur more commonly in hot weather and are usually found on the scalp, between the toes (athlete's foot) or fingers, in the groin and on the body (ringworm). You get ringworm (which is a fungal infection, not a worm) from infected animals or other people. Moisture encourages these infections.

To prevent fungal infections, wear loose, comfortable clothes, avoid artificial fibres, wash frequently and dry yourself carefully. If you do get an infection, wash the infected area at least daily with a disinfectant or medicated soap and water, and rinse and dry well. Apply an antifungal cream or powder like tolnaftate. Try to expose the infected area to air or sunlight as much as possible, and wash all towels and underwear in hot water, change them often and let them dry in the sun.

Hepatitis Hepatitis is a general term for inflammation of the liver. It is a common disease worldwide. Several viruses cause hepatitis and they differ in the way they are transmitted. The symptoms are similar in all forms of the illness, and include fever, chills, headache, fatigue, feelings of weakness and aches and pains, followed by loss of appetite, nausea, vomiting, abdominal pain, dark urine, light-coloured faeces, jaundiced (yellowed) skin and yellowing of the whites of the eyes. People who have had hepatitis should avoid alcohol for some time after the illness, as the liver needs time to recover.

The most common form, **hepatitis A**, is transmitted by contaminated food and drinking water. You should seek medical advice, but there is not much you can do apart from resting, drinking lots of fluids, eating lightly and avoiding fatty foods. Hepatitis E is transmitted in the same way as hepatitis A; it can be particularly serious in pregnant women.

There are almost 300 million chronic carriers of **hepatitis B** in the world. It is spread through contact with infected blood, blood products or body fluids, eg, through sexual contact, unsterilised needles and blood transfusions, or contact with blood via small breaks in the skin. Other risk situations include having a shave, tattoo or body piercing with contaminated equipment. The symptoms of hepatitis B may be more severe than type A and the disease can lead to long-term problems such as chronic liver damage, liver cancer or a long-term carrier state. Hepatitis C and D are spread in the same way as hepatitis B and can also lead to long-term complications.

There are vaccines against hepatitis A and B, but there are currently no vaccines against the other types of hepatitis. Following the basic rules about food and water (hepatitis A and E) and avoiding risk situations (hepatitis B, C and D) are important preventative measures.

HIV & AIDS Infection with the human immunodeficiency virus (HIV) may lead to acquired immune deficiency syndrome (AIDS), which is a fatal disease. Any exposure to blood, blood products or body fluids may put the individual at risk. The disease is often transmitted through sexual contact or dirty needles – vaccinations, acupuncture, tattooing and body piercing can potentially be as dangerous as intravenous drug use. HIV/AIDS can also be spread through infected blood transfusions; outside the major hospitals, blood used for transfusions may not have been adequately screened.

If you do need an injection, ask to see the syringe unwrapped in front of you, or take a needle and syringe pack with you. Fear of HIV infection should never preclude treatment for serious medical conditions.

Intestinal Worms These parasites are most common in rural, tropical areas of the Philippines. Some worms may be ingested on food such as undercooked meat (eg, tapeworms) and some enter through your skin (eg, hookworms). Infestations may not show up for some time and although they are generally not serious, if left untreated some can cause severe health problems later. Consider having a stool test when you return home to check for these and determine the appropriate treatment.

Rabies This fatal viral infection is found throughout the Philippines. Many animals can be infected (such as dogs, cats, bats and monkeys) and it is their saliva which is infectious. Any bite, scratch or even lick from an animal should be cleaned immediately and thoroughly. Scrub with soap and running water, then apply alcohol or iodine solution. Medical help should be sought promptly to receive a course of injections to prevent the onset of symptoms and death.

Schistosomiasis Also known as bilharzia, this disease is spread by tiny freshwater worms and is present in many parts of the Philippines, particularly on the southern islands (deforestation has made Mindanao a notable risk area). Avoid swimming or bathing in fresh water (ocean water and well-chlorinated swimming pools are OK) – even deep water can be infected. If you do get wet, dry off quickly and dry your clothes as well.

A blood test is the most reliable way to diagnose the disease, but it will not show positive until a number of weeks after exposure.

Sexually Transmitted Diseases STDs include gonorrhoea, herpes and syphilis; sores, blisters or rashes around the genitals and discharges or pain when urinating are common symptoms. In some STDs, such as wart virus or chlamydia, symptoms may be less marked or not observed at all, especially in women. Chlamydia infection can cause infertility in men and women before any symptoms have been noticed. Syphilis symptoms eventually disappear completely but the disease continues and can cause severe problems in later years. While abstinence from sexual contact is the only 100% effective prevention, using condoms is also effective. The treatment of gonorrhoea and syphilis is with antibiotics. Each STD requires specific antibiotics. There is no cure for herpes or AIDS.

Typhoid Typhoid fever is a dangerous gut infection caused by contaminated water and food. Medical help must be sought.

In its early stages casualties may feel they have a bad cold or flu on the way, as early symptoms are a headache, body aches and a fever that rises a little each day until it is around 40°C (104°F) or more. The casualty's pulse is often slow relative to the degree of fever present – unlike a normal fever, where the pulse increases. There may also be vomiting, abdominal pain, diarrhoea or constipation.

In the second week, the high fever and slow pulse continue and a few pink spots may appear on the body; trembling, delirium, weakness, weight loss and dehydration may occur. Complications such as pneumonia, perforated bowel or meningitis may occur.

Insect-Borne Diseases
Malaria This serious, potentially fatal disease is spread by mosquito bites. If you're travelling in rural parts of endemic areas (eg, the southern Philippines), it's important to avoid mosquito bites and to take tablets to prevent this disease.

Rural areas of many parts of the country, especially below 600m altitude, are a risk year-round. There's no reported risk in Metro Manila, on the islands of Bohol and Catanduanes or in Cebu province. Chloroquine resistant strains have been found on Basilan, Luzon, Mindanao, Mindoro and Palawan, as well as in the Sulu Archipelago.

Malaria symptoms range from fever, chills and sweating, headache, diarrhoea and abdominal pains to a vague feeling of ill-health. Seek medical help immediately if malaria is suspected. Without treatment malaria can rapidly become more serious and can be fatal.

If medical care is not available, malaria tablets can be used for treatment. You need to use a malaria tablet that is different from the one you were taking when you contracted malaria. The standard treatment dose of mefloquine is two 250mg tablets and a further two six hours later. For Fansidar, it's a single dose of three tablets. If you were previously taking mefloquine and cannot obtain Fansidar, then other alternatives are Malarone (atovaquone-proguanil; four tablets once daily for three days), halofantrine (three doses of two 250mg tablets every six hours) or quinine sulphate (600mg every six hours). There is a greater risk of side effects with these dosages than in normal use if used with mefloquine, so medical advice is preferable. Be aware also that halofantrine is no longer recommended by the World Health Organisation (WHO) as emergency standby treatment because of side effects, and should only be used if no other drugs are available.

Travellers are advised to prevent mosquito bites at all times. The main messages are:

- Wear light-coloured clothing.
- Wear long trousers and long-sleeved shirts.
- Use mosquito repellents containing the compound DEET on exposed areas (prolonged overuse of DEET may be harmful, especially to children, but its use is considered preferable to being bitten by disease-transmitting mosquitoes).
- Avoid perfumes or aftershave.
- Use a mosquito net impregnated with mosquito repellent (permethrin) – it may be worth taking your own.
- Impregnating clothes with permethrin effectively deters mosquitoes and other insects.

Dengue Fever This viral disease is transmitted by mosquitoes and is fast becoming one of the top public health problems in the tropical world. Unlike the malaria mosquito, the *Aedes aegypti* mosquito, which transmits the dengue virus, is most active during the day and is found mainly in urban areas, in and around human dwellings.

Signs and symptoms of dengue fever include a sudden onset of high fever, headache, joint and muscle pains and nausea and vomiting. A rash of small red spots sometimes appears three to four days after the onset of fever. In the early phase of illness, dengue may be mistaken for other infectious diseases, including malaria and influenza. Minor bleeding such as nose bleeds may occur in the course of the illness, but this does not necessarily mean that you have progressed to the potentially fatal dengue haemorrhagic fever (DHF). This is a severe illness, characterised by heavy bleeding, which is thought to be a result of second infection due to a different strain (there are four major strains) and usually affects residents of the country rather than travellers. Recovery even from simple dengue fever may be prolonged, with tiredness lasting for several weeks.

You should seek medical attention as soon as possible if you think you may be infected. A blood test can exclude malaria and indicate the possibility of dengue fever. There is no specific treatment for dengue. Aspirin should be avoided, as it increases the risk of haemorrhaging. There is no vaccine against dengue fever. The best prevention is to avoid mosquito bites at all times by covering up, using insect repellents containing the compound DEET and mosquito nets – see the Malaria section earlier for more advice on avoiding mosquito bites.

Cuts, Bites & Stings

Bedbugs & Lice Bedbugs live in various places, but particularly in dirty mattresses and bedding, evidenced by spots of blood on bedclothes or on the wall. Bedbugs leave itchy bites in neat rows. Calamine lotion or a sting relief spray may help.

All lice cause itching and discomfort. They make themselves at home in your hair (head lice), your clothing (body lice) or in your pubic hair (crabs). You catch lice through direct contact with infected people or by sharing combs, clothing and the like. Powder or shampoo treatment will kill the lice, and infected clothing should then be washed in very hot, soapy water and left in the sun to dry.

Bites & Stings In people who are allergic to bee and wasp stings, severe breathing difficulties may occur and require urgent medical care. Calamine lotion or a sting relief spray will give relief, and ice packs will reduce the pain and swelling. Some spiders are capable of uncomfortable bites as well.

Cuts & Scratches Wash well and treat any cut with an antiseptic such as povidone-iodine. Where possible, avoid bandages and Band-Aids, which can keep wounds wet. Coral cuts are notoriously slow to heal and if they are not adequately cleaned, small pieces of coral can become embedded in the wound.

Jellyfish Avoid contact with cone shells, sea snakes or jellyfish – seek local advice. Dousing in vinegar will deactivate any jellyfish stingers that have not 'fired'. Calamine lotion, antihistamines and analgesics may reduce the reaction and relieve the pain.

Leeches In damp rainforest conditions, leeches may become attached to you; do not pull them off – clean and apply pressure if the point of attachment is bleeding. An insect repellent may keep them away.

Snakes Cobras, including the king cobra, exist in the Philippines, but you're extremely unlikely to encounter one.

Less Common Diseases

The following diseases pose a small risk to travellers, and so are only mentioned in passing. Seek medical advice if you think you may have any of these diseases.

Chikungunya Fever Transmitted by mozzies, this viral infection occurs in the Visayas. Sudden pain in one or more joints, fever, headache, nausea and rash are the main symptoms. It is rarely fatal, though stiffness in the joints can last for weeks or months. No vaccine is currently available.

Cholera This is the worst of the watery diarrhoeas, and medical help should be sought. It occurs in many parts of the Philippines, though outbreaks are generally widely reported, so you can avoid such problem areas.

Filariasis This is a mosquito-transmitted parasitic infection that is prevalent in rural areas of the country. Possible symptoms include fever, pain and swelling of the lymph glands; inflammation of lymph drainage areas; swelling of a limb or the scrotum; skin rashes; and blindness. Treatment is available to eliminate the parasites from the body, but some of the damage already caused may not be reversible. Medical advice should be obtained promptly if the infection is suspected.

Japanese B Encephalitis This viral infection of the brain is transmitted by mosquitoes and is found throughout the Philippines. The risk to most travellers is extremely small, as most cases occur in rural areas, where the virus exists in pigs and wading birds. Symptoms include fever, headache and alteration in consciousness. Hospitalisation is needed for correct diagnosis and treatment. There is a high mortality rate among those who have symptoms; of those who survive, many are intellectually disabled.

Tetanus This disease is caused by a germ that lives in soil and in the faeces of horses and other animals. It enters the body via breaks in the skin. The first symptom may be discomfort in swallowing, or stiffening of the jaw and neck; this is followed by painful convulsions of the jaw and whole body. The disease can be fatal. It can be prevented by vaccination.

Tuberculosis TB is a bacterial infection usually transmitted from person to person by coughing but may be transmitted through consumption of unpasteurised milk. Milk that has been boiled is safe to drink, and the souring of milk to make yoghurt or cheese also kills the bacilli. Travellers are usually not at great risk, as close household contact with the infected person is usually required before the disease is passed on. You may need to have a

TB test before you travel, as this can help diagnose the disease later if you become ill.

Typhus Mite-borne typhus occurs in deforested areas of the country (eg, on Mindanao). Typhus starts with fever, chills, headache and muscle pains, followed a few days later by a body rash. There is often a large painful sore at the site of the bite and nearby lymph nodes are swollen and painful. Typhus can be treated under medical supervision.

Seek local advice on areas where ticks pose a danger and always check your skin carefully for ticks after walking in a danger area such as a tropical forest. An insect repellent can help, and walkers in tick-infested areas should consider having their boots and trousers impregnated with benzyl benzoate and dibutylphthalate. If a tick is found attached, press down around the tick's head (and *only* the head) with tweezers, grab the head and gently pull upwards.

Women's Health
Gynaecological Problems Antibiotic use, synthetic underwear, sweating and contraceptive pills can lead to vaginal fungal infections, especially when travelling in hot climates. Fungal infections are characterised by a rash, itch and discharge and can be treated with a vinegar or lemon-juice douche, or with yoghurt. Nystatin, miconazole or clotrimazole pessaries or vaginal cream are the usual treatment. Maintaining good personal hygiene and wearing loose-fitting clothes and cotton underwear may help prevent these infections.

Sexually transmitted diseases are a major cause of vaginal problems. Symptoms include a smelly discharge, painful intercourse and sometimes a burning sensation when urinating. Medical attention should be sought and sex partners must also be treated. For more details, see Sexually Transmitted Diseases earlier. Besides abstinence, the best thing is to practise safer sex using condoms.

Pregnancy It is not advisable to travel to some places while pregnant, as some vaccinations normally used to prevent serious diseases are not advisable during pregnancy (eg, yellow fever). In addition, some diseases are much more serious for the mother (and may increase the risk of a stillborn child) in pregnancy (eg, malaria).

WOMEN TRAVELLERS
As a rule, Filipino men are unfailing in their efforts to charm women, especially foreign women. Whether chauvinist or chivalrous, the approach taken to women travellers will involve a lot of compliments and attempts to get a conversation going. You may occasionally get the impression that you're being treated to a human version of a rooster ritual, but it's all pretty harmless.

Things get more interesting down south, where young men from conservative Muslim communities in particular have yet to come to grips with your very presence. The novel idea of a woman who may in principle have sexual relations with a man before marriage tends to send them into a rather aggressive form of confusion, and you can be subject to unwelcome verbal advances. It is extremely unlikely to go further than this, however, and one solution is to announce that you are in fact 'a widow' (being 'married' isn't a deterrent).

Filipinas will also shower you with questions. To minimise a sense of deja vu each time, it helps to appreciate the outlook of a family/group oriented culture where one's private individuality is not constantly on public display. Be prepared to share some stock answers to rote questions about your home country, marital status, family and so on. More familiar forms of conversation can be found with women professionals, and many interesting women work in the NGO sector.

Remember that you can make the machismo culture work for you, too – when dealing with male officialdom, for example, you'll find that a bit of lipstick works wonders in greasing the wheels.

GAY & LESBIAN TRAVELLERS
Gay Filipinos boast of their *gaydar*, or 'innate ability to spot another gay man no matter how well he hides it', but the sixth sense is seldom needed, as homosexuality is generally out in the open. *Bakla* (gay men) and

binalaki (lesbians) are generally accepted by society at large.

There are well-established gay cruising places or 'beats' in Manila, including Taft Ave and Makati Cinema Square, but you should still be wary of police and hustlers. Remedios Circle in Malate is the main gay area, and lodging in the area is considered gay-friendly. If you're in the Romblon islands in April, stick around for the Miss Gay Looc Festival, a week-long gay men's gala on Tablas.

For brilliant, up-to-date information about how to have a great time being gay, bisexual or lesbian in the Philippines, check out the Filipino Queer Directory Web site at www.tribo.org/bakla/bakla.html.

Kabaklaan is an interesting cyberzine 'for the queer in the Filipino you'. Its Web site is at www.tribo.org/badaf.html.

DISABLED TRAVELLERS

Like most 'third world' countries, the Philippines lacks the convenient infrastructure and services that make getting around easier for the disabled. Very rarely will you find disabled-friendly toilets or wheelchair ramps. However, the lack of provisions for independent travel won't leave you to fend for yourself – Filipinos will always offer assistance, without a fuss or an embarrassed pause.

SENIOR TRAVELLERS

Senior citizens get respect in the family-oriented Philippines and this will be extended to older visitors. The main issue for older travellers is the tropical heat, which is more quickly enervating than the climate you are probably used to – pace yourself and keep up the fluids.

The local tourism industry has yet to catch on to the concept of independent senior travel, so formal benefits are limited; PAL (see Seniors Cards earlier in this chapter) and Asian Spirit offer a 20% discount on domestic flights for persons 60 years of age or older.

TRAVEL WITH CHILDREN

Filipinos are simply crazy about kids, and rather fond of parents too – you and your offspring will be the focus of many conver-

sations, and your children won't lack for playful company.

You should supervise your children when swimming or playing on beaches, and make sure they understand not to touch coral. Bring plenty of sunscreen and light clothes for sun protection. It's important to keep small children well hydrated in a hot climate; Gastrolite helps prevent dehydration and also masks unpleasant tastes in the water. For more children's health information, see the Health section earlier in this chapter.

You will usually be able to buy disposable nappies (diapers), infant formula long-life milk in the main towns, but don't stray too far without buying everything you need or checking the local situation. The vast majority of hotels and resorts accept families with children.

Lonely Planet's *Travel with Children* by Maureen Wheeler has more useful advice for tropical travel with kids.

DANGERS & ANNOYANCES

Most Filipinos are honest folks who'll go out of their way to look after foreigners, and there's usually someone who'll keep an eye on you and your gear on transport and while queuing in the often crowded and chaotic transport offices. Still, it pays to be prudent, and you should watch (if not hold) your bags whenever possible. Beware of pickpockets in crowded areas of Manila or on tightly packed jeepneys and buses.

The Philippines has scams and rip-offs like anywhere else. Scams are a lot like slang – there's a local flavour to many, new ones pop up regularly and the classics stand the test of time. People who claim to have met you before probably haven't – a favourite line is 'I was the immigration officer when you came through'. Watch moneychangers for sleight-of-hand tricks, and stay out of card games for money.

Manila is a big city and you may encounter some hassles at night. Most of the time the attention paid is at worst uncomfortable, but women travellers in particular might feel more secure in mixed company or pairs.

Leaving aside the foreign tourists shuttling around in search of both adults and children, it's hard to ignore the street scene that centres on prostitution. A Philippine red-light zone doesn't exactly cast humanity in its best light, but a lot of the less-refined patrons are foreign guests. While a visit to a girlie bar is one thing, if you're anywhere out on the town you may encounter a few drunken dickheads desperate to buy relief from too much semen on the brain.

Finally, Filipinos have a unique greeting for male (and sometimes female) Westerners: 'Hey Joe!' or 'Hey Kano!' Both are hangovers from American colonial days and are used ad nauseam. Of course, if your name's Joe, you'll feel pretty special. If not, you may start to feel like a clown sent especially from the USA to give the locals a laugh.

LEGAL MATTERS

Unless you're a member of the US military serving under the controversial Visiting Forces Agreement (VFA), you'll have to obey the laws of the Philippines while you're there. This shouldn't prove to be too challenging, but be aware one legal nicety: drugs, including hash, are highly illegal and subject to hefty fines and/or imprisonment.

BUSINESS HOURS

Banks are usually open from 9 am to 3 pm Monday to Friday. Public and private offices typically function from 8 or 9 am to 5 pm, with a lunch break from noon to 1 pm on weekdays; a few private companies also work on Saturday morning. Department stores and supermarkets stay open until 7 pm, and smaller shops usually stay open until around 10 pm.

Museums are generally open from 8 am to noon and 1 to 5 pm on weekdays. Post office hours vary widely across the country, but should usually be open the same hours as museums. Embassies and consulates are open to the public mainly from 9 am to 1 pm Monday to Friday.

PUBLIC HOLIDAYS & SPECIAL EVENTS

Many businesses shut for the entire Easter week and for two weeks (or more) over Christmas and New Year. Expect overseas consulates and many embassies to take some time off during these periods as well.

In addition to the following fixed statutory holidays, National Heroes' Day is celebrated on the last Sunday in August. Maundy Thursday and Good Friday are also public holidays.

New Year's Day	1 January
Araw ng Kagitingan (Bataan Day)	9 April
Labour Day	1 May
Independence Day	12 June
All Saints' Day	1 November
Bonifacio Day	30 November
Christmas Day	25 December
Rizal Day	30 December
New Year's Eve	31 December

Filipinos certainly have a feel for fiestas. Festivals are plentiful, and range from simple village get-togethers to week-long rages – such as Kalibo's Ati-Atihan festival – that rival Rio.

As one would expect in a traditionally agrarian society shepharded by the Catholic church, festival seasons centre on Christmas, the Lunar New Year (January/February), the period of Lent and Easter (March/April), the May harvest and during the rainy season (June to September, though July is strangely quiet). Every town also has a patron saint, and every saint has a feast day, which means there's usually a fiesta on somewhere in the country. Whether Catholic priests converted a local ceremony or indigenous traditions used the new-fangled church calendar for their own purposes, the result is essentially the same: a celebration of communal life and its place in the cosmos.

Easter is doubtless the main religious festival, while the *moro-moro* verse extravaganza and *pasyon*, the week-long recital of Christ's Passion, exemplify the common ground between 'animism' and Christianity. For more details, see the Religion section in the Facts about the Philippines chapter.

Prodigal sons and daughters often return to their villages for festivals – if you're headed to a provincial area during a fiesta, you should arrange transport and accommodation as early as possible (though if you're not fussy, a place to sleep can usually be found). To hang out during the huge Ati-Atihan Festival in Kalibo, you'll want to book a hotel at least a month in advance.

Dates also change for a number of important holidays and festivals, notably Easter, Lunar New Year and events that follow the Islamic calendar.

Dates for Good Friday are 13 April 2001, 29 March 2002 and 18 April 2003. Lunar (or 'Chinese') New Year dates are 24 January 2001 (Year of the Snake), 12 February 2002 (Year of the Horse) and 1 February 2003 (Year of the Ram).

According to the Islamic calendar, the day actually begins at sunset, so holidays technically begin the evening before the date given here in the solar calendar. Dates may also vary a bit from what's written: the Islamic calendar is an approximation – the actual start of Ramadan, for example, is determined by the proper sighting of the moon.

Hijra New Year falls on 26 March 2001, 15 March 2002 and 5 March 2003. Hari Raya Hajj (Feast of Sacrifice) is the culmination of the Hajj (the pilgrimage to Mecca); the holiday may last up to four days. Dates are 6 March 2001, 23 February 2002 and 12 February 2003.

Maulod An Nabi is the prophet Mohammed's birthday, and a Muslim day of prayer and Koran readings in mosques. Dates are 4 June 2001, 25 May 2002 and 14 May 2003.

Ramadan dates are 17 November to 15 December 2001, 6 November to 4 December 2002 and 27 October to 24 November 2003. Hari Raya Puasa, the Feast of the Breaking of the Fast, begins on the last evening of Ramadan and may last for three days.

The following is a list of noteworthy festivals and special events around the country. For more details, see the relevant destination entry.

January

Three Kings Festival Celebrated in early January, this festival is a handy way to put off the holiday hangover till the new year; it is the official end of Christmas and is nationally celebrated (especially on the island of Marinduque).

Black Nazarene Procession The Quiapo Church, in Manila's Quiapo district, houses the Black Nazarene, a black wooden cross that is paraded through the streets in a massive procession on 9 January and again during Passion week (the week before Palm Sunday in Easter).

Kabankalan Sinulog Held on the second Sunday of the month in La Carlota on Negros, this is a wild street party in which dancers are daubed in black in honour of the island's Negrito people and a feast is held in honour of Santo Niño ('the child Jesus').

Ati-Atihan Festival Peaking on the third Sunday of the month, this week-long mother of all mardi gras rages from sunrise to sunset and is at its most riotous in Kalibo on Panay. Similar festivals are also held in the neighbouring towns of Batan (late January), Ibajay (late January), Makato (15 January) and Altavas (22 January). Cadiz on Negros celebrates its Ati-Atihan Festival in honour of patron saint Santo Niño (residents believe the holy infant protected the settlement from pirate attack) on the weekend nearest 26 January.

Vigan Town Fiesta This is held in the third week of January to commemorate the town's patron saint, St Paul the Apostle, with a parade and musical performances.

Dinagyang Festival Held in the fourth week of January in Iloilo City on Panay, this mardi gras-style festival celebrates Santo Niño with outrageous costumes and dances.

February

Nuestra Señora de la Candelaria On 2 February in Jaro, near Iloilo City on Panay, is the Feast of Our Lady of Candles; it's as much a good old-fashioned street party as it is a religious ritual.

Bamboo Organ Festival In the second week of February, organists from around the world gather in Las Piñas village, near Manila.

Balloon Festival This is a big event at Clark Special Economic Zone near Manila, with lots of colourful hot-air balloons and a race over Mt Pinatubo.

Guimaras International Mountain Bike Festival Guimaras Island hosts a three-day event centred around a 45km rough-road circuit.

Tawo-Tawo Festival The town of Bayawan on Negros celebrates its rice-relations with this Scarecrow Festival, which fills the streets with fantastic, fully choreographed street dances and parades.

Paraw Regatta On the third Sunday of the month is an exciting race from Iloilo City on Panay over to Guimaras Island by traditional sailing outriggers called *paraw*. Dating back to the 16th century, the race is a high-speed version of the trip supposedly taken by

Panay's ancient Malay settlers on their journey to the island from Borneo.

Kalilangan Festival This annual cultural festival runs from 22 to 27 February in General Santos on Mindanao.

March

Sinagayan Festival In mid- to late March, Sagay City on Mindanao holds this festival in honour of St Joseph.

April

Lenten Festival of Herbal Preparation During Lent in San Antonio on Siquijor, traditional healers strut their stuff to big crowds. The associated Tang-Alap ritual is a gloriously fun-loving gathering of herbs and roots used in a pagan form of holy communion and dawn prayers.

Crucifixion Re-Enactments Every Easter, morbid fascination drives the flocks to San Fernando (Pampanga) on Luzon to see fanatical Christians offering themselves up for crucifixion. At noon on Good Friday, a number of volunteers are physically nailed to wooden crosses in the barangay of San Pedro Cutud and whipped till they bleed by gangs of flagellants. A more sober affair is Ang Pagtaltal Sa Guimaras in Jordan on Guimaras; this usually features an amateur 'Christ' roped rather than nailed to his cross (and he's often helped up there with a few stiff drinks).

Moriones Festival During Easter's Holy Week, the country's most popular passion plays and processions take place on Marinduque.

Lami-Lamihan Festival In mid-April on Basilan Island, Yakan weavers hold the biggest of their elaborate festivals; this one is a mass of colourful parades, dances and horse races, and is held in the township of Lamitan.

Kamarikutan Pagdiwata Arts Festival First held in April 1999 in Puerto Princesa on Palawan, this festival is all set to become a regular event on the nation's cultural calendar. It features the work of traditional and contemporary Filipino artists through exhibits, performances and workshops.

Panaad Festival Held from April to May in Bacolod on Negros, this was originally a street festival, but now includes permanent displays of crafts, art and architecture from the various towns and cities in the area. In April you can also join in about a dozen individual minifiestas all going off at once in Bacolod.

Miss Gay Looc Festival Held in late April on Tablas in the Romblon islands, this week-long gay men's gala is sheer fun.

May

Pasalamat Festival On 1 May La Carlota on Negros holds a fun-filled, three-day thanksgiving ritual to honour the year's harvest and hard labour. A mardi gras atmosphere and homegrown drumbeats build up to a closing ceremony with dazzling native costumes and huge parade floats.

Viva Vigan In the first week of May, Vigan celebrates its heritage with, among other events, a *calesa* (horse-drawn carriage) festival, *zarzuelas* (operettas) and *abel* (weaving) exhibits.

Carabao Races In early May, Pavia, just outside of Iloilo City on Panay, is a good place to watch the water buffalo races.

Pahiyas On 15 May in Lucban, below Mt Banahaw on Luzon, is this annual harvest festival and feast of San Isidro Labrador, featuring giant papier maché effigies marched through the streets.

Pista'y Dayat On 1 May the coastal towns of the Lingayen Gulf on Luzon celebrate the area's foremost fiesta with water-borne parades.

Balibong Kingking Festival This fiesta is held from late May to June in the town of Loboc on Bohol.

Manggahan Sa Guimaras In late May, Guimaras Island's Mango Festival is held in San Miguel.

June

Araw ng Kutabato Festival In mid-June, the city of Cotabato on Mindanao suddenly becomes interesting, producing mammoth dance parades.

Pintados Held on 29 June, this 'painted festival' in Tacloban on Leyte celebrates the traditional tattooing practiced before the Spanish arrived (though nowadays water-based paints are used for the festival's body decoration).

August

Kadayawan sa Dabaw Festival During the second week of August, Davao on Mindanao showcases its Muslim, Chinese and tribal influences with costumed street parades, dances and performances, along with fantastic displays of fruit and flowers.

Lubi-Lubi Festival On 15 August, Calubian on Leyte celebrates the town's namesake, the coconut.

Bugoyan Festival Once held on 19 August in Abuyog on Leyte's south coast, there are plans to revive this 'bee festival', in which performers and dancers wear fabulous bee costumes.

September

Tuna Festival From 1 to 5 September, General Santos on Mindanao celebrates the king of all tinned creatures. Among the highlights is the competition for best-dressed tuna; there's also a parade of fishing floats and a sashimi night.

Kaamulan Festival For three days early in the month, Malaybalay, near Cagayan de Oro on

Mindanao, is the setting for this celebration of unity between the tribal people living in the area; activities include dance, song, storytelling, local food, and wine and ritual enactments.

Peñafrancia Festival Every third week of September thousands of devotees make a pilgrimage to Naga in south-eastern Luzon for the celebration of the Virgin of Peñafrancia, the Bicol region's patron saint.

October

Fiesta de Nuestra Senora Virgen del Pilar Held from 10 to 12 October, this is Zamboanga city's main festival. It's a Christian occasion, but also a great opportunity for street parties, parades, dances, markets and food fairs; there's also a big regatta featuring brightly coloured traditional sail boats.

Mt Bongao Festival In the second week of October, this sacred mountain in the Tawi-Tawi group is the site of a festival celebrated by Muslims and Christians alike.

MassKara Festival On the weekend nearest 19 October, Bacolod on Negros goes joyfully crazy with the 'many faces festival', which sees participants wearing elaborate, smiley face masks and dancing in the streets.

Lanzones Festival Around the third week of October, the island of Camiguin celebrates its most famous fruit.

November

Pintaflores Festival Held on 5 November in San Carlos on Negros is a famously frenetic street festival that harks back to the days when Filipinos would welcome foreign visitors by dancing en masse.

Lem-Lunay Festival In the second week of November at Lake Sebu on Mindanao is this celebration of T'boli culture, which culminates in horse-fights – the sport of royalty in local culture – when two stallions fight over a mare in heat.

Cañao Among the many celebrations of rice-planting season in the Central Cordilleras is *cañao*, a time of feasting, drinking and animal sacrifices.

December

Christmas Lantern Festival On the closest Saturday to Christmas, a number of truly gigantic Christmas lanterns are paraded through San Fernando (Pampanga) on Luzon; the lanterns remain on display till January.

Shariff Kabungsuan Festival This event in Cotabato city on Mindanao commemorates the arrival of Islam in the region and involves river parades of decorated boats.

ACTIVITIES
Diving & Snorkelling

The Philippines is widely touted as one the best diving destinations in Asia, though continuing fish feeding, pollution and dynamite-fishing tarnish the claim. Still, plenty of places invite you to put on your best rubber suit, throw on a tank and fall into the warm embrace of the Pacific. Some excellent reef-based dive sites can be found (mostly shallow coral-gardens with a lesser number of deeper coral walls, some with strong currents), as well as some of the best wreck diving in the world (mainly courtesy of the American-Japanese war). Due to extensive fishing, there is less of the big stuff (sharks, rays and turtles) in the waters off the Philippines than you might find in Australia, the Americas or the Red Sea, but there is still plenty of life around.

In general, you'll pay around US$60 for a day boat-trip with two dives and about P1000 for a complete set of scuba gear. Some resorts charge extra for boats (P500 to P1000); others charge an extra P500 for a dive master to accompany you. You can also do single dives for around US$20 to US$45, depending on the location, but you'll often pay as much for a few hours' use of a boat as you would for a whole day.

In almost all resorts, the boats won't go out for less than two people, or will charge hefty premiums for single divers, so you should try to get a group together if you can. This is because the resorts hire their bancas from fishermen who charge them elevated rates, knowing the resorts will make the money back off tourists. In the end, though, the cost is not much more expensive than anywhere else in the world.

Many resorts offer good-value dive and accommodation packages, which are probably the best way to dive in the Philippines; packages often include transport between the resort from the nearest major town (eg, Manila for resorts in Anilao). For an overnight stay with all meals and two dives, expect to pay from P3000 upwards. These packages can usually be booked in travel agents and dive shops in Manila and other major tourist cities.

Renting snorkelling and dive gear locally is often possible, but it's wise to check around if you're unsure of the dive outfit's quality and qualifications. If you want to buy scuba gear, see the Shopping section in the Manila chapter for Scuba World and Whitetip Divers, both in Ermita. These are reputable places to book and offer unbiased advice on good dive destinations.

Dive seasons vary across the islands, though many sites are accessible year-round. The dry season from November to the end of May generally brings the best and most reliable weather conditions for diving. *Bagyos* (typhoons) mainly target Luzon and the northern Visayas; they can occur at any time, though they are most common from April to November.

If you're hauling diving gear on planes, see the Baggage Allowance entry in the Getting Around chapter for details of weight limits and exemptions.

There is a decompression chamber in Subic Bay, and at least one other on Mindanao. Take very seriously expert advice on avoiding 'the bends'; considering the state of Philippine emergency services, there probably aren't many worse places to get decompression sickness.

The following are underwater highlights around the islands. Note that some dive sites are known by more than one name; if you're asking around, the name of the island's main dive resort or the nearest *barrio* (Spanish for district or neighbourhood) for access is often used to refer to the dive area.

Luzon & Around The main dive locations on Luzon are Anilao (at least 36 dive sites on coral gardens and walls), La Union/Bolinao (eight reef areas with a few huge drop-offs), Matabungkay and Nasugbu (similar to Anilao), and Subic Bay (wreck dives). Most of the reef dives off Luzon are relatively shallow coral gardens, suitable for almost all levels of diver. The region around Anilao and the islands of Sombrero and Maricaban has dozens of these sites, but gets rather crowded.

For the experienced diver, there are also some excellent deep-water dive sites in the area with strong currents and pelagics like

tuna, jacks, barracuda, mackerel, manta rays and even rare *butanding* (whale sharks). Matabungkay and Nasugbu are similar. La Union is an up-and-coming dive area with lots of dives suitable for novices and a few deeper sites with pelagics, plus good beaches. There are excellent wreck dives in Subic Bay, though it's not a great place to stay.

Other options include the Hundred Islands National Park, although much of the coral reef has been destroyed by dynamite and cyanide fishing, and further damaged by El Niño and bagyos. Locals claim the small island of Ivahos, west of Sabtang, has the best beaches in the area and excellent snorkelling.

Snorkelling with butanding *(Rhincodon typus)* has caught on in a big way (see the 'Sea Changes' boxed text). From February to May, large numbers of these huge, harmless plankton-feeders gather in the waters surrounding the village of Donsol near Sorsogon in South-East Luzon.

Gaspar Island off Marinduque is a marine reserve, with good snorkelling just off the northern beach. An old Chinese shipwreck lies offshore.

Mindoro Puerto Galera is an excellent snorkelling and year-round diving centre that has fallen behind nearby Sabang in the race to consume tourist dollars. Sabang itself is geared towards divers (dive-speak is the *lingua franca* of nearly every bar), with most hotels offering dive trips of varying standards and prices.

North Pandan Island is a paradise of prime dive spots. Its Eden is the Apo Reef Marine Nature Park (not to be confused with another Apo Island marine park off the south coast of Negros). There are also good dive sites off Ambulong and Apo islands.

Cebu Moalboal is considered *the* place on Cebu for diving, though experienced divers also rave about Olango Island. Mactan and Olango islands belong to one of the largest coral outcrops in the Philippines, but dynamite-wielding fisherfolk and the coral-munching crown of thorns starfish have been busy here. Dive companies from

Mactan make regular dive trips as far south as Cabilao Island, off nearby Bohol.

Around Capitancillo Island near Sogod, dynamite fishing has also shortened the life expectancy of marine life – and of the pricey dive tours sold by the famous Alegre Beach Resort. Off Malapascua there's excellent snorkelling and diving; the island's dive shop also has trips further afield, including to Manoc Manoc, where a well-preserved wreck lies.

Moalboal Island's Panagsama Beach is another good diving and snorkelling spot, and most of the resorts there rent gear. Tiny Pescador Island off Moalboal offers some of Cebu's most spectacular diving, with usually excellent visibility and depths of around 50m. The waters around this limestone outcrop are usually teeming with fish – and divers. Nearby Badian Island also has some good snorkelling and diving.

Bohol Bohol is blessed with numerous small offshore islands, many of which make wonderful dive destinations. At the beach near Bolod on Panglao Island, the Bohol Beach Club offers good snorkelling right out the front. Apart from trips to nearby marine meccas like Balicasag and Pamilacan islands, just south of Alona Beach, divers also use Panglao as a base for Cabilao Island to the north. Tiny Pamilacan Island, to the southeast of Panglao, is highly rated by divers, though hunting has reduced the chances of spotting once-common whales there.

Any season is diving season Bohol, though there can be some heavy rains between July and September.

Negros Diving is a year-round activity on Negros. The Sagay Marine Reserve protects one of the only areas in Negros still teeming with marine life, and the snorkelling is rewarding at Carbin Reef. Environmentally friendly Bais City, north of Dumaguete, is also popular for snorkelling, and has many other natural highs. The Apo Island Marine Reserve & Fish Sanctuary is a vital marine breeding ground and a favourite among divers. Other dive sites around Apo include Mamsa Point, Rock Point and Coconut Point.

Siquijor Diving is popular year-round here, and favourite spots include Paliton Beach (three submarine caves), Salag-Doog Beach (plenty of coral and the odd mako shark), Sandugan and Tongo, with colourful reefs. Larena is your likely port of entry to the island, and there are a couple of very pleasant beach resorts at nearby Sandugan Beach offering snorkelling and diving services. Another possibility is the Tulapos Fish Sanctuary, north of Enrique Villanueva.

Panay & Boracay The Far East Scuba Institute in Iloilo City does PADI open-water diving courses for P8000 and is the place to plan a diving trip to Guimaras and Nogas islands. Nogas has a marine sanctuary and one of Panay's best and most pristine coral reefs.

There's no problem finding ways into the water on Boracay: White Beach is awash with dive shops. The average dive with equipment costs US$25, while snorkelling gear rents for about P200 per day. Diving trips cost around P750.

Samar There's good snorkelling and diving in the Biri-Las Rosas islands, a marine-protected area, but you'll need your own equipment and no commercial accommodation is available. Borongan town is the jumping-off point for nearby Divinubo, a pretty island with good snorkelling. Around Guiuan there's Sulangan Beach for snorkelling; Kantican Island, also known as Pearl Island, has a pearl farm and clear water for snorkelling.

Leyte Southern Leyte may be the next big thing in Philippines diving. Around Panaon Island the waters and marine life in Sogod Bay have rebounded remarkably since dynamite and cyanide fishing ceased in the 1980s.

Limasawa Island offers rich reefs and drop-offs. Wall and cave diving are possible at Lungsodaan in Padre Burgos. At Son-ok in Pintuyan, at the southernmost point of Leyte, a locally managed fish sanctuary has seen the return of butanding, dolphins and whales. Blue Depth Dive Center in Padre Burgos is the only commercial dive operator in the area.

Mindanao Diving on Mindanao is just starting to take off, but there are some excellent sites around Camiguin, off the spur between Butuan and Cagayan de Oro on Mindanao.

Near Siargao is the hummock of Dako, with a beautiful beach and excellent snorkelling and diving. Samal Island offers snorkelling and diving, including wreck diving, though currents are strong there. Nearby Talikud Island is much less developed than its big sister and has some spectacular coral gardens off its west coast; since dynamite and cyanide fishing ceased in the late 1980s, the coral has made a heartening recovery.

Near General Santos there's good snorkelling and diving around Maasim and Glan on the edge of Sarangani Bay. Farther south are Sarangani, Balut and Ulanbani islands, with good dive spots.

Baliangao Wetland Park is quite out of the way, but worth the effort for its many attractions – among them is snorkelling offshore beside the marine protected area. The park is a Community-Based Sustainable Tourism (CBST) initiative.

Palawan Though there are better dives in less beautiful and picturesque locations in the Philippines, El Nido and Coron are the places everyone talks about. El Nido's setting is magnificent and the area has a reputation for being 'the unspoiled Philippines', which is true if you like your 'unspoiled' with air-con and cocktail bars!

Nearby, Coron town on Busuanga Island in the Calamian group is the main jumping-off point for wreck dives on the devastated support fleet for the Japanese invasion of Leyte (about 10 wrecks in all). There are also freshwater dives in Coron Lake, which has two thermoclines and unique flora and fauna.

Apulit Island in Taytay Bay is pricey, but it's a well-known dive destination in these parts. Flower Island is a very rustic place, although you'll find that prices are very modern. There's no electricity and divers will generally have to bring their own equipment.

Windsurfing

Windsurfing is possible all over the Philippines (Lake Taal on Luzon is an up-and-coming spot), but Boracay is the place to be seen and the island's wilder east coast has the best conditions for all levels of surfer. Parasailing is also popular on the island's beaches.

Sailing

The islands offer year-round sailing, with active yacht clubs in Manila and Subic Bay. Lake Taal near Manila is often hyped as 'a sailing mecca', while Puerto Galera on Mindoro has long been known to yachties as an excellent destination.

The Sail Philippines Web site at www .sailphi.org.ph has just about everything you need to know before you go, including events, sailing organisations and suppliers.

Surfing

The Philippines is getting a good reputation among surfers. The main attraction is good breaks at all levels of difficulty, which aren't (yet) crowded with fellow surfers. The main drawback is that waves don't break with the consistency of world-class beaches (such as in Indonesia) and you may be gazing at the horizon for a few weeks before tossing your board into the surf (in delight or disgust). Check with clued-in surfers to find out what you're paddling into – when some of the big waves roll in, reefs and shelfs can make for very challenging, and sometimes dangerous, runs.

On Luzon, popular destinations are San Fernando (La Union) and Bolinao on the Lingayen Gulf, and Daet in the island's south-east. Baler, on the east coast, is where the famous surfing scene in Francis Ford Coppola's *Apocalypse Now* was filmed – from October to February, surfers from around the world stand on the beach munching cigars and yelling 'Charlie don't surf!'. The best waves are actually said to be six hours north of Baler by jeepney.

Off Mindanao's north-east tip, Siargao Island is famed for the 'Cloud Nine' surf break, which many consider the world's best reef break. The Siargao Cup surfing competition is held in late September or early October; surfing can be good from April to October and great on the north-west coast during the

ahiyas, the annual harvest festival, Luzon.

B'laan children, South Catabato, Mindanao.

Mansaka woman, Compostela Valley.

All dressed up for a festival.

Everybody loves a parade...

The Philippines is a fruit-lover's paradise.

Rice for sale, Quiapo.

Green theme fruit display.

A lovely bunch of coconuts.

The markets in Quiapo stock everything from clothes to clocks – and of course, food.

Sea Changes

Despite serious and ongoing damage to marine ecosystems in the islands, the news isn't all bad: locals in a number of places have banded together to create fish nurseries and environmentally conscious organisations, and the national government has chipped in by declaring several marine protected areas. Where destructive fishing practices have been halted, coral and fish are making a remarkable comeback against the odds.

In Donsol, *butanding* (whale shark) watching is a big growth industry. In a scenario similar to Pagsanjan's famous rapids and aggressive touts, *banceros* (*banca*, or pumpboat operators) have been charging up to P5000 for a trip to see the giant fish. The local government and the World Wildlife Fund (WWF) are trying to impose a code of conduct on banceros so that the locals don't drive the fish away as they rush to exploit the opportunities offered by tourism. If it comes off, the money from tourism would at least be reaching a poor community, though the huge fish-barbecues put on to feed the tourists will put pressure on the other aquatic life in the area.

Divers and snorkellers can do their part as well. Following are some 'dos and don'ts' to help preserve the beauty and ecology of local marine life.

- Avoid touching living marine organisms or dragging equipment across the reef, and be conscious of the effects of your fins.
- Maintain proper buoyancy control to avoid colliding with coral.
- Spend as little time within caves as possible, as your air bubbles may be caught within the roof and thereby leave previously submerged organisms high and dry.
- Resist the temptation to feed fish.
- Take home all your rubbish and any litter you may find. Plastics in particular are a serious threat to marine life.

Mic Looby

north-east monsoon, but be prepared to wait for the right waves to roll in.

Caving

Volcanic islands make for great caves, and Luzon in particular is a spelunker's delight, with many interesting hole-in-the-wall sights to explore. The Callao Caves in Peñablanca, near Tuguegarao, are a major tourist draw, and there is also good caving around Sagada.

Bohol's best caving is done near Antequera at the Mag-aso and Inambacan Falls. Near Surigao on Mindanao is Silop Cave, with its 12 entrances that lead to a big central chamber. Spooky Siquijor is honeycombed with caves that have yielded many surprises, including ancient Chinese pottery.

Canoeing, Kayaking & Rafting

Shooting the rapids on the Pagsanjan River is one of Luzon's major tourist attractions. The town of Pagsanjan has become synonymous with the Magdapio Falls, which is the starting point for the famous canoe ride through the rapids.

The mighty Tibiao River on Panay churns up some healthy white water, and kayaking is popular out of the town of Tibiao. White-water rafting is reportedly good near Cagayan de Oro on Mindanao.

Resorts often rent kayaks and canoes for paddling about, and the natural wonders of places like Apulit Island off Palawan can be appreciated on kayaking tours. If you have your own equipment, sea kayaking is excellent off Naga in South-East Luzon.

Hiking & Trekking

Hiking is possible on nearly every island and most famously on Luzon, where a trek through the awesome rice terraces around Banaue and Batad is a highlight of any trip to the country. There are also pleasant hikes around Sagada and the Batanes offer rugged coastal strolls.

National parks offer networks of trails and plenty of variety. The 40km Leyte Mountain Trail is a treat, taking you past rainforest, lakes and waterfalls as it winds over the central spine of the island to one of two volcanic national parks.

Volcano climbing is a popular pastime, and ranges from short and sweet ascents to long and sweaty treks. Be aware of current conditions – not only are many of these volcanoes active, some (such as the tiny Taal Volcano) are notoriously so. The 2465m Mt Kanlaon volcano on Negros has been threatening to erupt in recent years and a 4km no-hiking zone has been imposed around it.

Hiking around the bizarre lahar formations of Mt Pinatubo rates highly on many visitors' lists, though the dormant volcanoes of Mt Banahaw and Mt Makiling offer fewer crowds and some of the best hiking on Luzon. Lake Taal also has several good hiking options. A two-day hike will get you superb views from Mt San Cristobal.

Hibok-Hibok volcano on Camiguin is a steep, full-day climb. Mt Apo (2954m) on Mindanao is the highest mountain in the Philippines; if you're in good shape, a three-day trek up the mountain is a rewarding adventure.

Cycling

The Philippines isn't all beaches and volcanoes, and mountain-biking is taking off as an activity in its own right on a number of islands – see the Bicycle section in the Getting Around chapter for details.

WORK

Nonresident aliens are not permitted to be employed, or theoretically look for work, without a valid work permit, while foreign residents require work registration. Both can be obtained from the Department of Labor & Employment (DOLE; ☎ 02-527 3585), Palacio del Gobernador, General Luna St, Intramuros, Manila.

Volunteer Work

Most NGOs in the Philippines work on ecological projects or programs to aid the poor. Major volunteer organisations active in the Philippines include Australian Volunteers International, United Nations Volunteers, the US Peace Corps and the UK-based Voluntary Service Overseas.

One program you can participate in while travelling is CBST – see the 'Breaking Down Barriers' boxed text in the Mindanao & Sulu chapter.

ACCOMMODATION

While there are plenty of places to stay in the Philippines, quality and cost vary enormously. On a few islands, formal lodging doesn't exist; on others it may be full for a festival or other occasion. In the former case, there's usually some resource for prearranging a place to sleep; in the latter, a polite visit to the mayor or *barangay* (small village or neighbourhood; the basic division of the Filipino social unit) captain will almost certainly find you a spot to rest your head for the night.

Advance booking for rooms is generally no problem, as someone will answer the phone, even in the small hotels and guesthouses, and your reservation will be honoured on arrival (do indicate if you're going to arrive late at night). It's also often worth asking for a discount or bargaining a little, as the price might come down.

Rental accommodation can be obscenely expensive in Manila's foreign ghettos and absurdly cheap in the provinces.

Camping

Formal camp sites are uncommon, though you can camp pretty much anywhere, including the beach – with permission if you are on private land, of course. Camping en route on treks is also common practice. Wherever you set up, be sure to take *all* your rubbish (from orange peels to condoms and sanitary napkins) with you when you move on.

Hostels

Manila's youth hostel is pleasant and good value, and there are a few hostels around the capital that make good bases for day trips or hikes. Other than that, hostels around the country aren't generally your best option.

Hotels

If your budget only stretches to P100 a night for a hotel, your options will be limited in most parts of the country. A reasonably clean single 'broom closet' can be found in many places for about P120, but

Gold-Diggers

It's now more than likely that before Japan's General Yamashita was captured and executed, he organised the burial of masses of gold plundered during WWII. This may have been done when the Philippines seemed a safe, Japanese-held storage spot, or it may have been done in desperate haste as American troops closed in – or perhaps it was a bit of both. In most cases, prisoners of war (POWs) were used to dig the often-complex tunnels and set antitheft booby traps. These POWs, and sometimes even fellow Japanese officers, were executed after burying the treasure – the total value of which has been estimated to be around US$3 billion – or US$100 billion by today's standards.

The vast majority of this loot was almost certainly dug up years later by one of the nastiest treasure hunters of all time – Ferdinand Marcos.

In 1998 a group of middle-aged Philippine soldiers filed a claim in California and Zurich against the Marcos estate for their efforts in unearthing an estimated 60,000 tonnes of gold and gemstones between 1973 and 1985. A joint affidavit, signed by around 100 alleged diggers, accompanied the claim. These men were apparently members of 'Task Force Restoration', formed primarily to undertake 'massive diggings and excavations', while ostensibly fighting communist rebels. This in turn spawned a secret government industry involved in melting down the gold to remove all traces of its origin, all helped by Marcos' martial law.

Whether Marcos carried out his massive gold fossicking in cahoots with other – possibly foreign – parties will probably remain a deeply embedded national secret. What is certain is that even this alleged grand theft by Marcos pales in comparison to the countless lives he stole during his time as leader.

As recently as 1999, 'Yamashita's Gold' claimed four lives in Lumban, near Laguna de Bay, southeast of Manila, when two treasure hunters were buried in a mine shaft they'd built. During the attempt to dig the men out, two emergency workers also died. Lumban, according to the recent revelations, was one of the first places where Marcos's men struck gold. It seems that searching for lost treasure will always remain a popular activity.

Mic Looby

you'll probably want to double that price to find anything liveable.

If you're not on a rock-bottom budget, take a look at mid-range hotels. The most expensive rooms in a budget hotel can be very ordinary and P600 or so won't seem worth it; for the same price, the cheapest rooms in a mid-range place are often far superior.

Hotel maintenance can be rather casual, so check the water and electricity are functioning before agreeing to take a room. Also, check that windows open and fire escapes are accessible – more than a few hotels appear to believe fire laws were made to be broken.

Homestays

There are plenty of homestay arrangements, many of them formal, others ad hoc. You may be invited to stay in someone's home, and be offered the best bed and food in the place, even if it's a financial burden to do so. If you wish to give money in repayment for the kindness, do it subtly.

A CBST initiative has created a unique homestay program with projects around the country – see the 'Breaking Down Barriers' boxed text in the Mindanao & Sulu chapter for more details.

FOOD

Filipino food isn't likely to become the next big thing in designer cuisine, but with strong Spanish, Malay and Chinese influences blended with typical Filipino creativity, a well-prepared dish can be delicious.

'Native' food, as it's often called, is laid out on view and dishes are eaten at the same time – and would often taste better if they were hot. Most Western palates find the everyday food served to be rather heavy, oily and liberally salted or sugared. Ordinary restaurants and foodstalls might be all right for a while, but it's definitely worth a splurge to try well-prepared, authentic Filipino cuisine for a change.

The bad news for lovers of animals and vitamins is that dishes tend to be long on intestines and short on greens. One of the few vegetables to make a regular appearance on plates in the southern Philippines, in particular, is *cassava* (bitter melon), though occasionally you'll find a tasty vegetable mix (pumpkin, potato, beans and eggplant) cooked in *ginataan* (coconut milk). One solution is to buy lots of fruit and peelable vegetables like carrots and cucumber at the many excellent street markets; another option is fish, which is on offer in a variety of dishes, some of them delectable.

Food is likely to be fresher and better prepared at stalls serving only three or four dishes; for a hit of protein, you can ask for a fried egg to be served with your rice. Note that an 'egg omelette' often means an omelette stuffed with pork mince; 'scrambled egg' is usually what Westerners call an omelette.

Snack food also tends to contain meat, though *kinilaw* (spiced and sliced raw fish or cuttlefish in lemon or vinegar) is one exception. Popular snacks include *tapa* (dried beef and onion rings) and *siopao* (a Chinese-style dough bun with pork or chicken filling). Tapa is a simple breakfast food; for dessert (or any time), *halo halo* is the most popular choice – it is shaved ice coloured with fruit, white beans and/or corn, and smothered in evaporated milk. Ice cream from street vendors is probably best avoided.

Self-catering at street markets is cheap – fruit is astonishing in its variety and affordable prices – and supermarkets are well stocked in cities. Eating out shouldn't strain your budget either, and you can save money by patronising *turo turo* (literally, point point) restaurants, where – you guessed it – customers point at selections on display. *Ihaw ihaw* grills are everywhere and serve the Filipino version of Japanese *yakitori* (chicken or pork on a stick). More expensive but still affordable are traditional *kamayan* restaurants, where food is eaten off banana leaves with fingers.

American and local fast-food outfits occupy many city street corners, and offer a fascinating array of 'Western food', from burgers to spaghetti and parfaits.

Local Food

Regional specialities are a real treat, especially if you're in a fast food rut or the allure of *adobo* (stewed chicken or pork, marinated in vinegar and garlic) is wearing thin. The best mix of local cuisine is probably in Luzon's Bicol region. *Cosido*, the Bicolano version of *sinigang* (sour soup), is made with young coconut milk. Other Bicolano specialties include *pinangat* and *laing* (gabi leaves cooked in coconut milk), and *Bicol express* (a hot and spicy pork and shrimp dish).

Main Dishes

Names of dishes often describe the way they are cooked, so it's worth remembering that adobo is stewed in vinegar and garlic, sinigang is sour soup, ginataan means cooked in coconut milk, *kiliwan* is raw seafood, *pangat* includes sauteed tomatoes and *inihaw* is grilled meat or fish. See also the Language chapter for details on food in the Philippines.

DRINKS
Nonalcoholic Drinks

Water in cities is generally safe to drink, but if you're unsure, stick to mineral or distilled bottled water. Water in rural areas is not reliable, as it often comes from dodgy wells or unknown sources.

Tea is served in Chinese restaurants; elsewhere instant coffee rules, except in the top-end hotels, where imported beans are often used.

Buko juice is young coconut juice with floaty flesh. It's usually sold in a presealed cup and is said to be good for staving off dehydration. *Guyanbano* juice is sweet but surprisingly refreshing and is made from the soursop. The popular little lemons known as *calamansi* are used to make a refreshing cordial or added to black tea. Wondrous curative powers are ascribed to them, so take a sip and see what happens.

Alcoholic Drinks

At around P12 to P30 a bottle, San Miguel must be one of the world's cheapest beers – and it's not bad, either. These days, 'San Mig' has stiff competition from the Danish brew Carlsberg and the domestic Manila brand beer; in response, San Miguel Light was launched with heavy fanfare in January 2000.

Palatable vodkas, whiskies and gins are domestically produced; Tanduay Rum is a perfectly drinkable travelling companion (P20 to P30 for a 375mL bottle) – and a handy antiseptic! Rural concoctions include *basi*, a sweet, port-like wine made from sugarcane juice. *Tuba* is a strong home-brewed palm wine extracted from the top of coconut trees; in its roughly distilled form it's called *lambanog*. Local firewater packs quite a punch – your stomach (if not your head) will thank you in the morning if you partake of the *pulutan* (small snacks) always served with alcohol.

ENTERTAINMENT
Bars

Nightlife mostly means bars, which come in two basic types: 'Western' and 'girlie'. These can be further divided into bars run by expats and those owned by locals, but the main issue, aside from the economics and ethics of the sex trade, is cost. An evening's drinking in a Western-style place will cost about P150 to P300; in a girlie bar it will be ten times that price since (for one thing) you're drinking for two. For more details, see the 'Wanted: GRO' boxed text in the Around Manila chapter.

Karaoke

Many Westerners would sooner remove their tonsils with pliers than spend an evening listening to inebriated amateurs pay homage to Celine Dion and Julio Iglesias. But when Filipinos want to unwind, they often do it around the *karaoke* machine. From coin-in-the-slot karaoke machines in Filipino canteens to huge neon KTV palaces, Filipinos are unabashed about belting out a tune, whether alone or in company.

Numerous venues offer cheap beer and song menus of Western and Philippine faves. Although most of these places offer

'ladies' drinks', the girls here are usually not required to do anymore than keep the customers drinking and singing.

Karaoke can be good fun, but it's also serious business in the Philippines. Criticising someone's performance is considered a grave insult, and every year arguments over karaoke are the cause of numerous murders and violent exchanges between Filipino men.

SPECTATOR SPORTS
Basketball

Basketball was first introduced by the American colonial administration as part of an orchestrated program to Americanise the locals (as English was to replace Tagalog as the national language, basketball was to replace cockfighting as the national sport). While neither of these objectives was really achieved, basketball found a place in the national psyche and a home on street courts from Anilao to Zamboanga.

Teams in the Philippine Basketball Association (PBA) are associated with sponsors rather than towns, with inspiring names like the Alaska Milkmen (sponsored by Alaska Milk), the San Miguel Beermen, Pop Cola and the Santa Lucia Realtors. The Metroball Basketball Association (MBA) league is more down to earth, with teams attached to major towns like Manila and Davao. Professional players in both leagues are scouted from the amateur teams at universities and colleges, as well as from overseas.

Very few pro opportunities exist, but basketball is widely perceived as a route out of poverty. In poor areas, teenagers dream of following in the footsteps of Pinoy basketball greats like Robert S Jaworski. The best way to find out about the many local leagues is to ask the kids on the village basketball court, though you'll probably find yourself talked into joining in the game.

Jai Alai

The fast-paced game of jai alai, or *pelota*, arrived from the Basque region of Spain with the explorer Magellan and remains one of the most popular national sports, if only because of the huge opportunities it offers for gambling.

Foul Play

Appealing to the Filipino obsession for gambling, cockfighting is still the No 1 sport in the Philippines. Select birds are raised on special food, treated with special medications and even washed with special shampoos before being taken to the local cockpit for what will almost certainly be the fight of their lives.

Combatants are fitted with a lethal three-inch blade on their ankles and are allowed to peck each other before a fight, in order to generate fighting spirit. With hundreds of peso riding on the outcome, the temptation for fight-rigging is high; just before the birds are released, the blades are wiped with alcohol to ensure they are free from poison.

The resulting squabble is usually brutally short. The winner is whisked away to a team of waiting surgeons, who stitch up any gaping wounds and dose the bird with antibiotics. The loser usually makes his way into the cooking pot. Incredibly, it is possible for a cock to have a fighting career; winning birds can be back in the ring in as little as two weeks!

Cockpits are found on the outskirts of most towns and villages in the Philippines, with Sunday being the most popular day for fights. The onlookers often take a gruesome pleasure in explaining the details of the sport to outsiders.

Jai alai is played by groups of six pelotaris on a *fronton*, which is similar to a squash court with wire mesh along one side. Players use a long crescent-shaped wicker basket *(cesta)* tied to one hand to launch a small hard ball against the far wall, which returns at a staggering speed (after several returns, the ball can be travelling at nearly 250km/h!). There are two pelotaris on court at any one time and if a player fails to catch and return the ball, he cedes a point and is replaced by the next player in line, which leaves the gamblers on the edge of their seats until the final ball.

SHOPPING

Manila's shops and markets see a wide range of authentic items from around the country, though lots of touristy trinkets are available as well. Handicrafts are popular and often high quality, including ornate wooden salad bowls and utensils, and hanging lamps and chandeliers made of shells.

Items made from shells are plentiful, but pose the problem of environmental damage through uncontrolled shell harvesting; trident shells and certain giant clams are in fact protected under the laws governing trade in endangered species. Another popular but problematic souvenir are the Balisong knives (fan or butterfly knives) produced in Taal in Laguna province, as these are illegal in many countries.

Happily, most types of clothing haven't figured out a way to hurt anyone, and you can pick up brand-name clothing at a fraction of its cost in the West. The Barong Tagalog, the traditional embroidered shirt worn by Filipino men, is also a good buy.

Traditional items can also be found in cities such as Cebu, Davao and Zambaonga; or, you could go to the source. Towns on tourist routes produce goods for tourists – for example, Banaue is running out of authentic products (and the wood to make them). The pickings are often better off the beaten track: Tacloban on Leyte is famous for the quality of its abaca products, Iligan on Mindanao has a good range of Muslim-produced handicrafts, while Lake Sebu is the heartland of the T'boli people and their weaving and betel-nut box-making.

Getting There & Away

AIR
Airports & Airlines

Since most people fly to the Philippines, and most flights land in Manila, Ninoy Aquino International Airport (NAIA) in Parañaque is likely to be your first taste of the Philippines. Too bad, but don't despair – most of the country is a lot better run than decrepit old NAIA. Doubtless as an incentive to fly with Philippine Airlines (PAL), the national carrier, its passengers get exclusive use of the cushy new Centennial Terminal II near NAIA.

Cebu City's Mactan-Cebu International Airport (MCIA) is the country's second busiest airport and is much better. Depending on your itinerary, Cebu's airport may also be a more practical entry/exit point. Airlines that fly into Manila usually also have flights to Cebu (eg, Singapore Airlines flies to Manila, while its feeder airline, Silk Air, flies to Cebu). Flights to MCIA can also be a cheaper option.

For more details on NAIA and MCIA, see the Getting There & Away entries in the Manila chapter and under Cebu City in the Visayas chapter.

Other airports with international flights include Davao on Mindanao and Laoag in North Luzon. Subic Bay has an international airport, but at the moment only pricey overseas charters use it. The international airport at the former Clark Airbase was yet to get off the ground at the time of writing.

Not so long ago, PAL ruled the red, blue and gold skies, but those days are over and the carrier has drastically cut back international and domestic services. For more on PAL, see the boxed text 'Up in the Air with PAL' in this section.

PAL currently flies between Manila and the following overseas cities: Hong Kong and Xiamen (China); Fukuoka, Osaka and Tokyo (Japan); Seoul (Korea); Dhahran and Riyadh (Saudi Arabia); Singapore; and Los Angeles and San Francisco (USA). PAL also flies from Cebu City to Osaka and Tokyo.

Up in the Air with PAL

Philippine Airlines (PAL), the 'national flagship' and the country's oldest airline, nearly didn't make it to the millennium party. Billions in debt, the airline was called to account by its overseas creditors in 1998 and escaped bankruptcy only by selling planes, laying off staff, and cancelling many domestic and international services. It took a few weeks to get the airline back in the air; in the meantime, passengers were finding happier alternatives to PAL's often-unreliable service.

A near-death experience like this might have made a lesser man humble, but PAL chairman Lucio Tan was soon making news once more. In October 1999 the Philippine government banned all Taiwanese carriers, which include China Airlines and EVA Air, from using Philippine facilities, rescinding a 1996 bilateral agreement on commercial landing rights. Critics claimed that the move was cynically timed for the holiday travel rush, since passengers between Manila, Hong Kong and Taipei seemed to prefer the more expensive services of the Taiwanese carriers to PAL's.

By this time, PAL was still US$2.2 billion in debt and Tan had already made noises about wanting to see the country's 'open skies' policy rolled back to stop its 'abuse' by foreign airlines. In announcing the ban, however, President Estrada admitted the move was made to shore up PAL's interests.

After much protest by international aviation organisations, the Philippine government lifted the ban a month later, but the Taiwanese side has since been in no hurry to sign a new agreement. One sticking point remains the so-called 'sixth freedom' rights, by which the Taiwanese would be allowed to ferry passengers from Manila to a third country, via Taipei.

By the time you read this, the dust should have settled in this case, but Tan's approach has made future skirmishes with other airlines a possibility.

Russ Kerr

For major airlines' local contact details, see the Getting There & Away section in the Manila chapter.

Buying Tickets

As airlines manoeuvre to fill gaps in services, the PAL financial fiasco of 1998 has probably improved your flying options to the Philippines – but it's also increased the number and complexity of deals on offer. Note that most air tickets are now valid for 35 days (sometimes 30 days) or one year – almost gone are the days of two- or three-month open return tickets. Prices given in this chapter are mainly for 35-day tickets.

With so many outfits trying for a bigger piece of the sky, you're as likely to find a cheap ticket in the so-called high season as in the low season, provided you do your research (or have a good travel agent do it for you) and book in advance. Many cheap tickets are promotional deals, and most are loaded with restrictions – you may be locked into a schedule and flying at odd hours, with no hope of a refund if your plans change. Be sure to check the fine print on tickets carefully.

Outside the Philippines, discount travel agents generally offer much better prices than what's quoted at airline offices. However, many airlines do offer some excellent fares to Net surfers. In addition to advertising in the travel sections of major newspapers and free 'what's on' guides, a lot of travel agents also have Web sites, which can make the Internet a quick and easy way to compare prices. Online ticket sales can work well if you are doing a simple one-way or return trip on specified dates. On the other hand, online super-fast fare generators are no substitute for a travel agent who knows all about special deals, has ways to avoid unwanted layovers and can offer advice on everything from which airline has the best vegetarian food to the best travel insurance to bundle with your ticket.

Book well in advance if you plan to arrive in December: Balikbayans (overseas Filipinos) and Filipino 'contract workers' (mainly toiling from Seoul to Saudi Arabia as maids, nannies and construction workers) flood the islands to visit their families during Christmas and New Year. If you're flying into Cebu, the lead-up to Lunar New Year in late January or early February can also get congested, as the city's sizeable Chinese population prepares to celebrate.

Round-the-World & Other Tickets Out of London, a good RTW deal is the British Airways Global Explorer ticket – UK£1100 gets you six free stops, including Manila, from where you can then fly to Australia and New Zealand. A RTW ticket from Frankfurt with British Airways and Qantas Airways via the Philippines costs around DM2500.

Qantas has a Multi-Asia ticket from Australia (A$1690), which allows a maximum of five stops (a minimum of two) in eastern Asia, including Manila. You have to stop at least once in what the airline considers 'south' and 'north' Asia; Manila is regarded as being in the north.

From the US west coast, a Circle Pacific ticket can be a convenient way to city-hop in Asia. For US$1330, you can fly from San Francisco to any or all of the following: Hong Kong, Guangzhou, Bangkok, Manila and Honolulu; then back to San Francisco.

Courier Flights Courier flights are a great bargain if you're lucky enough to find one. Air freight companies expedite delivery of urgent items by sending them with you as your baggage allowance. You are permitted to bring along a carry-on bag but that's all. In return, you get a drastically discounted ticket, though your schedule is fixed and you'll have difficulty changing it.

Courier flights stopping in Manila are occasionally advertised in the newspapers and on the Internet, or you could contact air freight companies directly. *Travel Unlimited*, PO Box 1058, Allston, MA 02134, USA, is a monthly travel newsletter that publishes many courier flight deals from destinations worldwide. A 12-month subscription to the newsletter costs US$25, or US$35 for residents outside the USA. Another possibility (at least for US residents) is to join the International Association of Air Travel Couriers (IAATC). The membership

Air Travel Glossary

Cancellation Penalties If you have to cancel or change a discounted ticket, there are often heavy penalties involved; insurance can sometimes be taken out against these penalties. Some airlines impose penalties on regular tickets as well, particularly against 'no-show' passengers.

Courier Fares Businesses often need to send urgent documents or freight securely and quickly. Courier companies hire people to accompany the package through customs and, in return, offer a discount ticket which is sometimes a phenomenal bargain. However, you may have to surrender all your baggage allowance and take only carry-on luggage.

Full Fares Airlines traditionally offer 1st class (coded F), business class (coded J) and economy class (coded Y) tickets. These days there are so many promotional and discounted fares available that few passengers pay full economy fare.

Lost Tickets If you lose your airline ticket an airline will usually treat it like a travellers cheque and, after inquiries, issue you with another one. Legally, however, an airline is entitled to treat it like cash and if you lose it then it's gone forever. Take good care of your tickets.

Onward Tickets An entry requirement for many countries is that you have a ticket out of the country. If you're unsure of your next move, the easiest solution is to buy the cheapest onward ticket to a neighbouring country or a ticket from a reliable airline which can later be refunded if you do not use it.

Open-Jaw Tickets These are return tickets where you fly out to one place but return from another. If available, this can save you backtracking to your arrival point.

Overbooking Since every flight has some passengers who fail to show up, airlines often book more passengers than they have seats. Usually excess passengers make up for the no-shows, but occasionally somebody gets 'bumped' onto the next available flight. Guess who it is most likely to be? The passengers who check in late.

Promotional Fares These are officially discounted fares, available from travel agencies or direct from the airline.

Reconfirmation If you don't reconfirm your flight at least 72 hours prior to departure, the airline may delete your name from the passenger list. Ring to find out if your airline requires reconfirmation.

Restrictions Discounted tickets often have various restrictions on them – such as needing to be paid for in advance and incurring a penalty to be altered. Others are restrictions on the minimum and maximum period you must be away.

Round-the-World Tickets RTW tickets give you a limited period (usually a year) in which to circumnavigate the globe. You can go anywhere the carrying airlines go, as long as you don't backtrack. The number of stopovers or total number of separate flights is decided before you set off and they usually cost a bit more than a basic return flight.

Transferred Tickets Airline tickets cannot be transferred from one person to another. Travellers sometimes try to sell the return half of their ticket, but officials can ask you to prove that you are the person named on the ticket. On an international flight tickets are compared with passports.

Travel Periods Ticket prices vary with the time of year. There is a low (off-peak) season and a high (peak) season, and often a low-shoulder season and a high-shoulder season as well. Usually the fare depends on your outward flight – if you depart in the high season and return in the low season, you pay the high-season fare.

fee of US$45 gets members a bimonthly update of air courier offerings, access to a fax-on-demand service with daily updates of last-minute specials and the bimonthly *Shoestring Traveler* newsletter. Contact IAATC on ☎ 561-582 8320 or visit its Web site at www.courier.org.

Travellers with Special Needs

Most international airlines can cater for people with special needs – travellers with disabilities, people with young children and even children travelling alone.

Special dietary preferences can be catered for with advance notice. If you are travelling in a wheelchair, most international airports can provide an escort from check-in desk to plane where needed, and ramps, lifts, toilets and phones are generally available.

Airlines usually carry babies up to two years of age at 10% of the adult fare, although a few may carry them free of charge. Reputable international airlines usually provide nappies (diapers), tissues, talcum powder and all the other paraphernalia needed to keep babies clean, dry and half-happy. For children between the ages of two and 12, the fare on international flights is usually 50% of the regular fare or 67% of a discounted fare.

Departure Tax

Departure tax for all international flights is P550, payable in cash only.

The USA

San Francisco is the 'consolidator' (North American discount ticket agent) capital of the USA, although some good deals can be found in Los Angeles, New York and other big cities.

Council Travel, the USA's largest student travel organisation, has around 60 offices in the country; its head office (☎ 800-226 8624 toll-free) is at 205 E 42nd St, New York, NY 10017. Call it for the office nearest you or visit its Web site at www.ciee.org. STA Travel (☎ 800-777 0112 toll-free) has offices in Boston, Chicago, Miami, New York, Philadelphia, San Francisco and other major cities. Check out its Web site at www.statravel.com.

Prices from the USA to the Philippines vary wildly from month to month as airlines battle for preferred spots on routes. Quoted here are the cheapest fares over the course of the year; note that the lowest one-way fares aren't a whole lot less than the cheapest return flights.

PAL offers Los Angeles–Manila tickets for US$740/920 one way/return. One-way tickets to Cebu (via Manila) from San Francisco or LA go for as little as US$660 on PAL.

From New York, Northwest Airlines flies from New York to Manila (via Detroit and Osaka) for US$900 return.

Canada

Travel CUTS (☎ 800-667 2887 toll-free) is Canada's national student travel agency and has offices in all major cities plus a Web site at www.travelcuts.com.

Flights from Ottawa to Manila (via Toronto and Hong Kong) are C$1700 return on Canadian Airlines or Cathay Pacific. Vancouver-Manila flights (via Seattle and Tokyo) are C$760/1400 one way/return with Alaska Air or Northwest Airlines, while Vancouver-Cebu tickets cost C$820/1330 on Alaska Air.

Australia

Two well-known agents for cheap fares are STA Travel and Flight Centre. STA Travel (☎ 03-9349 2411) has its main office at 224 Faraday St, Carlton, VIC 3053, and offices in all major cities and on many university campuses. Call ☎ 131 776 Australia-wide for the location of your nearest branch or visit its Web site at www.statravel.com.au. Flight Centre (☎ 131 600 Australia-wide) has a central office at 82 Elizabeth St, Sydney, NSW 2000, and there are dozens of offices throughout Australia. Its Web site is at www.flightcentre.com.au.

The high-season fare from Sydney to Manila is A$1339 return on Qantas; the low-season fare is A$1145 with Malaysia Airlines. From Sydney to Cebu, high-season fares are A$879/1405 one way/return on Malaysia Airlines; low-season fares (also on Malaysia Airlines) are A$695/1085. Fares from Melbourne are about the same as those from Sydney; flights out of Adelaide are often slightly cheaper.

Tickets from Brisbane usually cost a few dollars more, though Air Nauru offers some cheap deals on its Sunday and Thursday flights to Manila (via Nauru, Pohnpei and Guam) – on the Sunday flight you'll have to stay overnight in Nauru.

New Zealand

Flight Centre (☎ 09-309 6171) has a large central office in Auckland at National Bank Towers, on the corner of Queen and Darby Sts, and many branches throughout the country.

STA Travel (☎ 09-309 0458) has its main office at 10 High St, Auckland, and has other offices in Auckland as well as in Christchurch, Dunedin, Hamilton, Palmerston North and Wellington; its Web site is at www.statravel.com.au.

Currently there are no direct flights between New Zealand and the Philippines; the usual route is to fly to Sydney and pick up a direct flight from there.

The UK

Airline ticket discounters are known as bucket shops in the UK. Despite the somewhat disreputable-sounding name, there is nothing under-the-counter about them. Discount air travel is big business in London.

Popular travel agencies in the UK include STA Travel (☎ 020-7361 6161), which has an office at 86 Old Brompton Rd, London SW7 3LQ, and other offices in London and Manchester. You can also visit its Web site at www.statravel.co.uk. Usit Campus Travel (☎ 0870-240 1010), 52 Grosvenor Gardens, London SW1 WOAG, has branches throughout the UK and a Web site at www.usitcampus.com. Both agencies sell tickets to all travellers but cater especially to the under-26 age group and student crowd. Note that charter flights can work out cheaper than scheduled flights, especially if you do not qualify for the under-26 and student discounts.

Other recommended bucket shops include Trailfinders (☎ 020-7938 3939), 194 Kensington High St, London W8 7RG;

Bridge the World (☎ 020-7734 7447), 4 Regent Place, London W1R 5FB; and Flightbookers (☎ 020-7757 2000), 177-178 Tottenham Court Rd, London W1P 9LF.

From London to Manila, fares are UK£400 return with Kuwait Airways or UK£470 on Lufthansa Airlines (via Frankfurt). Other Philippine connections are a lot more expensive. On the London-Cebu route, the best student fare is UK£750 return with Singapore Airlines, Cathay Pacific and Malaysia Airlines; Singapore Airlines flies London-Davao for UK£630 return.

Continental Europe

Across Europe many travel agencies have ties with STA Travel, where cheap tickets can be purchased and STA-issued tickets can be altered (usually for a US$25 fee). Outlets in major cities include Voyages Wasteels (☎ 08 03 88 70 04 within France only, fax 01 43 25 46 25), 11 rue Dupuytren, 756006 Paris; STA Travel (☎ 030-311 0950, fax 313 0948), Goethestrasse 73, 10625 Berlin; Passaggi (☎ 06-474 0923, fax 482 7436), Stazione Termini FS, Galleria Di Tesla, Roma; and ISYTS (☎ 01-322 1267, fax 323 3767), 11 Nikis St, Upper Floor, Syntagma Square, Athens.

In the Netherlands, NBBS Reizen is the official student travel agency. You can find it in Amsterdam (☎ 020-624 09 89), Rokin 66, and there are several other agencies around the city. Another recommended travel agent in Amsterdam is Malibu Travel (☎ 020-626 32 30), Prinsengracht 230.

From Amsterdam to Manila, the cheapest return fare costs 1360 guilders with Kuwait Airways, valid for 12 months. This fare is available to everyone except Israeli citizens; it's 2100 guilders for a return ticket (three-month validity) with KLM-Royal Dutch Airlines.

Paris-Manila flights are cheapest with Vietnam Airlines at 5900FF return; a return ticket for the Paris-Cebu route is 6145FF on Cathay Pacific.

From Frankurt to Manila, a one-year return ticket is about DM1000 for students or travellers under 26 years of age; regular return fares hover between DM1100 and

DM1800. Kuwait Airways, Gulf Air and Royal Brunei Airlines currently offer the cheapest tickets.

Asia

Although most Asian countries are now offering fairly competitive air fare deals, Bangkok, Singapore and Hong Kong are still the best places to shop for discount tickets. Hong Kong's travel market can be unpredictable, but some excellent bargains are available if you're lucky.

China Hong Kong has a number of excellent, reliable travel agencies and some not-so-reliable ones. A good way to check on a travel agent is to look it up in the phone book: fly-by-night operators don't usually stay around long enough to get listed. Many travellers use the Hong Kong Student Travel Bureau (☎ 02-2730 3269), 8th floor, Star House, Tsimshatsui. You could also try Phoenix Services (☎ 02-2722 7378), 7th floor, Milton Mansion, 96 Nathan Rd, Tsimshatsui.

From Hong Kong to Manila, a typical PAL promotional fare (a 90-day ticket with loads of restrictions) is HK$2180 return; to Cebu it's HK$2380 return.

Cathay Pacific flies four times a week between Cebu City and Hong Kong. Cathay also has flights between Cebu City and Beijing, as well as between Hong Kong and Laoag.

Indonesia Bouraq Airlines flies twice a week between Manado on Sulawesi and Davao on Mindanao for US$156/262 one way/return.

Japan Flights from Japan to the Philippines are expensive, though discount travel agents in Tokyo do their best. Try No 1 Travel in Shinjuku (☎ 03-3200 8871), Shibuya (☎ 03-3770 1381) and Ikebukuro (☎ 03-3986 4291); STA Travel in Yotsuya (☎ 03-5269 0751), Shibuya (☎ 03-5485 8380) and Ikebukuro (☎ 03-5391 2922); Across Traveller's Bureau in Shibuya (☎ 03-5467 0077); and Just Travel in Takadanobaba (☎ 03-3362 3441).

PAL flies between Cebu City and Tokyo three times a week for ¥43,000/58,000 one way/return. PAL also flies from Manila to Osaka (via Cebu City) four times a week for ¥2,000 return. PAL also has flights between Cebu City and Fukuoka.

Korea In Seoul, Joy Travel Service (☎ 02-776 9871, fax 756 5342), 10th floor, 24-2 Mukyo-dong, Chung-gu (directly behind City Hall), offers good deals and has English-speaking staff. Cheap deals can also be found at Top Travel (☎ 02-739 4630) and the Korean International Student Exchange Society (KISES; ☎ 02-733 9494, fax 732 9568), both on the 5th floor of the YMCA building on Chongno 2-ga.

A Seoul-Manila ticket is around 285,000/570,000 won (US$250/500) one way/return with Korean Air (direct) and Cathay Pacific (via Hong Kong).

Malaysia Malaysia Airlines flies between Cebu City and Kuala Lumpur (via Kota Kinabalu in Sabah) on Thursday and Sunday for about RM1100 (US$280) return. Kuala Lumpur–Manila flights are about the same price.

Malaysia Airlines recently began flights twice a week from Zamboanga to Sandakan on Borneo.

Singapore Try STA Travel (☎ 065-737 7188) at 33A Cuppage Rd, Cuppage Terrace, Singapore. Check out its Web site at www.statravel.com.sg. Chinatown Point shopping centre on New Bridge Rd has a good selection of travel agents. Other agents advertise in the *Straits Times* classified columns.

Singapore Airlines flies daily between Manila and Singapore. Silk Air flies several times a week between Singapore and Cebu City (connecting with Davao on Wednesday and Thursday) for S$710/810 return in the low/high season.

Taiwan A long-running agent is Jenny Su Travel (☎ 02-594 7733, 596 2263), 10th floor, 27 Chungshan N Rd, Section 3, Taipei; Wing On Travel and South-East

Travel have branches all over the island. All three have good reputations and offer reasonable prices.

Direct air links between Taiwan and the Philippines were briefly suspended at the time of writing (see the boxed text 'Up in the Air with PAL' earlier in this chapter). Flights had resumed but carriers and capacities on routes were still uncertain at the time of this book's publication. You can fly between Taipei or Kaoshung and Manila, Cebu City or Laoag.

Thailand Khao San Rd in Bangkok is the budget traveller headquarters. Bangkok has a number of excellent travel agents, but there are also some suspect ones; ask the advice of other travellers before handing over your cash. STA Travel (☎ 02-236 0262), 33 Surawong Rd, is a good and reliable place to start.

Thai Airways International (THAI) does the Bangkok-Manila run for about 13,000B (US$350) return. The cheapest tickets to Manila are currently 6500/9000B (US$175/240) one way/return on Egypt Air. Singapore Airlines also flies daily to/from Cebu via Singapore.

South America

ASATEJ (☎ 011-4315 14570), Argentina's nonprofit student travel agency and the agent for STA Travel, is located on the 3rd floor, Officina 319-B, Florida 835, Buenos Aires. The best deals from Buenos Aires to Manila are vis Sydney and Singapore. Expect to pay around US$2100 for a return flight.

In Caracas, IVI Tours (02-993 60 82), Residencia La Hacienda, Piso Bajo, Local 1-4-Y, Final Avenida Principal de las Mercedes, is the agent for STA Travel in Venezuela and often has a range of good deals. Flights from Venezuala to Manila are via the USA, usually Miami and Los Angeles, and Tokyo (Japan). Fares start at around US$2300 return.

SEA

The current Brunei, Indonesia, Malaysia, Philippines East Asian Group Area (BIMP-EAGA) initiatives have made sea (and air) travel to/from Indonesia theoretically simpler, more reliable and open to all travellers. It is highly likely that the following details will change as demand, carriers and routes work themselves out.

Indonesia

EPA Shipping Line leaves General Santos for the deep-water port of Bitung, 55km from Manado (36 hours, P1800 one way) on Monday and Thursday. Schedules change, so check with the shipping line; the office is inside the port compound at Makar. This is a cargo boat that takes passengers; officially, there is no problem with foreigners making this trip, but you may want to check with the tourism office in General Santos first. You will need to finalise any Indonesian visa requirements with the consulate in Davao before leaving.

There is also a scheduled boat to Bitung from Davao (via General Santos) every Friday (see the Davao Getting There & Away section in the Mindanao & Sulu chapter for more details). At the time of publication, Pelni, the Indonesian national

Warning

The information in this chapter is particularly vulnerable to change: Prices for international travel are volatile, routes are introduced and cancelled, schedules change, special deals come and go, and rules and visa requirements are amended. Airlines and governments seem to take a perverse pleasure in making price structures and regulations as complicated as possible. You should check directly with the airline or a travel agent to make sure you understand how a fare (and ticket you may buy) works. In addition, the travel industry is highly competitive and there are many lurks and perks.

The upshot of this is that you should get opinions, quotes and advice from as many airlines and travel agents as possible before you part with your hard-earned cash. The details given in this chapter should be regarded as pointers and are not a substitute for your own careful, up-to-date research.

shipping line, had stopped operating on this route.

Malaysia

Aleson Lines leaves Zamboanga for Sandakan in Malaysian Borneo on Monday and Wednesday. Sampaguita Lines (☎ 062-993 1591 in Zamboanga) leaves Zamboanga for Sandakan on Monday and

Thursday. Fares from the Philippines are P500 to P1500 one way; the trip takes about 17 hours.

ORGANISED TOURS

The Department of Tourism (DOT) can help find a suitable tour (see Tourist Offices in the Facts for the Visitor chapter for DOT overseas offices).

Getting Around

AIR
Domestic Air Services

The main domestic airlines are Philippine Airlines (PAL), Air Philippines and Cebu Pacific. A host of smaller airlines have stepped up to fill in some of the gaps created by PAL's virtual implosion in 1998 (for more on PAL, see the boxed text 'Up in the Air with PAL' in the Getting There & Away chapter). Smaller domestic carriers include Air Ads, Asian Spirit, A Soriano Aviation, Golden Passage, Laoag International Airways, Mindanao Express and Pacific Airways (for Manila contact details, see the Getting There & Away section in the Manila chapter). Grand Air went bust in early 1999 after just a year in the air.

Size is important when it comes to Philippine air travel. Smaller airlines fly smaller planes, and smaller airports have fewer facilities (eg, no runway lights, so no flights after dark, and cancellations in low visibility). You're more likely to get on a flight during popular travel times with a bigger airline; on the other hand, the smaller planes often tend to land (or at least try) when the big planes turn back or stay on the ground. PAL flies the largest and generally newest planes: larger-model Boeing 737 and 747s, as well as several types of Airbus. Cebu Pacific fields a fleet of DC-9s, many of them older models.

Now that PAL has lost its domestic monopoly, it's worth shopping around for air fares. You may as well do this through the airlines directly, since local travel agents aren't going to get you any special deals.

Flight routes tend to be skewed towards the major airports, so planes fly from busy airport X to towns A, B and C, but not necessarily *between* A, B and C. Routes in the southern Philippines are particularly hit-and-miss.

Reasonably reliable flight information is available on the Internet from many of the airlines' Web sites. The government's tourism Web site lists current schedules of all domestic flights and airline contact details (follow the links from www.tourism.gov.ph); the Lakbay.Net site at www.lakbay.net also has online booking facilities.

PAL, Air Philippines and Asian Spirit have roughly comparable fares, while Cebu Pacific can be significantly cheaper and you can get discounts of 20% to 30% if you buy tickets four days in advance (seven days for Air Philippines flights). Asian Spirit often has promotions on specific routes.

Schedules and prices change, and promotions (as well as airlines) rapidly come and go. Currently, the full fare from Manila to Naga is P1140 on Air Philippines or Asian Spirit. Manila to Cebu fares vary from P1800 to P2200 depending on the airline; fares to Zamboanga are P1900 with Cebu Pacific, P3200 with Air Philippines or P3560 with PAL.

It's best to be flexible and to book in advance, but don't plan too tight a schedule – flight delays are a fact of life in the Philippines. During the wet season, schedules can be erratic due to the weather. If there is a typhoon warning, most flights will be grounded; few ferries will venture out of harbours, either, so you may just have to wait it out. You can also bank on the first few flights following a typhoon being massively overbooked. Smaller airlines in particular are fond of scheduling several flights, then cancelling one or more depending on how many passengers show up. If your flight is delayed or cancelled, you can enjoy a relaxing massage by one of the blind masseurs at the airport for about P150.

Christmas, New Year and Easter are the most heavily booked periods generally, and flights fill quickly to the scene of important festivals; with its sizeable Chinese population, Lunar New Year in Cebu City can also be busy. Be sure to reconfirm your seat on any flight, though it's not always a guarantee against being bumped.

In-Flight Entertainment?

Cebu's homegrown airline, Cebu Pacific, entertains passengers with in-flight minibasketball in the aisles – get the ball through the hoop and win a company baseball cap! But that's not half as attention grabbing as the special safety cards a select few passengers are asked to memorise ...

Passengers seated by exit doors must be able to assist cabin crew and perform the following in the event of an emergency: locate the emergency exit; assess outside conditions prior to opening the emergency exit; throw the exit door to free evacuation route; assess the condition of the escape slide, inflate the slide, and stabilise the slide after deploying; and assist passengers in exiting through the slide.

The small print on the card says that if you're under 12 years of age, or you wear eyeglasses, or you can't hear too well, or you just don't want to do it, then you *are* allowed to swap seats with someone more steely nerved.

Over at rival Philippine Airlines (PAL), you could be forgiven for thinking the airline's massive financial turmoil has seen its flight attendants ageing prematurely. Actually, when the airline laid off a massive slice of its staff in 1998, it chose to lop all its youngest crew members. The result is that the airline has the oldest flight attendants in the industry, with many of its former employees now flying with rival airlines.

Mic Looby

Baggage Allowance

Baggage allowance on small planes is usually limited – mostly to 10kg – and there's no pay-for-extra policy (if they let overweight gear on, the plane couldn't take off). Check this out when you book your flight, as you may need to store your bags.

On larger planes, you can pay to have your baggage limit increased. PAL offers a Flying Sportsman card for US$20 (or the equivalent in pesos, but it's best to get the card before you arrive), which allows the following limits on PAL flights: for golf, an extra 15kg (one golf set only allowed); for scuba diving, an extra 30kg (one cylinder without air and one dive bag/backpack only, plus assorted gear); and for sport fishing, an extra 20kg (in rod cases no longer than 5 feet, or 1.5m).

Domestic Departure Tax

Domestic departure tax varies from airport to airstrip and even from point to point. From Manila it is generally P140, while from distant El Nido it's P100. Domestic departure tax at most other small airports is P10. Mactan-Cebu International Airport has a curious pricing arrangement: departure tax from Manila to Cebu is P100; *to* Manila, and all other domestic destinations it's P53.

BOAT

Spend any length of time in the Philippines and you're bound to find yourself on a boat. Boats range from the high-class multidecked WG&A ferries and highly efficient luxury passenger catamarans (known as fastcraft or fast ferries) to the smallest of outriggers (called *bancas* or pumpboats), which shuttle between myriad beaches and piers.

Ferry & Fastcraft

Ferries of all descriptions and levels of seaworthiness ply the waters between islands. Ferries are often overcrowded and operators occasionally get collared by port inspectors, so the sailing is delayed while extra passengers are offloaded. Cramming every orifice of leaky tubs with passengers doesn't make them watertight – but it does increase the probability of the ship sinking, especially in heavy seas (see the boxed text 'That Sinking Feeling' in this section). You often have options as to which boat to travel on, so ask around locally about more reliable companies and ferries, and make travel plans accordingly.

Fastcraft are also increasingly common sights between islands. These are smaller, lighter and newer than the ferries, and well fitted, reliable and safe. They aren't called fast ferries for nothing, as they can cut the

MAIN SHIPPING ROUTES

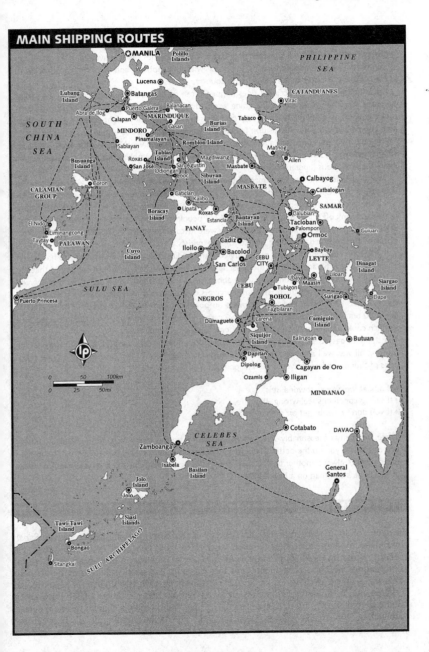

That Sinking Feeling

With 7000-plus islands and a mobile population, the Philippines relies heavily on ships of all descriptions to ferry folks around. Usually, this works without a problem, and there's no cause for alarm at the prospect of water-borne travel in the country.

Unfortunately, when an accident does happen it can be big, and major accidents receive major coverage. The chances of something going wrong doubles during holiday times, when people desperate to get home roll the dice and hop on ferries in conditions they might otherwise avoid. Shipping companies and port officials don't always mind the extra business, either.

The tales that emerged from a recent ferry sinking are instructive. Whatever the final verdict on what happened, it's worth considering the scenarios before scrambling onto any old boat just to make that ambitious itinerary work.

Two days before the last Christmas of the century, Trans-Asia Shipping's MV *Asia South Korea* was sailing from Cebu City for Iloilo City on Panay when it sank in rough waters near Bantayan Island. The accident occurred almost 12 years to the day since the ferry *Doña Paz* collided with a tanker and sank off Mindoro in 1987, killing 4341 people in history's worst peacetime shipping disaster. Though most of the passengers and crew were rescued from the 27-year-old *Asia South Korea*, at least 54 people died, including several foreign tourists.

It was soon apparent that a lot more survivors and bodies were recovered than should have been on the ship, at least according to the passenger and crew lists. Early evidence suggested that the ship struck a reef and questions also arose about the port inspection, when departure was delayed while some 80 people left the boat. Some survivors claimed they'd seen passengers moved to uninspected parts of the ship and more allowed on board before it finally set sail (four hours late) at about 10 pm; others also claimed that heavy cargo had been shifted away from the inspected area – which could dangerously unbalance the boat, especially in rough seas.

The ship had passed safety inspections a few months earlier and passengers could be forgiven for thinking all was well if a port inspection took place. Allegations in this case aside, here are three rules of thumb for ferry travel in the Philippines:

- If a boat looks overcrowded, it is.
- If sailing conditions feel wrong, they are.
- If you don't have to get on such a boat, don't.

There are plenty of reasonably safe options for getting from A to B – fastcraft are reliable, and locals can advise you on the better shipping companies on a given route. Remember: you're on holidays. There's always another boat – even if you may be stranded for a few days, there are worse places to be stuck than on a tropical island.

Russ Kerr

drudgery of long ferry rides by half the time. One modern convenience used to modern excess on these spiffy ships is air-conditioning, which is permanently set to 'blizzard' – take a sweater.

Three major shipping companies now handle interisland trips from Manila: Negros Navigation, Sulpicio and WG&A. These big players are reasonably reliable and safe, with disaster-defying names such as *Super-Ferry* and *Our Lady of Sacred Heart*. The pier at Batangas, a three-hour bus ride from Manila, is Luzon's main jumping-off point for popular Puerto Galera on Mindoro; see Getting There & Away under Batangas in the Around Manila chapter for more details.

For online shipping details between any ports in the country, try the *Sun-Star*

newspaper's shipping Web site at www
.esprint.com/~shipping/default.asp and the
WG&A Web site at www.wgasuper
ferry.com.

Though service on the main routes is
pretty reliable, be prepared for changes in
the itinerary. Adverse weather conditions
(especially during typhoon season) or renovation of a ferry can totally alter the sailing
times and boats used for various trips; un-
scheduled stops are also common. As with
planes, boats fill to overflowing during
Christmas, New Year and Easter, as well as
to the scene of major festivals.

On board, you can hang your hat on several levels of comfort and cost. Bunks on or
below deck on 3rd class should be fine, as
long as the ship isn't overcrowded. Some
women travellers on deck class prefer to
sail with a companion – as one female traveller put it, 'At least that way you know
what you'll wake up next to.'

Ferry prices vary widely but, as a guide,
the average fare between Manila and Cebu
City is around P700 on deck class for the
22-hour journey; between Manila and
Puerto Princesa it's about P550 (20 hours).
Inquire about student discounts: some shipping lines knock 20% to 30% off the regular fare.

Small Craft

Ferries may carry more weight, but the
backbone of interisland travel is supported
by bancas. In some areas, in addition to single rides, bancas can be hired for day trips
at a reasonable cost.

Bancas are powered by recycled Toyota
Corolla 1600 engines, so if you have an
aversion to sputtering smoke and fumes,
plant yourself near the bow. They are often
on regular schedules, but won't hit the surf
if seas are rough; banca pilots aren't always
crazy about night trips either.

Be wary of crossing fast-flowing rivers,
especially when swollen by floods. Locals
may attempt it, but they're usually on more
pressing business than sightseeing. Jury-
rigged and overloaded 'ferries' – often just
several bancas tied beneath a wooden platform – are particularly prone to capsizing.

BUS

So many potholes, so little time. An enormous number of bus services cover the
Philippines, and generally do it quite
cheaply and reliably. Island-hopping is even
an option on some bus routes; you can
travel from Manila to Davao, for example,
without getting your feet wet.

Departures are very frequent, although
buses sometimes leave early if they're full
– take care if there's only one bus a day!
People like to travel early, when it's cool, so
there are often more buses at this time, and
air-con buses almost always leave early in
the morning.

On Luzon, all roads lead to Manila and so
do all bus routes, so if you're headed from
the north down to say, the Bicol region,
you'll have to change buses at the appropriate Manila station (there is no central bus
station in the capital). The main companies
include BLTB, JAM, Victory Liner and
Philippine Rabbit.

As in most countries, it pays to mind
your gear while buses load and unload.
Mountainous roads such as those in the
Cordillera are noted for hairpin turns and
hair-raising, stomach-churning driving.
While most drivers on these WWII-era
tracks are just as interested in living as you
are, some are less adept at it than others. It
may be worth asking locals about the
current reputation of bus companies on
your route.

Reservations

As noted earlier, drivers get an itchy pedal
foot when the bus is full, and clutching a
reservation to your bosom as the bus zooms
away is cold comfort. That said, reservations are useful, especially on popular
routes and early morning buses where competition for a seat can be pretty stiff.

In bigger towns, reservations can be
made with the bus company by phone or in
person; in smaller centres, often a particular shop takes reservations on buses belonging to one or more companies. On
some routes you can also ring to request
that a bus stops for you at a designated time
and place; for example, BLTB buses to

Daet, Naga and Legaspi will stop in Lucena on request.

Costs

You can figure your fare roughly on distance and time. On regular buses you generally cover a bit under 2km per peso and the average speed is about 50km per hour. *Voila*! A 100km journey costs P50 or so and takes two hours.

On the other hand, you'd need a slide rule and a crystal ball to factor in chickens crossing the road, the number of flat tires, heart-stopping spurts of speed and so on, all of which seem to have been magically factored into the actual price you pay. It's a bit easier to take a look at the prices written on chalkboards wherever the buses depart.

Air-con buses are around 15% to 20% more expensive than ordinary buses, and trips on gravel roads are normally pricier than travel on sealed roads.

TRAIN

The route south from Manila to the Bicol region of south-east Luzon is the only remaining railway line in the country. It's so slow and unreliable that locals suggest taking the bus (they also claim to get pelted by stones as the train passes through the slums). There is, as the Filipinos say, *moro moro* ('just talk') about revamping the line.

JEEPNEY

For the basics of jeepney-hopping, see the Jeepney entry under Local Transport later in this chapter. Jeepney riding is generally efficient and hassle-free, though for trips out of town or in the countryside, it's wise to observe a few rules.

- Find out what the fare should be before you hop in. You can ask other passengers, or try a nearby shop.
- Try not to be the first person to get into an empty jeepney. If the driver suddenly takes off, you may have just bought a ticket on a pricey 'special ride' (which is probably the case if the driver doesn't stop for anyone else). If this happens, ask the driver to stop, and explain that you are only looking for a regular ride. Another possibility is perhaps cheaper but no less inconvenient: the driver may decide that it's not worth completing the journey with only one passenger and drop you off in the middle of nowhere.
- Take care if several men suddenly get in and all try to sit near you. Chances are you're being set up to be pickpocketed; get off and find another vehicle.
- On long trips it's worth trying to get a seat next to the driver – there's more leg room, and the time passes quicker if you can see where you're going.

Jeepneys are plentiful on most routes, but you may have to wait a while to get your ride: jeepney drivers need to make a living,

Jeep Thrills

The traditional recipe for this uniquely Filipino concoction is as follows: take one ex-US Army jeep, put two benches in the back with enough room for about 12 people, paint it every colour of the rainbow, add badges, horns, aerials, air fresheners, icons, lots of mirrors, a tape deck that only plays Filipino pop, a chrome horse (or a whole herd of them) and anything else you can think of. Then stuff 20 passengers on those benches, add four in front, hang a few more off the roof and drive like a maniac.

Alas, the old jeepneys are rapidly disappearing, victims of rust, wear and tear, and the desire to put a 'Made in the Philippines' stamp on this national institution. Products of a kinder, gentler international economy, blander vehicles are now mass produced from globalised automotive parts in cities like Cebu (though they're still hand-assembled here and there – see the Las Piñas entry in the Around Manila chapter). These roll off assembly lines pre-'jeepneyfied', leaving little room for the personal touches dear to purists.

This 'add chrome and stir' formula might sound like the automotive equivalent of microwaved *adobo*, but remember the basic ingredient of the original – it's unlikely we've seen the last incarnation of the tried-and-true jeepney.

Mic Looby & Russ Kerr

so they're not inclined to depart until they've got (at least) a full load. Or, you can have a jeepney (plus jeepney driver, of course) all to yourself for around P1200 a day.

MINIBUS

L-300 minibuses have become popular in many parts of the Philippines as rivals to regular buses. Operated privately, these vehicles usually hang around the car parks near bus depots and take passengers to popular destinations in air-conditioned comfort – normally at very competitive rates. The drawback is that drivers hate to head off with half-empty vehicles, so you may have to wait indefinitely or pay extra to leave straightaway. These vehicles are also known as 'FX vans' or 'air-con buses'.

CAR & MOTORCYCLE

If time is short, driving yourself is a quicker option than relying on jeepneys and other public transport, but it does come with caveats. Filipino driving is possibly at its most manic in and around Manila, as well as in Luzon's central mountains, though it is less life-threatening elsewhere, and verges on pleasant in and around cities such as Cebu.

Whatever you do, don't try to emulate the local style – driving in the Philippines is one area of 'cultural difference' where the 'when in Rome' principle doesn't apply.

Road Rules

Driving is on the right-hand side of the road (or at least it's supposed to be). If you do decide to hire a car or motorcycle, defensive driving is definitely the order of the day. Jeepneys and buses will stop at random to drop off and pick up passengers, and you should give way to buses in almost all situations, not least because of the devil-may-care attitude of their drivers.

In general, the outside lane is the safest place to be, though you can expect people to overtake on both sides if there's a gap in the traffic. On the expressways out of Manila, the hard shoulder is often used as an overtaking lane, so drivers should take extra care when exiting the highway.

Night driving holds its own particular hazards, quite apart from the issue of potential robberies in political trouble-spots (eg, certain parts of Mindanao). Tricycles, motorcycles and even large trucks are often driven without lights, while in small towns it's not unknown for families to put out tables and chairs and have dinner on the highway!

It's best to avoid driving at night if you can, but if you're on the road after dark, pay particular attention to school zones in small villages; these are frequently reduced to one lane. Also look out for burning cans of oil, which are used to mark broken-down vehicles, accidents and road works.

With the exception of the expressways out of Manila, most roads in the Philippines are single track, which can lead to some wild overtaking by local drivers. It's not uncommon for long-haul buses to overtake queues of five or six vehicles. Ignore the locals and only overtake if you're sure the road is clear; emergency services in the Philippines are few and far between.

Petrol is still cheap by North American or European standards, although prices are higher than in many South-East Asian nations (at the time of writing, the price was around P14 a litre). Shell, Caltex and the Petron corporation control the pipelines.

Rental

Car Rentals are generally offered on a daily or weekly basis, with or without the added expense of a driver. To rent a car, most places require you to be not less than 21 and not more than 65 years of age. Your home country's driving licence is legally valid for 90 days after you arrive in the country, but you're not likely to be asked for an International Driving Permit after that.

The rental agreement small print says cars can only be driven on surfaced roads. This rather cramps your style, especially if the main reason you want a rental is to get to those hard-to-reach spots on various islands. Some places also ask you to leave your passport as security, which is a bit awkward if you need to change money.

The big international car hire companies all have offices in Manila and at NAIA; see the Getting There & Away entry in the Manila chapter for details.

In the Visayas, local car hire companies in Cebu and Iloilo generally charge around P1000 per 12 hours, with special deals for longer periods.

If you're hiring a car, it's worth stopping into a car wash before you return the vehicle, or you will be charged an additional washing fee.

Motorcycle Motorcycles and motor scooters can be rented in just about every tourist spot and should be easy to find. For example, resort-happy Alona Beach on Panglao Island is lined with motorcycles for hire from P600 per day. In towns, popular guesthouses and cafes often have motorcycle-rental shops nearby. In more remote areas, just ask around.

As a rule, 125cc Honda or Suzuki cycles cost from P500 to P700 per day, or it's about P350 for smaller cycles. You should wear a helmet, but finding one can be difficult.

BICYCLE
Cycling in the Philippines is a seldom-explored option but, away from the treacherous traffic and exhaust fumes, it can be a great way to get around the quieter, less-visited islands such as the Batanes or Guimaras. Locals get around on bikes in many of these places, and the promise of peaceful rides along coastal and mountain roads to out-of-the-way villages makes lugging your bike (or renting one) well worth the effort.

Bicycles can travel by air. You *can* take them to pieces and put them in a bike bag or box, but it's much easier simply to wheel your bike to the check-in desk, where it should be treated as a piece of baggage. You may have to remove the pedals and turn the handlebars sideways so that it takes up less space in the aircraft's hold; check all this with the airline well in advance, preferably before you pay for your ticket.

You can take bicycles on domestic flights (you'll probably have to remove the front wheel), but take heed of the baggage allowance on small planes in particular (see the Baggage Allowance entry in the Air section in this chapter). If there's room, you can stow your bike on a bus or jeepney, usually for a small extra charge.

Rental
As guesthouses and resorts realise the virtues of hiring out bicycles, self-powered transport is getting easier to come by on many islands. Depending on where you are, mountain bikes go for anywhere from P100 (eg, on Boracay) to P300 per day (eg, on Guimaras, the home of a big mountain bike festival every February). In out-of-the-way areas, your lodging can usually help you rent a bicycle.

Purchase
If you are passing through Cebu, see Shopping under Cebu City in the Visayas chapter for branches of the Habagat Outdoor Store, which also sells bikes.

HITCHING
Petrol prices may be on the rise, but the cost of transport remains so low that hitch-hiking isn't worth the trouble, and you're seldom left stranded without a cheap and willing jeepney in sight. Filipinos won't resort to hitching, even if they don't have the money for transport. In any case, drivers expect a few pesos if they give lifts 'because of the high price of petrol' – a claim the domestic oil cartel is doing its best to legitimise.

Needless to say, hitching in the guerilla territory of Mindanao is positively suicidal.

WALKING
The myriad paths and trails criss-crossing nearly every island make walking an easy way to meet people, find hidden spots and generally discover the joys of nature. In fact, the hardest thing about walking is convincing solicitous tricycle and minivan drivers that you really are doing it by choice.

Pedestrians should note that zebra crossings are for decoration – never assume that cars will stop for you; also, drivers tend to regard traffic lights as negotiable requests.

LOCAL TRANSPORT
Bus
Although Manila has the country's only urban buses (see Getting There & Away in the Manila chapter for details), an efficient network of inexpensive jeepneys, tricycles, minibuses and other public utility vehicles more than makes up for the lack of buses elsewhere, and supplements the capital's overburdened buses as well.

LRT/Metrorail
Manila has a Light Rail Transit (LRT) system, an elevated railway also known as Metrorail. Part of the new MRT3 line to Quezon City opened in December 1999; with luck the southern part of the line, which links with EDSA, the main drag, will be open by the time you read this.

In Cebu City, plans are underway to develop an LRT system running throughout the city and as far north as Danao.

Jeepney
The main mode of public transport in most towns, jeepneys are the motorised version of people power (see the boxed text 'Jeep Thrills' earlier in this chapter).

The basic rules of jeepney riding are simple. Jeepneys can be flagged down anywhere, but usually prefer to stop where there is a crowd of potential customers. The Tagalog phrase 'Bayad to' (pronounced 'Bi-ye-to') translates as 'Here is my fare', and will get the driver's attention.

Jeepneys follow a set route and stop on demand, but it can be hard to see where you are from inside the vehicle – the best seats are up the front next to the driver. In big cities like Manila, jeepneys are festooned with signboards indicating where the vehicle goes; in other places, there's one sign in the front. Alternatively, the whole jeepney may be colour-coded according to its destination; occasionally they are unmarked and you'll have to ask the driver where it's going.

Jeepney drivers are generally as honest as Manila taxi drivers are crooked. Paying for a jeepney is straightforward – there's a price (ask other passengers if you're unsure) and you pay it, usually under the watchful eye of fellow riders, who will help if need be with translations. Outside the major urban areas (and seldom even there), there's little risk of fare hassles when you get off.

The average price for a short trip in town is P3. You pay at the end of the line, or anywhere along the way if you have a rough idea of the price. The driver usually has change, at least for smaller bills. When you want to get off, you can rap on the roof, hiss (you'll be joined by a chorus from the other passengers) or use the correct term 'pára', which is Tagalog for 'stop'.

Taxi
Manila is reputed to have South-East Asia's cheapest taxi fares, but since Manila is also reputed to have South-East Asia's most crooked taxi drivers, few of whom will stick to official metered rates (P20 plus P5 per kilometre), this would be difficult to verify. At least when they rip you off, they do it with a smile – with a few deep breaths, you should be able to manage a taxi ride from the airport. Manila also has a nice alternative: numerous air-con Toyota Tamaraw FX jeeps, known locally as Mega-Taxis. See Getting Around in the Manila chapter for more details.

By contrast, taxis in cities like Cebu are more like an out-take from *Night on Earth* than *Nightmare on Elm Street*. Airports seem to have a special effect on taxi drivers the world over, but beyond the gates of NAIA and MCIA, Filipino taxi drivers can be disconcertingly honest.

It's up to you whether you want to insist that drivers use the meter (in Manila, this will put you on the most roundabout course to your destination). If you do, watch that the meter works properly. Either way, keep your pack beside you or on your lap, and get out straightaway if you suspect you're being taken for a ride in more ways than one.

Tricycle
The tricycle is basically the Filipino rickshaw: a little roofed sidecar bolted to a motorbike or, less often, a bicycle. Tricycles are found in their various forms nearly everywhere and are useful – essential even – for short trips; in many areas, they can be

also rented by the hour (around P100 per hour is typical).

The flat fare in town is often officially the same for tricycles and jeepneys (usually P3; for longer trips, it's P3 for the first 2km plus 50c per additional 1km) and you may get away with the locals' rate in some towns; in most touristy areas, your chances of such a rate range from slim to none. In these areas, drivers of motorised tricycles will routinely quote P150 – especially if night is coming and/or the trip involves unsealed roads. Locals would pay a fraction of this price, so feel free to haggle.

Though often garishly done up in the mode of a jeepney, you'll likely hear a tricycle before you see one – if the smoke-belching two-stroke engine doesn't get your attention, the persistent call of 'Hey Kano!' will.

Tricyles for human transport in Manila (where they're also called pedicabs or sidecars) are mostly pedal-powered, and aren't especially cheap – depending on your bargaining power, a short trip costs from around P15 to P50.

Calesa

Ornate horse-drawn carriages are generally known by the Castilian word *calesa* (in Cebu City they're called *tartanillas*), and are still the main form of transport in a few rural areas. These two-wheeled, four-footed remnants of Spanish days are still in everyday use in Vigan; in Manila, calesas are mainly used to take tourists for a ride.

ORGANISED TOURS

For reliable local agencies offering a variety of tours, see Travel Agencies under Information in the Manila chapter. 'Live-aboard' dive tours are plentiful – see the Diving & Snorkelling section in the Facts for the Visitor chapter for more details.

The Green Travel Network has a Web site at www.greentravel.com and is a good online resource for legitimate, ecofriendly tours. Guided tours with international operators aren't cheap; for example, a five-day trip camping and trekking through the rice terraces of central Luzon will cost at least US$600.

Manila

History

Under Spanish rule, Manila was known as 'The Pearl of the Orient', the jewel of Spain's empire in the Pacific. Early tourists, like the 19th century traveller Fedor Jagor, described a splendid, fortified city of wide, cobbled streets and regal Spanish townhouses. Sadly, little remains of the Spaniard's splendid city today. Ravaged by US and Japanese bombing during WWII, modern Manila has grown up into a teeming metropolis, with huge tower blocks crowding the few surviving examples of Spanish and American colonial architecture.

History records that the city was founded by the Spaniard Miguel Lopez de Legazpi in 1571 although, in fact, a fortified Muslim settlement had already existed on the site for centuries. King Philip II of Spain hoped that the city would become known as Isigne y Siempre Leal Cuidad (Distinguished and Ever Loyal City), but the locals were neither loyal nor particularly keen to adopt the habits of their Spanish overlords. Within a few years, the city had reverted to its pre-Hispanic name of Maynilad (from the words *may* meaning 'there is', and *nilad*, a mangrove plant used to make soap), which was later corrupted to Manila.

For centuries, the hub of Manila was the walled city of Intramuros, (literally, 'within the walls'), which was exclusively reserved for the Spanish colonial government and later for wealthy American and Chinese-Filipino families, many of whom still play a prominent role in Philippine politics today. The nomadic Negrito people of the area were settled in nearby villages like Luneta, Paco and Santa Cruz, where they could be easily taxed. Metro Manila is actually a conglomeration of 17 towns and villages which were unified in 1976 as one of President Marcos' infamous presidential decrees.

The core of Metro Manila is formed by the districts of Intramuros, Ermita, Malate, Paco, Quiapo, Binondo and San Nicolas, which surround the mouth of the Pasig

HIGHLIGHTS

- Strolling through the weird and wonderful street markets in Quiapo, Binondo and Baclaran

- Paying your respects at the bizarre Chinese Cemetery, with its air-conditioned houses for the dead

- Checking out the new generation of happening Manila bars, nightspots and restaurants

- Touring Manila's excellent museums and art galleries

Metro Manila pp108-9
Intramuros & Rizal Park p114
Binondo & Santa Cruz p119
Ermita, Malate & Paco p122
Parañaque & Pasay City p124
Makati p128
Quezon City p130
Makati Avenue & Burgos Street p133
Adriatico & Mabini Streets p136

◆ MANILA

River. Apart from the walled city, important areas for tourists are Ermita and Malate (the main areas for budget accommodation and dining), Binondo and Quiapo (for Chinatown and the Quiapo markets) and North Harbour in San Nicolas (the departure point for most of the interisland ferries).

Around this central core are a number of other 'city centres' formed by villages that have grown together. In the north, Caloocan City and the Cubao district of Quezon City are important departure points for northbound buses, while the terminals for many south-bound buses are south of the centre in

MANILA

The Nilad, a mangrove plant used to make soap, supplies part of Manila's name.

Baclaran district, Pasay City. The international and domestic airports are further south in Parañaque (pronounced 'par-an-ya-kay'). Heading east from Pasay City, the remaining centres are Makati City (the main business district), Pasig City and Mandaluyong City.

The remains of the Spanish city, including some of Manila's most attractive and historic buildings, can still be seen in Intramuros. In contrast, few buildings in Makati, the business hub of Manila, are more than 40 years old. Fringing Makati are exclusive neighbourhoods like Forbes Park and Bel-Air, where Manila's wealthiest citizens live in private luxury, guarded from the rest of the population by their own private police forces.

The coastline north of the Pasig River is home to sprawling shantytowns, the most infamous being Tondo, where over 180,000 people are crammed into an area of only 1.5 sq km. Successive governments have tried to improve the statistics by demolishing the shantytowns, but the population of slum-dwellers continues to hover at about 1.5 million people.

Most people only use Manila as a base for a couple of days before heading north to the cooler highlands, or south to the beaches of Mindoro and other islands.

However, there's plenty to see and do in the capital if you're prepared to give it the time, from excellent museums and galleries to lively markets and cultural oddities like cockfighting and the Chinese cemetery, with its air-conditioned houses for the dead.

Orientation

The 'tourist belt' formed by Malate and Ermita is probably the best place to be based in Manila. Most of Manila's budget and mid-range accommodation can be found here, as well as many of the best restaurants. The area of most interest to tourists is bound by Roxas Blvd, Vito Cruz St, Taft Ave and the Pasig River.

Rizal Park, Intramuros, the main post office (known as the GPO) and immigration offices are all just north of the tourist belt, while long-distance ferries leave from the far side of the Pasig River at North Harbour. Nearby Divisoria is a major centre for cheap clothes. In the same area are the districts of Binondo (which includes Manila's colourful Chinatown) and Quiapo (where you'll find many of the most interesting street markets in Manila). All these destinations can be reached by jeepney from Mabini St in Malate or Ermita. The business centre of Makati is accessible by air-con public bus from Quiapo or Buendia/Gil Puyat Ave and EDSA in Pasay City. The elevated track of the Metrorail or Light Rail Transit (LRT) system runs all the way from Baclaran in Pasay City to Monumento in Caloocan City but it isn't particularly convenient for Makati, Quezon City or the tourist belt.

The traffic and smog make getting around Manila quite an ordeal. To add to the general air of confusion, many roads in Manila are known by two, or even three, names. Rizal Ave, the main road from Santa Cruz up to Monumento, is also known as Avenida and LRT; Arnaiz Ave in Makati is also Pasay Road; P Ocampo St, Malate is also known as Vito Cruz St; and Gil Puyat Ave, San Isidro is also known as Buendia. Street addresses in Manila are often given by the nearest street corner, eg, Pedro Gil St cor Mabini St.

Maps The excellent *E-Z Maps* published by United Tourist Promotions are widely available throughout the Philippines and cover Metro Manila, Makati and Quezon City in fine detail, though they lack a scale (P80). The Makati map is particularly useful as it features the names of all the high-rise buildings in the central business district. The Philippine Motor Association publishes a huge but very detailed 1:20,000 scale map of Metro Manila, which is available from the National Book Store (P145). Nelles Maps also publish a useful Manila map (scale 1:17,500) and a combined Philippines and Manila map (scale 1:1,500,000) which both show important buildings in the Metro Manila area.

Information

Tourist Offices The friendly tourist office (☎ 02-524 1703) is housed in a single room on the ground floor of the vast Department of Tourism (DOT) building in Rizal Park. The staff are knowledgeable about the whole of the Philippines and can provide computer printouts on areas you might like to visit. The office is open from 7 am to 6 pm daily. It's best to enter the building from Kalaw St. There's also a satellite kiosk in the arrivals lounge at Ninoy Aquino International Airport (NAIA) and another in the new Centennial Terminal II building. Both are open to meet incoming flights.

Upstairs in the DOT building, in Room 212, the office of the Corregidor Foundation (☎ 02-523 5605) handles hotel reservations and inquiries for the fortress island of Corregidor in Manila Bay.

Money It is not actually difficult to change money or travellers cheques in Manila, but many people fall foul of the rules governing foreign exchange. You will need your passport and the original receipts if you intend to change travellers cheques, and only a handful of banks and moneychangers can exchange travellers cheques in currencies other than US dollars. The greatest concentration of moneychangers can be found around the intersection of Mabini and Padre Faura Sts

in Malate. Generally, the rate is slightly lower than the rate for cash.

You should have no trouble changing US dollars cash and British pounds sterling. Deutschmarks, Canadian and Australian dollars are also widely accepted. Moneychangers usually offer the best rates, but you should be sceptical of unrealistically high offers, particularly from the 'fixers' who tout for various moneychangers in the tourist belt.

If you feel uncomfortable carrying large amounts of cash, credit cards can be used to get cash advances from hundreds of ATMs in the capital. AmEx and MasterCard are the most widely accepted, but Visa, Cirrus and Plus are also prevalent. ATMs are usually protected by an armed guard and the bank will a display an 'on-line' sign in the window if the ATM is working. Most ATMs have a P4000 or P5000 daily withdrawal limit.

Many of the banks will also change cash and travellers cheques. Opening hours are usually 9 am to 3 pm, Monday to Friday. The following is a list of useful banks and foreign exchange services in Manila:

American Express – Cash; AmEx travellers cheques (US and Australian dollars).
Branches: (☎ 02-526 8406 or 526 8408) On the corner of Mabini and Remedios Sts, Malate.
(☎ 02-869 4866) Ground floor, BSA Mansions, Benavidez St, Makati.
Bank of the Philippine Islands FOREX – Cash; AmEx and Thomas Cook travellers cheques; AmEx, MasterCard and Cirrus ATMs.
Branches: (☎ 02-818 5541) On the corner of Mabini and Remedios Sts, Malate.
(☎ 02-525 1829) On the corner of Mabini and Pedro Gil Sts, Ermita.
(☎ 02-819 7632) BPI Bldg, on the corner of Ayala Ave and Paseo de Roxas, Makati.
Citibank – Cash; Citibank travellers cheques; Visa and MasterCard ATMs.
Branches: (☎ 02-813 9177) Citibank Center Bldg, 8741 Paseo de Roxas, Makati.
(☎ 02-243 4111) San Fernando St, Binondo.
Equitable PCI Bank – Cash; AmEx travellers cheques (US dollars only); Visa, MasterCard and Plus ATMs.
Branches: (☎ 02-525 6108) On the corner of Mabini and Pedro Gil Sts, Malate.
(☎ 02-536 0331) Robinson's Place, Pedro Gil entrance, Ermita. Also open Saturday.
(☎ 02-886 0010) Equitable Bank Bldg, 8751 Paseo de Roxas, Makati.

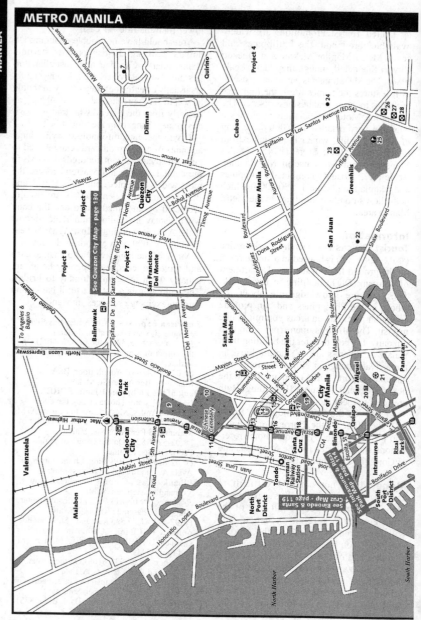

METRO MANILA

See Quezon City Map - page 130

See Intramuros, Binondo & Santa Cruz Map - page 119

Don Mariano Marcos Avenue

Quirino

Project 4

7

24

26
27
28

Diliman

Cubao

Epifanio De Los Santos Avenue (EDSA)

Ortigas Avenue

23

25

Greenhills

Visayas

Avenue

North Avenue

East Avenue

Quezon
City

Bohol Avenue

Timog Avenue

Aurora Boulevard

New Manila

San Juan

22

Shaw Boulevard

Project 6

Project 8

Project 7

Epifanio De Los Santos Avenue (EDSA)

West Avenue

San Francisco
Del Monte

E Rodriguez St

Doña Rodriguez
Street

Quirino Highway

To Angeles &
Baguio

North Luzon Expressway

Balintawak

6

North Luzon Expressway

Epifanio De Los Santos Avenue

Bonifacio Street

Del Monte Avenue

Quezon Avenue

Santa Mesa
Heights

Sampaloc

Antipolo Street

Magsaysay Boulevard

Pandacan

Valenzuela

Mac Arthur Highway

Grace
Park

5th Avenue

Rizal Avenue Extension

Mayon Street

Blumentritt

Dapitan St

España
St

Forbes St

City of
Manila

San Miguel

21

20 m

Mabini Street

C-3 Road

Juan Luna Street

Malabon

Caloocan
City

2
3

4

5

8

9

10

Chinese
Cemetery

11

13

16

12

14

15

17

18

19

Governor

Quezon Blvd

Rizal
Avenue

Recto

CM
Recto

Escolta St

Binondo

Quiapo

Intramuros

Rizal
Park

Bonifacio Drive

Tondo

North Port
District

José Abad Santos Street

Tayuman Railway
Station

Santa
Cruz

Homoratio Lopez Boulevard

North Harbor

South Port
District

South Harbor

MANILA

METRO MANILA

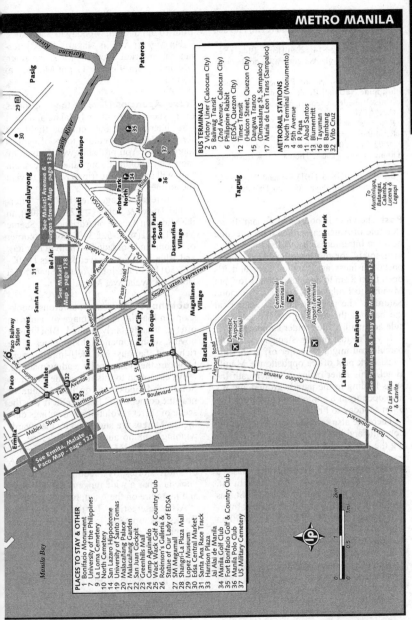

BUS TERMINALS
2 Victory Liner (Caloocan City)
5 Baliwag Transit
  (2nd Avenue, Caloocan City)
6 Philippine Rabbit
  (EDSA, Quezon City)
12 Times Transit
  (Halcon Street, Quezon City)
15 Dangwa Tranco
  (Dimasalang St, Sampaloc)
17 Maria de Leon Trans (Sampaloc)

METRORAIL STATIONS
3 North Terminal (Monumento)
4 5th Avenue
8 R Papa
11 Abad Santos
13 Blumentritt
16 Tayuman
18 Bambang
32 Vito Cruz

PLACES TO STAY & OTHER
1 Bonifacio Monument
7 University of the Philippines
9 La Loma Cemetery
10 North Cemetery
14 San Lazaro Hippodrome
19 University of Santo Tomas
20 Malacañang Palace
21 Malacañang Garden
22 San Juan Cockpit
23 Greenhills Mall
24 Camp Aguinaldo
25 Wack Wack Golf & Country Club
26 Robinson's Galleria &
   Statue of Our Lady of EDSA
27 SM Megamall
28 Shangri-La Plaza Mall
29 Lopez Museum
30 Edsa Central Market
31 Santa Ana Race Track
33 Harrison Plaza
34 Manila Golf Club
35 Fort Bonifacio Golf & Country Club
36 Manila Polo Club
37 US Military Cemetery

Manila Bay

To Las Piñas
& Cavite

To Muntinlupa,
Batangas,
Calamba,
Lucena &
Legaspi

HSBC – Cash; AmEx and Thomas Cook travellers cheques; Visa, MasterCard, Plus and Cirrus ATMs.
Branches: (☎ 02-814 5200) HSBC Bldg, on the corner of Ayala Ave and Paseo de Roxas, Makati.
(☎ 02-242 5888) Quintin Paredes St, Binondo.

Philippine National Bank – Cash; Visa and AmEx travellers cheques; Visa and MasterCard ATMs.
Branches: (☎ 02-525 6133) TM Kalaw St, Rizal Park, Ermita.
(☎ 02-242 8501) Escolta St, Binondo.

Thomas Cook – Cash; Thomas Cook travellers cheques.
Branch: (☎ 02-816 3701) Skyland Bldg, on the corner of Gil Puyat Ave and Tindaloo St, Makati.

Post The GPO is housed in a magnificent example of American colonial architecture near the Intramuros city walls. It's worth a visit solely for the building. All types of postal business are handled here and it's open from 8 am to noon and from 1 to 5 pm Monday to Friday and from 8 am to noon Saturday. The poste restante counter is at the back of the building on the left-hand side and mail is filed under surnames.

If you're just buying stamps or sending parcels you might be better off at the tiny Rizal Park post office opposite the Manila Hotel. This quiet office is underneath the steps leading to the parade ground and it's also open from 8 am to noon and from 1 to 5 pm Monday to Friday.

There are also satellite post offices at the domestic and international airports, including the new Centennial Terminal II.

Email & Internet Access The Classica Cristina Web Cafe, at 1565 Mabini St, Malate, near the corner of Pedro Gil St, has friendly staff and probably the fastest Internet connection in Manila. Rates are P70 an hour and it's open from 8.30 am to 11 pm Monday to Saturday.

Surf Service Web Cafe, at 506 Padre Faura St, Ermita, is another popular place, with Internet access for P80 an hour. It's open from 9 am to midnight daily except Sunday.

In the Park Square II mall, just off Arnaiz Ave in Makati, the Mail Station Net has

Internet access for P75 an hour. It's open from 10 am to 8 pm Monday to Saturday.

On Makati Ave in Makati, AMA Internet has Internet access for P75 an hour. It's open from 9 am to 11 pm Monday to Saturday.

Travel Agencies There are travel agencies everywhere in Ermita and Malate and most offer international and domestic flight and ferry bookings and guided tours of various tourist sites. You probably won't save any money by booking through these places, but they will save you the trip to Makati to visit the airlines in person.

Well-regarded agencies include: Inter-island Travel & Tours (☎ 02-522 1405), in the Midtown Arcade on Adriatico St; Scenic View Travel (☎ 02-522 3495), on the corner of Mabini and Soldado Sts (both in Ermita); and Blue Horizons Travel & Tours (☎ 02-813 5011), in the lobby of the Shangri-La Hotel, on Ayala Ave, Makati.

Bookshops There are numerous bookshops in Manila, but the range of books on offer is usually fairly limited. Blockbuster novels, slushy romances, biographies of the rich and famous and self-improvement books are the most popular reading material.

An exception to this rule is the excellent Solidaridad Bookshop, on Padre Faura St near the corner of JC Bocobo St. It was the scene of secret revolutionary meetings during the Marcos era and is run by the award-winning Filipino author F Sionil José. As well as the many Filipino (Tagalog) translations – the owner's *Waywaya*, a collection of short stories, is recommended – the bookshop has a wide range of travel books and literature on the Asian region.

Also interesting is the Tradewinds Bookshop, upstairs in the El Amenecer complex on General Luna St, Intramuros. It has a good selection of books on the Philippines and a wide assortment of modern and ancient maps.

The huge National Book Store chain has branches in most of the shopping malls in Manila, though the books on offer tend to be fairly lowbrow. Like most bookshops in the Philippines, it also doubles as a stationers. There are also branches in Robinson's Place in Ermita, Harrison Plaza in Malate, the Tutuban Center in Divisoria, the Araneta Center in Cubao and the Greenbelt Square mall in Makati.

The small Bookmark chain has contemporary novels as well as books on the Philippines. There's a branch on the corner of Greenbelt Dr and Makati Ave in Makati and another on Quezon Ave in Quezon City. Power Books, at 918 Arnaiz Ave (Pasay Rd), Makati, has a good selection of classic literature and international novels.

Libraries Several libraries in Manila are open to the public, though you need to leave photo ID with the guards on the door. The National Library (☎ 02-525 1314) is next to Rizal Park on TM Kalaw St, Ermita, and is open from 8 am to 5 pm Monday to Saturday. Also on TM Kalaw St, in the old Army & Navy Club, the Museo ng Maynila Library (☎ 02-536 7388) has reference books on the history of Manila. It's open from 8 am to 5 pm Tuesday to Saturday.

In the Ayala Triangle park in Makati, the Pilipinas Heritage Library (☎ 02-892 1801) has good resources on Filipino culture and ethnic groups, and there's also an Internet cafe (P100 per hour). It's open from 9 am to 4.30 pm Tuesday to Friday and from 10 am to 5 pm Saturday.

If you really want to get a feel for local history, the Lopez Museum (☎ 02-910 1009), on the ground floor of the Chronicle Building on Neralco Ave, Pasig, has an impressive archive of 13,000 Filipino books, including one of only three existing copies of Maximillianus Transylvanus' *De Moluccis Insulis* (The Mollucan Islands), which was printed in 1524 and contains the first published account of Magellan's trip to the Philippines. The museum is open from 8.30 am to 5 pm Monday to Friday and from 8 am to 4 pm Saturday. Admission costs P60.

Photographic Services Fast and reliable film processing is offered by the dozens of specialist film and camera shops on Hidalgo St, Quiapo, one street back from Quiapo Church. Expect to pay about P30 for one-hour processing, plus P3 per print for a 36-exposure film.

Cultural Centres Several nations have cultural centres in Manila. Most have their own libraries and stage regular cultural events like film screenings. Call the centres to find out what's on.

Alliance Française (☎ 02-813 2681) Keystone Bldg, Gil Puyat Ave, Makati
Australia Centre (☎ 02-754 6132 to 754 6135) 104 Paseo de Roxas, Makati
British Council Library (☎ 02-914 1011 to 914 1014) 10th floor, Taipan Place, Emerald Ave, Quezon City
Goethe Institut Manila (☎ 02-722 4671) 687 Aurora Blvd, Quezon City
Information Resource Center (☎ 02-523 1001, 897 1994) US Embassy, Roxas Blvd, Ermita

Laundry The friendly Laundryville, (☎ 02-450 1782), at 494 Soldado St, Ermita, offers free delivery to most hotels in Ermita and Malate. It charges P30 per kilogram of washing (2kg minimum) and it's open from 7 am to 7 pm Monday to Saturday and from 8 am to 5 pm Sunday.

Also recommended is the Sea Breeze Laundry (☎ 02-525 4971), at 1317 Adriatico St, near the corner of Padre Faura St. It also charges P30 a kilogram (3kg minimum). It's open from 8 am to 8 pm Monday to Saturday and from 8 am to 5 pm Sunday. If you drop your laundry off first thing in the morning, it should be ready that evening.

Swimming Only a few of the hotels in Malate, Ermita and Paco have their own pools, but visitors can (for a fee) use the swimming pools at the following private clubs, universities and hotels.

The Ninoy Aquino Memorial Stadium FB Harrison St, Malate; open from 8 am to 11.30 pm and from 1 to 5 pm daily except Monday; P20
Totalle Wellness & Fitness Center (☎ 02-526 8461) Philippine Women's University, Taft Ave, Malate; open from 5 to 9 pm Monday to Saturday; P60

The Park Hotel 1032 Belen St, Paco; open from 9 am to 9 pm daily; P75

The Old Army & Navy Club Seafood Wharf, Kalaw St, Ermita; open from 8 am to 8 pm Tuesday to Sunday; P100

The Manila Midtown Hotel On the corner of Adriatico and Pedro Gil Sts, Ermita; open from 8 am to 9 pm daily; P150

The Century Park Hotel Vito Cruz St, Malate; open from 7 am to 7 pm daily; P250

Medical Services If you need a doctor, reliable private medical services are provided by:

Makati Medical Center (☎ 02-815 9911)
   2 Amorsolo St, Makati
Manila Doctors Hospital (☎ 02-524 3011)
   677 United Nations Ave, Ermita
Manila Medical Center (☎ 02-523 8131)
   1122 General Luna St, Ermita

Alternative therapy is provided by the Balikatan Scientific Massage Center for the Blind in the Don Bosco mission on Arnaiz Ave. The blind masseurs offer sitting massages for P50, half-hour massages for P110 and hour-long massages for P220. It's open from 10 am to 7 pm Monday to Saturday.

Emergency Unfortunately, crime is a part of life in Manila and foreigners are popular targets for pickpockets and muggers. If the worst happens, the 24-hour Tourist Assistance Unit (☎ 02-524 1660, 524 1728) in the DOT building on TM Kalaw St, Rizal Park, may be able to help. The police emergency number for Manila is ☎ 166.

Dangers & Annoyances With a total population of close to 10 million people, Manila has a deserved reputation for being overcrowded. Traffic noise, crime and atmospheric pollution are also major annoyances, though the later plays a important part in producing Manila's legendary sunsets.

Things to See & Do
Perhaps because Manila is such an overpowering place, most visitors can't wait to leave the capital. However, there are plenty of attractions for those prepared to overlook Manila's flaws – from vibrant markets and

---

Antipollution Ride

Casual visitors might assume pollution is taken for granted in Philippine cities. But even in stinky old Manila, people are taking to the streets to demand a reduction in vehicle and industrial fumes. One of the most imaginative street protests is known as the Tour of the Fireflies. Held annually in late April, this 50km mass bike ride through seven cities of Metro Manila is a colourful call for clean air and the eventual return of the fireflies that once thrived in and around the city. Antipollution masks are worn by all riders and prizes are awarded for the best costumes and best adorned bikes. The ride starts at 7 am (a registration fee of P50 is payable from 5.30 am) from the Quezon Memorial Circle on North Ave in Quezon City. For more information contact Cycling Advocates via its Web site at www.mindgate.net/firefly/tour/html/commit .html, or drop into any Body Shop or participating bicycle shop.

Mic Looby

---

historic buildings to museums celebrating every aspect of the Philippines' cultural mix.

Rizal Park
Still widely known as Luneta, after the district that was demolished to build it, Rizal Park forms the lungs of Manila, with shady lawns, ponds, and monuments to almost every Filipino hero you care to mention. On evenings and weekends, hundreds of Filipinos gather to play music, stroll, watch the chess or martial arts displays, or just relax away from the swarming traffic.

The park sees its first visitors at dawn, when locals gather to practise t'ai chi or the traditional martial art of *arnis de mano* (a pre-Hispanic style of stick-fighting). There are formalised displays of arnis and other martial arts on Sunday afternoon. Right in the middle of the park is a small concrete skating ring, which is popular with Filipino teenagers (P5 admission, P30 skate hire).

The islands are recreated in miniature in the pond at the eastern end of the park and there are several ornamental gardens

From shantytowns...

To skyscrapers...

And the traffic in between.

JOHN PENNOCK

RICHARD I'ANSON

RICHARD I'ANSON

RICHARD I'ANSON

Transport options in chaotic, colourful Manila.

including the Orchidarium (P10), the mini-malist Japanese Garden (P5), and the ornate Chinese Garden (P10). The chess plaza is a shady spot where local grandmasters test their chess skills against each other and the clock (P8 for a board and pieces). All the gardens are open from 7 am to 7 pm daily.

The park is dedicated to the Philippine na-tional hero, Dr José Rizal, who was executed here by the Spanish on 30 December 1896 for inciting revolution. The dramatic last hours of Rizal's life are recreated in a series of statues which form part of a sound-and-light show in the evening. The **Diorama of the Martyrdom of Dr José Rizal** is open from 8 am to 5 pm Monday to Friday, and admission is P10. The sound-and-light show is given in Tagalog at 7 pm and in English at 8 pm (P50).

The Concert at the Park takes place most Sundays in the open-air auditorium near the Diorama, with a varied program of classical music, song and dance. Admission is free.

Also in the park are the huge DOT build-ing and the excellent Museum of the Pilipino People (see the later Museums section). **The Planetarium**, at the edge of the park on P Burgos St, offers projections of the stars at 9 and 9.30 am and 1.30 and 3.30 pm Monday to Saturday, but only if there are at least 15 interested visitors. Admission is P30.

Intramuros

If the Spanish had established their capital at nearby Cavite, the rest of the Philippines' history might have been very different, but Miguel Lopez de Legazpi chose to erect his fortress at the mouth of the Pasig River. De-spite the fortifications, the site was to prove notoriously difficult to defend, and the British, Americans and Japanese were all able to capture Manila with a minimum of force. Perhaps for this reason, the walled Spanish city survived until the end of WWII, when it was finally destroyed by US and Japanese bombing.

From its foundation in 1571, Intramuros was the exclusive preserve of the ruling classes. Within the walls were the luxurious houses of the Spanish feudal families, hospi-tals, numerous churches and broad cobbled plazas. The Filipinos were housed in nearby Luneta, in the area now covered by Rizal Park, while the 'troublesome' Chinese were kept under permanent supervision in a ghetto called Parian, which was the scene of wild riots and frequent massacres by the Spanish.

The number of vacant lots in Intramuros gives some indication of the ferocity of the Battle for Manila in WWII. As the USA gained the upper hand, the Japanese fell back to the walled city and Fort Santiago, with both sides destroying any buildings that provided cover for the enemy. By the end of the conflict, the city walls were almost all that remained of Intramuros, and nearly 100,000 Filipino civilians had died in the crossfire. Many of the museums in town have good collections of period photographs which show the old city in all its glory.

Despite the devastation, there are still a few impressive buildings, and the walled city is pleasantly quiet after the hectic pace of Ermita and Malate. Surrounding the re-stored city walls, the **Club Intramuros golf course** is open day and night for enthusias-tic local golfers.

San Agustin Church & Museum

The classically Spanish San Agustin Church on General Luna St is probably the most im-posing building to survive the firestorm. Built in 1599, this historic church was actu-ally the third church built by the Spanish on the site (the first two were destroyed by fire), and it has weathered seven major earth-quakes, as well as the Battle for Manila.

Following the 1863 and 1889 earthquakes, which destroyed one of the two church tow-ers, a pair of Italian artists were brought in to paint the elaborate trompe l'oeil patterns on the walls and ceilings. In the small chapel to the left of the main altar is the mausoleum of Miguel Lopez de Legazpi.

Spread over two floors of the adjacent Augustinian monastery is the excellent San Agustin Museum, which is devoted to the religious art of the Spanish colonial period, and includes whole altarpieces and screens rescued from Manila's churches during WWII. Opening hours are from 9 am to noon and from 1 to 5 pm daily. Admission is P45 and P20 (for students).

MANILA

INTRAMUROS & RIZAL PARK

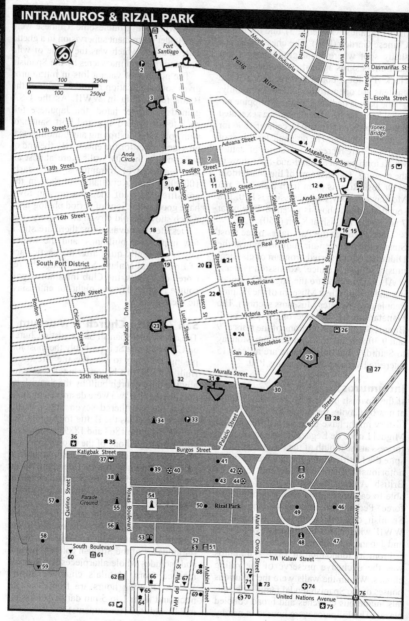

INTRAMUROS & RIZAL PARK

PLACES TO STAY
21 Hotel Intramuros de Manila;
    Casa Manila Museum; San
    Luis Complex
35 Manila Hotel
64 Bayview Park Hotel
66 Star Boulevard Inn
68 Mabini Mansion
73 Holiday Inn Manila

PLACES TO EAT
59 Golden Horizon Restaurant;
    Harbour Trips
60 Seafood Wharf
65 Barrio Fiesta
67 Maxim's
71 McDonald's
72 KFC

OTHER
1   Rizal Shrine
2   Club Intramuros Golf Course
3   Revellin de San Francisco
4   Immigration Office
5   GPO
6   Puerta Isabel II
7   Plaza Roma
8   Palacio del Gobernador
9   Puerta del Postigo
10 Archbishop's Residence
11 Manila Cathedral
12 Letran College

13 Bastion de San Gabriel
14 Saulog Transit; St Anthony
    Transit; Buses to Cavite &
    Ternate
15 Revellin del Parian
16 Puerta del Parian
17 Bahay Tsinoy Museum
18 Bastion de Santa Lucia
19 Puerta de Santa Lucia
20 San Agustin Church; Museum
22 Commission for Culture &
    The Arts
23 Fortin San Pedro
24 El Amanecer Building;
    Silharis; Tradewinds
    Bookshop
25 Bastion de Dilao
26 Alps Bus Terminal
27 Manila City Hall
28 National Museum
29 Revellin de Recoletos
30 Bastion de San Andres
31 Puerta Real Gardens &
    Aquarium
32 Bastion de San Diego
33 Golf Course
34 Ninoy Aquino & Legaspi
    Monument
36 Police Station
37 Rizal Park Post Office
38 Carabao Statue
39 Rizal's Execution Spot

40 Chinese Garden
41 Planetarium
42 Japanese Garden
43 Concerts in the Park &
    Open-Air Stage
44 Orchidarium
45 Museum of the Pilipino People
46 Philippines Model
47 Children's Playground
48 Department of Tourism
    (DOT); Tourist Office;
    Tourist Police
49 Agrifina Circle & Skating Rink
50 Central Lagoon
51 National Library
52 Philippines National
    Bank (PNB)
53 Rizal's Fountain
54 Rizal Memorial
55 Lorenzo Ruiz Statue
56 Tamaraw Statue
57 Quirino Grandstand
58 Children's Playground
61 Old Army & Navy Club;
    Museo ng Maynila
62 Museo Pambata
63 US Embassy
69 WG&A Office
70 Equitable PCI Bank
74 Manila Doctors Hospital
75 Western Police Station
76 United Nations Avenue Station

Manila Cathedral

The Manila Cathedral on General Luna St is the main Catholic church in Manila and is a popular venue for high-society weddings, which are often presided over by the Archbishop of Manila, the interestingly named Jaime Cardinal Sin. The original church was destroyed in WWII, but the Vatican donated considerable funds to its reconstruction, and the new cathedral, completed in 1958, looks suitably ancient. The church has a grand gilded altar and a huge 4500-pipe organ, and there is usually at least one wedding here every Sunday, where you can witness Manila's high society dressed in their finest.

Casa Manila

Also on General Luna St, the Casa Manila (or Los Hidalgos House) is a beautifully restored Spanish colonial home that offers a window onto the opulent, formal lifestyle of the Spanish gentry. The rooms are furnished

with period furniture and plaques explain which members of the household were allowed into which rooms at various times of day. Admission is P50/30 for adults/students and it's open from 9 am to noon and 1 am to 6 pm daily except Monday.

The new **Bahay Tsinoy** (or Museum of the Chinese in the Philippines), in the Kaisa Heritage Center, on the corner of Cabildo and Anda Sts in Intramuros, offers three-dimensional dioramas, interactive displays and a vast collection of period photos of the capital, all celebrating the huge role played by the Chinese in the growth of Manila. Admission is P50/30 for adults/students. It's open from noon to 5 pm Tuesday to Friday and from 9 am to 5 pm on the weekend.

Fort Santiago

The focus of Intramuros' defences was Fort Santiago, which at one time guarded the entrance to the Pasig River (the land west of here was all reclaimed from Manila Bay). While Fort Santiago proved to be almost impregnable, Manila Bay offered little protection to the Spanish fleet, a key factor in the victory of the US invasion forces. Many times in its history Manila has been declared an 'open city', in order to protect its people from the horrors of a sustained military siege.

Today the fort has been restored and stands as a memorial to the victims of WWII and the Philippine national hero José Rizal, who was imprisoned here in the final days before his execution. The Rizal Shrine at the centre of the fort contains audiovisual displays, a reliquary with one of Rizal's vertebrae, the first draft of Rizal's novel *Noli me Tangere* (Spanish: *Touch Me Not*) and the original copy of Rizal's farewell poem, which was smuggled out of his cell inside an oil lamp. It's open from 8 am to noon and 1 to 5 pm daily except Monday. On the way out, staff will request a donation and show you evidence of foreign visitors who have given hundreds of pesos. This is voluntary, so you shouldn't feel obliged to make a donation.

At the far end of the fort, the infamous cellblock where American prisoners of war were drowned by the rising tide is being restored after being ripped apart in 1988 by government-sanctioned treasure seekers looking for the war treasure of General Yamashita of Japan (see the boxed text 'Gold-Diggers' in the Facts for the Visitor chapter). Nearby, the cellblock where Rizal spent his last night has been turned into an open-air theatre and brass footprints set into the pavement mark his final steps to the execution spot in Rizal Park.

The gates to Fort Santiago are open from 8 am to 6 pm daily, though it's not really worth visiting when the shrine is closed. Admission is P40/15. The entrance is at the end of General Luna St, Intramuros, on the far side of Aduana St.

Cultural Center of the Philippines

The Cultural Center of the Philippines (CCP) was conceived as a celebration of Filipino culture by Imelda Marcos during the optimistic early years of her husband's regime. P40 million of the people's money was invested in the project, which sits on a plot of land reclaimed from Manila Bay. The whole thing was opened with great aplomb in September 1969.

The CCP never quite lived up to its promise, but the buildings here are grandly conceived and were designed by leading Filipino architect Leandro Locsin. The CCP itself houses an art gallery, a museum of musical instruments and a theatre that often has performances by the excellent Philippine Philharmonic Orchestra (☎ 02-832 3878 for details). Admission to the museum is free and it's open from 9 am to 5 pm Monday to Friday and from 10 am to 6 pm on weekends.

Dotted around the complex are the Folk Arts Theater (☎ 02-832 1120), the Philippine International Conference Center, the GSIS Building, the Westin Philippine Plaza hotel and the imposing Film Theater, which has sadly fallen into disrepair. Within the GSIS building, the **Museo ng Sining** is a huge museum of contemporary art. On display are sculptures, paintings and tapestries, including work by famous Filipino artists Fernando Amorsolo and Hernando Ocampo. It's open from 8.45 to 11 am and 1 to 4 pm Tuesday to Saturday and admission is free.

Also within the CCP complex, the stately **Coconut Palace** was built by the Marcos family to celebrate the Papal visit of 1981. Unfortunately for the dictator, Pope John Paul II refused to stay in such an ostentatious building while there was so much poverty on Manila's streets. The palace was eventually inaugurated by Brooke Shields. You can take a guided tour from 9 am to noon and from 1 to 4 pm daily except Monday (P100). Nearby are a number of permanent fairgrounds with roller coasters and other rides.

To get to the CCP from Malate or Ermita, take any Baclaran or Vito Cruz jeepney on MH del Pilar St to Harrison Plaza. On Vito Cruz St, at the end of the mall, you can pick up an orange Vito Cruz-CCP jeepney; they ply a circular route around the complex, passing most of the important buildings.

Museums

With the symbolic departure of the US forces from Subic Bay and Clark Airbase, the celebration of Filipino culture has become a national obsession. Tucked away in Manila's government buildings are some of the best museums in Asia, covering all periods of the Philippines' history. Whether you are interested in archaeology, tribal art or contemporary sculpture and painting, there should be something to take your fancy. Admission to government museums is often free, but you'll need to leave some ID when you sign in. Cameras are prohibited in all museums.

The centrepiece of the new National Museum network is the splendid **Museum of the Pilipino People** in the former Finance Building in Rizal Park. The best of the National Museum collection is housed here, including the skullcap of the Philippines' earliest known inhabitant, Tabon Man (actually a woman), who died around 24,000 BC. A large part of this excellent museum is devoted to the wreck of the *San Diego*, a Spanish galleon that sank off the coast of Luzon during a gun battle with the Dutch in 1600. As well as recovered artefacts, the wreck site has been painstakingly recreated within the museum. Other treasures include the anthropomorphic burial jars from the Maitan cave burial (sculpted to represent the faces of the dead) and a large collection of precolonial artefacts and musical instruments. Admission is free (ID required) and the museum is open from 9 am to 5 pm Tuesday to Sunday. Allow at least two hours for your visit.

With most of its treasures now in the Museum of the Pilipino People, the vast **National Museum** on Burgos Street, near Rizal Park, is a shadow of its former self. The few rooms that are currently open to the public house a small and drab collection of fossils, ethnological exhibits and ageing stuffed animals. The biggest attraction here is the vast painting 'Spoliarium', by the Filipino master Juan Luna. Admission is free (ID required) and the museum is open from 9 am to 5 pm Tuesday to Sunday.

Housed in the old Army & Navy Club on South Blvd, the **Museo ng Maynila** is devoted to the history of the capital. Among the interesting items on display are vintage postcards from the US colonial period and photographs taken during the Battle for Manila. It's open from 9 am to 6 pm Tuesday to Saturday and admission is free.

The excellent **Metropolitan Museum** in the Bangko Sentral ng Pilipinas is a bright, modern museum that showcases contemporary Filipino art. The exhibitions change regularly, so call ☎ 02-523 7855 to find out what's on. The basement houses a permanent exhibition of precolonial gold and pottery from the national bank collection. Admission is P50/30 and the museum is open from 10 am to 6 pm Monday to Saturday (the basement closes at 4.30 pm).

Next to the US Embassy on Roxas Blvd, the **Museo Pambata** is an interactive science museum for children, though adults can easily spend a few hours playing with all the levers and buttons. It's open from 9 am to 5 pm Tuesday to Saturday and from 1 to 6 pm Sunday. Admission is P50/30.

The **University of Santo Thomas Museum of Arts & Sciences** houses one of the oldest collections in Manila, with some items dating back to the original *Gabinete de Fisicia* (Natural History Room) of 1682. As well as stuffed animals, there are coins, instruments, paintings, religious images and ceramics. It's open from 10 am to 4 pm Tuesday to Friday and admission is P30. To get here, take a jeepney with 'UST' on its signboard.

The Ayala Foundation, which is devoted to fostering Philippine national pride, is responsible for Makati's **Ayala Museum** which features a series of miniature dioramas depicting the key events of the Philippine quest for independence. The museum provides a good overview of Philippine history, and there is also a collection of ethnic artefacts and model ships. It's open from 8 am to 6 pm Tuesday to Sunday.

Malacañang Palace

This attractive complex of colonial buildings, along José P Laurel St, San Miguel, is the seat of the Philippine government and also includes the **Museo ng Malacañang**, where you used to be able see Imelda Marcos' extravagant collection of shoes. Sadly, the shoes have now been replaced by a series of exhibits celebrating only the positive achievements of each Philippines president.

The museum is open from 9 am to 3 pm Monday to Friday, but Thursday and Friday are the best days to visit, as Malacañang is open for public viewing for only P40 (from Monday to Wednesday you'll have to pay P200 for the privilege of a guided tour). The entrance to the museum is through Gate 6, at the intersection of JP Laurel and San Rafael Sts. You can get there on the San Miguel/Malacañang jeepneys that leave from the Ilalim ng Tulay Market in Quiapo.

Nayong Pilipino

You can tour the Philippines in miniature at the Nayong Pilipino (Philippine Village) which attempts to reproduce the best of the islands in one spot. Dotted around the 45 hectare site are copies of famous landmarks, indigenous buildings and even a miniature version of the Mayon volcano, though a lot of the space is given over to souvenir shops.

There are numerous museums in the complex, including the excellent Philippine Museum of Ethnology, which showcases the colourful textiles, tools, weapons and instruments produced by the islands' various ethnic groups. Staff in traditional costume are often on hand to demonstrate how different items were used.

Other museums include the Museo ng Buhay Pilipino, with 19th century furniture, the Aguinaldo House, containing the DM Guevarra art collection, the Torogan House, with ethnic Muslim artefacts and the Bulwagan ng Kagandahan, which pays homage to Filipina beauty queens. Free jeepneys run between the various sections of the park.

The gates at the Nayong Pilipino are open from 7 am to 6 pm daily (to 7 pm on weekends), but the museums are only open between 9 am and 5 pm Tuesday to Sunday. Admission is P50. On weekends, traditional dances are performed in the Mindanao section of the Nayong Pilipino, beginning at 2.30 and 4 pm. There's also a Kamayan restaurant, where you can eat Filipino food with your hands. It's open from 7 am to 10 pm.

The entrance to the Nayong Pilipino is next to the Philippine Village Hotel and the new NAIA Centennial Terminal II, which can be reached by taking a 'Baclaran' jeepney from the tourist belt and changing to a jeepney heading to NAIA.

Chinatown

After centuries of suppression by the Spanish, Manila's Chinese population quickly rose to the top of the economic and social ladder under the more liberal US administration. Amongst Manila's famous Chinese *mestizos* (people of mixed Chinese and Spanish descent) are José Rizal, Ferdinand Marcos and Cory Aquino. The former Chinese ghetto of Parian is now buried under Manila City Hall, but the modern centre of the Chinese community is in Binondo, north of the Pasig River.

Ongpin St, which runs between the east and west friendship arches (or welcome gates), is the major thoroughfare in Chinatown. Here you'll find dozens of goldsmiths, herbalists, Chinese teahouses and shops selling incense and paper money to burn for the ancestors. The third welcome gate is on Quintin Paredes St, on the north side of Jones Bridge.

There aren't a great many sights here, but the streets are lively and there is a general atmosphere of industry and tradition. The numerous Chinese teahouses along Ongpin St are good for noodle or dim sum lunches.

Chinese Cemetery

As in life, so it is in death for Manila's wealthiest citizens, who are buried with every modern convenience in virtual houses in the huge Chinese Cemetery in Santa Cruz. With eternal addresses like Millionaires Row, there are tombs with crystal chandeliers, air-conditioning, hot and cold running water, kitchens and flushing toilets, in case the interred are caught short on the way to paradise.

The guards are well versed in local legends and offer tours of the most ostentatious tombs for P300. On 1 November, hundreds of Chinese-Filipino families gather to offer food and flowers to their ancestors.

The South Gate to the cemetery is open from 7.30 am to 7 pm daily. To get there take a 'Monumento' jeepney to Aurora Ave (where Rizal Ave becomes Rizal Ave Extension), and walk east to F Heurtes St, which runs up to the gate.

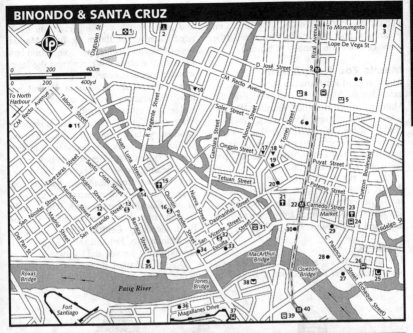

BINONDO & SANTA CRUZ

PLACES TO EAT
10 Quan Yin Chay
17 Maxim's
18 Hap Chan

OTHER
1   Tutuban Center Mall; Bodhi
    Vegetarian Restaurant
2   Seng Guan Buddhist Temple
3   Central Market
4   Manila City Jail
5   Cinemas
6   National Book Store
7   Philippine Rabbit Bus Terminal
8   Cinemas
11 Divisoria Market
12 Sulpicio Line Shipping

13 Citibank
14 San Fernando St Welcome
    Gate
15 Binondo Church & Plaza Ruiz
16 HSBC
19 Trial Court
20 Ongpin St Welcome Gate
21 Plaza Santa Cruz; Santa Cruz
    Church
23 Quiapo Church
24 PVP Buses to Makati
25 Globo de Oro Mosque
26 Jeepneys to Malacañang
27 Ilalim ng Tulay Market
28 Quinta Market
29 Hidalgo Street Photographic
    Shops

30 Royal Booking Office (Ferry
    Tickets)
31 Philippine Long Distance
    Telephone (PLDT) Office
32 Philippine National Bank (PNB)
33 THAI
34 Jones Bridge Welcome Gate
35 Manila Stock Exchange
36 Immigration Office
37 Buses to Cavite & Ternate
38 GPO
39 Metropolitan Theatre

METRORAIL STATIONS
9   D José
22 Carriedo
40 Central

Quiapo Church

The Quiapo Church, on Quezon Blvd in Quiapo, is a modern replacement for several older churches that were destroyed by fire, earthquake and bombing. Of interest here is the **Black Nazarene**, a black wooden cross which came to Quiapo from Spain in 1767. It's carried on the shoulder of a wooden statue of Christ, and devotees are allowed to fondle the cross and the heel of the statue though holes in the perspex case. The cross is paraded through the streets on 9 January and during Passion week (the week before Palm Sunday in Easter).

Manila Zoo & Aquarium

At the start of FB Harrison St, the southern extension of Mabini St, you will find the Manila Zoo and Botanical Gardens (the entrance is actually on Adriatico St), which includes some of the Philippines' rarer species but doesn't offer its animals much quality of life. It's open from 7 am to 7 pm daily and admission is P6.

Part of the Intramuros city walls, the Puerto Real Gardens & Aquarium has a small collection of tropical fish, including a few tiny sharks. It's open from 8 am to 6 pm daily and admission is P40.

Markets

The lively street markets around Carriedo St, Quiapo, offer hundreds of stalls selling clothes, fruit, alarm clocks, karaoke CDs and pretty much anything else you might need. Nearby, the **Ilalim ng Tulay Market**, under Quezon Bridge, has some good basketware and shell work amongst the tacky wooden models of *carabao* (water buffalo). Across the road, the **Quinta Market** is a busy 'wet and dry' market selling fish, vegetables and other foodstuffs.

Around Quiapo church are dozens of **apothecary stalls** selling all manner of herbal and religious medicines, as well as amulets (carved stones and other objects believed to have healing powers). The witches' brews on offer vary from health drinks like Noni juice, a nutritious plant extract, to infusions of toxic black mahogany seeds, which can be fatal in large doses. Further along Quezon Blvd, the dingy **Central Market** surrounds the Manila City Jail and sells clothes, military uniforms, knives and hardware.

Divisoria Market, on Santo Cristo St, is a major centre for bale clothing, with fake

Quiapo Church was built to replace older churches, ruined by various disasters.

examples of pretty much every brand name currently on the market. It's spread over several floors and there's a hectic 'wet and dry' market in the basement.

On CM Recto Ave, Binondo, in the direction of the harbour, are hundreds of stalls selling household goods and bale clothing and the **Tutuban Center mall**, which has similar brand-name clothes stalls to Divisoria Market.

The **Baclaran flea market** in Pasay City sells food, clothes, household goods and electronics. Prices are lower here than elsewhere in town and there are lots of canteens offering cheap and tasty local food. The market is busy until late in the evening.

In Malate, the **San Andres Market** has some of the most expensive fruit in Manila, though the produce is generally of a high quality. You can find many more unusual fruits here such as rambatan and *guybano* (soursop) here.

The **organic market** in the Greenbelt Square park takes place from 7 am to 3 pm every Tuesday and Saturday, with a good selection of organic fruit and vegetables.

Harbour Cruises

Golden Horizon Cruise & Travel (☎ 02-524 1571), based in the Golden Horizon Restaurant in Rizal Park, offers a number of one-hour cruises around Manila Harbour. All you will see are huge tankers in the bay, but the breeze is certainly refreshing after the lead-filled air of Metro Manila. The cruise leaves at 5.30 pm from Tuesday to Thursday (P70) to catch the sunset. At weekends, cheaper morning cruises are offered for P40.

Down the Drain?

At least 40 of the waterways that once helped flush out Manila Bay were officially listed as 'missing' by the Metropolitan Manila Development Authority after they started disappearing in the 1950s. Most of these creeks, or *esteros* – so vital in keeping the city's notorious floodwaters down – have been erased by construction projects and illegal rezoning, or clogged by squatters desperate for living space.

Mic Looby

Places to Stay

Manila has accommodation to suit all price ranges, from P300 box-rooms with fan and bed, to US$3000 penthouse suites with multiple rooms, private swimming pools and butlers. Prices given here are in pesos for the cheaper places, and in pesos or US dollars for the mid-range and top-end hotels.

Places to Stay – Budget

Accommodation in Manila is expensive compared to many countries in South-East Asia. Expect to pay P150 to P200 for a dorm bed, P300 upwards for fan rooms and at least P500 for air-con. Most of the cheap places are concentrated in Malate and Ermita, particularly along Adriatico, Mabini and MH del Pilar Sts.

Malate Malate is the main centre for budget travellers, and the area has undergone something of a renaissance in recent years, with the opening of numerous trendy bars and restaurants. However, many hotels have pushed up their prices to reflect their new, desirable surroundings.

The longest-standing travellers' centre in Malate is the *Malate Pensionne (☎ 02-523 8304 to 523 8306, 1771 Adriatico St)*, in the same complex as the Portico Restaurant. Set back from the road in a pleasant courtyard, it's something of an oasis in crowded Manila. Beds in slightly cramped dorms cost P242 with fan, or P275 with air-con, while singles/doubles start at P440/550 with fan and shared bathroom. Air-con doubles with cable TV, telephone and bathroom start at P1045.

Juen's Place (☎ 02-450 1265, 1775D Adriatico St), in an alley beside the Portico Restaurant complex, has basic facilities, but it's a good place to meet other travellers. The guesthouse is in the home of a Filipino family and guests have use of the kitchen. Beds in fan cooled dorms start at P165, with other rooms for P180/280.

Pension Natividad (☎ 02-521 0524, 1690 MH del Pilar St) is another friendly guesthouse set around a courtyard, with an inexpensive coffee shop that does good breakfasts. Beds in fan cooled single-sex dorms are P200, fan cooled rooms with common bathroom are P300/550. Unfortunately,

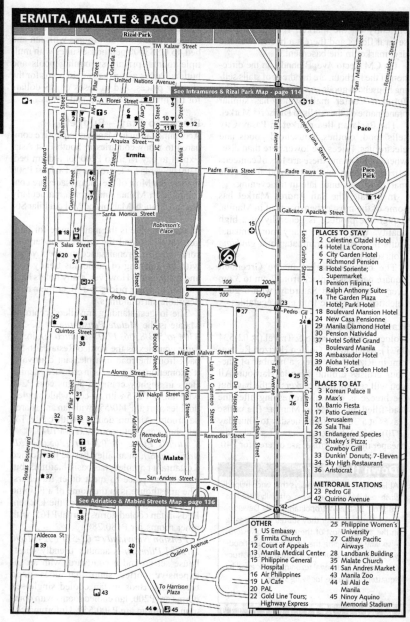

ERMITA, MALATE & PACO

See Intramuros & Rizal Park Map - page 114

See Adriatico & Mabini Streets Map - page 136

PLACES TO STAY
2 Celestine Citadel Hotel
4 Hotel La Corona
6 City Garden Hotel
7 Richmond Pension
8 Hotel Soriente;
   Supermarket
11 Pension Filipina;
   Ralph Anthony Suites
14 The Garden Plaza
   Hotel; Park Hotel
18 Boulevard Mansion Hotel
24 New Casa Pensionne
29 Manila Diamond Hotel
30 Pension Natividad
37 Hotel Sofitel Grand
   Boulevard Manila
38 Ambassador Hotel
39 Aloha Hotel
40 Bianca's Garden Hotel

PLACES TO EAT
3 Korean Palace II
9 Max's
10 Barrio Fiesta
17 Patio Guernica
21 Jerusalem
26 Sala Thai
31 Endangered Species
32 Shakey's Pizza;
   Cowboy Grill
33 Dunkin' Donuts; 7-Eleven
34 Sky High Restaurant
36 Aristocrat

METRORAIL STATIONS
23 Pedro Gil
42 Quirino Avenue

OTHER
1 US Embassy
5 Ermita Church
12 Court of Appeals
13 Manila Medical Center
15 Philippine General
   Hospital
16 Air Philippines
19 LA Cafe
20 PAL
22 Gold Line Tours;
   Highway Express
25 Philippine Women's
   University
27 Cathay Pacific
   Airways
28 Landbank Building
35 Malate Church
41 San Andres Market
43 Manila Zoo
44 Jai Alai de
   Manila
45 Ninoy Aquino
   Memorial Stadium

To Harrison
Plaza

the doubles with private bathroom at the back are next to a loud karaoke bar and are suitable for *very* heavy sleepers (P650 or P900 with air-con).

Right on Remedios circle, the tiny *Circle Pension* (☎ 02-522 2920, 602 Remedios St) offers clean, quiet rooms with fan, which sleep two to four people for P400, or larger rooms for P600.

The well-located *Joward's Pension House* (☎ 02-338 3191, 1730 Adriatico St, Malate) is not bad for the price, with clean rooms with fan at P220/308, and air-con rooms from P440. It's next door to the Joward's Hotpot Restaurant.

Next to Woods restaurant on Mabini St, the little *Soledad Pension House* (☎ 02-524 0706, 1529 Mabini St) has clean, basic rooms with fan from P150 to P180, depending on the size of the room. Better deluxe rooms are P290.

Ermita During the boom years of the sex trade, Ermita was awash with seedy 'inns' (bars with rooms upstairs), but very few of these places survived the clean-up campaign of Mayor Lim. There are a few cheap pension houses in the area if you're really watching the pennies.

Tucked away in a tiny street between A Flores and Arquiza Sts in Ermita, the friendly *Richmond Pension* (☎ 02-525 3864, 1165 Grey St) is a basic family run place with simple fan cooled singles/doubles at P240/410, fan cooled triples from P430 and air-con triples from P590.

Nearby, the little *Pension Filipina* (☎ 02-521 1488, 572 Engracia Reyes St) offers similar rooms for P300/400, or P500/600 with air-con.

Just south of Taft Ave, the recently refurbished *New Casa Pensionne* (☎ 02-522 1740), on the corner of Pedro Gil and Leon Guinto Sts, has very clean rooms and good security. Fan cooled rooms with shared bathroom are P350/460, and air-con doubles with bathroom cost P800.

Back on Mabini St, the long-running *Mabini Pension* (☎ 02-523 3930, 1337 Mabini St) has ageing rooms but it's still popular. Fan cooled rooms with shared bath cost P450/550, or P650 for doubles with bath. Air-con rooms are P950.

The *Ermita Tourist Inn* (☎ 02-521 8770, 1549 Mabini St, Ermita) has clean tiled rooms that aren't bad for the money at P660 to P890 for doubles with bath and air-con. They have a good travel agent downstairs.

Close to Robinson's Place, the *Fairmont Pension House* (☎ 02-526 1209), on the corner of Adriatico and Pedro Gil Sts, Ermita, has ordinary but clean rooms for P350 with fan and TV, P600 with air-con and TV and P700 with air-con, bath and TV.

At the far end of the mall, the *Midtown Inn* (☎ 02-525 1403, 551 Padre Faura St, Ermita) has passable rooms with air-con, bath and TV from P750, and slightly overpriced fan-rooms for P500/600.

Parañaque There are a couple of cheap places in Parañaque that are useful if you're connecting with an international or domestic flight. There are some good local food places in nearby Baclaran, although crime can be a problem in this part of town.

The *Manila International Youth Hostel* (☎ 02-832 0680, 4227-9 Tomas Claudio St) is pleasant, with friendly staff and spotless linen. Beds cost P120 (P140 for nonmembers) in the fan cooled dorm, or P170 (P200 nonmembers) in the coveted air-con dorm.

Located in one of the modern Parañaque housing estates, *The Townhouse* (☎ 02-833 1939, 31 Bayview Dr) is run by a friendly Balikbayan couple and has lots of communal areas. Beds in the dorm are P120, fan-rooms are P360/560, and air-con doubles with TV and private bathroom are P1000.

Places to Stay – Mid-Range

Most of the accommodation in Manila falls into this price range. Air-con, en suite bathroom, cable TV, phone and fridges are usually standard. Prices range from P1000 to P2000 (P3000 in Makati). In Ermita and Malate, most mid-range accommodation is along Mabini and Adriatico Sts. In Makati, Arnaiz Ave and Makati Ave are good places to start.

Malate & Ermita Just off Remedios circle, the *Cle D'Or Hotel* (☎ 02-524 0474,

MANILA

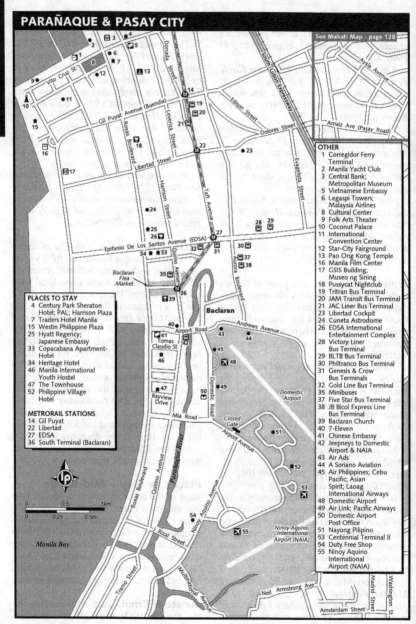

PARAÑAQUE & PASAY CITY

See Makati Map - page 128

PLACES TO STAY

4 Century Park Sheraton Hotel; PAL; Harrison Plaza
7 Traders Hotel Manila
15 Westin Philippine Plaza
25 Hyatt Regency; Japanese Embassy
33 Copacabana Apartment-Hotel
34 Heritage Hotel
46 Manila International Youth Hostel
47 The Townhouse
52 Philippine Village Hotel

METRORAIL STATIONS

14 Gil Puyat
22 Libertad
27 EDSA
36 South Terminal (Baclaran)

OTHER

1 Corregidor Ferry Terminal
2 Manila Yacht Club
3 Central Bank; Metropolitan Museum
5 Vietnamese Embassy
6 Legaspi Towers; Malaysia Airlines
8 Cultural Center
9 Folk Arts Theater
10 Coconut Palace
11 International Convention Center
12 Star-City Fairground
13 Pao Ong Kong Temple
16 Manila Film Center
17 GSIS Building; Museo ng Sining
18 Pussycat Nightclub
19 Tritran Bus Terminal
20 JAM Transit Bus Terminal
21 JAC Liner Bus Terminal
23 Libertad Cockpit
24 Cuneta Astrodome
26 EDSA International Entertainment Complex
28 Victory Liner Bus Terminal
29 BLTB Bus Terminal
30 Philtranco Bus Terminal
31 Genesis & Crow Bus Terminals
32 Gold Line Bus Terminal
35 Minibuses
37 Five Star Bus Terminal
38 JB Bicol Express Line Bus Terminal
39 Baclaran Church
40 7-Eleven
41 Chinese Embassy
42 Jeepneys to Domestic Airport & NAIA
43 Air Ads
44 A Soriano Aviation
45 Air Philippines; Cebu Pacific; Asian Spirit; Laoag International Airways
48 Domestic Airport
49 Air Link; Pacific Airways
50 Domestic Airport Post Office
51 Nayong Pilipino
53 Centennial Terminal II
54 Duty Free Shop
55 Ninoy Aquino International Airport (NAIA)

Baclaran

Domestic Airport

Closed Gate

Ninoy Aquino International Airport (NAIA)

Manila Bay

0   0.5   1km
0 0.25 0.5mi

612 Remedios St, Malate) has a good location but fairly ordinary rooms. Air-con rooms start at P800 with shared bath. More expensive rooms have bath and TV.

A few blocks south on Adriatico St, **Bianca's Garden Hotel** (☎ 02-526 0351, 2139 Adriatico St, Malate), formerly the True Home, is probably the most charismatic mid-range hotel in town. The rooms contain local furniture and works of art and there's a lovely pool. Fan rooms with shared bath are P700, and excellent air-con rooms with bath and TV cost from P1300 to P1700.

The **Rothman Inn Hotel** (☎ 02-523 4501 to 523 4510, 1633 Adriatico St, Malate), in the heart of the restaurant district, is better than many more expensive places. Good-value rooms with air-con, bath, phone and TV are P1500 (P1600 with fridge), while apartment-style rooms with small kitchen are P2500.

Palm Plaza (☎ 02-521 2502 to 521 2510), on the corner of Pedro Gil and Adriatico Sts, is a popular, modern hotel with good business facilities in the lobby. Rooms with air-con, bath, cable TV, phone and fridge start at US$65 for singles, or US$75 for doubles and twins. It also has an outdoor pool.

Around the corner, the **Las Palmas Hotel** (☎ 02-524 5602), on the corner of Mabini and Pedro Gil Sts, Malate, is a fairly middle-of-the-road hotel. Slightly ageing singles/doubles with air-con, TV and bathtubs start at US$55/65.

The modern **City Garden Hotel** (☎ 02-536 1451, 1158 Mabini St, Ermita) has a no-nonsense corporate atmosphere and smart air-con rooms with bath, cable TV and phone from US$54/64. Discounts are often available and there's a good coffee shop and bar in the lobby.

The **Royal Palm Hotel** (☎ 02-522 1515, 1227 Mabini St, Ermita), is a well-maintained hotel with a friendly, personal atmosphere. Comfortable rooms with air-con, bath, cable TV and phone start at US$40/50.

In a new building on Mabini St, the **Citystate Tower Hotel** (☎ 02-400 7351, 1315 Mabini St, Ermita) is a well-run business hotel that offers air-con rooms with TV, phone and bath from P1150 to P1550.

The owners also run a bus that connects with the boats to Puerto Galera.

The rooms at the **Centrepoint Hotel** (☎ 02-521 2751 to 521 2761, 1430 Mabini St, Ermita) are a little run-down compared to the lobby, but are OK for the price. Rates range from P1150 to P1600 for doubles and twins with air-con, bath, phone and cable TV. You can book the Si-Kat coach and ferry to Puerto Galera from here.

The three-star **Hotel Frendy** (☎ 02-526 4211 to 526 4214, 1548 Mabini St, Ermita) is clean, quiet, and well run. Comfortable, nicely furnished rooms with air-con, bath, cable TV, phone and fridge start at P1650/2090, including breakfast.

Owned by the Mansion group, the **Riviera Mansion** (☎ 02-523 4511 to 523 4525, 1638 Mabini St, Ermita) is a neat modern apartment-style hotel, with well-furnished doubles and twins with kitchenette for P2000 (P1600 without).

La Corona Hotel (☎ 02-524 2631 to 524 2638, 1166 MH del Pilar St, Ermita) is owned by the American chain Best Western, and has ordinary but comfortable rooms with air-con, bath, cable TV, phone and minibar for P1500. Reduced rates are available for longer stays.

Off the main drag, the **Celestine Citadel Hotel** (☎ 02-525 2789, 525 3347, 430 Nuestra Señora de Guia St, Ermita) is a quiet, modern place with clean, slightly futuristic rooms with air-con, cable TV, phone and minibar, starting at P1000 a double.

The **Star Boulevard Inn** (☎ 02-536 1448, 536 1775, 415 United Nations Ave, Ermita) has a central location and tastefully furnished rooms with wooden floors. Prices start at P1200 for doubles or P1500 for twins, all with air-con, bath, phone and cable TV.

Right by Robinson's Place in Ermita, the **Cherry Blossom Hotel** (☎ 02-524 7631) has very clean air-con rooms with bath, phone, cable TV and comfortable furnishings for P1150. Larger rooms with a round king-size bed are P1573.

Away from the noisy part of Ermita, the large **Hotel Soriente** (☎ 02-523 9456, 545 A Flores St, Ermita) has spacious, wood-furnished rooms with air-con, bath and TV for P999 or P1099 with cable TV. There's a small supermarket and restaurant in the same building.

At the opposite end of the tourist belt, the long-established *Ambassador Hotel* (☎ 02-524 6011, 2021 Mabini St, Malate) is a little overpriced. Slightly tired air-con rooms with bath, TV and fridge are P2032/2372.

Nearby, the *Aloha Hotel* (☎ 02-526 8088, 2150 Roxas Blvd, Malate) has seen too many heavy smokers. Without a view, air-con rooms with bath, TV and phone are P1400. With a view of the bay, you'll pay P1875.

Intramuros There really is only one accommodation option within the walled city. The *Hotel Intramuros de Manila* (☎ 02-524 6730 to 524 6732, Plaza San Luis), on the corner of Cabildo and Urdaneta Sts, is in the same complex as the Casa Manila Museum and offers smartly furnished air-con singles/doubles for P1600/2000 and deluxe rooms with fridge and TV for P2200/2600.

Paco Surrounding the tiny Paco Park are a couple of quiet foreign-owned hotels with pleasant rooms.

The Swiss-owned *Garden Plaza Hotel* (☎ 02-522 4835, 1030 Belen St) has a small pool and good air-con rooms with TV, bath and phone that are slightly overpriced at P1800.

Next door, the newer *Park Hotel* (☎ 02-521 2371, 1032 Belen St) is Australian-owned and has a lovely secluded pool. Rooms start at US$30, or there are suites with jacuzzi for US$75.

Makati Cheap accommodation is pretty thin on the ground in Makati, but there are a number of mid-range hotels dotted around the place. The area around Burgos St is Makati's *zona caliente* (red-light district) but the hotels are reasonably priced, the restaurants are good and you aren't obliged to spend your time in the seedy bars.

One of the better hotels in this area is the friendly *Robelle House* (☎ 02-899 8209, 4402 Valdez St), behind the International School. It has a quiet location and a lovely

pool. Rooms vary in quality, with ordinary fan-rooms with shared bath at P650/750 a single/double, and spacious air-con rooms with bath from P1078/1225. See the Makati Avenue & Burgos Street map.

The *Jupiter Arms* (☎ 02-890 5044, 102 Jupiter St) is a newish business hotel, with good air-con rooms and the usual mod cons from P1780/2080.

On the corner of Kalayaan Ave and Makati Ave, the *Millennium Plaza Hotel* (☎ 02-899 4718) is nicely maintained and has a good restaurant. Rooms aren't cheap though, starting at US$88 for a studio and US$130 for a one-bedroom suite. Air-con, phone and cable TV come as standard.

Nearby, on the corner of Kalayaan Ave and Mercado St, the *Primetown Century Tower* (☎ 02-750 3010) has the usual high Century standards, with air-con rooms with bath, TV and phone starting at US$85.

The *Century Citadel Inn* (☎ 02-897 2370, 5007 Burgos St) is another Century-owned place with well-equipped air-con rooms from US$75.

On the corner of Makati Ave and Durban St, the *Sunette Tower Hotel* (☎ 02-897 1804) has a variety of air-con rooms with bath, phone and cable TV from US$75, which is a bit expensive for what you get.

The rooms aren't bad for the price at the friendly *Pensionne Virginia* (☎ 02-844 5228, 816 Arnaiz Ave). This old-style pension offers doubles or twins with air-con, TV and fridge for P1045, with larger rooms from P1375.

Nearby, the *El Cielito Inn* (☎ 02-815 8951, 804 Arnaiz Ave) has clean rooms with air-con, bath and cable TV from P1300/1620. It also has a quiet coffee shop and restaurant.

The new *Copa Businessman's Hotel* (☎ 02-844 8811, 912 Arnaiz Ave) has nicely furnished but pricey air-con rooms with fridge, cable TV and phone from P1980, or suites from P2310. The hotel also has weekly rates.

Quezon City Tomas Morato Ave is the most desirable address in Quezon City. Many of the upmarket restaurant chains have branches here and it's also convenient for the big 'disco-theatre' nightclubs.

The **Rembrandt Hotel** (☎ 02-373 3333, 26 T Morato Extension) is a classy independent hotel with a TGI Friday in the lobby and probably the finest ballroom in the city. Attractively furnished air-con rooms with bath, cable TV and phone start at P2700 a night.

Standards are high at the **Century Imperial Palace Suites** (☎ 02-411 0116), on the corner of T Morato Ave and Timog St. It has suites with air-con, bath, phone and cable TV at US$90 for studios, US$100 for one-bedroom suites and US$120 or more for two-bedroom suites.

On a quiet residential street, the **Villa Estela Hometel** (☎ 02-371 2279, 33 Scout Santiago St) has a nice pool and a mixture of new and old rooms with air-con, bath and TV. The old rooms are true to their name and cost P990, the better, new rooms cost P1430.

The bizarre **Camelot Hotel** (☎ 02-373 2101 to 373 2110, 35 Mother Ignacia Ave) is housed in a fake chateau, and has numerous suits of armour and medieval weapons. Air-con doubles and twins start at P1200 and P1420. It also has the Dungeon Bar and Hall of King Arthur ballroom.

In the business heart of Quezon City, the **Metropolitan Apartment Hotel** (☎ 02-921 4241, 131 Malakas St) has well-maintained rooms. Doubles with air-con, bath, TV and phone are P1400, similar twins are P1500, and suites start at P1850. It's around the corner from the Philippine Heart Center.

The **Sulo Hotel** (☎ 02-924 5051), on Matalino St, is an upmarket business hotel with several restaurants and a pool. Very good rooms with air-con, bath and all mod cons start from P3300/3700 a single/double. There are discounts for long stays.

Places to Stay – Top End

Like most international hotels in South-East Asia, Manila's top end places strive to recreate the colonial decadence of places like Raffles in Singapore. Marble-floors, fountains, palms and jazz ensembles are the norm, though only a few places bring it off

with real style. Rates quoted are in US dollars and are for the high season (November to March). Outside this period, reductions of 25% to 50% are commonplace. It's also cheaper if you book these places through a travel agent.

Malate & Ermita The standard by which other hotels are judged in Manila is the sumptuous **Pan Pacific Hotel** (☎ 02-536 0788), on the corner of Adriatico and General Malvar Sts, Malate. As well as the usual luxuries, rooms have a computer and personal butler trained by members of the House of Windsor in England. Singles/doubles start at US$350/370, though low-season rates can be as low as US$115.

Also impressive is the **Manila Diamond Hotel** (☎ 02-526 2211), on the corner of Roxas Blvd and Dr J Quintos St, Malate, which has an excellent pool and great views of the city from the Sky Lounge bar on the top floor. Rooms with all mod cons start at US$240/260, running all the way up to US$2000 for the Presidential Suite. Discounts of 50% are available in the off season.

The **Hotel Sofitel Grand Boulevard Manila** (☎ 02-526 8588, 1990 Roxas Blvd, Malate) is a little too old to be truly luxurious, but the facilities are impressive and it has a popular casino. Rooms start at US$160/180.

In Ermita, the huge **Manila Midtown Hotel** (☎ 02-526 7001), on the corner of Pedro Gil and Adriatico Sts, has a lovely pool that's open to the public, as well as the usual luxury facilities. Standard rooms start at US$150/160, while suites are available from US$220. Cebu Pacific and Gulf Air both have offices in the lobby.

On the corner of United Nations Ave and Maria Y Orosa St, Ermita, the **Holiday Inn Manila** (☎ 02-526 1212) offers the same experience as staying in a Holiday Inn anywhere in the world. Rooms start at US$133/144.

The appealing **Bayview Park Hotel** (☎ 02-526 1555, 1118 Roxas Blvd, Ermita) is owned by the Century group and has correspondingly high standards. The building is probably the cleanest in Ermita and room

MANILA

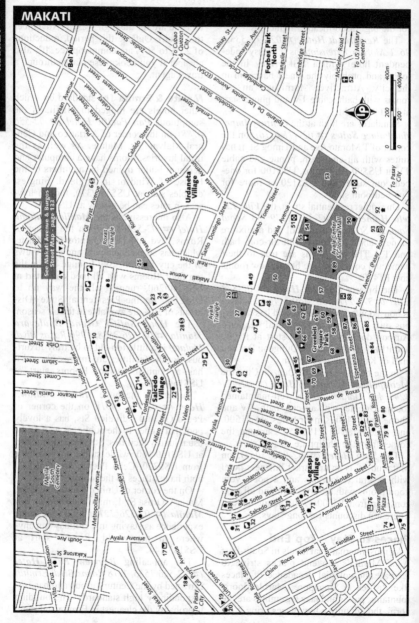

MAKATI

MANILA

MAKATI

PLACES TO STAY

25 Mandarin Oriental
45 Charter House; Asian Spirit
49 The Peninsula Manila
50 The Shangri-La Hotel & Blue Horizons Travel & Tours
53 Hotel Inter-Continental
73 Amorsolo Mansions
78 El Cielito Inn
79 Pensionne Virginia; Kashmir Restaurant
84 Copa Businessman's Hotel
86 New World Renaissance Hotel
92 Dusit Hotel Nikko & Japan Airlines

PLACES TO EAT

2 Don Henrico's
4 Max's Restaurant
5 Baan Thai Restaurant
19 Maxim's Tea House
23 Top of the Citi
54 Outback Steakhouse
56 Furusato
58 Verandah Grill
59 Le Soufflé Restaurant; Padi's Point
60 Shakey's Pizza
61 Tia Maria's Restaurant; Strumm's Nightclub
63 Schwarzwälder Restaurant; Tony Romas' Ribs
64 Mario's & Italianni's
65 New Orleans
67 Flavors & Spices Restaurant; Max's
69 Prince of Wales Pub & Restaurant

74 Kamayan Restaurant; Saisaki
80 Gold Ranch
87 Pizza Hut & Bookmark Bookshop
89 Kimpura Restaurant; Peking Garden; Supermarket

OTHER

1 Scuba World
3 Padi's Point
6 Equitable PCI Bank
7 French Embassy & United Airlines
8 Cathay Pacific
9 New Zealand Embassy
10 Air France
11 Thai Airways International
12 Spanish Embassy
13 Malaysia Airlines
14 Malaysian Embassy
15 Singapore Airlines
16 Swissair
17 Makati Central Post Office
18 Thomas Cook
20 Alliance Francaise
21 Makati Medical Center
22 Korean Air
24 Citibank
26 Filipinas Heritage Library
27 Makati Stock Exchange
28 Equitable PCI Bank
29 German Embassy
30 Ninoy Aquino Monument
31 Alitalia
32 Indonesian Embassy
33 Equitable PCI Bank
34 Aeroflot
35 British Airways; Qantas

36 Egypt Air
37 Canadian Airlines
38 International Asiana Airlines
39 Thai Embassy
40 Lufthansa Airlines
41 Bank of the Philippine Islands (PCI)
42 HSBC
43 Australian Embassy
44 PAL
46 Korean Air
47 Canadian Embassy
48 UK Embassy
51 Rustan's Department Store
52 San Antonia Church
55 Hard Rock Café
57 The Landmark Department Store
62 Ayala Museum
66 San Mig Pub
68 United Supermarket
70 Greenbelt Mall
71 Singapore Embassy
72 KLM - Royal Dutch Airlines
75 Balikatan Scientific Massage Centre for The Blind
76 Makati Cinema Square
77 Vietnam Airlines
81 Negros Navigation
82 American Express
83 El Al Israel Airlines
85 Power Books
88 Ayala Center Bus Terminal & Park Square II
90 National Book Store
91 SM Department Store
93 Mail Station Net & Universe Cybercafe

rates start at US$95/110 without view, or US$110/130 overlooking Manila Bay.

The first **Manila Hotel** (☎ 02-527 0011), in Rizal Park, Ermita, was destroyed during WWII, but the new building has the same sense of style as the original. The hotel boasts French, Italian, Japanese and Chinese restaurants and some of the most expensive rooms in Manila. The Presidential Suite, which has 10 rooms, a private butler and its own pool, costs a cool US$2500 a night. Less ostentatious rooms start at US$200/250.

Close to the CCP, the **Traders Hotel Manila** (☎ 02-523 7011, 3001 Roxas Blvd, Malate) is another large business-class

hotel with a bar, restaurant and pool. Rooms start at US$140/160. Unless you can afford the Traders Club rooms at the top of the hotel, you can get more for your money elsewhere.

Next to Harrison Plaza, the Japanese-owned **Century Park Hotel** (☎ 02-528 8888, 599 Vito Cruz St) comes close to the Raffles vision; the lobby is splendid, the concierges courteous and the rooms luxurious. Rooms start at US$210/220. The Top of the Century piano bar on the top floor offers stunning views over Manila Bay.

In this company, the **Westin Philippine Plaza** (☎ 02-551 5555) is looking slightly old, and it's location in the depths of the CCP

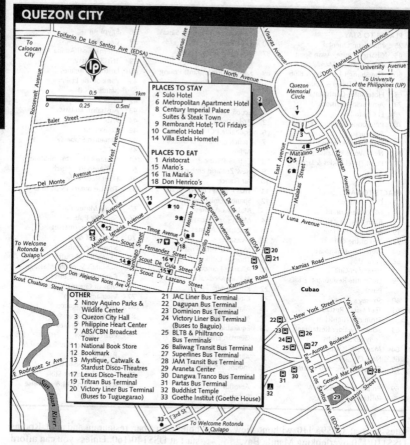

QUEZON CITY

To Caloocan City

Epifanio De Los Santos Ave (EDSA)

0 0.5 1km
0 0.25 0.5mi

Roosevelt Avenue

Baler Street

West Avenue

Del Monte   Avenue

Quezon Avenue

To Welcome Rotonda & Quiapo

Mother Ignacia Avenue

Scout Santiago

Scout De Guia

Scout Dr Lazcano Street

Don Alejandro Roces Ave

Scout Chuatuco Street

E Rodriguez Sr Ave

San Juan River

Mindanao Ave

North Avenue

Visayas Avenue

Don Mariano Marcos Avenue

University Avenue

To University of the Philippines (UP)

Quezon Memorial Circle

East Avenue

Kalayaan Avenue

Matalino Street

Malakas Street

V Luna Avenue

Sgt Esguerra Avenue

Mo Ignacia Avenue

Timog Avenue

Fernandez Street

Scout Street

Scout Torillo

Scout De Los Santos Avenue (EDSA)

Kamias Road

Kamuning Road

Cubao

New York Street

Yale Avenue

Aurora Boulevard

East De Los Santos Ave (EDSA)

General Mac Arthur Ave

Tuazon Street

3rd St

To Welcome Rotonda & Quiapo

PLACES TO STAY
4 Sulo Hotel
6 Metropolitan Apartment Hotel
8 Century Imperial Palace Suites & Steak Town
9 Rembrandt Hotel; TGI Fridays
10 Camelot Hotel
14 Villa Estela Hometel

PLACES TO EAT
1 Aristocrat
15 Mario's
16 Tia Maria's
18 Don Henrico's

OTHER
2 Ninoy Aquino Parks & Wildlife Center
3 Quezon City Hall
5 Philippine Heart Center
7 ABS/CBN Broadcast Tower
11 National Book Store
12 Bookmark
13 Mystique, Catwalk & Stardust Disco-Theatres
17 Lexus Disco-Theatre
19 Tritran Bus Terminal
20 Victory Liner Bus Terminal (Buses to Tuguegarao)
21 JAC Liner Bus Terminal
22 Dagupan Bus Terminal
23 Dominion Bus Terminal
24 Victory Liner Bus Terminal (Buses to Baguio)
25 BLTB & Philtranco Bus Terminals
26 Baliwag Transit Bus Terminal
27 Superlines Bus Terminal
28 JAM Transit Bus Terminal
29 Araneta Center
30 Dangwa Tranco Bus Terminal
31 Partas Bus Terminal
32 Buddhist Temple
33 Goethe Institut (Goethe House)

complex, off Roxas Blvd, isn't particularly convenient. Rooms start at US$225/245.

Pasay City & Parañaque Across the road from the new Centennial Terminal II, the *Philippine Village Hotel* (☎ 02-833 8080), at Nayong Pilipino Park, Pasay City, is a huge airport hotel with hundreds of rooms, several restaurants, a ballroom and extensive conference facilities. The Nayong Pilipino is also right on the doorstep. Singles/doubles cost US$135/155.

On the corner of EDSA and Roxas Blvd, the *Heritage Hotel* (☎ 02-891 8888) is an-

other huge business hotel, with standard rooms from US$220/240. For US$290, the Millennium Club rooms allow you to use the exclusive bar, restaurant and business facilities on the top floor.

Nearby, the *Hyatt Regency* (☎ 02-833 1234, 2702 Roxas Blvd) is a standard Hyatt property with shell chandeliers in the lobby and a casino. Rooms start at US$220, but discounts of up to 60% are available in the low season.

Makati Predictably, Makati's top-end places to stay tend to be more expensive than their Ermita or Malate counterparts. Many of the hotels here offer rooms with great views over Makati, particularly those around Ayala Triangle.

The **Shangri-La Hotel** (☎ 02-813 8888), on the corner of Ayala Ave and Makati Ave, is probably the best traditional luxury hotel in Manila. Its Presidential Suite is certainly the most expensive room in town at US$2900 a night. Other rooms start at US$250/275 a single/double. Zu, one of Manila's more popular nightclubs, is also here.

Across the road, the vast **Peninsula Manila** (☎ 02-887 2888), also on the corner of Ayala Ave and Makati Ave, boasts 500 rooms and takes up an entire city block. Rooms start from US$295 a night. The Nielsen's Seafood Restaurant here does an excellent seafood buffet on Friday evenings.

The **Mandarin Oriental** (☎ 02-750 8888), on the corner of Makati Ave and Paseo de Roxas, has an atmospheric blackstone interior and rooms from US$290/310. Suites start at US$490.

Right in the middle of the Ayala Center, the Thai-owned **Dusit Hotel Nikko** (☎ 02-867 3333), on the corner of EDSA and Arnaiz Ave, offers good service and rooms from US$260 a night.

Covering similar ground, the **New World Renaissance Hotel** (☎ 02-811 6888), on the corner of Esperanza St and Makati Ave, by the Greenbelt Square mall, charges US$145 for good executive rooms.

The **Hotel Inter-Continental** (☎ 02-815 9711, 1 Ayala Ave) is well located for the restaurants in the Ayala Center/Greenbelt Square mall areas. Rooms start from US$220/240. The Cats Nightclub here is quite popular.

Places to Stay – Apartments

Malate & Ermita For longer stays, it may be worth renting an apartment. Several places in town offer fully furnished suites with kitchens, air-con, cable TV and bathrooms for not much more than the cost of a hotel room. The prices listed do not include telephone, electricity or water bills.

Cheap but basic apartments are available at **Victoria Mansions** (☎ 02-525 9444, 600 JM Nakpil St, Malate). All rooms have air-con and prices start at P600 for one person per day, P700 for two per day. Cheaper monthly rates are available for longer stays.

On Adriatico St, the **Dakota Mansion** (☎ 02-521 0701, 555 Gen Malvar St, Malate) is one of five apartment hotels in Manila belonging to the Mansion chain. Standards are high and studio apartments cost P1700/23,500 daily/monthly. One-bedroom apartments cost from P2200/35,0000 and two-bedroom apartments cost from P3000/37,000.

The **Pearl Garden Apartel** (☎ 02-525 9461, 1700 Adriatico St, Malate) has quite comfortable suites with air-con, cable TV and kitchen. Studios cost P990/24,000, while one-bedroom suites cost P1386/32,890.

Opposite the Robinson's Place mall, **Casa Blanca I** (☎ 02-523 8251, 1447 Adriatico St, Ermita) has passable fully furnished apartments with kitchen, bath and phone. One-bedroom apartments that sleep two people cost P1100/12,870.

Pacific Place Apartelle Suites (☎ 02-521 2279, 526 1254, 539 Arquiza St, Ermita) is a clean, modern place with a good variety of apartments. All suites have air-con, kitchen, bath and cable TV. Daily rates range from P1708 to P2318, depending on the size of the apartment (from P30,500 to P37,820 monthly).

Close to Rizal Park, **Mabini Mansion** (☎ 02-521 4776 to 521 4789, 1011 Mabini St, Ermita) is another hotel belonging to the Mansion chain. Good one-bedroom apartments start at P1700/23,500.

The **Boulevard Mansion Hotel** (☎ 02-521 8888, 1440 Roxas Blvd, Ermita) is another Mansion hotel and has studio apartments from P1850/24,000 and one-bedroom apartments from P2000/25,000.

Away from the busy part of Ermita, **Ralph Anthony Suites** (☎ 02-521 1107, 521 5590), on the corner of Maria Orosa and Arkansas Sts, offers slightly more upmarket accommodation. Air-con studio apartments with bath start at US$45 daily, while much better one-bedroom suites with kitchen range from US$55 to US$80 daily (from US$1400 to US$2000 monthly).

Makati The *Amorsolo Mansions (☎ 02-818 6811, 130 Amorsolo St, Makati)* is another good Mansion-chain hotel, with air-con suites with phone, kitchenette and cable TV. Studios are P2700/34,000 daily/monthly and one-bedroom suites are P3100/37,000.

Also central, the *Charter House (☎ 02-817 6001, 114 Legaspi St)* offers air-con one-bedroom apartments a step away from the Greenbelt Square mall for P2200/52,800. Rooms have cable TV and phone and there's a pool on the roof.

Near Burgos St, the *Travelers Inn (☎ 02-895 7061, 7880 Makati Ave)* has large air-con rooms with bath, slightly mismatched furniture, cable TV, phone and kitchenette. Rates are P1800/11,330 daily/weekly.

On the other side of Makati Ave, *Regine's Hotel (☎ 02-897 3888)*, on the corner of Makati Ave and Kalayaan Ave, has OK studios with air-con, bath, phone and TV from P2300/50,000 daily/monthly. One-bedroom apartments start at P3500/70,000.

Pasay City & Parañaque Convenient for the airports and EDSA, the *Copacabana Apartment-Hotel (☎ 02-831 8711, 264 EDSA Extension)* has good apartments with air-con, phone, cable TV, kitchens and full sets of kitchenware. Studios start at P1485/30,580 daily/monthly, while one-bedroom apartments are P1760/40,150. Two and three-bedroom apartments are also available.

Places to Eat

A huge range of cuisine is represented in Manila, from Chinese, Korean and Filipino food to Mexican tacos and European specialities like pizza, pasta and paella. The meals on offer are generally of a high quality, and prices are moderate compared to Europe or the USA, although slightly higher than in other South-East Asian countries.

The following prices are generally for mid-range dishes on each menu. Snacks will be cheaper, luxury items like *lapu-lapu* (grouper) will cost significantly more. More

expensive restaurants will often add a 10% service charge.

Fast Food Cheap snack stalls are conspicuously absent from the streets of Manila, but you can eat cheaply at Filipino canteens. These basic restaurants are tucked away on the sidestreets and display a selection of dishes in the window, usually including *adobo* (meat cooked in vinegar and garlic), *sinigang* (sour fish soup) and *inihaw na bangus* (char-broiled milkfish). Ordering is pretty much a case of pointing at whatever takes your fancy.

Captain Nook's, on Pedro Gil St, Malate, is a popular canteen and there are several good places on Santa Monica St, between MH del Pilar and Mabini Sts in Ermita. Less adventurous types can choose the same food from labelled pots at *Woods Restaurant* on Mabini St. Two dishes with steamed rice and chicken broth should set you back about P60.

If you don't mind eating in a shopping mall, the food courts of most of the large shopping centres offer fast food interpretations of a remarkable variety of Asian cuisines, including Filipino, Chinese, Thai, Vietnamese and Japanese. A standard meal of meat or fish, rice and soup costs around P50. *Robinson's Place* mall in Ermita and the *Ayala Center* in Makati have the best selections.

The usual fast food players like *McDonalds*, *Burger King*, *KFC* and *Pizza Hut* have branches here, and local competitors include Jollibee (burgers), *Chow-King* (Chinese), *Max's* (fried chicken), *Racks* (steaks), *Greenwich Pizzapasta* and *Shakey's Pizza*, all of which have branches throughout town.

Filipino For Filipino food in more comfortable surroundings, *Zamboanga Restaurant*, on Adriatico St, offers a dinner show of traditional Filipino dance at 7 and 8.30 pm daily. The show isn't particularly cultural but it's good fun and a good variety of Filipino dishes are available for about P200 (P300 to P400 for seafood). It's open from 10 am to 11 pm daily.

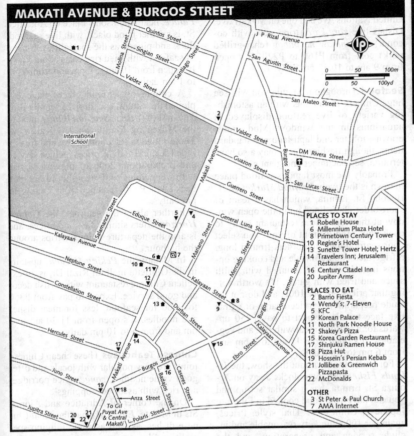

MAKATI AVENUE & BURGOS STREET

International School

PLACES TO STAY
1 Robelle House
6 Millennium Plaza Hotel
8 Primetown Century Tower
10 Regine's Hotel
13 Sunette Tower Hotel; Hertz
14 Travelers Inn; Jerusalem Restaurant
16 Century Citadel Inn
20 Jupiter Arms

PLACES TO EAT
2 Barrio Fiesta
4 Wendy's; 7-Eleven
5 KFC
9 Korean Palace
11 North Park Noodle House
12 Shakey's Pizza
15 Korea Garden Restaurant
17 Shinjuku Ramen House
18 Pizza Hut
19 Hossein's Persian Kebab
21 Jollibee & Greenwich Pizzapasta
22 McDonalds

OTHER
3 St Peter & Paul Church
7 AMA Internet

On Remedios circle, ***Ang Bistro sa Remedios*** serves a good selection of dishes from Pampanga province which is noted for its cuisine. A meal of *sinigang na baboy* (sour tamarind broth with pork) and rice will cost around P250. It's open from 6 am to 2 pm and from 5 pm to 2 am Thursday to Saturday.

On Padre Faura St, Ermita, ***Kamayan*** is a successful chain, where you eat with your hands, in the traditional Filipino style. Meals from around the islands cost from P300, though there is a good value lunch deal for P240. Before and after dining, you can wash your hands in the huge pots of water at the back of the room. It's open from 11 am to 2 pm and from 6 to 10 pm daily. There's another branch on Arnaiz Ave, Makati.

The 24-hour ***Aristocrat***, on Roxas Blvd, Malate, is always full of locals and has good Filipino food and reasonable prices. Dishes like inihaw na bangus with garlic rice cost around P200 while specialities like crispy *pata* (fried pork knuckle) start at P300. There's a satellite branch in the Quezon Memorial Circle, Quezon City.

Barrio Fiesta is a large chain that offers a good range of Filipino food. There's a branch on the corner of Maria Orosa and E

Reyes Sts, Ermita, another nearby on United Nations Ave and one on Makati Ave. Dishes like *kare-kare* (tripe stew with coconut) and *inihaw na baboy* (char-grilled pork) cost from P160 to P220. It's open from 9 am to 10.30 pm daily.

Seafood Throughout Manila you will see huge Chinese restaurants with an astonishing variety of live seafood displayed in aquariums in the window. Mud crabs, prawns, lobster and lapu-lapu are standard items, though flashier places may also have terrapin, sea cucumber and giant eel.

Probably the most famous seafood place in town is the lively *Seafood Market* on JC Bocobo St, Ermita, which has a team of short-order chefs lined up in the open window at the front of the restaurant ready to cook your food in front of you. You select your seafood and side orders from a long, refrigerated counter inside and cooking options include steamed, sauteed with chilli sauce and fried with garlic. It's worth noting that prices are per 100g, and do not include preparation, service charge or extras like face towels. Expect to pay P450 upwards for a seafood meal with rice and vegetables. It's open from 11 am to 3 pm and from 6 pm to 1 am daily.

For better food without the show, the *Islands Fisherman*, two blocks away on Arquiza St, Ermita, has a similar set-up and you can have your food cooked in Filipino, Japanese, Chinese or Thai style. Prices, again per 100g, are very reasonable and include service and preparation, and the house band will serenade you while you eat. Expect to pay P300 for a meal. It's open daily from 11 am to 2 pm and from 6 to 10 pm daily.

For the full Chinese seafood experience, the *Sky High Restaurant*, opposite the Malate Church, on Remedios St, Malate, has anything and everything from the sea – from conch shells to terrapins and poisonous rock-fish, which are killed and prepared in front of the restaurant. Expect to pay P350 to P500 for a seafood dish with vegetables and rice. It's open from 11 am to 2 pm and from 5.30 pm to midnight daily.

The huge, neon-lit *Amity Seafood Palace*, near Robinson's Place on Adriatico St, is another good place, with live seafood, duck and pigeon as the specialities. A meal of seafood with fried rice costs about P300. It's open from 10 am to 2 pm and from 6 pm to 1 am daily.

A couple of seafood places have exploited the natural backdrop of Manila Bay. The best of these is *Seafood Wharf*, next to the Museo ng Manila on TM Kalaw St. There's a good selection of live and freshly killed seafood and the prices include service and preparation; 200g of prawns or fish with vegetables and rice should set you back about P350. It's open from 7 am to 10 pm daily.

Further along the seafront, the *Golden Horizon* offers similar fare and prices, and is also the departure point for trips around the harbour.

In Makati, the *Peking Garden*, upstairs in the Glorietta mall on Rizal Dr, is an excellent Chinese restaurant with stylish decor and good service. Expect to pay from P350 to P660 for seafood, less for meat dishes and noodles. It's open from 11.30 am to 2 pm and from 6 to 10 pm daily.

Chinese Teahouses These cheap Chinese joints are very popular with locals and offer good value noodles, *congee* (rice porridge) and rice with assorted 'toppings'.

On the corner of Adriatico and Alonzo Sts in Malate, *East Lake* has the usual Chinese dishes, as well as some Filipino specialities like *carne con ampalaya* (meat with bitter melon). Rice toppings and noodle dishes range from P70 to P100. It's open from 9 am to 3 am daily.

One of the better teahouses, *Hap Chan* on Ongpin St, Binondo, specialises in hotpot dishes but also serves rice and noodles. It's popular with locals, and most dishes cost P140. It's open from 10.30 am to 3 am daily. There's another branch on GM Malvar St, Malate.

Another successful teahouse chain is *Maxim's*. The original branch is at 965 Ongpin St, Binondo. Specialities are *mami* (noodle soup), siopao and dim sum in the

P50 to P80 range. It's open from 6 am to 10 pm daily. There's also a branch on the corner of United Nations Ave and MH del Pilar St, Ermita, and another on the corner or Urban Ave and Chino Roces St, Makati.

On Makati Ave in Makati, the *North Park Noodle House* has possibly the best range of Chinese noodle dishes in Manila. Prices range from P50 to P100. It's open from 10.30 am to 3 am daily.

Japanese On North Dr in the Ayala Center, *Furusato* is easily the classiest Japanese restaurant in Manila. The waitresses wear kimonos and the food is served at traditional Japanese low tables. The sushi and sashimi is excellent; expect to pay at least P500 for a freshly prepared tray of sushi, P800 for sashimi. Tempura costs from P250 to P350 and noodle dishes start at P250. It's open from 11.30 am to 2 pm and from 5.30 to 10 pm daily.

Upstairs in the Glorietta mall on Rizal Dr, *Kimpura* is a swish-looking Japanese place with surprisingly reasonable prices. Tempura and teppanyaki dishes cost from P150 to P300, while a set of sushi and sashimi will set you back P250 to P400. Opening hours are from 11.30 am to 2 pm and from 6 to 10.30 pm daily.

In the Islands Fisherman restaurant on Padre Faura St, Ermita, *Saisaki* offers an excellent Japanese buffet, with a sushi/sashimi bar and an excellent selection of tempura and teppanyaki dishes. At lunchtime, the buffet costs P352; in the evening it's P440. It's open from 11 am to 2 pm and from 6 to 10 pm daily. There's another branch on Arnaiz Ave, Makati.

On Makati Ave, Makati, the *Shinjuku Ramen House* has good, inexpensive ramen noodles for P200 and tempura for P200 to P300. Opening hours are from 10 am to 1 am daily.

Korean Manila has a number of excellent Korean barbecue restaurants, where you barbecue your own food on a gas-fired hotplate in the centre of the table. Marinated meats and seafood are served with interesting side dishes such as beansprouts,

peanuts in syrup, seaweed and kim-chi (pickled cabbage).

Best of the bunch is probably the tasteful *Korean Palace*, on the corner of Adriatico and Remedios Sts. A meal of marinated meat or seafood, numerous side dishes and rice costs about P220. It's open from 9 to 1 am daily. There's another branch on the corner of MH del Pilar St and Plaza Nuestra Señora de Guia in Ermita and a third on Kalayaan St, Makati, which is only open from 4 pm.

Also good is the huge *Korean Village Restaurant*, at 1783 Adriatico St. The service is good, beer is cheap, and a steak barbecue with rice and side dishes costs only P110. Japanese tempura and hotpot meals are also available for around P120. It's open from 11.30 am to 2.30 pm and 5.30 to 10 pm daily (only from 5.30 to 10 pm Sunday).

The *Korea Garden Restaurant* on Burgos St, Makati, offers the usual barbecue fare and tempura dishes for around P250. It's open from 11.30 am to 2.30 pm and from 5.30 to 11 pm daily.

Thai There is less Thai food in Manila than you might expect, as Filipinos are not generally fond of spicy cooking. Perhaps the best in town is *Flavors & Spices*, beside the Greenbelt Square mall in Makati. Salads are P200 and seafood or meat curries with rice range from P250 to P400. It's open from 11 am to 2.30 pm and from 6.30 to 11 pm daily. There's another branch in the Pan Pacific Hotel in Malate.

Baan Thai, on the corner of Makati Ave and Jupiter St, has authentic Thai food and nice decor. There's a lunchtime buffet for P297, while the usual curries with rice cost around P150. It's open from 11.30 am to 2 pm and from 6.30 to 10 pm daily.

In Malate, but on the far side of Taft Ave, the friendly *Sala Thai*, on JM Nakpil St, is one of the longest-established Thai places in Manila. It uses freshly prepared herbs, and prices are reasonable at P100 to P150 for a Thai curry with meat or seafood and plain rice. It's open from 10 am to 2.30 pm and from 6 to 10 pm daily except Sunday.

MANILA

Spanish The long-established *Patio Guernica*, on the corner of JC Bocobo St and Remedios Circle, specialises in Spanish dishes such as paella and *callos* (tripe), as well as seafood and pasta. Most dishes fall into the P300 to P500 range. It's open from 11.30 am to 2 pm and from 5.30 to 11 pm or later daily (from 5.30 to 11 pm Sunday). There's another Patio Guernica on MH del Pilar St, Ermita.

The popular *Casa Armas*, on JM Nakpil St, has a dedicated following and a good selection of paella (try the paella negra with squid) as well as *calderata* (spicy stew) and callos. Most mains cost from P350 to P500. They also serve excellent omelettes. It's open from 11 am to 2 am Monday to Saturday and from 6 to 11 pm Sunday.

Ilustrado is a stylish Spanish restaurant in the El Amenecer complex on General Luna St, Intramuros. Exotic mains like blackened sea bass cost from P250 to P600. Opening hours are from 11.30 am to 2.30 pm and from 6 to 10 pm daily.

In the Greenbelt Square mall in Makati, *Mario's* offers Spanish dishes like callos and *chorizo* (sausage) soup for around P350. There's a good Sunday buffet for P395. It's open from 7 to 10 am, from 11.30 am to 2.30 pm and from 5.30 to 11 pm daily. There's another branch on T Morato Ave, Quezon City.

Italian *Italianni's* is an upmarket Italian chain with branches in Robinson's Place in Ermita and the Greenbelt Square mall on Legaspi St, Makati. In addition to the usual pasta and pizza from P200 to P300, mains like chicken parmesan start at P400. There is an authentic (if pricey) wine list. It's open from 11 am to midnight daily.

Bravo, on the corner of JM Nakpil and Adriatico Sts, is a stylish new Italian place. The emphasis is on authentic Italian food, from thin-crust pizza to minestrone soup. Most mains are in the P200 to P300 range. It's open from 10 am to midnight daily (till 2 am Friday and Saturday).

On the corner of Pedro Gil and Mabini Sts in Malate, *Don Henrico's* has an excellent range of pizza and some of the friendliest staff in Manila. Pizzas start at P184 for

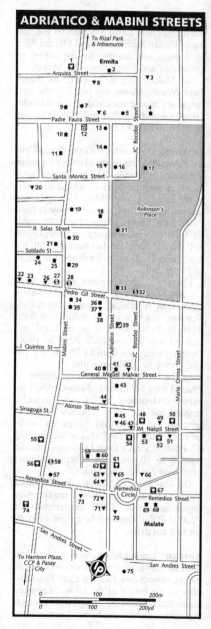

ADRIATICO & MABINI STREETS

PLACES TO STAY		PLACES TO EAT		7	Whitetip Divers
2	Pacific Place Apartelle Suites	3	Seafood Market	12	Surf Service Web Cafe
4	Midtown Inn	6	Kamayan Restaurant;	13	7-Eleven
9	Royal Palm Hotel		Kashmir Restaurant; Jollibee	14	Sea Breeze Laundry
10	Citystate Tower Hotel	8	The Islands Fisherman; Saisaki	16	Midland Plaza; JB Rent-a-Car
11	Mabini Pension	15	Amity Seafood Palace &	23	Peñafrancia Tours
17	Cherry Blossom Hotel		Teahouse	24	Laundryville
18	Casa Blanca I	20	Cheap Filipino Canteens	27	Equitable PCI Bank; Classica
19	Centrepoint Hotel; Si-Kat	22	Captain Nook's Restaurant		Cristina Web Cafe
	Ferry Office	26	Don Henrico's	28	Bank of the Philippine Islands
21	Soledad Pension House;	37	Zamboanga Restaurant		(BPI) FOREX
	Woods Restaurant	42	Hap Chan Teahouse	30	7-Eleven
25	Ermita Tourist Inn &	44	East Lake Restaurant	31	Interisland Travel & Tours;
	Scenic View Travel	46	Steak Town Restaurant;		Midtown Arcade
29	Hotel Frendy		Chronicle Cafe and Bravo	32	Equitable PCI Bank;
33	Manila Midtown Hotel,		Restaurant		National Bookstore;
	Gulf Air & Cebu Pacific	47	Casa Armas Restaurant		Outback Steakhouse
34	Riviero Mansion	49	Three Amigos Restaurant	39	Kim Luan Taoist Temple
35	Las Palmas Hotel	51	Gotham Restaurant; Common	48	Verve Room; Episode Bars
36	Palm Plaza Hotel;		Ground Café; Sala Restaurant	50	Jazz Rhythms & 617 Nakpil
	KEI Rent-a-Car	63	Korean Village Restaurant	52	Insomnia
38	Rothman Inn Hotel	64	Korean Palace	54	Politixx Bar; The Lobby
40	Pan Pacific Hotel; Flavors &	65	Cafe Adriatico	55	Republic of Malate
	Spices	66	Patio Guernica	56	Hobbit House
41	Dakota Mansion	70	Café Adriatico 1900;	57	American Express (AmEx)
43	Pearl Garden Apartel		In The Mood Ballroom	58	Bank of the Philippine Islands
45	Joward's Pension House &	71	Ang Bistro sa Remedios		(BPI) FOREX
	Joward's Hot Pot Restaurant	72	Cafe Havana	61	Ten Years After;
53	Victoria Mansions	73	Tia Maria's Mexican		Padi's Point
59	Juen's Place		Restaurant	62	Library Bar
60	Malate Pensionne;			67	Pipeline Bar
	Portico Restaurant	**OTHER**		74	Malate Church
68	Cle D'or Hotel	1	Cowboy Grill	75	San Andres Sports
69	Circle Pension	5	Solidaridad Bookshop		Complex

small, P329 for medium and P446 for large. It's open from 11 am to midnight daily. There are two branches on Jupiter St and in the Glorietta 4 mall, Makati and on T Morato Ave, Quezon City.

Western European For German cuisine in impressive surroundings, try the *Schwarzwälder*, on Makati Ave in Makati. Mains like schnitzel are around P500 and hearty German sausages cost P280. Opening hours are from 7 to 10 am, from 11.30 am to 2.30 pm and from 5.30 to 11 pm daily.

Nearby, on the corner of West Dr and Makati Ave, *Le Soufflé* is an excellent French restaurant with a very good wine list and authentic dishes. Soufflé is the speciality here and there are also some interesting salads. Mains cost from P300 to

P400. Opening hours are from 11 am to midnight daily.

With two branches on Remedios circle, *Cafe Adriatico* was one of the original Adriatico restaurants and offers a wide range of European dishes, including seafood, steak, pasta and fondue. Pasta dishes cost P200, while other mains start at P300. The *Cafe Adriatico Premiere* is open from 10 am to 6 am daily. Opposite, the *Cafe Adriatico 1900* is open from 11 am to 2 pm daily.

In you want to dine on top of Manila, the impressive *Top of the Citi* is on the 34th floor of the Citibank Tower at 8741 Paseo de Roxas in Makati. Pasta dishes cost P250, seafood and steaks are P500. It's open from 7 am till 10 pm Monday to Friday. The entrance is actually around the corner on Valero St.

Indian & Middle Eastern The main Indian option in town is the upmarket *Kashmir Restaurant* on Padre Faura St, Ermita. The north Indian curries here are good but expensive, particularly when you add the 30% tax and service charge. It's open from 11.30 am to 11 pm daily. There's also a branch in Makati on Arnaiz Ave.

The *Jerusalem* restaurant on MH del Pilar St, Ermita offers excellent *shwarma* (kebabs in a rolled pitta bread) for P50 and a good range of main courses like *salona* (spicy stew). It's open from 7.30 am to 3 am daily. There's another branch on Makati Ave, Makati.

Also on Makati Ave is *Hossein's Persian Kebab*, which offers a good range of kebabs and north Indian curries. Vegetable dishes are P130, biryani (curried rice) dishes are P200 and shish kebabs are P250. It's open from 11 am to 1 am daily.

Mexican & Latin American The best Mexican place in town is the *Three Amigos* on trendy JM Nakpil St. The portions are generous, the food authentic and all dishes come with salad, rice, beans and salsa. Most dishes cost between P150 to P200. Opening hours are from 6 pm to 2 am Sunday to Thursday and from 6 pm to 3 am Friday and Saturday.

Cafe Havana is a very upmarket Cuban restaurant on the corner of Adriatico and Remedios Sts, with unusual mains like banana pizzas and fiery *encendido* stews. Tapas dishes cost from P100 to P200, pizzas are around P200 and other mains cost from P400. It's open from 11 am to 2 am daily.

Tia Maria's is a popular Mexican restaurant chain that offers live music and authentic Mexican food, though the portions are a little small. Tacos and enchiladas cost around P150. It's open from 4 pm to at least 3 am. There's also a branch on Makati Ave, Makati and another on T Morato Ave, Quezon City.

Steaks You can get good steaks in Manila, but the meat on offer is usually genuine Black Angus beef, air-freighted from the USA. Expect to pay at least P350 to P500 for a 300g steak.

One of the longest-established places, *Steak Town*, on Adriatico St, Malate, has a good selection of steaks for P350, including tea or coffee, soup, garlic bread and bottomless salad from the salad bar. The *Chronicle Cafe* next door is the smoking wing of the same restaurant. It's open from 11 am to midnight daily. There's another branch on T Morato Ave, Quezon City.

Above the Schwarzwälder restaurant on Makati Ave, *Tony Roma's Ribs* offers steaks, burgers and of course, ribs – cooked in smoky, pepper or chilli sauces. Portions are generous and most dishes cost from P300 to P500.

Nearby on Legaspi St, in the Greenbelt Square mall, *New Orleans* offers good steaks and Creole cooking in the P300 to P500 range. The three course executive lunch is good value at P195. The doors are open from 11 am to 2 pm and from 6 to 11 pm daily.

On Arnaiz Ave in Makati, the *Gold Ranch* is a popular steakhouse, with Angus beef cooked a variety of ways for around P500 and pasta dishes at P250. It's open from 11.30 am to 2.30 pm and from 6.30 to 10.30 pm daily.

Australian steaks are showcased at the pricey *Outback Steakhouse*, on the 2nd floor of the Robinson's Place mall in Ermita, for around P500. It's open from 11 am to 11 pm Monday to Friday and from noon to 2 am on weekends. There's another branch in the Glorietta mall in Makati's Ayala Center.

Vegetarian Vegetarian options are limited in the capital. Restaurants with vegetarian dishes include *Three Amigos* on JM Nakpil St and *Tia Maria's* on Remedios St, with tasty cheese enchilada, and *Endangered Species* on MH del Pilar St with salad and vegetarian pastas. All of the Korean restaurants in town offer bean curd instead of meat in most of their dishes. Italian places like *Don Henrico's*, *Italianni's* and *Bravo* offer good vegetarian pizza and pasta options.

For dedicated vegetarians, a few restaurants in Binondo cater to the Chinese Buddhist community, with lots of tofu and soya protein-based dishes. In the Tutuban Center mall on CM Recto Ave, *Bodhi* offers vegetarian health food with soya in place of meat. Soups, noodles and mains cost from P30 to P70 and it's open from 10 am to 8 pm daily.

In Chinatown on Soler St, *Quan Yin Chay* is another tiny vegetarian canteen with a wide choice of vegetarian dishes. Meals with rice cost from P50 to P80. It's open from 7 am to 9 pm daily.

Vegetarian-friendly local foods include *lumpia sariwa* (vegetable spring rolls), *torta* (fried eggplant with egg) and *atsara* (pickled unripe papaya).

Breakfast From 7 am, the *Seafood Wharf* restaurant offers a P65 continental breakfast and a P130 American breakfast overlooking the bay.

The *Sabungan Coffeeshop* in the Manila Midtown Hotel has a good breakfast buffet with local and foreign food for P400 (all inclusive), from 6 to 10 am daily.

From 6 to 10 am daily, the Manila Hotel offers a P465 buffet breakfast in its *Cafe Ilang-Ilang* with a suitably impressive selection of American and Filipino items (tax and service not included).

The Shangri-La Hotel in Makati has a sumptuous breakfast buffet for P560 in its *Island Café*, from 6.30 to 10.30 am daily.

For a fast, unsophisticated breakfast, *Mister Donut* and the American chain *Dunkin' Donuts* have branches all over town. A breakfast of two donuts and a coffee works out at about P30.

Entertainment

With the vigorous clean-up campaign of Mayor Lim, Manila is beginning to shake off its traditional connotations of the term 'entertainment'. A few girlie bars still manage to cling on in Ermita and Malate, but the money is now in chic American-style bars for Manila's wealthy twenty-somethings. If you want to see what Ermita was like five years ago, the 24-hour *LA Cafe* on MH del Pilar St is representative of the scene throughout the country, with international food, teenage girls and a 'single white male' customer base.

Bars JM Nakpil St is the centre of the new youthful bar scene in Manila. Most of the bars here are open till 2 or 3 am weekdays and as late as 5 am Friday and Saturday.

The place to be seen is currently the *Common Ground Cafe* at the Gotham Restaurant. This bar wouldn't look out of place in London or New York, with live music, DJs and a lively young crowd It has P200 consumable cover on weekends. Nearby, *Insomnia* is a popular gothic-themed place with live music. It has a P200 consumable cover on weekends. Across the street, the *Verve Room*, above the minimalist *Episode Bar* has good international DJs and a throbbing sound system. *Politixx* sees a slightly older crowd and has cabaret, stand-up comedy and live music. Other options include *Jazz Rhythms*, with jazz music, the balcony bar at *617 Nakpil*, the *Lobby* and *Joy*.

The new *Republic of Malate* complex on Mabini St, Malate, has the stylish *Survival Cafe* bar, decorated with an eclectic collection of cameras, survival gear and radios (open from 8 pm to 3 am). Nearby, on Remedios Circle, the *Pipeline* is a loud music bar with regular live bands. Admission is usually about P250, which includes two drinks.

On the corner of Mabini and Arquiza Sts in Ermita, the *Cowboy Grill* is a very popular music venue, with pitchers of beer, sizzling snack meals and at least three live bands a night, from country-and-western acts to note-perfect Filipino versions of the big 'boy bands'. It's open until 3 am daily. There's another branch on Remedios St, near Malate Church.

There are several old favourites that are still going strong. The curious *Hobbit House* is a long-running folk club which is owned and run by a cooperative of dwarfs. The acts here range from flawless Filipino versions of Bob Dylan to expat folksingers. It's open from 7 pm till about 3 am daily (P150 cover).

On Remedios Circle, *In the Mood* is probably the most popular of the ballroom dancing clubs, with dinner dances till 3 am daily except Sunday. The consumable cover charge is P200 Monday to Thursday and P250 on Friday and Saturday.

Padi's Point is a bar chain, with branches on Adriatico St, Malate, Jupiter St, Makati and the Greenbelt Square mall. Pitchers of beer and sizzling Filipino snacks are the main attraction. It's open till 5 am daily and there's a consumable P150 cover charge on Friday and Saturday.

Also on Adriatico St, Malate, *Ten Years After* has a plane sticking through the roof and offers beers, snacks and rock videos from 5 pm to at least 2 am Monday to Saturday. Across the road, the tiny *Library Bar* is a stand-up comedy venue that's popular with the gay crowd (P350 consumable cover charge).

In the Greenbelt Square mall in Makati are the long-running *San Mig Pub* on Legaspi St and the British-themed *Prince of Wales Pub & Grill*, both offering beer and snack foods. A nicer place to drink is the open-air *Verandah Grill*, overlooking the peaceful Greenbelt Square park, with the usual sizzling Filipino dishes and cold beer till late.

Hotel Bars If you don't mind dressing up, the rooftop bars at some of the top end hotels are great places to watch sunset over Manila Bay and the views are worth the slightly elevated prices.

The *Sky Lounge* at the Manila Diamond Hotel has stunning views and live music from 8.30 pm till late. The *Top of the Century*, at the Century Park Hotel, is another swish bar with a jazz quartet and the 'Singing Lovelies' from 6 pm to 1 am.

Nightclubs & Karaoke Huge videoke TV lounges are more popular than nightclubs in Manila, but there are a few old-style nightclubs at some of the large hotels. *Zu*, at the Shangri-La Hotel on Makati Ave, Makati, is a long-running favourite of the expat crowd. Other choices include *Cats*, at the International Hotel on Arnaiz Ave and *Strumm's* in Greenbelt Square, Makati.

For the full 'KTV experience', there are dozens of disco-theatres around the intersection of Quezon Ave and Timog Ave in Quezon City, including *Stardust*, *Catwalk*,

Mystique and *Lexus*. The EDSA International Entertainment Complex in Pasay City also offers a variety of KTV choices.

Cinemas Manila boasts over 200 movie screens, just counting the theatres in the malls, so finding a film to watch should not be a problem. All of the local newspapers have extensive film listings.

If you're feeling more adventurous, the Filipino film industry is prolific, though all-action gangster movies are the mainstay. All of the mall theatres show a few Tagalog films and there are numerous independent film theatres around the intersection of Rizal Ave and CM Recto Ave in Santa Cruz and along Pedro Gil St in Paco.

Theatres There are a several theatres in Manila, which mainly play host to cultural performances of classical music and dance. The William Shaw Theater in the Shangri-La Plaza mall is a good place for plays and comedy events. Call the DOT office (☎ 02-524 1703) or the theatre box offices for information about performances. The theatres include:

The Cultural Center of the Philippines (CCP) (☎ 02-832 3878) Roxas Blvd, Malate
The Folk Arts Theater (☎ 02-832 1120) CCP Complex, Roxas Blvd, Malate
The William Shaw Theater (☎ 02-633 4821) 5th floor, Shangri-La Plaza mall, EDSA, Mandaluyong
The Rajah Sulayman Theatre (☎ 02-527 2961) Fort Santiago, Intramuros

Spectator Sports
Cockfighting Bloodthirsty cockfights take place at several venues around Manila and the atmosphere is always highly charged (see the 'Foul Play' boxed text in the Facts for the Visitor chapter). The huge Libertad cockpit on Dolores St in Pasay City is close to the tourist belt, and there is action here every afternoon except Thursday and Saturday, though Sunday is the best day to visit (P30). To get here take a jeepney or the LRT to Libertad station in Pasay City and change to an east-bound Evangelista-Libertad jeepney.

Other cockpits include the Philippine Cockers Club in Santa Ana, the Olympic Stadium in Grace Park, Caloocan City and La Loma on Calavite St, Quezon City.

Jai Alai The huge Jai Alai de Manila *fronton* (court), next to Harrison Plaza, is regularly closed following raids by government inspectors. If it's open, the atmosphere is great, with peso flying around as fast as the balls. Opening hours are from 5 pm till about 1 am daily except Sunday and admission is free. Bags, alcohol and cameras are prohibited.

Basketball The Cuneta Astrodome (☎ 02-833 7333) on Roxas Blvd, Pasay City, is the venue for professional basketball games. The league is run by the Philippine Basketball Association and hundreds of local fans cram into the bleachers (concrete bench seats) every Tuesday, Friday and Saturday. Games start at 5 pm and 7.30 pm, and courtside seats are P220 (P20 for bleachers).

The smaller San Andres Sports Complex (☎ 02-400 3950), on San Andres St, Malate, is the home of the Manila Metrostars, part of the new Metroball Basketball Association, with games on Saturday at 1.30 pm (call for details).

Horse Racing A day at the races is a popular bonding ground for Filipino men and Manila's main racetrack is the San Lazaro Hippodrome on Felix Huertas St in the Santa Cruz district. The all-weather track is made of charcoal and soft rock topped with a thick layer of sea sand. Nearly half a million dollars worth of bets are placed at San Larazo every week. Afternoon races are held on Wednesday, Thursday, Saturday and Sunday, and admission is P5. Tayuman is the nearest Metrorail station.

Shopping

Handicrafts Manila has a reputation as an arts and crafts centre and some attractive handicrafts can be found here, though there are a lot of tourist trinkets. Ornate wooden salad bowls, carved from a single piece of wood, are a good buy, as are baskets and carved wooden utensils and boards for the

traditional Asian game of *sungka*, which is played by moving cowrie shells between hollows on a carved piece of wood.

Hanging lamps and chandeliers made of wafer-thin shell panels are also popular buy, as are the shell lanterns that Filipinos traditionally hang outside their houses at Christmas. Along MH del Pilar St and in the Sining Pilipino complex on Mabini St, are dozens of shops selling Filipino paintings. The standard is often quite high and the subject matter varied, even though the artists turn these things out at an alarming rate.

Silharis, in the Plaza San Luis complex on General Luna St, Intramuros, has an excellent selection of superior-quality handicrafts, as do Galeria Andrea and Galeria de las Islas in the same building. The museum shop in the Museum of the Pilipino People has a good selection of authentic tribal artefacts.

The Ilalim ng Tulay Market, underneath Quezon Bridge in Quiapo, is a good place to pick up handicraft bargains, though you'll have to haggle to get the best prices. Fixed prices are available in the handicraft sections of the major department stores; Robinson's Place mall in Ermita and Landmark, in the Ayala Center in Makati, are good places to look.

Clothing You can buy authentic brand-name clothes in Manila for a fraction of the prices charged in Europe, Australia or the USA. The department stores are divided up into areas for the different brands. For even less, you can pick up copies of most big names in the bale-clothing markets in Divisoria and Baclaran and the street markets along CM Recto Ave in Binondo.

The Barong Tagalog, the traditional dress shirt worn by Filipino men, is a popular purchases. The best Barong are made from *piña*, a fabric woven from pineapple fibres. Many of the examples for sale in department stores and shops in Malate and Ermita were made in the village of Lumban, near Pagsanjan in Laguna province.

Other Souvenirs Shells are a popular purchase and the Pacific Ocean produces a startling variety of colours and forms. However, environmentalists have serious concerns about the impact of uncontrolled shell harvesting. In particular, trident shells and certain giant clams are protected under the laws governing trade in endangered species.

The *balisong* (fan or butterfly knives) produced in Taal in Laguna province are popular souvenirs, though you should be aware that these are illegal in many countries. There are numerous knife stalls in the Central Market, on Quezon Blvd, Quiapo.

For scuba diving equipment, Scuba World (☎ 02-895 3551), at 1181 Vito Cruz Extension, Makati, is recommended. In Ermita, Whitetip Divers (☎ 02-526 8190), in the small arcade at 1362 Mabini St, has a good range of gear and offers advice on diving in the Philippines.

Shopping Centres Robinson's Place, on Adriatico St, Ermita, is a modern mall with lots of clothing boutiques, restaurants, a bowling alley and eight cinema screens. There's also a good supermarket and department store. It's open from 10 am to 9 pm daily (the entrance on Pedro Gil St is open till 2 am).

The vast Ayala Center in Makati has malls within malls and you can walk around for hours without leaving the air-conditioned corridors. The covered Glorietta Center has three floors and four wings meeting on a huge atrium, with cinemas, numerous food courts, expensive antique shops and Japanese dance-karaoke machines (like a giant version of the computer game Simon-Says). It's open from 10 am to 8 pm daily.

Nearby, the Greenbelt Square mall includes the usual shops, restaurants and cinemas plus there's a pleasant park with some excellent restaurants and an open-air church. The mall is open from 10 am to 8 pm daily.

By the intersection of Ortigas Ave and EDSA in Quezon City is another huge shopping mall, with restaurants, cinemas, shops, condominiums and hotels. The huge SM Megamall, Shangri-La Plaza and Robinson's Galleria are the main malls here and the British Council Library is also here.

Nearby, Greenhills, on Ortigas Ave, is another popular mall.

In Divisoria, the Tutuban Center on CM Recto Ave is an unusual mall housed in a mock-up of a Chinese warehouse. The main building has shops and restaurants, while the two annexes are devoted to bale clothing and fake brand names. Just south of Malate on FB Harrison St, Harrison Plaza is a slightly ageing air-con mall with several cinemas and numerous souvenir stalls.

Getting There & Away

Air With the exception of Philippine Airlines (PAL), the national carrier, international flights to/from Manila use the ageing NAIA in Parañaque. International or domestic PAL passengers get to use the plush new Centennial Terminal II, which is close to NAIA on MIA Rd. See the Getting Around section for details of transport options to/from NAIA and Centennial II terminals.

A P550 departure tax is payable for international departures. Call NAIA on ☎ 02-877 1109 for information on arrivals and departures.

The offices for most of the international airlines are in Makati, but a few have satellite branches in Ermita and Malate. Security guards in Makati are some of the most officious in Asia; you'll need to leave ID with the guard on the door to visit many of the airline offices listed below.

Aeroflot (☎ 02-817 7737) 2nd floor, YL Holding Bldg, on the corner of Salcedo and Herrara Sts, Legaspi Village, Makati

Air France (☎ 02-887 7581) 18th floor, Trident Tower Bldg, 312 Gil Puyat Ave, Salcedo Village, Makati

Alitalia (☎ 02-893 9761) 6th floor, Don Jacinto Bldg, Dela Rosa St, Legaspi Village, Makati

Asiana Airlines (☎ 02-892 5681) Ground floor, I-Care Bldg, Dela Rosa St, Legaspi Village, Makati

British Airways (☎ 02-817 0361, 815 6656) Ground floor, Filipino Merchants Bldg, on the corner of Dela Rosa and Legaspi Sts, Makati

Canadian Airlines International (☎ 02-8923 4889) Golden Rock Bldg, Salcedo St, Salcedo Village, Makati

Cathay Pacific Airways (☎ 02-525 9367) on the corner of Pedro Gil and Dr Vasquez Sts,

Ermita; (☎ 02-848 2747) 24th floor, Trafalgar Plaza Bldg, 105 Dela Costa St, Salcedo Village, Makati

EgyptAir (☎ 02-815 8476) Ground floor, Windsor Tower Bldg, Legaspi St, Legaspi Village, Makati

El Al Israel Airlines (☎ 02-816 2387, 816 4121) 3rd floor, Rajah Sulayman Bldg, Benavidez St, Legaspi Village, Makati

Japan Airlines (☎ 02-812 1591) Mezzanine, Dusit Hotel Nikko, on the corner of Arnaiz Ave and EDSA, Makati

KLM-Royal Dutch Airlines (☎ 02-815 4790) La Paz Centre, on the corner of Salcedo and Herrera Sts, Legaspi Village, Makati

Korean Air (☎ 02-893 4909) Ground floor, LPL Plaza Bldg, Alfaro St, Salcedo Village, Makati; (☎ 02-893 4909) Ground floor, SGV Bldg, Ayala Ave, Makati

Lufthansa Airlines (☎ 02-810 4596) Ground floor, Collonade Bldg, on the corner of Legaspi and C Palanca Sts, Legaspi Village, Makati

Malaysia Airlines (☎ 02-525 9404) Ground floor, Legaspi Towers, 300 Vito Cruz St, on the corner of Roxas Blvd, Malate; (☎ 02-867 8767) 25th floor, World Centre, Gil Puyat Ave, Makati

Qantas Airways (☎ 02-812 0607) Ground floor, Filipino Merchants Bldg, on the corner of Dela Rosa and Legaspi Sts, Makati

Singapore Airlines (☎ 02-810 4951 to 810 4959) Ground floor, 138 Dela Costa St, Salcedo Village, Makati

Swissair (☎ 02-818 8351) Zuellig Bldg, Malugay St, Makati

Thai Airways International (THAI) (☎ 02-243 2645, 243 2652) Ground floor, Escolta Twin Towers, 288 Escolta St, Binondo; (☎ 02-812 4744) Ground floor, Country Space I Bldg, Dela Costa St, Salcedo Village, Makati

United Airlines (☎ 818 7321 to 818 7328) Ground floor, Pacific Star Bldg, on the corner of Gil Puyat Ave and Makati Ave, Makati

Vietnam Airlines (☎ 02-893 2083, 810 3653) Ground floor, Colonnade Bldg, 132 C Palanca St, Salcedo Village, Makati; (☎ 02-812 7794) Ground floor, 152 Xanland Corporate Bldg, Amorsolo St, Legaspi Village, Makati

Domestic flights on PAL leave from the new Centennial Terminal II at NAIA, while Cebu Pacific, Asian Spirit and Air Philippines operate from the old domestic terminal, just north of NAIA. All of these companies have express ticket offices, where you can buy tickets for same-day travel at the Domestic Terminal.

Around the terminal are ATMs for MasterCard, AmEx and Cirrus, and there is a P100 terminal fee for domestic departures (charter companies have individual terminal charges).

Useful airline addresses include:

PAL (☎ 02-523 7046) Ground floor, Century Park Hotel, Vito Cruz St, Malate; (☎ 02-816 6691) S&L Bldg, 1500 Roxas Blvd, Ermita, open from 8 am to 5 pm Monday to Friday, from 8 am to noon Saturday; (☎ 02-855 8888, information ☎ 855 9999) Express Office, Centennial Terminal II, NAIA, open from 2 am to 8 pm daily

Asian Spirit (☎ 02-840 3811 to 840 3816) Ground floor, LPL Towers, 112 Legaspi St, Makati; (☎ 02-514 4310) Express Office, Domestic Terminal, Pasay City, open from 3 am to 6 pm daily

A Soriano Aviation (☎ 02-833 3852) Andrews Ave, Pasay City

Air Ads (☎ 02-833 3264) Andrews Ave, Pasay City

Air Philippines (reservations hotline ☎ 02-843 7770); (☎ 02-524 0540) 472 Padre Faura Center, on the corner of Padre Faura and MH del Pilar Sts, Ermita; (☎ 02-843 7001) Ground floor, MB Center, 6805 Ayala Ave, Makati; (☎ 02-551 2177) Express Office Domestic Terminal, Pasay City, open from 2 am to 8 pm daily

Cebu Pacific (reservations hotline ☎ 02-636 4938); (☎ 02-526 5516) Ground floor, Manila Midtown Hotel, Adriatico St, Malate; (☎ 02-893 9607) Ground floor, Collonade Bldg, 132 C Palanca St, Makati; (☎ 02-551 1218) Express Office, Domestic Terminal, Pasay City, open from 1 am to 8 pm daily

Golden Passage Travel (☎ 02-725 4485) 403 Tower B, Wack Wack Twin Towers, Mandaluyong City

Laoag International Airways (☎ 02-551 9729) Domestic Road, Domestic Airport, Pasay City

Pacific Airways (☎ 02-891 6252) Domestic Road, Domestic Airport, Pasay City

One important thing to remember about domestic air travel in the Philippines is the volatile nature of pricing – and the fact that there are often many promotional deals available from the airlines.

Luzon There are numerous short flights around Luzon. PAL flies to Naga at 6.30 am daily except Saturday and to Legaspi at 10 am daily. There's an extra flight to Legaspi at 3.10 pm Monday, Tuesday, Friday and Saturday. There's a flight to Tuguegarao at 7 am Monday, Wednesday and Saturday.

Air Philippines flies to Legaspi at 9.15 am and Naga at 2.45 pm daily, to Laoag at 10.45 am Wednesday, Friday and Sunday, and to Baguio at 10.30 am Tuesday, Thursday, Saturday and Sunday.

Asian Spirit flies to Naga at 6 am daily, and to San Fernando (La Union) at 11 am Monday, Wednesday, Friday and Saturday.

Laoag International Airways has flights to Laoag at 6 am Tuesday and at 9.55 am Friday (P1600). Golden Passage has charter flights to San Fernando (La Union) at 7.30 am Tuesday and Friday and at 1 pm Sunday (P1600).

Batanes Islands Laoag International Airways has a flight to Basco on Batan Island at 6 am Tuesday and at 9.55 am Thursday (P3600).

Catanduanes Air Philippines and Asian Spirit both fly to Virac on Catanduanes Island at 7 am daily.

Marinduque Asian Spirit has a flight to Santa Cruz at 6 am daily except Tuesday and Saturday.

Mindoro Pacific Airways is *supposed* to have flights between Sablayan and Manila. Pacific Airways' Mamburao-Manila flights are slightly more dependable.

Pacific Airways flies from Manila to Mamburao and back at around 10 am Monday, Wednesday and Friday (P1600, 30-45 minutes). See also the Mamburao Getting There & Away section in the Mindoro chapter.

Air Philippines flies from Manila to San José (P1400, one hour) at 6.30 am Tuesday, Wednesday, Friday and Sunday. At 7.20 am Monday, Thursday, Saturday and Sunday, Asian Spirit has a flight to San José (P1000, one hour).

Bohol Asian Spirit flies to Tagbilaran on Bohol at 5.30 am daily (P2430).

Cebu PAL has daily flights to Cebu City (P1400, one hour) about every two hours from 5 am to 5.30 pm, with an extra flight at 8.30 pm Wednesday, Thursday and Sunday, and return flights on the same day. Cebu-Manila flights go from 7.10 am to 10.25 pm.

Air Philippines flies four times daily from Manila to/from Cebu City (P1400, one hour), leaving Manila at 6 and 10 am and 2 and 6 pm. Cebu-Manila flights go daily at 6.50 am and 1.20, 3.40 and 7.10 pm (P2100).

Cebu Pacific flies daily – on the hour, every two hours – between Manila and Cebu City (P1600, one hour). Manila-Cebu City flights go from 5 am to 5 pm. Cebu City-Manila flights go from 7 am to 7 pm. You get a discount of about P300 for taking the early flight (5 am) from Manila to Cebu, or the late flights (5 and 7 pm) from Cebu to Manila.

Leyte PAL flies to Tacloban at 5.30 am and at 2 pm daily except Tuesday. Air Philippines flies to Tacloban at 5.30 am daily, returning at 7.15 am. Cebu Pacific flies to Tacloban at 6.10 am, 12.20 pm and 2.40 pm daily.

Masbate Asian Spirit flies to Masbate town at 5 am daily (P1750, one hour). Flights from Masbate town to Manila leave at 6.50 am daily. Laoag International Airways has a flight to Masbate town at 6 am Monday, Wednesday and Friday and at 12.15 pm Sunday (P1750).

Masbate Express (Corporate Air) flies at 8.30 am daily (P1620, one hour) to Masbate town. Flights from Masbate town to Manila leave at 10.30 am. Masbate Express (Corporate Air) (☎ 02-832 2316 or 0917 925 1112) has an office opposite Manila's domestic terminal on the 6th floor, Unit L, Ding Velayo Building and a desk at the Masbate town airport.

Negros PAL flies to Bacolod at 5.10 and 9.55 am and 3 pm daily.

Air Philippines flies to Bacolod City at 12.25 pm daily, and to Dumaguete City at 6 am daily. There's also a flight to Dumaguete at 3 pm Monday, Wednesday, Friday and Sunday.

Cebu Pacific has flights to Bacolod (P2040, one hour) at 10.30 am and 4.20 pm daily. There's also a flight at 5.30 am Monday, Tuesday, Thursday and Saturday, and another at 7.30 am Wednesday, Friday and Sunday. Bacolod-Manila flights depart at 11.30 am, 4.30 pm and 6.40 pm daily.

Panay PAL flies to Roxas at 5.45 am daily, to Iloilo at 5.20 and 9.45 am and 2.30 and 5.40 pm daily, and to Kalibo at 9.30 am and 3.25 pm daily.

Air Philippines flies to Iloilo City (P1500, one hour) at 5.15 am, 2 pm and 4.45 pm daily, and to Kalibo at 1.45 pm daily. Iloilo-Manila flights go at 7 am, 3 pm and 6.30 pm daily.

Cebu Pacific flies to Roxas City at 5.30 am, and to Iloilo at 9.50 am and 4 pm daily. It flies Roxas-Manila at 7.10 am daily (P1800, one hour). At 5.20 am Monday, Wednesday, Friday and Sunday there's an extra flight to Iloilo. The same airline flies four times daily from Iloilo to Manila at 7.40 and 11.30 am, 4 and 6.30 pm (P1950).

Asian Spirit has flights to Caticlan (for Boracay Island) at 8.45 am and 1, 2.30 and 3 pm daily (P1550). Caticlan-Manila flights go at 10.15 am, 1.30 pm and 5 pm daily.

Golden Passage flies to Caticlan at 7.30 am and 3.30 pm Wednesday, Friday and Sunday (P2000). Pacific Air has Caticlan flights at 7 and 10.30 am and 2.30 pm daily (P1650).

Romblon Laoag International Airways has a flight to Romblon at 9.30 am Monday and Thursday (P1140).

Samar Asian Spirit flies to Calbayog at 11 am Tuesday, Wednesday, Friday and Sunday (P1885), returning the same days; and to Catarman at 10 am daily except Monday and Friday (P1830), returning the same days.

Palawan For Palawan, PAL has a flight from Manila to Puerto Princesa at 11.50 am daily, while Air Philippines flies there at 10 am daily.

From Manila to Sandoval, Seair flies at 7 am daily (or just about daily). This is offi-

cially a charter flight, with bookings organised in Manila through Asia Travel (☎ 02-752 0307, fax 894 5725), or Noah's Century (☎ 02-810 2623). For Manila-Coron town flights you should contact Seair at their office at the domestic airport in Manila (☎ 02-891 8709).

A Soriano Aviation offers daily charter flights from Manila to El Nido at 7.30 am and 3.30 pm for US$141/230 one way/return. In the opposite direction, flights leave El Nido at 9.30 am and 5 pm. When booking, you need to give four days' notice from Manila and one day's notice from El Nido (in El Nido, you can book at the Ten Knots travel office, also known as the White House).

Golden Passage has charter flights to El Nido at 11.30 am Friday and Sunday (P4485) continuing to Puerto Princesa. Flights back to Manila leave Puerto Princesa at 1 pm and El Nido at 3 pm. There are rumours that this may become a daily flight. There is also a flight to Puerto Princesa via Busuanga at 7.30 am Monday, returning the same day. From Manila to El Nido, there's also a daily charter flight available with Corporate Air (☎ 02-832 2316 or 0917 925 1112).

For the diving resort of Coron on Busuanga Island in the Calamian Group, Asian Spirit has a flight at 9.45 am daily. Golden Passage flies to Busuanga at 7.30 am Monday, Thursday and Sunday. Air Ads flies to Busuanga at 7.30 am daily. Pacific Air has flights to Coron at 8 am daily.

Mindanao PAL flies to Cagayan de Oro at 5 and 10 am and 1.10 pm daily, and to Davao at 5.10 and 11 am daily. There's another flight to Davao at 2.50 pm daily except Wednesday. There are also daily flights to General Santos City at 6.30 am, Butuan City at 10.30 am, and Zamboanga at 4.50 am. There is an extra flight to Zamboanga at 2.10 pm daily except Friday and Sunday. PAL has a 9.50 am Monday, Tuesday, Thursday, Saturday and Sunday flight to Cotabato. There's also a flight to Dipolog at 6 am Tuesday, Thursday, Saturday and Sunday and at 9.20 am Friday.

Air Philippines has daily flights to Zamboanga at 10.15 am, to Cotabato at 9 am, to Cagayan de Oro at 5.45 and 10.15 am, to General Santos City at 7 am and to Davao at 5 am and 3 pm.

Cebu Pacific flies to Davao at 5 and 10 am and 1.20 and 3.20 pm daily, and to Cagayan de Oro at 5.10, 9.30 and 11.40 am. There's also a 6 am flight to Zamboanga.

Boat The port of Manila is divided into two sections, South Harbour and North Harbour. Unfortunately, all the passenger ferries from Manila use the hard-to-reach North Harbour, on the far side of the Pasig River. It's probably best to take a taxi, as the port area isn't a place to be wandering around with luggage. On the meter from Malate or Ermita, a taxi should cost P50. In the opposite direction, you'll have to be a very hard bargainer to pay less than P100.

There are now only three major shipping companies handling interisland trips from Manila. Negros Navigation has numerous trips to Palawan, Mindanao and islands in the Negros. Sulpicio Lines and WG&A cover the same ground, and also offer trips to smaller islands like Masbate. All three companies have ticket offices at North Harbour and smaller offices in town. Note that schedules for the shipping companies are very vulnerable to change; adverse weather conditions or renovation of a ferry can totally alter the sailing times and boats used for various trips.

Negros Navigation (☎ 02-245 0601) Pier 2 and Pier 8, North Harbour. All boats except the MV *Don Claudio* leave from Pier 2.
Destinations: Panay, Negros, Cebu and Bohol islands, Mindanao, Palawan
Offices: (☎ 02-818 3804) Loyola Bldg, 849 Arnaiz Ave, Makati
(☎ 02-733 3895) Royal Booking, on the corner of C Palanca St and Quezon Blvd, Santa Cruz
Sulpicio Lines (☎ 02-245 0616) Pier 12 and Pier 16, North Harbour. All boats except the MV *Dipolog Princess* leave from Pier 12.
Destinations: Cebu, Leyte, Samar, and Masbate islands, Mindanao
Offices: (☎ 02-241 9701) 415 San Fernando St, Binondo

(☎ 02-733 3895) Royal Booking, on the corner of C Palanca St and Quezon Blvd, Santa Cruz
WG&A (☎ 02-245 0693) Pier 4 and Pier 14, North Harbour
Destinations: Cebu, Negros, Panay, Bohol and Masbate islands, Mindanao
Offices: (☎ 02-525 6373) 2nd floor, Trinidad Bldg, on the corner of Mabini St and United Nations Ave, Ermita
(☎ 02-894 3211) Twin Cities Condominium, Makati

Bohol, Cebu & Panay Destinations and journey times include: Cebu City (18-22 hours); Bacolod and Dumaguete on Negros Island (19-22 hours); Iloilo, Roxas and Dumaguit on Panay Island (18-25 hours); and Tagbilaran on Bohol Island (28-31 hours).

For Cebu City, Negros Navigation's MV *Mary Queen of Peace* leaves at 9 pm Tuesday (direct). The MV *St Peter the Apostle* leaves at 9 am Friday (direct).

For Bacolod, the MV *St Joseph the Worker* leaves at 2 pm Monday (via Iloilo), at 7 pm Wednesday and at noon Saturday (direct). The MV *St Peter the Apostle* leaves at 9 pm Monday, while the MV *St Ezekiel Moreno* leaves at 5 pm Sunday.

For Iloilo, the MV *St Joseph the Worker* leaves at 2 pm Monday (direct) and at noon Saturday (via Bacolod). The MV *San Lorenzo Ruiz* goes directly to Iloilo at 8 pm Wednesday, the MV *Mary Queen of Peace* leaves at 11 pm Friday, the MV *Santa Ana* leaves at 2 pm Sunday and the MV *St Ezekiel Moreno* leaves at 5 pm Sunday (via Bacolod).

For Panay, the MV *Princess of Negros* leaves for Roxas at noon Tuesday, continuing to Dumaguit. The same ship leaves for Dumaguit at 6 pm Thursday, continuing to Roxas.

At 9 am Friday, the MV *St Peter the Apostle* goes directly to Tagbilaran on Bohol. The MV *San Paolo* goes to Dumaguete on Negros at midnight Friday. At 8 am Wednesday, the same ship leaves for Tagbilaran, stopping at Dumaguete.

From Pier 8, the MV *Don Claudio* leaves at 10 am Wednesday for Estancia on Panay (20 hours, direct) and San Carlos on Negros (52 hours).

For Cebu, Sulpicio Lines' MV *Princess of the Ocean* leaves 10 am Wednesday, the MV *Princess of the Universe* leaves at 10 am Tuesday, the MV *Princess of New Unity* leaves at 4 pm Thursday and the MV *Filipina Princess* leaves at 10 am Sunday (all direct). The MV *Cebu Princess* leaves for Cebu at 10 pm Friday (42 hours, via Masbate Island and Ormoc on Leyte).

The MV *Princess of the Pacific* goes directly to Iloilo at 10 am Tuesday. From Pier 16, the MV *Dipolog Princess* leaves for Cebu at noon Wednesday (65 hours, via Tagbilaran on Bohol, and Dipolog and Iligan on Mindanao). Also bound for Cebu, the MV *Princess of the Caribbean* leaves at noon Wednesday (65 hours, via Dumaguete on Negros and Ozamis on Mindanao), and the MV *Princess of the Ocean* leaves at 8 pm Saturday (48 hours, via Cagayan de Oro on Mindanao).

The WG&A MV *Superferry XII* leaves Pier 4 for Cebu at 3 pm Tuesday, at 7 pm Thursday and at 9 am Sunday. The MV *Superferry I* or MV *Superferry VIII* goes directly to Cebu from Pier 4 at 8 pm Monday, to Iloilo from Pier 14 at 10 am Wednesday, and to Bacolod from Pier 4 at 9 am Friday. From Pier 14, the MV *Superferry VI* or MV *Superferry X* goes to Cebu at 9 am Friday and to Iloilo at 9 am Saturday.

The MV *Superferry II* or MV *Superferry IX* goes directly to Iloilo from Pier 14 at noon Tuesday, to Dumaguete from Pier 4 at midnight Wednesday and to Bacolod from Pier 4 at 8 pm Sunday. For Panay, the MV *Lipa* leaves for Dumaguit and Roxas at 6 pm Monday (Pier 4), at 2 pm Wednesday (Pier 4) and at 2 pm Saturday (Pier 6).

The MV *Superferry III* leaves Pier 4 at midnight Monday for Tagbilaran, continuing to Dumaguete. The MV *Sacred Heart* or MV *Medjugorje* leaves for Tagbilaran at 9 pm Friday (direct).

Leyte & Samar The Sulpicio Lines' MV *Tacloban Princess* leaves for Tacloban on Leyte at noon Wednesday (40 hours, via Catbalogan in Samar), and at noon Saturday (30 hours, direct). The MV *Cebu Princess* leaves for Ormoc on Leyte at 10 pm Friday

(50 hours, via Masbate Island). For Calubian, Baybay and Maasin on Leyte, the MV *Palawan Princess* leaves at 8 pm Wednesday (47 hours to Maasin).

Masbate The Sulpicio Lines' MV *Cebu Princess* leaves for Masbate on Masbate Island at 10 am Friday (23 hours, direct). Its MV *Palawan Princess* leaves at 8 pm Wednesday (19 hours, direct). WG&A's MV *Sacred Heart* or MV *Medjugorje* leaves Pier 6 on Monday at 11 pm (28 hours, direct).

Mindanao Destinations and journey times include: Cagayan de Oro (29-48 hours); Cotabato (45-57 hours); Davao (52-74 hours); Dipolog (42 hours); Iligan (46-53 hours); Nasipit (31-40 hours); Ozamis (40 hours); Surigao (32-53 hours); General Santos (48-70 hours); and Zamboanga (43 hours).

To Cagayan de Oro, Negros Navigation's MV *St Peter the Apostle* leaves at 9 pm Monday (via Bacolod) and the MV *Mary Queen of Peace* leaves at 11 pm Friday (via Iloilo). For Ozamis, the MV *Santa Ana* leaves at 2 pm Sunday (via Iloilo), continuing to Iligan. To Surigao, the MV *San Paolo* leaves at midnight on Friday (via Dumaguete). The MV *Mary Queen of Peace* leaves for Nasipit at 9 pm Tuesday (via Cebu).

For Zamboanga, Negros Navigation's MV *St Ezekiel Moreno* leaves at 5 pm Sunday (via Bacolod and Iloilo), continuing General Santos City and Davao. The MV *San Lorenzo Ruiz* leaves for Zamboanga at 8 pm Wednesday (via Iloilo), continuing to Cotabato and General Santos City.

Sulpicio Lines' MV *Princess of the Pacific* leaves for Zamboanga at 10 am Tuesday (via Iloilo). The MV *Princess of the Ocean* leaves for Cagayan de Oro at 8 pm Saturday (direct), and for Nasipit at 10 am Wednesday (via Cebu).

For Surigao, the MV *Palawan Princess* leaves at 8 pm Wednesday (via Masbate and Leyte) and the MV *Filipina Princess* leaves at 10 am Sunday (via Cebu), continuing to Davao. The MV *Princess of New Unity* leaves for Davao at 4 pm Thursday (via Cebu), while the MV *Princess of the*

Caribbean leaves for Ozamis at noon Wednesday (via Dumaguete).

MV *Dipolog Princess* leaves Pier 16 for Dipolog at noon Wednesday (via Tagbilaran on Bohol), continuing to Iligan.

WG&A's MV *Superferry I* or *Superferry VIII* goes to Surigao from Pier 4 at 8 pm Monday (via Cebu), to Davao from Pier 14 at 10 am Wednesday (via Iloilo and General Santos City), and to Cotabato from Pier 4 at 9 am Friday (via Bacolod and Zamboanga).

The MV *Superferry VI* or MV *Superferry X* goes to Zamboanga and Davao from Pier 14 at 2 pm Monday, to Cagayan de Oro from Pier 14 at 9 am Friday (via Cebu), and to General Santos City from Pier 14 at 9 am Saturday (via Iloilo), continuing to Davao.

The MV *Superferry II* or MV *Superferry IX* goes to Zamboanga from Pier 14 at noon Tuesday (via Iloilo), continuing to Cotabato, and to Cagayan de Oro from Pier 4 at midnight Wednesday (via Dumaguete). For Iligan and Ozamis, one of the two boats leaves Pier 4 at midnight Thursday, and the other at midnight Saturday. One of the boats also leaves Pier 4 at 8 pm Sunday for Cagayan de Oro (via Bacolod).

The MV *Sacred Heart* or MV *Medjugorje* goes to Dipolog from Pier 4 at 9 pm Friday (via Bohol), and to Surigao from Pier 6 at noon Thursday, continuing to Nasipit.

Mindoro Boats to/from Mindoro use the port at Batangas (see that entry in the Around Manila chapter).

Palawan & Busuanga The Negros Navigation MV *Santa Ana* leaves for Puerto Princesa at 2 pm Thursday (24 hours, direct). WG&A's MV *Superferry III* leaves Pier 14 for Coron at 4 pm Friday (14 hours), continuing to Puerto Princesa (27½ hours).

Bus Getting out of Manila by bus is harder than you might expect as there is no central bus terminal. The dozens of private operators in town have their own terminals scattered across the city, but most are close to EDSA (Manila's ring road), which connects the highways north and south of the capital. Many south-bound services leave from terminals in Pasay City, while north-bound services frequently leave from Caloocan City, or Cubao in Quezon City.

The bus schedules listed are generally for daytime services, though there may be later buses. All the terminals listed below are easy to reach by public transport.

It should also be noted that bus drivers in the Philippines are among the most maniacal on the face of the earth – you may well be in for a white-knuckle ride and crashes are frequent.

Malate Several companies have air-con buses to Legaspi, via Naga City, which leave from the DHL offices on the corner of Pedro Gil and MH del Pilar Sts in Malate. Peñafrancia Tours (☎ 02-450 1122), at 483 Pedro Gil St, has a 7 pm bus for P400 (P330 to Naga). Around the corner, Gold Line Tours (☎ 02-450 0506), on the corner of MH del Pilar and Pedro Gil Sts, has a bus at 8 pm for P410 (P325 to Naga). Next door, Highway Express (☎ 02-450 1615) has a 7.30 pm bus to Naga City only (P395).

There are also useful buses that meet the boats to Puerto Galera. A bus leaves the Centrepoint Hotel on Mabini St at 9 am daily, connecting with the 11.45 am MV *Si-Kat II* to Puerto Galera (P350 one way). Alternatively, a bus leaves the Citystate Tower Hotel on Mabini St at 8 am daily, connecting with the MV *Super 85* ferry (P360/695 one way/return). Both buses can be booked in the hotels.

Intramuros & Santa Cruz There are informal terminals for several bus companies very close to the tourist belt, with destinations like the pier in Batangas (for ferries to Puerto Galera), Cavite, Ternate, Angeles and the Bataan peninsula.

1 Alps Transit, at the Concepcion St (Bastion de Dilao) entrance to Intramuros, across from City Hall, has buses to the pier in Batangas every 20 minutes (three hours). Any north-bound jeepney from Taft Ave or Mabini St will pass by City Hall.

2 Saulog Transit and **St Anthony Transit**, at the Anda St (Bastion de San Gabriel) entrance to Intramuros, have buses to Cavite and Ternate every seven minutes. 'Divisoria' jeepneys pass here; get off just before the Jones bridge.

3 Philippine Rabbit (☎ 02-734 9836), on the corner of Oroquieta St and Rizal Ave, Santa Cruz (Avenida Terminal), has buses every 20 minutes to Angeles in Pampanga province, and Balanga and Mariveles in Bataan province. All buses go via San Fernando (Pampanga province).

Sampaloc North-east of the centre are a number of useful bus companies for northern destinations such as Bangued and Vigan in Ilocos Sur province, Laoag in Ilocos Norte province, Tuguegarao in Cagayan province, Banaue in Ifugao province and Baguio in Benguet province. Jeepneys from Taft Ave or Mabini St heading to 'Blumentritt' via 'Dimasalang', or 'Dapitan' will bring you close to all these stations.

4 Autobus Transport Systems (☎ 02-743 6870), on the corner of Dimasalang and Laong Laan Sts, Sampaloc, has a daily bus to Banaue at 10 pm, and regular buses to Tuguegarao, Vigan and Laoag. To get here take any jeepney going to Blumentritt via Dimasalang from Taft Ave or Mabini St.

5 Dangwa Tranco (☎ 02-731 2859), 1600 Dimasalang St, Sampaloc, has buses to Baguio every few hours. To get here take any jeepney going to Blumentritt via Dimasalang from Taft Ave or Mabini St.

6 Dominion Transit (☎ 02-743 3612), on the corner of Blumentritt and Laong Laan Sts, Sampaloc, has buses every two hours to Vigan and Bangued, via San Fernando (La Union). To get here take any jeepney going to Dapitan from Taft Ave or Mabini St in the tourist belt. The terminal is next to the Caltex gas station on Blumentritt St.

7 Fariñas Trans (☎ 02-743 8580 to 743 8582), at 1238 DH Lacson St, Sampaloc, has half-hourly buses to Laoag via Vigan. To get here take any jeepney going to Blumentritt via Dimasalang from Taft Ave or Mabini St.

8 Maria de Leon Trans (☎ 02-731 4907), on the corner of Geliños and Dapitan Sts, Sampaloc, has hourly buses going north to Laoag via San Fernando (La Union) and Vigan. Jeepneys going to Dapitan from Taft Ave or Mabini St pass close to here.

Caloocan City Caloocan City is an important departure point for north-bound buses. Destinations include Olongapo in Zambales province, San José del Monte and Baliwag in Bulucan province, Cabanatuan in Nueva Ecija province and Dagupan in Pangasinan province, as well as Bangued, Vigan, Laoag and Baguio. All terminals in Caloocan City can be reached by Monumento jeepney or the LRT.

9 Baliwag Transit (☎ 02-364 0778), at 199 Rizal Ave Extension, Caloocan City, has buses every 40 minutes to Cabanatuan, which is a jumping-off point for the surfing beaches of Baler. The company also has regular services to Baliwag and San José del Monte. Jeepneys from Mabini St to Monumento will take you here; get out near the Equitable PCI bank on the corner of 2nd Ave. The terminal is midway between the Fifth Ave and R Papa Metrorail stops.

10 Philippine Rabbit (☎ 02-363 6264), on EDSA, Balintawak, Caloocan City, has hourly buses to Baguio and Bangued, and buses every few hours to Laoag and Vigan. To get here take a jeepney or the Metrorail to Monumento, then take a south-bound local bus bound for Cubao.

11 Victory Liner (☎ 02-361 1506), at 713 Rizal Ave Extension, Caloocan City, has four daily buses to Baguio and hourly buses to Dagupan. There are half-hourly buses to Olongapo, Iba and Santa Cruz in Zambales province. Take a jeepney or the Metrorail from the tourist belt to Monumento; the terminal is just before the Monumento roundabout.

Cubao North-Bound Most buses from Cubao head north, to Cabanatuan, San Fernando (La Union), Baguio, Bangued, Tuguegarao, Vigan, Laoag or even Aparri, at the top of Cagayan province. All terminals in Cubao can be reached by taking a 'Cubao' jeepney to either the Aurora Blvd or Quezon Ave junctions with EDSA, and transferring to a north or south-bound local bus from there.

12 Baliwag Transit (☎ 02-912 3361), on EDSA, Cubao, Quezon City, has buses north to Tuguegarao (via Cauayan) every two hours, and buses to Aparri at 5 am and 5.50 pm. A few doors away is a second Baliwag terminal with buses every 20 minutes to Cabanatuan via Baliwag. Buses to San José del Monte leave regularly from both terminals.

13 Dagupan Bus Co (☎ 02-727 2330), on the corner of EDSA and New York St, Cubao, Quezon City, has buses every hour to Dagupan, Alaminos and Lingayen in Pangasinan province. There are also hourly buses to Tuguegarao and Baguio.

BUS DESTINATIONS FROM MANILA

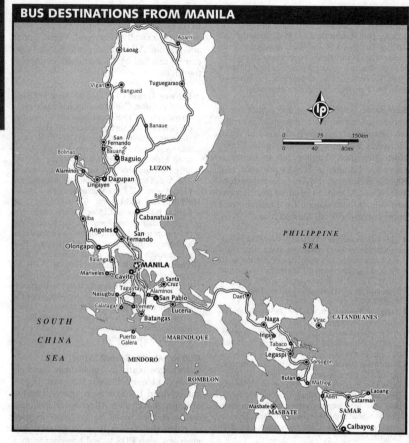

[map labels: Aparri, Laoag, Tuguegarao, Vigan, Bangued, Banaue, San Fernando, Bauang, Bolinao, Baguio, LUZON, Alaminos, Dagupan, Lingayen, Baler, Cabanatuan, Iba, Angeles, San Fernando, PHILIPPINE SEA, Olongapo, Balanga, Mariveles, MANILA, Cavite, Santa Cruz, Tagaytay, Alaminos, Nasugbu, San Pablo, Daet, Calatagan, Lemery, Lucena, Naga, Virac, CATANDUANES, Batangas, MARINDUQUE, Iriga, Tabaco, Puerto Galera, Legaspi, SOUTH CHINA SEA, MINDORO, Sorsogon, Bulan, Matnog, Laoang, ROMBLON, Allen, Catarman, SAMAR, Masbate, MASBATE, Calbayog]

0   75   150km
0   40   80mi

14 Dangwa Tranco (☎ 02-410 1991), at 832 Aurora Blvd, Cubao, Quezon City, has two morning and two evening buses to Baguio. There is also a bus to Banaue at 7.30 am daily.

15 Dominion Transit (☎ 02-727 2350, 727 2334), on EDSA, Cubao, Quezon City, has hourly buses to San Fernando (La Union), Bangued and Vigan.

16 Partas (☎ 02-725 7303, 725 1740), on Aurora Blvd, Cubao, Quezon City, has hourly buses to Bangued, Vigan and Laoag. Most buses stop in San Fernando (La Union).

17 Victory Liner (☎ 02-727 4688), on EDSA, Cubao, Quezon City, has buses to Alaminos, Dagupan and Lingayen in Pangasinan province every 40 minutes. There are also hourly buses to Baguio.

18 Victory Liner (☎ 02-921 3296), on the corner of EDSA and East Ave, Quezon City, has at least eight buses daily to Tuguegarao and buses to Aparri at 4.30 am and 6.30 pm. Most buses stop in Cabanatuan, on the way up to Cagayan province.

Cubao South-Bound A few services run south from Cubao, including buses to Batangas and Lucena, Daet and Naga in Camarines Norte province and Legaspi in Albay province.

19 BLTB (☎ 02-913 1525), in Alimall I, Araneta Center, Quezon City, has buses every half-hour

BUS DESTINATIONS FROM MANILA

Destination (Town)	Km	Duration of Journey (Hours)	Bus Company Number
Alaminos (Laguna)	78	1.30	19,20,21,22,27,31,33
Alaminos (Pangasinan)	254	6.00	15,17,18
Angeles	83	1.30	3
Aparri	596	13.00	12
Baguio	246	6.00	5,10,11,14,26
Balanga	123	2.30	3,29
Baler		7.00	29
Banaue	348	9.00	4,14
Bangued	400	8.00	5,6,10,15,16
Batangas	111	3.00	1,19,21,22,27,33,35
Bolinao	283	6.00	25
Cabanatuan	115	2.30	9,12,18,25
Calatagan		4.00	27
Calbayog		12.00	27,30,34
Catbalogan		16.00	27,30,34
Cavite		1.00	2
Catarman		20.00	27,34
Daet	350	7.00	23,24,27,30,34
Dagupan	216	5.00	11,13,17,25,26
Iba	210	5.00	11
Laoag	487	10.00	4,7,8,10,16
Lemery		3.30	19,20,21,27,31,33
Lingayen	227	5.30	13,17
Legaspi	550	12.00	24,27,30,32,34
Lucena	136	3.00	19,20,21,22,27,30,32,33,34,35
Mariveles		3.30	3,29
Matnog	670	17.00	27,30,34
Maasin		28.00	27,30,34
Naga	449	9.00	24,27,30,32,34
Nasugbu	102	2.30	27,28
Olongapo	126	3.30	26
Ormoc		26.00	27
San Fernando (La Union)	269	7.00	5,8,11,15,16
San Fernando (Pampanga)	66	1.00	3,26,29
San Pablo	87	2.00	19,20,21,22,27,30,32,34,35
Santa Cruz/Pagsanjan	101	2.30	19,21,27
Sorsogon	604	14.00	27,30,34
Tacloban		24.00	27,30,34
Tagaytay	56	1.30	28
Tuguegarao	483	9.00	4,12,13,18
Vigan	407	9.00	4,5,6,7,8,10,15,16

to Dalahican (for ferries to Marinduque) and Batangas, and buses every two hours to Santa Cruz in Laguna province.

20JAC Liner (☎ 02-928 6140, 929 6943), on the corner of EDSA and East Ave, Quezon City, has buses going south to Lucena every 20 minutes.

21JAM Transit (☎ 02-414 9925), on the corner of EDSA and Monte de Piedad St, Cubao, Quezon City, has buses every 30 minutes to Batangas, Lucena and Santa Cruz.

22Tritran (☎ 02-925 1759), on the corner of EDSA and East Ave, Quezon City, has half-hourly buses to Lucena and Dalahican, and buses to Batangas every 20 minutes.

23Philtranco (☎ 02-913 3602), in Alimall, Araneta Center, EDSA, Cubao, Quezon City, has buses to Daet (via Lucena) every few hours.

24Superlines (☎ 02-414 3319), at 670 EDSA, Cubao, Quezon City, has at least 16 buses a day to Daet via Lucena, and less frequent buses continuing to Naga and Legaspi.

Pasay City North-Bound A couple of bus companies head north from Pasay City for destinations like Baguio, Cabanatuan, Dagupan and Olongapo.

25Five Star Bus Lines (☎ 02-833 4772), Aurora Blvd, Pasay City, has regular buses to Cabanatuan and Dagupan. There are also buses to Bolinao in Pangasinan every half-hour.

26Victory Liner (☎ 02-833 5019), on EDSA, Pasay City, has hourly buses to Baguio and Dagupan, and a half-hourly service to Olongapo.

Pasay City South-Bound Most buses out of Pasay City head south, with some even connecting by ferry to other islands. Useful destinations include Batangas, Lucena, Nasugbu and Santa Cruz. A few buses go further afield to Daet, Naga, Legaspi and to the islands of Samar and Leyte.

27BLTB (☎ 02-833 5501), on EDSA, Pasay City, has buses every 15 minutes to Batangas City and Nasugbu and Lucena. There are also hourly buses to Dalahican Port, Calatagan (near Matabungkay beach) and Santa Cruz. Long-haul trips include Naga (8.30 and 9.30 am and 8 pm), Legaspi (8.30 am and 8 pm) and Matnog (2.30 am and 2.30 and 3.30 pm). For Samar, there's a 10 am bus to Catarman and a 12.45 pm bus to Tacloban. For Leyte, there's a 12.15 pm service to Ormoc, and an 11 am service to Maasin. To get here take a Baclaran jeepney

from MH del Pilar St or the LRT to EDSA and change to an east-bound bus.

28Crow Transit (☎ 02-551 1566, 804 0616), at Gizelle's Park Plaza, Pasay rotonda (roundabout), on the corner of Taft Ave and EDSA, Pasay City, has buses to Nasugbu every 30 minutes and buses to Tagaytay (for Lake Taal) every 15 minutes. To get here, take a jeepney or the LRT along Taft Ave to EDSA station.

29Genesis (☎ 02-551 0842), at Gizelle's Park Plaza, Pasay rotonda, on the corner of Taft Ave and EDSA, Pasay City, has buses to Mariveles in the Bataan peninsula via San Fernando (Pampanga) and Balanga, leaving every 15 minutes. There are also several early morning buses to the surfing beaches of Baler in Aurora province. To get here, take a jeepney or the LRT along Taft Ave to EDSA station.

30Gold Line Tours (☎ 02-831 9737), on the corner of EDSA and Taft Ave, Pasay City, has a bus to the islands of Samar and Leyte at noon daily. Stops include Calbayog, Catbalogan, Tacloban and Maasin. To get here, take a jeepney or the LRT along Taft Ave to Gil Puyat station.

31JAC Liner (☎ 02-831 8977), on Taft Ave, Pasay City, has buses every 30 minutes to Lucena (via Alaminos) and to Lemery. To get here, take a jeepney or the LRT along Taft Ave to Gil Puyat station.

32JB Bicol Express Line (☎ 02-833 2950), on Aurora Blvd, Pasay City, has hourly buses to Legaspi in Albay province, via Lucena and Naga. To get here take a Baclaran jeepney from MH del Pilar St or the LRT to EDSA and change to an east-bound bus.

33JAM Transit (☎ 02-831 4390), on the corner of Taft Ave and Gil Puyat Ave, Pasay City, has buses every 15 minutes to Batangas, Lucena and Santa Cruz de Laguna. There are also half-hourly buses to Dalahican and buses every 15 minutes to Lemery. To get here take the LRT to Gil Puyat station, or a Baclaran jeepney to Buendia/Gil Puyat Ave and change to an east-bound bus.

34Philtranco (☎ 02-833 5061, 832 2456), on EDSA, Pasay City, has a 4.15 am daily bus to Davao (three days) and to Cagayan de Oro at 6 pm daily (three days), both in Mindanao. There are also buses to Tacloban in Eastern Samar at 9, 9.30 and 10.30 am and 2 pm, stopping in Calbayog and Catbalogan. At 9, 10 and 11 am there is a bus to Catarman in Northern Samar. Most buses also stop in Daet, Naga, Legaspi and Sorsogon.

35Tritran (☎ 02-831 4700), at 2124 Taft Ave, Pasay City, has buses every 30 minutes to Batangas and Lucena (via San Pablo). To get here take the LRT to Gil Puyat station, or a Baclaran jeepney to Buendia/Gil Puyat Ave and change to an east-bound bus.

Minibus A number of brightly painted minibuses leave for various destinations from Quirino Ave in Baclaran, Pasay City. GSIS is one of several companies with regular services to Tagaytay. Buses leave every few minutes from about 5 am to 8 pm (P35) also stopping in Las Piñas. Minibuses to Cavite, Zapote and Alabang also leave from here.

Car & Motorcycle Your first experience of Manila traffic may put you off the idea of renting a car permanently, but if you don't mind the traffic jams and unorthodox local driving habits, a rental car is probably the best way to visit the attractions around Metro Manila. Remember though, that you are prohibited from driving your car in the capital on certain weekdays: number-plates ending in 1 and 2 are banned on Monday, 3 and 4 on Tuesday etc.

The North Luzon and South Luzon toll expressways offer the fastest and easiest routes out of the capital, while EDSA is a convenient connecting route between the two. Toll charges vary depending on where you enter and exit the system; from EDSA in Pasay City to Calamba it's P16.

The big international car hire companies all have offices in town and at NAIA and charge around P2500 a day for air-con Toyota Corollas. Budget (☎ 02-816 6682) has offices at NAIA, the Peninsula Manila and the Hotel Inter-Continental in Makati. Hertz (☎ 02-897 5151) has offices at NAIA and the Sunette Tower, on the corner of Durban St and Makati Ave, Makati.

There are also several good independent car rental places in Ermita and Malate. JB Rent-a-Car (☎ 02-526 6288), inside the Midland Plaza Hotel complex on Adriatico St, is recommended, with the usual Toyota Corollas from P1200 daily and Honda hatchbacks for P7000 a week. At the Palm Plaza Hotel, KEI Transport (☎ 02-524 6834) offers air-con Toyota Corollas for P1300 a day or P7700 a week.

Getting Around

To/From the Airport For most visitors, the first point of contact with the Philippines is NAIA, about 10km south of central Manila. These days, progress through the airport is relatively smooth; baggage trolleys with porters are available for P40, and free telephones in the baggage-claim area allow travellers to call ahead to confirm or arrange accommodation in the Metro Manila area. Beyond the customs hall there are several exchange counters which offer differing exchange rates – shop around for the best deal. It's a good idea to ask for a few smaller bills when you change money, as taxi drivers will rarely admit to having change.

Also in the arrivals area are a small DOT counter and ATMs for MasterCard, Cirrus and AmEx. The offices for most of the airlines are upstairs in the departures area. A P550 departure tax is payable for international departures. Call NAIA on ☎ 02-877 1109 for information on arrivals and departures.

Getting through NAIA is the easy part. From the airport to central Manila, it's 'uphill' all the way. A line of booths in the arrivals lounge offer coupons for taxi rides to the centre, which cost pretty much whatever the drivers feel like charging. P280 is a fairly standard fare to Ermita or Malate, or P300 to Makati, though requests for far more are not uncommon. On the meter, the same journey costs P60 to P70. Drivers often work in collaboration with hotels, so it's best to have a good idea of where you want to go before you get into a cab.

It used to be possible to go upstairs to the departures concourse and find a metered taxi that was dropping off passengers, but these days the drivers will make a big fuss of offering you a special deal and charge you P200 anyway. You could always walk down to Ninoy Aquino Ave and flag a taxi, but the fare is unlikely to be much cheaper and travellers have been robbed and even murdered on the way from the airport in unlicensed cabs.

In the opposite direction, you may be able to get a cab to use its meter. Otherwise, the flat fee charged by most drivers for the trip from Ermita/Malate to NAIA is only slightly elevated at P100 to P150.

For Makati, Cubao, Quezon City or other destinations along EDSA, you can pick up a local bus on the road immediately outside the airport. As you leave the NAIA terminal, walk past the eager taxi drivers waiting in the car park and go under the flyover to your right. Fares cost from P4 to P14. Buses also pass the domestic airport and Centennial Terminal II.

Jeepneys on the 'Baclaran–Domestic–MIA' route run from the bridge by the 7-Eleven in Baclaran to Centennial Terminal II, NAIA and then to the domestic airport, finishing back in Baclaran. The fare for any journey along this route is P3.

From the bridge in Baclaran, it's a 400m walk north to the Metrorail terminal along Quirino Ave, or you can take a tricycle (pedicab) for about P20. The Metrorail charges a flat rate of P10 to Pedro Gil station in Malate or United Nations Ave station in Ermita.

Jeepneys to Malate and Ermita leave from opposite the modernist Iglesia ni Cristo church, which is another 100m beyond the Metrorail station. Jeepneys with a 'Mabini' signboard run right through the middle of Malate and Ermita, passing close to almost all of the accommodation in the area.

If you fly with Philippine Airlines (PAL) on a domestic or international flight you will end up at the Centennial Terminal II, which has the same facilities (and scams) waiting for arriving passengers, including expensive coupon taxis. If you're transferring from NAIA to Centennial Terminal II for a prebooked PAL flight, there's a free shuttle bus. Alternatively you can pick up a jeepney in front of the airport (jeepneys on the 'Baclaran–Domestic–MIA' route pass the domestic airport and Baclaran before looping back to Centennial Terminal II).

There are taxis waiting in front of the domestic airport but they demand absurdly elevated rates. If you flag a taxi on Domestic Rd outside the terminal, you may get meter rates and they'll certainly charge less than the taxis inside the gates.

Buses to destinations along EDSA also pass by here, or you can pick up jeepneys to Baclaran and Centennial Terminal II and NAIA.

Bus Local buses are only really useful to get to places along EDSA or Taft Ave, as they are prohibited from most streets in the centre of town. Depending on the journey, ordinary buses charge from P4 to P10; air-con buses charge from P7 to P14.

Like jeepneys, buses have their destinations on signboards in the windows, for example 'NAIA', 'Ayala' (for the Ayala Center in Makati) and 'Monumento' (for Caloocan City). Probably the most useful local bus is the air-con PVP Express bus from Quiapo Church to the Ayala Center in Makati. The fare is P14 and buses run day and night. Any 'Quiapo' jeepney from Malate or Ermita can drop you off at Quiapo Church.

Taxi Manila is rumoured to have the cheapest taxi fares in Asia, but few taxi drivers are willing to stick to the official metered rates. Instead most will quote wildly exaggerated figures for just about any destination you care to mention. It's a matter of personal choice whether you want to push the issue and insist that the driver uses the meter (in which case you will end up taking the most circuitous route to your destination) or just accept the system and pay up. The official flag-down rate is P20 plus P5 per kilometre travelled.

Jeepney For the uninitiated, Manila jeepneys can be a challenging experience. The long wheel-base jeeps offer a bewildering array of destinations on signboards in the window, and few people arrive exactly where they intend to on their first jeepney ride.

The list of destinations written on the side of the jeepney will often give a more accurate picture of the route than the signboards in the window. Heading south from Ermita/Malate along MH del Pilar St, jeepneys to 'Baclaran' pass close to Harrison Plaza, the CCP, the Jai Alai de Manila stadium and many of the south-bound bus terminals. They also provide easy access to the south end of EDSA, where you can pick up buses to the north-bound long-haul bus terminals and Makati.

Heading north from Baclaran, jeepneys pass along Mabini St or Taft Ave, heading off in various directions from Rizal Park. 'Divisoria' jeepneys take the Jones Bridge, passing close to the immigration office; 'Santa Cruz' and 'Monumento' jeepneys take the MacArthur Bridge, passing the GPO; and 'Quiapo' and 'Cubao' jeepneys take the Quezon Bridge, passing Quiapo Church and the markets.

Useful final destinations include: 'Divisoria' for the Divisoria Market; 'Monumento' for Santa Cruz, the Chinese Cemetery or the bus terminals in Caloocan City; and 'Cubao' via 'España' for the bus terminals on EDSA. See the entries under individual bus companies for details of useful jeepneys to the bus terminals.

Mega-Taxi Manila has numerous air-conditioned Toyota Tamaraw FX jeeps, also known as Mega-Taxis, which follow similar set routes to the jeepneys, picking up and setting down passengers en route. The fare is about P20 for longer rides, or P10 for short hops. They can also be used as taxis, and offer flat-rate or metered fares to places like the airport or Makati.

LRT/Metrorail Known interchangeably as the Metrorail or Light Rail Transit (LRT), the elevated railway system runs from Baclaran in Pasay City to Monumento in Caloocan City, following Taft Ave and Rizal Ave. Avoid peak times, from about 8 to 10 am and 3 to 6 pm, when the trains are packed to capacity and there are many opportunities for pickpockets. Tokens for the automatic gates are valid for one ride of any distance along the route (P10). Trains run from 5.30 am to 10.30 pm daily except Good Friday. Stations/stops on the north to south route are:

Monumento For the Philippine Rabbit and Victory Liner terminals in Caloocan City.

Fifth Ave For the Baliwag terminal in Caloocan City.

R Papa For the Baliwag terminal in Caloocan City.

Abad Santos For the Chinese Cemetery.

Blumentritt For the Chinese Cemetery.

Tayuman For the San Lazaro Hippodrome and Sampaloc bus terminals.

Bambang For the Sampaloc bus terminals and University of Santo Thomas.

D José For the Philippine Rabbit terminal in Santa Cruz and cinemas on CM Recto St.

Carriedo For Quiapo Church, the markets and Chinatown.

Central For City Hall, the National Museum, Intramuros, the GPO and Rizal Park.

United Nations Ave For the hospitals, Rizal Park and the DOT office.

Pedro Gil For Ermita and Malate hotels and restaurants.

Quirino Ave For Malate and the San Andres Sports Complex and market.

Vito Cruz For the CCP complex, Harrison Plaza, Jai Alai de Manila stadium and Ninoy Aquino stadium.

Gil Puyat For south-bound bus terminals in Pasay City and buses to Makati and Cubao.

Libertad For the Libertad cockpit and Cuneta Astrodome.

EDSA For south-bound Pasay City bus terminals and buses along EDSA to Makati and Cubao.

Baclaran For the Baclaran Market, jeepneys to the airport and south-bound minibuses.

Calesa Ornate horse-drawn carriages known as *calesas* are still the principal form of transport in some rural areas, but in Manila, they're mainly used to take tourists for a ride. If you use the carriages, agree a firm price for the trip before you board. Even if everything stays above board, you can expect to pay slightly more than a cab for the same journey.

Tricycle Manila's rickshaw system is predominantly pedal-powered. Tricycles (also known as pedicabs and sidecars) are bicycles with sidecars, which are useful for short hops, though they aren't the cheapest way to get around. Short journeys, from the Malate Pension to Robinson's Place mall for example, will cost about P15 to P50, depending on how well you bargain.

Around Manila

The regular transport links to/from Metro Manila allow a huge range of day or overnight trips to the surrounding area. Whether you're interested in beaches, scuba diving, historic churches or volcanoes, there should be something here that appeals, and many places see surprisingly few tourists, despite their proximity to the capital.

The principal tourist attractions in the area are Lake Taal and the Taal Volcano, the rapids on the Pagsanjan River, historic Corregidor Island in Manila Bay, the hot springs at Los Baños, trekking around the Mt Pinatubo volcano, near Angeles, and scuba diving off the coast near Nasugbu. All of these places have their merits, and all see large numbers of tourists, particularly in the high season.

As an alternative, the dormant volcanoes of Mt Banahaw and Mt Makiling and the historic Bataan Peninsula offer the chance to get away from the crowds and do a little exploring for yourself.

Most of these destinations can be visited in a day, but others, particularly the hikes around the many volcanoes in the area, really deserve an overnight trip. Transport is frequent and there are several attractions which can be visited as half-day trips from Manila, or combined to make a whole day trip. Las Piñas, Cavite and Calamba could all be visited in a day, as could Tagaytay and Nasugbu or Los Baños and San Pablo or Pagsanjan.

LAS PIÑAS

The tiny village of Las Piñas, 20km south of Manila, has long been swallowed up by Metro Manila, but it still has a pleasant village atmosphere and many of its buildings have been restored using traditional building methods.

The principal attraction here is the **bamboo organ** in the San José Church on Quirino Ave. The famous organ was built in 1821 by the Spanish priest Padre Diego Cera during a lean period for church funds. To save money, bamboo was used instead of

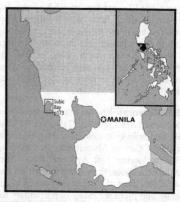

HIGHLIGHTS

- Trekking through the impressive landscape created by the Taal and Mt Pinatubo Volcanoes
- Exploring the forested slopes of mystic Mt Banahaw, near San Pablo
- Unwinding in the relaxing hot springs at Calamba and Los Baños
- Scuba diving on the coral reefs off Anilao and wreck-diving in Subic Bay

metal for 832 of the 954 organ pipes. Aside from being an impressive feat of engineering, the organ has a unique sound, which the custodians will demonstrate for you when you visit.

In the second week of February, organists from around the world gather here for the Bamboo Organ Festival. You can visit the organ from 8 am to 12 pm Monday to Friday. Admission costs P10.

Also of interest in Las Piñas is the huge **Sarao Jeepney Factory**, where most of Manila's jeepneys are assembled entirely by hand. The management and staff welcome tourists to come in and take a look at the creation of a jeepney, from the bare aluminium

AROUND MANILA

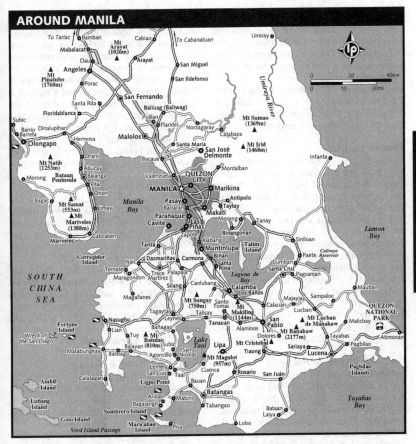

chassis to the peacock-like finished product. The factory is open from about 9 am to 4 pm daily except Sunday.

Getting There & Away
Minibuses to Cavite from Baclaran stop in Las Piñas, or you can pick up a Saulog or St Anthony bus to Cavite from near the Intramuros city walls. Zapote jeepneys also pass Las Piñas.

CAVITE
The protected harbour of Cavite, 35km southwest of Manila, was the site of the destruction of the Spanish fleet during the US invasion of Luzon in 1898. The Spanish admiral Montojo pulled his flotilla back to the Cavite Peninsula to save Manila from a direct attack, but General Dewey's forces destroyed all but one of his ships in only seven hours.

The city is now the home of the Philippine Navy and has a few resorts strung along the unimpressive beaches on the west side of the peninsula. The main reason to come here is to visit the **Aguinaldo House**, where the revolutionary army of General Aguinaldo proclaimed the Independence of the Philippines on 12 June 1898. The proclamation was short lived – the Americans quickly stepped in and quashed Aguinaldo's forces – but the event holds a special place in Filipino consciousness. The house is now a shrine and you can tour Aguinaldo's private rooms and visit his mausoleum in the gardens. It's open from 8 am to noon and from 1 to 5 pm daily except Monday (free admission). Hats must be removed as a sign of respect.

Places to Stay

Cavite isn't really worth an overnight stay, but there are a couple of luxury resorts about 40km south of here, in Ternate, that are far enough away from Manila to have clear water and clean beaches.

The luxurious *Calbayne Bay Resort* (☎ 02-813 8519) in Ternate has good beaches, tennis courts, a golf course and a big pool and hires out water sports equipment like minicatamarans. Air-con rooms with bath start at P3888 (P4860 in high season).

Also in Ternate, the long-running *Puerto Azul Resort* (☎ 02-525 9248) has similar facilities, including tennis and squash courts and a pool, and offers air-con rooms with bath for P2300, and suites for P3000.

Getting There & Away

Saulog and St Anthony have air-con buses to Cavite and Ternate via Las Piñas leave every few minutes from just outside the Intramuros city walls. Alternatively, colourful minibuses leave from Baclaran in Pasay City.

Marilag Transport Systems has boats every 15 minutes between the Cultural Center of the Philippines (CCP) complex in Manila and Cavite Harbour from 6 am to 6 pm Monday to Friday (P45). There are hourly services from 7 am to 5 pm Saturday, but only two ferries at 9.15 am and 5 pm Sunday.

CALAMBA

Calamba, south-east of Manila on the shores of the Laguna de Bay, was the birthplace of the Philippine national hero José Rizal, and the Spanish-colonial house where Rizal was born is now venerated as the **Rizal Shrine**. On display are numerous items of Rizal memorabilia. The house is

open from 8 am to noon and from 1 to 5 pm daily except Monday (free admission). Calamba also has a number of spa resorts with natural **hot springs** and swimming pools open to day-trippers, for a fee.

Near the Santa Rosa exit from the South Luzon Expressway, **Enchanted Kingdom** is probably Luzon's most popular theme park, with a good selection of roller coasters and other thrill rides. It's open from 10 am to 5 pm Wednesday and Thursday, from 10 am to midnight Friday and Saturday, and from 10 am to 10 pm Sunday. Admission is P300.

Places to Stay

On the highway towards Los Baños, the impressive *Crystal Springs Waterworld* (☎ 049-545 2496) boasts eight swimming pools, open to the public from 7 am to 5 pm (P240). Double rooms with air-con, bath and private spa pool cost P1450.

Also on the highway, near the 55km marker, the *Bato-Bato Mountain Resort* (☎ 049-545 1777), in Pansol, Calamba, has six pleasant pools and is open 24 hours. Day-trippers pay P50 (P75 at night) and comfortable air-con rooms with private bath cost P1000 a single/double.

Getting There & Away

BLTB buses from Manila to Santa Cruz pass through Calamba. Only get out at the Calamba bus terminal if you want to visit the Rizal Shrine, as the resorts are all on the highway, on the far side of town.

Coming from Santa Cruz or Batangas, most Cubao or Pasay City buses stop at the Calamba terminal on the way up to Manila. To continue to Los Baños, either take a bus or pick up a south-bound jeepney marked 'UP'; they run to the University of the Philippines campus in Los Baños, 24 hours a day.

LOS BAÑOS

Los Baños (literally, 'The Baths'), a few kilometres south-east of Calamba, trades heavily on its natural hot springs, with numerous resorts offering water slides, Olympic-sized pools, jacuzzis and even hotel rooms with their own private spas. Splash Mountain and the Monte Vista resort complex, both on the national highway towards Calamba, are recommended for day-trippers.

If you get tired of the water, the University of the Philippines Los Baños (UPLB) campus is the starting point for **treks** up to the top of 1144m Mt Makiling, an old volcano with some impressive forest on its upper slopes. It takes about two hours to walk the 8km from the UPLB campus to the summit. Jeepneys to the College of Forestry come up to the start of the trail.

The UPLB College of Forestry has a small **natural history museum**, open from 8 am to 5 pm Monday to Saturday, and the **Makiling Botanic Gardens**, which has a captive breeding program for the endangered Philippine eagle and a peaceful swimming pool in the middle of the forest (open from 8 am to 4.30 pm, P10 admission, P50 for swimmers).

Places to Stay

The cheaper resorts are all in the suburb of Bayan just north of Los Baños proper. The main road through Bayan branches off the highway as it turns inland just outside of town; look out for the green Region Bank sign.

The *Los Baños Lodge* (☎ 049-536 3171, 145 Villegas St) has the usual collection of swimming pools and offers simple fan-rooms for P455 and clean air-con rooms with bath for P875, or P1200 with spa pool.

Nearby, the *City of Springs* (☎ 049-536 0731, 147 Villegas St) has a good main pool and restaurant and a wide variety of rooms. Dormitory beds cost P275, fan-rooms start at P660, and air-con rooms with bath start at P1258 (P1313 with pool).

Owned by the same people as City of Springs, the *Splash Mountain Resort* (☎ 049-536 0731), on the National Highway, has numerous waterslides, some of the best pools in Los Baños and it's open 24 hours. Day-trippers pay P70, night-trippers P80. Smart, attractively furnished air-con rooms cost P1774 with pool, P1358 without.

On the highway in the direction of Calamba, the impressive *Monte Vista Hot Springs Resort* (☎ 049-545 1259) is owned

by one of the biggest mineral water companies in the Philippines (the bottling plant is in the same complex). There are numerous pools, spas and water slides here and the facilities are open 24 hours. Good air-con rooms with bath cost P1500 (P1900 at weekends) and rooms with private pool cost P2000 (P2500). Day-trippers pay P95 Monday to Thursday and P125 Friday to Sunday.

Getting There & Around

From Pasay City and Cubao there are regular BLTB buses to Santa Cruz which stop in Los Baños (1½ hours). From Santa Cruz, or to get back to Manila, take a bus marked 'Cubao' or 'Pasay' from the highway.

Jeepneys run from Calamba to Los Baños and up to the UPLB campus 24 hours. Jeepneys up to the UP College of Forestry (for Mt Makiling) leave from the Jollibee restaurant on the national highway. The last trip downhill leaves at about 5 pm.

ALAMINOS

The owners of **Hidden Valley** near Alaminos knew they were onto a good thing when they opened their property as a jungle resort. The private retreat boasts lush tropical flora, hot springs and numerous natural pools for swimming, though the price tag for all this getting 'back to nature' is a very contemporary P1550 per head for day-trippers, including a buffet lunch of native Filipino food.

As well as swimming in the springs, guests can hike in the resort's pristine forests; the trek up the valley to the Hidden Falls is a popular route. Numerous Pilipino (Tagalog) films have used Hidden Valley as the backdrop for romance scenes and the resort is popular with wealthy residents of Manila, who come here at the weekend to wind down away from the smog. Despite the price, it can get pretty full at weekends.

Places to Stay

The *Hidden Valley Springs Resort* offers overnight packages including all meals and admission to the springs for a cool P5356 for a single or P8225 for doubles. The rooms are clean and have air-con and bath, but you could get a lot more for your money almost anywhere else. You can book with its office in Manila (☎ 02-818 4034).

Getting There & Away
Tritran, BLTB and JAM Transit all have regular buses from Pasay City which pass by Alaminos on the way to San Pablo, Lucena, Daet, Naga or Legaspi. From Los Baños or Santa Cruz on Laguna de Bay, it's best to take a jeepney to San Pablo and change to a Manila-bound bus or a jeepney.

SAN PABLO
San Pablo, 15km east of Alaminos, is known for its seven volcanic lakes, which offer some pleasant walks. Closest to the centre is the appealing Sampaloc Lake on Schetelig Ave. You can walk around the lake and there are several restaurants on stilts which sell the tasty *tilapia* (carp) that are raised here. Across the road is the small Bunot Lake, and further north are the lakes of Calibato, Palacpaquen, Mohicap, Yambo and Pandin. The youth hostel in town is a quiet base from which to explore the lakes. The town is also the jumping-off point for hikes up the sacred slopes of Mt Banahaw (see the Mt Banahaw section later).

About 10km south of San Pablo, on the outskirts of Tiaong, is the Villa Escudero an exclusive resort with an artificial lake, a lovely swimming pool and a native restaurant with tables in the water. The estate doubles as a coconut plantation and houses an eclectic museum of handicrafts and curios. Admission is P636 (P728 on Friday, Saturday and Sunday). You can get here by Tiaong jeepney from San Pablo.

Places to Stay
The very pleasant **Sampaloc Lake Youth Hostel** *(☎ 093-562 3376, Doña St, Efarca Village)* overlooks peaceful Lake Sampaloc and has steps down to the road around the lake. Fan-cooled dorm beds with a view cost P200, or P150 in the dorm without the view. To get here, follow Schetelig Ave, the main road to the lakes.

In Tiaong, the **Villa Escudero** *(☎ 02-523 2944)* offers cottages with fan and bath starting at P2176 for a single, including

admission and all meals. Doubles start at P1651 per person with the same inclusions.

Getting There & Around
Numerous buses from Manila pass through San Pablo on the way to places like Lucena, Daet, Naga and Legaspi. Most buses stop on Schetelig Ave, close to the San Pablo church. BLTB has a terminal just outside of town on the road to Alaminos and Manila.

Jeepneys run from San Pablo up to Santa Cruz and Los Baños. You can pick them up anywhere along the highway. Tiaong jeepneys leave from the bus stop by the San Pablo church.

For the lakes, jeepneys run up Schetelig Ave to Nagcarlan and Liliw, passing close to Sampaloc and the other six lakes in the area. Jeepneys to Dolores (for Kinabuhayan and Mt Banahaw) leave from the public market (ask a tricycle to take you to 'public market').

MT BANAHAW
The vast dormant volcanic cone of Mt Banahaw, 15km east of San Pablo, is almost always prefixed by the term 'mystic'. Obscure religious sects like the Rizalistas gather in the silent depths of the Banahaw crater to wash in the 'River Jordan' and pray for the rebirth of José Rizal. Every Easter, up to 30,000 devotees can descend on the tiny village of Kinabuhayan to begin the ascent of the holy mountain.

For the sceptic, Mt Banahaw offers some of the most impressive hiking in southern Luzon. The weather is an important consideration however, as the awe-inspiring views from the rim down into the 600m deep crater can vanish entirely in low cloud. Even in the dry season cloud can suddenly rise up from the crater bottom, adding to the spooky atmosphere.

The trek up to the crater rim (2177m) and down into the crater, returning via the canyon on the south side of the volcano, takes two to three days, but the crater rim can be visited as an overnight trek. The path is well-worn, but guides are available in Kinabuhayan who can point out some of the sites of importance to the various religious sects. The village is also

JOHN PENNOCK

Manila's pollution makes for an incredible sunset over Manila Bay.

JOHN PENNOCK

Taal Lake – the home of Taal Volcano, south of Manila.

Jesus, Mary and Joseph! Religious figurines for sale.

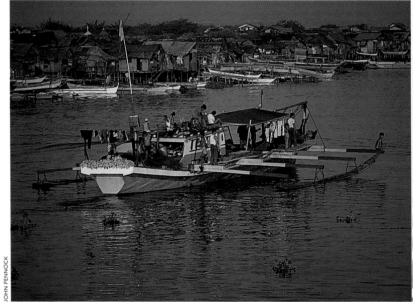

Filipino life often revolves around fishing.

the starting point for treks up to Mt San Cristobal, another two-day hike, with good views over the Visayan Sea.

Getting There & Away

Jeepneys to Dolores leave from the public market in San Pablo every few minutes during daylight hours (ask a tricycle for 'public market'). From Dolores you can pick up another jeepney to Kinabuhayan. It's best to get an early start so you can reach the crater rim in daylight.

LUCBAN

Hidden away in the foothills of Mt Banahaw, the quiet mountain town of Lucban comes alive on 15 May for *Pahiyas*, the annual harvest festival and feast of San Isidro Labrador. All the houses in town are adorned with multicoloured rice-starch decorations called *kiping* and giant papier-mâché effigies are marched through the streets up to the town church.

The air here is pleasantly cool and the narrow streets are full of atmosphere, with a number of old Spanish townhouses. The moss-encrusted Church of St Louis of Toulouse dates from 1738, though, as usual, it sits atop the ruins of several far older churches. Among other things, Lucban is known for its *longanisa* (Chinese-style pork sausages) and *pancit* (fried noodles). There are also a few little handicraft shops around the plaza.

Places to Stay

Unfortunately, the only accommodation in town is the *Banahaw Hotel*, a noisy disco-hotel with piped music in the rooms. You'll pay P610 or P750 for air-con and bath. It's next to the petrol station on Quezon Ave.

The *Nawawalang Paraiso Hotel* (☎ 042-373 6575), on the way to Tabayas, is a pleasant resort with the usual array of swimming pools and picnic huts. Fan-cooled cottages start at P540, while air-con rooms start at P1540.

Getting There & Away

There are regular jeepneys and minibuses from Grand Central Terminal in Lucena. In the reverse direction, jeepneys leave from the Lucban Academy near the Rizal Monument, but you can pick up minibuses and jeepneys on Quezon Ave. Heading on to Pagsanjan, jeepneys run along Rizal St.

TAYABAS

Approximately halfway from Lucena to Lucban, Tayabas is another typical mountain town, with the delightful St Michael Archangel Church, which was built in 1856 over the ruins of a 1585 church. It's painted inside like a Victorian opera house. About 4km from Tayabas, on the dirt road to Sampaloc, the stone Malagunlong Bridge was built by the Spanish in the 16th century and is a popular picnic spot. You can get here by tricycle.

PAGSANJAN

The town of Pagsanjan (pronounced 'pag-san-han'), 20km north-east of Lucban, has become synonymous with the **Magdapio Falls**, which are the starting point for the famous canoe ride through the rapids of the Pagsanjan River. Shooting the rapids is one of Luzon's major tourist attractions and boat trips along the river form a huge part of the income for the town. On the down side, competition for passengers is fierce, with dozens of wannabe boatmen shouting out 'Pagsanjan Falls! Pagsanjan Falls!' at any passing foreigner.

A few years ago things got really out of hand, with *banceros* (the boatmen who paddle the canoes upstream against the current) demanding up to 12,000 peso for the trip and persecuting passengers who refused to pay handsome tips on top. Fortunately, falling tourist numbers have prompted the government to stamp out some of the bad practices at Pagsanjan.

The official rates have now been raised to P580 per person, or P1080 for a solo passenger, as a bit of a sweetener for the banceros, though life jackets and cushions will cost you extra. Businesses that display the 'Tourist Information Satellite Office' sign are committed to protecting their passengers from harassment. This said, booking a trip through your accommodation is still the best way to ensure a hassle-free journey.

For the ride upstream, two banceros paddle each canoe up to the Magdapio Falls against the fearsome flow of the river. At the top, the banceros will take you under the falls on a bamboo raft for an additional P50 fee. From here, you let the water do the work. The trip downstream is fast and exhilarating. Some of the final scenes of Francis Ford Coppola's epic Vietnam War movie *Apocalypse Now* were filmed along this stretch of river and a few relics from the movie can still be seen along the banks as you shoot downstream.

The height of the wet season (August to September) is the best time to ride the rapids. At any time of year it's best to avoid weekends, as half of Manila seems to descend on Pagsanjan. You should bring a plastic bag for your camera, as it's a pretty damp ride. It's still not unheard of for travellers to face requests for extra money halfway up the river, but if you book through your accommodation, you should be able to avoid this scam.

Places to Stay

West of the town plaza on General Taiño St, the *Pagsanjan Rapids Hotel* (☎ 02-834 0403) has good facilities, including a pool and a bar overlooking the river. Comfortable air-con rooms with bath are P1200, or P1560 with a view.

In the middle of town at 39 Rizal St, the *Camino Real Lodging House* (☎ 049-645 2086), has nice, large rooms for P300 with fan and P600 with air-con, and charges government rates for the boat trip.

Behind the municipal hall at 821 Garcia St, *Willy Flores Guesthouse* is a friendly family-run place that has its own boat. Clean rooms with common bath and table fan are P200 (P250 with private bath). Also on Garcia St, the *Riverside Bungalow* (☎ 049-828 4039, 792 Garcia St) has two fan-cooled rooms for P400, and a two-bedroom air-con house for P1200.

North of town on the highway, the *Pagsanjan Falls Lodge* (☎ 049-808 4209) has a strange mix of facilities, including a sandy-bottomed swimming pool, a restaurant overlooking the river and a disco. Fan-rooms are overpriced at P1100, while passable air-con rooms with TV are P1500. Day-trippers can use the pool for P100. Nearby, the *Pagsanjan Garden Resort* (☎ 02-810 3655) is owned by the Department of Tourism (DOT) and has dorm beds at P187 a head, fan-rooms with common bath for P308 and air-con rooms with bath that sleep three for P693.

A few kilometres further north of Pagsanjan, the large *La Corona de Pagsanjan Resort* (☎ 02-524 2631) has three pools and tasteful rooms starting at P750 with air-con and bath and P1000 with air-con, bath, TV and VCR (cheaper rates are available in the low season).

Places to Eat

One block back from the plaza on Mabini St, *Me-Lin* has good Chinese food and a few Western dishes (like pizza) for around P100. On General Taiño St, *Dura-Fe* has good Filipino food at low prices but it closes at 8 pm.

A few minutes' walk from the plaza, the pretty *Gallery 85 Cafe* offers local handicrafts and Filipino meals for about P150. *Revelations*, at 55 Rizal St, is a surprisingly happening place for a town like Pagsanjan and has good live bands on weekends and sizzling Filipino meals.

Getting There & Away

There are no direct buses to Pagsanjan, but there are regular services from Manila to nearby Santa Cruz. The bus terminal is on the highway, about halfway between the two towns; jeepneys to Santa Cruz and Pagsanjan pass by every few minutes. BLTB and JAM Transit have buses at least once an hour to Cubao (a district of Metro Manila in Quezon City) and Pasay City (2½ hours). On the highway, in the direction of Los Baños, Supreme has regular buses to Lucena.

Jeepneys run regularly between Santa Cruz and Pagsanjan along P Guevarra Ave, passing the bus terminals on the highway. For San Pablo or Los Baños, jeepneys leave from the plaza in front of Santa Cruz's city hall. For Calamba, you can pick up a jeepney next to the unappealing modern Church of Santa Cruz.

From Pagsanjan you can take a jeepney to the pretty mountain town of Lucban, and connect from there to Lucena. Jeepneys also head north along General Taiño St to the craft villages of Lumban and Paete.

AROUND PAGSANJAN

There are a few interesting spots in the immediate vicinity of Pagsanjan. **Lumban** is a small village on the edge of the Laguna that is famous for its Barong Tagalog shirts and embroidery. A little further around the lake, Paete is known for its papier-mâché sculptures and woodcarving.

Up on the hillside overlooking the Laguna, **Lake Caliraya** is an artificial lake produced by the hydroelectric plant at the foot of the hill. You can hire water sports gear from the Caliraya Recreation Center and Caliraya Country Club. Jeepneys run up here occasionally from Santa Cruz and Pagsanjan.

TAAL LAKE & TAAL VOLCANO

One of the world's smallest and deadliest volcanoes, Taal boasts over 47 craters and 35 volcanic cones. As recently as 1977, the calm of this peaceful spot was shattered by explosive phreatomagmatic (gaseous) eruptions as subterranean magma flows tried to find a new route to the surface. The action is far from over at Taal; every few years, there are ominous rumbles from the crater, and a team of vulcanologists keep a 24-hour vigil from the village of Talisay on the lake shore.

The picturesque volcanic island sits in a lake in the middle of a vast crater, itself blasted out by prehistoric eruptions. There are splendid views over the volcano from Tagaytay and other towns that follow the ridge.

The bulk of the island emerged from the lake during the savage eruption of 1911, which claimed hundreds of lives in the area. Over the next 66 years, a series of phreatomagmatic and strombolian (lava-producing) eruptions has sculpted and resculpted the island's appearance.

The main Taal crater is in the middle of the island (the obvious cone visible from the ridge is actually Binitiang Malaki, which last erupted in 1715). Within the Taal crater is a yellow sulphurous lake (itself containing a small island), which is about an hour's hike from the shore.

The most active crater is Mt Tabaro on the west side of the island, which saw some dramatic lava flows in 1968 and 1969 and erupted explosively in 1970, 1976 and 1977. Since then, Taal Volcano tours have become a popular activity with several villages on the lake's shore offering motorised *bancas* (pumpboats) across to the island and horses up to the main crater and lava flows.

TAGAYTAY

Sprawling along the crater rim north of the volcano, Tagaytay offers the classic view of Taal Lake; from here, the fishing village of Laurel, Binitiang Malaki and Taal Volcano itself are perfectly lined up in the direction of Mt Maculot. November to March is the best time to visit, as Tagaytay is often covered by low cloud during the wet season.

The viewing gallery at the Taal Vista Hotel on the main highway offers the best view of Taal, but a long-running industrial dispute has left the future of the hotel in question. Next best is the view from the DOT-owned Tagaytay Picnic Grove, 8km from Tagaytay on the road to Mt Sungay, which also has a skating rink and horse riding. It's open from 6 am to midnight daily (P15).

For great views over the whole area, the **Peoples Park in the Sky** is perched on top of 750m Mt Sungay and includes a shrine, restaurant and walking trail. To get here, take a jeepney marked 'Peoples Park' from the Olivarez mall near the Silang rotonda (roundabout).

With an elevation of 600m, Tagaytay is pleasantly cool after the heat of Manila, and exclusive country clubs are springing up all along the ridge. The next eruption of Taal may destroy some of the most expensive real estate in the Philippines.

Places to Stay

Most of the accommodation is out of town on the Aguinaldo Highway.

If it's open, the *Taal Vista Hotel* (☎ 046-413 1223) is the place to stay in Tagaytay, though rooms with a lake view cost a steep P2900. Comfortable rooms without the view are P2700. Also here is the Casino Filipino (P100 admission).

The cottages at the *Tagaytay Picnic Grove* (☎ 046-860 0216) have good views but are frequently booked out by groups. Singles/doubles start at P1320/2195. Prices are 30% cheaper in the off season.

On the far side of the Silang rotonda are a number of reasonably priced places that are convenient for the jeepneys down to Talisay. Right next to the turn-off, *Fortune Duck* (☎ 046-860 0166) has immaculately clean, spacious rooms with fan for P800, P1000 with TV.

Nearby are *Keni Po* (☎ 046-860 1035), with air-con rooms with bath and TV at P1500, and *5R*, which has good fan-rooms with TV and bath starting at P800.

Places to Eat

Probably the nicest place to eat in Tagaytay is the long-established *Josephine*, between the Taal Vista Hotel and the Silang rotonda. Meat and seafood can be cooked in a variety of traditional styles, including *inihaw* (grilled), *halabos* (steamed) and *sinigang* (in sour soup). Expect to pay about P250 for a meal. It's open from 7.30 am to 10.30 pm daily.

Getting There & Around

Coming from Manila, the BLTB and JAM Transit buses to Nasugbu and Calatagan pass through Tagaytay; you can continue on to Nasugbu by bus or jeepney from Tagaytay.

Minibuses to Baclaran in Pasay City leave from the highway just north of Tagaytay every few minutes and there are also regular jeepneys to Zapote.

To Lemery/Taal village, jeepneys leave when full from the junction of the Diokno and Aguinaldo Highways, about 10km south of Tagaytay near the 'Nasugbu' sign.

To get here, take a Nasugbu-bound bus and hop out at the junction.

Coming from Manila, you should get off at the Silang rotonda for the Tagaytay Picnic Grove, Talisay or the Peoples Park in the Sky. Jeepneys for 'Peoples Park' leave from the Olivarez shopping mall near the roundabout every few minutes.

TALISAY

The small town of Talisay on the edge of Lake Taal is the start of a string of small *barangays* (villages or neighbourhoods) which offer banca trips out to Taal Volcano. The business has become quite commercialised, with dozens of operators vying for the attention of arriving tourists. Depending on where you hire them, motorised bancas to the island vary from P800 to P1000. It's best to get a group together as the rate is for the whole boat. Most places charge an extra P15 to P30 for life jackets.

The volcanic island offers several hikes; easily the most popular is the trip up to the main crater with its evil-looking yellow pool and island. The walk takes about an hour, or you can hire horses for P300. Although most boat trips come with a guide, you don't really need one for this walk. Other options include the neat cone of Binitiang Malaki and the longer hike to the active cone of Mt Tabaro, which is probably the most impressive part of the island. For all the walks, it's wise to bring plenty of drinking water and a hat, as the craters are hot and dusty and there's little shelter on the island.

A swim in the lake is the ideal way to finish off a trek. The coast of the island offers some attractive entry points, or you can swim at any of the beach resorts around the coast. In barangay Santa Maria, the Taal Lake Yacht Club (☎ 02-811 3183) has a good selection of water-sports equipment for hire and charges P100 admission. It's open from 8 am to 5 pm daily.

If you want to find out more about the volcano, the **Philippine Institute of Volcanology & Seismology** (PHILVOLCS), in barangay Buco, houses the volcano-monitoring station and an interesting museum that gives a breakdown of the volcano's many eruptions. Also here are the seismographs that monitor activity on the volcano. You can visit the facility from 8 am to 6 pm.

Places to Stay

In Leynes, close to the turn-off for the dirt road to Tagaytay, *Gloria de Castro's* (☎ 043-773 0138) has one of the cheapest boats to Taal (P800 with guide) and fairly comfortable rooms with bath and fan for P400 and P500.

Also in Leynes, *Natalia's Guest House* (☎ 0918-873 7217), also known as the Taal Lake Guest House, has boats with guide for P1000 and passable rooms with bath and fan for P500 and P700. Nearby, the *San Roque Beach Resort* (☎ 0918-290 8384) is a friendly place with nipa huts with bath for P750 and a house with three bedrooms, air-con and kitchen for P3000. Taal boats are P1000.

Close to the Taal Lake Yacht Club in Santa Maria, the *Talisay Green Lake Resort* (☎ 043-773 0247) has pleasant facilities for day-trippers (P70 admission) and good air-con rooms with bath and TV for P1500. Boats are P1000.

Rosalina's Place (☎ 043-773 0088) in Banga, close to the main road to Tagaytay, is across the road from the beach but it has a good restaurant with a fish-and-crab buffet at noon daily (P100) and cheap boats to Taal for P700. Fan-cooled singles good for two cost P200, while larger rooms that sleep three are P300.

Getting There & Away

There are regular jeepneys to Talisay and Laurel from Tanauan, which is on the main bus route between Manila and Batangas. BLTB and JAM Transit both pass through here on their way from Pasay City to Batangas. It takes about an hour and a half to reach Tanauan from either end. The last jeepney trip back to Tanauan from Laurel leaves at 4 pm (6 pm from Talisay).

Coming from Tagaytay, the road to Talisay branches off the road to the Peoples Park, a few kilometres from the Silang rotonda. Jeepneys run downhill from the junction to Talisay until about 6 pm (P50).

NASUGBU

About 50km west of Tagaytay is Nasugbu, which has some of the most popular beaches close to Manila. They run the gamut from broad strips of dark brown sand to small white-sand coves. The sand on the main beach in Nasugbu is almost black, while a few kilometres north, **White Sands** is a private bay with fine white sand. There are also good beaches at Natipuan, Munting Buhangin and on the so-called **twin islands** near the exclusive Punta Fuego country club. A banca to the beaches from the Wawa pier in Nasugbu will cost about P500. Wawa is also the departure point for the exclusive Fortune Island Resort on nearby Fortune Island.

The tourist trade is very commercialised though, and most of the resorts carry posters warning guests to 'Beware of self-style tourist guides, hopping local canvassers or vehicle-chasing molesters or fixers who sow fear and confusion among tourists'. It's not as bad as all that, though you'll probably be approached by a few fixers during your time in Nasugbu. You don't need any help to find the resorts in town; they're all on the Boulevard, two streets down from the highway.

Places to Stay

The lovely *White Sands Resort* (☎ 02-833 5608) has a peaceful, secluded cove with fine yellow sand and shady cottages on the hillside. Admission for day-trippers and guests is P300 including a Filipino lunch, while overnight packages start at P1694 for pleasant nipa huts that sleep up to six, or P4300 for air-con cottages, plus the admission fee.

The *Maya-Maya Reef Resort* (☎ 0912-322 8550) in Natipuan is a popular destination for yachting buffs and has a private marina, water sports, a dive school and smart air-con cottages arranged around a lovely pool. Rates for cottages start at US$50 (US$75 on public holidays). Scuba dives cost US$30 with all gear. The road to the resort passes some palatial summer houses.

The plush *Fortune Island Resort* (☎ 02-818 3458) charges a steep P1250 for day-trippers, including transfers from Wawa pier, lunch and use of the beaches and swimming pool. The island has good snorkelling and diving and you can hire gear from the island's dive school. Accommodation packages start at P4644 for two persons, including transfers.

In Nasugbu proper, the *Maryland Beach Resort* (☎ 043-216 2277) has fan-cooled nipa huts from P800 and air-con rooms that sleep four from P2800. There's also a good pool. The admission fee is P40.

Nearby, the large *Vitug Beach Resort* (☎ 043-931 1367) is a well-run family resort with nice lawns, a pool, jacuzzi and a variety of fan-cooled and air-con rooms starting at P1200 a double (P1000 from July to October). Admission for day-trippers is P60.

Places to Eat

The best place to eat in town is the well-regarded *Kainan sa Dalampasigan* on Ruiz Martinez St, which offers excellent and reasonably priced seafood in a peaceful pavilion set back from the seafront. A generous meal of fried shrimp with garlic and French fries or rice costs about P150. The restaurant is open from 7 am to 9 pm.

On the Boulevard, the *Nayon ni Rebekah* restaurant offers sizzling Filipino meals and cold beer 24 hours a day and often has live music.

Getting There & Around

BLTB has buses from Pasay City to Nasugbu every 15 minutes, while Crow Transit covers the same route every 30 minutes. The BLTB terminal is by the park in the middle of Nasugbu; Crow has a terminal on the highway in the direction of White Sands. Crow also has buses to the pier in Batangas every 45 minutes (two hours).

Jeepneys in Nasugbu are not marked with destinations; you'll have to ask the driver to make sure you're heading in the right direction. From Nasugbu, jeepneys to Tali beach leave from the highway until about 5 pm, passing White Sands and the other resorts.

For Matabungkay, take a jeepney to Lian and change at the Shell petrol station to a bus or jeepney bound for Calatagan. From Nasugbu you can get jeepneys to Lemery

that connect with jeepneys to Tagaytay, via the Diokno Highway.

MATABUNGKAY

Matabungkay is touted as the finest beach around Manila, but White Sands near Nasugbu is just one beach that is better and less crowded. The beach at Matabungkay isn't bad though, and there are regular buses from Manila to Calatagan that pass the junction down to the beach. The water is clean and it's possible to hire floating bamboo picnic huts anchored out over the reef, which are good bases for snorkelling (P400).

It's a popular spot for Manila residents, so the usual fixers abound. Tricycles charge at least P40 for the short trip to the beach, but the resorts are all close together so you don't need any help finding a place to stay when you get there.

Places to Stay

The best place to stay in Matabungkay is the *Matabungkay Beach Resort & Hotel* (☎ 0912-392 5048), with a good pool, a restaurant, well-maintained grounds and a tidy strip of beach out front. Air-con rooms with bath are P1500, P1760 with fridge, or P1960 with fridge and TV. There's a branch of Philippine Divers here and it charges P1200 for one dive with all gear. The resort is about 500m south of the pier.

Nearby, the inexpensive *Greendoors Cottages* (☎ 0912-360 6944) is clean and quiet, with leafy grounds and large fan-cooled singles and doubles for P300/700 a single/double.

North of the pier, the *Coral Beach Club* (☎ 0912-318 4868) is popular with older holiday-makers and has a secluded pool, restaurant and bar. Tasteful air-con rooms with TV and bath cost P1375 (P1980 with fridge). The resort picks up guests from Lian.

The exclusive *Punta Baluarte Resort* (☎ 043-892 4202) in Calatagan is a genuine retreat, with a secluded location, salt water pool, tennis courts, golf course and horse riding. Rooms with air-con, TV, phone and bath start at P2700, or P3000 on the ridge above the resort. You can book in Manila on ☎ 02-899 4546.

Getting There & Away

BLTB buses leave Manila for Calatagan every few hours, passing the junction to Matabungkay, but you could also take a bus to Nasugbu and change to a Calatagan-bound jeepney at Lian. From Batangas pier, Crow buses to Nasugbu pass through Lian. A tricycle from the Matabungkay junction to the beach is P40.

TAAL

Taal is an appealing old town with a number of old Spanish-colonial buildings, but the atmosphere is marred slightly by Lemery, the modern township across the river. Taal is famous for its embroidery and *Balisong* or fan-knives, and the truly massive Basilica ng Taal church, built between 1849–1865. JAM Transit and JAC Liner buses to Cubao and Crow buses from Batangas to Nasugbu pass through Lemery every few minutes.

There are also occasional jeepneys up to the junction of the Diokno and Aguinaldo Highways, where you can pick up a bus into Tagaytay. Destinations aren't marked, so you'll need to ask the driver to find the right jeepney. Most services leave from near the McDonald's on the main road through Lemery.

ANILAO

Anilao, 20km south of Taal on a small peninsula, is a popular diving centre and has a good reputation around Asia, though the practice of fish-feeding and other bad diving behaviour is an environmental black mark. There are dozens of dive resorts strung out along the coastal road south of the village; most of the dive sites are coral gardens, though there are some walls with strong currents further from the shore.

There are 36 dive sites in Balayan Bay and around Sombrero and Maricaban islands that can be visited from Anilao. In general, the further you go from shore, the more chance you have of getting a dive site to yourself. Some resorts offer free beach dives, and you can explore the shallow area close to the shore for a long time without reaching your decompression limit.

The attractions here are all below the water. There isn't much of a nightlife in Anilao and the beaches are rocky and poorly maintained.

Places to Stay

The best dive resorts are outside of Anilao in the small barangays along the edge of the peninsula. Almost all have telephone numbers in Manila.

In barangay Ligaya, *Aqua Tropical Sports* (☎ 02-523 2126) is a no-nonsense dive resort and the leafy grounds are very attractive. Clean air-con rooms with TV, fridge, hot water and balconies start at P2100. Dives are P1450 for two tanks, plus P1000 gear hire.

Nearby in barangay Solo, the *Dive Ocean Beach Resort* (☎ 0912 883 6368) is run by a friendly Korean team and offers free beach dives to the sites just off shore. One-day, one-night packages including food and accommodation start at P1500; twoboat-dives are P1500.

In barangay San José, the *Vistamar Beach Resort* (☎ 02-821 8332) is a friendly Catholic resort, with spacious double rooms with fan for P1400 and air-con rooms from P1600. The resort has a nice pool, a dive shop and restaurant, and admission for day-trippers is P50.

Just outside Anilao town, the *Anilao Seasports Center* (☎ 02-897 6622) offers full board only in clean rooms overlooking a quiet bay. The package rate is P1450 including meals, and dives are P500 each, plus a boat fee of P1200.

Getting There & Away

From Batangas, regular jeepneys run out to the tiny cocoa-producing town of Mabini, where you may have to change jeepneys to continue to Anilao. The journey takes about 20 minutes, passing the huge Petron and Union Carbide plants in Bauan. You can pick up a jeepney on P Burgos St in Batangas.

BATANGAS

The capital of Batangas province boasts a busy port and numerous chemical plants and oil refineries, but the town itself isn't

AROUND MANILA

particularly attractive. Most people only come here to pick up a boat to Puerto Galera on the beach island of Mindoro or further afield to the island of Romblon in the Visayas.

With a hire car Batangas is a possible base for trips up to Lake Taal, Anilao or even Nasugbu, as well as nearby Bauan Beach and the rugged coast near Tabangao, which offers some remote diving and snorkelling if you have your own gear.

Places to Stay

On the outskirts of town in the direction of Manila, the *Alpa Hotel* (☎ 043-723 1025), at Kumintang Ibaba, has a quiet location near the Batangas Provincial Capitol. There's a nice pool and elegant air-con rooms with bath range from P1120 to P3750. To get here, turn off the highway near the Mabini monument. Jeepneys to the suburb of Balaytas pass nearby.

The best of the cheap hotels in Batangas is the new *Travellers Inn* (☎ 043-723 6021) on Rizal Ave Extension. It's on the way to the ferry terminal and offers clean, comfortable rooms with air-con and bath starting at P425 (P475 with TV).

On the other side of Padre Burgos St, the *Avenue Pension House I* (☎ 043-300 1967, 150 JP Rizal Ave) is a short-stay place that has passable fan-rooms with bath for P300 and air-con rooms with bath for P400. There is a second Avenue Pension House at 163 MH del Pilar St.

Getting There & Away

Bus In Batangas, BLTB and JAM Transit both have terminals on the road to Bauan, with buses every 15 minutes to Cubao and Pasay City (three hours). You can get here by 'Bauan' jeepney from the McDonald's on Padre Burgos St in Batangas.

From the pier to Manila, BLTB and JAM Transit have buses to Pasay City, while Tritran serves Cubao; buses leave for both destinations every few minutes. Crow Transit has buses from the pier to Nasugbu about every 45 minutes. Alps Transit runs to its terminal near the walls of Intramuros in Manila every 20 minutes.

Boat Batangas is the main jumping-off point for the extremely popular resort town of Puerto Galera on Mindoro, and there are also boats to Calapan, Abra de Ilog, Sablayan and San José, and to Romblon Island. Batangas pier is at the end of Rizal Ave.

All of the boat companies operating out of Batangas have desks in the terminal building and the competition is quite fierce, with rival boat companies shouting out their destinations at arriving tourists. The terminal fee is P10, payable at the counter just outside the departures gate.

Mindoro Ferries and outriggers operate all day (until about 6 pm) between Batangas and Puerto Galera (or Sabang). The crossing takes one to two hours, depending on the craft, and prices range from P65 for outriggers to P150 for air-conditioned catamarans.

There are also a few combined bus-and-boat trips from the tourist belt in Manila to Puerto Galera. A bus leaves the Centrepoint Hotel (☎ 02-521 2751), on Mabini St, Ermita, at 9 am daily, connecting with the 11.45 am MV *Si-Kat II* to Puerto Galera. The combined bus-and-boat fare is P350 one way (P150 for the boat only) and you can book at the hotel. Alternatively, a bus leaves the Citystate Tower Hotel (☎ 02-526 2733) on Mabini St at 8 am daily, connecting with the MV *Super 85* ferry for P360/695 one way/return.

Viva Shipping Lines' (☎ 043-723 2986) has boats from Batangas to several ports on Mindoro. Boats leave for Calapan every 15 minutes from 2.30 am to 10 pm (P150), and to Puerto Galera at 8.30 am, 12.20 pm and 5 pm (P150). For Sablayan and San José, the MV *Santa Maria* leaves at 7 pm Tuesday, Friday and Sunday and the MV *Marian Queen* leaves at 5 pm Monday, Wednesday and Saturday (P160). The MV *Penafrañcia VIII* leaves for San José at 5 pm daily except Thursday.

Montenegro Shipping Lines' (☎ 043-723 7698) car and passenger ferries sail from Batangas to San José in the south at 6 pm Tuesday, Thursday and Saturday (P200 to P300, 10 hours). From San José to

AROUND MANILA

Batangas, ferries sail at 6 pm Sunday, Wednesday and Friday.

There are also boats from Sablayan to Batangas, between 7 and 8 pm Tuesday, Thursday and Sunday (P175 to P265, nine hours).

Datinguinoo Shipping Lines (☎ 0912 306 5332) operates the pumpboats MV *Princess Kay*, MV *Sabang Princess I*, MV *Sabang Princess II* and MV *Super Gigi*, which leave Batangas Sabang Beach at 9.30 and 10.30 am, 12.15 and 2.30 pm (P75 to P80, 1½ hours). From Sabang, boats set sail at 6, 7, 8, 9 and 11.30 am, and 3 and 4 pm. Times mat vary depending on weather conditions, and loading and unloading delays.

Super Diamond Shipping (☎ 0917 927 7745, 0917 306 5332) has the air-con MV *Blue Eagle* which leaves for Puerto Galera at 11.30 am and 3.30 pm daily (also at 9 am Thursday to Sunday), charging P110.

Romblon For the Romblon group of islands, the Viva Shipping Lines' MV *Penafrañcia IV* leaves for Odiongan at 4 pm Tuesday, Thursday and Saturday (P160). The MV *Penafrañcia III* leaves for Odiongan (P220), Romblon town (P220) and Sibuyan (P230) at 7 pm Monday, Thursday and Saturday.

Shipshape Shipping (☎ 043-723 7615) has boats to San Agustin (P250), Romblon town (P250) and Sibuyan (P275) at 6 pm Monday, Thursday and Saturday, and to Odiongan (P180) at 6 pm Wednesday, Friday and Sunday. The routes are shared by the MV *Princess Camille* and the MV *Princess Colleen*.

Montenegro Lines' MV *Don Francisco* goes to Odiongan at 6 pm Sunday and Wednesday (P120).

CORREGIDOR

The scene of fierce fighting during WWII, the island of Corregidor became the last bastion of resistance by American forces during the Japanese invasion of Luzon in 1941. Following the Japanese capture of Manila, General Douglas MacArthur masterminded his operations from Corregidor until March 1942, when he left to spearhead the defence

Once the scene of ferocious WWII fighting, Corregidor is now the site of the Pacific War Memorial.

of Australia. His successor, General Jonathan Wainwright, finally surrendered to the Japanese in May 1942. Huge numbers of American and Filipino prisoners of war died on the Death March from Mariveles to the concentration camp in Tarlac.

Corregidor was occupied by the Japanese until January 1945, when MacArthur arrived to liberate the island, honouring his promise to return to Corregidor (see the boxed text 'I Shall Return'). The second battle for Corregidor was no less bloody than the first, and as American forces gained a foothold on the island, the Japanese detonated an underground arsenal, killing 2000 of their own troops and countless American soldiers.

At the island's highest point is the American-built **Pacific War Memorial**, a shrine to the thousands from both sides who died in the conflict. The structures here include a symbolic metal flame and an open-topped dome that catches the sun on 6 May, the day on which the island fell. Elsewhere, the jungle is quietly reclaiming the ruined buildings and heavy artillery guns.

Things to See & Do

The Corregidor Foundation has opened the island as a tourist attraction to anyone interested in the battles of WWII. The admission fee of P100 includes a guided jeepney tour of the devastated military buildings and rusting heavy armaments, as well as the numerous war monuments on the island. Significant sights include **General MacArthur's**

'I Shall Return'

As the USA's most famous soldier, General Douglas MacArthur is also credited with one of the most famous war-time quotes: 'I Shall Return.' Contrary to popular opinion, 'Dugout Doug' – as he was christened by the embittered troops on the Bataan Peninsula – didn't come up with these words himself. Nor did he say them until he was safely docked in Australia and facing an adoring throng of reporters. Reading from a prepared statement, the general said:

The President of the United States ordered me to break through the Japanese lines for the purpose, as I understand it, of organising the American offensive against Japan, a primary object of which is the relief of the Philippines. I came through and I shall return.

Long before this, Macarthur's chief of staff had proposed the slogan 'We Shall Return' – 'we' meaning the USA. This was then modified at the urging of the Philippine diplomat and writer Carlos P Romulo, who felt that his people wanted an assurance from MacArthur himself, not from a faceless country that had betrayed them so badly. The famously egocentric general happily obliged and the rest is history.

Mic Looby

HQ, the **mile-long barracks**, the **gun batteries** and the **Spanish lighthouse**, which offers good views over Manila Bay. There is also a small museum.

Another attraction is the sound and light show in the **Malinta Tunnel**, a bomb-proof bunker that was used as a hospital during the conflict (P150). If you want to explore the island by yourself, there's a regular bus service from 9 am to 5 pm (P60 for the day), or you can hire bikes from the jetty for about P200.

Places to Stay

The accommodation options on the island are only available as part of package tours,

which include meals, tours and boat transfers from Manila. You can book through the Corregidor Foundation office in the DOT building on TM Kalaw St in Manila (☎ 02-523 5605) or with Sun Cruises (☎ 02-831 8140).

The upmarket hotel and resort is a bit pricey for the average traveller. Groups of 10 or more can hire out the *Corregidor Youth Hostel* for P1775 per head including meals and transfer from Manila, but the hostel doesn't accept individual guests or drop-ins.

Rooms at the attractive *Corregidor Hotel* aren't cheap, but they're fitted with traditional rattan furniture and have aircon, TV and bath. Double rooms are P2950 including transfers and meals, while twin rooms start at P2300 per head with the same inclusions.

The *Beach Resort* near the Japanese Garden of Peace has problems with garbage washing in from Manila Bay. It's currently closed until the owners can work out a way around the problem.

Getting There & Away

A good way to see the island is the day tour offered by Sun Cruises (see Places to Stay earlier), which includes boat transfers, the entrance fee, a guided tour and a buffet lunch at the Corregidor Hotel (P1500). The cruises depart from the jetty within the CCP complex on Roxas Blvd in Manila between 7.30 am and 8 am, returning at 2.30 pm (departing between 10 am and 10.30 am, returning at 6 pm on weekends). There is a P5 terminal tax. You can book at the jetty or with any of the travel agents in town.

You can also visit Corregidor by banca from Cabcaben, near Mariveles, on the Bataan Peninsula. Bancas cost about P800 return for the whole boat, but if you can hook up with a group of local tourists, the rate drops to P200 per head. Buses run from Mariveles to Balanga and Olongapo every few minutes, stopping in Cabcaben. You can pick them up near the Jet Ferries terminal in Mariveles and the Mt Samat Ferry Express terminal in Orion.

BATAAN PENINSULA

For WWII veterans, few places have such bitter associations as the Bataan Peninsula. Both sides saw some of their darkest moments in the jungles around Mt Mariveles. The Dambana ng Kagitingan (Shrine of Valor) atop nearby Mt Samat is a monument to the grim battles that were fought here before the US finally surrendered to the Japanese on Corregidor Island in 1942.

Since the war the majority of tourists to the area have been returning servicemen, but there are opportunities for hiking on the upper slopes of **Mt Natib** (1253m) and some sites, like the shrine on Mt Samat, can easily be visited as a day trip from Manila.

Getting There & Away

From Mariveles, Genesis Transport has buses to Pasay City every 15 minutes and hourly buses to Baguio. Philippine Rabbit also goes to Manila. You can pick up a minibus for Cabcaben or Balanga on the highway by the Jet Ferries terminal (one hour). For Mt Samat, take a jeepney bound for Bagac.

From Manila, Jet Ferries (☎ 02-831 9976) has daily boats from the CCP complex to Mariveles at the tip of the peninsula (P170, one hour) at 8 am, noon, 3 and 6.30 pm, returning to Manila at 6 and 10 am and 1.30 and 5 pm. At the CCP jetty there is a P5 terminal tax.

Mt Samat

Every 9 April, American and Japanese veterans gather at the **Dambana ng Kagitingan** (Shrine of Valor), on top of Mt Samat, and pay tribute to the thousands of their comrades who fell in the surrounding jungles. The centrepiece of the shrine is a **90m-high crucifix** with battle scenes carved around its base. There is also a memorial wall, an open-air chapel and a small **museum of weapons** captured from the Japanese.

If it's working, you can take the lift up to the crossbar of the massive crucifix, where there is a long viewing gallery with stunning views out over Mt Mariveles, Manila Bay and the South China Sea. If you need reminding of the fact that you're suspended in mid-air, the guards will open the windows to allow the wind to roar through and shake the building.

After the hectic pace of Manila, the atmosphere here is quiet and reverential and the 7km walk from the highway junction to the shrine passes through some pleasant woodland. The complex is open from 8 am to 5 pm daily, but you can only climb the crucifix from 10 to 11 am and from 3 to 4 pm Monday and Tuesday, from 9 to 11 am and from 2 to 4 pm Wednesday to Friday, and from 9 to 11 am and from 1 to 4 pm on weekends. Admission is P20.

Getting There & Away Ferries from Manila to the village of Orion are run by Mt Samat Ferry Express (☎ 02-551 5290). The *Ok Ka Ferry I* and *Ok Ka Ferry II* leave Manila at 7.40 and 10.30 am and 1.30 and 4.55 pm; in the reverse direction, boats depart Orion at 6.15 and 9.05 am, noon and 3.15 pm (P110 plus P5 departure tax, one hour). You can pick up a jeepney to Bagac from the highway.

From Balanga, jeepneys to Bagac leave from the Victory Liner bus terminal on Paterno St. Ask to be dropped off at the junction to Mt Samat. A tricycle directly to the Mt Samat junction will cost about P40 from Orion or Balanga.

Balanga

The provincial capital of Bataan is a friendly little place with a few hotels, a cathedral, a busy town market and a couple of good restaurants. It's a good base for hikes up to the summit of nearby Mt Natib or the WWII shrine at Mt Samat and there are a few interesting churches in the area, most notably in Orion and Abucay (the church here dates to at least 1610 and housed the first printing press in the Philippines). The trail to Mt Natib starts from the village of Abucay, just north of Balanga on the way to Olongapo; it's a long day or an easier overnight climb to the summit.

Places to Stay & Eat The better of the two hotels in town is the *Elison Hotel* (☎ 047-237 2942), formerly the Alitaptap Hotel, on Lerma St near the cathedral.

Clean air-con rooms with bath and TV are P650/800 a single/double.

Close to the terminal for Mariveles minibuses, the **Hotel Samat** (☎ 047-237 2860), on Camacho St, offers clean air-con rooms with bath for P700 (P500 without TV).

The **Plow & Harrow** is a plush steak restaurant with English dishes like roast beef and fish and chips for P300 and steaks for P400. It's open from 11 am to 10.30 pm.

On St Joseph's St, behind the mall, **Sam's Pizza** is a small pizza chain that offers tasty square pizzas and live music in the evenings. For local food, there are dozens of little canteens around the market.

Getting There & Away From its terminal on Paterno St, Victory Liner has buses to Olongapo (hourly from 3 am to 6 pm, one hour). Jeepneys to Bagac also leave from here.

Out of town on Capitol Rd, Philippine Rabbit has buses to Rizal Ave in Manila every hour from 2.30 am to 4.20 pm (3½ hours). There are also buses to San Fernando in La Union province (seven hours), and Tarlac City (three hours).

Minibuses to Mariveles leave when full from Camacho St near the Caltex station from 5 am to 8 pm, taking one hour (40 minutes to Cabcaben).

Jeepneys run up and down the coast to places like Orion, Abucay and Orani.

OLONGAPO & THE SUBIC BAY MARINE AUTHORITY

Until recently, the natural deep-water harbour of Subic Bay was the base for the huge 7th Fleet of the US Navy. Olongapo and the other communities along the coast were entirely dependent on the naval base, generating much of their revenue from the sex industry.

America's last possession in the Philippines was returned to the islands in 1992, after 12 Filipino senators made the bold decision to reject the extension of America's lease of the facility. A monument on the wharf here displays the prints of the twelve hands that 'freed the nation'.

Rechristened the Subic Bay Marine Authority, the former naval base is evolving into a busy industrial zone and resort, with numerous luxury hotels and casinos, and charter flights bringing in gamblers from across Asia.

The sex industry was already in decline when Kate Gordon, the mayor of Olongapo, closed down all the girlie bars a few years ago. Today, most tourists come here to scuba dive on one of the 27 shipwrecks that lie on the bottom of Subic Bay, or to tour the Jungle Environment Survival Training (JEST) Camp. With a hire car, Olongapo is also a good base from which to explore Bataan, the area around Mt Pinatubo or the Zambales coastline.

Information

The Tourist Information Centre (☎ 047-252 4154) is on the second floor of Building 662, Taft St, SBMA, close to the waterfront. It's open from 8 am to 5 pm daily. You can check your email at Ann Raquel's Internet Café on Magsaysay Drive, upstairs next door to Ann Raquel's Hotel.

Barrio Barretto & Subic Village

During the lifetime of the naval base, the whole strip of coast from Olongapo to Subic village was the *Sin-upon-Sea* to Angeles' *Sin City*, with dozens of seedy restaurants, nightclubs and girlie bars. Today, the bubble has definitely burst and fishing is once again becoming the main industry in the villages, though there is still enough action here to attract the Angeles crowd at weekends.

Baloy Long Beach, at the north end of barrio Barretto, is probably the best beach for a day trip. You can get here by blue jeepney from the Victory Liner terminal.

Diving & Other Activities

Of the seven **wrecks** commonly visited by divers, the USS *New York* (27m) is probably the most impressive. The battle cruiser was built in 1891 and was scuttled by American troops in 1941 to keep it out of Japanese hands; the wreck is a haven for fish and the huge cannons are still intact.

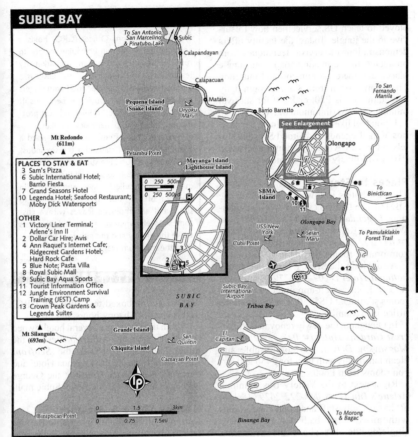

SUBIC BAY

PLACES TO STAY & EAT
3 Sam's Pizza
6 Subic International Hotel;
   Barrio Fiesta
7 Grand Seasons Hotel
10 Legenda Hotel; Seafood Restaurant;
   Moby Dick Watersports

OTHER
1 Victory Liner Terminal;
   Arlene's Inn II
2 Dollar Car Hire; Avis
4 Ann Raquel's Internet Cafe;
   Ridgecrest Gardens Hotel;
   Hard Rock Cafe
5 Blue Note; Pasta Villa
8 Royal Subic Mall
9 Subic Bay Aqua Sports
11 Tourist Information Office
12 Jungle Environment Survival
   Training (JEST) Camp
13 Crown Peak Gardens &
   Legenda Suites

AROUND MANILA

Other wrecks include the *Oryoku Maru* (20m), the *Seian Maru* (27m), the *El Capitan* (20m) and the 1898 wreck of the *San Quintin* (16m), as well as several small patrol boats and landing craft.

Moby Dick Watersports (☎ 047-252 3773), across from the Legenda Hotel, and Subic Bay Aqua Sports (☎ 047-252 3005), further along Waterfront Drive, both charge about US$60 for two dives, which includes all equipment. The latter company has half-hour flights over the Mt Pinatubo lahar flows for US$150 (with a maximum of three passengers). Both com-

panies offer half-hour bay cruises for about P1300.

The beaches here are fairly undesirable; probably the best are those on Grande Island in the bay (day-trippers are charged a P15 admission fee). Motorised bancas leave every hour from the SBMA Telecommunications Department on Waterfront Rd (P60). There are also beaches in the red light districts of barrio Barretto and Subic if you don't mind the seedy company.

The other highlight in the SBMA is the **Jungle Environment Survival Training (JEST) Camp** (☎ 047-252 2313), where the indigenous Ayta people of the area were employed to teach US servicemen how to survive in the jungle. Today, the facility offers demonstrations of survival techniques from producing fire to making soap from jungle plants, and there's a minizoo and museum. The camp is open from 8 am to 5 pm daily and admission is P20, or P250 for survival training sessions (minimum of five persons).

If you feel like testing your luck, the **casinos** at the Legenda and Grand Seasons Hotels in the SBMA (open 24 hours, admission P100) will gladly take your money.

Places to Stay

The best hotels in town are all within the SBMA. The Legenda group owns the luxurious *Legenda Hotel* (☎ 047-252 1888), on Waterfront Rd, and *Grand Seasons Hotel* (☎ 047-252 2888), on Canal Rd, with smart, comfortable rooms starting at US$86.

Also within the SBMA, the *Subic International Hotel* (☎ 02-843 7794), on Santa Rita Rd, has well-appointed executive rooms starting at US$150. The reservations office is in Manila.

In Olongapo, the newly renovated *Ridgecrest Gardens Hotel* (☎ 047-222 2006, 15 Magsaysay Drive), has comfortable and clean fan-rooms with bath for P450 and air-con rooms from P600.

Right next to the Victory Bus terminal, *Arlene's Inn II* (☎ 047-222 2629, 18/18th St) has friendly staff and good clean rooms with air-con and bath for P600/800 a single/double. It's above the Chowking fast-food restaurant.

Places to Eat

Probably the friendliest of the dozens of pizza places in town is *Sam's Pizza*, on Magsaysay Drive, which has live music in the evenings and good square pizzas in the P150 to P200 price range. It's open from 6 pm to 1 am daily.

Further south on Magsaysay Drive, *Pasta Villa* has a good selection of pizza and pasta in the P100 to P200 price range. It's open from 11 am to midnight.

The big disco-theatres like the *Blue Note* and *Hard Rock Café* all offer live music,

---

Wanted: GRO

The Guest Relations Officer (GRO) holds a controversial position in Philippine society. In rural communities and in many upmarket city restaurants and karaoke bars, the GRO is a glorified waitress, employed to sit with singers and coerce them into buying expensive soft drinks known as 'ladies' drinks' to boost profits from these traditionally slow drinkers.

However, the system has also provided a convenient opt-out clause for the sex industry. As a way around the strict antiprostitution laws, sex workers take some of their payment in the form of ladies' drinks, and the rest in the form of 'bar fines', which are payable to the bar if an employee leaves with a customer. As elsewhere in the world, the bars make the money and the girls take home less than the minimum wage.

Joe Bindloss

GROs (see the boxed text 'Wanted: GRO' in this chapter), happy hours and pizza.

Within the SBMA are several hotel-owned restaurants including a *Barrio Fiesta* at the Subic International Hotel, the *Seafront Restaurant* opposite the Legenda Hotel and the *Hollywood Steak House* at the George Dewey complex, near the Royal Subic mall.

Getting There & Around

Currently all the flights into Subic Bay international airport are expensive international charters. Victory Liner has buses at least once an hour from Rizal Ave in Olongapo to Baguio, Pasay City, Caloocan City and Balanga.

Jeepneys in Olongapo are colour-coded. Yellow jeepneys run along Rizal Ave to the main gate to the SBMA. Blue jeepneys leave for Subic from the street behind the Victory Liner terminal.

For hire cars, Dollar (☎ 047-223 2394) and Avis (☎ 047-223 3256) both have offices in the Subic Sports Plaza on Perimeter Rd, one block back from Magsaysay Drive. All companies charge about P1600 a day for air-con Toyota Corollas.

SBMA shuttle buses depart from the Park-n-Shop car park next to the main gate for the waterfront, the Royal Subic Mall, the airport and Upper Cubi (for Crown Peak Gardens, returning via the JEST camp). There are buses every few minutes from 8 am to 6 pm, then hourly till midnight.

SAN FERNANDO (PAMPANGA)

The busy industrial town of San Fernando – not to be confused with San Fernando (La Union) north-west of Baguio – is the capital of Pampanga province and was right in the line of fire when the liquid mud from Mt Pinatubo came sliding down the Pasig-Potrero River in 1996. The entire suburb of Bacolor vanished under the mud flows, though you can still see a few rooftops sticking out of the reeds on the road to Olongapo. Vast dikes have been constructed just west of town to funnel the next flows away from downtown San Fernando.

One of the main reasons people come here is for the dubious attraction of seeing fanatical Christians offering themselves in a **crucifixion ceremony** every Easter. At noon on Good Friday, a number of volunteers are physically nailed to wooden crosses in the barangay of San Pedro Cutud, and whipped till they bleed by gangs of flagellants. For the participants, it's a spiritual recreation of Christ's journey on the Via Crusis ('Way of The Cross'), but most of the onlookers gather for the novelty value.

The other big event in San Fernando is the annual **Christmas Lantern Festival**. On the closest Saturday to Christmas at about 8 pm, a number of truly gigantic Christmas lanterns are paraded through the town and up to the Paskuhan Village park, accompanied by the usual fiesta shenanigans. The lanterns remain on display till January.

The Paskuhan Village houses the tourist office, the Pinatubo House (built from the material that rained down on the town) and a public swimming pool. The complex is shaped like a Christmas star, and houses numerous stalls selling lanterns and other souvenirs. Admission is P15 (plus P20 if you want to use the pool).

Information

The tourist office (☎ 045-961 2665) is in the Paskuhan Village on the Expressway.

Places to Stay

The new *Hotel Grace Lane (☎ 045-860 1234, 860 6060)* is just off the MacArthur Hwy on the way into town. Comfortable air-con rooms with bath start at P950 a single or double (P760 in the low season) or P1100 for larger rooms (P880 in the low season). Suites start at P2600.

The *Boliseum Motel (☎ 045-961 2040),* in the Juliana subdivision on the outskirts of San Fernando, is a passable short-stay place that offers clean, quiet rooms with air-con, TV and bath for P550.

Getting There & Away

Buses from Manila to Olongapo pass through San Fernando; Philippine Rabbit goes to Olongapo from its Avenida terminal, while Victory Liner has regular Olongapo buses from Pasay City and Caloocan. There are also buses north from San Fernando (La Union) and Baguio.

Alternatively, a jeepney ride north to Angeles, and a second trip on to Dau will get you to the Mabalacat Terminal, which is a stop for buses on most of the main routes north.

ANGELES

If it wasn't for the destruction caused by the eruption of Mt Pinatubo, there would be little reason to visit the strip of girlie bars and cheap hotels known as Angeles. The dusty highway outside the perimeter fence of the former Clark Airbase has seen nearly a century as the centre of the sex industry in the Philippines, but Angeles is a one-trick town and there's not much here to delay the traveller.

Most people mean Balibago district in Dau when they talk about Angeles. Angeles is actually a small village 2km south of the red light district. The sex industry first took hold here in the 1900s when US servicemen began taking 'R&R' in the villages surrounding the US military base. Today, the young girls who work the bars along Fields

AROUND MANILA

Ave cater mainly to middle-aged Australian, American and European men who are ferried in from Manila, barrio Barretto and Subic by highly profitable international sex-tourism cartels.

Pinatubo can easily be visited as a day trip from Manila, particularly if you have your own transport, so there isn't really any need to contribute your tourist dollars to this place.

Orientation & Information

You don't need much help finding your way around Angeles. Balibago doesn't consist of much more than Fields Ave and its extension Don Juico Ave. Philippine Rabbit buses stop on Henson St, which meets the MacArthur Hwy near Balibago. Dau is 2km north along the highway.

The Angeles business community runs a small tourist information office (☎ 045-322 0507) on Don Juico Ave. It's open from 9 am to 5 pm daily.

Places to Stay & Eat

There are dozens of cheap hotels along Fields Ave and Don Juico Ave, but unless you're here for the 'entertainment', it's a fairly dispiriting place to stay.

If you do stop over, the business hotels at the far end of Fields Ave from the MacArthur Highway are probably the most discreet, though the *Oasis Resort Complex* (☎ 045-322 6121) seems to be the only hotel where conferences actually take place. Rooms here start at P1500 with air-con, bath and cable TV.

Nearby, the *Clarkton Hotel* (☎ 045-322 3424) is one of several generic mid-range hotels on Don Juico Ave with pools and air-con rooms with bath and TV. At the Clarkton rooms start at P900. The nearby *America Hotel* and *Europhil International* charge slightly less.

Of the cheapies, the *Vistillana Hotel* (☎ 045-322 0519), on Charlotte St, a side street off the MacArthur Hwy, is clean and sees less action than the Fields Ave hotels because of its location. Rooms with fan and bath are P270, or P330 with air-con, bath and TV.

It can be hard to find a meal in Angeles without receiving unwelcome attention; the fast-food places are probably your best bet. Despite its location, the only entertainment at *Rick's Cafe* on Fields Ave is usually movies on the VCR and it also has cheap burgers and sandwiches. You can also access the Internet and rent motorcycles here.

Getting There & Around

From Manila, Philippine Rabbit has regular air-con buses from Rizal Ave (Avenida) to its terminal on Henson St in Angeles village (1½ hours). Most north-bound buses from Manila take the North Luzon Expressway, stopping at the Mabalacat Bus Terminal in Dau, a few kilometres north of Angeles. Yellow jeepneys run between Dau and Angeles village 24 hours a day.

You can hire off-road motorcycles from several moneychangers on Fields Ave for P500 a day. Rick's Cafe on Fields Ave has smaller motorcycles for P350 a day.

CLARK SPECIAL ECONOMIC ZONE

After the 1991 eruption of Pinatubo, the USA finally ceded to the Philippine government's demands and vacated the Clark Airbase. Like Subic Naval Base, Clark has now been given special economic status in an attempt to encourage industrial development, but this hasn't been a resounding success. The international airport has yet to see a scheduled flight after eight years of negotiations and the Expo-Pilipino cultural theme park is dogged by management disputes and is usually closed. One of the few profitable tenants here is the Philippine Air Force.

Every February, Clark holds a large **Balloon Festival**, with lots of colourful hot-air balloons and a race over the volcano. Regular air-con buses around the Special Economic Zone leave from the main gate.

MT PINATUBO

For centuries, the residents of Angeles took the nearby volcanoes of Mt Pinatubo and Mt Arayat for granted. That was to change suddenly on 15 June 1991, when Pinatubo, the larger of the two volcanoes, literally blew itself apart, sending a column of ash and rock 40km into the air. The mountain lost 300m in height and the vaporised material rained down on nearby Angeles, Clark Airbase and Subic Bay as fine dust and fist-sized fragments of rock.

The eruption was caused by magma superheating pockets of water within the rock, creating an explosive force akin to a nuclear detonation. Earthquakes shook the ground, lightning and thunder boiled in the sky and everywhere ash fell in unbelievable quantities. The main centres of the sex industry were right in the path of the destruction, prompting many church groups to draw biblical conclusions. As if to support this, a savage typhoon chose this moment to lash northern Luzon, turning the ash into lethal *lahar* (mobile volcanic mud).

Warnings of the eruption came as early as April 1991, when gentle clouds of steam begin rising from the hitherto-dormant crater. It wasn't long before the seismographs placed on the mountain by the US military were registering dangerous levels of pressure within Pinatubo. Despite the pyrotechnics of the main eruption, it was the resulting lahar flows that were to do the most damage. Liquid mud flooded downhill from the volcano, burying 1000 hectares of prime farmland and claiming over 1000 lives.

Pinatubo is unlikely to erupt again in the near future, but the lahar deposits are prone to remobilisation by the annual rains and continue to cause fresh devastation every year. In September 1995, the suburb of Bacolor in San Fernando was entirely swallowed up by new lahar flows.

The sex industry quickly bounced back in Angeles, but the economic impact of the eruption can still be felt across Pampanga. Pinatubo tours were conceived as a way to revive the fortunes of some of the worst-affected areas, but a lot of the money has ended up in the pockets of Angeles businessmen.

Touring Pinatubo

The easily eroded lahar flows have created a stunning landscape around the volcano.

The Abacan and Pasig-Potrero rivers continually cut new channels through the sediment, leaving towering pinnacles of lahar, hanging valleys and steep-sided canyons. In the dry season it's possible to wander for hours through the canyons or even trek all the way up to the volcano itself.

Many people book guided tours through travel agents in Angeles, but it's easy to arrange the trip yourself, bypassing the Angeles tourist machine and ensuring that the money goes directly where it's needed.

The starting point for the trip is the village of Sapang Bato, about 8km west of Angeles. Jeepneys leave from opposite the Philippine Rabbit terminal on Henson St until 5 pm, or you can reach the village by hire vehicle from the end of Don Juico Ave (Fields Ave). At Sapang Bato you'll need to register at the barangay hall and pay for a Pinatubo permit (P50).

The trek proper begins at Target, a resettlement project for displaced Aeta people, 2km west of Sapang Bato (you can either walk or hire a tricycle). At Target, you'll need to register at the village store, where you can pick up a local guide for P300. Tips or donations are gratefully received and go into a communal pot to pay for road repairs and loans to farmers in the village.

From Target it's about an hour's walk before you hit the lahar canyons. If you do the trip without a guide, the best policy is to stick to the main channel of the river. It's best not to attempt the trek if there's a chance of rain.

You can hike all the way to the summit (1760m) in the dry season, but it will be a very long day or an overnight trip. Trekking through the lahar is hot and dusty work, so bring plenty of water.

Road Tours & Scenic Flights With a hire vehicle you can easily do a circuit from Angeles to Porac and on to the vanished suburb of Balocor, returning by San Fernando. The route crosses the Mega Dike project outside Porac, where you can still see the ruins of buildings sticking out of the lahar. You can also do the first part of the trip by public transport. Jeepneys leave for Porac from Rizal Ave Extension near the Angeles public market.

One-hour scenic flights over Pinatubo are available from Clark Aerial Services (☎ 045-322 2890) on Fields Ave (P2500). Book the day before you want to fly.

MT ARAYAT

Many people arriving in Angeles mistake the towering volcanic cone of 1026m Mt Arayat for Pinatubo, as it dominates the skyline. The volcano affords several half-day hikes to peaks on the crater rim, from where there are stunning views over Pampanga province. Also here are a network of swimming pools fed by a natural spring which, legend has it, produces the purest water on earth.

You can hire a Department of Environment guide for around P500 at the Mt Arayat National Park complex in Arayat Village. There is a P20 fee to climb the mountain, which also allows you to use the pools.

Getting There & Away

Arayat is about 25km east of Angeles. Jeepneys to Arayat leave from Plaridel St near the Angeles public market. The last trip back to Angeles leaves at about 6 pm. A tricycle from Arayat market to the national park costs about P20.

LUCENA

Most people only pass through Lucena, 120km south-east of Manila, on the way to the port of Dalahican, which is the departure point for boats to Marinduque, but the capital of Quezon province is a pleasant enough place to overnight before catching a boat in the morning. The port is quite a lively place in the morning as dozens of boats unload their cargoes of squid, *lapu-lapu* (grouper) and tuna.

Also of interest is the **Museo ng Quezon** in the Provincial Health building in the Quezon Capitol compound on Quezon Ave. Housed here are numerous items of memorabilia from Manuel L Quezon, the dapper first president of the Philippines. It's open from 8 am to 5 pm Monday to Friday.

Quezon Ave is the main shopping street in Lucena. Here you'll find numerous banks and restaurants, the **San Ferdinand Cathedral** and the **Geek Station Internet cafe**, which is open till midnight. North of town, Quezon Ave forms the road to Tayabas and Lucban. Follow P Gomez St for the highway to Atimonan and Dalahican port.

Places to Stay

The *House of Halina Hotel* (☎ 042-710 2902, 104 Gomez St) has a variety of reasonably priced rooms, a good open-air restaurant and secure off-street parking. Spacious fan-rooms with private bath are P200, while air-con rooms range from P600 to P1000.

On the road to Manila, the *Lucena Fresh Air Hotel* (☎ 042-710 2424) is a clean conference hotel and resort with a good swimming pool and a restaurant. Fan-rooms are P175 with shared bath and P250 with private bath, while air-con rooms start at P460.

Across the road, the *Travel Lodge Chain Motel* (☎ 042-710 4482) has a secluded pool and gardens and fan-rooms with bath from P200. Air-con rooms with cold water only are P450, or air-con suites with patio, hot and cold water and TV start at P715 (P650 without TV).

Getting There & Away

Bus BLTB, JAC Liner, JAM Transit and Tritran have regular services from Cubao and Pasay City to Lucena Grand Central Terminal or the port of Dalahican. Heading south, BLTB buses to Daet, Naga and Legaspi will stop in Lucena if requested (call BLTB on ☎ 042-710 3291 to make a reservation). Regular jeepneys connect Dalahican and Grand Central.

Atimonan minibuses leave Grand Central every half hour, passing through Quezon National Park. Out of town on the road to Manila, Supreme Lines has buses to Batangas (3½ hours) and Santa Cruz (three hours).

Boat Several shipping lines have offices on the dock at Dalahican. The biggest operator here is Viva Shipping Lines (☎ 042-373

5112) which has five express boats and two car-ferries daily to Balanacan/Boac (P150/75 express/*roro* (car ferry), 2½ hours), leaving between 3 am and 3 pm. For Santa Cruz, there's an express boat at 8 am and a car-ferry at 7.30 am (P175/50, three hours).

Viva also has a service to Masbate on Masbate Island, leaving Dalahican at 6 pm Saturday, Monday and Thursday (P350, 14 hours).

Other operators include Aleson Shipping Lines (☎ 042-373 4953), with boats to Balanacan (P60) and Santa Cruz (P80), both leaving at 8.30 am, and Montenegro Shipping Lines (☎ 042-373 3992), which leaves for Balanacan at noon (P60).

North Luzon

The Zambales Coast runs north of Subic up to Santa Cruz and is dotted with small beach resorts. If you're heading into the Cordilleras and want to spend a couple of days on the beach along the way, this stretch of coastline is worth a brief stop. The coast surrounding the Lingayen Gulf and its two provinces (Pangasinan and La Union) is home to many of North Luzon's most well-known beach resorts – Hundred Islands National Park and San Fernando. Don't expect fine white-sand beaches with turquoise water though. The beaches here are pleasant enough, but they don't compare with Luzon's southern neighbours.

The Cordillera region is the Philippines' largest mountainous area. The impressive Banaue rice terraces are the most famous sight of the Central Cordilleras, but more pristine scenery is found farther afield in Batad, Sagada and Kalinga. Tourists flock to blissfully relaxed Sagada to see its famous hanging coffins, though the unspoiled town is itself worth a trip. Fans of the afterlife shouldn't miss Kabayan's spooky mummy caves, though the area is also a pleasant place to explore the here and now.

Not far from the commercial town of Tuguegarao in Cagayan province are the Callao Caves, as well as other caves to keep casual spelunkers occupied. Isabela province is home to the Palanan Wilderness Area, one of the few remaining rainforests in the Philippines.

Ilocos province is home to the charming city of Vigan, the oldest surviving Spanish-colonial city in the Philippines. On the north coast of Luzon, Pagudpud is easily the most gorgeous beach in this part of the country.

The Philippines' most isolated province, Batanes is a mini-archipelago 280km north of Luzon and 190km south of Taiwan, where the Pacific Ocean meets the South China Sea. The archipelago has three inhabited islands – Batan, Sabtang and Itbayat. The landscape here is striking: Batan,

HIGHLIGHTS

- Hiking around Sagada's tranquil mountain-top setting
- Enjoying the limestone villages, magnificent coastline and rolling hills of Batanes (particularly Sabtang)
- Feasting your eyes on the beautiful amphitheatres of rice terraces at Batad and Banaue
- Taking a *calesa* (horse-drawn carriage) ride through Vigan's cobblestone streets

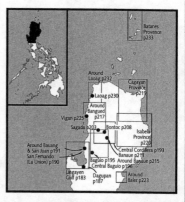

with its rocky coastline and gently rolling, Bermuda-grass covered hills, is ideal for hiking, as is Sabtang, with its timeless limestone villages, and Itbayat, the most rugged and remote of the three.

Zambales Coast

The beaches along this stretch of coast, to the west of Mt Pinatubo, are better than those farther north in San Fabian and San Fernando (La Union). But don't come expecting palm-fringed, gleaming white-sand beaches: the sand is grey and there's not

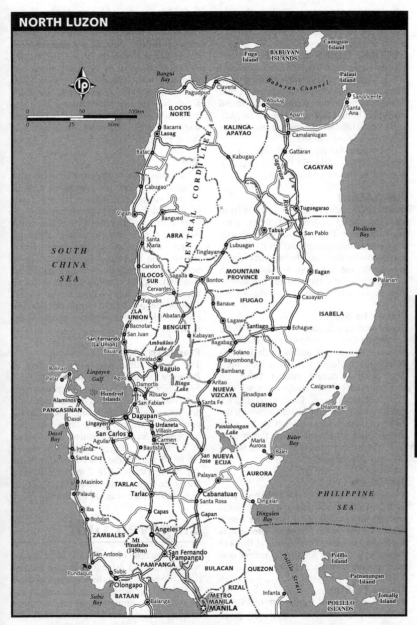

NORTH LUZON

much shade. However, the aqua-blue water is good for swimming.

GETTING THERE & AWAY

Victory Liner has a frequent bus service between Manila and Olongapo, and between Alaminos and Olongapo (five hours). From Olongapo there are frequent Iba-bound buses (2½ hours) that pass through San Antonio and Botolan. There are also direct buses from Manila to Iba.

From San Antonio there's sporadic a jeepney service to barrio Pundaquit (P10), or you can hire a tricycle (P40).

PUNDAQUIT

Down a mostly dirt road, 5km south-west of San Antonio, is a stretch of pretty, wide beach in barrio Pundaquit. From here you can hire a *banca* (pumpboat) for P350 a day to take you to the small, uninhabited outlying islands, the most well known of which is Capones, where the beaches are said to have superb white sand.

Places to Stay

Capones Beach Resort (☎ 0918 816 4816, fax 047-654 694), on Pundaquit beach, has pleasant beachfront accommodation, although the building itself is a bit motel-like, with concrete rooms lined up alongside each other. Doubles are P900/1250 with fan/air-con. There's a restaurant that looks out onto the beach, although the view is somewhat obstructed by nipa sheds lined up closer along the beach. Still, the resort manages to maintain a cheerful atmosphere.

BOTOLAN

A one hour drive up the Zambales Coast from San Antonio brings you to the small town of Botolan, where a few more beach resorts dot the shore. The beach here is narrower than those at Pundaquit and Iba, but the water is shallow for several metres out, making it an easy place to swim.

Places to Stay

West Coast Beach Resort (☎ 0918 229 9477, fax 047-811 1042) is a friendly place

with well-kept, air-con rooms for P850. Fan-cooled rooms with splendid ocean views cost P650. Nearby is *Rama International Beach Resort (☎ 0918 371 0300, fax 047-811 1042)*, with similarly plain but pleasant rooms. The dorm rooms for P200 and doubles with shared bath for P500 aren't bad for the price. Rooms with sea views are more expensive, with cottages starting at P995 and rooms with bath and fan at P695.

IBA

A half-hour drive up the coast from Botolan brings you to Iba, the province's capital, where a couple of kilometres north of town you'll find the largest concentration of resorts along the Zambales Coast. The beach here is similar to Pundaquit, although longer – it also attracts larger crowds. From Iba you can take day hikes into the Zambales mountain range. A road runs inland from Palauig, the next town north of Iba, to barrio Salasa, from where a trail to Mt Tapulao begins. The tourism office in Iba can provide more information about hiking in the area.

Places to Stay

The most attractive resort in Iba is *Palmera Garden Beach Resort (☎ 047-811 2109, fax 811 1886, ✉ palmera@mozcom.com)*. Cottages are attractively positioned alongside a small swimming pool, and Palmera has a large but cosy restaurant. Small fan-cooled rooms start at P350, and cottages and air-con rooms are P880. Larger and less cosy is *La Playa del Norte (☎ 047-811 2364, fax 02-894 5668)*, built to accommodate large groups. Doubles/cottages start at P770/880.

Lingayen Gulf

Despite the brownish sand and often murky water (Hundred Islands being an exception), the beach resorts here manage to draw in tourists, including those seeking to escape Manila's smog-choked streets, those keeping the sex trade alive and surfers.

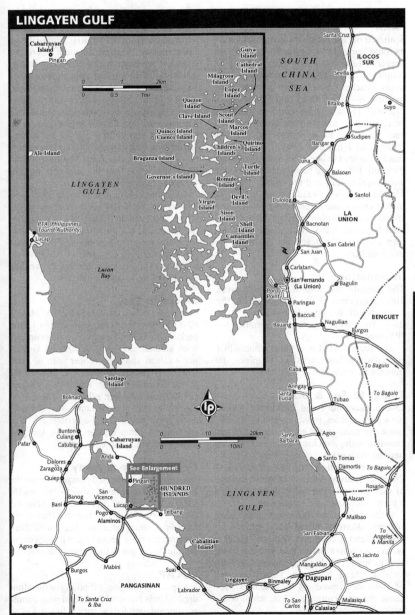

LINGAYEN GULF

HUNDRED ISLANDS NATIONAL PARK

Scattered off the coast of Lucap, this small national park (1844 hectares) consists of over 100 little limestone islands. While a couple of dozen of the islands have tiny sandy beaches, the majority are basically mushroom-shaped rocky outcrops with no beaches. There's some good snorkelling here, although much of the coral reef has been destroyed by dynamite and cyanide fishing. El Niño and *bagyos* (typhoons) that hit the area in late 1998 have also taken their toll. Efforts are being made to protect what coral is left, and the nearby Bolinao Marine Laboratory is cultivating giant Australian clams and regenerating local coral species and transplanting them to the area. Islet-hopping and kicking back on your own private little beach are the main attractions here.

Information

The friendly and informative Philippines Tourist Authority (PTA) is at the end of the Lucap wharf. It's open from 8 am to 5 pm daily. You can pay your park entrance fee (P5) here.

The nearest ATM is at the Equitable PCI Bank (which has Cirrus) in Alaminos, 10 minutes by tricycle from the wharf.

Things to See & Do

Quezo, Governor's and Children's islands have picnic tables, pavilions and grills. Because the beaches are small, they often get crowded with picnicking families. If you're here on the weekend, you're better off asking your boatman to drop you off at one of the other islands. An easy climb to the top of Governor's Island will reward you with a pretty view over the whole park.

A few other islands have some interesting features: Marcos Island has a blowhole, Scout Island a cave and Quirino Island a water cave where, at low tide, you can sit on the 'picnic rock'. It's in a cavern and bats swirl overhead. Notice the stubby remains of stalactites sawed off by poachers. Because the cave entrance is low, small boats with no canopy can enter.

There are some protected areas with good **snorkelling** but you must have prior permission from the tourist authority in Lucap before entering the area. There are staghorn, cabbage, rocky and other corals, schools of tiny tropical fish, thousands of fluorescent blue-rimmed giant clams and, if you look closely, edible green 'sea-grapes' (they go well with raw tomatoes). The area around Claves Island is said to have good snorkelling and is not a protected area. You can rent snorkelling equipment for P250 a day from The Last Resort (☎ 075-551 2440) or the souvenir shop in front of Maxine by the Sea.

Dive sites here have seen better days: even 15m down, coral has been damaged or destroyed by cyanide fishing. Areas surrounding Braganza, Kagaw and Cathedral islands reputedly have the best diving. The closest place to rent dive equipment is in San Fernando (La Union), although the tourist office here has plans to open a dive shop.

Places to Stay

The tourist office (☎ 075-551 2505, Manila 02-812 1984) rents accommodation in the park. There is a two-bedroom stone *cottage*, with kitchen and bath (P2000) on Governor's Island and a basic *hut* with no bath (there's a public bath on the island) for P500. There is a larger *hut* with a kitchen (P1300) on Children's Island. There's no electricity but kerosene lamps are provided, as is fresh water for showering. It's also possible to camp on the islands, but you must have your own equipment.

Getting There & Away

You can hire a motorised pumpboat from the Lucap wharf or from Maxine by the Sea for P300 a day, or P600 if you plan to spend the night on an island. The tourist office regulates boat rental rates, so check with them for current prices. From Lucap it takes about 20 minutes to get to the closest islands.

LUCAP

Lucap is the jumping-off point for the Hundred Islands National Park, and where most accommodation for the park is found. Lucap

NORTH LUZON

itself is an unexciting one-road town made up primarily of a row of hotels. Although it's on the shore, there's no beach here.

Places to Stay

On the road from Alaminos, the first place you'll come to (and the most inexpensive in Lucap) is *Kilometer One* (☎ 075-551 2510), 1km from the wharf. Quiet, clean, well-kept doubles with fan and shared bath are P200. Closer to the centre of things is *Ocean View Lodge* (☎ 075-551 2501), with clean, dimly lit rooms with fans starting at P300. There's a restaurant on the ground floor.

Maxine by the Sea (☎ 075-551 2537) has no-frills singles/doubles with bath starting at P300/400 (if you don't use the air-con). You'll be made to feel at home at the *Island Hostel* (☎ 075-551 2842). You can eat home-cooked meals with the owners, or use the kitchen to cook for yourself. On the top floor there's a light and airy double with bath, air-con and stereo for P700; smaller doubles with air-con are P500. *LS Marina 100* has a nice homely atmosphere. Doubles in the A-frame house start at P1000. There are also clean, tasteful huts with bath and fan on the waterfront for P500.

If you're coming with a big group, *Hundred Islands View* (☎ 075-551 2465) has a clean and spacious two-bedroom, two-bath cottage with a kitchen, cable TV and veranda for P4500. Lucap's most upmarket lodging is *Vista del Mar* (☎ 075-551 2492), with a pretty white adobe exterior. All rooms have air-con, hot water, a refrigerator and TV, and they start at P1500.

Places to Eat

On a pier, *Maxine by the Sea* has a popular restaurant, where you can dine on delicious seafood dishes such as *lapu-lapu* (grouper, P70). Across the road, the restaurant at the *Last Resort* has a similar, more reasonably priced menu. Here you can linger over a beer for as long as you want, and most people do just that.

Vista del Mar specialises in Chinese-style seafood dishes. The second-storey restaurant has indoor and outdoor seating with a view of the Hundred Islands. *Hun-*

dred Islands View has a couple of tables on the waterfront and specialises in seafood, including crab and red snapper. *LS Marina 100* has a nice restaurant in the back that serves typical Filipino food.

For a quick and inexpensive meal, head for the row of *souvenir stands* on the wharf, which serve tasty local dishes.

Getting There & Away

From Alaminos to Lucap, take a tricycle for P25 (P35 at night). The 5km ride north to Lucap takes about 10 minutes.

Victory Liner, Five Star and Dagupan Bus all have hourly services between Manila and Alaminos (P180, five hours). Philippine Rabbit plies this route with less frequency. From Manila you can also take a Dagupan-bound bus and change at Tarlac to an Alaminos-bound bus.

From Alaminos to Dagupan, the Victory Liner bus leaves hourly and the Dagupan Bus leaves every 20 minutes.

BOLINAO

A fishing town on the extreme northwestern tip of the Lingayen Gulf, Bolinao is a buzzing and pleasant provincial town that doesn't see many tourists. Bolinao was once a prosperous trade centre, attested to by sunken Chinese junks and Mexican galleons said to be lying just offshore. There is also a Japanese munitions ship sunken just off nearby Santiago Island. Underwater visibility is usually poor, so the area hasn't developed as a diving destination. Surfing, on the other hand, is rumoured to be good just offshore, near the Bolinao lighthouse.

Things to See & Do

Built by Augustinians in 1609, the **Church of St James** in the town plaza is a rarity, given its Mexican influence. On its antique altar are two tongue-protruding, Aztec-like statues said to be brought to Bolinao by the early traders. Also rare are the wooden *santos* (religious statues) on the church's facade, which, unlike many churches in the Philippines, have not been snatched by collectors.

The small and rather unimpressive **Bolinao Museum** (☎ 075-554 2065), on Rizal St, is the province's sole museum. It houses archaeological finds from the area, although the best articles have been moved to the National Museum in Manila.

Across the street from the lighthouse is the **University of the Philippines Marine Service Institute** (UPMSI; ☎ 0912 604 3916). Visitors are welcome to view the laboratory, where researchers cultivate near-extinct indigenous species with the aim of transplanting them into their natural environment; the lab also aims to transfer the technology to other parts of the Philippines. Among other species, they cultivate various coral species, giant clam, abalone and sea urchin.

A few beaches dot Bolinao's coast, although the one closest to town, Guiguiwanen Beach, is small and unimpressive, and in recent years has been plagued by murky water. Much more inviting but less accessible is **Patar Beach**, 12km (45 minutes by tricycle; P300 round-trip) from town. To get there take A Celino St (between the church and museum, across from Bolinao Central School) to Balingasay. Beyond Balingasay the road turns to dirt. Keep following it past the coconut farms, and bring your own food and drink.

Places to Stay & Eat
Celeste Sea Breeze Inn & Restaurant (☎ 075-554 2035), on the waterfront, has basic but cheerful rooms with bath and fan for P375/450 a single/double. Its affable proprietor is a good source of local knowledge. The restaurant here is the best place to eat in town. Next door is *El Piscador Village Inn & Restaurant* (☎ 075-554 2559), where plainly furnished doubles with fan/air-con are P300/500. It has a pleasant thatch-roofed restaurant. *Tummy Teasers*, on A Celino St, has tasty pizza, spaghetti and tacos, as well as more authentic Filipino food, served in clean outdoor surroundings.

About 4km from Patar beach on the road from Bolinao is the small and beautifully landscaped *Dutch Beach Resort* (☎ 0912 311 6540), where immaculately kept whitestone cottages with air-con and refrigerator are P1000/1600. Next door is the *Tropical Hut Beach Resort*, where you can get back to nature in a no-frills thatched hut for P500. There's a common bathroom, and a tap from which you can bathe.

Entertainment
Bolinao is renowned in the province for its prowess in breeding exceptional fighting roosters, called 'Boltex' or 'Bolinao Texas.' Fights take place on weekends, starting around noon at the cockfighting stadium just outside of town, on the road to Alaminos.

Getting There & Away
Five Star and Victory Liner operate buses every hour between Alaminos and Bolinao (P20, one hour); Philippine Rabbit has a less frequent service. Five Star has hourly buses from Manila to Bolinao (P188). The last bus to Alaminos from Bolinao leaves at 4 pm.

There's also jeepney service (P20) until 5 pm. Jeepneys to Bolinao leave from the acacia tree opposite the main church in Alaminos.

LINGAYEN
The provincial capital of Pangasinan, Lingayen is much quieter than neighbouring Dagupan. The town is divided into two parts: the commercial centre with its central plaza, which was originally built by the Spanish, and, about 1km away, the spacious, orderly Capital Building area, built by the Americans. On the Capital Building grounds is the small open-air **Lingayen Gulf War Memorial museum**. It has interesting photos with detailed captions on the US beach landing (9 January 1945), the Japanese military and Filipino guerrilla forces. There's also a Japanese fighter plane, artillery and tanks.

The beach here, similar to most others along the gulf, is not particularly captivating. However, the coastline comes alive with a fluvial parade each 1 May, in celebration of Pista'y Dayat. This is the province's foremost fiesta.

Places to Stay & Eat
Across from the Capital Building *Hotel Consuelo* (☎ 075-542 8933), on the corner

of Alvear St and Maramba Blvd, has modern, clean rooms for P650/750 a single/double. The restaurant in the hotel, which serves seafood and Chinese cuisine, is recommended by locals. Close by, but fronting the beach, is the PTA-run *Lingayen Gulf Resort Hotel (☎ 075-542 6304),* with clean, standard rooms for P715/935. Dorm beds with fans are P165, and it has a pleasant little pool and an outdoor restaurant.

Getting There & Away

Five Star and Dagupan Bus both have hourly services to/from Manila (five hours).

From Dagupan, there are frequent jeepneys to Lingayen (P7, 50 minutes); you can catch them opposite the CSI shopping centre on AB Fernandez Ave.

DAGUPAN

Dagupan is a fairly typical exhaust fume-ridden commercial centre, with not much of interest for travellers. Three kilometres

north of town (a 15 minute ride) is the so-called **Bonuan Blue Beach**, although the only thing blue is the sky. The beach in nearby San Fabian is a better option.

You can connect to the Internet at Bitstop (☎ 075-522 1264), on the 2nd floor, New Sim Too Bldg, 29 AB Fernandez Ave, on top of the Jade Movie House, for P60 an hour. It's open from 8 am to 6.30 Monday to Friday. Queenbank, next to Star Plaza Hotel, has an ATM that accepts Plus and MasterCard.

Places to Stay & Eat

The recently opened *Value Star Inn (☎ 075-522 8381)* on AB Fernandez Ave, has modern, neat and clean (albeit small) singles with fans for P250, or more spacious doubles with air-con and cable TV for P550. It's best to make a reservation as rooms are often full. *Floren Hotel (☎ 075-522 0666),* on Rizal St, is another good option. Doubles with air-con and cable TV are

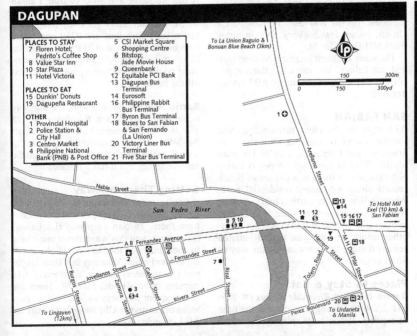

DAGUPAN

PLACES TO STAY	5	CSI Market Square
7	Floren Hotel;		Shopping Centre
	Pedrito's Coffee Shop	6	Bitstop;
8	Value Star Inn		Jade Movie House
10	Star Plaza	9	Queenbank
11	Hotel Victoria	12	Equitable PCI Bank
		13	Dagupan Bus
PLACES TO EAT		Terminal
15	Dunkin' Donuts	14	Eurosoft
19	Dagupeña Restaurant	16	Philippine Rabbit
			Bus Terminal
OTHER	17	Byron Bus Terminal
1	Provincial Hospital	18	Buses to San Fabian
2	Police Station &		& San Fernando
	City Hall		(La Union)
3	Centro Market	20	Victory Liner Bus
4	Philippine National		Terminal
	Bank (PNB) & Post Office	21	Five Star Bus Terminal

To La Union Baguio &
Bonuan Blue Beach (3km)

0   150   300m
0   150   300yd

Arellano Street

Nable Street

San Pedro River

To Hotel Mil
Exel (10 km) &
San Fabian

Herrero Road

M.H. Del Pilar Street

AB Fernandez Avenue

Fernandez Street

Burgos Street

Jovellanos Street

Zamora Street

Calvan Street

Rizal Street

Rivera Street

Tolero Road

Perez Boulevard

To Lingayen
(12km)

To Urdaneta
& Manila

NORTH LUZON

P650. Although it's a bit run-down, the staff at *Hotel Victoria*, on AB Fernandez Ave, are friendly and the rooms clean. Rooms with air-con start at P400. The most upmarket hotel in town is *Star Plaza* (☎ 075-523 4888), on AB Fernandez Ave, where rooms start at P850.

The elegant *Dagupeña Restaurant* (☎ 075-522 2752), on AB Fernandez Ave, serves excellent traditional food for around P100.

Sampaguita Disco, on Rizal St, has live music every night. Get there by 8.30 pm to catch the start of it.

Getting There & Away
Five Star, Victory Liner and Dagupan Bus all run frequent trips to/from Manila (P125/169 nonair-con/air-con, five hours). Philippine Rabbit, Victory Liner and Byron Bus all go to Baguio (P50, 2½ hours). These three companies also have frequent buses to Alaminos (two hours) and Bolinao (three hours) via Lingayen (45 minutes, 12km). To San Fabian (15 minutes, 10km) and San Fernando, La Union, buses leave every five minutes from MH Del Pilar St.

There are frequent jeepneys to Lingayen and San Fabian. You can catch them opposite the CSI shopping centre on AB Fernandez Ave.

SAN FABIAN
Although the beaches surrounding San Fabian are more inviting than those in Dagupan and Lingayen, they're far from idyllic. Next to the town proper is barrio Nibaliw, where there is a cluster of beach resorts along a pleasant residential road. About 3.5km farther north is barrio Bolasi, where there are a few more resorts, and another 3km north in barrio Alacan is another resort. In fact, you'll find isolated resorts dotting the coastline all the way to San Fernando.

Places to Stay & Eat
Barrio Nibaliw *Riverside Resort* (☎ 075-511 2229) was being renovated at the time of writing. It has large, plainly decorated

doubles for P650. There's also a small restaurant overlooking a pretty view of the river and the beach is a short walk across the road. Down the road is *Charissa's Beach Houses* (☎ 075-523 6860), where small air-con huts are P792 and two-bedroom cottages cost P1980. There is also a small swimming pool. *The Lazy 'A' Beach Resort* (☎ 075-511 5014) has small cottages with fan/air-con starting at P800/1200. There's also a swimming pool.

The nicest place to stay, and the most expensive, is at the end of the road. The *Sierra Vista Beach Resort* (☎ 075-511 2023, ℮ asiatravel.com), has clean, cheerful doubles with air-con starting at P1750. It has a swimming pool, and a restaurant that serves good food and elaborate tropical fruit cocktails. Also on this road is the *San Fabian Yacht Club restaurant*, specialising in US-style dishes.

Barrio Bolasi Set back from the highway is the attractive and isolated *San Fabian PTA Beach Resort* (☎ 075-523 6502), where you can really get away from it all. Dorm beds with fans are P250 and clean, comfortable rooms start at P1200. The spacious grounds include an attractive swimming pool and a children's pool, and it's just off the beach.

Barrio Alacan Visible from the highway is the *Windsurf Beach Residence* (☎ 918 380 1666), where basic huts with fans cost P430/495 weekdays/weekends. It's next to a small rocky beach that's not very suitable for swimming and it has a restaurant.

Getting There & Away
If you're going to Manila or Baguio, you should go back to Dagupan and catch a bus from there. To San Fernando (La Union) (1½ hours), you can wave down one of the frequent buses on the National Highway. To get to San Fabian, take any bus from Dagupan (15 minutes). Buses leave every five minutes from MH del Pilar St. There are also frequent jeepneys to San Fabian; they leave opposite the CSI shopping centre on AB Fernandez Ave.

AGOO

Agoo gained fame throughout the Philippines when, in September 1993, hundreds of thousands of Filipinos gathered here to behold an apparition of the Virgin Mary, which was predicted to appear by a local 13-year-old boy. Although the much-publicised spectacle failed to take place, many did claim to see the sun twirling around and emitting extraordinary colours. Today the young prophet (now a she) has her own chapel on a hill overlooking the town. She welcomes visitors the first Saturday of each month.

Worth a look is the **Museo Iloko**, which houses various Ilocano artefacts. Across the street is the **Agoo Basilica**, an impressive Mexican-baroque structure, which houses the image of Our Lady of Charity, believed to have miraculously survived an 1892 earthquake that destroyed the church in which it was then kept. During Holy Week, the basilica is a favourite pilgrimage destination.

Places to Stay & Eat

On the beach, about a 10-minute ride from the town centre, is *Agoo Playa Hotel* *(☎ 072-521 0889)*. Its nice rooms (although showing signs of wear) in prettily laid-out grounds and start at P1171/1351 a single/double. There's also a large swimming pool. In the town centre, on National Hwy near the Agoo Basilica, is *Iceland Bakeshop & Restaurant*, where you can get inexpensive Filipino and Chinese meals.

Getting There & Away

Buses from San Fernando en route to Manila pass through Agoo. From Manila (five hours), take any bus bound for San Fernando, Vigan or Laoag.

SAN FERNANDO (LA UNION)

The provincial capital of La Union, San Fernando is surrounded by dozens of beach resorts dotting the coastline both north and south of the city. This stretch of beach is narrow, with brownish sand. It's lined with fishing boats and pretty much devoid of swimmers and sunbathers.

Bauang (pronounced 'ba-**wahng**'), which encompasses the stretch of coastline south of the city, sprung up around Poro Point, which until 1991 was the sight of the US military's Wallace Air Station.

Like Angeles and other former sites of US military bases, prostitution here is rampant – as are tourists in search of it. Sadly, San Fernando made headlines in recent years when it was exposed as a bastion for paedophiles. A few local resort operators were prosecuted and imprisoned, but the problem is ongoing. Some resorts have 'nightclubs' that don't allow 'unaccompanied women' to enter, but others are genuinely friendly.

Information

There are several banks on Quezon Ave, including Equitable PCI Bank and Bank of the Philippine Islands (BPI), which have ATMs with international access.

For P40 an hour you can surf the Web at Internet Cafe, on the 3rd floor, Lassam Building on Governor Luna St; it's open from 9 am to 6.30 pm Monday to Friday.

Things to See & Do

The striking Taoist and Catholic Chinese **Ma-Cho Temple** sits atop a hill just north of San Fernando. The original image of the Virgin of Caysasay, the patroness of San Fernando's Filipino-Chinese community, is brought here every second week of September as part of the week-long activities in celebration of the Feast of the Virgin (the rest of the year a replica is on display). **The Museo de La Union** displays archaeological finds from the area. In front of the museum is **Freedom Park**, where statues of Filipino national heroes and presidents line the steps leading to the park. The large grounds of the **Botanical & Zoological Garden**, 6.5km east of the city, has a variety of plant life and pavilions.

You can **scuba dive** in the area, where you can see two Japanese tanks (at 41m). Ocean Deep (☎ 072-414 440, ✉ oceand@ net.com.ph) offers dives for US$35 per dive. They also offer scuba certification courses for US$270.

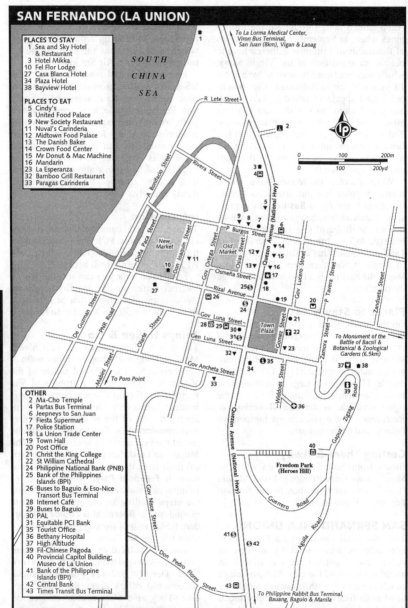

SAN FERNANDO (LA UNION)

PLACES TO STAY
1 Sea and Sky Hotel & Restaurant
3 Hotel Mikka
10 Fel Flor Lodge
27 Casa Blanca Hotel
34 Plaza Hotel
38 Bayview Hotel

PLACES TO EAT
5 Cindy's
8 United Food Palace
9 New Society Restaurant
11 Nuval's Carinderia
12 Midtown Food Palace
13 The Danish Baker
14 Crown Food Center
15 Mr Donut & Mac Machine
16 Mandarin
23 La Esperanza
32 Bamboo Grill Restaurant
33 Paragas Carinderia

OTHER
2 Ma-Cho Temple
4 Partas Bus Terminal
6 Jeepneys to San Juan
7 Fiesta Supermart
17 Police Station
18 La Union Trade Center
19 Town Hall
20 Post Office
21 Christ the King College
22 St William Cathedral
24 Philippine National Bank (PNB)
25 Bank of the Philippines Islands (BPI)
26 Buses to Baguio & Eso-Nice Transort Bus Terminal
28 Internet Café
29 Buses to Baguio
30 PAL
31 Equitable PCI Bank
35 Tourist Office
36 Bethany Hospital
37 High Altitude
39 Fil-Chinese Pagoda
40 Provincial Capitol Building; Museo de La Union
41 Bank of the Philippine Islands (BPI)
42 Central Bank
43 Times Transit Bus Terminal

SOUTH CHINA SEA

To La Lorma Medical Center,
Viron Bus Terminal,
San Juan (8km), Vigan & Laoag

R Lete Street

Rivera Street

A Bonifacio Street

Doña Paca Street

New Market

Don Joaquin Street

Gov Ortega Street

Olas Street

Old Market

P Burgos Street

Quezon Avenue (National Hwy)

Osmeña Street

Gov Lucero Street

P Tavera Street

Zandueta Street

Rizal Avenue

Gov Luna Street

Gen Luna Street

Town Plaza

Gomez Street

Zamora Street

To Monument of the Battle of Bacsil & Botanical & Zoological Gardens (6.5km)

Gov Ancheta Street

De Guzman Street

PNR Road

Olarte Street

Mabini Street

To Poro Point

Widdees Street

Quezon Avenue (National Hwy)

Gov Nisce Street

Don Pedro Flores Street

Capuz Zigzag Road

Freedom Park (Heroes Hill)

Guerrero Road

Aguila Road

Provincial Capitol Building; Museo de La Union

To Philippine Rabbit Bus Terminal,
Bauang, Baguio & Manila

0   100   200m
0   100   200yd

Surfing was first introduced to the Philippines by US servicemen based here in the 1960s. The stretch of coastline around San Juan, 8km north of San Fernando, draws surfers from November to February, when the surf is ideal for amateurs. It's a 10-minute jeepney ride to Urbiztondo beach, which is particularly popular with Australian and Japanese surfers. The Surf Shop (☎ 072-242 4544) offers lessons by Filipino, Japanese and Australian instructors, and also rents equipment: surfboards (P100 an hour), boogie boards (P50), windsurfers (P150) and a hobiecat (P300). Unfortunately, the water here isn't ideal for swimming, as the currents are quite strong.

Places to Stay
Bauang has the largest concentration of resorts; it's 6km south of San Fernando. San Juan, 8km north of San Fernando, and the coastline just north of San Juan is also dotted with places to stay. San Fernando has some accommodation, but be sure to ask for a room that's not facing the road, which roars with traffic day and night.

San Fernando *Hotel Mikka* (☎ 072-415 737) has clean standard rooms with air-con, cable TV, phone and hot water for P625/750 a single/double. A short distance up the street is the city's best hotel, *Sea and Sky Hotel & Restaurant* (☎ 072-415 279). Rooms with beautiful views cost P800, and have air-con, cable TV and hot water; for P1200 there's a gorgeous 2nd floor attic room. Basement rooms are P600 and rooms with highway views P700. Book ahead, as it's often full.

Bauang Dozens of resorts line the beachfront here, several of which are openly engaged in the sex trade. The following selection do not have 'nightclubs' and they do welcome female travellers; unfortunately, these tend to be more pricey. Peak season rates (October-May or June) are given; during the rest of the year rates drop by up to 20%.

Long Beach Resort Hotel (☎ 072-242 5673) has decent, if drab, rooms starting at P525/600 with fan/air-con. It also has a large restaurant on the waterfront. The smaller *Blue Lagoon* (☎ 072-412 531) has better, more cheerful rooms for P850, and a restaurant overlooking the water.

One of the biggest and most well-known resorts here is *Bali Hai Beach Resort* (☎ 072-242 5679, @ balihai@net.com.ph). Well-kept, clean rooms are P975/1250 with fan/air-con. It has a pool and a pretty beachfront restaurant. Another good, large resort in the area is *Cabaña* (☎ 072-242 5586), where rooms start at P1100 and there's a beautiful pool. The elegant *Villa Estrella*

AROUND BAUANG & SAN JUAN

SOUTH CHINA SEA

To Vigan
Cabaroan
Bacnotan
LA UNION
To San Gabriel
Baroro
Baroro River
Potteries
Santa Rosa
Tabok
Carusipan
Illi Norte
San Juan
Urbiztondo
Lingsat
La Lorma Medical Center
Carlatan
San Fernando

See San Fernando (La Union) Map – page 190

White Beach
San Francisco Airport
Canaoay
San Vicente
Pagudpud
Pagdalagan Norte
Pagdalagan Sur
Paringao
To Bauang (1km) & Manila

PLACES TO STAY & EAT
1 Scenic View Tourist Inn; German Sunset Beach Resort
2 Casa del Mar
3 Las Villas
4 Monaliza Beach Resort
5 Hacienda
6 Se-bay
7 La Union Surf Resort
10 Oasis Country Resort
11 Blue Lagoon
12 Tunuan Ti Bauang Restaurant
13 Bali Hai Beach Resort; South Pacific Resort; Sea Breeze
14 Cabaña
15 Coconut Grove Resort
16 Villa Estrella Resort Hotel
17 Long Beach Resort Hotel; North Palm Beach Resort

OTHER
8 Surf Shop
9 Tomb of the Unknown Soldier

NORTH LUZON

Resort Hotel (☎ 072-413 793) has large rooms (showing signs of wear) starting at P1450. On the highway is the area's newest hotel, *Oasis Country Resort*. It has clean, tasteful rooms with cable TV from P1695.

San Juan *Monaliza Beach Resort* (☎ 072-414 892) is a nice little place that has breezy rooms overlooking the sea for P300/600 a single/double. On Urbiztondo beach is *Hacienda* (☎ 072-242 1109), where slightly run-down rooms start at around P250. *Sebay* (☎ 072-242 5484) is a popular and friendly place with a large restaurant overlooking the beach. Dorm beds are P200, rooms with fan/air-con are P350/600. *La Union Surf Resort* (☎ 072-242 4544) has small cottages with fans for P500.

A couple of kilometres north of San Juan are a handful of isolated and well-managed resorts that are much nicer than those in Bauang, as is the beach. Exceptionally attractive is *Las Villas* (☎ 072-242 3770), where doubles start at P650. *German Sunset Beach Resort* (☎ 072-414 719) also has well-kept rooms with fan/air-con for P450/550. Next door is the large *Scenic View Tourist Inn* (☎ 072-413 901), which has a family atmosphere. Pleasant, clean rooms start at P525/690 with fan/air-con.

Places to Eat

San Fernando On the town plaza, *La Esperanza* is an open-front restaurant that serves reasonably priced Filipino food, pasta and delicious baked goods; try the fresh *lumpia* (vegetables wrapped in a rice pancake). For good Chinese-Filipino dishes try *Mandarin* on Quezon Ave. *United Food Palace*, on P Burgos St, serves cheap and tasty standard Filipino fare. The best streetside eatery in town is *Paragas Carinderia*, a couple of stalls down a small street, across from the Plaza Hotel.

Bauang Well-heeled Filipinos dine at some of the more upmarket resorts along the beach (which are also nice places to watch a sunset). The elegant *Villa Estrella* has a refined seaside restaurant with a good salad bar, as does *Cabaña*. Fans of red

meat should head to *Bali Hai* for a barbecue. *Oasis* has an inexpensive 24-hour outdoor roadside restaurant with daily specials for P50.

Entertainment

On a hill overlooking San Fernando is *High Altitude*, the most happening disco in town. The more refined *Villa Estrella* has bands starting around 8 pm most nights. *Cabaña* and *Long Beach Hotel*, often feature bands from Manila and also have shows. The area surrounding Poro Point junction is the main red-light district.

Getting There & Away

Asian Spirit flies from Manila to San Fernando at 11 am Monday, Wednesday, Friday and Saturday. Golden Passage has charter flights from Manila (P1600) at 7.30 am Tuesday and Friday, and at 1 pm Sunday.

Buses to Baguio (1½ hours) leave from Gov Luna St every 15 minutes, with the last one leaving around 6.30 pm. Philippine Rabbit has hourly buses to Baguio. The last bus departs at 11.30 pm. To Manila (seven hours), Philippine Rabbit has hourly buses 24 hours a day. Partas Bus has air-con buses (P206) from 2 am until 12.30 pm. If you're heading to Vigan (P108, four hours), Philippine Rabbit has regular buses from 1 am to 7 pm, and Partas Bus has air-con buses leaving every 30 minutes (24 hours).

Central Cordillera

The Cordillera is comprised of Baguio City and five provinces: Benguet, Ifugao, Mountain Province, Abra and Kalinga-Apayao. There are no passable roads connecting Abra with other Cordillera provinces.

The Igorot people of the area pride themselves on having a strong sense of community and culture, and on having resisted assimilation relatively successfully. The environment, however, has been less successful against modern life: gold and copper mining have resulted in much deforestation, especially in the southernmost provinces.

April and May show the rice terraces at Banaue, in the Central Cordilleras, at their best.

Waterfall near Sagada, North Luzon.

Hundred Islands National Park, North Luzon.

Woodcarving, Banaue.

The extraordinary hanging coffins of Sagada, North Luzon.

Calesas (horse-drawn carriages) are still widely used in Vigan, North Luzon.

Cathedral in Vigan, North Luzon.

Paoay Lake, North Luzon.

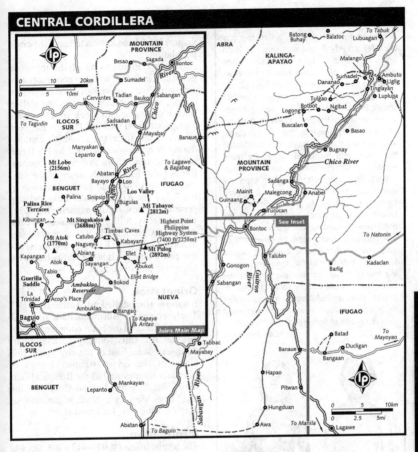

CENTRAL CORDILLERA

The best time to visit is in the dry season, from November to May. Rice planting season, which begins in November, is a good time to see festivals and celebrations, including *cañao*, a time of feasting and drinking, during which animal sacrifices take place. In December and January, especially at higher altitudes (eg, Sagada), it's not unusual for the temperature to drop below 10°C, perfect for hiking. In February the weather begins to warm. March through to May are the warmest and driest months. April and May are the best months to see the Banaue rice terraces.

BAGUIO

Baguio (pronounced 'ba-gee-oh') was originally constructed by US military forces as a mountain retreat in the early 1900s. Nicknamed the 'Summer Capital', its cool climate attracts Manila's wealthy when the lowlands are sweltering. The area's original inhabitants are the Ibaloi and Kankana-ey. Much of the Igorot ancestral land in this region has been developed, and members of these tribes assimilated into present-day society. Although most foreign travellers stay only overnight en route to Sagada or Banaue, Filipinos make this a destination.

Bulol Carving

According to tribal legend, an Ifugao boy once fell gravely ill and was close to death when he looked up from his sickbed to see two branches of a *narra* tree (the yellow-flowered national tree of the Philippines) entwining before his eyes. From these branches sprang Bugan and Wigan, the husband-and-wife team whom the Ifugao believe first populated the earth. Instantly, the boy was cured, and ever since Ifugao boys have celebrated their entry into manhood by carving these deities, known collectively as *bulol* (or *bulul*).

Such figures are often used to keep evil spirits away from Ifugao rice stores, or even to increase rice yields after poor harvests. Usually carved as a male and female pair, the bulol were – according to Ifugao mythology – first fashioned from a narra tree by the spirit god, Humidhid. Genuine bulol are carved from the hardy core of the narra tree, ensuring resistance against the elements of the earth-bound world and the spiritual world. To ensure maximum bulol power, Ifugao carvers try to use the wood of a narra tree growing near the house of the intended bulol patrons.

Caroline Liou

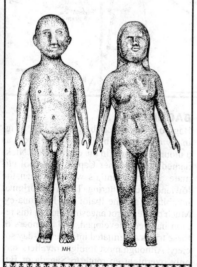

MH

From March to May, Baguio experiences a population surge, and during Holy Week visitors have been known to triple the city's population.

Baguio's appeal as an idyllic mountain getaway has faded, with the construction of a massive mall, the lack of good accommodation, water shortages, smog and traffic-ridden streets and the lack of convenient transportation to the city. The city has been rebuilt twice since the mid-20th century: during WWII it was flattened by US forces staging bombing raids to drive out Japanese forces (who had already deserted the city) and then in 1990 by an earthquake measuring 7.7 on the Richter scale. Gold and copper mining (now hardly existent) has led to water scarcity. Still, Baguio makes a worthwhile stop, particularly if you're interested in handicrafts, local food (eg, dog meat) and the city's active nightlife, propelled by a large student population.

Orientation

Baguio was modelled on Washington, DC. The rectangular Burnham Park is in the city's centre, and the main commercial hub, Session Rd, runs roughly parallel to its north-east side. East of the city you'll find many of the lavish summer homes of Manila's elite, as well as the Botanical Gardens, Wright Park, Baguio Country Club and Mines View Park. North of Baguio is its neighbouring city, La Trinidad.

Information

The tourist office (☎ 074-442 6708, fax 442 8848) is on Governor Pack Rd and is open from 8 am to noon and from 1 to 5 pm daily.

There are several branches of Equitable PCI Bank along Session Rd, where the ATMs accept MasterCard and Cirrus. Also on Session Rd is Bookmark, which has a small selection of travel guides and some Philippines classics, including the works of José Rizal.

Check your email at Cyberspace, Inc (☎ 074-443 8734) on the ground floor of the Mount Crest Hotel. Rates are P100 an hour on weekdays (P60 for students) and P50 an hour on weekends. It is open from 8 am to 1 am daily.

BAGUIO

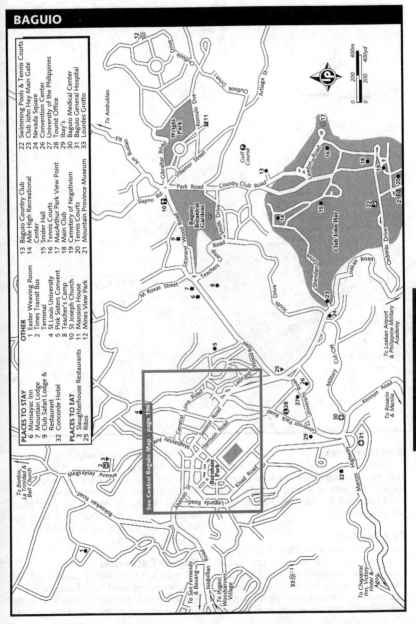

PLACES TO STAY
6 Munsayac Inn
7 Mountain Lodge
9 Club Safari Lodge & Restaurant
32 Concorde Hotel

PLACES TO EAT
3 Slaughterhouse Restaurants
25 Ritos

OTHER
1 Easter Weaving Room
2 Times Transit Bus Terminal
4 St Louis University
5 Pink Sisters Convent
8 Teacher's Camp
10 St Joseph Church
11 Mansion House
12 Mines View Park
13 Baguio Country Club
14 Mile High Recreational Center
15 Snider Hall
16 Tennis Courts
17 MacArthur Park View Point
18 Main Club
19 Cemetery of Negativism
20 Tennis Courts
21 Mountain Province Museum
22 Swimming Pools & Tennis Courts
23 Club John Hay Main Gate
24 Nevada Square
26 Convention Center
27 University of the Philippines
28 Tourist Office
29 Ibay's
30 Baguio Medical Center
31 Baguio General Hospital
33 Lourdes Grotto

See Central Baguio Map – page 196

NORTH LUZON

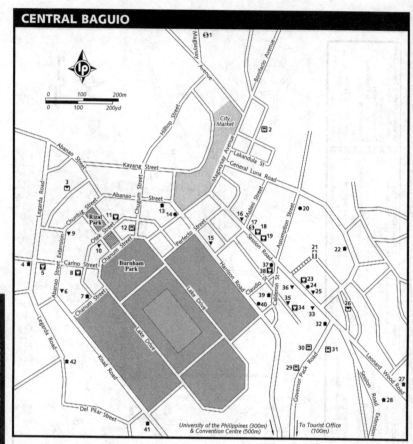

CENTRAL BAGUIO

Burnham Park

Centrally located, Burnham Park is named after the American architect who planned Baguio. The park is centred around an artificial lake, and is a pleasant place to stroll and people-watch.

City Market

Just north of Burnham Park, City Market is a maze covering three sq km. You'll find vendors selling everything from fruit, vegetables, meat, dozens of varieties of rice, coffee, tobacco and the ubiquitous peanut brittle and strawberry jam. As well

as food it has a large selection of handicrafts, including silver jewellery, weavings and woodcarvings. Although the handicrafts are of the mass-produced-for-tourists variety, the market is a great place to get lost for a few hours. The sight and smell of the food alone is reason enough to spend time here.

Baguio Cathedral

Set on a hill overlooking Session Rd, the twin-spired cathedral served as a barter centre and refuge for 5000 locals during the heavy bombing of the city during WWII.

CENTRAL BAGUIO

PLACES TO STAY
4   Mount Crest Hotel;
    Cyberspace Inc; Gimbal's
7   Benguet Pine Tourist Inn
13 Baguio Hotel Ambassador
22 Citylight Hotel
27 El Cielito Inn
28 Casa Vallejo
32 The Baden Powell Inn
37 Prime Hotel; Benguet
    Supermarket
39 Burnham Hotel; Cook's Inn
    Restaurant
41 Inn Rocio
42 Baguio Palace Hotel

PLACES TO EAT
6   Kamimura
9   Cafe by the Ruins

10 O'Mai Khan
15 Rose Bowl Restaurant
16 Star Cafe
25 Don Henrico's
33 Mario's Steakhouse
35 Ritos
36 Sizzling Plate

OTHER
1   Equitable PCI Bank
2   Dangwa Tranco Bus
    Terminal; Lizardo Trans Bus
    Terminal
3   Post Office; City Hall
5   Alberto's
8   Spirits
11 Wild West
12 Eso-nice Transport Bus
    Terminal

14 Maharlika Livelihood
    Center
17 Equitable PCI Bank
18 Rumours
19 TP Kafe
20 St Louis Filigree Shop
21 Bagio Cathedral
23 Ionic Cafe
24 Bookmark
26 Post Office
29 Philippine Rabbit Bus
    Terminal
30 Byron Bus Terminal Dagupan
    Bus Terminal; Partas Bus
    Terminal
31 Victory Liner Bus Terminal
34 Backstreet
38 Cafe San Luis
40 Avis Rent-a-Car; PAL Office

You can get to the cathedral from the concrete stairs off Session Rd.

Lourdes Grotto
Established by Spanish Jesuits in 1907, the small grotto sits at the top of 252 steps (if you don't want to climb the steps, you can also drive to the grotto). There's a nice view from here of the city's rooftops.

Camp John Hay
Formerly a US military rest and recreation facility, Camp John Hay is currently being renovated into an upmarket vacation resort. Although the US' lease on the land expired in 1991, the US ambassador to the Philippines still has a summer house here. WWII in the Philippines began and ended here: the first bomb to hit the Philippines was dropped here by the Japanese in 1941, and this is where General Yamashita signed the Japanese surrender four years later. The sprawling, 360-hectare, pine-covered grounds include hiking trails and a golf course. Worth a look is the prettily landscaped **Bell amphitheatre**, just across from the **Cemetery of Negativity**, where peculiar epitaphs are engraved on mock gravestones (eg, 'Knot A Teemplayer, Born a Star, Lived a Meteor, Died in Flames'). The **Mile High viewpoint** here has a nice vantage point,

without having to wade through loads of souvenir stalls.

Baguio Botanical Gardens
North of Camp John Hay, off Leonard Wood Rd, is the Botanical Gardens, where you'll find souvenir stalls, some Igorot houses and a few Igorot people in tribal costume, who, for a few pesos, will pose for a photo. The park is also becoming a place for the homeless.

Wright Park & Mansion House
East of the Botanical Gardens is Wright Park, where parents come to bring their kids to ride ponies around a track. Across the street from Wright Park is Mansion House, the president's summer home. The ostentatious gate is modelled on that of Buckingham Palace.

Mines View Park
Baguio's most well-known viewpoint, Mines View Park, is basically a small viewing platform at the end of a long row of souvenir stalls. Still, there's an interesting view of the mines (no longer operational) carved into the Benguet mountain range. Within walking distance is the **Good Shepherd Convent**, where the sisters sell the best strawberry jam, *ube* jam and peanut brittle

NORTH LUZON

in the city. Proceeds go towards advocacy programs for unwed mothers.

To get here from Baguio, take the Plaza-Kias-PMA jeepney.

Philippine Military Academy

Referred to as the 'West Point of the Philippines,' this is a popular tourist destination for Filipinos. The visitor centre houses a small **museum** with an eclectic collection of military memorabilia. There are also nice views of the Benguet mountain range from here.

From Baguio, take the Plaza-Kias-PMA jeepney for about 30 minutes.

Tam-awan Village

Created by the originators of Cafe by the Ruins (see Places to Eat later), Tam-awan (literally, 'vantage point') is a 'village' of eight Ifugao houses transplanted from Banga-an (near Banaue) to Baguio's suburbs. It has been laid out to resemble a traditional Ifugao village, and aims to be a living museum that fosters a deeper understanding of the Cordillera people's cultural heritage. It has a pleasant cafe/art gallery where you can sip native coffee and buy quality souvenirs, and if you're lucky, there may also be some artists at work.

Bell Church

The Bell Church is a cluster of small, ornate, pagoda-roofed temples set on a hill near La Trinidad. Though originally a Buddhist temple, the priest here practises a mix of Buddhism, Taoism, Confucianism and Christianity. You can also get your fortune told.

La Trinidad

Baguio's neighbouring city and the capital of Benguet province, La Trinidad has a few interesting sights. Farmers from remote regions deliver their mounds of vegetables, packed tight into every crevice of their jeepney, to the **vegetable market**, and it's from here that the produce is distributed to other markets in the area. **Benguet State University** has a food processing and training centre where you can watch bread, strawberry jam and ube jam being made.

Locals say this is the best and cheapest place for these items, and you can also pick strawberries here.

The tourist office, in the Provincial Capitol Building grounds, can help arrange climbs up nearby **Mt Pulog**. There's also a small **museum** here, displaying native farming implements and traditional costumes. It's open from 8 am to noon and from 1 to 5 pm Monday to Friday.

Places to Stay – Budget

Good budget accommodation in Baguio is limited. If you're arriving on a weekend or holiday, it's best to reserve ahead. Although not very clean, the *Benguet Pine Tourist Inn* (☎ 074-442 7325, 82 Chanum St), on the corner of Ortek St, has some of the cheapest accommodation in town. Dorm beds are P220, and standard doubles with shared/private bath are P415/690, breakfast included.

Casa Vallejo (☎ 074-442 3045 or 442 4601, ✉ vallejo@mozcom.com, 111 Session Rd) has clean, spacious rooms with shared bath for P475/725/875 a single/double/triple, including a hearty breakfast. Try to get a room not facing the road as the traffic is pretty noisy. The chic and hip *Citylight Hotel* (☎ 074-444 7544, 245 Upper General Luna Rd) is less cosy, but you can get a tiny single for P280, with shared bath, cable TV and phone. Doubles are from P850 to P2800; the Bachelor's Pad includes a living room, bar and balcony.

The Baden Powell Inn (☎ 074-442 5836), on the corner of Governor Pack and Session Rds, has decent dorm beds for P300 including breakfast; rooms with private bath are P850. The rooms are quiet and the hotel has a cosy bar and restaurant with an outdoor deck.

Places to Stay – Mid-Range

Away from the bustle of Session Rd, on a small hill among pine trees, is *Inn Rocio* (☎ 074-442 6535, 63 Kisad Rd). Small but clean and well-maintained doubles with cable TV are P750. The restaurant here is famous for its Blum pie, a tasty concoction of cappuccino and chocolate mousse.

Another good option is the friendly *Baguio Hotel Ambassador* (☎ 074-442 5078, 25 Abanao St), where plain but clean doubles cost P680. The conveniently located *Burnham Hotel* (☎ 074-442 2331, 20 Calderon St) is cosy, and nicely decorated with native handicrafts. Doubles are P980.

Away from busy Session Rd, *Munsayac Inn* (☎ 074-442 6897) has doubles with TV and refrigerator for P950. There's a good handicraft shop downstairs, a cosy restaurant that serves free coffee. Next door is *Mountain Lodge* (☎ 074-442 4544, 27 Leonard Wood Rd), where clean, comfortable rooms are P700/800. The first thing you'll notice at *Club Safari Lodge & Restaurant* (☎ 074-442 2419, 191 Leonard Wood Rd) is the huge elephant head on the wall – right next to the rhino head, the boar head, the lion head and the leopard head. Rooms here start at P1000. The Plaza-Mines View jeepney travels between Club Safari and the town centre.

Places to Stay – Top End
Baguio's newest and most swanky hotel is *Concorde Hotel* (☎ 074-443 2058), in Europa Center on Legarda Rd. Tasteful standard rooms are P1485 and the hotel has a gym, 24-hour coffee shop and several restaurants. Closer to town is *El Cielito Inn* (☎ 074-442 8743, 50 North Dr), where rooms with a phone start at P1296/1548 a single/double.

The well-known *Baguio Palace Hotel* (☎ 074-442 7734), on Legarda Rd, is a well-kept, convention-type hotel with large, clean rooms starting at P1500. Similar, and just down the street, is *Mount Crest Hotel* (☎ 074-443 9421), where rooms are P1300/1400. The centrally located *Prime Hotel* (☎ 074-442 7066), on the corner of Session Rd and Calderon St, is no longer in its prime, but has acceptable rooms for P1200.

Places to Eat
A favourite of locals, *Rose Bowl Restaurant* serves Filipino-Chinese food, such as chop suey (P130), steamed shrimp (P180) and some American dishes. Also very popular is *Cafe by the Ruins*. It's touted as an artists' hang-out, although you're just as likely to see teens with cell phones. The food is excellent and the surroundings elegant. Try Auntie Cecile's Chicken Adobo (P145), the eggplant flan (P105) or chocolate rice porridge served with smoked fish (P90). The Ruins coffee with cinnamon is delicious.

Ritos serves delicious *bulalo* (beef bone soup; P85 for two), perfect on a chilly day, and great *pinakbut* (P50). Ritos has two locations (both on back streets away from the exhaust fumes): behind the district engineer's office, a short stroll from Casa Vallejo on Upper Engineer's Hill; and on Diego Silang St, a small street parallel to Session Rd. Another local favourite is *Kamimura*, (literally, 'we're cheap'), where you can get good tempura (P105), teppanyaki (P95) and teriyaki (P95). If you're in the mood for Mongolian barbecue (P145) and white table cloths, *O'Mai Khan* won't disappoint.

Carnivores will appreciate the *slaughterhouse restaurants*, next to the slaughterhouse on Magsaysay Ave, where authentic home-cooking is served in a setting that isn't as bad as it sounds. The best is *Balahadia's*, a plain but pleasant eatery with bamboo furniture. *Inihaw* (roast pork) is roasted right in front of the restaurant. *Kambing* (goat intestines; P40) and *papaitan* (beef) are also tasty, or if you're really adventurous try dog meat, a specialty here.

There are several good places to eat along Session Rd, including the popular *Don Henrico's* for pizza, and *Sizzling Plate*, where you can get sizzling plates of tasty meat for reasonable prices, such as pork chops (P50), fillet mignon (P130) or BBQ chicken (P69). Also worth a try is *Star Cafe* for Chinese food; try the *pancit* canton (stir-fried noodles with vegetables and meat).

For fine dining, *Mario's Steakhouse* is known for its paella and steak.

Entertainment
As well as being a retreat for Manila's elite, Baguio is a college town, and consequently there's no shortage of nightlife. A great place see live music is *Wild West* (48 Otek St), a grungy, cavernous country and western bar

NORTH LUZON

near the Eso-nice bus station. Even if you're not a country music fan, this is a fun place to experience the Benguet cowboy phenomenon. Other places to listen to live bands are *Gimbal's*, in the Mount Crest Hotel; and *Alberto's*, across the street. *Cafe San Luis*, just off Session Rd, has pop and new-wave bands nightly.

The spiffy but laid-back *Backstreet* is a pleasant bar to relax and have a drink. It's off the main road, so you get a break from the exhaust fumes. *Rumours*, on Session Rd, is a good down-to-earth bar to relax and have a beer or two. It also has good fruity drinks. Next to Rumours, on the second floor, the long and narrow *TP Kafe* starts jumping late at night and stays open till 4 am. Also on Session Rd, *Ionic Cafe* is a smoky, dimly lit place where you can have a coffee or a beer and appetisers. The trendiest place in town is at *Citylight Hotel*, on General Luna Rd.

Spirits is an upmarket disco, complete with red-velvet furniture and a P150 cover charge. On the third floor is *E3* (no cover), where you can surf the Internet for P120 an hour, which includes one drink.

Shopping

Baguio is a good place to buy local handicrafts, including weavings, wood-carvings, baskets and reasonably priced silver jewellery. The city market sells mostly low-quality handicrafts; for higher-quality weavings (at higher prices), try the Easter Weaving Room. A *tapis* (traditional wrap skirt) costs P710.

Good places to buy silver are St Louis Filigree and Ibay's. St Louis sells silverware sets, jewellery, picture frames and even intricate silver nativity scenes. You can see artisans at work in the building next door. Ibay's has a wider and more modern selection, and you can also watch items being made. For one-stop shopping, Munsayac Inn has a large shop with a good selection of wood-carvings and other souvenirs. For legitimate antiques, try Teresita's, on Upper General Luna St, Christine's Gallery, on Chanum St, or Sabado's, on Outlook Dr.

Other famous Baguio products are strawberry jam and peanut brittle. See the Mines View Park and La Trinidad entries earlier this section. Pink Sisters Convent also sells delicious cookies and other homemade goodies.

Getting There & Away

Air At the time of writing PAL had discontinued services to Baguio. Asian Spirit flies from Manila once a day, departing at 9.30 am and arriving in Baguio at 10.30 am (P1098). To Manila, the flight departs Baguio at 11 am, arriving at noon. The Asian Spirit (☎ 074-442 5838) office is in Nevada Square. Air Philippines flies from Manila to Baguio at 10.30 am Tuesday, Thursday, Saturday and Sunday.

Bus There are three main roads to Baguio: Kennon Rd (aka Zigzag Rd), which is only open to light vehicles; the Marcos Hwy, which buses to/from Manila take; and if you're coming from San Fernando, the Naguillian Rd.

Frequent Philippine Rabbit, Victory Liner, Dagupan Bus and Dangwa Tranco buses go from Manila to Baguio (six hours) via Angeles. From Dagupan, Philippine Rabbit, Victory Liner and Byron Bus make frequent trips (P50, 2½ hours). From San Fernando, buses to Baguio leave from Governor Luna St every 15 minutes, with the last one leaving at 6.30 pm (1½ hours). Philippine Rabbit has hourly buses to Baguio, the last leaving at 11.30 pm.

From Sagada to Baguio, buses leave hourly from 6 to 10.30am. To Sagada (P136, seven hours), Lizardo Trans buses depart from the Dangwa terminal hourly between 6.45 and 11.45 am each day. From Bontoc to Baguio, a Dangwa bus leaves at 6 am, and a D'Rising Sun bus at 2 pm. To Bontoc, D'Rising Sun buses depart from next to the Times Transit terminal hourly from 4.45 am to 3 pm.

For buses to/from Kabayan and Banaue, see those sections later in this chapter.

To Cabanatuan (en route to Baler), Summerbloom Bus departs from near the Dagupan bus terminal at 7.30 am and 1 and 3 pm.

MT PULOG

Rising 2892m, Mt Pulog is the second highest peak in the Philippines, after Mt Apo in Mindanao. Most climbers start from Baguio (and overnight there) and complete the climb in two days. From Baguio, Ambangeg (the starting point at the base of the mountain) is a six hour drive (60km). From here it's an eight to nine hour climb to the top; from the rangers' station it takes hours. The climb is more challenging if you start from just outside Kabayan central. For climbing information contact the Benguet tourist office or Department of Environment & Natural Resources (DENR) in Baguio.

KABAYAN

A quiet vegetable-farming town nestled in a broad valley, Kabayan was catapulted to fame in the 1970s when mummies were 'discovered' by the outside world. The mummies, believed to be over 500 years old, are unique to this region, and only nine other cultures practise mummification worldwide. Found in caves, the mummies are placed in foetal position in short coffins made from hollowed-out tree trunks.

Soon after the mummies were found, they began disappearing from their burial places, and have reportedly been spotted in private museums in Hawaii and Australia. Some of the caves are now locked and the locations of others are fiercely guarded. If you visit the caves, consider whether you're willing to disturb the burial place: locals customarily make offerings of gin and *pinikpikan* (a special chicken dish) before entering the caves.

Mummies aside, Kabayan is a nice place for scenic hiking and clean air. After dark the town quietens, and the stars are a remarkable sight. Kabayan is believed to be the site of the first Ibaloi settlement, and Ibaloi is the main dialect spoken here. The area is also known for producing excellent, strong Arabica coffee and aromatic and tasty *Kinto-man* (red) rice.

Things to See & Do

To get a good overview of the area's history and culture, your first stop should be the Kabayan branch of the **National Museum**, in a small house just beyond the bridge leading west from town. It has some mummies on display, including one in a carabao-shaped wooden coffin and another with its tattooed skin still intact. Also on display are artefacts of local tribes, the Ibaloi, Kankanai and Ikalahan, and descriptions of some of their rituals. The friendly curator may be able to guide you to some of the surrounding caves. The museum is open from 8 am to noon and from 1 to 5 pm Monday to Friday.

Behind the building next to Kabayan Farm Supply is the **Opdas Mass Burial Cave**. The cave contains hundreds of skulls and bones believed to be between 500 and 1000 years old. There's a gate at the cave entrance; you can ask for the key at the small *sari-sari* (convenience) store nearby.

About 3km from town is the **Tinongchal Burial Rock**, a large rock bored with eight holes into which several coffins have been placed. A footpath next to the museum leads here.

The **Bangao Cave** is about 6km from Kabayan. The hike (approximately six hours return) takes you past some beautiful views of the vegetable fields. From the town of Bangao, a 40-minute climb up a steep trail leads to the cave, which contains five coffins.

Bulalacao Lake, about 12km from town at the foot of Mt Pulog, is a pristine mountain lake. To visit Bulalacao you should have a guide, as the trails are not marked. Juliet Igloso, curator at the Kabayan National Museum, may guide you or be able to help you find a guide. It's also possible to drive most of the way to Bangao and Bulalacao, but the road is rough and you'll need a 4WD. A ride to Bangao is about P500, or P1000 to Bangao and Bulalacao.

Places to Stay & Eat

Kabayan Coop Lodge is the only place to stay in the area. Clean but rustic rooms are P100 night, all with shared bath. Next door is the *Brookside Cafe*, where you can get good, strong Arabica coffee and if you're lucky, Kinto-man rice. There are a couple of other places to eat about 50m down the road.

NORTH LUZON

If you plan to eat later than 7 pm let the restaurant know, as things shut early here.

Getting There & Away

The Norton Trans bus leaves Baguio for Kabayan (P70, five hours) at 9 and 10 am and noon daily. The terminal is next to the Times Transit terminal. Bring a bandanna as most of the road is unpaved and the trip gets extremely dusty. From Kabayan to Baguio, there are three Norton Trans buses daily. There is no fixed schedule, but they usually run between 7 am and noon.

You can go from Kabayan to Abatan, and meet a bus going to Sagada or Bontoc. From Kabayan, you must hire a private jeep to Soysoyesen, Gujaran (P200, about 40 minutes) and from there catch the bus to Abatan, Bugias, which leaves at 6.30 am (P40, about two hours, one trip daily). From Abatan you can catch one of several buses travelling from Baguio to Sagada (P60) or Bontoc, the last passing through Abatan around 3pm.

SAGADA

Sagada is a tranquil mountain-top town (population 3000, altitude 1500m) where you can walk down the middle of the road and only rarely be disturbed by a lone passing vehicle. Pine trees and rice terraces dominate the landscape, and the beautiful scenery and cool climate make this an excellent place to hike and just appreciate nature.

Despite its popularity, Sagada has for the most part managed to stave off changes that would detract from its appeal as an 'ecotourism' destination – there are no massive luxury hotels or blaring discos, and for many Sagadans, the traditional way of life remains intact. Sagadans are of Kankanay ancestry, and their native language is Kankanay, although, as in the rest of the Cordilleras, Ilocano and English are widely spoken.

Sagada's claim to tourism fame is its hanging coffins, seen on cliffsides surrounding the town and in limestone caves. Sagada's appeal also lies in its relaxed atmosphere. In addition it has some good restaurants serving great food, friendly, laid-back locals and reasonably priced accommodation.

Sagada gets chilly at night, especially from December to February, when temperatures drop as low as 4°C. From March to May temperatures rise as high as 30°C in the day. The rest of the year is the wet season, during which it rains most afternoons and the Halsema Hwy (the road between Baguio and Sagada) becomes difficult to negotiate.

Information

The tourist information centre is in the municipal building. It requests a P10 fee, which goes towards environmental protection and the restoration of tourist sights. It sells a detailed map (P7.50) of the area and arranges guides to the Sumaging Cave or Bomod-ok Waterfall. The post office is also in this building.

In the lower level of the building is the Sagada Rural Bank, which will change travellers cheques and cash (US dollars only) at a poor exchange rate. You're best off changing money in Bontoc or before you arrive in Sagada. It's open from 8 to 11.45 am and from 1.15 to 4.30 pm Tuesday to Saturday. Across from the bank there's a small store that sells domestic newspapers, including the *Inquirer*, and lends books.

There is no phone line in Sagada, although there are plans to install a public phone. You can send telegraphs from the municipal building.

Dangers & Annoyances

In mid-1999, two women, in separate incidents and both hiking alone in broad daylight, were reportedly robbed while in the Lumiang Cave/Sumaging area. This (female) author did most of the hikes alone and had no problems, but it's obviously safer if you can find someone to hike with.

When exploring Sumaging Cave you need a guide to show you the way and to provide gas lanterns and rope, which may be necessary in some areas. Recently a tourist fell 53m to his death in the Matangkib Burial Cave (currently closed) while exploring without a guide. Check with the tourist information centre for areas to avoid.

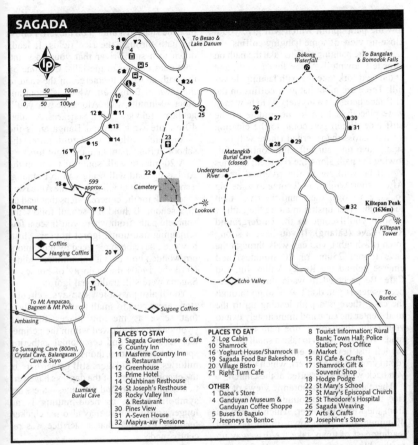

SAGADA

PLACES TO STAY
3 Sagada Guesthouse & Cafe
6 Country Inn
11 Masferre Country Inn & Restaurant
12 Greenhouse
13 Prime Hotel
14 Olahbinan Resthouse
24 St Joseph's Resthouse
28 Rocky Valley Inn & Restaurant
30 Pines View
31 A-Seven House
32 Mapiya-aw Pensione

PLACES TO EAT
2 Log Cabin
10 Shamrock
16 Yoghurt House/Shamrock II
19 Sagada Food Bar Bakeshop
20 Village Bistro
21 Right Turn Cafe

OTHER
1 Daoa's Store
4 Ganduyan Museum & Ganduyan Coffee Shoppe
5 Buses to Baguio
7 Jeepneys to Bontoc
8 Tourist Information; Rural Bank; Town Hall; Police Station; Post Office
9 Market
15 RJ Cafe & Crafts
17 Shamrock Gift & Souvenir Shop
18 Hodge Podge
22 St Mary's School
23 St Mary's Episcopal Church
25 St Theodore's Hospital
26 Sagada Weaving
27 Arts & Crafts
29 Josephine's Store

Hiking

It's an interesting one-hour hike through **Echo Valley**, a sacred burial area where you'll see many **hanging coffins** high on the surrounding limestone cliffs. There are many intersecting paths through the valley and it's tricky to figure out which way to go. Following is one route, which takes about an hour, taking you past some interesting scenery.

Walk past St Mary's Episcopal Church, then up the steps to the left. At the top of the steps (don't enter the gate) follow the path left to the cemetery. Most Sagada natives are now buried, although some members of the older generation are still put to rest in burial caves or hanging coffins. At the cemetery go left to the top of the hill, then down the path leading to the right. Walk between the rocks to the path on the right leading down. Continue to the right when the path intersects with others. When you come to the lone pine tree on the edge of the rockface, take the path going down. From here you should be able to see hanging coffins across the valley both in front of you and on your right side. Go through the broken wooden gate and at the next fork go left. At the fork after that go right, then follow the path uphill, which will give you a close-up view of some hanging coffins.

From the hanging coffins take the path on your left downhill. At the fork go left, and at the next fork take the path leading downhill. There are more hanging coffins on the cliff face here; it's a mystery as to how they were placed so high in the middle of the cliff face. When you come to the clearing go left. Cross the riverbed (there will be a small cave on your left) and continue following the path along the riverbed; at times you'll be walking in the riverbed itself. After a short while you'll come to some big rocks; cross over these and the river, then follow the river upstream along the path.

Soon you'll come to the **Underground River Cave (Latang)**. If you have a strong torch (flashlight), you can walk through the cave (about 250m, or 20 minutes) and emerge behind the Rocky Valley Inn and Cafe. Be prepared to wade through knee-deep water. If you don't want to go through the cave, there is a path leading up to the road – enter the cave and immediately exit to your right, then follow the path up to the road. A third option is to take a small path on the left just before the entrance to the cave (don't cross over the river), which will bring you back where you started at the church.

There are superb panoramic views of the rice terraces and surrounding mountains from the **Kiltepan tower**, which is about a 40-minute hike from town. From the road leading east of town, take the driveway up to the Mapiya-aw Pensione. Before you reach the pensione take the stone path on your right going uphill (don't go through the gate). At the top of the ridge the path forks; go left. When you see the fence on your left, walk right along the better-marked grass path to a dirt road and follow this uphill. If you don't want to take the same route back, follow the dirt road down to the main road; from there it's a longer walk back to town (although you may get lucky and be able to hitch a ride).

About a half-hour walk outside of town are the small **Bokong Waterfalls**, where on a hot day you can take a refreshing dip.

From town, walk past Sagada Weaving and take the steps just after it on the left. Follow the path through the rice fields. It leads down to a small river that you cross and continues upriver to the falls. Continue on the path and you'll emerge on the road to the town of **Banga-an**, which is about another 40-minute walk. Along the way you'll get beautiful views of rice terraces. Another 40-minute walk beyond Banga-an is the picturesque village of **Aguid** (after the school in Banga-an, take the right fork).

A 20-minute walk south of town on the Ambasing road will bring you to **Demang**, a small traditional village. On the Ambasing road, look for the concrete steps that lead up to a school. Behind the school follow the concrete path, from where you'll see a few remaining traditional **Igorot houses**. Most, however, have been replaced by more modern wooden houses with aluminium siding. Until the 1960s the majority of houses in Sagada were still traditional Igorot.

You'll also pass a few **dap-ays** – circular stone areas next to small thatched-roof huts that serve as meeting places for men (women are not allowed within the perimeter), as spiritual and ceremonial gathering spots, as well as courthouses and even dormitories. Male villagers still gather here in the evenings. Some of the dap-ays have vertical sculptures around the edges – these are symbolic heads, as head-hunting is no longer practised. You may also see chicken feathers, evidence that a sacrifice was recently made.

Continue on the concrete path and you'll pass through some rice paddies, emerging from the paddies at a patch of land where no houses are built. This is the site of a massacre in the 19th century, in which the neighbouring tribe, the Bontocs, reputedly killed close to 100 Sagadans. The path will lead you back up to the main road, next to Dao-Angan Enterprises (near the Yoghurt House).

Less than a 1½-hour walk from town is **Mt Ampacao**, from where there are also beautiful views of rice terraces, surrounding towns and Mt Polis. On the road south from town continue past the Right Turn Cafe till you see some concrete steps on the right side of the road. Go up the steps to the school, and behind it (to the right of the elementary school building), take the dirt path on the left, which leads to the mountain top. You can continue from here to **Lake Danom**, which you can also reach by taking the road to Besao; it's about an hour's walk from town.

Bomod-ok Falls (Big Waterfall) were off-limits to tourists without a guide at the time of writing, due to a tribal land dispute between two villages. To get there, take the road to Banga-an, and from there it's a one-hour hike up to the waterfall, which is surrounded by rice terraces.

Caving
On the road to Ambasing, just before the Right Turn Cafe, you can catch a glimpse of the **Sugong coffins** from the road. A short distance after the Right Turn, you'll see a paved road going off to your left. Follow the paved road and you'll see a path to your left. This path leads down to the **Lumiang Burial Cave**, where over 100 coffins are stacked in the entrance. The oldest is believed to be about 500 years old, and there are longer coffins (which aren't carved from tree trunks) that are only 15 years old. From the main road you can see more coffins off the right-hand side of the road.

A short distance further down the road is the path leading to **Sumaging (Big Cave)**. You must have a guide to explore this cave, who will likely take you to 'King's Curtain', from where you can go down to the 'swimming pool' (freezing but crystal clear). Just above the pool you can see some interesting fossilised shells. Also, don't miss the 'rice terraces'.

You can descend further to smaller pathways, where you'll have to negotiate some very small entrances. The rocks in the cave have been worn smooth, giving them an otherworldly look. They're made of limestone and calcium bicarbonate, which gives them a glittering effect. It's a good idea to wear shorts when exploring the cave as you'll have to wade through knee-deep water at times. Before you get to the wet part of the cave, your guide will advise you

to remove your shoes, so you can grip the rocks better. The tourist information centre has fixed prices for guides (P300 for up to five people), so arrange a guide through it.

Loko-ong (Crystal Cave) is closed indefinitely, due to looting of stalactites, and **Matangkib Burial Cave** is also closed (see Dangers & Annoyances earlier).

Other Attractions
On the outskirts of town is the **St Mary's Episcopal Church**, first established in 1905 by a US Episcopalian priest. The church is a stone building with stained-glass windows, and the grounds include a basketball court, co-op store, hospital, high school and cemetery. Most Sagadans are now buried in this cemetery, rather than in hanging coffins.

Well worth a look are the photos of Sagada-born photographer Eduardo Masferre, on display in the **Masferre Inn** and in his **studio** (although it's open infrequently) just outside town. His photos, which have been exhibited worldwide, including at the Smithsonian Institute in Washington, DC, depict Cordillera natives during the mid-20th century.

You can watch weavers at work at **Sagada Weaving**, where traditional Bontoc patterns are woven into backpacks, money belts and other practical items. Prices are a little steep (about P475 for a large backpack), but the quality is high and they're cheaper here than outside Sagada.

Places to Stay
Lodging in Sagada is basic but clean, comfortable and inexpensive. Unless otherwise mentioned, there's no hot water, although upon request most places will heat a big bucketful for bathing.

Set on a hill amid pine trees on the outskirts of town is the serene *St Joseph's Resthouse*, a former convent converted in the 1970s. Tiny singles with a shared bath are P75, doubles with private bath are P500 and cottages with hot shower are P1000. (For an additional P20 you can use the hot shower in one of the cabins.) It also has a restaurant, although prices, especially for breakfast, are a little steep. You can arrange

NORTH LUZON

here a full-body massage by a blind masseuse for P120.

About a 20-minute walk from town is *Mapiya-aw Pensione*, attractively set in what resembles a Chinese rock garden. Singles/doubles with a shared bath are P150/450. Try to get the double with a balcony, for fine views of the mountains. The bus from Baguio or Bontoc passes the pension before reaching Sagada; ask the driver to drop you off.

In town, the *Sagada Guesthouse & Cafe* has small, basic rooms for P75/150 with a shared bath. It can be a bit noisy, as buses and jeepneys leave from across the street (they start beeping their horns at 6 am). *Country Inn* has spacious rooms for P200 (try to get the room with the fireplace) and *Ganduyan Inn* has rooms showing a little wear and tear for P75/150.

Greenhouse has four rooms and is like staying in someone's home. Basic rooms are P100/150 and you can also arrange a massage here. Across the street is *Masferre Country Inn & Restaurant*, with clean, spacious doubles with shared bath for P250. About a 10-minute walk east of town is *Pines View*, which has two rooms for P80 per person. You can use the kitchen here. Nearby is *A-Seven House*, with rooms for P75 per person. It has no restaurant or cooking facilities.

Slightly more upmarket and more hotel-like is *Olahbinan Resthouse*, with rooms for P200/500 with shared bath, P800 for a double with private bath.

Conspicuously larger than any other building in town, and hopefully not a sign of things to come, is Sagada's most upmarket lodging, the *Prime Hotel*, where doubles with private bath and hot shower are P1000. It's difficult to get a room here though, as attendants seem to be forever absent.

Places to Eat

Most restaurants prefer reservations. If you don't reserve, some places may turn you away or not offer much choice.

Log Cabin serves excellent Western-style food in a pleasant, relaxed atmosphere (dinner only). In addition to hearty dishes

such as pork tenderloin with mashed potatoes, it has vegetarian and pasta dishes, as well as good French wine (P290 per bottle).

Masferre's also serves good food; try the beefsteak or vegetable chop suey. *Village Bistro*, about a 15-minute walk south of town, has a full menu and two outdoor tables. *Shamrock* has the liveliest atmosphere in town and serves simple dishes, as well as more hearty meals.

For a quick, tasty and inexpensive lunch try one of the small *eateries* along the plaza or next to the municipal hall. The best place in town for breakfast is *Yoghurt House/Shamrock II*, where you can get tasty, creamy homemade yoghurt (P35) with granola, excellent ginger tea and native coffee. You can get good lunches and dinners here, and if you reserve ahead they can even prepare pinikpikan (P200), an Igorot delicacy. *Tapey* (rice wine) is sometimes sold here at P120 per bottle. Good for breakfast is *Ganduyan Coffee Shoppe*, which opens at 5.30 am – a good option if you're leaving on the early jeepney to Bontoc. Try the maple syrup crepes.

Entertainment

There's a pretty strictly enforced 9 pm curfew here. Good places to pass the time until then are *Shamrock*, *Shamrock II* and *Log Cabin*.

Shopping

Souvenir stores in the area sell baskets, woodcarvings and other traditional Cordillera handicrafts. However, if you're going to

---

Hash Hunting

If you're looking for it (and aren't concerned about the police looking for you), pot and hash are pretty easy to come by in Sagada. If you're not interested, you probably won't even be aware of its presence. Be aware that, legalities aside, its use can be perceived as disrespectful to native Sagadans, especially if it's used in sacred areas, such as in the burial caves.

Caroline Liou

Banaue there's a much larger selection there. Sagada is well-known for its weaving, and this is a good place to buy good-quality woven items. The Ganduyan Museum has a small shop that may sell some antique baskets, as well as reproductions.

Sagada is not a good place to buy warm clothing so bring your own, especially if you are here in January or February.

Getting There & Away
From Manila, the quickest way by bus to Sagada is via Banaue. From Manila to Banaue (P160, nine hours) a Dangwa Tranco bus leaves at 7 am daily; you can also take the Autobus, which arrives in Banaue at around 5 am. From Banaue to Sagada, either take the 7.30 am jeepney or the noon bus to Bontoc (2½ hours), and connect with a jeepney to Sagada (40 minutes, hourly from 8.30 am to 4.30 pm).

A more scenic option is via Baguio. From Baguio to Banaue you must take the famous Halsema Hwy – six hours of bumpy, mostly unpaved and very dusty road (unless it's just rained), that twists and turns and passes through magnificent Cordillera scenery. Be sure to get a seat on the right-hand side of the bus. To Sagada (P136, seven hours), Lizardo Trans buses depart from the Dangwa terminal hourly from 6.45 to 11.45 am each day. From Sagada to Baguio buses leave hourly from 6 to 10.30 am.

From Sagada to Bontoc (40 minutes), jeepneys leave hourly (or as they fill up) from 6 am till noon. To Banaue, take a jeepney to Bontoc, from where jeepneys leave for Banaue at 7.30 and 9 am and noon (or as soon as they fill up). You can also take a bus from Bontoc to Banaue: an Immanuel Trans bus leaves from the Dangwa Tranco terminal at 8 am and Afuvel and Von Von buses leave at 8.30 am.

BONTOC
Bontoc is the capital of Mountain Province and the major commercial centre for the area. In contrast to serene Sagada, Bontoc's streets teem with tricycles and jeepneys. Most travellers pass quickly through Bontoc en route to Sagada or Banaue. However,

it's worth stopping at Bontoc at least for a few hours to visit the museum. It's also the best place for up-to-date information on trekking in Kalinga and a good starting point for treks in the area, such as to the Malegcong rice terraces.

Information
There is no tourist information centre in Bontoc; Pines Kitchenette is the best place to get information and find a guide.

Landbank and Philippine National Bank (PNB) have branches in Bontoc that will change cash and travellers cheques. Landbank gives slightly better exchange rates.

You can make long-distance telephone calls from the Smart Phone next to Zander's Cafe (from 8.30 am to 7 pm Monday to Friday and from 9 am to 6 pm Saturday), or at D'Sister's (from 7 am to 8 pm daily).

Bontoc Museum
Definitely worth a look is the **Bontoc Museum**, housed in replicas of traditional Ifugao, Sagada and Bontoc dwellings (open from 8 am to noon and from 1 to 5 pm daily). It has an interesting array of Igorot artefacts, including Ibaloi, Kalinga and Ifugao baskets, brass gongs with human jawbones as handles (proof the owner has taken a head) and traditional woven clothing. There are also several Masferre photos depicting life in the area from the 1930s to 1950s, as well as photos of headhunters and their bounty. Outside the museum is a model of a traditional village, including an *ato* (the religious and political centre for the men of the village).

Hiking
There are some good hikes in the area through rice terraces and small villages, as well as one to a hotspring (in Mainit). A recommended two-day trek is **Bontoc-Malegcong-Guinaang-Mainit**, where you can spend the night at the Odsey Guesthouse, and then back to Bontoc.

For a good day trip from Bontoc, catch a jeepney to **Malegcong**. It will drop you on the roadside, from where it's a half-hour hike to the spectacular stone-walled rice terraces and small village, which still has

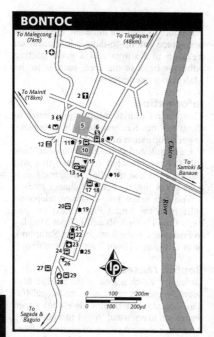

BONTOC

PLACES TO STAY
11 Pines Kitchenette
18 Eastern Star Hotel Extension
19 Eastern Star Hotel & Restaurant
21 Village Inn
25 Lynda's

PLACES TO EAT
15 Shekinal
26 Tchaya-Pan

OTHER
1 Hospital
2 Church
3 Philippine National Bank (PNB); Provincial
   Capitol Building
4 Post Office
5 Town Plaza
6 Landbank; Mountain Province Trade Centre
7 Massage Center
8 Jeepneys to Tinglayen; Bus to Banaue
9 Jeepneys to Malegcong
10 Market
12 Bontoc Museum
13 D'Sister's Long-Distance Telephone
14 Jeepneys to Mainit
16 All Saints Mission Elementary School
17 Jeepneys to Sagada
20 Zanders Cafe & Smart Phone
22 D'Rising Sun Bus to Baguio
23 Police Station; Municipal Hall
24 Jeepneys to Banaue
27 Von Von Bus to Banaue
28 Petron Petrol Station
29 Dangwa Tranco Bus Terminal

some traditional houses. It's a steady two-hour, downhill walk back to Bontoc.

Trekking guides can be hired for about P500 per day. While there is a tour guides association in Bontoc, they have no centre. Rita Bagwan at Pines Kitchenette is an excellent source of local information. Locals also recommend Francis Pa-In, Juliet Soria, Kinad and Ferdie. Most hotels can help you find these or other guides. In Bontoc you can also hire a guide for trekking in Kalinga, although you can do this once you get to Tinglayen (Kalinga).

Places to Stay
The best place to stay is *Pines Kitchenette*, with rooms with shared bath for P100/200 a single/double, or P500 with private bath. Another decent option is *Eastern Star Hotel & Restaurant*, where basic but clean rooms are P70/140 with shared bath. It has an extension where rooms with private bath are P300/600. Other basic but acceptable places in Bontoc are *Golden Dawn Hotel* (P70 per person), *Lynda's* (P100) and *Village Inn* (P100). The latter can also help arrange car rentals. Across the river in Samoki, *Ridge Brook Hotel & Restaurant* has good rooms for P100 per person.

Places to Eat
Tchaya-pan, near the municipal hall, serves good, reasonably priced meals, as does *Shekinal*, close to the public market. Also good is the restaurant at *Pines Kitchenette*. All serve the usual chicken and pork *adobo* and vegetable chop suey-type dishes.

Shopping
Woven goods made in nearby Samoki are sold in the Bontoc public market on Sunday.

The Mountain Province Trade Center in the Multipurpose Center has a handicraft showroom with traditional wares from around the region.

Getting There & Away

From Manila you must pass through either Baguio or Banaue to get to Bontoc. From Banaue to Bontoc (2½ hours), there's a 7 am jeepney or a noon bus. To Banaue, jeepneys leave at 7.30 and 9 am and noon (or as soon as they fill up). An Immanuel Trans bus leaves from the Dangwa Tranco terminal at 8 am and a Von Von bus leaves at 8.30 am.

From Baguio to Bontoc D'Rising Sun buses depart hourly from 4.45 am to 3 pm. From Bontoc, D'Rising Sun buses depart for Baguio hourly from 9.30 am to 2 pm.

Jeepneys to Mainit leave at 1 and 2 pm daily (one hour, 18km) and to Malegcong at 10am and noon (30 minutes, 7km).

See the Sagada section earlier for transport to/from Sagada. For transport to/from Tinglayen see the later Kalinga Province section.

AROUND BONTOC

Farther afield from Bontoc, there are other areas of magnificent rice terraces that are becoming more accessible to trekkers, including **Kadaclan**, **Barlig** and **Natonin**. In Kadaclan you can stay at the *Kadaclan Tourists' Homestay* (ask for Grace Chungalan).

Jeepneys from Bontoc leave for Natonin (six hours) via Kadaclan (four hours) at 11 am and 2 and 4 pm daily.

KALINGA PROVINCE

Kalinga is the most pristine and ruggedly beautiful of all the Cordillera provinces.

Trekking is the main draw for tourists. You'll get your first glimpse of the area's awesome scenery as the bus follows the winding Chico River. Hanging bridges, waterfalls and carefully tended rice terraces are common features of the landscape. This is not a place for those hoping to snap a few photos of natives in traditional clothing (which, sadly, you can do in Banaue, where

---

The Kalinga & the Outside

The Kalinga, who were traditionally head-hunters (although the practice no longer exists), have a fierce sense of culture and community, and have been successful in shunning outsiders intent upon exploiting the province's natural resources. The area was considered risky for travellers over the past couple of decades, chiefly due to plans by the lowland (ie, national) government to construct the Chico Valley dam. If completed, the entire Kalinga Valley would have been flooded, destroying centuries-old villages and leading to the resettlement of tens of thousands of Kalinga.

The New People's Army (NPA), together with the Kalinga, joined forces to halt the dam, resulting in often-violent fighting against the Philippine military. Although the project has been stopped, the Kalinga are understandably wary of outsiders, especially as rumours of plans to mine the area constantly circulate. Another reason for outsiders to be cautious is due to the large marijuana fields being cultivated in the area.

Caroline Liou

---

for a fee locals will don their tired and dusty traditional costumes and pose).

Tinglayen

A good starting point for treks in Kalinga is Tinglayen, 48km (or a 2½ hour ride) from Bontoc. There's one guesthouse here, run by the current mayor, who can also help you find a guide – a necessity for hiking in this area. Just across the hanging bridge from Tinglayen is the *barangay* (neighbourhood) of LupLupa, where the legendary Victor Baculi, the barangay captain of LupLupa, resides. Victor is an excellent source of information and well-known throughout the region.

Trekking You'll need a guide in Kalinga to show you where to go and to give you indispensable advice on culturally appropriate behaviour and gifts. Villagers commonly request matches, so stock up. A guide will also advise you on which areas are safe – tribal peace pacts are frequently made and just as frequently broken. If you haven't arranged a guide in Bontoc, Victor Baculi is the best person to show you around, or his family can suggest other guides. You can also ask at the Sleeping Beauty Resthouse.

A good two-hour walk in the immediate vicinity is **Tinglayen-Ambuto-Lilig-Tinglayen**, which takes you through some small rice terraces and villages, where a few native houses remain. You may also come across some village elders with tattooed arms. More commonly you'll see women with tattooed arms, meant as decoration; occasionally you'll see men with tattooed arms, an indication that they were once headhunters.

An excellent one-day hike is **Tinglayen-Ngibat-Botbot-Buscalan-Bugnay-Tinglayen**. You have to be reasonably fit, and be prepared to negotiate a few precariously narrow sections with steep drop-offs on one side. Take the 7 am jeepney from Tinglayen to Bontoc, and get off a few kilometres south of Tinglayen, from where the path starts (in the vicinity of Basao). If you miss the jeepney, it's a one-hour walk along the road to the path. From here it's a steep one-hour climb to Ngibat, and another hour's climb to Botbot. From Botbot it's an easy 40-minute walk to the beautiful village of Buscalan, which is surrounded by pretty stone-walled rice terraces where there are still many traditional houses. From Buscalan to Bugnay is the most striking section – it's mostly flat – taking you past some rolling, grassy mountain scenery, and if you're lucky, you'll get a good view of the Sleeping Beauty mountain chain, so-called because it's said to resemble a sleeping woman. You should be in Bugnay by 3.30 pm, to catch the jeepney back to Tinglayen. Otherwise, it's a long 14km walk back to Tinglayen; to hire your own ride will set you back about P400.

A two-day hike, or three days at a more relaxed pace, takes you through **Tinglayen-Malango-Sumadel-Dananao-Tulgao-Botbot-Buscalan-Bugnay-Tinglayen**. The scenery and villages are similar to the hike described above. There are waterfalls and hotsprings between Dananao and west Tulgao, which are worthwhile detours if you have the time.

Places to Stay & Eat In poblacion Tinglayen, *Sleeping Beauty Resthouse* (☎ *078-872 2212*), owned by Fernando Abay, Tinglayen's mayor, has some basic rooms for P100 per person. You can also try looking for *Victor Baculi* in LupLupa (get off the bus a few minutes prior to reaching poblacion Tinglayen, then cross the hanging bridge over the Chico River). There is no set fee to stay in his home, but you should offer some money upon departure (around P100 per person per night) and bring your own food. It's also good to bring some gifts, such as a chicken, fruit or a bottle of gin. Be prepared to sleep on the floor. There are no toilets in the village, so it's a good idea to bring a small shovel to dispose of waste. Take any rubbish you accumulate out with you.

There is a *restaurant* across the street from Sleeping Beauty Resthouse. You may want to stock up on food before coming here, although Tinglayen does have a small *store* that sells instant noodles, water, rice and canned goods.

Getting There & Away The most common route to Tinglayen is from Bontoc. A bus leaves at 7.30 am (P45, three hours), and there are jeepneys at 8 and 8.30 am (two hours). All leave from the circle. From Tinglayen to Bontoc, a jeepney leaves at 7 am. A jeepney also travels between Tinglayen and Tabuk.

BANAUE

Northern Luzon's most famous site, the Banaue rice terraces (altitude 1200m) are truly stunning – not only for their magnitude but because they were carved more than 2000 years ago by the Ifugao, using simple wooden tools. This highly sophisticated irrigation system was a remarkable innovation, using bamboo tubes and elaborate mud channels to transport water from its source to the terraces. These mud-walled terraces

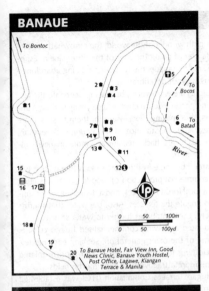

BANAUE

To Bontoc

To Bocos

To Batad

River

To Banaue Hotel, Fair View Inn, Good News Clinic, Banaue Youth Hostel, Post Office, Lagawe, Kiangan Terrace & Manila

BANAUE

PLACES TO STAY
1 Terraceville Inn
2 Cozy Nook
3 Halfway
4 Stairway Lodge & Restaurant
7 New Wonder Lodge
8 Greenview Lodge; Las Vegas Restaurant
9 People's Lodge & Restaurant; Bakery
11 Sanafe Lodge & Restaurant
15 Banaue View Inn
18 Spring Village Inn
20 J&L Pension

PLACES TO EAT
10 Valgreg's
14 Cool Winds
19 Green Meadows Restaurant

OTHER
5 Church
6 School
12 Town Hall; Tourist Information; Post Office
13 Market
16 Banaue Museum
17 Autobus Terminal

with bright green rice shoots. In Banaue, one rice crop per year is planted: terraces are repaired and seeds are sown in small terrace plots in December and January; the terraces are plowed and the sprouting seedlings are transplanted into the newly prepared and flooded terraces in February and March; and rice is harvested in June and August. If it has been a particularly cold winter, planting begins later.

Especially if you've just come from pristine Sagada, the town of Banaue gives the impression of being an unattractive collection of dilapidated tin buildings. Many opt to spend only a short amount of time in Banaue, quickly heading to Batad, Bangaan, which have more well-maintained rice terraces.

Information

There is a small, usually unstaffed, tourist information centre in the town hall. You're better off asking for information at your hotel or at Hygie's, next to Cool Winds. You can buy detailed maps of the area for P10 at most hotels. Official rates for tricycle and jeepney trips to local sights are posted at various locations around town (including at the tourist information centre). The post office is in the town hall.

If possible, change money before arriving in Banaue, as the exchange rate is low. Many hotels will change cash, albeit at a low rate, and the Banaue Hotel also changes travellers cheques (bring the original purchase receipt and your passport).

Guides are not necessary for hikes to Batad, Bangaan, Cambulo and even Pula, as the paths are pretty clear. However, a well-informed guide can help make your trek more interesting. Charlie Dumpit (ask for him just outside the gates of the Banaue Hotel) and Hygelac 'Pelac' Cayong (he has a small shop next to Cool Winds) are both very good.

To hike to destinations farther afield, secure yourself a guide, who will also arrange accommodation in small villages. If you're in a village without a guide and need accommodation, ask to see the barangay captain, who should be able to help.

NORTH LUZON

were not built by slave labour but by village co-operatives.

The best time of year to see the terraces is in April or May, when they are flourishing

The Decline of a Wonder

Often (justly) called the eighth wonder of the world, the renowned rice terraces are currently in danger of going the way of the other seven. Especially in the immediate area of Banaue, the terraces are being abandoned and are showing serious signs of deterioration.

The most oft-cited culprits are earthworms burrowing deep into the terraces; the low-yielding indigenous rice varieties (whose yearly harvest is unable to sustain farmers, thus making it necessary for them to seek more profitable work elsewhere); the absence of the younger generation, who have left the fields for less back-breaking and more financially rewarding jobs; and tourism.

Tourism is regarded by some as the most serious threat, as it has encouraged the commercial production of woodcarvings, resulting in the depletion of local forest resources, and a dwindling water supply with which to irrigate the terraces. Also, the water that tourists (and tourist services) use contributes further to water scarcity.

Tourism is also cited as having commercialised Ifugao culture. For example, some of the older generation, seeking easy money, don traditional clothing for tourist cameras, and tourism-related jobs have become more attractive than tending the fields.

In 1994 the Ifugao Terraces Commission (ITC) was established with the mission of saving the rice terraces, which are a Unesco World Heritage Site. It has proposed establishing a trust fund for farmers from tourism-related industries, and has pledged to work with woodcarvers to restore watersheds, and to research methods of alleviating the earthworm menace. However, many of the farmers have yet to benefit from the ITC programs and are even unaware of the commission's existence.

Caroline Liou

The tourist centre has official rates for guides: for example, a guide to Bangaan is P300, to the viewpoint P150, to Batad P500 and to Hapao P300.

The Viewpoint

A 10-minute ride north-east of Banaue on the road to Bontoc brings you to the Viewpoint, from where (after you wade through throngs of souvenir stands) there are magnificent views of the surrounding rice terraces. Unfortunately, the view is interrupted by shabby tin buildings (despite efforts by the tourist board to spruce them up) and the town of Banaue below. From the viewpoint it's a strenuous three-hour hike through the terraces back to Banaue – you must balance along the edges of rice terraces for much of the way. The path is clear most of the way, aside from the section between Bocos and Matanglag where the trail is less obvious, so you don't need a guide. It's a shorter hike if you head back to the road from Bocos, skipping Matanglag.

Banaue Museum

The Banaue Museum, next to the Banaue View Inn, houses a good collection of Ifugao, Kalinga and Bontoc artefacts. There's also an excellent collection of photographs of the region and people from the early 1900s. It's open from 8 am to 5 pm daily (entry P25); if closed, ask at the Banaue View Inn and they will usually open it for you.

Tam-an, Poitan & Matanglag Villages

Tourist brochures tout these as artists' villages, however, more likely you'll see a few people 'knitting' grass around the edges of wooden bowls. Still, the two-hour hike from Tam-an (down some concrete steps a short distance behind the Banaue Hotel) through Poitan and back to Banaue will take you past some traditional Ifugao houses and pretty views of small rice terraces. Much of the path follows an irrigation canal that's over a century old. On reaching the road from Poitan, the steps on the opposite side (a little towards Banaue) lead up to Matanglag (30 minutes). There are still a couple of bronzesmiths in Matanglag, and there's also one on the roadside close to where the steps begin.

Places to Stay

On a small hill overlooking the town is *Banaue View Inn* (☎ 073-386 4078). Spacious, clean rooms with shared, hot-water bath are P150 per person, P600 with private bath.

There are several places in town, but all are noisy, either from tricycles and jeepneys or from the river below. *People's Lodge & Restaurant* (☎ 073-386 4014) has acceptable singles/doubles with shared bath for P100/200 (singles have been known to rise to P200); rooms with private bath start at P300.

Across the street, *New Wonder Lodge* has similar rooms for P100, P350 with private bath or P450 with private hot-water bath. *Greenview Lodge* (☎ 073-386 4021), has rooms with shared bath for P100 (plus P20 for a hot shower), or P400 for a room with private, hot-water bath. *Cozy Nook* is quieter and more homey, with a nice common space and balcony. Rooms are P100, all with shared bath (P15 for hot water). *Halfway* has acceptable rooms but small rooms, for P75/400 for shared bath/private hot-water bath.

Stairway Lodge & Restaurant is a bit run-down. Rooms with a shared/private bath are P75/250. *Sanafe Lodge* (☎ 073-336 4085) has basic but clean rooms for P450/650 single/double, as well as dorm

rooms for P150. The single rooms all face the road, so it's noisy.

Heading out of town *J&L Pension* (☎ 073-386 4103) has good, airy rooms for P250/350/450 a single/double/triple (shared hot-water bath). Its traditional huts just across the road accommodate three and are P450 (you can use the main hotel's hot shower for an extra P20). *Spring Village Inn* (☎ 073-386 4037) has clean and nice rooms for P350/400 (shared bath), as does *Terraceville Inn* (☎ 073-386 4069) at P400 per room. *Fair View Inn* (☎ 073-386 4002) also has good rooms for P300/500 with private bath.

The most upmarket accommodation in town is the large *Banaue Hotel* (☎ 073-386 4087, fax 386 4048), where rooms with balconies are P2850/3160, or P6194 for a suite. The hotel also has a swimming pool, which nonguests can use for P50.

Places to Eat

Although the food is mediocre and prices slightly high, *People's Lodge & Restaurant* is a pleasant and popular place to hang out. Right next door, *Las Vegas Canteen & Restaurant* has slightly better service and food. *Cool Winds* serves similar food; for a filling dinner try Cool Winds Rice (P85). Cool Winds is also open a little later than other restaurants (till 10 pm if there are customers).

A good, reasonably priced restaurant is *Hidden Valley Restaurant*, just past the gates of the Banaue Hotel, a 10-minute uphill walk from town (P10 tricycle ride). Try their chicken *tinola* (P50). Just outside of town is the no-frills but pleasant *Green Meadows Restaurant*. *Valgreg's*, near People's, has a good selection of baked goods.

Banaue Hotel has the best restaurant in town, and prices are only slightly higher than other restaurants here. It also has an evening buffet.

Entertainment

Banaue quietens down pretty early, and there are no bars or late-night hang-outs to speak of. *Banaue Hotel* (☎ 073-386 4087) puts on traditional Ifugao dance performances at around 8.30 pm once or twice a week. Performances are usually scheduled only when large tour groups are staying at the hotel, so call ahead for the schedule.

Shopping

Handicraft shops are everywhere in Banaue, though finding quality items isn't easy. Woodcarvers traditionally used ebony and other hardwoods, but because the wood is now difficult to find (the few forests where these trees still grow are now protected) most carvers use softwoods, then paint or stain them dark. Inspect woodcarvings for signs of cracking, and be aware that in a dry climate your souvenir will very likely develop cracks. Bronze and silver (or a mixture of the two) jewellery is also made here. The *buong*, a symbol of good luck and fertility, is hung on necklaces. You'll also find plenty of woven goods and baskets for sale.

Getting There & Away

From Manila, Dangwa Tranco and Autobus have direct buses to Banaue (10 hours). If you arrive on the 6 am Autobus, the New Wonderlodge, takes guests in the wee hours (you could also try the Banaue View Inn).

From Banaue to Manila, a Dangwa Tranco bus leaves at 7 am (P200) and an Autobus at 5 pm. Reserve your ticket the afternoon before; Dangwa Tranco tickets can be reserved at Niclyn's store, near the town hall, and Autobus tickets at Esther's, near Cool Winds. You can also take a jeepney to Bagabag, then a bus or jeepney to Solano. From Solano there are frequent Manila-bound buses, or if you're lucky you might be able to get on a Manila-bound bus from Bagabag.

From Baguio to Banaue, Dangwa Tranco has direct buses (the southern route via Bayombong) departing at 7 am and 7 pm (P150/190 nonair-con/air-con, nine hours). Autobus has direct buses, departing at 7.30 pm (P185, air-con), as does JBL Trans, departing 7 pm (P185 nonair-con). To Baguio, a Dangwa bus leaves at 7 am and an Autobus at 6 pm.

For travel to/from Sagada and Bontoc, see those sections earlier.

To Bontoc, a jeepney leaves from near the Sanafe Lodge at 7 am. There are also two buses daily, one that passes through Banaue around 10 am (except Sunday), and another at around noon. Walk up the steps just past Cool Winds, and wait for the bus in the concrete shed at the top of the stairs.

AROUND BANAUE

In addition to those at Banaue, four other Ifugao rice terraces are included on Unesco's World Heritage List: at Batad, Mayoyao, Hapao and Kiangan. With the exception of Batad, which requires a 1½ hour hike to reach it, these terraces can be viewed from the road.

Batad & Around Batad

It's an easy 1½-hour hike to Batad from Bangaan, or a shorter (but steeper) hike from Batad junction. From Bangaan to Batad, go left any time you come to a fork in the path (ie, stick to the mountain). The magnificent sight of the beautifully contoured amphitheatre of rice terraces surrounding Batad village is something to remember. The village itself is still mostly made up of traditional Ifugao wood and *cogon* (grass-thatched) houses, and the rice terraces are well cared for and beautifully sculpted. It's worth spending a night or two here and hiking around the area.

The **Tapplya Waterfall** is about a 40-minute hike from Rita's or Simon's in Batad. Walk down to the village and then up to Mountain Inn, from where some stones steps (next to the shed) lead down to the waterfall (stay on the left when the path starts going up). You don't need a guide, but parts of the path are steep and slippery, so use caution. The falls themselves are about 30m high and the pool is a cold and refreshing place for a dip.

If you feel like a longer hike to/from Batad, try one of the following routes:

Batad Junction or Bangaan–Batad–Cambulo–Kinakin From Batad junction to Batad it's about 1½ hours, from Batad to Cambulo it's another 1½ hours and from Cambulo to Kinakin (13km) it's 3½ hours. There are some steep sections, and the hike is exhausting in parts. At the

AROUND BANAUE

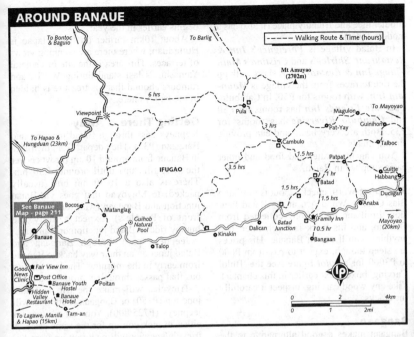

- - - - - Walking Route & Time (hours)

time of writing, the path from Cambulo to Kinakin was being made into a road. There is accommodation in the more remote Cambulo (see
Places to Stay & Eat), but the town is nowhere
near as beautiful as Batad.

**Batad Junction or Bangaan–Batad–Cambulo–
Pula–Banaue Road** From Cambulo to Pula is
about three hours and from Pula to the road it's
about six hours. If you take this route, you
might plan on spending one night in Batad and
one in Pula. There is no accommodation in Pula,
so try to arrange a place to stay before leaving
Banaue; otherwise, ask Pula's barangay captain
if he can help. The hike from Cambulo to Pula
follows a winding river, with rice terraces
carved high into the mountains on either side.
Much of the hike is through rice terraces, and
about halfway there you'll cross over a small
hanging bridge. Pula is a tiny collection of Ifugao houses on a hilly outcrop. Just outside of
Pula on the way back to Banaue, there's a waterfall and deep swimming pool, just under a
bridge. The path from Pula to the road back to
Banaue (six hours) is through lush forest, a nice
change after so many rice terraces!

A guide is not necessary for these hikes, as
the path is pretty clear, though finding the
right path out of the village can be confusing (ask a local for directions). Alternatively, you could hire a local just to help you
through the rice terraces out of the village,
then continue alone once the path is clear.
Guides are available in Cambulo and Batad
for P200 per day.

Places to Stay & Eat Accommodation in
Batad is very basic, with squat toilets and no
hot water (although a bucket of hot water
can be heated). Unless mentioned, all places
have attached restaurants and rooms are P35
per person. If you're coming from Batad
junction or Bangaan, the first places you'll
come across are *Hillside*, *Rita's*, a nice and
very friendly place, and *Simon's*, the largest
and most popular place (its restaurant serves
good pizza with tasty cheese). All have great
views of the rice terraces and picturesque
Batad village. Heading down towards the

NORTH LUZON

village, you'll see signs for *Batad Pension*, another nice and friendly place (it also has a modern toilet).

In Batad village is *Foreigner's Inn & Restaurant*, *Shirley's* and *Cristina's Main Village Inn & Restaurant*. A short walk up the rice terraces from the village is *Mountain Inn*, with rooms for P50. In Cambulo, *Cambulo Friends Inn* has rooms for P50 and *Cambulo Riverside* has rooms for P35. Both are very basic and can provide simple meals.

You can buy water and food and other basic supplies in Batad.

Shopping Worth checking out is Emiliano Blas Quality Wood Art, at the Batad Pension. Emiliano uses ebony collected from Quezon, and his work is much finer than anything you'll see in Banaue. His prices are steep though; expect to pay from P600 to P3000 for a *bulol* figure (see the 'Bulol Carving' boxed text earlier in this chapter). Like any wood carving, inspect it carefully for cracks.

Bangaan

Bangaan makes a good alternative to the Batad hike, as the small village is an easy 15-minute walk from the terraces. The rice terraces here are beautiful and better-kept than those surrounding Banaue. You can stay overnight at the *Family Inn* for P150 per person.

Mayoyao

Some 40km (three hours) north-east of Banaue are the Mayoyao rice terraces. The town is spread out over the valley, detracting from the attractiveness of the terraces. Still, these stone-walled terraces are an impressive sight, and even more extensive than those in Banaue.

Hapao

About 15km south-west of Banaue is Hapao, the site of yet more stunning rice terraces, which (unlike Banaue) are stone-walled. The turn-off to Hapao is about halfway between Banaue and the viewpoint. If you're in Banaue in February, the trip to Hapao may be especially worth-

while, as the planting season here usually begins earlier in the year.

About 10km farther on from Hapao is **Hungduan**, where there are stunning views of terraces. This area is the site of General Yamashita's last stand during WWII, and rumours abound that his treasure is hidden in the valleys here.

Getting There & Away

Jeepneys pass through Batad junction and Bangaan (P35). They depart from the plaza in Banaue from around 10 am (or whenever the first fills up) until around 4.30 pm. There is also a 10.30 am bus (usually packed) to Mayoyao that goes via Batad junction and Bangaan (wait for this bus in front of People's). Expect a dusty and bumpy ride to Batad junction or Bangaan.

Jeepneys pass through Bangaan and Batad junction on their way back to Banaue from early in the morning. The last trip is a bus that passes through at around 9 am.

Tricycles will make the trip to Batad junction (P150) or Bangaan (P200), as will jeepneys (P725/800). You can arrange for either to pick you up for the same price. A tricycle/jeepney will pick you up from Kinakin for P120/440. If you don't arrange a pick-up, it's long walk back to Banaue, as vehicles are few and far between.

There's one jeepney trip a day from Banaue to Hapao, and only one trip per day back to Banaue, passing through Hapao in the early morning. To make the trip in one day, you must hire a jeepney. Check at the tourist office in the town hall for the current official rate.

BANGUED

Bangued is the commercial centre of Abra, one of Luzon's least-travelled and most economically depressed provinces. There isn't much in the way of sights in the town itself, although it's the jumping-off point for highland towns populated by the Itneg (also known as the Tingguian). Bangued itself is in a valley, so it doesn't enjoy the cooler climates of Abra's higher altitude towns.

You can enjoy simple pleasures in Bangued, such as watching the sun rise over

AROUND BANGUED

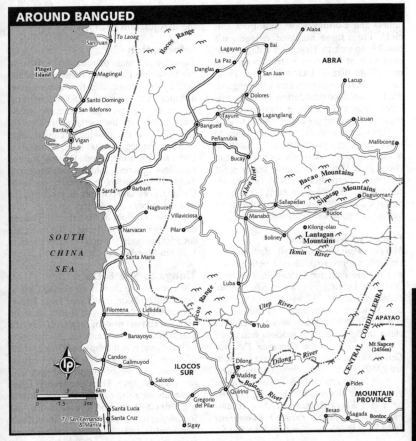

the Cordilleras from the banks of the Abra River in Callaba, or taking a stroll up to **Victoria Park**, from where you can get a view of the famous Sleeping Beauty mountain range and the town below. However, Bangued is a pretty typical commercial town, with tricycles and jeepneys whizzing by emitting loads of exhaust fumes (that get trapped in the valley) and the usual amounts of noise.

A 10-minute tricycle ride from town is the little Itneg village of **Peñarrubia**. You can walk across a precarious hanging bridge to the village, or continue along the road the

tricycle takes from Bangued, which also leads to the village.

The village recently began reviving the indigenous art of natural dyeing. Mang Luis is one of the few Itneg artists still versed in this dying art. The Luis family embroidery is known as *kinamayan*, with traditional designs representing rice, hands, caterpillars, horses and other traditional symbols. Their weavings and other handicrafts from around the region are sold in the trade centre across from the capital building.

From Bangued, jeepneys make daily trips to the villages of **Sallapadan** (three hours),

Bucloc (six hours), **Daguioman** (seven hours) and **Boliney** (one hour from Bucloc). From these highland villages, it's possible to trek to Tingguian villages. The road ends at Daguioman, from where it's possible to hike to **Licuan** in a day. From Licuan, there are jeepneys back to Bangued. There's no accommodation in these villages; upon arrival, pay a courtesy call to the mayor and inquire about a place to stay.

There are no roads connecting Abra to other Cordillera provinces. Before setting out into Abra's backwoods, its important to check in at Bangued's capital building for the latest information on NPA (known locally as the Nice People's Army) activity in the area. Joji Guillen-Crisologo in the media bureau is a good source of information.

Places to Stay & Eat
Marysol Pension has small, dark but acceptable rooms with shared bath/air-con and private bath for P250/400. The most upmarket lodging in town is *King David Palace Hotel* (☎ 752 8404), on Capitulacion St, where rooms with bath and fan/air-con are P450/650. The rooms are plain but clean in this standard, modern hotel. It's possible to stay at the *Diocesan Pastoral Center*, where rooms with air-con and bath are P350. Inquire at the church on the plaza.

Next to the capital building on the plaza you can get decent, inexpensive Filipino food at *3 Kings Restaurant*. Also recommended by locals is *Prince's Restaurant* and *Uncle Pete's Fastfood*, both on Taft St.

Getting There & Away
Philippine Rabbit and Partas Bus each have an hourly service to Manila (nine hours). Partas has three buses daily to Baguio (P154, five hours). There are frequent minibuses to/from Vigan (P30, 1½ hours).

Cagayan & Isabela

TUGUEGARAO
The capital of Cagayan province, Tuguegarao is a busy commercial centre with little of interest for travellers. The city does,

however, make a good base for exploring the sites just outside of town.

Information
Tuguegarao's main thoroughfare is Bonifacio St, where the tourist office, banks and market are located, and from where long-distance calls can be made. The tourist office is on the 2nd floor above the public market, although the tourist office (☎ 078-844 0203) at the provincial capital, 7km south of Tuguegarao, has more information about activities in the area. On staff are two excellent guides, Johnper Sanchez and Teddy Babaran, who can guide you in the Callao Caves, and possibly on hikes into the Sierra Madres.

On the 2nd floor of the Citimall, you can check your email at Albert's Internet Cafe for P50 per hour. It's open from 9.30 am to 8.30 pm Monday to Friday.

Things to See & Do
The main tourist draw is the **Callao Cave** in Peñablanca, 24km (one hour) from Tuguegarao. Along the way you'll pass beautiful views of endless rows of cornfields, with the Sierra Madre mountains in the distance. Callao Cave, is at the top of a 206-step flight of stairs. Inside the cave, below a natural skylight, is a beautiful little chapel with pews and an altar. There are several other, more adventurous, caves in the area, including **Odessa Cave**, said to contain the most interesting rock formations, and **Sierra Cave**, which also contains amazing stalactites and stalagmites. Except for Callao Cave, you'll need a guide to explore the caves, as well as a flashlight or headlamp (not necessary for Callao Cave), extra clothes (you'll get extremely muddy crawling through passages) and mosquito repellent. Consider sticking around to watch the tens of thousands of bats stream out of the caves over the Pinacanauan River at around 5.30 pm daily.

The **Pinacanauan River**, a freshwater tributary of the Cagayan River, is worth a visit for its beautiful clear green water and limestone cliffs. There's a fine pebble beach a short way upstream from the caves from where you can swim. Canoes transporting

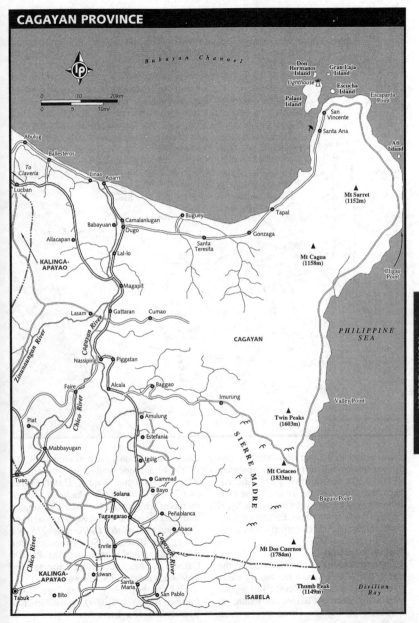

CAGAYAN PROVINCE

Babuyan Channel

Don Hermanos Island
Gran Laja Island
Lighthouse
Palaui Island
Escucha Island
Escaparda Point
San Vincente
Santa Ana
Ati Island

Mt Sarret (1152m)

Abulug
Ballesteros
To Claveria
Linao
Aparri
Lucban
Babayuan
Camalaniugan
Buguey
Tapal
Dugo
Allacapan
Lal-lo
Santa Teresita
Gonzaga
KALINGA-APAYAO
Magapit
Mt Cagua (1158m)
Illigau Point
Lasam
Gattaran
Cumao
Zimunaungan River
Cagayan River
CAGAYAN
PHILIPPINE SEA
Nassiping
Piggatan
Chico River
Faire
Alcala
Baggao
Imurung
Piat
Amulung
Valley Point
Mabbayugan
Estefania
Iguig
Twin Peaks (1603m)
SIERRE MADRE
Tuao
Gammad
Bayo
Mt Cetaceo (1833m)
Solana
Tuguegarao
Peñablanca
Baguio Point
Enrile
Abaca
Chico River
Cagayan River
Liwan
Mt Dos Cuernos (1784m)
KALINGA-APAYAO
Tabuk
Bito
Santa Maria
San Pablo
ISABELA
Thumb Peak (1149m)
Divilian Bay

NORTH LUZON

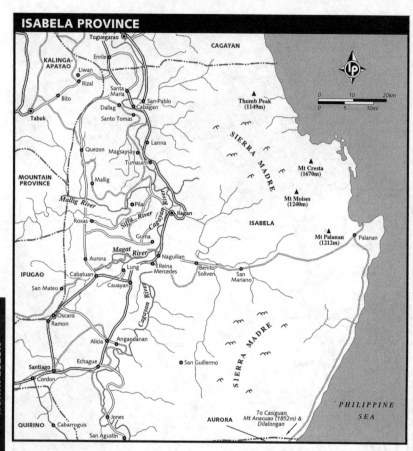

ISABELA PROVINCE

residents and all manner of belongings (including horses and furniture) to upstream villages make several trips a day. The village closest to the caves, Tungi, is one hour upstream, and the farthest village, Baclay, is 1½ days' walk from Tungi. Farther on from Baclay are some Aeta (Negrito) settlements.

Places to Stay

Budget accommodation tends to be on the grotty side; if you want a reasonably clean place, expect to spend at least P400 night.

Although dreary, *Pension Abraham*, on Bonifacio St, has the cheapest rooms in town. Basic rooms with shared bath are P100/140 a single/double, or with air-con P390/440 (no hot water). *Hotel Elinas* (☎ 078-844 2198, 133 Bonifacio St) has better rooms with air-con for P380/450; singles with no air-con are P220. Showing signs of wear and tear, *Hotel Delfino* (☎ 078-844 1314), on Bonfacio St, has rooms for P400/500. *Hotel Lorita* near St Peter's Cathedral, has acceptable rooms for P550/605 (air-con, TV, hot water).

The two best places to stay are *Hotel Candice* (☎ 078-844 2001), on the corner of Blumentritt and Luna Sts, where good, clean rooms start at P650 (air-con, TV, hot water), and nearby *Pension Roma*, where singles start at P390, or P670 with TV, hot water and air-con.

Callao Caves Resort, on the banks of the Pinacanauan River, has dorm beds/basic rooms for P80/200. If you want to see the bats (around 5.30 pm) consider staying here, as you'll have missed the last jeepney back to town.

Places to Eat

Pampenguana, on Bonifacio St, is a local institution since 1956, and has an excellent bakery with a huge variety of cakes. Service is friendly and prices are reasonable. A little more upmarket is *Adrinels Restaurant* on Rizal St. Try the grilled *tanguigui* (P100), fresh lumpia (P18) or beefsteak Tagalog (P80). For the best *pancit* in town, try *629 Restaurant*.

Getting There & Away

PAL has flights to/from Manila each Monday, Wednesday and Saturday (P1600, one hour). You can fly from Tuguegarao to Basco on Monday (P2000, plus P103 airport tax. To fly to/from Palanan see that section later.

Autobus, Baliwag Transit and Victory Liner all have daily services to/from Manila (12 hours). From Banaue, take any jeepney to Solano or any Manila-bound bus and change at Bagabag (about two hours), from where you catch a Tuguegarao-bound (five hours) bus from the junction. The buses are usually jam packed, so expect to stand for a while.

To get to the Callao Caves (about one hour) catch a jeepney from in front of the market on Bonifacio St. There are several jeepneys between 6 am and 3.30 pm daily, leaving as they fill up. The last trip back is at about 4 pm.

PALANAN

This remote Isabela province settlement is only accessible by cargo ship from Baler in Aurora province, light aircraft from Tuguegarao or a trek of several days across the Sierra Madre mountains.

The Palanan Wilderness Area is home to several threatened bird species.

The town of Palanan has a couple of small paved roads, no electricity (unless provided by a backyard generator) and only one motorised vehicle. The Dumagat, a seminomadic Aeta group, inhabit the Palanan coastline. Because of the area's inaccessibility, the Dumagat lifestyle has remained relatively unchanged for generations. As with other remote areas in the Philippines, especially where there is no accommodation, you should pay a courtesy call to the mayor upon arrival.

Getting There & Away

One option is to take a light aircraft to/from Tuguegarao. At the time of writing the 45-minute flight was P6000 one way. Call Chemtrad Airlines (☎ 078-844 3113) at the Tuguegarao domestic airport for details.

Cargo ships to Palanan leave Cemento Wharf in Baler, Aurora, on an irregular schedule (sometimes weekly, sometimes monthly). The trip is about 14 hours, with a stop in Casiguran. You might have to wait a month for the next boat to bring you back from Palanan.

If you want to hike to Palanan, Ilagan (Isabela province) is said to be the place to find a guide.

SANTA ANA & PALAUI ISLAND

Five hours by bus from Tuguegarao is the small town of Santa Ana, on the northeasternmost tip of Luzon. The town itself isn't of much interest, but there are some unspoiled, beautiful white-sand beaches nearby, such as **Angib Beach**, accessible by boat from San Vicente (20 minutes), or a 1½-hour walk from the end of the road. Reminiscent of Hundred Islands National Park, the long, white-sand beach and crystal clear water is surrounded by a dozen or so rocky outcrops. The area has not been developed; bring your own food and drinks.

San Vicente (a barangay of Santa Ana) is the jumping-off point for **Palaui Island**, 15 minutes by motorised *lampitao* (small boats). Although the beach isn't as pretty as at Angib, the small island village of **Punte Verde** is a nice place to relax and experience a slower pace of life. There are no roads, motorised vehicles or electricity on the island. You can do a three-hour hike across the island to beautiful **Cape Engano** and **Siwangag Cove**, where there is an old lighthouse, originally built by the Spanish, and a gorgeous white-sand beach.

The rainy season is from November to late February, during which it can rain every day. March to July is fishing season, when deep-sea fishers from around the world come in search of sailfish, blue marlin, barracuda and others.

There is no accommodation in the area, although the DENR on Palaui has some extra beds they may let you use. In Santa Ana, friendly Mayor Rodriguez should also be able to help arrange accommodation. The Naval Base here sometimes allows travellers to stay in its guesthouse.

Plans are in the works to develop Port Irene, a short distance east of Santa Ana, as an international shipping port. This entire area has been earmarked as a special development zone and land ownership disputes are a source of local tension. Upon arriving in Santa Ana, pay a courtesy call to the mayor's office in the municipal hall, indicating you plan to travel in the area.

Getting There & Away
Don Domingo has a direct bus from Tuguegarao to Santa Ana, leaving at 6 am daily.

Florida Liner buses to Manila leave Santa Ana at 11 am and 3 pm daily, via Tuguegarao. Buses for Tuguegarao leave at 2 and 8 am. There are frequent jeepneys to Aparri (two hours) between 6 am and 2 pm. To Laoag and Vigan, take a jeepney to Magapit (85km), from where there are frequent bus connections.

CLAVERIA
In the north-west of Cagayan province, the small coastal town of Claveria has a long, pretty and clean beach, nicely framed by a couple of small mountains on one side and hills on the other. It is four hours from Santa Ana, and three hours from Laoag. Two small, beachside resorts have recently been established here, each providing a pleasant

place to enjoy the friendly, relaxed, small-town ambience.

Places to Stay
A short walk out of town, along the beach, the *Claveria Bayview Inn & Beach Resort* is a converted home. Nicely furnished rooms with bath and fan, right on the beach, start at P350 and delicious home-cooking is available. A few doors down, the pleasant *Casa Grande Inn* has dorm beds for P60, although the owner is often not around and the place is closed.

Getting There & Away
From Santa Ana to Claveria take any bus to Laoag or Vigan, or take a jeepney to Magapit, and then transfer to any Laoag or Vigan bus. Get off at the Petron station as you enter Claveria (the town centre isn't visible from the highway), and take a tricycle (P3) to the accommodation at the beach.

There are frequent direct buses from Claveria to Laoag and Vigan that leave from the town centre. They pass Pagudpud, which is 1½ hours from Claveria. There are also frequent buses from Claveria to Manila and Tuguegarao.

BALER
The commercial centre of Aurora, Baler draws surfers from around the world from October to February. Its claim to fame is the surfing scene in Francis Ford Coppola's *Apocalypse Now*. **Sabang Beach**, where most of the area's accommodation is concentrated, is a narrow brown-sand beach. It's OK for swimming, but not exceptionally attractive, and is a five-minute tricycle ride (P5) from the town centre. **Cemento Beach**, where surfers say the waves are better, is 8km south-east of Baler, about 30 minutes by tricycle (P40) or jeepney. From Cemento it's a 30-minute hike to **Digisit**, where there are some small hot springs near the beach. The best waves are rumoured to be six hours north of Baler by jeepney, then by boat to the reef.

There's a nice white-sand beach at **Dicasalarin Cove**. To get here you can hike or hire a fishing boat (30 minutes) from the bridge

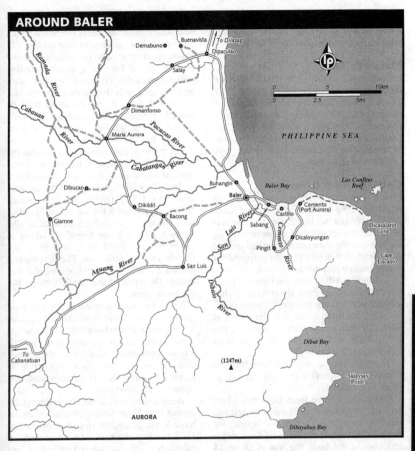

AROUND BALER

PHILIPPINE SEA

NORTH LUZON

AURORA

just outside Baler on the road to Sabang. Further south is **Dibut Bay**, about a two-hour boat ride from Sabang. The beach here is similar to Sabang Beach, and the town is mostly populated with Aeta descendants.

Inland from Baler is San Luis, with the **El Pimentel (Calisetan) Falls**, where you can swim. San Luis can be reached by tricycle (about 45 minutes) from Baler.

Places to Stay

With the exception of *Amihan Hotel*, in Baler, all accommodation is in Sabang. *Tita Guding's Beach Resort* has very basic,

plain singles for P200, or a room with three beds for P500 (both with shared bath). *Bay's Inn* has fancier rooms for P250 with bath and fan, or P200 with shared bath. There are a couple of discos across the road, so it's pretty noisy late into the night. A couple of doors from Bay's Inn is a two-room *beachside cottage* for P300.

Angarra Beach House & Restaurant, has good, clean rooms that open onto a pretty backyard garden for P250/300 a single/double. *DSB Lodge* has plain but clean beachside rooms with nice views for P250. You have to go to the building next door for running water. The imposing three-storey *Amco Beach Resort* has plainly decorated doubles with fan/air-con for P300/500.

Places to Eat
In the town centre, the friendly *R&F Restaurant* serves tasty, inexpensive food. Try the *sotanghon* (chicken, vegetable and noodle soup, P25). *Melly's Restaurant*, on Quezon St, has good self-serve food, and roasts chicken (P180 for a whole chicken) out front of the restaurant. It also has a good selection of ice cream.

Getting There & Away
From Cabanatuan to Baler, Genesis has two buses daily, the last leaving at around 9 am. ABC Trans' last bus is at 3 pm. You can also make the five-hour trip by jeepney (P80), the last leaving the central terminal around 4 pm (earlier if it fills up). Be prepared for a very bumpy and dusty ride.

To Manila, ABC Trans and Genesis Trans have regular buses from Baler. Genesis has a direct bus, leaving at 6 am; all other buses go via Cabanatuan, the last departing at noon. The last jeepney leaves around 2 pm (P75). Five Star has frequent buses from Cabanatuan to Manila (P93).

There are regular jeepneys from Baler to Dilasag (eight hours) in the north, as well as south to Cemento.

Cargo ships leave from Cemento wharf on an irregular schedule (sometimes weekly, sometimes monthly) bound for Palanan, in Isabela province. If the captain lets you on the boat, the trip is about 14 hours, with a stop in Casiguran. As boat trips are infrequent, you may have to wait a month for the next boat to bring you back from Palanan; a much more expensive alternative is to take a light aircraft to/from Tuegegarao.

Ilocos

VIGAN
Vigan, with its narrow cobblestone streets, antiquated ancestral homes and *calesas* (horse-drawn carriages), is a rare remnant of Spanish-era Philippines. Its river location, near where the river meets the South China Sea, made it a convenient stop on the Silk Route connecting Asia, the Middle East and Europe, and it become a thriving trading post where gold, logs and beeswax were bartered for goods from around the world.

In 1572 Spanish conquistador Juan de Salcedo (grandson of Legazpi), took possession of the bustling international port. Salcedo became the Lieutenant Governor of the Ilocos region, and Vigan became the centre of the political, religious and commercial activities of the north. It became a hotbed of social dissent against the Spanish when, in 1762, Diego Silang captured Vigan and named it the capital of Free Ilocos. He was eventually assassinated (the Spanish paid a close friend of Silang to shoot him in the back), and his wife, Gabriela Silang, took over. The first woman to lead a revolt in the Philippines, she was eventually captured and publicly hanged in the town square.

Vigan has been nominated for inclusion in the Unesco World Heritage List. Unlike Manila and Cebu, whose colonial buildings were pretty much destroyed in WWII, Vigan remained relatively unscathed. Today, however, the city is struggling to achieve a balance between economic development and preservation.

A good time to visit the city is during the annual Viva Vigan festival, organised by the Save Vigan Ancestral Homes Association. Held the first week of May, it includes a calesa festival, *zarzuelas* (operettas) and *abel* (weaving) exhibits. The Vigan town fiesta, held the third week of January, commemorates the town's patron saint, St Paul the Apostle, with a parade and musical performances.

Information
The tourist information office, in the Leona Florentina Building, has very little to offer in the way of tourist information.

Just off Plaza Burgos is PNB, where the ATM accepts Cirrus, Plus, MasterCard and Visa cards. Nearby is Equitable PCI Bank, which has an ATM with MasterCard and

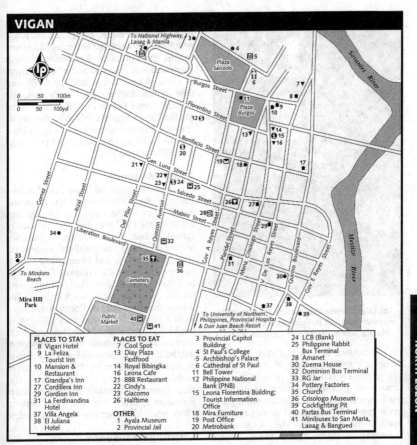

VIGAN

To National Highway, Laoag & Manila

Soventes River

Burgos Street

Florentino Street

Bonifacio Street

Gen Luna Street

Salcedo Street

Mabini Street

Liberation Boulevard

Gomez Street

Rizal Street

Del Pilar Street

Quezon Avenue

Gov A Reyes Street

Plaridel Street

Mena Crisologo Street

V De Los Reyes Street

Quirino Boulevard

Gov E Reyes Street

Mestizo River

Plaza Salcedo

Plaza Burgos

Archbishop's Palace

Cemetery

Public Market

Mira Hill Park

To Mindoro Beach

To University of Northern Philippines, Provincial Hospital & Don Juan Beach Resort

PLACES TO STAY	PLACES TO EAT	3 Provincial Capitol Building	24 LCB (Bank)
8 Vigan Hotel	7 Cool Spot	4 St Paul's College	25 Philippine Rabbit Bus Terminal
9 La Feliza Tourist Inn	13 Diay Plaza Fastfood	5 Archbishop's Palace	28 Amanet
10 Mansion & Restaurant	14 Royal Bibingka	6 Cathedral of St Paul	30 Zuema House
17 Grandpa's Inn	16 Leona Cafe	11 Bell Tower	32 Dominion Bus Terminal
29 Cordillera Inn	21 888 Restaurant	12 Philippine National Bank (PNB)	33 RG Jar
29 Gordion Inn	22 Cindy's	15 Leona Florentina Building; Tourist Information Office	34 Pottery Factories
31 La Ferdinandina Hotel	23 Giacomo	18 Mira Furniture	35 Church
37 Villa Angela	26 Halftime	19 Post Office	36 Crisologo Museum
38 El Juliana Hotel	OTHER	20 Metrobank	39 Cockfighting Pit
	1 Ayala Museum		40 Partas Bus Terminal
	2 Provincial Jail		41 Minibuses to San Maria, Laoag & Bangued

Cirrus. There are also a number of banks on Quezon Ave, the city's modern commercial thoroughfare.

Amanet, at 32 Gov A Reyes St, offers Internet access for P60 an hour; open from 8 am to 8.30 pm daily.

Mestizo District

Recently dubbed 'heritage village', and popularly known in the past as 'Kasanglayan' (literally, 'where the Chinese live'), this is Vigan's **old town** – where ancestral homes and other colonial architecture buildings are concentrated. The area runs roughly south of Plaza Burgos, with Gov A Reyes St on the west to Quirino Blvd on the east, down to Abaya St on the south. It is centred around spiffed-up Crisologo St, where most of the tourist shops are located, and Plaridel St, which runs parallel.

The **colonial mansions** here were built by Chinese merchants who settled, intermarried and, by the 19th century, had become the city's elite. Although generally considered Spanish, the architecture is actually a combination of Mexican, Chinese and Filipino styles (eg, the sliding *capiz* shell windows are Filipino design). Walking along

CAROLINE LOU

The calesa (horse-drawn carriage) is a valid mode of transport in Vigan as opposed to in Manila, where its more of a tourist 'trap'.

the cobblestone streets, you have the sense of being transported back in time, though you're quickly reminded you're in the 21st century as a massive Coca-Cola delivery truck squeezes past or a smog-emitting tricycle zooms by. Ancestral homes that are open to the public are Villa Angela and Quema House (at the time of writing Sequia Mansion was closed).

Plaza Salcedo & Plaza Burgos

Vigan has two main squares – Plaza Salcedo, dominated on one end by the Cathedral of St Paul, and the more lively Plaza Burgos, where locals stroll and where, in the afternoons, stalls sell delicious local delicacies. The interesting Cathedral of St Paul is built in 'earthquake baroque' style (ie, thick-walled and massive). Originally constructed in 1574, the cathedral that stands today was completed in 1800. Note the Chinese Fu dogs carved into the facade's pilasters. The octagonal bell tower is south of the church,

across Burgos St. Next to the church is the Archbishop's Palace, completed in 1783, which once housed the ecclesiastical court. During the Philippine Revolution/Spanish American War it served as the headquarters of General Emilio Aguinaldo in 1898, and then as headquarters for US forces under Colonel James Parker in 1899. Inside is the Museo Nueva Segovia, which houses ecclesiastical artefacts and relics. It's open from 8.30 to 11.30 am and from 2 to 5 pm weekdays (P10 admission).

Ayala Museum

Housed in the ancestral home of Father José Burgos is an extensive collection of Ilocano artefacts, including a series of 14 paintings depicting the 1807 Basi Revolt by the locally famed painter Don Esteban Villanueva. Weavings, Tingguian jewellery, musical instruments, pottery, and farming and fishing implements are also on display. On the second floor is the Ilocano Hall of Fame, with photos of and captions describing the achievements of famous Ilocanos. It's open from 8.30 to 11.30 am and from 1.30 to 4.30 pm Monday to Friday (P10 admission). Next door to the Ayala Museum is the provincial jail, built in 1657. Several leaders of dissent against the US forces in 1899 were detained in this jail, including Mena Crisologo, Enrique Quema and Estanislao Reyes. Former President Quirino was also born here in 1890, while his father was the jail's warden.

Crisologo Museum

The Crisologo Museum houses a charming, albeit ragtag, collection of memorabilia of the Crisologo family, one of Vigan's prominent families from which the area's former governor and congressman descend. Wooden *santos* (saints), intricately carved furniture, Madame Crisologo's collection of butterfly dresses, scrapbooks and newspaper clippings, Ming vases and church vestments are on display. Open from 8.30 to 11.30 am and from 1.30 to 4.30 pm daily.

Public Market

Well worth a few hours' visit is Vigan's sprawling public market. It's a good place to shop for *abel* (weaving) and to sample delicious local snacks such as *bibingka, tinopig, patopat* or *sinuman* (different variations of rice cake). It's also a good place to pick up fruits that are in season, such as *kaimito* (star apple).

Potteries

There are a couple of large pottery factories on Liberation Blvd, near the corner of Gomez St. They mostly make large *burnay* clay jars, in which *basi* (sugarcane wine) and *bagoong* (fish paste) is fermented. The craft was introduced to the region by Chinese artisans. The 50m-long dragon kilns, which are over 100 years old, are an amazing sight; it takes seven full-grown trees to fire up the kiln, which happens about once a month. On weekdays, you can watch well-known local potter Banong at work on his huge potter's wheel at RG Jar on Gomez St. You can also see Kevin the *carabao* (water buffalo) at work, mixing the clay as he walks on it. In addition to burnay jars, you can buy all types and sizes of beautiful brown clay vases and other knick-knacks at very reasonable prices.

Weaving

In Camanggan and Naguilian, in Caoayan (barangays of Vigan), about a 10-minute tricycle ride from town, you can watch weavers at work in their homes. They mostly make practical items, such as bathrobes, placemats and stoles for priests. You might also try barangay Mindoro, where there may still be weavers making *binakol,* weavings that incorporates a traditional psychedelic-looking, geometric design.

Other Attractions

About 4km outside of town, south down Quirino Blvd, is the small, picturesque fishing village of **Pandan**, Caoayan. On the way you'll pass the Mestizo River, with its milkfish farms, and a small wharf where local fishers sell crab, shrimp and milkfish in the wee morning hours. The village, with bougainvillea and other flowers sprouting everywhere, is a great place to stroll around. From the Vigan public market take the Caoayan jeepney, or better yet, hire a calesa.

Also in the vicinity is a **beach**. Before reaching the wharf, take a right to Manget. Along the way you'll pass the opulent home of the current governor, complete with shooting range and boa constrictor zoo (not open to the public). At the end of the road is the Don Juan Beach Resort, from where you can access the shore. The sand here is greyish-brown and the surf not particularly inviting. Still, it's a nice place for a stroll and to get away from the bustle of town.

Places to Stay

Vigan hotels are generally on the run-down side. Most accommodation is mid-range and of mediocre value. The following hotels are all in and around Vigan's Mestizo District.

The best place to stay in Vigan is *Villa Angela* (☎ 077-722 2914, fax 722 2351, 26 Quirino Blvd), the majestic old Vigan mansion now converted into a hostel. It only has a few rooms, so reserve in advance. A double/triple is P500/900 and a room that fits four to five people is P1200 (all with shared bath). They also have a double with air-con for P1000. Unfortunately, large loading trucks nearby begin work early in the morning, so bring earplugs.

The most modern hotel in the area is *Gordion Inn* (☎ 077-722 2526, fax 722 2840, 15 Salcedo St), where well-kept, air-con doubles start at P880. Nearby is *El Juliana Hotel* (☎ 077-722 2994, 5 Liberation St), where not-so-great doubles with air-con, TV and bath start at P475; better-kept doubles are P575 and P700. There's a pool here, which even hotel guests must pay to use (P30).

Cordillera Inn (☎ 077-722 2727, fax 722 2739), on beautiful Mena Crisologo St, has good but plain doubles (fan and shared bath) for P475, and better doubles with bath and air-con for P1100 up. It's owned by the prominent old Vigan family, the Crisologos. On Mabini St, off of Crisologo St, is *La Fernandina Hotel* (☎ 077-722 2964), with plain, rather run-down doubles for P450, and better ones for P600.

On a corner of Plaza Burgos is *Mansion* (☎ 077-722 2383, 1 Mena Crisologo St), where plain but satisfactory doubles are P650 and P850 (with TV and hot water). Just off the plaza is *La Feliza Tourist Inn* (☎ 077-722 2926, 8 V de los Reyes St), with decent but plain rooms for P660. Nearby is the *Vigan Hotel* (☎ 077-722 1906, fax 722 3001, ✉ viganhtl@iln.cyberspace.com.ph), on the corner of Burgos and V de los Reyes Sts. Plain but clean rooms with fan are P395/495 a single/double, with air-con P695/795. *Grandpa's Inn* (☎ 077-722 2118, 1 Bonifacio St) has plain doubles with fan and shared bath for P165, with private bath for P275 and with private bath and air-con for P440.

Outside of town in Managat, Caoayan, is the well-kept *Don Juan Beach Resort* (☎ 077-722 2362). Bamboo huts with fan/air-con are P900/1200, and there's a restaurant here.

Places to Eat

Leona Cafe on Plaza Burgos is the place to eat Ilocano specialties. If you're not worried about cholesterol, try *bagnet* (pork belly deep-fried till crispy, P120) or *longanisa* (sausage, P72). The *street stalls* on Plaza Burgos, open from about 3 to 7 pm, serve cheap, tasty snacks such as *empanadas* (deep-fried flour tortillas filled with shrimp, cabbage and egg) and *okoy* (deep-fried shrimp omelette). Also on Plaza Burgos is *Diay Plaza Fastfood*, a cafeteria-style restaurant that serves good, cheap Filipino food, and is a good place to cool off in the afternoons with a *halo-halo* (a dessert of shaved ice, condensed milk and fruit) or mango shake. Also on the plaza is *Royal Bibingka*, where you can get excellent fresh-from-the-oven *bibingka* (rice cake).

On the outskirts of the Mestizo district is *Halftime*, a disco with an outdoor restaurant that serves typical Filipino dishes. *Cool Spot*, also with outdoor seating, was once the place to go but is now little frequented. There are several air-con fastfood joints on Quezon Ave, including *Cindy's*, which serves decent Filipino-style fastfood, and *Giacomo*, which specialises in pizza.

Shopping

There are several antique shops in the Mestizo District, which are fun to browse in but mostly carry reproductions. Ornate wooden furniture is produced in Vigan, and shops such as *Mira Furniture* on the corner of Bonifacio and Plaridel Sts, take orders for custom-made furniture. Abel, or weaving, can be found in the *public market*, as well as at *Rowilda's* on Crisologo St and *Hi-Q* on Salcedo St. Pure cotton mosquito nets, difficult to find in other parts of the Philippines, are also available here. The locally produced pottery is also worth checking out. Try *RG Jar*, on Gomez St, where you can buy metre-tall clay burnay jars for around P100, or smaller pieces.

Getting There & Away

Philippine Rabbit has hourly buses to/from Manila (P312 air-con, nine hours), as does Partas Bus. Partas and Philippine Rabbit have hourly buses from Vigan to Baguio (P152, five hours) that pass through San Fernando.

Philippine Rabbit makes frequent trips to Laoag (P62, 1½ hours). You can also go to Bantay (on National Hwy), and wait for a Laoag minibus at the Caltex station. Frequent minibuses to Bangued leave from next to the public market.

Getting Around

Vigan is one of the few remaining towns in the Philippines where calesas are still in use. If you stay in the city centre, the cost of a calesa ride is the same as a tricycle ride (P3). If you go out of the city centre, negotiate a price beforehand. Tricycles are the easiest, although most noisy, way of getting about, as they are motorised in this part of the country. Jeepneys going to various barangays leave from the public market.

AROUND VIGAN
Santa Maria Church

Worth the one-hour trip south is the Santa Maria Church. Designated a World Heritage site by Unesco in 1990, this massive Baroque (1769) structure sits atop a hill overlooking the town of Santa Maria. The church was used as a fortress during the Philippine Revolution in 1896. Stairs on one side lead down an overgrown path into an old walled cemetery with a crumbling altar – the perfect setting for a Dracula film.

Also worth a visit is the architecturally interesting primitive baroque-style Church of San Vicente, just south of Vigan and not far from Santa Maria. Chinese and Japanese missionaries were once housed here. Inside the church the holy-water pits are Qing dynasty blue-and-white ware.

Magsingal

There is a branch of the **National Museum** in Magsingal, 11km north of Vigan, where Ilocano relics are on display. The two-storey museum houses pottery, porcelain, baskets, farming equipment and a wooden sugarcane crusher used for making sugarcane wine. It's open from 8.30 to 11.30 am and from 1.30 to 4.30 pm Monday to Friday. Next door is the **Magsingal Church** (1827), which houses two rather interesting sculptures of pregnant-looking angel mermaids.

LAOAG

The capital of Ilocos Norte, Laoag (pronounced 'lo-**ahg**') remains loyal Marcos country: Imee Marcos, daughter of Ferdinand and Imelda, is a congresswoman here, and her brother Ferdinand R ('Bong Bong') Marcos is the current governor.

There's not much to see and do in Laoag, although it attracts a fair number of tourists from Taiwan, most of whom stay at the Fort Ilocandia Hotel, which is also a casino. Laoag has an interesting sinking (and leaning) bell tower, of which only the upper half of the front door is visible.

The main commercial street is Rizal St; here BPI has an ATM that accepts AmEx, MasterCard and Cirrus. Cyberspace, on General Segundo St, has fast Internet connections for P50 per hour (open from 9 am to 10.30 pm daily).

Places to Stay

Centrally located *Hotel Del Norte* (☎ 077-772 1171, 26 Fonacier St), has clean and cheerful rooms with shared bath for P225/400 a single/double, and doubles with air-con and TV for P600. The pastel-coloured, Art Deco *Tiffany Hotel*, has modern, clean rooms with TV and air-con for P480/600. A short walk from the commercial centre *La Elliana Hotel* (☎ 077-771 4876), near the corner of Rizal and Ablan Sts, has clean, modern rooms for P550/600. Nearby is *Starlight*, where acceptable, rooms are P270, P395 with air-con. The upmarket *Palazzo De Laoag Hotel* (☎ 077-773 1842, 27 P Paterus St), a 10-minute tricycle ride from the centre of town, has very nice rooms starting at P1080.

Some 9km south of town, on the beach, is the sprawling, upmarket *Fort Ilocandia Resort Hotel* (☎ 077-772 1166), originally built by the Marcoses for their daughter Irene's wedding reception. Today the resort is heavily marketed to Taiwanese tourists. Standard rooms start at P3400/3710. Amenities include a casino, golf course and disco.

Places to Eat

La Preciosa is the place to go for delicious Ilocano specialties in cosy but elegant surroundings. Try the *puqui-puqui* (P55). The more casual, neon-lit *Fiesta Ilocana Restaurant*, in the Isabel Building just off Rizal St, also serves good local cuisine, such as *dinengdeng* (bean, eggplant and horseradish soup, P45) and crispy *pata* (pork) for P120. *Macy's Diner*, under Tiffany Hotel, is modelled on an American 1950s diner and serves hamburgers and shakes. Although a little pricey, *Golden Cow* serves excellent, authentic Chinese food, such as *mapo tofu* (spicy tofu) for P105.

Shopping

A visit to Sarusar is a must for anyone interested in handicrafts and Ilocano food. More like a museum than a store, Sarusar (meaning 'storage place') is a nonprofit organisation that assists Ilocano producers in marketing their products. There's a beautiful collection of quality local weavings, as well as locally produced food. It's open from 9 am to 6 pm Monday to Friday and from 1 to 5 pm Saturday.

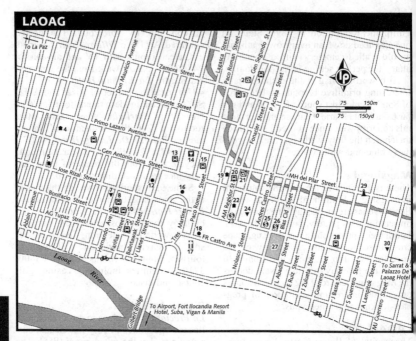

LAOAG

The public market is good for abel at reasonable prices, including the locally produced, geometric-patterned weavings called *binacol*.

Getting There & Away

Laoag International Airlines (☎ 077-772 1888, 772 1793, 772 1795; in Manila 02-551 9729) has regular flights to/from Manila (P1600) and to/from Basco, Batanes (P2000). Cathay Pacific has flights direct from Hong Kong and Taiwan. Jeepneys to the airport leave from Fonacier St (P10, 10 minutes). If you have an early flight take a tricycle as jeepneys don't start filling up till mid-morning.

Fariñas Trans, Maria Del Leon, RCJ, Philippine Rabbit, Autobus and Partas all have frequent buses to/from Manila (11 hours).

Minibuses to Pagudpud (P37, 1½ hours, 75km) leave every half hour or so. You can also take any Tuguegarao-bound bus and

get off at Pagudpud, although you'll have to get off the bus on the highway and take a tricycle into town. Florida, Autobus and RCJ have frequent buses to Tuguegarao.

Frequent minibuses leave from behind the Capitol Building for Vigan (1½ hours). Philippine Rabbit and Partas also have bus service to Vigan. Philippine Rabbit has hourly buses to Baguio (P158/214 nonaircon/air-con, 6½ hours).

Jeepneys to Batac and Paoay leave from Hernando at Rizal St. Callayab-bound jeepneys go to Fort Ilocandia.

AROUND LAOAG
Batac

In Batac, the **Marcos Museum** makes an interesting stop, if only to view the refrigerated body (although now looking suspiciously like plastic) of the late Ferdinand E Marcos, on display in a glass coffin next door to the main museum. The museum is in Marcos' boyhood home. You

LAOAG

PLACES TO STAY
4 Starlight
5 La Elliana Hotel; Autobus Bus Terminal
19 Tiffany Hotel; Macy's Diner
22 Hotel Del Norte

PLACES TO EAT
7 La Preciosa
24 Fiesta Ilocana Restaurant
30 Golden Cow

OTHER
1 Florida Liner Bus Terminal
2 Cyberspace
3 Partas Bus Terminal
6 Philippine Rabit Bus Terminal
8 Jeepneys to Paoay & Batae
9 RCJ Bus Terminal
10 Fariñas Trans Bus Terminal
11 Maria Del Leon Bus Terminal; Jeepneys to Callayab (Fort Ilocandia)
12 Sarusar
13 Minibuses to Pagudpud
14 Harmony & Rhythm
15 Minibuses to Vigan
16 Provincial Capital Building
17 St William's Cathedral
18 Sinking Belltower
20 Jeepneys to Airport
21 Amanet
23 Bank of the Philippine Islands (BPI)
25 Equitable PCI Bank
26 LBC Bank
27 Market
28 Jeepneys to Sarrat
29 Mt Del Pillar

might want to hurry over here though, as the Bureau of Internal Revenue constantly threatens to 'evict' the late dictator to help pay off the Marcos' P23.5 billion tax debt. Open from 9 am to noon and from 1 to 4 pm daily. Batac is about 63km north of Vigan.

Paoay

About 4km west of Batac, off the main highway is Paoay (pronounced 'pow-**why**'). The town's massive, fortress-like **Paoay Church** – built in 'earthquake baroque' style (with Gothic elements, as well as Chinese and Japanese influences) – is included on Unesco's World Heritage List. The church is built of thick coral blocks and stucco-plastered bricks, sealed with limestone mor-

tar mixed with sugarcane juice; with its 26 external buttresses, it has the appearance of a fort. Construction began in 1804, and was completed 90 years later. A few metres away is a three-storey coral stone belltower, dating from 1793.

Overlooking Paoay Lake, on the border of Laoag City, is the **Malacanang of the North**, the opulent former residence of the Marcoses. Legend holds that the lake was once the site of a town submerged as divine condemnation of the inhabitants' extreme materialism. It's open from 9 am to noon and from 1 to 4 pm Tuesday to Sunday (P20 admission includes a guide). From Laoag, take the Laoag-Suba jeepney.

Nearby is the road to **Suba Beach**, a long, desolate brown-sand beach surrounded by sand dunes. There's no public transport to the beach; from Laoag you can take a tricycle for about P100 return.

PAGUDPUD

The palm-tree lined, white-sand beach and azure blue water of Pagudpud is achingly beautiful. Unfortunately, the overpriced accommodation snaps you back into reality. If you're looking for a lively beach resort atmosphere, this isn't it, but if you're looking for a quiet place to get away from it all, Pagudpud fits the bill.

Places to Stay

Terra Rika Beach Resort (☎ 077-772 1845) is a small, well-maintained, family-run place with a few rooms (from P1000 to P2500). Budget travellers can camp for P700, including tent with mattress and bedding for two (P1000 for four). Next door is the *Villa Del Mar Ivory Beach Resort* (☎ 02-928 8296), where dark and poorly maintained doubles start at P1400. Slightly better rooms are P1700. You can rent tents here for P300/700 for two/four people. It also has a swimming pool.

The most upmarket accommodation is at *Saud Beach Resort*, where guards at the gate demand P50 just to enter. Standard doubles start at P2384, although if it's not high season you can negotiate this down to P1200. Nicer doubles in the main building

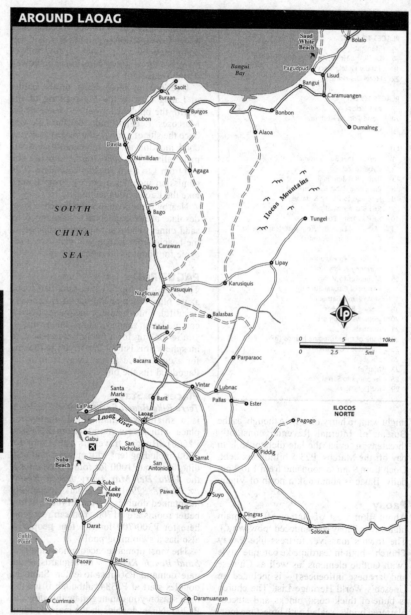

AROUND LAOAG

NORTH LUZON

Bangui Bay

South China Sea

Saud White Beach
Bolalo
Pagudpud
Lisud
Bangui
Caramuangen
Bonbon
Dumalneg
Alaoa
Saoit
Buraan
Burgos
Bubon
Davila
Namilidan
Agaga
Dilavo
Bago
Carawan
Ilocos Mountains
Tungel
Lipay
Naglicuan
Pasuquin
Karusiquis
Balasbas
Talatal
Parparaoc
Bacarra
Vintar
Lubnac
Pallas
Ester
Santa Maria
Barit
Pagogo
La Paz
Laoag
ILOCOS NORTE
Laoag River
Gabu
San Nicholas
Piddig
Suba Beach
San Antonio
Sarrat
Nagbacalan
Suba
Lake Paoay
Pawa
Suyo
Darat
Anangui
Parlir
Dingras
Culih Point
Solsona
Paoay
Batac
Currimao
Daramuangan

0   5   10km
0 2.5 5mi

are P2384 year-round. The atmosphere is relaxing and the rooms are nicely done. Space under the shades is P500 per day.

Getting There & Away
From Tuguegarao, any Laoag or Vigan-bound bus passes Pagudpud. From Laoag, see that section earlier.

Batanes

Batanes' natives are called the Ivatan (literally, 'place where boats are cast ashore'). The native dialect of this island-group province, 280km north of North Luzon and consisting of 10 islands (population 14,180 for the three inhabited islands), is a combination of several Philippine dialects; English and Tagalog are also widely spoken. The average income here ranks among the lowest in the country, though people barter to meet their daily needs. Most people subsistence farm, and garlic is the only commercial crop.

The sea is all-important to the Ivatan way of life, and if the weather is conducive, you'll eat well in Batanes. Flower pots are made from plastic fishing buoys that have floated to shore; metal buoys are cut open and used as pots, and pretty green, blue and yellow glass buoys are used as decorations.

Central to daily life is the weather. The traditional, typhoon-safe houses are built with metre-thick limestone walls, strong cogon roofs and small, narrow windows and doors. If the winds are blowing from the north, no boats leave shore and no planes take off or land. Typhoon season is from July to December, and it's not uncommon for six typhoons to hit the archipelago in one year alone. The best time to visit the islands is from March to May, when the weather is relatively hot and dry. Because the weather is so unpredictable, you need time and flexibility to visit Batanes.

BATAN ISLAND
Basco
Basco (population 5000), on the island of Batan, is the largest town in Batanes. It's a

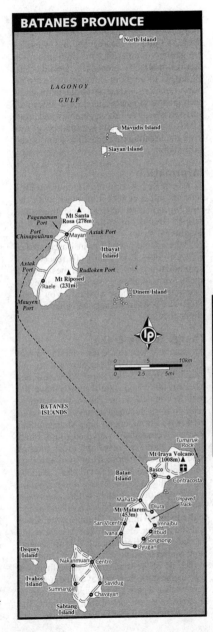

BATANES PROVINCE

NORTH LUZON

very friendly, modern-looking town, where most people get around on foot or by bicycle, although motorcycles and tricycles are gaining popularity. This tidy little town has 12 hours of electricity per day. In Basco, as throughout Batanes, there are no public markets. Abad St is the main commercial street, where there are a few small sari-sari stores selling vegetables and fruit. The island's main road (National Hwy) follows the breathtaking coastline from Basco to Imnajbu.

Information

Elizabeth Reyes and Lory Tan put out *Trek Batanes,* an excellent mini-guide with detailed information on treks, available at the Filipino Bookstore in the Glorietta mall in Manila.

There is one phone/fax in Basco (☎/fax 632-533 3444, 533 3456). To reserve accommodation, call and leave a message. To speak with someone, leave a message letting that person know what time you'll call back. The PNB in Batanes can change travellers cheques.

Things to See & Do

An excellent way to see the island is to rent a mountain bike (P100 per day; ask at your lodging). Because there are so few automobiles on the island, you'll mostly have the road to yourself. From Basco, the National Hwy follows the coast around the island to the town of Imnajbu, passing Mahatao, San Vicente, Ivana and Uyagan en route. From Imnajbu take the gravel and grass interior road through **Marlboro Country** that brings you back to Mahatao. The ride isn't exceedingly strenuous, but it takes about six hours.

A couple of kilometres before you reach Mahatao, you'll see a paved road and a sign to the fishing village of Diura, Crystal Cave and the Spring of Youth. The village is inhabited only during Dorado fishing season, from March through to June. From Diura, go to the end of the road, from where there's a path to the dark, narrow cave (about a half-hour walk). There's a municipal cottage in Diura where you can spend the night. Inquire at the municipal hall in Mahatao.

Beaches in Batan mostly have brownish sand, or are strewn with pebbles or boulders. The surf can be rough, so check with locals which beaches are safe. The beach in Mahatao, and White Beach, just south of Mahatao, are generally considered safe for swimming. There is a beautiful boulder beach at **Songsong Bay** (not to be confused with Songsong, the deserted village) north of Basco.

Mt Iraya (1008m), at the northern end of Batan, can be climbed (from Basco) in about five hours and descended in about three, though the summit is usually covered in clouds.

The surfing is said to be good off the coast of Mahatao. You can also explore war tunnels built by the Japanese, who occupied the islands during WWII.

Places to Stay & Eat

A very pleasant place is *Mataw Inn*, behind Builder's Bank next to the wharf on the National Hwy. More like a homestay than a lodge, the owners will make you feel at home and will feed you till you burst. Walk-ins are welcome, but it's best to book (see Information earlier). Rooms with shared bath are P150 per person, and room and board is P450.

Another excellent option is *Mama Lily's*, right on the plaza. Immaculate rooms with shared bath are P150 per person, P500 with meals. Large portions are seafood are served at Mama Lily's, so arrange to have some meals here. Around 5 am each morning loudspeakers hooked up to the church blast prayers.

Iraya Lodge offers good, clean lodging. It's just off the plaza, near the municipal hall.

Getting There & Away

The airport is a 10-minute walk north of the plaza in Basco, Batan, or you can take a tricycle into town (P10, plus P10 per bag).

From Manila, Laoag International Airlines (☎ 02-551 9729 in Manila, 077-772 1888 or 772 1793, fax 773 1888 in Laoag, ☎ 078-844 5518, fax 844 0988 in Tugegarao) has regular flights to Basco on at 6 am Tuesday and 9.55 am Thursday (P3600, plus P103 terminal fee). You can also fly from Tuguegarao on Monday (P2000, plus P103 terminal fee).

A nine-seater plane flies Tuesday, Thursday and Saturday from Laoag (P2000, plus P103 terminal fee). There's a 10kg maximum baggage weight (which sometimes includes carry on). It's an additional P44 for each extra kilogram. Once in Batanes, you can book your return flight at the Basco airport.

Book planes about a week in advance, as flights can fill up quickly.

There are no passenger boats to Batanes. It's possible to get here on cargo ships, but there's no regular schedule. From Manila it's about a four-day boat ride to Batanes.

Getting Around

Jeepneys regularly ply the road from Basco to Imnajbu from around 4.30 am to around 4 pm. From Basco, wait for the jeepney in front of Builder's Bank, near the wharf. A few tricycles can be hired for special trips. They're usually parked on Abad St, or ask your accommodation if they can help arrange one. The island also has a few bicycles for rent; ask at your accommodation.

SABTANG ISLAND

Sabtang's villages feel as if they've stopped in time. Its small limestone-house villages, magnificent rocky coastline and rolling hills – even more striking than Batan – makes it ideal for hiking.

You can do a round-trip hike around the island. From Centro (where the ferry docks), you can hike south on the road to **Savidug** in about an hour (6km). Just outside of town is an *idjang*, a large rocky hill. In pre-Hispanic times Ivatan villages were built next to idjangs, from where villagers defended themselves by hurling rocks at their attackers.

From Savidug it's another 2km to picturesque **Chavayan**. There's a beautiful pastel-coloured church just next to the beach. From Chavayan it's a two-hour walk through the island's interior to **Sumnanga**, also known as 'Little Hong Kong', because its little houses are crammed right up to the shoreline. Follow the road from Sumnanga

to **Nakanmuan** and back to Centro. **Ivahos Island**, a small, uninhabited island west of Sabtang, can be accessed from Nakanmuan or Sumnanga if you can find someone with a boat to take you. Locals say Ivahos has the best beaches and excellent snorkelling.

Although you can do this hike in a day, you'll probably miss the last boat back to Basco, which leaves at 3 pm, so plan on spending the night in Centro. The *School of Fisheries* has a nice dormitory for P50 per person; there's a canteen downstairs. There are also a few sari-sari stores in Centro.

You may very well meet friendly Ivatans who will open their homes to you; bring along a few gifts, such as reading material (eg, books on fishing), hooks and lines, to show your appreciation for their hospitality.

Getting There & Around

It's possible to hire a jeepney (P1200 per day) in Centro (ask the mayor), to get to Sabidug and Chavayan. The jeepney must then backtrack to Centro to go to Nakanmuan and Sumnanga. There are also a couple of jeepneys that make regular trips from Centro-Sabidug-Chavayan, then back to Centro and on to Nakanmuan and Sabtang.

To get to Sabtang from Batan, there's a ferry at around 6.30 am and one at 9 am. They leave from across the church on the outskirts of Ivana. These ferries also make return trips to Batan in the morning. There is one afternoon ferry from Sabtang to Batan at around 3 pm; check the departure time when you get to Centro.

ITBAYAT ISLAND

Some 40km north of Batan is the island of Itbayat (population 3060), the Philippines northernmost inhabited island. Electricity was introduced here only in 1997, and there is no TV or telephone service.

The only way to get here is on a very rocky four-hour boat ride from Basco. Because the island is completely surrounded by tall rocky cliffs, the ports are precarious, narrow concrete ledges carved into the cliffs; to disembark you have to time your jump onto the port for when the wave is at an equal height. Itbayat's ports are connected by gravel road (with the exception of the road from Port Chinapuliran to Mayan, which is paved) to the main town of **Mayan**, at the bottom of the bowl-like island. Port Chinapuliran is 3km from Mayan. There is no coastal road.

Raele is about 9km south of Mayan. The area here is rolling grass hills, with the occasional lone palm to remind you that you're in the tropics. The island is crisscrossed with trails, making it a great place for trekking during good weather. To the east of Raele is **Mt Riposed** (231m), from where there are nice views.

From Mayan it's a beautiful half-hour walk along a grassy road with native flowers to **Paganaman port**, where at around 5 pm you'll see farmers on their way back from the fields. Many older woman still wear *soots* (raincaps made from reeds that trail all the way down the back). You'll also see fishermen coming back with their colourful catch of the day. If you arrive at the port at low tide, soak in a little natural swimming pool in the rocks next to the port.

There are is no lodging house on the island, but the mayor will let you stay in the *guesthouse* (P100 per person), which has a kitchen you can use. Upon arrival, call on the mayor at the municipal building and inquire about accommodation.

There are a few sari-sari stores that sell food and drinks, but you're best to bring some food and water with you. Unlike Batan Island, the water here must be boiled before drinking. Try to buy some coconut crabs, which are caught on the island's cliffs.

Getting There & Around

It's a gruelling four-hour ride from Basco to Port Chinapulitan, departing Basco at around 8.30 am (P200 one way). If you get motion sick, take medication before the trip. Here the Pacific Ocean and the South China Sea converge, causing strong currents. The boat is a small wooden motorboat, which will most likely be loaded with goods and livestock. Come prepared to stay on Itbayat longer than planned, as you can't be certain when you'll be able to make the return trip. During typhoon season, boats have been known to not be able to make the crossing for a month at a time. The boat leaves Itbayat for Basco shortly after it arrives, usually at around 1 pm. There are no boats to or from Itbayat on Sunday (or, of course, if the weather is bad, the wind is from the north, the moon is full...).

There is an airstrip with a dirt runway, although all flights ceased after an plane accident three years ago in which the mayor was killed. There are plans to pave the runway so flights can resume.

There's no public transport around the island. A few residents have motorbikes.

South-East Luzon

Outdoors-lovers will find plenty to do in the little-travelled southern Luzon peninsula known as Bicol, home to the Mt Mayon volcano and its perfectly symmetrical cone. The main attractions for visitors are hiking, surfing, swimming (with friends, loved ones or whale sharks) and doing your bit for the environment by soaking up those harmful UV rays on gorgeous beaches.

The largely undeveloped island of Catanduanes offers peace, quiet and the beautiful bay at Puraran.

The island province of Marinduque, also unspoiled, lies between Bicol and Mindoro. Here you can join a passion play during the island's popular Moriones Festivals, hang with the bats in caves near Santa Cruz or (should you feel the urge) repent your sins in Boac's lovely church.

Bicol

Bicol technically includes the provinces of Albay, Camarines Norte, Camarines Sur and Sorsogon, and the islands of Catanduanes and Masbate, but this section of the chapter covers peninsular Bicol only. (Catanduanes is covered in a separate section later in this chapter, and Masbate is included in the Visayas chapter).

Mt Mayon, Mt Isarog, near Naga, and Mt Bulusan in Sorsogon offer great hiking opportunities. Daet, in Camarines Norte, is well known for surfing. Caramoan, in Camarines Sur, has a stunning shoreline and crystal clear blue water, which is great for swimming. Donsol, with its *butanding* (whale sharks; see the boxed text 'Sea Changes' in the Facts for the Visitor chapter), offers an amazing opportunity to swim with the world's largest fish. Bicol is also known for its delectable, fiery food, laden with hot peppers and coconut.

The New People's Army (NPA) is still active in some of the more remote regions, notably in Sorsogon, so you may need to

HIGHLIGHTS

- Swimming with the glorious *butanding* (whale sharks) in Donsol
- Climbing to the knife edge of Mt Mayon
- Sampling the fiery cuisine of Bicol
- Relaxing and waiting for the surf to kick in at wide and wild Puraran Bay in Catanduanes

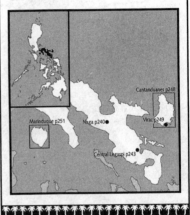

travel with caution in some parts of those areas (see Sorsogon later).

Getting There & Away

Boat Ferries bound for Masbate depart from Bulan. The trip takes about 3½ hours and tickets are P47.

Bus From other parts of Luzon, the best way to travel to Bicol is by bus. A number of companies have frequent bus services throughout the region, including BLTB, Philtranco, JB Bicol Express Line, AMA and Superlines.

Train It's also possible to take a train from Manila to Naga and Legaspi and points along the way. A new train station is expected to

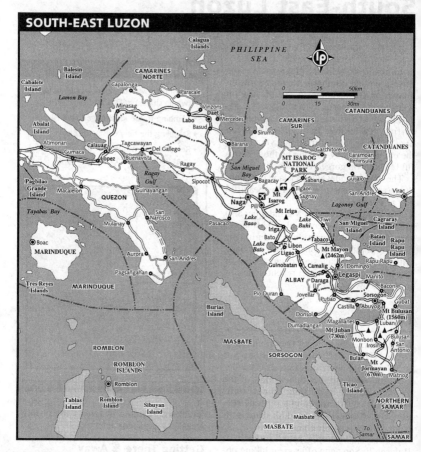

SOUTH-EAST LUZON

open in Manila in June 1999, with improved service. There are only two long-distance trains per week: Train 517 leaves at 6 pm Thursday for Naga (P234, 11 hours) and Legaspi (P297, 14 hours); train 577, with deluxe service, leaves at 4 pm Thursday for Naga and Legaspi.

DAET

The capital of Camarines Norte, Daet is a busy commercial centre. Its main attraction is the big waves at **Bagasbas Beach**, 4km from town. Other nearby beaches known for surfing are **Mercedes** and **San José**.

Alvin Obusan, of Alvino's Pizza House (see Places to Eat later), is the president of the Camarines Norte Surfing Association, and is a good source of information about surfing in the area. He can also set you up with a surf guide, who can take you to the best waves further afield. The narrow, brown-sand beaches aren't good for swimming, as the current is strong and the shoreline is littered with wood and other debris that has floated to shore.

Mercedes is a ragtag but charming little fishing village from where you can hire a boat to explore the islands in **San Miguel**

Bay. **Apuao Grande Island** is a private island with a cosy little resort run by Swagman Travel (see Places to Stay following).

Places to Stay

Lodging in Daet is basic. There are a couple of decent places to stay, but aside from these, all other lodging is of the dank and run-down variety.

In Daet, the cleanest place to stay is **Dolor Hotel** (☎ *054-721 2167*), on Vinzon's Ave. Rooms are spacious and the staff is friendly. There's also a coffee shop and restaurant. Rooms with fan and bath are P220/350 a single/double, and with air-con P450/650. The hotel is on the 3rd floor.

Nearby is the **Kariligan Hotel**, on Moreno St, where run-down rooms with fan and bath are P150/200 and slightly better-maintained rooms with air-con are P400. The **Sampaguita Lodging House**, on Vinzon's Ave, has similar rooms for P75/150 with common bath, P150/250 with fan and bath and P300/395 with air-con.

Off Bagasbas Beach, the **Travellers Hotel** has simple but clean and well-kept spacious rooms with bath and fan for P200, or P400 with air-con. It also has some nicely done cottages for P150. Also on Bagasbas, across the street from the beach, **Alvino's Pizza House** has some bunk beds for P150 per head.

On Apuao Grande Island, **TS Resorts** (☎ *054-721 1545*) has well-kept, comfortable cottages on the beach for P600/800. The resort has tennis courts, a golf course and swimming pool. The pretty island has a nice beach and gentle waves great for swimming. However, the small community of condos being developed here could reduce the resort's appeal. The resort has a private boat which can bring you to the island. Call ☎ 054-721 1604 for reservations and to arrange the boat.

Places to Eat

As with accommodation, Daet is pretty limited when it comes to good places to eat. The cavernous **Ocean Garden Restaurant**, on the 3rd floor across from the Philtranco bus terminal, serves Chinese-style dishes.

The seafood here, at more than P200 a dish, is pricey. Just around the corner, the **Golden House** is less spiffy, but serves similar food at similar prices. On the corner of Moreno St and F Pimentel St, **Sandok at Palayok** serves typical Filipino dishes.

Possibly the best place to eat in the area is **Alvino's Pizza House** (see Places to Stay earlier), on Bagasbas Beach. The open-air restaurant serves delicious pizzas for about P140.

Getting There & Away

Air There's a small airport at Bagasbas Beach. At the time of writing PAL had discontinued flights from Manila.

Bus Phil Tranco, AMA and Highway Express have hourly buses from Manila to Daet (P257, eight hours). Buses to Naga (P56, two hours) and Legaspi leave from the Central terminal.

NAGA

Naga, in Camarines Sur, is one of Luzon's more pleasant commercial centres. At its core are two plazas, both surrounded by shops and restaurants. Naga's prosperity is evident in its large number of banks, shops and restaurants. It's also a college town, with a student body active in the area's outdoors scene.

Every third week of September thousands of devotees make a pilgrimage to Naga for the Peñafrancia Festival, in celebration of the Virgin of Peñafrancia, Bicol's patron saint.

Naga is the jumping-off point for **Mt Isarog**, Bicol's second-highest volcano (now dormant), and the **Caramoan Peninsula**, with its stunning shoreline; it's great for camping, swimming and, if you have your own equipment, sea kayaking.

Information

There are a couple of places to check email in Naga: Internet Naga in Traders Square above Dunkin' Donuts (open till 7.30 pm) and NetAmbayan above the Bicharra Cinema (open from 9 am to 8 pm, P80 per hour).

SOUTH-EAST LUZON

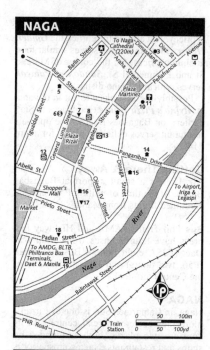

Kadlagan Outdoor Shop (☎ 054-472 3305, ✉ kadlagan@hotmail.com), at 17 Dimasalang St, leads guided trips to Mt Isarog and Caramoan. If possible, contact the shop before arriving in Naga so it can make arrangements for your trip. It can also organise tents and other camping gear. The manager, Jojo, is an excellent source of information about mountaineering and other outdoor activities in the area.

Places to Stay

A short distance from Plaza Rizal is the friendly *Moroville Hotel* (☎ 054-474 1411), where clean but worn rooms start at P250 with fan and bath or P350 with air-con, bath and cable TV. It also has slightly more expensive rooms that are a bit better. The *Sampaguita Tourist Inn* (☎ 054-473 8896) has grotty singles with common bath for P100, and better (but still mediocre) rooms with air-con and bath for P350/450.

Located on the plaza and a bit better-kept is the *Naga Crown Hotel* (☎ 054-473 8305, fax 473 9730), where clean but basic rooms with air-con and bath are P600/900 a single/double. The *Aristocrat Hotel* (☎ 054-473 8832) has a complicated collection of rooms ranging from dank and small with fan and common bath for P270/295 – to better with air-con and bath, but overpriced, for P676/731. The *Grand Imperial Hotel* (☎ 05421-473 6535) is very overpriced (although it quickly offers a 25% discount) with basic and slightly run-down rooms with air-con and bath (no TV) for P930/1380. A short way outside of town is the new *Lucky Fortune Hotel* (☎ 054-472 0324), where good, basic singles are P400 with fan and bath or P850 with air-con, bath and TV. Doubles start at P1200.

Villa Caceres (☎ 054-473 6530 to 473 6533, fax 473 9327), a 10-minute ride out of town, is Naga's most upmarket lodging. Its rooms are still pretty basic though; standards start at P750/1000.

Places to Eat

Popular with locals, *Oyster Villa* has a large array of Chinese dishes, most priced over P160. It also has budget meals for P65, like sweet-and-sour fish fillet or chicken curry. Open 24 hours a day is the modern and stylishly decorated *Chinoy*. It has a similar menu with similar prices to Oyster Villa, as well as sizzling plates and snacks such as fresh *lumpia*. Several fast-food joints are found around the plaza, including *Geewan*, which serves local food, cafeteria-style. There's a 20% discount if you arrive after 8.30 pm.

Getting There & Away
Air Asian Spirit, Air Philippines and Philippine Airlines (PAL) have flights from Manila to Naga and vice-versa (around P1100).

Bus From Manila, AMDG and Tritran buses go to Naga (10½ hours) and Legaspi. Naga is 2½ hours from Daet. From Naga's Plaza Rizal, you can catch a Diversion-bound jeepney to the terminal in front of Jollibee.

A Philtranco bus goes directly to Donsol, passing through the Philtranco bus terminal (at Diversion) between 10 pm and 1 am (six hours).

CARAMOAN PENINSULA
A four-hour journey from Naga brings you to the isolated Caramoan Peninsula, in Camarines Sur, where you can kick back on the unspoiled, gorgeous white-sand beaches. As at Hundred Islands National Park, a short way offshore there are several limestone islets with small beaches. The limpid, turquoise water is great for swimming, and it's possible to rent a *sabit-sabit* (small fishing boat) and paddle from island to island. About 4km from town is **Gota Beach**, a pretty white-sand beach excellent for swimming. The beach is divided in the centre by a rocky outcrop, where a concrete shed has been built (hopefully not a sign of things to come). There are fishing boats on one side; ask a local if you can hire one. You could also try going to Paniman to hire a boat, and from there head to Gota or one of the outlying islands.

The scenery inland from the beach is stunning, with rice paddies reaching right up to towering limestone cliffs. Further inland is mostly coconut farms in rolling green hills. There are several small dirt roads around the area that would be good for hiking. The mountainous interior of the Caramoan Peninsula still sees some insurgency, so check at the Caramoan Municipal Hall for the latest news if you plan to head into the interior.

Despite its isolation, the population of Caramoan Peninsula is almost 40,000. Although jeepneys and tricycles ply the streets of its *poblacion* (town centre), it's still a pretty quiet place. There are a couple of small eateries where you can buy meals, but there is no accommodation. You're best off bringing your own camping equipment (or arranging this with Kadlagan in Naga; see Information earlier) and camping on Gota Beach. Alternatively, check with the mayor once you reach town, to see if she can help you find a place to stay. Plans are under way to build accommodation in the area; check with tourist information in the Grand Imperial Hotel in Naga for the latest developments.

Getting There & Away
From Naga, take a bus or jeep from the Central terminal (across from Tito George Eatery at the Diversion road) to Laganoy (P30, one hour). Get off the bus or jeep in San José or Gota, then complete the last 15 minutes to Sabang in another jeepney. The first trip leaves Naga at 4.30 am. From Sabang, there are four regular boats to Guijalo from 10 am to 1 pm, leaving as they fill up (P50, two hours). You can also hire your own boat for P500. From Guijalo, it's a 10-minute jeepney or tricycle ride to Caramoan's poblacion. There is no road that connects Sabang to Guijalo and Caramoan to Garchitorena, although it's possible to bike to Caramoan from Naga on dirt paths.

From Manila, Philtranco buses go direct to Sabang.

MT ISAROG NATIONAL PARK
Dominating Camarines Sur's landscape is Mt Isarog (1966m), Bicol's second-highest volcano, now dormant. From *barangay* (small

village or neighbourhood) Panicuason (pro-nounced 'pan-ee-**kwa**-sone'), Carolina, a half-hour walk along a well-maintained dirt path leads to the entrance of the Mt Isarog National Park. The park consists solely of the mountain, which stands alone and isn't part of a mountain range. From the entrance, a short walk down some stone steps leads to **Malabsay Falls**. If it's not too crowded (it's a popular picnic spot for city dwellers in the area), it's a nice place to swim. On clear days, if you're facing the falls, there are beautiful views of Mt Isarog rising up behind the falls. Along the same stairs, before reaching Malabsay Falls, a smaller path from the first concrete shed leads to **Yabo Falls**.

From the entrance, a path to the left leads to **Nabuntan Falls**, about 1km away.

If you plan to hike any further, you must get a permit from the Department of Environment & Natural Resources (DENR) in Naga. Guides are available at the Kadlagan Outdoor Shop in Naga. You can reach Mt Isarog's summit in two days and descend in one. Trails are well-maintained and there are camps with water sources along the way.

Getting There & Away
From Naga, take a jeepney to Panicuason (P8, 45 minutes). Ask the driver to let you off at the road leading to Mt Isarog. From where the jeepney drops you off, it's an easy half-hour walk to the entrance of the park. The last jeepney back to Naga leaves Panicuason around 4 pm.

LEGASPI
The capital of Albay province, Legaspi is a friendly town situated at the foot of the striking Mt Mayon, one of the world's most active volcanoes. The town itself is pleasant enough, with some good restaurants where you can try the region's spicy cuisine, but there are no sights really to speak of. Most travellers come here to climb Mayon and head to Donsol, in Sorsogon, to swim with the mighty whale sharks.

A short drive outside of Legaspi there are a few minor tourist sights, including the **Cagsawa Ruins**, site of the church submerged by volcanic ash when Mt Mayon

erupted in 1814. Santo Domingo's shoreline has a few mediocre but pleasant **beaches** and resorts. There are also some spectacular views of the shoreline along the **coastal road to Joroan**.

Information
Worth visiting is the friendly and informative Department of Tourism (DOT; ☎ 052-482 0712, 214 3215, fax 482 0811), Regional Center Site, located on the outskirts of town. From Peñaranda St (Legaspi's main commercial street) take a Rawis-bound jeepney, and get off just after the bridge, about a 10-minute ride from town. The office offers packages to climb Mt Mayon that include guide, porter and food.

You can rent a car at Tropical Tours (☎ 052-480 7291, ✉ tropical@binfonet .com), in the V&O Building, Lapu Lapu St, starting at P700 for four hours or P1750 for 12 hours (includes driver). It also offers package tours to sights around the area.

There are a couple of places to check your email in Legaspi: GlobaLink Internet Cafe, on the 2nd floor of the AMA building on Lapu Lapu St, is open from 8.30 am to noon and from 1.30 pm to 6 pm; P60 per half-hour. Catsnet, near the Graceland fast food restaurant, by the Capital building in Albay also has Internet connections. You can make long-distance calls at Matelco, behind the JB bus terminal. The Bank of the Philippine Islands (BPI), on Quezon Ave, has ATMs that accept Cirrus, MasterCard and AmEx cards. Equitable PCI Bank on Rizal St handles cash advances on Visa cards.

PAL has an office in the Legaspi airport. For reservations call ☎ 052-245 5024. Also near the airport is the Philippine Institute of Volcanology & Seismology (PHILVOLCS), where Mt Mayon is monitored.

Places to Stay
The best moderately priced accommodation in town is the modern **Legaspi Tourist Inn** (*☎ 052-480 6147, fax 480 6148, 3rd floor V&O Building), where clean and well-kept standard rooms with bath and fan are P450/510 a single/double, or with air-

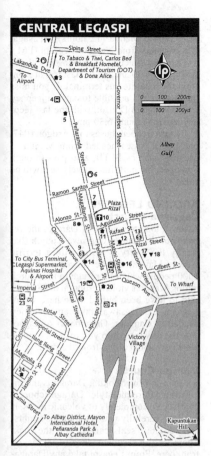

CENTRAL LEGASPI

PLACES TO STAY
3 Albay Hotel
5 Casablanca Hotel
7 Catalina's Lodging House
11 Rex Hotel
12 Hotel La Trinidad
20 Legaspi Tourist Inn
24 Tanchuling Hotel

PLACES TO EAT
1 Waway Restaurant
17 'Hilton'
18 Boklan

OTHER
2 Caltex Petrol Station
4 BLTB Bus Terminal
6 Shell Petrol Station
8 Bicharra Entertainment Center
9 Bank of the Philippine Islands (BPI)
10 St Rafael Church
13 Philippine National Bank (PNB)
14 LCC Department Store
15 JB Bicol Express Line Bus Terminal
16 Matelco
19 Post Office
21 GlobaLink Internet Cafe; AMA Computer
22 Equitable PCI Bank
23 Philtranco Bus Terminal

con P650/710. It also has a small and friendly cafe.

Near the cathedral is *Catalina's Lodging House* (☎ 052-480 7841, 96 Peñaranda St), Legaspi's best budget accommodation. It has clean and basic rooms for P110/160 with shared bath or P170/270/370 for singles/doubles/triples with bath. Rooms with bath and air-con are P320/420/530.

Across from the cathedral, *Rex Hotel* has reasonably priced, although slightly run-down, rooms with fan and bath for P240/275, and slightly better rooms with air-con and TV for P540.

One of the nicest places to stay in the area is in Rawis, at the *Carlos Bed & Breakfast Hometel* (☎ 052-482 0738), where nicely decorated and very clean rooms with air-con are P650. 'Hometel' aptly describes this place – although larger than a regular house, its common areas include a living room with TV and dining room. Roosters being raised nearby for cockfighting are sure to rouse you early in the morning.

A bit outside the city, but easily accessible due to the constant flow of Legaspi-Daraga jeepneys that pass near the hotel and plaza, *Tanchuling Hotel* (☎ 052-480 6003) has good, plain singles/doubles with bath and air-con for P550.

The quiet and dark *Hotel La Trinidad* (☎ 052-480 7469, fax 214 3148) has worn rooms starting at P870/970. A much better option in this price range is *Casablanca Hotel* (☎ 052-480 8334, fax 480 8338, ✉ lee@globalink.net.ph), where modern, well-kept and clean rooms start at P960. A bit further down the road is the *Albay Hotel*, with similar (and therefore overpriced) rooms starting at P2000.

At the time of writing, and at an altitude of 810m, the *Mayon Skyline Hotel* (☎ 052-431 1201) is located over halfway up the north-west side of Mt Mayon. Portions of the road up here can be rough and there is no public transport, so you must hire your own car to get here (one hour by car from Legaspi). Unfortunately the rooms here are in a state of disrepair. Rates are P500 for a room that can accommodate up to three people. Most people who spend the night here do so to climb Mayon; a guide can be arranged through the hotel for P1500.

Far and away the most luxurious hotel in the area is the *Mayon International Hotel* (☎ 052-480 1655, fax 245 5064, ✉ tesa@ globalink.net.ph), which is located about a 15-minute ride outside of the city, on a hill overlooking the city, ocean and the majestic Mt Mayon. It has a swimming pool and several restaurants. Rooms here start at P1526. The hotel can arrange packages to Donsol, including transportation and boat.

Places to Eat

Dona Alice, in Rawis, about 10 minutes' jeepney ride from town (with great views of Mt Mayon along the way), serves good native dishes and seafood, including Bicol Express (P40), blue marlin (P80) and *tanguigui* (P100). It has a tropical atmosphere, with bamboo and rattan furniture. On the same road but a bit closer to town is *Waway Restaurant*, also well-known in the area for native dishes. Waway is closed on Sunday.

For a taste of homemade local food try the *'Hilton'*, nicknamed by locals because of its rather upscale prices. It's in a bit of a dodgy neighbourhood, behind *Boklan*, a Chinese restaurant that also serves good food. Hilton's speciality is *cosido*, the Bicolano version of *sinigang* (sour fish soup), made with young coconut milk.

Getting There & Away

Air PAL and Air Philippines have daily flights to/from Manila. At time of writing there were no direct flights to Cebu.

Bus BLTB and JB buses have frequent service to/from Manila (12 hours) via Naga. It's 2½ hours from Naga to Legaspi (P61).

There are direct buses to Donsol, with the first trip at 4.20 am and the last trip at 2 pm from the Satellite bus terminal. If you miss the last trip it's possible to catch a jeepney from Daruga to Donsol, with the last jeepney leaving around 6.30 pm.

JB runs frequent buses to Sorsogon (P47, one hour). Buses headed from Manila to Matnog, such as BLTB, also pass through Sorsogon, but most likely every seat will be filled.

AROUND LEGASPI
Cagsawa Church

A few kilometres north of Daraga, the remains of the sunken Cagsawa Church (basically the belfry – along with a terrific view of Mayon), can be viewed here. Over 1000 people who took refuge in the church during Mayon's violent eruption in 1814 are said to have been buried alive here. From Legaspi to Cagsawa, take any jeepney headed to Camalig, Guinobatan or Ligao. Ask the driver to drop you off at the ruins, which are about 500m from the road.

Daraga Church

Set on a hill overlooking Daraga is the interesting Baroque-style Daraga church, constructed completely of volcanic rocks. If you look carefully you'll see *santos* (saints) and religious seals carved into the rock. There are also excellent views of Mt Mayon from here. From Legaspi take any Daraga-bound jeepney.

Hoyop-Hoyopan Caves

A popular tourist destination among locals, this series of caves near Camalig, 8km from Legaspi, includes the easy-to-traverse Hoy-op-Hoyopan Caves, where 2000-year-old artefacts have been found. Nearby is the more challenging Calabidongan Cave (literally, 'Cave of the Bats'). To explore the caves you must have a guide; Fred Nieva in Camalig should be able to make arrangements.

From Legaspi to Hoyop-Hoyopan take any jeepney headed to Camalig, Polangui,

Guinobatan or Ligao. Get off at Camalig and take a jeepney to Cotman (40 minutes).

Santo Domingo

About 30 minutes north from Legaspi is a stretch of black-sand beach with a few beach resorts, the nicest of which is the *Mayon Spring Resort*. It's prettily laid out, with orchids planted everywhere, and the grounds include a swimming pool. Rooms are P550 with air-con, or you can use the resort's facilities for the day for P50. Much more basic is the *Reyes Beach Resort*, where rooms with fan are P195/530 a single/double. To Santo Domingo, take any jeepney from the Legaspi public market (30 minutes).

Mt Mayon

One of the Philippines' most photographed sights, Mt Mayon (2420m) is renowned for its perfectly symmetrical cone. You can see the slopes of Mt Mayon dramatically rising from the flat Albay terrain surrounding it, from as far away as Naga. It is truly a mesmerising sight; in fact, the volcano's name derives from the Bicolano word meaning beauty.

Mayon is considered one of the most dangerous volcanoes in the world, due to its relatively frequent eruptions. The last time it erupted was in March 2000, and in a previous eruption in 1993 a team of American volcanologists who were doing research on its slopes were killed. At the time, equipment monitoring Mt Mayon had temporarily been moved to Mt Pinatubo, which had recently erupted. Other recent eruptions of Mayon occurred in 1968, 1978 and 1984.

At time of writing Mayon was off-limits to trekkers following the March eruption, but in quiet times it is a popular climb. You don't need to be an experienced mountain climber to ascend Mayon, although you should be in good shape. First go to the DOT in Legaspi to arrange a guide. The cost is P4500 for up to two climbers, which includes a guide, porter, food and camping equipment. Additional people are an extra P1500 each. Ask if your guide has a radio so they can keep in constant touch with PHILVOLCS, who monitors Mayon's activity. If you can't get a

guide with a radio, be sure your guide has checked with PHILVOLCS just prior to starting the climb. A highly recommended guide is Alan Velasco. There are two ways to reach Mayon's crater: via Buyuan, on Mayon's south-east slope, or from the Mayon Skyline Hotel on the north-west side. Local guides and the tourist office advise climbing the south-east side because it's less risky. Although it takes only one day to climb the north-west side (starting from the Mayon Skyline Hotel), it requires traversing dangerously narrow ledges and there have reportedly been more accidents here.

Plan on two days to climb Mayon's south-east slope. From the golf course, where the jeepney will drop you off, it takes about three hours to reach Camp One, where there is a fresh water source. The climb to Camp Two, where you'll spend the night, is about another three hours. There is no fresh water source here, but there is usually rainwater that you can purify. The path from Camp One to the summit is a hardened lava gulch, basically increasingly steep black rock and boulders with no shade. From Camp Two to the knife edge, where you can look down into the crater, is about 2½ hours. Flash floods often occur near the summit, which basically turn the lava gulch (ie, the path you're hiking in) into a waterfall. Your guide should advise you on what to do depending on how strong the flood is. Basically don't panic! The climb is especially difficult if it rains, as the rocks become really slippery.

Rubber-soled shoes with good traction are necessary; the guides all wear Teva-type shoes. You should also bring a waterproof jacket, to protect you from rain as well as keep you warm at the summit, which gets quite chilly. The best time to climb Mayon is in March or April, after which it gets unbearably hot.

DONSOL

Until the recent 'discovery' of whale sharks off the coast here, Donsol, about 25km south of Legaspi, was an obscure, sleepy fishing village in one of Sorsogon's more remote areas. Then in 1998 out-of-town divers shot a video of the whale sharks, and

Whale Sharks

Known as the largest fish in the world, the *butanding* (whale shark) can grow up to 18m long, although it's more common to see them about half that size. No-one knows why the sharks gather in such large numbers near the shore of Donsol; the only other places in the world where they're found in similar numbers are off the shores of Ningaloo (Australia) and the Galapagos Islands. The gentle creatures are considered harmless and friendly, and don't seem to mind humans swimming alongside them (as long as you don't touch them).

Caroline Liou

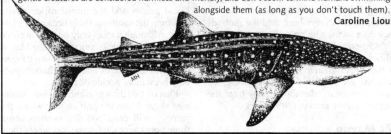

a newspaper carried a story about Donsol's butanding (the local word for whale shark). Days after the story was published, poachers from other provinces arrived in the area. The local and central governments quickly drafted a municipal ordinance prohibiting the catching of whale sharks and the poachers were arrested (although illegal poaching still occurs). Since then Donsol has quickly become one of Bicol's most well-known towns, with travellers and media from around the world descending on the town to see the famous creatures.

It's truly an exhilarating experience swimming along with these huge blue-grey, silver-spotted creatures. You need to be a decent swimmer and in relatively good shape to keep up with the sharks, although if you're lucky your crew will be able to position your boat close to a shark so you don't have to swim far to see one. Only snorkelling equipment is allowed; scuba diving is prohibited.

It's difficult to predict your chances of seeing a whale shark. The peak months are February to May, although sharks migrate here as early October and November. There is no snorkelling equipment for rent in Donsol, so bring your own mask and fins.

The World Wide Fund (WWF) For Nature and the Sorsogon Provincial Tourism Council have established well-organised guidelines for swimming with the whale sharks. Upon arrival in Sorsogon, stop in at the Visitor Center next to the Municipal Hall. It will arrange a boat, spotter and a Butanding Interaction Officer (BIO) for you. The cost is P2200 plus a P300/100 foreigner/Filipino registration fee per person per day. The boat can accommodate up to six people. If you turn up alone there's a good chance there might not be anyone to share a boat (and the hefty cost) with. It's possible to make a reservation by calling Donsol's only phone line at ☎ 056-411 1109 and leaving a message for Becky Razo in the Visitor Center.

Places to Stay & Eat

Santiago Lodging House, next to the visitor centre, has a few good, clean rooms available for P150 per person per night. This is basically a homestay; its friendly owner, Iderlina Santiago, used to be a schoolteacher in Donsol.

Another option in town, although not nearly as nice, is the *Travellers Inn*. To get here from the Visitor Center, walk two blocks north-west on San José St and turn left; it's just above the pharmacy. Basic, dank rooms are P150 per person per night.

Although it's not in town, the *Amirevic Agrala Farm Beach* resort has nice, well-kept cottages on the beach for P300 night. There's no road: from Donsol you must hire a boat to get here. It's about a 10-minute boat ride north-west of Donsol.

Emiliano's is Donsol's only restaurant; it serves basic fare at affordable prices. Early in the morning you can get delicious *puto* (rice cakes with toasted coconut) at the city market.

Getting There & Away
Donsol is about two hours from Legaspi and two hours from Sorsogon. From Legaspi there are direct buses to Donsol, with the first trip at 4.20 am and the last trip at 2 pm from the Satellite bus terminal. If you miss the last trip it's possible to catch a jeepney from Daruga to Donsol, with the last jeepney leaving around 6.30 pm. The last bus from Donsol to Legaspi leaves at 3.30 pm.

If you can't get a direct bus, you can take a bus to Putiao (a town about halfway between Legaspi and Sorsogon), and from there catch a bus or jeepney bound for Donsol. From Putiao to Donsol is just over an hour.

SORSOGON
The capital city of the province of the same name, Sorsogon doesn't have any tourist sites to speak of. However, it's a good place to arrange a guide for exploring **Mt Bulusan**, an active volcano, or to arrange other outdoor activities, such as diving or mountain biking. Note that the NPA is still sometimes active in the region, so check on the latest conditions before setting out into Sorsogon's more remote areas.

Information
The active and informative Sorsogon Tourism Council is in Fernandos Hotel (☎ 056-211 1573, fax 211 1357, ✉ fernan dohotel@hotmail.com). It can help you arrange a guide for climbing Mt Bulusan as well as provide information on other outdoor activities in the area.

There is an Equitable PCI Bank on Rizal St with an ATM that accepts MasterCard and Cirrus cards.

Places to Stay
Accommodation in Sorsogon is not cheap. The newly opened *Villa Kasanggayahan* (☎ 056-211 1275) has modern, nicely decorated rooms with air-con for P650. It can also arrange mountain-biking tours and whale-watching tours in Donsol for P1000 per person. *Fernandos Hotel* (☎ 056-211 1573, fax 211 1357, ✉ *fernandohotel@hotmail.com*), on N Pareja St, also has good but aging rooms for P796/971 a single/double.

Getting There & Away
Philtranco and JB Line have buses to/from Manila (14 hours). From Legaspi, JB has frequent service with the last bus leaving at 6 pm. A BLTB bus to Sorsogon passes through Legaspi around 8 pm, although usually every seat is full. It's about two hours from Legaspi to Sorsogon.

The first trip from Sorsogon to Donsol (two hours) leaves at 5.30 pm and the last trip leaves at 3 pm. You may have to get off the bus at Putiao and switch to another bus to get to Donsol.

MT BULUSAN
Known among local climbers for its interesting and varied terrain, Mt Bulusan's (1560m) slopes are covered in dense forest. The climb is mostly through woods but eventually leads to an open field where there are excellent views of the Bicol Peninsula and out to the sparkling blue sea. Note that Mt Bulusan is an active volcano that last erupted in 1983.

The path begins at Lake Bulusan, about 12km west from the town of Bulusan. From here, you can climb to the summit and descend the same day to San Benon Hot Springs (also known as Mateo Hot & Cold Springs Resort), at the foot of Mount Bulusan, for a refreshing soak.

A hiking guide will cost about P500 (see the earlier Information entry under Sorsogon). Bring gloves and wear long sleeves to protect yourself from leeches that drop down on you after it's rained. From Sorsogon, you can take a jeepney to the town of Bulusan, but from there you must hire a tricycle to get to Lake Bulusan.

SOUTH-EAST LUZON

Places to Stay

The pretty, bed-and-breakfast-style *Villa Luisa Celeste* (☎ *056-211 2999, 211 1667*), located just outside the town of Bulusan, has well-kept, tastefully decorated rooms and a small pool. The surrounding scenery – rice fields and lush coconut trees – is gorgeous. Also in the area is Masacrot Springs, where for P10 you can soak in a natural mineral water pool. Although it's a little run-down, it's a nice place to spend the day. There is no overnight accommodation here, although you can rent a hut for the day for P50.

Just outside of Irosin is the *San Benon Hot Springs*, at the foot of Mt Bulusan. The pretty and well-maintained grounds include natural hot, warm and cool pools. You can spend the night here in a native-style cottage for P300, or rent a shade for the day for P50. The resort is 2km from the highway, down a dirt road surrounded by lush green scenery and coconut trees. Look for the sign pointing to the resort in Monbon, Irosin.

RIZAL BEACH

About 45 minutes from Sorsogon, 4km outside of the town of Gubat, is a stretch of nice brown-sand beach with a few small resorts. The *Rizal Beach Resort* (☎ *056-211 1056*) has basic but clean rooms with fan for P580, or P850 with air-con. Next door there's a better option for similar rates: *Veramaris Resort* is a pleasant and well-kept villa-style resort with a small swimming pool.

MATNOG

At the southernmost tip of Luzon is Matnog, a one-road town leading to the ferry terminal, from where you can catch a ferry bound for Samar. If you miss the last ferry, there are a couple of dilapidated places to stay, including *AG Primo Lodging House*, next to the Bayantel across from the ferry terminal. Rooms are P200. Nearby is *Leah's Rest & Lodging House*, with similarly dank rooms for P150.

Getting There & Away

Philtranco, JB, AMA and BLTB all have buses that go direct from Manila to Matnog.

Ferries depart Matnog for Allen on Samar (1½ hours) and possibly to San Isidro (also on Samar).

Catanduanes

A rugged and rural island, with its east coast open to the Pacific Ocean, Catanduanes has a narrow coastal strip rising abruptly to a range of mountains running north to south. Beyond the capital (Virac) the island is little developed. Buffalo sleds are common transportation in the smaller villages, and stands of native forest remain in the centre of the island.

Catanduanes is the wettest place in the Philippines, with less rain falling between April and June. Its exposed position makes it *bagyo* (typhoon)-prone, and it is still recovering from the big wind of 22 October 1998, when all the coastal communities, including Virac, were flattened and many

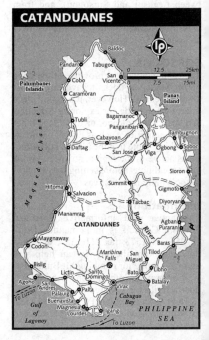

CATANDUANES

people died. The small tourist infrastructure was likewise destroyed and is mostly still under reconstruction. Phone lines are a problem too.

The Bicol-speaking islanders are welcoming, and the island has a safe, unsophisticated, unhurried atmosphere in which to relax for a few days.

Getting There & Away
Air Catanduanes can be reached from Manila and Tabaco on Luzon. Asian Spirit and Air Philippines fly daily to Virac from Manila (70 minutes). Both airlines' offices are on San Juan St in Virac.

Boat A boat leaves Virac for Tabaco at 9.30 am daily (P52, 3½ hours). A boat also leaves San Andres for Tabaco daily around 1.30 pm (P52, 3½ hours).

Getting Around
The airport is 2km from town; a tricycle ride will cost P20.

The terminal for buses and jeepneys is at the market in Virac. Buses are faster and less bumpy than jeepneys. They leave around 7 am and 11 am, connecting with boats arriving from Tabaco, for the three main routes of Pandan, Gigmoto and Viga.

Tricycles operate locally around the towns for about P5 per trip, or around P100 per hour to hire. Eli Zafe is a helpful tricycle driver who speaks good English and will take you almost anywhere; ask for him at the airport or call him on ☎ 052-811 1205.

Rodino Molina hires out his jeep and driver, with the cost depending on destination. A return to Puraran on the east coast, for example, will cost P1500. Ask for him at the small restaurant opposite the Provincial Capitol Building.

VIRAC
This is a compact town and everything is within easy walking distance. It is still recovering from the typhoon of 1998 and there are few buildings of interest, though it makes a good base for day trips around the island.

You can change US dollars only at the Philippine National Bank; there are no ATMs.

Places to Stay & Eat
Best value and variety is at *Marem Pension House* (☎ *052-811 1104*, @ *MaremPensionHse@hotmail.com*), on Rafael St, where

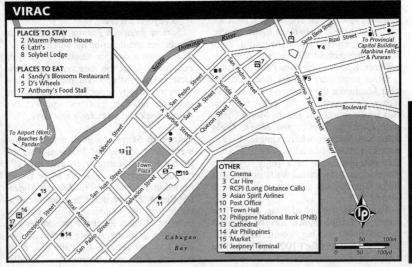

VIRAC

PLACES TO STAY
2 Marem Pension House
6 Latri's
8 Solybel Lodge

PLACES TO EAT
4 Sandy's Blossoms Restaurant
5 D's Wheels
17 Anthony's Food Stall

OTHER
1 Cinema
3 Car Hire
7 RCPI (Long Distance Calls)
9 Asian Spirit Airlines
10 Post Office
11 Town Hall
12 Philippine National Bank (PNB)
13 Cathedral
14 Air Philippines
15 Market
16 Jeepney Terminal

To Provincial Capitol Building, Maribina Falls & Puraran

To Airport (4km), Beaches & Pandan

Santa Elena Street
Rizal Street
Domingo River
Santo
San Pedro Street
Surtida Street
San José Street
Quezon Street
Geronimo Tabuco Street
Boulevard
Wharf
M. Alberto Street
Surtida Street
San Juan Street
Town Plaza
Salvacion Street
Rizal Avenue
Conception Street
San Pablo Street
Cabugao Bay

0   50   100m
0   50   100yd

SOUTH-EAST LUZON

prices range from P150 for tiny rooms with fan and share bath to P775 for air-con family rooms with bath. Of the budget lodgings try *Solybel Lodge*, where dark, basic rooms with fan and share bath cost P85 to P150, but there is a pleasant communal veranda. At *Latri's*, on Geronimo Tabuzo St, tiny plywood rooms cost from P125 with fan and share bath to P650 for air-con and bath.

Try *Anthony's food stall* near the bus terminal and *D's Wheels* at the roundabout for good fresh fish and vegetable dishes for around P25 a serve. *Sandy's Blossoms Restaurant*, also at the roundabout, has a nice terrace for eating out and good food for around P100 per person. You can get simple dishes at Marem's Pension.

AROUND VIRAC

Maribina Falls (formerly Binanuahan Falls) is 5km west of town and 200m walk off the road. The falls thunder down in the wetter months but there is usually safe swimming from March to June. There is no caretaker at present so the surrounding area is a bit grotty, but the water itself remains clean.

The beach resorts west of Virac, all with gorgeous views across to Mt Mayon in Luzon, were devastated by the 1998 typhoon and most were hoping to be fully operational again by the end of 1999. Best and closest of these is *Twin Rock Beach Resort*, with a lovely garden, a beautiful 'twin rocks' formation in the bay and coral just offshore. Rooms range from P400 to P1000.

Other resorts are *Bosdok Beach Resort* near Magnesia; the expensive and isolated *Kosta Alcantara*, on the coast between Bosdok Beach Resort and the Monte Cielo, with rooms at P2000; and *Monte Cielo* near San Andres, where simple, breezy rooms right on the beach cost P450 and air-con cottages with bath (ugly concrete exteriors, but fine rattan walls inside) cost P750. The day-use rate for each resort is around P20.

Two kilometres east of Virac, on the river mouth, is *Dolly's Beach Resort*. It's a bit run-down but has big, comfortable, self-contained cottages for P1000 and looks like a quiet base for day trips.

THE WEST COAST

The road from Virac to **Pandan** is bumpy, beautiful and sometimes hair-raising as it follows the coast. It's a good way to see rural island life, with great views across Maqueda Channel to the islands of southern Luzon. There is no commercial lodging in Pandan, so you'll need to ask locally if you want to stay overnight.

Day-trip options could be to arrive on the early bus, ask the driver to drop you at Pandan's pretty little beach for a few hours, and walk the few hundred metres back into town to pick up the later bus to return to Virac. Alternatively, get off in Caramoan or one of the beaches overlooking the Palumbanes islands on the way, and ask the driver to pick you up a couple of hours later on the return journey.

THE EAST COAST
Puraran

The stunning wide Bay of **Puraran** is about 30km north of Virac on the east coast, along an extremely bumpy and beautiful road; look out for the monumental ruins of the **Spanish church** at Bato on the way. There is coral reef just offshore with good snorkelling and safe swimming inside the reef, but beware of dangerously strong currents beyond the reef.

Surfers gather at Puraran from May to September and describe the surf as 'fickle', often waiting days or weeks for the right conditions. Once the monsoon hits around October, almost constant rain makes the water too choppy for good surfing. Puraran is simple, relaxing, quiet and a perfect spot to kick back and relax for a few days.

Places to Stay Two small resorts almost merge into one on the beach at Puraran. Both have rebuilt attractively after the 1998 typhoon; electricity was due to be reconnected in September 1999. *Elena's Majestic Beach Resort* describes the scenery, rather than the simple and pretty bamboo cottages. It costs P350 per person per day including all meals. *Puting Baybay Resort* next door has cottages for P300 plus P200 per person per day for meals. Allegedly, both rates have been known to vary according to a traveller's nationality (!) so check rates on arrival. Apart from food, bring all extras you need, including your own surfing and snorkelling gear; it's a long way back to Virac for supplies.

Getting There & Away There is a jeepney from Virac to Gigmoto via Puraran at around 11 am (P20, 2½ hours) and a jeepney to Virac from Puraran at around 3 am (going to the early market). There may be others; ask at the terminal in Virac. Otherwise get a more regular jeepney from Virac to Baras and hire a tricycle (P50, 30 minutes) to Puraran.

You can charter a tricycle from Virac for P300 one way (two hours) or P500 for a one-day return; you may also be able to negotiate the hire of a car and driver from the schoolteacher in Puraran.

THE NORTH

There is no public transport on the undermaintained road sections from Pandan to Bagamanoc and from Tambugnon to Gigmoto; you will need to charter a jeep or walk. Buses run between Virac and Viga (P50, three hours), travelling through steep hilly country, native forest and small inland villages. There are still occasional rumours of NPA activity in the central north-east, so check locally if you plan any solo hikes.

Marinduque

Marinduque is a gem of an island province; its 100km coastal strip rising to a spine of hills. Its income is based on copra production, and many people fish for a living or are subsistence farmers. This rural economic base has kept the countryside green and the coast and most of the ocean relatively healthy. The notable exception is near Santa Cruz, where toxic seepage from a copper mine has resulted in the mine's closure. Environmental groups are working hard, in a test case for environmental protection in the Philippines, to call those responsible to account.

The island is famous as the setting for the Three Kings Festival in early January and the Moriones Festivals during Holy Week. Visitors are welcome to watch the passion plays and to join in the processions around the island. During Moriones, the local government has information booths in each town, matching visitors with the mostly Tagalog-speaking Marinduqueños who provide additional homestay accommodation. There is a flood of tourists at that time of year, but at present Marinduque is generally experiencing a tourism lull, following the closure of several resorts and the use of only small aircraft to service the island.

Information

The Philippines National Bank (PNB) in Boac seems to be the only place to change money on the island. It accepts US dollars only. In late 1999 there was no public access to Internet in Marinduque.

For a great account of the lives of island fishing and farming communities read James Hamilton-Paterson's *Playing with Water,* a superb meditation on his time spent in the pseudonymous island of Tiwarik. Could this be Marinduque?

Getting There & Away

Air Asian Spirit has a flight between Manila and Santa Cruz at 6 am daily except Tuesday and Saturday. The Asian Spirit booking office is in the Boac Hotel.

Boat Several vessels go from Balanacan to Manila's Dalahican Port. Monte Negro Shipping Lines' MV *Maria Theresa* leaves at 9 am, 4 pm and midnight daily (P50 to P75 air-con, two hours).

From Buyabod the fast boat MV *Santa Cruz* leaves for Manila at 5.15 am and noon daily (P150, two hours). Slower boats take four hours.

A boat leaves Gasan at 8.30 am daily (P70, three hours) for Pinamalayan on Mindoro.

Getting Around

Marinduque airport is 12km south of Boac. A jeepney to Boac costs P30 per person; a charter tricycle costs P100.

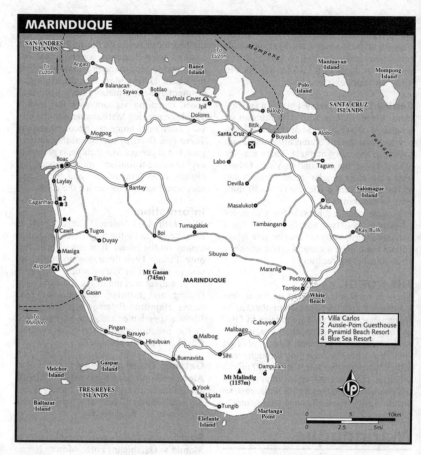

MARINDUQUE

1 Villa Carlos
2 Aussie-Pom Guesthouse
3 Pyramid Beach Resort
4 Blue Sea Resort

Jeepneys run frequently over the island in all directions. Tricycles usually make local runs but can be chartered for local half-day rate of P350, and for about P300 for the 30km or so between major towns.

BOAC

Boac is Marinduque's capital. It is a pretty, tatty town, with pot plants everywhere and many attractive, dilapidated **Spanish-era wooden houses**. The beautiful **church**, built in 1792 on the hill in the centre of town, and its attached convent are the focal points. Inside, a **carved Black Christ** lies under a glass dome on a massive wooden carriage that is pulled through the streets during Moriones.

The dusty **museum** (open from 8 am to noon and from 1 pm to 5 pm Monday to Saturday, entry free), on the Plaza, houses a good collection of Marinduque's history and an extraordinary selection of Moriones masks and costumes.

Places to Stay & Eat

Easily the best value in town is the *Tahanan sa Isok* (☎ *042-332 1231*) on Canovas St. All rooms have air-con and great bathrooms; prices start at P700. There

A traditional house in Luzon.

is a pretty garden restaurant with books and newspapers supplied.

The *Boac Hotel* on Nepomuceno St has passably clean rooms with fan and bath from P250, with air-con and bath from P600. It has a restaurant and a good bakery.

Cely's Lodging House (☎ 042-332 1519, 10 de Octobre St) and attached restaurant has dingy rooms with fan for P150.

Krisna's Restaurant and *ALB Food-world*, on opposite sides of the Boac Hotel, serve good Filipino dishes for lunch and dinner.

Kusina Sa Plaza, opposite the museum, is clean and bright and serves pasta dishes and coleslaw as well as Filipino food at lunchtime.

AROUND BOAC

There is a selection of **beach resorts** south of Boac, but most are unprepared for visitors in the June to December off-season. Take your own snorkel equipment. Resorts that function year-round include *Villa Carlos* (☎ 042-332 1881), just outside Boac over the bridge, where all rooms have air-con and bath and prices range from P1200 to P1500.

The water may be cleaner for swimming near the *Aussie-Pom Guest House*, about 4km south of town, where airy rooms with fan cost P200. Rooms have slatted floors and are unscreened.

Next door is the *Pyramid Beach Resort* (☎ 042-332 1328), where tidy rooms with fan cost from P250, and with air-con from P800. The garden sitting area is ordinary at best.

The *Blue Sea Resort* (☎ 042-332 1334), 6km south of Boac, has pleasant landscaped gardens leading to the beach. Rooms with fan and bath cost P360 and rooms with air-con and bath cost P515.

MOGPOG

Mogpog is a pretty hillside town at the junction of the roads to Balanacan and Santa Cruz. It holds a **Moriones Festival** smaller than that of Boac and Gasan. The town's only hotel is the *Hill Top Lodge* (☎ 042-332 3074), which has balconies and beautiful views across the hills. Fan rooms cost P250, air-con rooms cost P600, and all rooms have share bath. This is the nearest hotel to Balanacan if you arrive late at night by boat.

BALANACAN

This is the small port area in the north-west of the island servicing Luzon. Jeepneys meet all boats and deliver from, and go directly to, all parts of Marinduque.

SANTA CRUZ

Santa Cruz is set on a ridge in the hills, and you can walk quickly out of the bustle of town into countryside. It holds a **Three Kings Festival** in January and a **Moriones Festival**. Its quiet **church** was built in 1714; go and see if the hundreds of bats hanging from the walls and rafters are in daytime residence. A beautiful **wooden former convent building** is beside the church and there is a green and shady forecourt. Behind the church is the **undertakers' street**, with opulent white hearses, coffins and silk drapes on display. Saturday is market day.

Places to Stay & Eat

Rico's Lodging House (☎ 042-321 1085) – and karaoke bar – is opposite the PNB. You can ask for a *room* in the family house of the owner of Rico's, Mr Ricohermoso, around the corner. It's noisy, friendly and just clean enough. Both lodgings cost P150 per room with fan.

The bland *Santa Cruz Hotel* has all air-con rooms with private bath. They cost P600 to P700.

The *restaurant* at Rico's (see earlier) serves decent Filipino and Western food and a meal will cost up to P100. *Laica's Restaurant* on Palomares St has a garden setting but dull food. *Tita Digs* tatty restaurant on Claudio St serves cheap and tasty dishes of the day for around P30. The elderly Tita Amie, who cooks, is a delight.

Getting There & Away

There is a regular jeepney service from Boac, and a less regular service in the direction of Torrijos. A boat runs twice daily between Santa Cruz's port at Buyabod and Luzon.

AROUND SANTA CRUZ

The privately owned **Bathala Caves** beyond Ipil are terrific. Clambering a bit, you can explore two or three of the 26 caves in a couple of hours. With luck, you'll see thousands of bats and swifts, and several enormous rock pythons. Cool off afterwards in the natural pool behind the caretaker's house. A guided tour costs P100 plus P50 entry fee. Take a flashlight and charter a tricycle for the bumpy 10km trip from Santa Cruz. Half-day charter costs P350.

The **Santa Cruz Islands** offer good snorkelling and fishing and white-sand beaches. The only accommodation is on Maniuayan Island, where Luceta Perlada rents *rooms* on the beach for around P200. *Bancas* (pumpboats) leave from Buyabod when they're full enough. The trip takes 30 minutes on a calm day, and costs P20 per person. A banca can be chartered for P300 one way.

The beach on **Salomague Island** can be reached by boat from Suha in an hour, but there is no accommodation.

POCTOY

Visit **White Beach** in Poctoy, the longest stretch of sandy beach on the island. From here there are wide views of **Mt Malindig**, the dormant volcano that is the highest point on Marinduque.

At *Rendezvous Cottages* on White Beach itself, simple rooms cost P100. To rent a fan costs P20 per day, to have washing water delivered costs P20 per day and all meals will cost around P200 per person. Bancas can be hired.

Quiet *Jovita's Paradise*, just to the north of White Beach, has a beautiful private stretch of sand with garden and cottages along the shore. Bancas can be hired for P50 per hour. Rooms with fan and bath cost P500; rooms with air-con and bath cost P800.

Getting There & Away

From Santa Cruz to Torrijos the irregular jeepney service costs P15 per person. It is more frequent at the weekend.

BUENAVISTA

This small town in the south of the island is reached along a scenic and sometimes hair-raising road along the coast from Torrijos and over the ridge beside Mt Malindig. The **Malbog hot springs** (entry fee P15 per person) are a pretty 2km walk or jeepney ride out of town. Access is gained through the Susanna Hot Spring Resort.

Places to Stay

Susanna Hot Spring Resort, 2km out of Buenavista, at Malbog, has three small hot pools and a pleasant garden, but the restaurant is not always open. Bright rooms with fan and bath cost P400; there are tiny single rooms with share bath for P200.

Dingky Chua offers *rooms* with his family in town for P150 per person and can arrange half-day fishing trips for around P1000; ask for him at the market in Buenavista.

Getting There & Away

Jeepneys are infrequent from Torrijos and cost P15 per person. There is a more regular daily service from Boac.

AROUND BUENAVISTA

Small **Elefante Island** can be visited by banca from Lipata (P300 return). It is a privately owned resort that is presently closed, but visitors can use the beach.

The **Tres Reyes Islands** can be visited by banca from Pingan Beach. To visit Gaspar takes 15 minutes and costs P500 return including waiting time; to Melchor takes 30 minutes and costs P500 return; to Baltazar takes one hour and costs P700 return. Gaspar Island is a marine reserve and there is good snorkelling just off the northern beach. An old Chinese shipwreck lies offshore and some of its ceramics, dating from the late 16th century, can be seen in the museum in Boac.

GASAN

Gasan thrives on its **Three Kings Festival** and **Moriones Festival** and there are many souvenir shops in town, especially along Rizal Street, selling wooden masks and basketware.

Places to Stay & Eat

There are some lodging houses in town, but these appear to be closed except for Moriones.

Sunset Garden Resort (☎ 042-342 1004, fax 342 1003, @ sunsetgarden@vasia.com), 2km north of town, has a great beach setting. Cottages with fan and bath cost P530; with air-con and bath P730. Diving with qualified dive instructors can be arranged and equipment can be hired. There is a comfortable restaurant and bar with Filipino and Western food.

In Gasan the *People's Restaurant*, opposite the sports complex on the waterfront, is clean and serves good simple dishes.

Getting There & Away

There is a regular jeepney service between Buenavista and Boac via Gasan. Boats run daily between Gasan and Pinamalayan on Mindoro.

Mindoro

A great mountainous chunk of an island just south of Luzon, Mindoro is packed with resorts along its north coast. Its premier spots are Puerto Galera and Sabang, though some of the country's most idyllic offshore islands, brilliant diving, excellent hiking and mountain climbing can be found beyond these two places.

Even in the touristy northern areas, Mindoro's roads are stunningly bad. Our record in one day was three flat tyres – on a bus that had to be push-started to begin with. The laughter that erupted when the third tyre blew was pure Filipino. Roads connecting quite large towns can often be no more than vague scratches on a flood plain. In any other country, you'd pay a lot of money for this sort of cross-country, 4X4 adventure. Here, you get it for less than P100!

Mindoro is a good place to really discover the joys of travelling by *banca* (pumpboat). Puttering from beach to beach, particularly around Puerto Galera and Sabang, is a wonderfully worry-free way to travel, relax and get your bearings all at the same time.

Mindoro's indigenous Mangyan people inhabit forests and coastal areas throughout Mindoro, including Puerto Galera, Mt Halcon, Mansalay and San José.

HIGHLIGHTS

- Revelling in Puerto Galera's coastal amenities and atmosphere – close to Manila yet light-years away
- Submerging youself in superb diving and snorkelling
- Soaking up the sun on local beaches, before partaking in excellent food and drink

White Beach p264
Puerto Galera Beaches p263
Puerto Galera p260
Sabang Beach p267
Big La Laguna & Small La Laguna p270
San José p277

GETTING THERE & AWAY
Air
Luzon Poor cash-strapped PAL no longer flies between Manila and Mindoro. For flights to Mindoro's main airports at Mamburao and San José, you'll need to fly Air Philippines or Asian Spirit. Pacific Airways is supposed to have flights between Sablayan and Manila, but these flights may or may not be happening by the time you read this book. Pacific Airways' Mamburao–Manila flights are slightly more dependable.

Pacific Airways has flights from Manila to Mamburao and back at around 10 am Monday, Wednesday and Friday (P1600, 30 to 45 minutes). See also the Getting There & Away entry for Mamburao, later in the chapter.

Air Philippines flies from Manila to San José (P1400, one hour) at 6.30 am Tuesday, Wednesday, Friday and Sunday. Asian Spirit has a flight to San José at 7.20 am Monday, Thursday, Saturday and Sunday (P1400, one hour).

Palawan Pacific Airways (☎ 036-288 3162) in Caticlan can organise a charter flight between Caticlan and Busuanga's Coron town airport (P4500 per person, minimum of four). Remember that Pacific Airways needs a few days' notice and that flights are subject to the availability of aircraft.

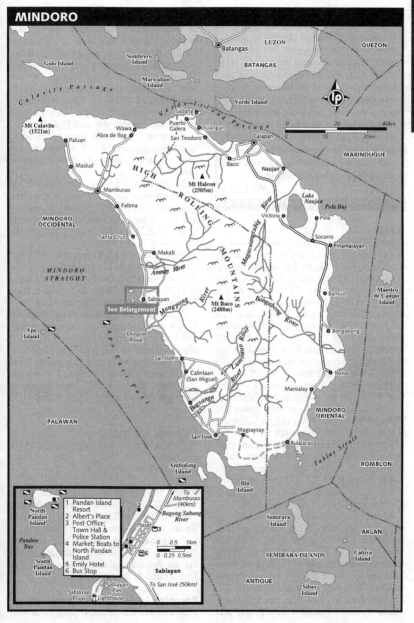

MINDORO

LUZON

QUEZON

Golo Island

Sombrero Island

BATANGAS

Batangas

Calavite Passage

Maricaban Island

Verde Island Passage

Verde Island

Mt Calavite (1521m)

Wawa

Abra de Ilog

Sabang

Puerto Galera

Dulangan

Calapan

Paluan

San Teodoro

MARINDUQUE

Maslud

HIGH

Baco

Naujan

Mamburao

Mt Halcon (2505m)

Fatima

ROLLING

River

Lake Naujan

Pola Bay

MINDORO OCCIDENTAL

Victoria

Pola

Santa Cruz

Magasawangtabig

Socorro

Pinamalayan

MINDORO STRAIGHT

Makati

Amnay River

MOUNTAINS

Bansud

Maestro de Campo Island

Apo Island

Sablayan

See Enlargement

Mongpong River

Mt Baco (2488m)

Bongabong River

Bongabong

Dongon Point

Apo East Pass

San Isidro

Lumintao River

Calintaan (San Miguel)

Bugsanga

River

Mansalay

Roxas

PALAWAN

San José

Magsaysay

MINDORO ORIENTAL

Bulalacao

Tablas Strait

Ambulong Island

Ilin Island

ROMBLON

0   20   40km
0   10   20mi

AKLAN

Semirara Island

SEMIRARA ISLANDS

Caluya Island

ANTIQUE

Sibay Island

Sablayan enlargement

North Pandan Island

Pandan Bay

South Pandan Island

To Mamburao (40km)

Bagong Sabang River

Plaza

1 Pandan Island Resort
2 Albert's Place
3 Post Office; Town Hall & Police Station
4 Market; Boats to North Pandan Island
5 Emily Hotel
6 Bus Stop

0   0.5   1km
0   0.25   0.5mi

Sablayan

Sablayan Pier

Sablayan Point ★ Lighthouse

To San José (50km)

MINDORO

The Mangyan

The indigenous people of Mindoro are collectively known as Mangyan, and comprise tribes including Alangan, Buid, Iraya, Hanunoo, Tagaydon and Tatagnon. Among the least 'modernised' of the Philippine indigenous groups, the 80,000 or so Mangyan were originally a coastal people, but with the arrival of new settlers they were forced to relocate to the rugged interior of Mindoro. The basket-weaving Mangyan communities on Mindoro's north coast are often visited by tourists from nearby Puerto Galera and Sabang.

Mic Looby

Boat

Luzon The typical route to Mindoro is from Batangas, on Luzon, to Puerto Galera (or Sabang) or Calapan. Ferries and outriggers operate all day (until about 6 pm) between Batangas and Puerto Galera (or Sabang). The crossing takes one to two hours, depending on the craft, and prices range from P65 for outriggers to P350 for the swish Si-Kat ferry. The Si-Kat fastcraft departs every morning from Puerto Galera to Batangas to connect with a bus to Manila (P350, 2½ to three hours).

There are also a few combined bus and boat trips from the tourist belt in Manila to Puerto Galera. A bus leaves the Centrepoint Hotel (☎ 02-521 2751) on Mabini St, Ermita at 9 am daily, connecting with the 11.45 am MV Si-Kat II to Puerto Galera. The one-way fare is P350 and you can book at the hotel. Alternatively, a bus leaves the Citystate Tower Hotel (☎ 02-526 2733) on Mabini St at 8 am daily, connecting with the MV Super 85 ferry for P360/695 one way/return.

About 3km west of Puerto, Balatero is served by the large Viva Shipping Lines (☎ 043-723 2986 in Batangas). Viva has boats to several ports on Mindoro. Boats leave for Calapan every 15 minutes from 2.30 am to 10 pm (P150), and to Puerto Galera at 8.30 am, 12.20 and 5 pm (P150). For Sablayan and San José, the MV Santa Maria leaves at 7 pm Tuesday, Friday and

Sunday and the MV Marian Queen leaves at 5 pm Monday, Wednesday and Saturday (P160). The MV Penafrañcia VIII leaves for San José at 5 pm daily except Thursday.

Montenegro Shipping Lines' car and passenger ferries sail from Batangas to San José in the south at 6 pm Tuesday, Thursday and Saturday (P200 to P300, 10 hours). From San José to Batangas, they sail at 6 pm Sunday, Wednesday and Friday.

There are also boats from Sablayan to Batangas, between 7 and 8 pm Tuesday, Thursday and Sunday (P175 to P265, nine hours).

Datinguinoo Shipping Lines (☎ 0912 306 5332) operates the MV Princess Kay, MV Sabang Princess I, MV Sabang Princess II and MV Super Gigi, which leave for Puerto Galera at 9.30 am, 10.30 am, 12.15 pm and 2.30 pm (P75 to P80).

Super Diamond Shipping (☎ 0917 927 7745, 0917 306 5332) has the air-con MV Blue Eagle, which leaves for Puerto Galera at 11.30 am and 3.30 pm daily (also at 9 am Thursday to Sunday), charging P110.

Pumpboats come and go all day from Sabang's central shore. Many are running back and forth to Batangas, while others are taking trips to Puerto Galera (P180) or elsewhere. From Batangas to Sabang, pumpboats leave at 9.30 am, 10.30 am, 12.15 pm, 1.30 pm and 2.30 pm (P65, 1½ hours). From Sabang to Batangas they set sail at 6, 7, 8, 9, and 11.30 am, and 3 and 4 pm. Times may vary.

Palawan A pumpboat sails from San José to Concepcion, on Busuanga Island at 4 am on Tuesday and Thursday. This can be a particularly rough voyage.

Panay Big pumpboats from Roxas (Mindoro) to Caticlan leave at 10 am Monday and Friday (P200, 5 to 7 hours). From Caticlan to Roxas, the boats leave at 9 am Wednesday.

Pumpboats also operate between San José and Libertad (east of Caticlan), going via the Semirara Islands. These leave San José around 11 am, usually daily.

Romblon Large ferry-type pumpboats operate between Roxas and Odiongan, as well as between Roxas and Looc. Boats from Roxas to Odiongan leave between 10 and 11 am Tuesday, Friday and Sunday (P85, three hours), and from Odiongan to Roxas between 10 and 11 am Thursday, Saturday and Monday. From Roxas to Looc, boats leave between 10 and 11 am Tuesday, Friday and Sunday (P85, 3 to 3½ hours), and return between 10 and 11 am Thursday, Saturday and Monday.

Larger pumpboats operate between San José and Libertad (east of Caticlan on Panay), going via the Semirara Islands. These head off around 11 am.

GETTING AROUND
After even moderate rainfall, well-worn roads linking places such as Puerto Galera and Sabang can become almost impassable. Remember too that precious few jeepneys or tricycles will head off anywhere after dark. Pumpboat drivers are usually OK about night rides.

You couldn't do a complete circuit of Mindoro by road even if you wanted. To the north, there's no passable road linking Puerto Galera and Wawa (Abra de Ilog), and to the south there's little more than a jungle path linking San José with Bulalacao. Beware: on some maps, both these routes are marked as main roads. In both cases, there are good alternative sea routes.

Boat
With a fleet of outriggers of all shapes and sizes, the island is one of the few bold enough to advertise official pumpboat rates (at Puerto Galera pier and at Big La Laguna Beach). Standard pumpboats are licensed to carry six people. Trips should be priced per boat, rather than per person, and the average day trip costs from P600 to P700.

Bus & Jeepney
Jeepneys, bless their overheated hearts, brave some very rugged roads in Mindoro. For many of the more popular routes, the driver may offer to head off before the jeepney is completely packed – but you'll pay at least twice as much as normal for the privilege. In more remote areas, drivers will regularly attempt world records in overloading (see the later Getting There & Away entry for Roxas). Buses generally cover the same routes as the jeepneys (one exception is the jeepney-only run between Puerto Galera and Calapan). Mindoro's fleet of durable, nonair-con buses are often a little cheaper than the jeepneys.

An alternative to the bus and jeepney is the FX van, which operates along the east coast of Mindoro, between Calapan in the north and Bulalacao in the south. Similar vans (L-300s) operate on islands such as Mindoro and Cebu. Waiting stations for these speedy, 12-seater air-con minibuses are usually next to where the buses terminate, and marked with the sign of the operating company – Oriental Trans Services Association Inc (OTSAI). At the Calapan pier, you're bound to get the hard sell from an FX van driver. These vans come and go just about all day, with departures usually based on the number of passengers available. Prices are often higher than jeepney and bus fares, but the trips are quicker. The official route is Calapan–Bongabong–Roxas–Mansalay–Bulalacao.

Tricycle
In Mindoro's two great tourist haunts, Sabang and Puerto Galera, foreigners soon find there are basically three tricycle rates: local rate, tourist rate, and the outrageous tourist rate. Tricycle riders of the motorcycle variety will quote P150 as a matter of course – especially if night is coming on and/or the trip involves unsealed roads. Locals would pay a fraction of this price, so feel free to haggle.

For the record, the official tricycle rates are: P3 for every 2km, 50c for every kilometre after that, or P50 per hour.

PUERTO GALERA
In recent years, the excellent sailing and snorkelling spot of Puerto Galera (pronounced 'pw-air-toe gal-**air**-ah') has been outgunned by nearby Sabang. Now something of a haven for foreign, alcoholic retirees, beautiful little Puerto Galera is very quiet compared to its lively young neighbour. With no nightlife beyond a few beers

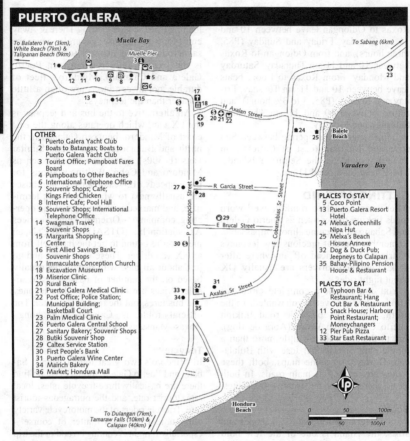

PUERTO GALERA

To Balatero Pier (3km),
White Beach (7km) &
Talipanan Beach (9km)

Muelle Bay

Muelle Pier

To Sabang (6km)

OTHER
1 Puerto Galera Yacht Club
2 Boats to Batangas; Boats to Puerto Galera Yacht Club
3 Tourist Office; Pumpboat Fares Board
4 Pumpboats to Other Beaches
6 International Telephone Office
7 Souvenir Shops; Cafe; Kings Fried Chicken
8 Internet Cafe; Pool Hall
9 Souvenir Shops; International Telephone Office
14 Swagman Travel; Souvenir Shops
15 Margarita Shopping Center
16 First Allied Savings Bank; Souvenir Shops
17 Immaculate Conception Church
18 Excavation Museum
19 Miserior Clinic
20 Rural Bank
21 Puerto Galera Medical Clinic
22 Post Office; Police Station; Municipal Building; Basketball Court
23 Palm Medical Clinic
26 Puerto Galera Central School
27 Sanitary Bakery; Souvenir Shops
28 Butiki Souvenir Shop
29 Caltex Service Station
30 First People's Bank
31 Puerto Galera Wine Center
34 Mairich Bakery
36 Market; Hondura Mall

Balete Beach

Varadero Bay

PLACES TO STAY
5 Coco Point
13 Puerto Galera Resort Hotel
24 Melxa's Greenhills Nipa Hut
25 Melxa's Beach House Annexe
32 Dog & Duck Pub; Jeepneys to Calapan
35 Bahay-Pilipino Pension House & Restaurant

PLACES TO EAT
10 Typhoon Bar & Restaurant; Hang Out Bar & Restaurant
11 Snack House; Harbour Point Restaurant; Moneychangers
12 Pier Pub Pizza
33 Star East Restaurant

H Axalan Street
R Garcia Street
E Brucal Street
L Axalan Sr Street
P Concepcion Street
E Cobarrubias Sr Street

To Dulangan (7km),
Tamaraw Falls (10km) &
Calapan (40km)

Hondura Beach

0   50   100m
0   50   100yd

and a wall-mounted TV, this place is often fast asleep by 9 pm.

There's talk of making Balatero pier, roughly halfway between Puerto Galera town and White Beach, the main point of entry to the area by sea.

Web sites specific to Puerto Galera and surrounding areas include www.puerto galera.net and www.mindoro.com.ph.

Information
Tourist Offices The tourist office is on the pier, next to the board advertising pumpboat fares. It's open from 9 am to 5 pm Monday

to Saturday. Pick up the yearly *Puerto Galera Travel Guide Map* (P80 to P100).

From the tourist office and other tourist haunts, you can pick up the free *Puerto Galera Fortnightly* newspaper, which includes local news, tourist information and events calendars.

Money The Rural Bank changes cash, as does the Swagman Travel office (☎ 0912 319 9587). As in Sabang, the Swagman office also does cash advances on major credit cards (8% commission). You'll need your passport as well as your card to get cash this way. The process takes about 10 minutes, as the staff shout your credit card number through a two-way radio and await approval from headquarters. You can have flights reconfirmed and arrange visa extensions too. It's open from 8 am to 5 pm daily.

Post & Communications The Puerto Galera post office is in the Municipal Building, near the Rural Bank on H Axalan St (the road to Sabang).

No land lines mean Puerto Galera and surrounding areas are only connected to the outside world by cell phones. There's an international telephone office on the Puerto Galera pier, and a similar office just up the street (on the left heading up the hill from the pier). The Swagman Travel office, and many resorts, also offer international phone services. The average deal is P400 to P500 for the first three minutes, and P100 to P150 per subsequent minute.

And just as there's no land line for the phone, there are few satellite dishes for TV. The town of Calapan has cable TV.

Email & Internet Access At the time of writing, a tiny but ambitious Internet cafe was about to open on the pier. One thing's for sure – the cell phone line it must use will make connections even less reliable than your average cell phone.

Medical Services The Palm Medical Clinic (☎ 043-442 0250) is just out of Puerto Galera proper, on the road to Sabang. The 24-hour Puerto Galera Medical Clinic (☎ 043-442 0117) is on H Axalan St, next to the Municipal Building. The Miserior Clinic is on the corner of P Concepcion St and H Axalan St.

Emergency The area's police station, at the Municipal Building, has no telephone. A cell phone is on the way apparently, and might be in operation by the time you read this.

Things to See & Do
The small **Excavation Museum** has ancient Chinese and Thai burial jars on display, as well as Filipino pottery dating back more than 2000 years. There's no entry fee, but

the donation box always appreciates P10 or so. The museum is in the grounds of the Immaculate Conception Church, and is open from 8 am to noon and from 1 to 5 pm daily. Enter the church grounds through the gate in front of the belltower, then turn right.

About 2km from Puerto Galera proper, on the right-hand side heading for Calapan, a hiking trail heads inland and upwards for 2km to a **Mangyan tribal village**, where you may see these expert basket weavers at work. Another 1km along the road (before the asphalt runs out), also on the right heading for Calapan, a 2km unsealed road snakes its way up to the **Python Cave**. This really is home to a 2m python, along with a colony of bats. Back on road, about 100m further, near the basketball court, a rough driveway leads to a **hot spring**. Entry fees vary according to whether the waters are flowing. Tricycles can take you all the way, or at least some of the way, to these three places for P10 to P30.

The quiet town of **Dulangan** (pronounced 'doo-lang-an') is on a beautiful beach about 7km south-east of Puerto Galera town, on the road to Calapan. It's home to quite a few foreign blokes avoiding the tourist hordes. In early 1999, *something* measuring about 7m in length was spotted by fisherfolk off Dulangan Beach, and identified as a *bulik-pating* (tiger shark). But local marine biologists reckoned the description fitted a *butanding* (whale shark) better. Dulangan residents just called it a big, scary fish and have more or less avoided swimming here ever since. From Puerto Galera to Dulangan, it's P10 by jeepney (marked 'Calapan'), or P20 to P30 by tricycle.

The mighty **Tamaraw Falls** are a rough, scenic ride from Puerto Galera. Cool mountain water plummets into a natural pool from high above the road, gushes down to two man-made swimming pools, and disappears into a deep valley below. Several swimmers have slipped while climbing the rocks around the top pool, hence the 'no entry' sign in this section. The falls are popular on the weekend, but during the week you can just about have this brilliant place to yourself. The gates to the main swimming holes are open from 7 am to 5 pm daily (entry is P10 for adults, P5 for children). Small shelters, perched on the edge of the pools, are available for picnicking. No food is sold here, but drinks are sometimes carted in by vendors. To get here from Puerto Galera, catch a Calapan-bound jeepney from next to the Dog & Duck Pub (P15, 40 minutes). Puerto Galera tricycle riders tend to demand hundreds of pesos for the trip to Tamaraw Falls. Sure, the road is bad but it's not *that* bad. P50 per hour is the official rate for tricycle hire. If you have your own motorcycle, this trip is a must.

Places to Stay

Rooms in Puerto Galera are generally cheap. Right at the wharf, *Coco Point* has OK rooms with fan and bath for P400. Up the hill, the modest *Melxa's Greenhills Nipa Hut* has small, basic rooms with fan and private bath for P200. Rooms in the beachside annex are rougher, but the bay view is good.

The *Dog & Duck Pub*, not far from the market, has basic rooms upstairs with common bath starting at P200 (see the later Places to Eat entry). Nearby, the *Bahay-Pilipino Pension House & Restaurant* (☎ 043-442 0266) has similar rooms, with a common balcony overlooking the busy street, for P200 to P250 (see also Places to Eat following).

Prominently placed above the pier, the *Puerto Galera Resort Hotel* (☎ 02-525 4641) sits oddly among the rest of the town's budget accommodation. All rooms are P987 from Monday to Thursday, and P1382 from Friday to Sunday. The good showers, air-con, TV and fridge make these rooms pretty good value – four days a week. Room prices are for one person only (for two, add P200 to P300). All prices include breakfast at the hotel's restaurant.

Places to Eat

The row of *restaurants* along the pier offer relaxed dining with great views of the harbour. Meaty Western meals are a speciality here and breakfasts cost around P100. Exceptions include the *Typhoon Bar & Restaurant*, which does a tasty chilli fish

with rice for P130. The *Hang Out Bar & Restaurant* has American breakfasts for P95, and the *Harbour Point Restaurant* does chicken for P140.

At the end of the pier, right where most boats from Batangas dock, the *Pier Pub Pizza* has well-priced Filipino and Western dishes. Thick, fruity pancakes are P38, tasty pizzas are P120 to P195 and *calamares* (squid) with fries and salad is P150.

The *Puerto Galera Yacht Club* (☎ 043-442 0136) is also something a little different. It has a cafe and bar, with happy hour from 3 pm to 6 pm daily. A free shuttle service boats you there and back from the pier (a few minutes each way), and operates from 8.15 am to 9 pm daily.

Down the other end of town, the *Dog & Duck Pub* cooks up beef and chicken curries for around P140. Spaghetti costs P60 to P110. The nearby *Bahay-Pilipino Pension House & Restaurant* does a shrimp omelette for P125 and fruit shakes for P45. It also specialises in German and Filipino dishes.

Opposite the Dog & Duck is the humble *Star East Restaurant*, serving a wide range of fine Filipino dishes for P40 to P60.

Getting There & Away

Boat The most popular route to Puerto Galera is from Batangas, on Luzon, to Puerto Galera's Muelle Pier. Buses run directly to Batangas from the BLTB terminal in Manila (P74, three hours). Ferries and outriggers operate all day (until about 6 pm) between Batangas and Puerto Galera (or nearby Balatero or Sabang). The crossing takes one to two hours, depending on the type of boat. See the Getting There & Away entry for Mindoro at the beginning of the chapter.

About 3km west of Puerto Galera, Balatero is served by the lumbering Viva car and passenger ferry.

Pumpboats can be hired for the trip to Sabang (P180) or any other beach you fancy. From Puerto Galera to Small La Laguna Beach it's P120, to Big La Laguna Beach P150. For a hefty P1650, you can avoid the long jeepney ride to Calapan, and go by pumpboat instead.

If you want to head west to Wawa (Abra de Ilog) from Puerto Galera, there's no road between these two towns. A rented pump-boat to Wawa will cost you P1500. A cheaper, less direct option is to go to Batangas and catch a boat to Wawa (see the later Getting There & Away entry for Batangas).

Jeepney & Tricycle Jeepneys leave for Sabang when full from just above the pier (P10), and tricycles can also be hired for the ride (P60 to P150). A jeepney in the other direction, to Aninuan and Talipanan beaches, is P15 (15 to 20 minutes). Further afield, jeepneys to Calapan cost P30 (two hours).

AROUND PUERTO GALERA

About 1km from Puerto Galera town, on the road to Sabang, is a choice bunch of places to stay for those seeking privacy and panoramic views. The *Franklyn Highland Beach Resort* (☎ 0912 314 8133) is a friendly new place on the high ridge above the main road. Roomy nipa huts here cost from P500 to P700. The restaurant and pool here have great views of Varadero Bay to the south.

Next door, on a vast plot of prime land, is the luxurious *Tanawin Bay Resort* (☎/fax

526 0117), featuring such crazed architectural delights as the Snail House and the Circle House. Great views and weird cottages cost from P1200 to P1600.

Just to the north, on a point overlooking Port Galera, is *Kalaw Place* (☎ 0912 301 4778). As unique for its low-key approach to tourism as it is for its stunning position and accommodation, it has several cottages and one vast timber villa. Rates range from around P650 to about P2400.

Nearby, the top value *Pirate Cove Beach Resort* (☎ 0912 270 9428) has comfortable cottages for P500. Carl, the Swedish part-owner, can pick you up from any beach in the area if you ring ahead.

The *Encenada Beach Resort* (☎ 0912 312 9761), on the beach of the same name, is in a lovely spot. But the rooms and cottages hardly deserve their US$60 to US$80 price tags. One reader felt a little misled when he arrived to find that this place, despite it's beachy position, has no good diving nearby.

On Boquete Island, clinging to Mindoro by a narrow land bridge, is the *Sandbar Beach Resort & Clubhouse* (☎ 0912 385 1904). Big, well spaced-out cottages complete with kitchen, bath and chunky

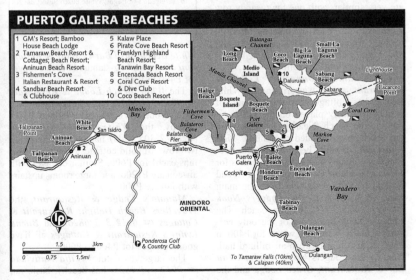

PUERTO GALERA BEACHES

1 GM's Resort; Bamboo House Beach Lodge
2 Tamaraw Beach Resort & Cottages; Beach Resort; Aninuan Beach Resort
3 Fishermen's Cove Italian Restaurant & Resort
4 Sandbar Beach Resort & Clubhouse
5 Kalaw Place
6 Pirate Cove Beach Resort
7 Franklyn Highland Beach Resort; Tanawin Bay Resort
8 Encenada Beach Resort
9 Coral Cove Resort & Dive Club
10 Coco Beach Resort

MINDORO

furniture cost a hefty P1500. Nearby, back on the main road, the *Fishermen's Cove Italian Restaurant & Resort (☎ 0912 306 8494)* comes with a secluded beach and pretty nipa hut cottages for P750.

White Beach

A cheaper, simpler alternative to Sabang, White Beach also offers more sand and more interaction with locals. There are also no girlie bars here, and you don't necessarily need to hold a diving licence to hold a conversation. The beach's dazzling expanse of sand can make it extremely hot compared to Sabang or Puerto Galera. There are regular games of volleyball on the sand in front of the Travellers Beach Delight Restaurant & Cottages.

International calls can be made via cell phone from several resorts, including White Beach Nipa Hut and Travellers Beach Delight Restaurant & Cottages.

Places to Stay Many places to stay have mosquito nets 'just in case' (there have been several unconfirmed reports of dengue fever here). While there are plenty of places to stay in White Beach, prices and standards are very similar, with one long, sandy row of resorts offering cheap rooms and cottages, with fan, bath and balcony for P400 to P600. The air-con rooms are tidy, plain, and quite pricey at around P1200. Exceptions are mentioned as follows.

The *Summer Connection Lodge & Restaurant*, at the western end of White Beach, has cottages for P500, some of which are nicely placed on the hill overlooking the beach. Nearby, set back from the beach in a secluded compound, *Villa Anastacia* has solid, brightly painted, freestanding cottages with kitchen facilities for a very reasonable P400. There's a dirt road leading to Villa Anastacia from the main road, as well as to the *Lodgers Nook (☎ 0912 305 7011)*, by the beach. The Lodgers Nook has some of the only cottages actually facing the water, for P400 to P600. It also has an open-air billiard hall. Next to the Lodgers Nook, *Cherry's Inn Bar & Restaurant*, *Grace Lodge* and the

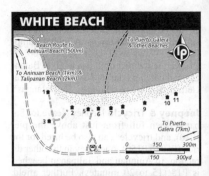

WHITE BEACH

1 Summer Connection Lodge & Restaurant
2 Cherry's Inn Bar & Restaurant; Grace Lodge;
   White Beach Basil Bar Lodging & Restaurant
3 Villa Anastacia
4 Waiting Shed; Jeepneys to Puerto Galera
5 White Beach Nipa Hut; White Beach Lodge &
   Restaurant
6 Manalo's Lodge & Restaurant; Travellers Beach
   Delight Restaurant & Cottages
7 Buena Lynne's Restaurant & Cottages; Sailors
   Shack Bar & Restaurant
8 Villa Natividad
9 Lenly's Beach Resort Bar & Restaurant
10 Delgado's Cottages; White Beach Resort Bar &
   Restaurant
11 Mylah's Nipa Hut & Restaurant

White Beach Basil Bar Lodging & Restaurant offer your bog-standard beach cottages for P400 to P500.

The *White Beach Lodge & Restaurant (☎ 0912 311 6127)* has a larger than usual open layout, and cottages for P400 to P500. Nearby, the *White Beach Nipa Hut (☎ 0912 305 9343)* has no nipa huts, but two rows of solid cottages (some with two fans each) for P600. Similar cottages with air-con are P1200, and large rooms upstairs with fan are P800.

Manalo's Lodge & Restaurant, the *Travellers Beach Delight Restaurant & Cottages (☎ 0912 312 6826)* and *Buena Lynne's Restaurant & Cottages* all have good cottages for P400 to P600.

The large, two-storey *Villa Natividad (☎ 0912 391 1825)* has beachy, basic fan rooms for P500 (P1200 with air-con). Nearby, *Lenly's Beach Resort Bar & Restaurant*, *Delgado Cottages*, *White Beach Resort Bar & Restaurant*, and *Mylah's Nipa Hut & Restaurant* all offer OK cottages, for P400 to P500.

Places to Eat Just as there are no exceptional places to stay here, there are no really outstanding restaurants either. There are, however, heaps of good, honest eateries. Many of these places are attached to the aforementioned places to stay.

Food at the *White Beach Lodge & Restaurant*, set back from the beach, is a tasty combination of Western and Filipino. Prices range from P70 to around P140.

The *Travellers Beach Delight Restaurant* is noted for its big, cheap breakfasts (P40 to P75) and pancakes (P30 to P45), and pizzas (including vegetarian) for P100 to P135. A nice touch is the ginger tea, at P15 a cup.

Buena Lynne's Restaurant & Cottages has great fruit shakes for P25, American breakfasts for P70, and good pizzas for P140.

The *Sailors Shack Bar & Restaurant* offers dishes from P45 to P100. It does a good vegie curry, as well as spaghetti bolognese and *adobo calamares* (squid marinated in vinegar and garlic). The whole fish dishes are also well worth trying. There's live music here several times a week.

Getting There & Away While it's an easy enough 10 to 15 minute jeepney ride from Puerto Galera town (P10), White Beach is at its most attractive when approached by boat (P400 to P450 from Sabang).

Aninuan Beach
White Beach's western neighbour is Aninuan Beach, just the place if you find White Beach too heavily populated. The low lights and pristine surrounds makes this a good spot for fireflies – watch their nightly dancing around the big *talisay* tree next to the Aninuan Beach Resort. And if you think you saw some of the shells around here moving, you're not necessarily crazy – hermit crabs are fond of this beach too.

Places to Stay & Eat Accommodation choices are concentrated along the eastern end (ie, the end closest to White Beach) of this gorgeous beach.

Just around the rocks from White Beach, there's an as-yet unnamed family-run *resort* with a loud, aqua-coloured main building. This building has spotless tiled rooms with private bath and fan for P600. Similar rooms with air-con cost P1200. There's a shared balcony overlooking the water. Out the front, a shack-style cafe offers sandwiches (P35 to P60) and brewed coffee (P25). In front of the cafe, try out the beach shower that's masquerading as a fake tree.

Next door, stretched out along the beach, the *Tamaraw Beach Resort & Cottages* (☎ 0912 304 8769) offers a great location and good value. Nipa hut-style cottages with balcony, bath and fan cost P500. Excellent, small Filipino dishes (around P100 per dish) can be served to you under thatched-roof shelters right on the sand.

A little further along, the *Aninuan Beach Resort* (☎ 0912 330 8683) has overpriced fan rooms and cottages for P1200. Big, comfortable air-con rooms with equally spacious balconies are better value at P1500. The food is very good, and can be served at tables on the sand, next to the bar. Big breakfasts cost P60 to P140 and fine seafood dishes cost P120 to P210.

Aninuan is a 15-minute walk from White Beach, along the main road, or a five-minute scramble around the rocky point. Jeepneys run fairly regularly between Aninuan and Puerto Galera (P20). The resorts here can also arrange boats to/from Puerto Galera or Sabang (P500 to P600).

Talipanan Beach
Taking the tropical seclusion one big step further, the bright and breezy *GM's Resort* (☎ 0912 354 3997) is on Talipanan Beach, the western extension of Aninuan Beach. It has a 2nd floor, open-air eating area with wonderful ocean views. Tidy rooms with balcony and fan are P500. Ageing duplex cottages with balcony and fan are poorer value for the same price. Well-run and friendly, its restaurant serves breakfasts

from P60 to P75, vegie curry for P45, and Filipino-style dishes for P75 to P100.

To get to Talipanan Beach, you can organise a pumpboat through GM's Resort (P700 from Puerto Galera), or you can take the road around from White Beach. For a beautiful beach trek, you can simply walk from Aninuan Beach along the sand, following the trails up and over the rocky outcrops along the way. It takes about half an hour.

SABANG BEACH

Sabang's beachfront is jam-packed with hotels, restaurants and dive shops. Rowdier than anywhere else on the island, Sabang still has plenty of quiet patches of paradise if you look hard enough. The place tends to be geared towards divers, with most hotels offering dive trips of varying standards and prices. The average single dive with all equipment included is US$50.

If you don't dive, it's still worth hiring a snorkel and mask for the day (P50 to P100) to check out the coral at nearby places such as Long Beach. But if the sight of dead or dying coral upsets you, stay on dry land.

Information

Cash advances are available on credit card from the Swagman Travel office by the water (8% commission). Several of the bigger resorts also do cash advances on credit cards for guests.

The Swagman Travel office, several telephone offices, and a number of resorts, offer international telephone services via cell phone. The average rate per minute is P100 to P150 (P400 to P500 for the first three minutes).

A newspaper seller roams Sabang's beachfront most mornings.

Places to Stay

Most of Sabang's accommodation is along the beach. And, generally speaking, the places at the east end of the beach (with the dividing line being the street where jeepneys come and go from) are cheaper than those to the west. The east side has signs along the sand saying 'Segregated

Trash' but don't take this personally – it's to do with rubbish collection, not budget travellers.

At the far eastern end of Sabang Beach is *Tina's*, where the friendly manager Sergio will proudly tell you it's the cheapest place in town. No-frills cottages, some with good views of the beach, start at P200.

Next to Tina's, *Villa Sabang & Octopus Divers* (☎ 0917 903 9645) is a popular place with powder-blue air-con rooms for P990. Cottages with kitchenette (fan only) cost P650. There's also a restaurant, bar and swimming pool.

Gold Coast has two rows of solid, brightly painted cottages for P350 to P500. All have a balcony, private bath and fan. The pricier cottages have a kitchen.

Next door, the *Sabang Inn Beach Resort* offers tidy rooms with private bath and fan for P500, and the *Seashore Lodge* (☎ 0912 304 9340) has a leafy compound with balconied huts going for P800 with air-con, bath, fridge and cable TV.

The *VIP Dive Resort & Action Divers* has rooms above the dive shop with private bath, fan and views for P500 to P600. *At Cans Inn*, a few doors along, is big, plain and good value, with balconied rooms right on the water. Rooms cost P350 with fan, P800 with air-con.

Next door to the Sunshine Coast Restaurant, the newly christened *Garden of Eden Cottages* are stretching the truth a little. OK cottages with balconies, fan and private bath cost P400 to P500.

On Sabang's main street, towering over the Tropicana Restaurant, is the over-the-top *Tropicana Pirate Fortress Beach Resort* (☎ 02-528 5141, ☎/fax 0912 306 8102, ✉ ctropicana@pacific.net.ph), which has a Web site at www.pacific.net.ph/~ctropicana. This artificial castle has several levels of outrageously plush rooms with air-con, four-poster beds and marble bathrooms. Prices start at around P2000.

On the western side of Sabang's main street, *Capt'n Gregg's Divers Lodge* (☎ 0912 306 5267, ✉ email capt_greg@epic.net) is much loved by divers, and has rooms over the water from around P450 (fan and bath) to

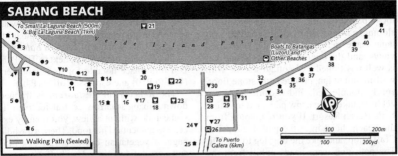

SABANG BEACH

To Small La Laguna Beach (500m) & Big La Laguna Beach (1km)

Verde Island Passage

Boats to Batangas (Luzon) and Other Beaches

To Puerto Galera (6km)

Walking Path (Sealed)

0   100   200m
0   100   200yd

SABANG BEACH

PLACES TO STAY
1 Kokomo Inn
3 Paradise Inn
6 Terraces Garden Resort
8 Atlantis Resort Hotel
13 Big Apple Dive Resort
14 Red Coral Cottages;
    Island Trekking Office
15 Jovimel's Inn
20 Capt'n Gregg's
    Divers Lodge
25 Tropicana Pirate Fortress
    Beach Resort; Tropicana
    Restaurant
34 Garden of Eden Cottages
35 At Can's Inn
37 Juling's Place
38 Seashore Lodge
39 Sabang Inn Beach Resort;
    Gold Coast

40 Villa Sabang & Octopus
    Divers
41 Tina's

PLACES TO EAT
4 Diner
7 Angelyn's Restaurant
10 Tamarind Restaurant &
    Music Pub
16 Relax Thai
    Restaurant
17 Le Bistrot
24 Sabang Fastfood
27 Lucky's Saloon
30 Traveller's Restaurant;
    Scuba World
31 Janelle's Fastfood
32 Deco Stop
33 Sunshine Coast Bar &
    Restaurant

OTHER
2 The Craft Shop
5 General Store
9 Asia Divers & Swagman
    Travel
11 South Sea Divers
12 Swagman Travel;
    Cocktail Divers
18 It's OK Bar; Fruit & Vegetable
    Stalls
19 The Pub
21 Anaconda Floating Bar
22 Dutch Coffee Shop;
    Umbrella Disco
23 Sabang Disco
26 Jeepneys, Tricycles to Puerto
    Galera
28 International Telephone Office
29 Sunset Disco
36 Action Divers; VIP Dive Resort

P600 (with air-con). See also the later Places to Eat entry.

The ***Big Apple Dive Resort*** (☎ *0912 308 1120,* 📧 *info@bigapple.com.ph*) starts at the beach and stretches a long way back. Cottages with fan and bath are P550, and P750 to P900 with kitchen and TV. This place includes a very popular dive centre, restaurant/bar and a swimming pool. It also has a Web site at www.dive-bigapple.com.

The ***Atlantis Resort Hotel*** (☎ *0912 308 0672,* 📧 *atlantis@vasia.com*) has a Web site at www.atlantishotel.com and is the area's most upmarket place to stay. With barely a right angle in sight, this terraced building looks almost organic, with rooms

set into a lush, green hill. The Ristorante da Franco (see the later Places to Eat entry) out the front is a high-roofed hut-style hall affectionately known as 'The Wool Shed'. Rooms with fan and private bath are a pricey US$35. All other rooms have air-con, starting with deluxe at US$45, and moving steadily up to suites with huge balconies for US$55 to US$65. All prices are for single occupancy only – an extra person adds US$10 to the price. A dip in the swimming pool is P50 for nonguests.

The ***Terraces Garden Resort*** (☎ *0912 306 6543*) is Sabang's best kept secret – and its lack of signage and tricky access should keep it that way. Cute, thatched-roof cottages (P600), decorated inside with local basketry, are set among beautiful, sloping gardens. Individually named cottages have generous balconies and good views, and the open-air restaurant and bar is well positioned. All cottages come with wall-mounted fan, private bath, stone floor, comfy double bed, and bedside lamp. To get here, take the narrow path next to Angelyn's Beach Resort. If you're coming from the beach, head in at the path beside The Craft Shop, and take the dog-leg to the left. The path you want heads uphill from the little open-air, diner-style Filipino eatery, then past a makeshift basketball court and a general store.

To the south-east of Sabang, the **Coral Cove Resort & Dive Club** (☎ 0973 771 571) has cute, well-kept rooms with fan for P800. This sleepy, secluded place has a restaurant with great views and a pool table. Dive trips are a speciality, and there's a private jeep or boat to pick you up from Sabang.

Places to Eat

To start the day in style, the **Sunshine Coast Bar & Restaurant** offers the 'Feeling Shitty Breakfast' (one coffee, one Coke, cornflakes, and two cigarettes – all for P50). English breakfasts are P150, as are Japanese breakfasts (miso soup, fish and rice). Thai red curries and Indian dishes are also around P150. This place is right on the beach where the boats pull in and has a great little eating area under the generous shade of a talisay tree.

The nearby **Deco Stop** is a French-flavoured bar and cafe, right on the water. Breakfasts are around P95, and dishes such as chicken adobo (chicken marinated in vinegar and garlic) are P125. **Janelle's Fastfood** is a friendly, open-air eatery serving fine, basic Filipino food for P40 to P50. Nearby, **Sabang Fastfood** offers similar fare for around the same price.

The big, timber **Tropicana Restaurant**, on the main drag heading up the hill, has a giant menu. Breakfasts range from P90 to P145. Mains include fresh seafood and Italian dishes, with imported wines to wash it all down. A spicy Madras fish curry will set you

back P145. Videos are screened most nights, and there's an upstairs eating area if you want to avoid the movie. Nearby is the popular little upstairs steakhouse of **Lucky's Saloon**.

The **Dutch Coffee Shop**, next to The Pub, is a little place notable for its hamburgers (P40 to P50) and espresso coffee (P40).

The **Relax Thai Restaurant** is trapped down Sabang's narrow central footpath. If you can do without a view, you'll enjoy excellent, authentic Thai food. There's a whole page of vegetarian dishes (P120 to P145) and a great, five-course Thai buffet is served every Saturday from 6.30 to 10 pm (P295 per head). A word of warning when ordering: 'spicy' here means gum-achingly spicy.

Le Bistrot is a big place squeezed in along Sabang's central footpath. Tasty Filipino dishes are P150 to P180, and exotic Swiss cheese dishes are P230 to P440.

On a prime spot by the water, the **Tamarind Restaurant & Music Pub** has a meat-heavy menu with most dishes around P200.

Ristorante da Franco, under the same, high roof as the Atlantis Resort Hotel, has authentic Italian dishes that aren't cheap but are worth every peso. Other fine food includes a *lapu-lapu* (grouper) fillet with vegetables (P295) and good pizzas (P125 to P145). French wines are P85 per glass. Big breakfasts range from P95 to P195.

For peaceful, open-air dining and garden views, the **Terraces Garden Resort Bar & Restaurant** is worth the short climb up from Sabang's central footpath (see the earlier Places to Stay entry). Large breakfasts are P120, and seafood offerings such as shrimp are P210. Chicken *apritada* (a spicy, tomato sauce) costs P175.

Capt'n Gregg's Divers Lodge has a 2nd floor, open-air restaurant right on the water. The American breakfast is good value at P85. Big eaters might like to take up the 'Pizza Challenge'. The kitchen needs four hours' notice for this. A long-time diver's favourite, this place has ancient Chinese bowls and other ocean-floor finds on display.

Angelyn's Restaurant, also by the water, has good daily seafood specials. Filipino and international dishes range from

P80 to P130. The vegetable omelette with toast (P65) makes for a filling, meat-free breakfast.

Entertainment

Sabang's reputation as a seedy, girlie-bar sort of place has faded as more straightforward, diver-oriented drinking holes have gained ground. The surviving 'exotic dancer' venues tend to pass themselves off as discos. Huddled around the beach end of the main street, they certainly don't dominate Sabang's nightlife like they once did.

A short walk along Sabang Beach towards the neighbouring Small La Laguna Beach is *The Point*, a beautifully breezy bar perched above the walking path. It's open till midnight, does bar snacks and has a big, eclectic CD collection and cocktail list. Happy hour is from 5.30 to 6.30 pm.

Opposite the Relax Thai Restaurant, *The Lounge* is an indoorsy, air-con bar with frozen cocktails and a sporty theme. It has a happy hour from 5 to 7 pm.

If you really want to drink like a fish, there's the double-decker *Anaconda Floating Bar*, moored off Sabang's central shore. Take plenty of protection against the sun – you can almost smell the foreign flesh roasting. It's open from 9 am to 6 pm daily, and a free shuttle boat will take you there and back from Capt'n Gregg's Divers Lodge.

Getting There & Away

Pumpboats chug between Sabang and Batangas (Luzon) daily. Other boats and ferries to/from Batangas are found at Puerto Galera and Balatero. Jeepneys and tricycles to Puerto Galera head off from the steep main road inland (P10 to Puerto Galera by jeepney, P50 officially by tricycle).

AROUND SABANG
Small La Laguna Beach

An easy stroll from Sabang is Small La Laguna Beach, where the *El Galleon Beach Resort* (☎/fax 865252) has spacious poolside hut-style rooms with fan for P950 (P1500 with air-con). The stylish, open-air restaurant has simple treats – like jaffles

(P65), right up to Thai combination curry (P160) and even *coq au vin* (P230).

Roelyn's Restaurant, opposite the Tropical Massage rooms, has tasty Filipino and Western dishes for around P100.

Next door, beside the Scuba World Dive Center, the *Sunsplash Restaurant* does European specials such as goulash for P155. Behind the restaurant, the *Sunsplash Cottages* are in a pretty, quiet garden setting. The cottages are solid, with bath, thatched roofs, small balconies, fridge and TV for P750.

The *Havana Moon Restaurant & Beach Resort* has good, standard cottages for P600, or air-con ones for P800.

Next door, the *Full Moon Restaurant & Resort* does Thai curries for P150, and balconied cottages for P700. The restaurant screens videos most nights, and promises lots of scintillating gossip.

Nick & Sonia's Cottages, beside Action Divers, offer simple cottages for P400. Next door, the *Marelex Beach Resort* has rooms with shared balcony and a small garden for P500.

Portofino (☎ 02-776 704) is Small La Laguna's answer to Sabang's stylish Atlantis. Less well organised, this expensive, comfortable villa has air-con rooms starting at P2000. Its fan cooled room – a shoebox with a bunk bed and bathroom – is a sick joke at P1500. The hotel doesn't accept guests for less than two nights.

Next door, *Carlo's Inn* (☎ 0912 301 0717) is a fun, friendly place with eclectic decor. Rooms here are stacked all the way up the steep hill, ensuring great views and firm calf muscles. Good rooms start at P450, climbing to P850 for deluxe with air-con.

A pumpboat between Puerto Galera and Small La Laguna Beach is P150 (20 minutes). If you're feeling really lazy, you can even get a pumpboat between Small La Laguna and Sabang (P50, five minutes).

Big La Laguna Beach

Next to Small La Laguna, Big La Laguna has plenty of accommodation options, including *Nick & Sonia's Cottages* and *Full Moon*, which both have pleasant, quite

BIG LA LAGUNA & SMALL LA LAGUNA

To Batangas,
Puerto Galera
& other Beaches

1 Big La Laguna
Beach

2 Small La Laguna
3 Beach
4
5
6
7 8

See Sabang Beach Map – page 267

Sabang Beach

0   250   500m
0   250   500yd

PLACES TO STAY
1 Miller's Corner
3 La Laguna Beach Club;
5 Carlo's Inn; Portofino
6 Marelex Beach Resort;
    Action Divers; Nick
    & Sonia's Cottages
7 Havana Moon Restaurants
    & Beach Resort; Scuba
    World Dive Center; Full
    Moon Restaurant & Resort;
    Sunsplash Cottages & Resort

PLACES TO EAT
8 Roelyn's Restaurant;
    Tropical Massage;
    El Galleon
    Beach Resort;
    Asian Divers;
    The Point

OTHER
2 Pumpboat Fares
    Board
4 Penman's Pass

comfortable cottages from P350. The *Paradise Lodge* (☎/fax 375 6348) has rooms for P550, and the *La Laguna Beach Club* (☎ 0973 855 545, ✉ La Laguna@epic.net) has a swimming pool and comfortable rooms with fan and bath for around P700 (P1100 for air-con).

West of Big La Laguna is the exclusive *Coco Beach Resort* (☎ 0917 890 1426), with about 90 meticulously finished nipa huts hidden among the palms of a big, beautiful beach. Huts start at US$38 per person (US$48 per person for two nights) and there's no air-con, but prices includes round-trip transport (Manila-Coco Beach-Manila) and buffet breakfast.

A pumpboat between Puerto Galera and Big La Laguna Beach is P120 (18 minutes).

Between Big La Laguna and Sabang, a pumpboat should cost about P70 (less than 10 minutes).

East Coast

Mindoro's High Rolling Mountains have sliced the island into two provinces. The eastern province is known as Mindoro Oriental, with the north-eastern city of Calapan as its capital.

CALAPAN

Calapan (pronounced 'kal-ah-pan'), the busy capital of Mindoro Oriental, is about 40km from Puerto Galera via a rough, winding road with spectacular views across Verde Island Passage. The city hosts the annual Sanduguan Festival and is a good base for hiking trips to Mt Halcon (see following Things to See & Do section).

JP Rizal St is the main drag of Calapan, and it's this street that jeepneys and buses crawl along, before terminating at the market, just off JP Rizal St on Juan Luna St. Around the intersection of Juan Luna and JP Rizal Sts you'll find a Metrobank and an Equitable PCI Bank, the Calapan Doctor's Clinic, and PT&T and RCPI telephone offices.

Things to See & Do

While there's not a lot to see in Calapan, there's plenty of adventure nearby – and that's where Calapan's Base Camp Outdoor Shop (☎ 288 8445) comes in. As the headquarters of the **Halcon Mountaineers**, the shop has the unmistakable stench of well-worn hikers' boots. Just as strong is its reputation for hardcore hiking and climbing trips on Mt Halcon, about 30km south-west of Calapan. At 2505m, Halcon is the country's fourth highest mountain but – according to these lads – it's the toughest one to climb.

The standard trip is two days up, two days down, taking in the perilous 'Monkey Bridge' (a tangle of tree trunks spanning the Dulangan River), the breathtaking 'Knife Edge' ridge walk, and finally the peak, which often juts well above the clouds. The mountaineers have an arrangement with the local Mangyan tribespeople, who are employed as porters on request (a few days notice is appreciated). There's no set price for the trip, you tend to just pay as you go. Costs along the way are likely to include tent rental

The Tamaraw

The tamaraw (Bubalus mindorensis), one of the world's most endangered land mammals, is found only in Mindoro. The stout little native buffalo has fallen victim to hunting, disease and, most recently, large-scale deforestation. Its numbers have dropped to a near-disastrous 300, from an estimated 10,000 in 1900. Now clinging to survival in remote corners of reserves such as Mt Iglit-Baco National Park, the tamaraw has so far failed to breed in captivity.

Mic Looby

(P300), hiking registration (P40), porter (P150 per day plus meals), guide (P700 total plus meals), and jeepney hire (P350 total, not per head). The maximum number of people per guide is five. For more information, contact Randy at the shop – one block from JP Rizal St, on MH del Pilar St, between the Riceland I Inn, and the Riceland II Inn.

Places to Stay

On JP Rizal St, around the corner from the market and public transport terminal, is the multistorey **Riceland I Inn**. Rooms here are tiled and tidy, and range in price from P150 to P600. There's a P150 room key deposit on all rooms.

Diagonally opposite is the slightly taller **Hotel Mayi** (☎ 288 4437), which has good, smallish, double and twin rooms with fan and common bath for P250 and P350. Doubles and twins with private bath and cable TV are P400. For air-con and cable TV, you'll pay P650.

For quieter lodgings, you can wander down nearby MH del Pilar St, over the bridge, to the **Riceland II Inn** (☎ 288 5590). A single-storey, grey complex houses rooms ranging from P220 (twin with private bath and fan) and P280 (twin with private bath and overhead fan), to air-con rooms with private bath for P340 to P500. In the rear annexe building, larger rooms with one double bed are P285 (with fan), P400 (with air-con) to P625 to P800 (air-con, cable TV and extra beds).

Places to Eat

Calapan has an excellent **market**, strong on fruit and fish. It's on Juan Luna St, just around the corner from the Riceland I Inn on JP Rizal St. On JP Rizal St, there's a **Mister Donut** and **Jollibee**, as well as the Hotel Mayi's 2nd floor **Samara Restaurant**, specialising in seafood and steak.

On MH del Pilar St, diagonally opposite the Riceland II Inn, is the cute little **Kawayan Restaurant**, a shining monument to bamboo (kawayan means bamboo). The friendly family running this place offer a small, tasty range of mostly Filipino dishes. Excellent camaron rebasado (deep-fried shrimp) is P90, beef tapa (dried, a popular snack or breakfast food) is P50, and vegetable chop suey is P65. The halo-halo (shaved ice coloured with fruit, white beans and/or corn, and smothered in evaporated milk, P25) special is a meal in itself.

Within the Riceland II Inn's compound you'll find **Fiesta Beeranda Fast Food**, a low-key, open-air cafe serving sandwiches for P25 to P45 and simple Filipino fare for around P50.

Getting There & Away

Boat A tricycle between JP Rizal St, in central Calapan, and the pier should be P10 to P15. From here, it's a quick and easy ride between Calapan and Batangas, now that SuperCat/SeaAngels fastcraft do the trip daily (P150, 45 minutes). From Calapan to Batangas, they leave frequently between 5 am and 6.30 pm. From Batangas to Calapan, there are numerous departures between 4.30 am and 6.30 pm.

In Calapan, you can buy tickets at the pier, or at the small Aboitiz Shipping office, in the Tamaraw Centre on JP Rizal St.

Montenegro Shipping Lines has bigger, slower boats from Calapan to Batangas approximately 12 times a day from 1 am to 6.30 pm (P60 to P70, two hours). From Batangas to Calapan, they also set off about 12 times daily, from 4.30 am to 9.30 pm. And as if that wasn't enough, Aquajet fast-craft are due to start a daily service between Calapan and Batangas as of April 2000.

For P1650, you can travel between Calapan and Puerto Galera by pumpboat.

Bus & Jeepney Jeepneys from Puerto Galera to Calapan leave approximately hourly from around 6 am to 2 pm daily (P30, two hours). These jeepneys can be found on P Concepcion St, next to the Dog & Duck Pub in Puerto Galera. From Calapan to Puerto Galera, the official jeepney times are 8.30 am and 3 pm, but there are usually additional trips being made. The jeepneys wait at the market on Juan Luna St. Buses don't operate between Calapan and Puerto Galera.

Like jeepneys, small buses leave Calapan from the market on Luna St. They depart, until about 2 pm daily, to Bongabong (P50, three hours) via Pinamalayan (P25, 1½ hours).

Large buses operate from the Calapan pier to Roxas (P100, four hours) via Pinamalayan (P40, 1½ hours), and to Mansalay (P120, 4½ hours). These buses run from around 6 am to around 2 pm daily. FX minibuses compete with the large buses at the pier for passengers, operating throughout the day but only heading off when full. To Roxas it's about three hours and costs P100.

BONGABONG

Bongabong (pronounced 'bong-**ah**-bong') is a compact little fishing town on a mangrove-fringed inlet, about 20km north of Roxas. Apart from challenging nearby Roxas for the title of medical clinic capital of Mindoro, Bongabong has a good range of eateries. Also, next to the market, at the parking bay for buses (on General Segundo

St), there's a concrete statue in honour of a big, colourful fish. Elsewhere around town, concrete sharks and flying fish are mounted on pedestals.

International calls can be made at the PLDT Bongabong Telephone Exchange, oppsite the OTSAI waiting station on Governor A Umali St.

Places to Stay & Eat

The *D & G Pension House & Restaurant* is one block from the water, on the corner of Baltazar and Umali Sts. Brightly decorated in aqua and white, it has a nice shared balcony on the 2nd floor and a restaurant with a large menu, including seafood dishes for P70 to P100. The rooms, all good for two, are a bit of a letdown. Standard rooms with fan and common bath are P150, or P200 with bath. These are more inviting than the windowless air-con rooms for P500.

One block on, heading away from the market, Governor A Umali St has plenty of good food places. These include the sweet-smelling *Five Star Bakery & MC Levin Restaurant* (directly opposite the OTSAI waiting station), the *Chinatown Restaurant*, and *Gneto's Pizza House*. Gneto's, past the school, has home-made pizza for around P70.

Getting There & Away

By bus or jeepney to Roxas, it's P20 to P30 (one hour), and to Calapan it's P50 to P90 (three hours) depending on the type of bus. The buses and jeepneys come and go from a large parking bay on General Segundo St, next to the market. FX minibuses will pick you up from the OTSAI waiting station on Governor A Umali St. They charge P30 to Roxas (30 to 45 minutes), and P90 to Calapan (2½ to 3 hours).

You may be able hire a pumpboat to take you from here to Tablas Island (Romblon), or there may be one heading there – but don't count on it.

ROXAS

If you happen to be in urgent need of medical advice, Roxas (pronounced 'raw-hahs') will suit you nicely. This dusty little town is

Rice drying on the roadside, South-East Luzon.

The Philippines is predominantly Catholic.

The famous symmetrical cone of Mt Mayon, South-East Luzon.

A Mangyan structure in Mindoro.

Talipanan Beach, Puerto Galera, Mindoro.

Tropical waters beckon in Mindoro.

Discover the joys of the *banca* (pumpboat) in Mindoro.

packed with pharmacies, dentists and medical clinics. If you're fit and healthy, you'll probably be keen to hop on one of the regular boats to Panay or Romblon out of here as soon as possible. On Morente Ave, the main drag, the town's brand new market is centrally placed and full of life. If travelling by jeepney between Roxas and Bulalacao (around the town of Mansalay), you may be lucky enough to share a ride with Mangyan tribespeople who are often in these parts to trade goods. If they take a shine to you, you might just get a guided tour around their nearby mountain villages.

Information

There's an unofficial tourist office on the ground floor of the Santo Niño Hotel, opposite the market. Run by the attentive Ador Villaluna, the office has details about getting to/from Roxas. There's also a small selection of Mangyan *ramit* (sarong) for sale (P250), as well as woven bags and coin purses (P15 to P100). Ador also has information on visiting the Mangyan people.

Next door to the Santo Niño Hotel, on the ground floor of the Villa Roxas Hotel & Restaurant, is the PLDT Roxas Telephone Exchange Office, which has an international telephone service. There's also a Globelines international phone office on Morente Ave, on the other side of the market.

Places to Stay & Eat

The town's three central hotels stand shoulder to shoulder, facing the market, on Administration St. This street alone includes one pharmacy and three medical clinics.

The *Hotel Dannarose* is a creaky, timber establishment with narrow corridors and quite OK old single rooms with fan for P100. Doubles with bathrooms cost P200. Front rooms can be noisy. The shared terrace is a good place to watch the goings on at the market across the street.

Right next door, the *Santo Niño Hotel* (☎ 036-453 0056) is big, old and dark, with polished floorboards and box-like single rooms with fan and common bath for P100. In the main building, spacious rooms with three to five beds (P100 per person) are a

good deal. The friendly restaurant on the ground floor has good Filipino food for around P60.

One more door along is the newish *Roxas Villa Hotel & Restaurant* (☎ 036-453 0017, ✉ roxasvillahotel@yahoo.com). With its reception desk hidden down the covered drive, this place has clean, simple rooms with good showers, ceiling-mounted fan, and rock-hard beds for P250. Some of these rooms are windowless and airless – others are more inviting. For bigger rooms, with air-con and TV, you'll pay around P750. The hotel's restaurant menu includes a decent vegetable chopsuey with beef (P55), and *pancit bihon* (thick or thin noodle dish, P40).

The large *Native Food Restaurant*, on the road between the pier and Roxas proper, serves fine local cuisine for P50 to P150.

Getting There & Away

Boat Roxas' pier is a P15 tricycle ride from the centre of town. If you want to buy tickets in Roxas for the Calapan-Batangas boat trip, there's a SuperCat/SeaAngels fastcraft ticket office on Magsaysay St, near the Morente Ave intersection.

For Panay, boats from Roxas to Caticlan leave at 10 am Monday and Friday (P200, 5 to 7 hours). From Caticlan to Roxas, the boats leave at 9 am Wednesday.

For Romblon, big pumpboats operate between Roxas and Odiongan, as well as between Roxas and Looc. Boats from Roxas to Odiongan leave between 10 and 11 am Tuesday, Friday and Sunday (P85, three hours), and from Odiongan to Roxas between 10 and 11 am Thursday, Saturday and Monday. From Roxas to Looc, boats leave between 10 and 11 am Tuesday, Friday and Sunday (P85, 3 to 3½ hours), and return between 10 and 11 am Thursday, Saturday and Monday.

Bus & Jeepney Large buses operate between Calapan and Roxas (P100, four hours) via Pinamalayan (P40, 1½ hours), and to Mansalay (P120, 4½ hours). They run daily from around 6 am to around 2 pm, between the pier at Roxas and the pier at Calapan.

FX minivans, operated by OTSAI, operate between Roxas and Calapan pier (P100, two hours), as well as between Roxas and Bulalacao (P150, 2 to 2½ hours). In Roxas, they leave from the corner of Morente Ave and Magsaysay Ave.

A bus from Roxas to Bulalacao (via Mansalay) leaves from Magsaysay Ave at 9 am daily (P30, 2½ hours). In theory, this should get you to Bulalacao in time for the pumpboat to San José at 11 am daily. From Bulalacao to Roxas, buses also head off at 9 am daily.

Jeepneys from Roxas to Bulalacao leave at 5 and 7 am daily (P30, two to three hours). From Bulalacao, a Roxas-bound jeepney waits for passengers arriving by pumpboat from San José at around 2 or 3 pm. The road between Roxas and Bulalacao can be extremely dusty – but if you're tackling it by jeepney you'll probably be shielded from the dust by all the passengers piled on top of you.

BULALACAO

The remote fishing town of Bulalacao (pronounced 'bull-**ah**-la-cow') is a vital link for anyone wanting to round the rugged southern coast of Mindoro. There are plenty of buses and jeepneys running between Bulalacao and Roxas, but between Bulalacao and San José it's boats only. Apparently, there *is* some sort of road between Bulalacao and San José, but if Mindoro's go-anywhere jeepneys don't attempt it, it must be one hell of a road.

The town itself is nestled into a rise above a large beach. Dominated by a church-like basketball stadium, it has a couple of general stores and one or two small, no-name eateries.

Getting There & Away

Boat The pumpboat to/from San José must moor in the deeper waters outside a breakwater. Small boats shuttle passengers back and forth from the shore (P10 one way).

One pumpboat leaves San José at 11 am daily (P100, three hours), and another leaves Bulalacao, also at 11 am daily. There may occasionally be a 1 pm pumpboat from San José and/or Bulalacao as well.

Bus & Jeepney From Bulalacao to Roxas, buses head off at 9 am daily (P30, 2½ hours).

A jeepney waits right on Bulalacao's beach for passengers from the boat, and heads for Roxas when its very, very full (P30, two to three hours).

The most comfortable and expensive mode of transport between Bulalacao and Roxas is the FX minivan. These air-con minibuses cost P150 and take around two hours. Departures times vary, depending on the number of passengers willing to pay the high price.

West & North-West Coast

The province of Mindoro Occidental, representing the island's western half, makes for some particularly rough riding. The road between Mamburao and Sablayan is a doozy. In April 1999 it involved a detour across the flood plain of the Amnay River.

WAWA (ABRA DE ILOG)

If you catch a boat to remote Wawa (pronounced 'wah-wah') on the north-west coast you'll see why there's no useable road west of Puerto Galera. A cloud-scraping wall of jagged mountains runs right to the shore. Little more than a bundle of small buildings around a sagging pier, Wawa works just fine as the northern gateway to Mindoro's west coast, and is well served by boats from Batangas (see the Getting There & Away entry for Mindoro, at the beginning of the chapter).

Officially, Wawa is the coastal outersuburb of Abra de Ilog (pronounced 'ah-bra de ill-og'), a nondescript town about 5km inland. The road between here and Mamburao is rough and mostly unsealed, but it takes you through some attractive rice and corn farming land.

Places to Stay & Eat

Abra de Ilog has no places to stay, and Wawa's accommodation consists only of the *L & P Lodging House* – it's on your left if you're standing on the pier gazing out to sea. No-frills fan rooms are P120. A couple of small *eateries* by the pier should help get you through the night.

Getting There & Away

Although you'll dock at Wawa, as far as the shipping lines are concerned, your destination is Abra de Ilog. Montenegro Shipping Lines operate car and passenger ferries from Batangas to Wawa (Abra de Ilog) at 1, 3 and 8 am and 2 pm daily (P70 to P90, 2½ hours). From Wawa (Abra de Ilog) to Batangas, the boats sail at 4.30, 6.30 and 11 am and 5 pm daily.

A special ride by pumpboat between Wawa (Abra de Ilog) and Puerto Galera should cost around P1500.

When boats dock at Wawa, there are usually several jeepneys waiting to take passengers south to Mamburao (P40, one hour). Be prepared for a bone-shaking ride.

MAMBURAO

Capital of the western province of Mindoro Occidental, Mamburao (pronounced 'mambor-**ow**') is a quiet, relatively undeveloped town. Fishing and boat building are the main industries, and there's a good beach just north of town.

Places to Stay

On National Rd, which runs through the centre of town, is the *La Gensol Plaza Hotel (☎ 711 1072)*. Formerly the Tamaraw Hotel, this place is pretty fancy by Mamburao standards. All rooms are on the 2nd floor, where plain, tidy singles/doubles start at P250/350 with fan and private bath. Roomier air-con doubles and twins with cable TV are a bit overpriced at P850.

Nearby is the *Travellers Hotel & Restaurant*, also on National Rd, near the Iglesia Ni Cristo Church with its three-pronged facade. It's a rambling, two-storey place where small doubles and twins with fan and bath start at P150. The floral wallpapered, air-con doubles for P500 are a little cramped.

The quiet *Tayamaan Palm Beach Club Resort* is about 4km north of town (P10 to P20 by tricycle), on the edge of a pretty, beach cove. Concrete cottages are nicely laid out among rows of palm trees on a large lawn. Complete with bath, murals, fan and balcony, the cottages are P600 with one room, or P800 to P900 with two rooms. A simple European Breakfast is P135, and Filipino dishes are P110 to P140.

Places to Eat

The *Travellers Hotel & Restaurant* serves Filipino favourites such as pancit Canton for P40. Out the front of the hotel, *Allejna's French Fries Corner* is a little stall selling deep-fried goodies. Next to the church, the *Sandwich Station* has hamburgers and fried egg and cheese rolls. About 300m past the Traveller's Hotel, opposite the 'Slightly Used Appliances' Store and a karaoke bar, the truckstop-style *Stop Over Restaurant* is popular with bus drivers. It serves Filipino dishes for around P40.

Getting There & Away

Air Mamburao's airport is about 1km from the centre of town (there's a turn-off 100m from the Caltex service station). It may look abandoned, but at the time of writing, Pacific Airways flies three times a week to/from Manila (see the Getting There & Away entry for Mindoro, at the beginning of this chapter). The ticket office and check-in counter is in a private house in Mamburao – where you'll have your luggage weighed using grocery scales. The 'office' is well hidden, so take a tricycle (P5 to P10 from National Rd).

Note that Pacific Airways flights to/from Mamburao may not happen if passenger numbers are low.

Bus & Jeepney Buses between Mamburao and Sablayan take about three hours (P50). In Mamburao, they leave from the Stop Over Restaurant.

Jeepneys between Wawa (Abra de Ilog) and Mamburao run all day, usually in synch with boats to/from Wawa pier (see Getting There & Away for Wawa, earlier). On the potholed old road, the 32km trip takes at least one hour (P40).

SABLAYAN

A welcome sight after the long road journey from the north or south, Sablayan (pronounced 'sab-**lay**-an') sits astride the Bagong Sabang River. It has a lively market, and boats of all shapes and sizes strung out along its river-mouth port. For most travellers, its beauty lies in its proximity to North Pandan Island.

Places to Stay & Eat

Next to the market, the river, and boats to North Pandan Island, the *Emily Hotel* is a well-run, single-storey place with small, basic singles/doubles with fan and bath for P80/160. The restaurant does budget meals for P40.

Over the river (P2 by boat), *Albert's Place* has slightly fancier rooms from P250 to P500. There's also a restaurant.

Getting There & Away

Boats to North Pandan Island wait for customers in front of the market. The standard one-way fare is P100 per boat (P20 minutes).

Ferries from Sablayan to Batangas dock at the Sablayan Pier, south of the town centre (P5 by tricycle). See the Getting There & Away section for Mindoro, at the beginning of the chapter.

Buses and large jeepneys go via Sablayan on their way north to Mamburao (P50, three hours) or south to San José (P40 to P50, 3 to 3½ hours). Most can simply be flagged on National Rd running along the town's eastern edge, but you can also catch regular JRS buses from the company office in town.

NORTH PANDAN ISLAND

This slice of paradise is as close to tropical perfection as you can get without buying your own island. It has a curvaceous, white sand beach to the south and untamed forest stretching across to its northern shore. All around the island are prime dive spots, and there are at least two enchanting, easy hiking trails across the island to the gloriously named Spaniard's Nose Point and beach cove. North Pandan Island is the ideal base from which to explore nearby Apo Island, part of the exceptional divers' sanctuary of the **Apo Reef Marine Nature Park** (not to be confused with the Apo Island Marine Reserve and Fish Sanctuary of *another* Apo Island, off the south coast of Negros).

Pandan Island Resort includes **Whitetip Divers** (fax 526 6065, ✆ amo@info.com .ph), which charges US$25 for 'fun dives' with all equipment provided. Six days of diving, with equipment, is US$230. It has a Web site at www.schifauer.com/pandan.

Apart from dives around the island, the dive shop offers package **boat trips** to: Mahai on Apo Island (US$85 for two, with picnic, one day); Amas on Apo Island (US$93 for two, with breakfast and lunch, one day); Busuanga (US$554 for two, two nights/three days); and Boracay via Ambulong Island.

The resort's minimal lighting makes the beach an ideal place for **star-gazing**. Other pursuits include **snorkelling** (snorkel gear P100 per day), **waterskiing**, **wakeboarding** and **monoskiing** (P1100 per hour, including instructor), and **ocean kayaking** (US$10 per day).

Places to Stay & Eat

An idyllic combination of simple living and pure, tropical decadence, the *Pandan Island Resort* is the sole occupant of the island. This laid-back, smoothly run place has budget singles/doubles with common bath for US$10/12, standard bungalows for US$18, and deluxe cottages for one to four persons at US$30 to US$36. All have balconies and sliding, bamboo doors. Security is low here – there are no locks or room keys. The nightly buffet dinner is a feast that would outdo any five-star restaurant. Breakfast is a flat US$3, and main meals are US$6.

Getting There & Away

Strange, deafeningly loud, box-like launches will ferry you back and forth between Sablayan and North Pandan Island for P100 per boat (20 minutes). Standard pumpboats will do the same. Both types can be hired from in front of the market in Sablayan. The resort can sort out a boat for you for the trip back to Sablayan.

South-West Mindoro

South-west Mindoro takes in a lively bunch of towns and some excellent diving. More adventurous travellers will enjoy the challenging lack of roads, while the less adventurous will enjoy the luxurious hotels.

SAN JOSÉ

On Mindoro's south-west coast, San José (pronounced 'san ho-**say**') is notable for taking its videoke sessions very seriously. It's possible to boat out to the good dive spots off both Ambulong and Apo Islands from here, but if you need to rent equipment, you'd be better off doing the trip from North Pandan Island, halfway up the west coast (see North Pandan Island, earlier). It's also possible to reach the **Mt Iglit-Baco National Park** from San José, but recent reports suggest that deforestation has taken its toll on all but the upper-most reaches of this, the last refuge of the *tamaraw* (native buffalo). You can get there by jeepney from San José, heading north and

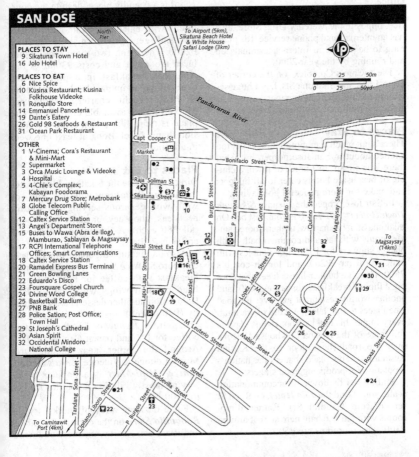

SAN JOSÉ

PLACES TO STAY
9 Sikatuna Town Hotel
16 Jolo Hotel

PLACES TO EAT
6 Nice Spice
10 Kusina Restaurant; Kusina Folkhouse Videoke
11 Ronquillo Store
14 Emmanuel Panceteria
19 Dante's Eatery
26 Gold 98 Seafoods & Restaurant
31 Ocean Park Restaurant

OTHER
1 V-Cinema; Cora's Restaurant & Mini-Mart
2 Supermarket
3 Orca Music Lounge & Videoke
4 Hospital
5 4-Chie's Complex; Kabayan Foodorama
7 Mercury Drug Store; Metrobank
8 Globe Telecom Public Calling Office
12 Caltex Service Station
13 Angel's Department Store
15 Buses to Wawa (Abra de Ilog), Mamburao, Sablayan & Magsaysay
17 RCPI International Telephone Offices; Smart Communications
18 Caltex Service Station
20 Ramadel Express Bus Terminal
21 Green Bowling Lanes
22 Eduardo's Disco
23 Foursquare Gospel Church
24 Divine Word College
25 Basketball Stadium
27 PNB Bank
28 Police Sation; Post Office; Town Hall
29 St Joseph's Cathedral
30 Asian Spirit
32 Occidental Mindoro National College

inland. Coming from Sablayan, there's a signposted road to the sanctuary 6km north of Calintaan.

In December, San José locals donate food and clothes to the Mangyan tribespeople, who head into town at this time.

Information

Don't expect to find ATMs here, but the Metrobank and the PNB bank will both change travellers cheques.

On the corner of C Liboro and Rizal Sts you'll find an RCPI International Telephone Office, as well as a Smart Communications Office.

The Globe Telecom Public Calling Office, opposite the Mercury Drug Store, also has an international phone service. It's planning to have several Internet terminals up and running by the year 2000.

The 4-Chie's Complex, on the corner of Lapu-Lapu and Sikatuna Sts, has a huge selection of Philippine newspapers, as well as some international news magazines.

Places to Stay

There's not much accommodation to get too excited about in San José proper, but what there is is cheap. Just north of town, a couple of beachside hotels cater to all budgets and make for more peaceful holidaying.

In San José proper, the friendly *Sikatuna Town Hotel* (☎ 491 1274) is your best bet. On Sikatuna St, it has narrow, timber-floored single rooms with fan and common bath (with bucket shower) for P120. For doubles with bath you'll pay P260, and for air-con it's P500. There's a bunker-like canteen that does big Filipino breakfasts for around P40, and another worthy restaurant just over the road (see Places to Eat, later). A word of warning: every night, this hotel's front rooms cop the full force of the Kusina Folkhouse Videoke over the road (next door to the Kusina Restaurant). This place shatters the nation's reputation for producing good singers.

Sliding swiftly down the accommodation scale, you'll find the *Jolo Hotel*, on Rizal St (enter from Gaudiel St). Rather dingy rooms with fan and bath here start at around P300. Air-con rooms are P500.

A P5 tricycle ride north of town will bring you to two beachside hotels well out of earshot of San José's videoke bars. The hotels are next door to each other, both facing the brown-sand beach.

The *Sikatuna Beach Hotel* (☎ 491 2182) is the budget option. In an annexe building, it has drab but fairly roomy singles with bath and fan for P240. Doubles and twins cost P260. Deluxe rooms cost P660. In the main building, the restaurant does barbecued chicken with rice, salad and soft drink for P55.

The *White House Safari Lodge* (☎ 491 1656) is a friendly place, despite the doorbell security entrance. Luxurious standard rooms with balcony, private bath, fridge, TV and generous furnishing start at P2000. The giant, two-room family suite faces the water and costs P3000. A big, American breakfast in a dining room overlooking an immaculately kept garden is P168. Yacht charter, fishing and snorkelling are available on request. This place is more like a rich relative's mansion than a hotel. Book at least one week in advance.

Places to Eat

Directly opposite the Sikatuna Town Hotel, the *Kusina Restaurant* will look after you well, with generous servings of sizzling beefsteak, chopsuey, or garlic mushrooms (all P80 each). A Filipino breakfast with coffee is P35.

Also on Sikatuna St, on the other side of C Liboro St, *Nice Spice* does a big Filipino breakfast with coffee for P45, and spicy fried chicken wings with rice for P55. Halo-halo and other desserts are a speciality (P40 to P60). Just down the street, the cheap little *Kabayan Foodorama* does coffee for P5, and pancit Canton for P25. Around the corner, near the big Orca Music Lounge & Videoke, *Cora's Restaurant & Mini-Mart* is a popular place, serving mostly Filipino favourites for P60 to P100.

For a dazzling array of snacks, try the *Ronquillo Store* on the corner of C Liboro and Rizal Sts. Nearby, the more traditional

Dante's Eatery serves fresh Filipino dishes straight out of the pot (P20 to P40). Around the corner, the *Emmanuel Panceteria* is a friendly, sit-down eatery.

In the eastern part of town, on Rizal St, the popular *Ocean Park Restaurant* is a fairly big place serving good Filipino dishes (P40 to P80). Despite the name, it's not so big on seafood. Not far away, on MH del Pilar St, the *Gold 98 Seafoods & Restaurant* does good Filipino-style seafood for around P80 to P100 per dish.

Entertainment
The *Orca Music Lounge & Videoke*, three-storeys high, lit with fairylights, and on the main drag of C Liboro St, is hard to miss. It has a happy hour from 2 to 5 pm daily, when beers cost P14.

Just down the street, you can catch a movie at the *V-Cinema*, or go tenpin bowling at the *Green Bowling Lanes* at the other end of the street. Nearby is the exceptionally seedy *Eduardo's Disco*.

Getting There & Away
Air San José's airport is about 5km northwest of town (P10 by tricycle).

PAL and Asian Spirit have daily flights between San José and Manila. There's an Asian Spirit office (☎ 491 4151) in the Santos Building near St Joseph's Cathedral, or you can contact the San José airport (☎ 491 4154).

Boat Boats to/from San José dock at Caminawit Port, 4km south of town (P10 by tricycle). Pumpboats use the area just to the south of the pier. Crowded with small boats and stores, this spot is a cross between a port, a beach, and a garbage dump.

Pumpboats to Bulalacao leave at 11 am daily (P100, three hours). While travelling this route, we saw a couple of sea turtles swimming along right beside the boat, about 5km south of Bulalacao. For other pumpboat destinations available from here see the Getting There & Away entry for Mindoro, at the beginning of the chapter.

Bus & Jeepney Several buses make the trip between Mamburao and San José (P90, 6 to 7 hours) up until about midday daily, but it's a bum-numbingly long stretch. This journey is best broken by a refreshing stop in Sablayan (see the Sablayan and North Pandan Island entries, earlier). Buses between Sablayan and San José leave regularly up until about midday (P33 to P40, three hours).

Jeepneys also battle the long, flat rubbly road linking Sablayan and San José. For some reason, they cost more than the buses, but take longer (P50, 3½ hours).

The Visayas

The Philippines' main island-group is the Visayas. Situated between Luzon (and Mindoro) to the north, Palawan to the west and Mindanao to the south, the main islands and major sub-groups of the Visayas are Cebu, the Camotes Islands, Bohol, Negros, Siquijor, Panay, Boracay, the Romblon Group, Masbate, Samar, Leyte and Biliran. Scattered among these are numerous small islands – so many, in fact, that it looks like you can literally 'island hop' around the region without getting your feet wet.

Getting around requires a bit more preparation than that, but a virtual navy of regular fastcraft and reliable *bancas* (pumpboats) makes it manageable, especially if you're not in a hurry. If time is short, there are numerous flights (and an ever-changing number of airlines doing them) between many of the islands. For island-hopping ideas, see Suggested Itineraries in the Facts for the Visitor chapter.

Cebu

Cebu City is a major gateway to the Visayas (and an attractive alternative to entering the country at Manila's manic airport), but there's more to Cebu than its main airport.

With a long, bare backbone of a central mountain range, Cebu's north and south coasts are where most travellers head for beach beauty. To the north, the offshore island of Bantayan is an increasingly popular backpackers' haunt, while to the south, Moalboal is *the* place for diving and budget hedonism. Divers and birdwatchers rave about Olango, a reef-ringed outcrop not far from Mactan.

Cebu's main cities are Cebu City, Toledo, Danao, Mandaue and Lapu-Lapu (on Mactan). All five are strapped around the island's waist in a broad belt – so avoiding them, if that's your aim, is fairly straightforward.

HIGHLIGHTS

- Deciding for yourself whether Bohol's spooky Chocolate Hills are under- or over-rated
- Being spell-bound by Siquijor's beachy beauty and its unique traditions of herbal medicine and religious festivals
- Slurping on one of Guimaras' fantastic mangoes after a vigorous mountain-bike ride
- Luxuriating or bumming around on Boracay's gorgeous beaches
- Remote Guiuan's natural beauty and interesting human history
- Tacloban's dusty and decaying Santo Niño Shrine and Heritage Center, with it's eclectic collection of arts and crafts

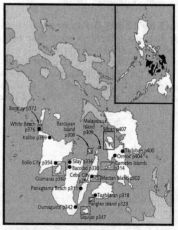

Getting There & Away

You can wing or sail your way to Cebu – whatever takes your fancy – from destinations Philippine and abroad. You'll find transport information in the individual destination entries in this section. When planning your route from A to B, however, it's very important to remember that schedules and fares change like the breeze. It's well worth checking to make sure you've got the latest-model information.

CEBU CITY

Like some ageing screen siren, Cebu City somehow manages to seem young and innocent after all these years – just don't look too closely. To think, this place is older than Manila, has the nation's busiest port and a population nearing one million. But then again, what city wouldn't look good compared to Manila?

The story goes that the beaches of what is now Cebu City were once so broad and shallow that visitors by boat had to wade ashore. This gave the area its original name – Sugbo, which is Visayan for 'walk on water'.

Chinese, Cambodians and Arabs are thought to have been wading ashore at Sugbo as early as the 15th century, to trade gold, cotton, opium and slaves. So when European explorer Ferdinand Magellan turned up here in 1521, he was a late arrival.

Orientation

As far as most visitors are concerned, Cebu City is Manila minus the mayhem. Its traffic is chaotic, but not insane. Its size and layout can actually be understood, rather than merely endured. And – sigh – hardly any of the taxi drivers here are employed by Satan.

The city's centre has shifted inland in recent years, and locals now refer to the newer precinct around Fuente Osmeña as 'uptown' and the older district around Colon St as 'downtown'. The boundary is blurry – for our purposes, we've divided uptown from downtown at Del Rosario St. Beyond the uptown area is Lahug, which includes the upmarket Beverly Hills.

Cebu City has a long history of changing its street names, with many of the old names living on, either in the minds of taxi drivers or on street signs yet to be removed. If you find yourself squinting up at a street sign with black lettering on a yellow background, it's an old sign – and the name *may*

have since changed. Up-to-date signs are those with white, or reflective, lettering on a bright green background. The most commonly confusing streets are: Manalili St (formerly V Gullas St); Maria Cristina St (formerly N Rafols St); Don F Sotto St (formerly Jasmin St); Salinas Dr (formerly Cebu Airport Rd); and Osmeña Blvd (formerly Second Ave 13th *and* MacArthur Blvd). There are also many streets, avenues, drives and boulevards using the same name, such as Osmeña, or Ramos – often all that differentiates them is a first name or initial (eg, J Osmeña St, S Osmeña St and so on).

Maps Decent enough tourist maps can be picked up free from the airport, the Department of Tourism (DOT) office (see Tourist Offices later), and most hotels. For the full, huge picture, pick up the pink-and-blue Geoplan Cebu Foundation map (P150) sold at the National Bookstore in the SM City shopping mall. It has a scale of 1:20,000 and takes in the city surrounds, including Mactan. Be warned that this map requires a PhD in origami and cartography to fold it up – don't open it in strong winds unless you're suitably qualified.

For nautical and topographical maps and charts, set a course for the National Mapping and Resource Authority (Namria) office (☎ 032-412 1749), in the downtown area. It's on the 3rd floor (Room 301) of the Osmeña Building, on the corner of Osmeña Blvd and Jakosalem St. In the uptown area, Morbai Maps & Charts (☎ 032-232 2965) may also have what you're looking for. It's at 36 Gorordo Ave.

Information

Tourist Offices The tourist office (☎ 032-254 2811) is on the ground floor of the LDM Building on Lapu-Lapu St, next to Amway.

The Cebu City branch of Swagman Travel (☎ 032-254 1365, 412 5709, fax 254 1382) is at 301 F Ramos St. Fly the Bus coaches stop here on their way to and from Moalboal (the Moalboal & Panagsama Beach section is under South of Cebu City, later). This is the place to book tickets for

Fly the Bus, organise tours and pick up the latest travel information.

Immigration Offices The immigration office is on the 4th floor of the Philippines Commercial & Industrial Bank (PCI) Building, on the corner of MC Briones and P Burgos Sts, behind City Hall. As we went to press, there had been a merger between PCI and Equitable Bank, so the building name may have changed. You can extend a 21-day visa to 59 days here, but you'll have to produce your passport and an onward ticket. In the great tradition of bureaucracy, you'll also be asked to photocopy your passport, your visa, your ticket and – afterwards – your receipt (there's a photocopier in the hallway, but it's not always working). This all adds up to a 'visa waiver', and it costs P150. Passports dropped off here in the morning can be retrieved in the afternoon. For longer visa extensions, your passport will be sent to Manila to languish for around two weeks – less if you pay the express fee. See Visas & Documents in the Facts for the Visitor chapter for more details.

By the way, rumours about this office's tough dress-code are true – you may well be refused a visa extension if you turn up in your sweat-soaked tourist garb. If you have no choice, a smile and a joke might just save you.

Money Bank hours are from 9 am to 3 pm weekdays. The Equitable Bank issued cash advances on Visa and JCB credit cards, and the PCI Bank generally handled other major credit cards, and Cirrus. The merger may have resulted in both banks handling all the cards. Many banks have credit card-friendly ATMs, but the most dependable is the one at HSBC, near Maxilom Ave. There's a 24-hour security guard on duty beside the machine, and cards accepted include Visa, MasterCard, Cirrus and Global Access.

Post The city's main post office is in the downtown area, near Fort San Pedro, with another branch nearby at City Hall. Hole-in-the-wall sub-branches can be found at many of the universities around town. Of

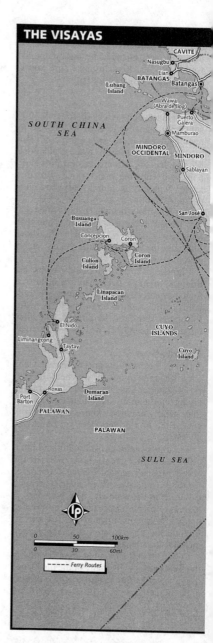

THE VISAYAS

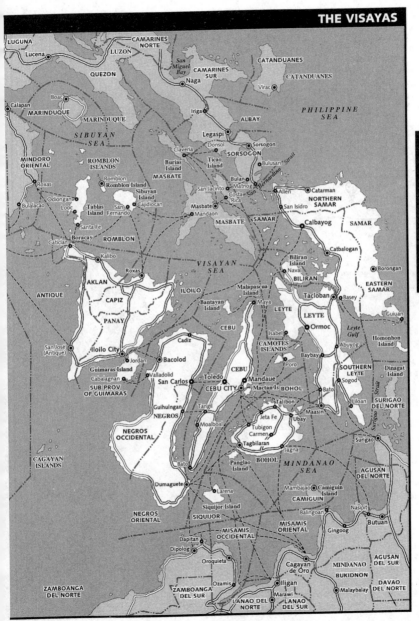

THE VISAYAS

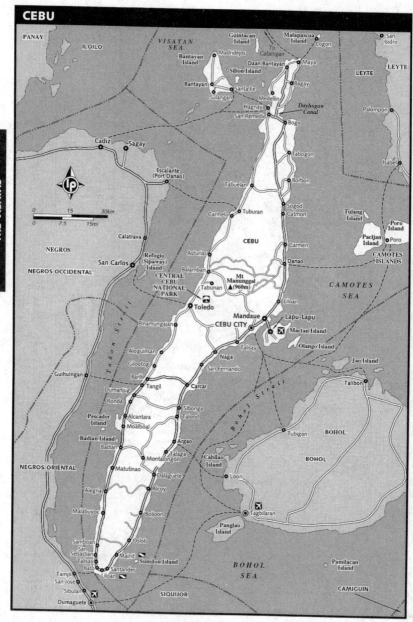

course, if you just want to send a postcard or two, your hotel should handle it for you.

Email and Internet Access Dotted around town, but concentrated around the universities and colleges, the city's cyber-cafes are cheap, and full of students – but there's usually a terminal or two vacant. Cebu City is one of the cheapest Internet cities in South-East Asia. In theory, the more you pay, the faster the computers and the better the air-con. The majority of 'cafes' don't serve food or drinks. Business hours vary, but all are open seven days a week. The rates in this section are per hour.

In the downtown area, there's the relatively long-established Ruftan Internet Cafe & Pensione (P25) on Legaspi St. It can get a little sticky here, as there's no air-con.

Sky Net Computer Internet Services (P25) is a little place on Sanciangko St. Its hours are usually from 9 am to around 9 pm. Microbagz (P30) is on Colon St, upstairs, among a bunch of doctors' offices (Room 3, Binamira Building). It has about eight terminals and is open from 9 am to 11 pm.

By the time you read this, Cyberscape, on Pelaez St, should have opened its doors. Watch this cyberspace?

The little @netdepot cafe (P30), way over on Sikatuna St, is open from 11 am to 10 pm. Bizdepot (P30), on Del Rosario St, stays open till around midnight and is fiercely air-conditioned.

Elicon House, the budget hotel on Junquera St (see Downtown under Places to Stay later), is surrounded by Internet cafes. Directly opposite the hotel, the futuristic-looking Internet Café (P30) has just opened. Its opening hours weren't set at the time of writing. On the same side as Elicon House, you can't miss Cybernet Café (P30) and Digital Shack (P20). Cybernet is the bigger of the two, with about 30 terminals. It serves snacks and drinks and is open 24 hours. Digital Shack is open from 9 to 3 am.

In the uptown area, the 24-hour @4th-Media.net (P25) is on the Fuente Osmeña central circle. Heading up J Osmeña Blvd, which runs off Maxilom Ave, you'll find Internet, Etc (P35), open from 9 am to 9 pm.

Next to Jollibee on Maxilom Ave, the aptly named Microhouse (P25) has only four terminals. It's open from 9.30 am to midnight. Behind the same Jollibee, through the shopping mall on F Ramos St, is the much larger Moscom (P40), open from 9 to 2 am. Chatzone (P20), on Maxilom Ave, is open from 9 to 6 am.

Internet Cebu (P35) is a stylish 24-hour joint on Queen's Rd, diagonally opposite the Lone Star Saloon Bar and KFC, behind Maxilom Ave.

Bookshops There's a large National Bookstore uptown on Maxilom Ave, as well as at the SM City shopping mall over on Juan Luna Ave. Both stores have huge stocks of local and international fiction and nonfiction, magazines, stationery and maps.

There's a secondhand bookshop, Bargain Books – Old San Francisco Bookstore, on Del Rosario St, downtown. On sale here is an eclectic range of pre-loved books (P20 to P80). The shop is air-conditioned, and is open from 9 am to 5 or 6 pm.

Medical Services Cebu's three main medical centres are in the uptown area. Cebu Doctors Hospital (☎ 032-253 7511) is on President Osmeña Blvd, near the Capitol Building. Farther south on the same street is the Metro Cebu Community Hospital (☎ 032-253 1901). The Cebu (Velez) General Hospital (☎ 032-253 1871) is nearby, on F Ramos St.

Emergency For emergency tourist assistance, call the 24-hour Task Force Turista (☎ 032-254 4023) or Cebu City Police Station (☎ 032-253 5636).

Basilica Minore del Santo Niño

This magnificent church and convent is one hell of a survivor. Built in 1565 and burnt down three times, it was rebuilt in its present form in 1737. Almost makes you afraid to go near it, lest it burst into flame while you're busy admiring the heavenly ceiling murals and ornate altar. A souvenir shop inside the church sells tiny bottles of holy

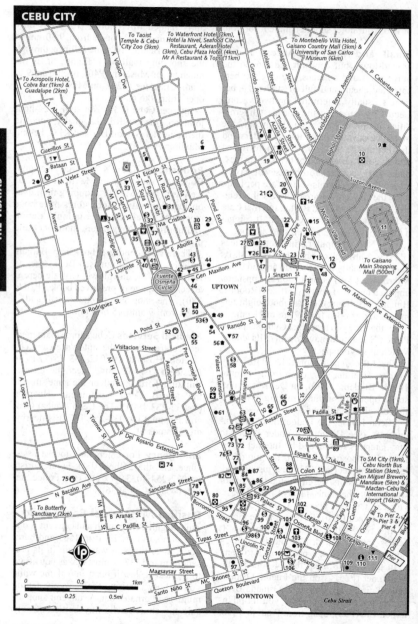

THE VISAYAS

CEBU CITY

To Taoist
Temple & Cebu
City Zoo (3km)

To Waterfront Hotel (2km),
Hotel la Nivel, Seafood City
Restaurant, Aderan Hotel
(3km), Cebu Plaza Hotel (4km),
Mr A Restaurant & Tops (11km)

To Montebello Villa Hotel,
Gaisano Country Mall (3km) &
University of San Carlos
Museum (6km)

To Acropolis Hotel,
Cobra Bar (1km) &
Guadalupe (2km)

To Gaisano
Main Shopping
Mall (500m)

UPTOWN

Fuente
Osmeña
Circle

To Butterfly
Sanctuary (2km)

To SM City (1km),
Cebu North Bus
Station (3km),
San Miguel Brewery
(5km) &
Mactan-Cebu
International
Airport (16km)

To Pier 2,
Pier 3 &
Pier 4

Pier 1

DOWNTOWN

Cebu Strait

0   0.5   1km

0   0.25   0.5mi

CEBU CITY

PLACES TO STAY
5 Mayflower Pension House
6 Cebu Pensione Plaza; Caltex
  Service Station
8 Kukuk's Nest Pension House
  & Restaurant; Philippines
  National Bank (PNB)
9 Marriott Hotel
18 Pensionne La Florentina
19 West Gorordo Hotel;
  Family Choice Restaurant
22 Richmond Plaza Hotel;
  Soccer Pitch
25 Eddie's Hotel & Beverly
  Room Bar & Restaurant
31 Cebu Mintel
35 Jasmine Pension House;
  Verbena Pension House
42 Park Place Hotel
49 Residencia Ramos; Swagman
  Travel; Velez General Hospital
56 Diplomat Hotel & Diplomat
  Garden Restaurant; European
  Delicatessen & Butcher Shop
  Restaurant
60 Teo-Fel Pension House &
  Café Felicidad
64 Elicon House & Elicon Café;
  Digital Shack; Cybernet Café
68 Harbor View Hotel
83 Cebu View Tourist Inn
86 Century Hotel; New Cinema
  Theater
87 Hotel de Mercedes; Javy's
  Café; McSherry Pension House
90 Hotel de Victoria de Cebu;
  Visayan Restaurant
91 Ruftan Internet Café &
  Pensione

PLACES TO EAT
1 Bistro Buanevista Bar &
  Restaurant
13 Jollibee
17 Royal Concourse
26 Swiss Chalet Restaurant
33 Persian Palate; Wheels Bike
  Shop
37 KFC
40 Italia Ice-Cream Parlour
45 McDonald's; Bank of the
  Philippine Islands (BPI);
  Caltex Service Station
46 Jollibee; Moscom; Microhouse

47 Shakey's Pizza
48 Lighthouse Restaurant
51 McDonald's
57 Café Adriatico
72 Fruit Stalls
73 Jollibee; Santa Rosario Church
77 Our Place
78 Fruit Stalls; Sky Net
  Computer Services
79 Bakeshops
81 Snow Sheen Restaurant
84 Pete's Kitchen; Cyberscape;
  RCPI Telephone Office;
  Equitable PCI Bank
85 Golden Crust Bakery;
  Cinerama Cinema
95 Fruit Stalls
111 Food Stalls

OTHER
2 Guadalupe Market
3 Caltex Service Station
4 Capitol Building
7 Aboitiz Express &
  SuperCat/SeaAngels Shipping
10 Ayala Center Shopping Mall;
  Cebu Business Park
11 Hippodromo (Cemetery)
12 Petron Service Station
14 Morbai Maps & Charts Office
15 Tinder Box Cigar Shop
16 Chapel of Our Lady of the
  Miraculous Medal; Metrobank
20 Caltex Service Station
21 Perpetual Soccour Hospital
23 Chatzone
24 Iglesia Church
27 Internet Cebu
28 Lone Star Saloon Bar; KFC
29 Habagat Outdoor Store
30 Internet, Etc
32 Equitable PCI Bank;
  Cebu Doctors Hospital
34 Philippine Chinese Spiritual
  Temple
36 Harley's Entertainment Pub
38 Philippines National Bank (BPI)
39 Rizal Memorial Library;
  Red Cross
41 @4th-Media.net
43 HSBC & ATM
44 National Bookstore
50 Thunderdome Bar; Volvo Bar
52 Shell Service Station

53 Equitable PCI Bank
54 24-Hour Convenience Store
55 Metro Cebu Community
  Hospital
58 Metrobank
59 Police Station
61 Cebu State College
62 Bizdepot
63 Internet Café
65 Bargain Books - Old San
  Francisco Bookstore
66 Caltex Service Station
67 Caltex Service Station
69 Police Station
70 @netdepot
71 Post Office; San Carlos
  University
74 Cebu South Bus Terminal
75 Caltex Service Station
76 Bank of the Philippine
  Islands (BPI)
80 Gaisano South Shopping Mall
82 Post Office; University
  of Cebu
88 Post Office; University of
  The Visayas
89 Casa Gorordo Museum
92 Negros Navigation;
  Colonnade Mall; Supermarket; Jollibee; Oriente Cinema
93 Microbagz; KFC
94 Gaisano Metro Shopping Mall
96 Equitable PCI Bank
97 Carbon Market
98 Equitable PCI Bank
99 Equitable PCI Bank
100 PAL
101 Namria Map Office
102 Cebu Cathedral; Religious
  Souvenir Stalls; Petron
  Service Station
103 Basilica Minore del Santo
  Niño; Religious Souvenir Stalls
104 Equitable PCI Bank
105 Post Office; Cebu City Hall
106 Equitable PCI Bank;
  Immigration Office
107 Magellan's Cross
108 Tourism Office
109 Cebu Port Authority;
  Food Stalls
110 Department of Tourism; Fort
  San Pedro; Public Toilets

THE VISAYAS

water (P20), but you might want to buy a larger bottle just in case. Holy souvenirs are also available at stalls outside the main gate, on President Osmeña Blvd.

Butterfly Sanctuary
The Butterfly Sanctuary (☎ 032-261 6884) is west of the downtown area, where you wouldn't expect butterflies to hang around.

But hang around they do, from branches and leaves all over Rene Jomalon's garden. Rene regularly opens his home to school groups, but tourists are just as welcome. There's no charge, although a small donation would be appreciated. The best time of day for viewing is the morning, and the best time of year is from June to February. On view also are artworks made from butterfly wings (Rene assured us the owners of the wings died of natural causes) – even a presidential portrait! Ring first to make a booking.

To get there, catch a jeepney (P2.50) from N Bacalso Ave, which turns into Cebu South Rd and hop off at Macopa St (after the second pedestrian overpass). Walk up Macopa St, and take the first left after Basak Elementary School. The sanctuary is on the corner at the end of this street. A taxi will get you there for around P40.

Casa Gorordo Museum

Downtown, at 35 L Jaena St, not far from Pier 3, the Casa Gorordo Museum (☎ 032-255 5630) is one of the hidden gems of Cebu City. Originally a private home, it was built in the 1860s by the Gorordos, a merchant family. The lower part of the house has walls of Mactan coral stone, cemented using tree sap. The stunning upper-storey living quarters are pure Philippine hardwood (known as *tugus*), held together not with nails but with wooden pegs. Items on display include gorgeous wooden kitchenware, antique photos and a collection of *berso* (hand cannons) used for launching fireworks. The museum is open from 9 am to noon and from 2 to 5 pm daily. Admission is P15. To arrange special group-tours, contact Ferelyn Canoy during business hours at the museum.

Cebu City Zoo

When the German-based Quantum Conservation group cast an expert eye over the Cebu City Zoo in 1997, its diagnosis was grim:

We found the worst situation we had ever encountered at any zoo anywhere regarding animal housing, feeding, animal care and management. The one positive factor, apart from the location of the zoo, was the friendliness of the people working at the zoo.

In 1997–98, Quantum Conservation, Cincinatti Zoo and Melbourne Zoo donated funds and lent their expertise, but the helping hands withdrew in mid-1998, frustrated by the lack of government support for the zoo and its overachieving, understaffed managing body, the Philippines Wetlands and Wildlife Conservation Foundation (PWCF).

The zoo currently has reptiles, birds and monkeys, and its hoped that a special aviary can one day house the endangered endemic Cebuano bird, the black schama (locally known as the *siloy*).

The zoo is in the upmarket Beverly Hills area, a few blocks from the Taoist Temple (see later in this section). Its grounds total about seven hectares of prime, man-made forest. To get there, take a jeepney from the city centre to Calunasan, which drops you right at the zoo (P3, five minutes). A taxi from the city centre should cost P30 to P40.

Entrance is P5/3 for adults/children. The zoo is open from 6am to 6pm daily.

It's estimated that the zoo needs at least US$750 per month to feed its animals, but with gate receipts falling woefully short of this target, malnutrition, sickness and death remain a tragic reality. Donations are best directed to the PWCF's Perla Magsalay at the zoo (☎ 032-419 8240), and you should stipulate how you want your money used. For more information, contact Quantum Conservation, Effektive Artenschutz – effective species conservation (☎ 05441-82133, fax 82132, ✆ quantum@t-online.de, Heeder Dorfstrasse 44, 49356 Diepholz, Germany), or visit its Web site at www.quantum-conservation.org. Alternatively, visit the Fauna & Flora International Web site at www.ffi.org.uk.

Fort San Pedro

Built in 1565 to keep a lookout for pirates, Fort San Pedro has since served as an army garrison, a rebel stronghold, a prison camp and the city zoo. These days, it's in retirement as a peaceful, walled garden and handsomely crumbling ruin. Officially, entry is P10. It's closed Monday.

Magellan's Cross

Magellan's cross? Wouldn't you be if you'd sailed all the way from Europe only to die in a soggy heap on the island of Mactan? Ferdinand's Catholic legacy, a large wooden cross, is housed in a stone rotunda (built in 1841) across from Cebu City Hall. The crucifix on show here apparently contains a few splinters from a cross Magellan planted on the shores of Cebu in 1521. A painting on the ceiling of the rotunda shows Magellan erecting the cross (actually, the locals are doing all the work – Magellan's just standing around with his mates).

Motorcycle Races

If you happen to be at Cebu North bus station on a Saturday night at around 11.30 pm, watch how you cross the street. Every week at this time, the city's motorcycle riders rev up their machines and race them around five designated blocks in Mandaue, in the North Reclamation Area. It's not exactly legal, but police have been known to be among the enthusiastic spectators, sometimes even acting as race officials. One local newspaper has reported that individual bets of up to P25,000 are laid on some of these races.

Philippine Chinese Spiritual Temple

A colourful, multitiered maze of dragons, pergolas and carefully crafted gardens, this haven from the hustle and bustle is within surprisingly easy walking distance of uptown's busy Capitol Building area. Regular prayer meetings are held here. To find it, head west along J Avila St and look for the distinctive roof at the end of the street.

Taoist Temple

Overlooking the city, in the ritzy Beverly Hills residential area, the magnificent Taoist Temple shares its serene aspect with the Cebu City Zoo (see earlier in this section). It's also a symbol of the city's large and influential ethnic Chinese population. To get to the temple take a Lahug or Calunasan jeepney and ask to stop at the Taoist Temple or Beverly Hills – you've then got a short walk uphill. Alternatively, take a taxi for about P30 to P40.

Tops Lookout Area

Nearby Mt Busay makes a mighty backdrop for Cebu City, but the best view is from the mountain itself, where you'll find the Tops Lookout Area. Better known simply as 'Tops', this modernist fortress-like viewing deck provides spectacular views, especially at sunrise or sunset. Entry is P25. There are food stalls up here, but you can also wander over to the stylish Mr A (see Lahug under Places to Eat later).

Many Lahug jeepneys get within about 500m of the lookout (you may have to change at La Nivel Hotel or Cebu Plaza Hotel and ask for another jeepney to Tops), and a taxi will go all the way from downtown for around P80.

University of San Carlos Museum

Perched on the 5th floor of the university, this captivating collection of specimens would be the envy of any museum. A mixture of marine biology, entomology and natural history, the collection features thousands of carefully bottled beasties, some positively alien bat species, and a morbidly fascinating six-legged *carabao* (native buffalo). There's also a fine collection of pottery from the archaeology department nearby. There's no admission fee; just climb the stairs and start browsing. Opening hours are from 8 am to noon and from 12.45 to 4.45 pm weekdays, and from 8 am to noon Saturday. The university is on Archbishop Reyes Ave, east of the uptown area (P2.50 by University jeepney, P40 to P50 by taxi).

San Miguel Brewery

Free tours of the San Miguel Brewery (☎ 032-345 7246) happen at 9 am every Monday, Tuesday and Wednesday. Although aimed at school students, anyone else is welcome to tag along and no bookings are needed. Tours cover the entire brewing process and take about 2½ hours – yes, you have to wait that long for the free beer-tasting. The plant is in the city of Mandaue, which is fast becoming an outer suburb of Cebu City. It's roughly halfway between downtown Cebu City and the airport, so if your timing's right you could drop in for a beer on your way through. A taxi from downtown to the plant should cost from P40 to P50.

Waterfront Hotel & Casino Filipino

Yes, it's a hotel, and it's not even an *old* hotel, but this one is special. The enormous foyer of the Waterfront Hotel is dominated by a spell-binding ceiling mural – a 50m-by-30m recreation of explorer Ferdinand Magellan's world map, so high and so detailed that you'd need Ferdinand's telescope to read it properly. So pull up a big comfy chair, order a drink from the roving bar staff, and gaze in air-con comfort. Each corner of the mural depicts a Filipino forefather: local hero Chief Lapu-Lapu, 1940s president Manuel Roxas, revolutionary martyr José Rizal, and visionary painter Juan Luna.

The hotel's Casino Filipino is worth a look while you're here, if only for the mechanical horse-racing betting machine and the fake night-sky of the main gaming room. There's no real dress code, but you can expect to be frisked by security guards. You should rug up, too – the place is kept at arctic temperatures to keep the punters fresh and lively.

Activities

Interesting, energetic tours in and around Cebu City are organised by Swagman Travel (☎ 032-254 1365, 412 5709), at 301 F Ramos St. These include a four- to five-hour trek through the mango plantations of Guadalupe, north-west of town (P2000, maximum of five people), and a kayak tour of Olango Island (the Olango Island entry is under Around Cebu City, later) for US$25 per person (minimum of three).

Places to Stay

You certainly won't suffer from a lack of accommodation choices in Cebu City.

Downtown *Ruftan Internet Cafe & Pensione* (☎ 032-79138) is a glimpse of the future of low-end accommodation in South-East Asia: shabby, no-frills rooms without air-con or bath (P165), but with email on tap in the foyer (P25 per hour). Better, quieter rooms facing away from noisy Legaspi St range from P220 to P440.

For the price, *McSherry Pension House* (☎ 032-52749) is all right despite a tiny, dingy reception area and laneway entrance. Large rooms with fan and bath are P250/300 a single/double, and P350/450 with air-con. It's a central, multistorey place, shoe-horned down a lane off Pelaez St, beside Hotel de Mercedes.

The faded *Century Hotel* (☎ 032-255 1341, fax 255 1600, @ kenneth@gsilink .com), also on Pelaez St, has cheap but windowless air-con singles/doubles with private bath and telephone for P385/485. Cable TV costs an extra P54.

Hotel de Victoria de Cebu (☎ 032-254 1331), on Manalili St, isn't as grand as its title suggests, but it has OK rooms for P420/532. It's a few doors from the cheap-eat Visayan Restaurant.

Despite the awning entrance and the brochures promising great value, the rooms at *Elicon House* (☎ 032-253 0367), on Junquera St near the corner of Del Rosario St, seem a little overpriced. Standard rooms with air-con and private bath (P400/500) are small and windowless. Attached is the Elicon Café, which serves Filipino dishes for P20 to P30. Good *halo halo* (shaved ice coloured with fruit, white beans and/or corn, and smothered in evaporated milk) is P30. There are several Internet cafes around the hotel (see Email & Internet Access under Information, earlier).

With its central location and recently refurbished rooms, *Hotel de Mercedes* (☎ 032-253 1105, fax 253 3880, 7 Pelaez St) is a little shabby around the edges but an excellent budget option. Big, bright deluxe rooms with private bath (hot water's a little reluctant), air-con, telephone and cable TV go for around P600 to P700 (often negotiable). It's opposite Pete's Kitchen.

Another of the best new budget places to stay is just around the corner from Hotel de Mercedes. The friendly *Cebu View Tourist Inn (☎ 032-254 8333, 254 9777, 200 Sanciangko St)* has tidy, welcoming rooms with private hot-water bath, air-con, phone and cable TV for P600 to P700 (discounts are possible). At the time of writing, the hotel was offering 20% off all rooms, indefinitely.

Over on MJ Cuenco Ave, not far from the dock area, is the large *Harbor View Hotel (☎ 032-233 0210, fax 233 0218)*. This is a light industrial area on the fringe of Cebu's shantytowns. Carpeted standard rooms are P650/P850 and come with air-con and private bath. Deluxe rooms (P1550) and suites (P1880) are overpriced. Don't get a room near the lift (elevator) – it chimes loudly every time it stops on your floor.

Uptown *Mayflower Pension House (☎ 032-253 7233, fax 412 4741, ✉ mayflwer@cebu.weblinq.com)*, on Villalon Dr, near Escario St's impressive Capitol Building, has smallish singles/doubles/triples for P210/275/340 with fan and common bath, or P435/540/675 with air-con, bath, phone and cable TV. There's a tricycle parking bay right outside.

Kukuk's Nest Pension House (☎ 032-412 2026, 157 Gorordo Ave) is a tired old meeting place with singles/doubles with fan and common bath for P224/392. You'll pay P616 for air-con, bath and cable TV. Despite its advanced years, the rooms are all right, but you can get tidier, cleaner rooms for the same price elsewhere. Some bathrooms are mildewy, but most have showers with very high water pressure (but no hot water). There's a small library in the main building, and a popular restaurant out the front with local artworks alongside its barbecued chickens, but traffic noise and fumes can spoil the mood a little. The Fly the Bus coach stops here on its way to and from Moalboal, and bus tickets can be booked here (see Getting There & Away under Moalboal & Panagsama Beach, later).

A fine alternative to Kukuk's is the tall, thin *Pensionne La Florentina (☎ 032-231 3318, 18 Acacia St)*, around the corner. Get a room upstairs, facing the front, and you'll have nice views, private bath, air-con and cable TV for a top-value P500/550.

Not far away, on F Sotto Dr, the big *Richmond Plaza Hotel (☎ 032-232 0361, fax 232 1974)* has tidy rooms, with a view, for P650/750. For your money you get private bath, air-con, cable TV and telephone. Not as snooty as it first appears, this place is aimed at the business crowd and has its own restaurant.

Tucked behind the Swagman Travel office at 301 F Ramos St, the older-style *Residencia Ramos (☎ 032-253 6249)* has a relaxed atmosphere and budget rooms at P449/505. These have air-con, cable TV and private cold-water bath. For hot water, try the premium rooms at P561/617.

As its brochure says, *Teo-Fel Pension House (☎ 032-253 2482, fax 253 2488)* is 'conveniently located at the hub of downtown-uptown Cebu'. On a leafy, relatively quiet stretch of Junquera St, this place offers smallish, aqua-coloured, rattan-furnished rooms with air-con and private bath for P400/600. Deluxe rooms are P700/800. The cheaper rooms lack hot water, telephone and TV – but some have a view of the street from the bathroom window. On the ground floor is the little Café Felicidad. A rooftop bar is apparently on the way. This place is a little pricey for what it offers, and discounts for long-term stays can be difficult to get.

Near the northern end of Osmeña Blvd, *Jasmine Pension House (☎ 032-54559)* has basic rooms with air-con, bath and cable TV starting at P480. Jasmine's near-neighbour on G Garcia St, *Verbena Pension House (☎ 032-253 3430)*, has big, simple rooms for P360/410. A room for four is a bargain at P530. All rooms have air-con and bath.

Hidden behind the Cebu Doctors Hospital on Osmeña Blvd, *Cebu Mintel (☎/fax 032-254 6200)*, also known as the Austrian Pension Haus, is a well-run place with tidy rooms for P600/700. All rooms have air-con, private bath and telephone. Optional extras are cable TV (P50) and fridge (P80).

To find it, head east from Osmeña Blvd on M Cristina St, and take the second left – an unlikely-looking dead-end street called F Ramos Extension. The hotel is on the right, past the car park.

Cebu Pensione Plaza (☎ 032-254 6300), on N Escario St, near the Caltex service station, has plain, clean doubles from P650 to P900. All rooms come with air-con, private bath, telephone and cable TV.

In a relatively quiet part of town, *Diplomat Hotel* (☎ 032-254 6341, fax 254 6346) is a good choice for the gourmet – the hotel complex includes the Diplomat Garden Restaurant and the European Delicatessen & Butcher Shop (see the Uptown entry in Places to Eat, later). Nicely furnished standard rooms are well priced at P700. Swankier rooms are upwards of P900. All rooms come with air-con, private bath, telephone and cable TV.

There's a distinctly squeaky-clean feel to *West Gorordo Hotel* (☎ 032-231 4347). Single men will be politely told when checking in that no 'guests' are allowed, and either gender may find the intense floral wallpaper and pastel decor a little overpowering. That said, it's a quiet place with doubles at P840. Next door is the Family Choice Restaurant, very popular with – yes – families.

Eddie's Hotel (☎ 032-254 8570, fax 254 8578), just off lively Maxilom Ave, is a new place that's been getting good reviews. Standard singles and doubles are the one high price of P1290 (deluxe single/doubles/triples cost P1380), but for that you get air-con, telephone, private bath, cable TV and a dinky little two-seater balcony. *And* it promises discounts of up to 20% if you're staying a while. Also popular, especially for steaks, is the hotel's 24-hour Beverly Room Bar & Restaurant.

Park Place Hotel (☎ 032-253 1131, 253 0118) is right on Fuente Osmeña, Cebu City's central-circle hub. It's a swish, multistorey place offering rooms with a view from P1250, and a leafy rooftop terrace.

Marriott Hotel (☎ 032-232 6100) is set amid a little parkland, near the Ayala Center shopping mall and Cebu Business Park.

As you might expect, rooms are comfortably classy. Doubles with good views start at P3000, with discounts of up to P500 possible on weekends and Monday.

A rooftop Jacuzzi may just make the five-storey *Acropolis Hotel* (☎ 032-253 1911, fax 253 2305) worth the extra effort to get to. It's on V Rama St in the northern suburb of Guadalupe, a P20 to P30 taxi ride from President Osmeña Blvd. Standard/deluxe rooms are plush but a little pricey at P1320/1680. There's a restaurant attached, and next door you'll find the swish Cobra Bar nightclub.

Lahug The cheekily named *Waterfront Hotel & Casino Filipino* (☎ 032-232 6888, fax 232 6880) is more than 2km from the water, in the hilly eastern outskirts of the city centre. At the time of writing, the hotel was offering a discount 'for an indefinite period'. This means you can get singles/doubles for a quite reasonable P1800/2300 (with breakfast). Even if you don't plan to stay here, you might like to drop in for a drink and a peek at the amazing foyer (see the Waterfront Hotel & Casino Filipino entry earlier).

By comparison, the Waterfront's main rival, *Cebu Plaza Hotel* (☎ 032-231 1211, fax 231 2071) is positively morgue-like – except for a couple of lively eateries and a nice swimming pool. And, like the Waterfront, it's offering an indefinite 'value rate' for rooms, starting at P2400 (with breakfast). A taxi from downtown should cost you about P60.

Montebello Villa Hotel (☎ 032-231 3681) has a wonderful, well-established garden, complete with birdhouses, two swimming pools and a tennis court. At P999/1380, standard/deluxe rooms aren't as special as the surrounds, but if you can have breakfast at the poolside restaurant (for around P200), who cares? The hotel is behind the big Gaisano Country Mall, a P50 taxi ride from downtown, on Archbishop Reyes Ave.

Heading for the hills of Lahug, *Aderan Hotel* (☎ 032-231 4832) is a reasonably priced mid-range place. Rooms rates start at P600 (air-con, telephone, private bath and bar fridge). There's also a great stretch of fruit stalls out the front. Its rival across the road is the more upmarket *La Nivel* (☎ 032-232 7271, 1 Salinas Dr). Comfy rooms are P960/1128. A taxi from downtown to here should be about P50.

Places to Eat

Cebu has good, but not great, restaurants. And alas, for those hoping to find a culinary gem hidden down some quiet back street, many of the city's worthwhile eateries are to be found in hotel complexes or shopping malls. The invasion of fast-food outlets has taken a heavy toll on Cebu's homegrown cuisine.

There's a generous serving of street stalls set up at regular spots around town. The biggest stall of them all is the *Carbon Market*, in the downtown area – a great place to explore. Many stalls around town sell fruit during the day and switch to freshly cooked fritters or traditional flame-grilled kebabs (P5 to P10) by night.

Still in snack mode, Cebu City is full of *bakeshops* (bakeries). These offer a reliable and intriguing source of fresh bread rolls, cakes and buns. For dessert, most restaurants will happily whip up a halo halo ice cream delight, while *Italia Ice-Cream Parlour*, just off President Osmeña Blvd on J Llorente St, uptown, offers your more standard ice cream treats.

Unless otherwise stated, opening hours for the eateries listed below are from 8 or 9 am until 10 pm and beyond, although many of the specialist seafood restaurants don't open their doors until 6 pm.

Downtown While truly great restaurants are rare in Cebu City, they're virtually nonexistent in the downtown area. Fast-food joints and uninspiring Filipino-style diners are the norm.

Golden Crust Bakery, on Colon St, sells the biggest sweet *mammon* (P12) in town. These are like obese Twinkies or sponge cupcakes. Golden Crust's other distinction is that it doubles as a karaoke bar, making it one of the only bakeries in town that stays open late.

For a light breakfast or snack, and a browse of the Web (see Email & Internet Access earlier), the scruffy old *Ruftan Internet Cafe & Pensione* on Legaspi St is ideal. It serves a spectacular tuna-and-egg special sandwich for P70.

Snow Sheen Restaurant, on Osmeña Blvd, is typical of what's on offer in the downtown area restaurant-wise. It has OK, low-priced Chinese and Filipino food for around P70. It's no better or worse than any of the more anonymous restaurants in the area.

Pete's Kitchen, on Pelaez St, opposite Hotel de Mercedes and McSherry Pension House, is actually two restaurants sharing *three* shopfronts. Brighter, breezier and busier than most, these twin eateries offer small, cheap Chinese and Filipino dishes (around P30 per dish) smorgasbord-style. The cooks wave flies away with custom-made swatters. There's very little for vegetarians here – unless you include the medical texts on sale in one of the windows. *Cancer of the Colon & Rectum* (seriously!) is a bargain at P350.

Over the road, the very plain *Javy's Café*, next to Hotel de Mercedes, does a set menu or regular dinner deal for P162. This gets you a soft drink and three courses-of-the-day. Top value, but don't bother trying to swap one of these items for something from the normal menu – they won't budge.

Visayan Restaurant, down on Manalili St near Hotel Victoria de Cebu, offers big portions of Filipino food (P60 to P70) and friendly service. Vegetarians should note: the bean-curd soup has meat in it, the fried rice has meat in it …

Our Place, upstairs on the corner of Pelaez and Sanciangko Sts, is a favourite haunt of foreign blokes. It's a cosy, colourful, old-style place with a well-stocked bar and a menu ranging from breakfast omelettes (P60) to hearty steaks (P70). The dinner menu is as antivegetarian as they come. It's open Monday to Saturday, all day till late.

Uptown Opposite the Capitol Building at the northern end of President Osmeña Blvd,

THE VISAYAS

Persian Palate dishes up large helpings of excellent Indian and Middle Eastern food. Its menu includes a rarity in Cebu City – a vegetarian section (good curries for P60 to P80, great big pappadams for P10). Its front window advertises spicy food, but even the 'hot' curries are quite mild. If anything's going to have you sweating here it's the lack of air-con. There's another, smaller, air-con Persian Palate in the Ayala Center shopping mall (on level 3).

Bistro Buanevista Bar & Restaurant is near the Capitol Building (follow Escario St around the side of the Capitol Building, where it turns into M Velez St, head over the bridge, turn right at E Osmeña St, and it's on the corner of the first street on your left!). This well-hidden drinking hole does a good meal deal (steak, rice and soft drink) for P205.

Over on Gorordo Ave, **Royal Concourse** looks like a ritzy hotel, but is in fact a ritzy food-court. It has fresh selections of Filipino and Japanese food, mixed grills, sweets and more. Romantic it is not, but the combination of good food, a pianist, a giant TV screen and a disco ball makes it pretty special. For a plate of four huge tempura prawns (shrimp), two mixed-vegetable dishes, plain rice and a giant jug of iced melon juice, you'll pay a piffling P215.

Sizzling Chef, in the Ayala Center shopping mall, serves big steaks (T-bone P65), as well as traditional favourites such as sizzling *sisig* (a stew often made with pork and spiced liver), *bangus* (milkfish) and *gambas* (shrimp) – P45 each.

On leafy F Ramos St, Filipino and Chinese cuisine is served at **Diplomat Garden Restaurant**, directly behind the Diplomat Hotel. It's a big, bright, friendly place, popular with large groups.

At the front of the Diplomat Hotel, you'll find **European Delicatessen & Butcher Shop Restaurant**. It sells imported cold meats, cheeses and wine downstairs (Australian wines are around P300) and upstairs, offers a menu you could get lost in. Imported salmon (P242), imported steaks (from P400 to P900), even imported onion rings (P80)! Only the pianist, the waiters

and the orchids appear to be homegrown. The average backpacker may feel a little underdressed here, but as long as you can afford to pay around P800 for dinner, you'll be most welcome.

Over the road, there's great service and old-world charm aplenty at **Café Adriatico**. Again, you may feel a little out of place if you're a sweaty mess of shorts and sandals, but no-one's going to object. The food is Filipino- and Italian-style, with a strong Cuban flavour. The pepper steak is good value at P185, as are the various Filipino dishes. Vegetarians be warned: the garlic bread is sprinkled with bacon. A lunch or light dinner for one should cost around P350. Oh, and if you've got a thirst, order a bottomless glass of iced tea, or turn up for the happy hour (8 pm till closing), when all drinks are half-price.

The tranquil **Swiss Chalet Restaurant**, on Maxilom Ave, has an impressive range of tasty, meaty European dishes (around P150), as well as imported wine and cheese.

Lahug **Lighthouse Restaurant**, on the second level of the Gaisano Country Mall, is a seafood specialist with a twin on Maxilom Ave. **Wunderbar Kaffee Haus**, near the main entrance to the Gaisano Country Mall, is open 20 hours a day and features Germanic delights. To get there, grab a cab (P50 from downtown), or jump on a northbound jeepney marked 'Talamban-Carbon', or 'Labangon via Escario' (P2.50).

At 1 Salinas Dr (underneath Hotel la Nivel), **Seafood City Restaurant** serves some of the best seafood in town. The nautical decor and the large selection of wines is a winner. It's a P50 taxi ride from downtown.

Farther up the hill, the classy **Café Tartanilla** does a lavish buffet three times daily for around P200. You'll find it inside the swanky Cebu Plaza Hotel complex, overlooking the city. A taxi up here costs around P60.

Follow the road past the Cebu Plaza Hotel, towards the lookout area known as Tops (see the Tops Lookout Area entry earlier), and you'll reach **Mr A**. A favourite with the city's young professionals, it has a cool, open-air pub feel and fine Filipino and Western dishes (around P100). The views are fantastic.

Entertainment

Harley's Entertainment Pub, in the uptown area on President Osmeña Blvd, has live bands every weekend, which kick off at 9.30 pm. Admission is P100 (with one drink). A Philippine-style Planet Hollywood, Harley's is open all day during the week and offers cheap drink-and-meal deals (eg, four San Miguel beers for P99, burger with soft drink for P32).

At 15 Queens Rd, *Lone Star Saloon Bar* is in the girlie-bar precinct around Maxilom Ave. It's a popular drinking spot open from noon to 3 am, with a happy hour from 7 to 10 pm.

Up at the Cebu Plaza Hotel complex in, *Pards Bar & Restaurant* is a groovy place decorated with drawings by Fine Arts students from the local University of San Carlos. A different band plays here every night (except Sunday), from 9.30 pm to around 1 am. Prime-beef burgers (P190) and good local specialities such as *chicharon bulaklak* (deep-fried pig intestines; P100) are available, as are free chess sets.

A long-time favourite place for party animals is *Bai Discotheque*, also in the Cebu Plaza Hotel complex. It's open from 9 pm to 3 am (5 am on the weekend). The action on the dance floor revs up around 11 pm most nights.

Shopping

Adventurers looking for inspiration should drop into the Habagat Outdoor Store (☎ 032-232 0742). There's one uptown on Don Ramon Aboitiz St, and one in the SM City shopping mall. Both are packed with hiking, biking and camping gear (including top-quality sports sandals), and they're also the unofficial headquarters for regular outdoor-adventure activities in and around Cebu City.

For the more relaxed types, there's the Tinder Box cigar shop on Gorordo Ave, selling good quality local and imported to-bacco products in a variety of flavours, shapes and sizes. High-class coffee and spirits are also available. There's a smaller Tinder Box shop in the shopping arcade at Pier 4 (SuperCat/SeaAngels ferries' main port of call).

The New Cool Breeze barber shop, on Pelaez St, opposite Pete's Kitchen, has a wide range of services. Open from 9 am to 9 pm, its services include 'ordinary haircut' (P50), shave (P40), manicure (P45), and 'blackheads removing' (P55).

Getting There & Away

Air If you've got the option and it fits your itinerary, flying into Cebu City rather than Manila has its advantages. Cebu City's Mactan-Cebu International Airport (MCIA; ☎ 032-340 2977) is second only to Manila in terms of air traffic, but way ahead in terms of user-friendliness. The domestic giant Air Philippines hopes to one day fly to San Francisco, Los Angeles, Hong Kong and other international destinations. Let's hope the airline does all air travellers a favour by using Cebu City as a regular entry/exit point.

One domestic airline that won't be flying to any airport is GrandAir, which fell in a financial heap in early 1999, after only a year in the air.

Airport departure tax *from* Manila is P100. *To* Manila, and all other domestic destinations, its P53, and P550 for international flights.

The following airlines have offices either at MCIA on Mactan, or in Cebu City itself, or both:

Cathay Pacific (☎ 032-254 0821, 254 0746, airport office 340 0729, fax 253 8417) Rivergate mall, Gen Maxilom Ave, Cebu City

Cebu Pacific (☎ 032-225 0201, fax 225 0206, ✉ beegee@gsilink.com)

Malaysia Airlines (☎ 032-231 3887, 232 0904, airport office 340 2978) Unit 312, 3rd Floor, Ayala Center, Cebu Business Park, Cebu City

Mindanao Express (☎ 032-340 0201) c/- U-Freight Cebu, Mactan international airport, Cebu
Web site: www.mindanao.com/mindanao-express/offices.html

Pacific Airways (☎ 032-340 3500, fax 232 2116)

Philippine Airlines (PAL; 24-hour Manila hotline ☎ 02-816 6691, 032-340 0191 to 340 0199)
Web site: www.philippineair.com

Singapore Airlines (SilkAir) (☎ 032-232 6211, 232 6218, airport office 032-340 0042) Suite 302, 3rd Floor, Cebu Holdings Center, Cebu Business Park, Cebu City

Luzon PAL has daily flights to Cebu City (P1400, one hour) about every two hours from 5 am to 5.30 pm, with an extra flight at 8.30 pm Wednesday, Thursday and Sunday, and return flights on the same day. Cebu City–Manila flights go from early morning to late evening.

Air Philippines flies from Manila to Cebu City (P1400, one hour) at 6 and 10 am, and 2 and 6 pm daily. Flights leave Cebu City at 6.50 am, and 1.20, 3.40 and 7.10 pm.

Cebu Pacific flies daily – on the hour, every two hours – between Manila and Cebu City (P1600, one hour). Manila–Cebu City flights go from 5 am to 5 pm. Cebu City-Manila flights go from 7 am to 7 pm. You get a discount of about P300 for taking the early flight (5 am) from Manila to Cebu, or the late flights (5 and 7 pm) from Cebu to Manila.

Mindanao PAL flies to Davao (P1800, one hour) twice daily, with extra flights on Monday and Friday. Davao–Cebu City flights go at 10 am and 5 pm.

Cebu Pacific flies from Cebu City to Davao (P1800, one hour) at 7.30 am and 12.10 pm daily. Its Davao–Cebu City flights are at 9 am and 1.40 pm daily.

Air Philippines flies daily to General Santos City (P1700, one hour) at 10.20 am, returning the same day at 11.50 am. It also has a Cebu City–Zamboanga flight (P1700, one hour).

Mindanao Express has flights from Cebu City to Zamboanga (via Ozamis), as well as flights from Cebu City to Iligan and to Camiguin.

Negros PAL flies once daily from Cebu City to Bacolod and back at noon Monday,

Tuesday, Friday and Saturday. Flights from Bacolod to Cebu City depart at 1.40 pm.

Cebu Pacific has a daily mid-morning flight to Bacolod (P1100, 30 minutes), as well as a Bacolod–Cebu City flights.

Palawan PAL dropped its flights from Cebu City to Puerto Princesa in 1998. At the time of writing, smaller airlines hadn't filled the hole, so unless someone's stepped up in the meanwhile, travellers must get from Cebu to Palawan via Manila.

Panay PAL flies to Iloilo City four times a day on Monday, Tuesday, Friday and Saturday, with return flights to Cebu City the same day.

Cebu Pacific has mid-morning flights to Kalibo (P1300, one hour) on Tuesday, Friday and Sunday, and flies from Kalibo to Cebu City on the same days. Cebu Pacific also flies to Iloilo (P1300, 30 minutes) at 3 pm daily, with daily early-morning flights to Cebu City.

The newly expanded Mindanao Express flies to Kalibo (one hour) on Monday, Wednesday, Thursday, and Friday, returning on the same days. It also has flights from Cebu to Roxas.

Asian Spirit flies from Cebu City to Kalibo (P1500, one hour) and back, once a day.

China Cathay Pacific flies from Cebu City to Hong Kong on Tuesday, Thursday, Friday and Sunday. Flights from Hong Kong to Cebu City are on the same days. Cathay Pacific also has flights between Cebu City and Beijing.

Japan PAL flies from Cebu City to Tokyo on Wednesday, Thursday and Sunday, with return flights on the same days. PAL also flies from Manila to Osaka (via Cebu City) on Wednesday, Thursday, Saturday and Sunday, with return flights to Manila (via Cebu City) on the same days. PAL also has flights to Fukuoka.

Malaysia Malaysia Airlines flies from Cebu City to Kuala Lumpur (via Kota

Kinabalu) on Thursday and Sunday afternoons, and from Kuala Lumpur to Cebu City in the morning.

Singapore Singapore Airlines' Silk Air flies several times a week between Singapore and Cebu City.

Boat Cebu City's multipiered port throngs with boats heading to Philippine islands and to international ports. Larger passenger-ferry companies, such as Philippine Fast Ferry (operators of SuperCat/SeaAngels), have high-speed ferries, known as fastcraft, to and from Cebu City every day of the year except Good Friday (it's generally business as usual on Holy Thursday, Black Saturday and Easter Sunday).

Ticket prices for passenger liners quoted in this section apply to the cheapest fare, usually known as 'economy' or 'budget'. More expensive categories available are usually 'tourist', and 'cabin' (air-con), which cost around 20% and 30% more, respectively – and are often well worth it if you plan to get some sleep.

There's a 20% discount on round trips with SuperCat/SeaAngels and several other fastcraft companies between Cebu City and Ormoc, Tagbilaran and Dumaguete. Also, most passenger liner companies offer discounts of around 20% for bookings made four days in advance. This information is very vulnerable to change – make sure you have the most current schedules and fare information before you make your plans.

For on-line shipping details, go to the *Sun-Star* newspaper's excellent shipping Web site at www.esprint.com/~shipping/default.asp; and the WG&A/SuperFerry Web site at www.wgasuperferry.com. You can also contact the combined booking offices of WG&A/SuperFerry, SuperCat/SeaAngels and Aboitiz Express on a Cebu City booking hotline (☎ 032-233 1944) from 8.30 am to 7 pm Monday to Saturday.

Cebu City passenger-ship companies and their details are as follows:

Aboitiz Express (☎ 032-231 9136) SM City shopping mall

ACG Express Liner (Seacat; ☎ 032-253 5973) Pier 5, Port Area

Bullet Express (Fast Ferries; ☎ 032-255 1383) CPA Bldg, Pier 1, Port Area

Cebu Ferries (☎ 032-253 1181, hotline ☎ 232 0490 fax 232 3436, **☉** cfc@cebu-online.com) Pier 4, Reclamation Area Web site: www.wgasuperferry.com/cebu_ferries

Cokaliong Shipping Lines (☎ 032-253 2262) Pier 1, Port Area

Delta Fast Ferries (☎ 032-232 6295) Water Jet Terminal, Pier 4, Port Area

George & Peter Lines (☎ 032-75598) Corner of Jakosalem St and Quezon Blvd

Maypalad Shipping (☎ 032-70005) 39 R Palma St

Negros Navigation (☎ 032-255 6583, hotline ☎ 262 4943) Ground Floor, Colonnade Mall, Colon St

Palacio Shipping (☎ 032-255 5492) Corner Mabini and Zulueta Sts

Philippine Fast Ferry – see SuperCat/SeaAngels

San Juan Shipping (☎ 032-232 6277) Opascar Bldg, Benedicto St, Reclamation Area

Seacat – see ACG Express Liner

Socor Shipping Lines (☎ 032-419 0647, fax 255 7767) Pier 1, Warehouse Bldg, Port Area

Starlite Shipping (☎ 032-253 7776) Pier 1, Reclamation Area

Sulpicio Lines (☎ 032-232 5361) 1st St, Reclamation Area

SuperCat/SeaAngels (☎ 032-232 2345) Pier 4, North Reclamation Area

Trans-Asia Shipping Lines (☎ 032-254 6491, fax 255 7899) Corner of MJ Cuenco Ave and Quezon Blvd

Water Jet Shipping (☎ 032-232 3888, fax 232 1358) Water Jet Terminal, Pier 4, Reclamation Area

WG&A/SuperFerry (☎ 032-232 0490) Pier 4, Reclamation Area

Bantayan Palacio Shipping has nightly boats from Cebu City to Santa Fe, except on Sunday and Monday, and from Santa Fe to Cebu City, except on Monday and Tuesday.

Biliran San Juan Shipping ferries sail from Cebu City to Naval (P160, eight hours) on Monday, Wednesday and Friday nights.

Bohol Aboitiz Express and SuperCat/SeaAngels offer a popular two-day 'Skip Trip'

THE VISAYAS

Bohol package deal taking in several Bohol destinations. Contact Aboitiz Express (☎ 032-231 9136), or visit its Web site at www.esprint.com/~skiptrips. See Boat in the introductory Getting There & Away entry in the Bohol section for details.

Cokaliong Shipping liners go from Pier 1 to Tagbilaran every night. Fast Ferries (Bullet Express) fastcraft sail to Tagbilaran and back to Cebu City three times daily. Lite Shipping boats cover the same route, leaving nightly.

Palacio Shipping has boats to Tagbilaran on Monday, Wednesday and Friday afternoons, and from Tagbilaran to Cebu City very early in the morning on the same days.

Seacat fastcraft go from Pier 5 to Tubigon (P200, one hour) and back to Cebu City four times daily between about 7 am and 7.30 pm. Socor Shipping Lines' fastcraft service the same route each morning.

SuperCat/SeaAngels fastcraft sail between Cebu City and Tagbilaran six times daily (P220, 1½ hours), and between Cebu City and Dumaguete (P290) via Tagbilaran once daily. Starlite Shipping has a nightly boat to Tagbilaran (P60), and daily boats to and from Cebu City and Tubigon (P50).

Trans-Asia Shipping Lines ferries go to Tagbilaran daily at 7.30 pm and from Cebu City to Cagayan de Oro (Mindanao) via Tagbilaran at noon Monday.

Water Jet fastcraft travel five times daily from Cebu City to Tagbilaran (P220, 1½ hours) and back.

Camiguin Cebu Ferries has a boat from Cebu City to Camiguin (P205, 10 hours) on Saturday night.

Camotes Islands Palacio Shipping has a daily boat to Poro town and back, as do Socor Shipping Lines.

A SuperCat/SeaAngels fastcraft leaves Pier 4 for Poro town (P150, 1¼ hours) at 8.30 am. At 10 am, this boat goes on to Ormoc on Leyte. It leaves Ormoc at 4 pm and goes via Poro town (departing at 5.15 pm) on its way back to Cebu City. Another fastcraft goes from Poro town to Cebu City every morning.

Leyte Cebu Ferries has boats from Cebu City to Tacloban (P200, 12 hours) on Monday and Wednesday evenings and back to Cebu on Tuesday and Thursday afternoons; to Ormoc (P95, 10 hours) on Friday and Sunday afternoons; and to Palompon (P90, eight hours) on Friday evening and back to Cebu on Saturday morning.

Cokaliong Shipping liners go from Pier 1 to Maasin on Monday, Tuesday, and Thursday evenings and at noon Sunday.

San Juan Shipping has ferries to Ormoc at 11 am daily, and to Palompon at noon. Sulpicio Lines ferries go from Cebu City to Ormoc via Masbate on Monday night.

SuperCat/SeaAngels has five fastcraft (in each direction) daily between Cebu City and Ormoc (P360, two hours). Some of these boats go via the Camotes Islands (see that entry earlier in this section). Fastcraft also sail each morning to Maasin (P330, two hours), and back to Cebu City around noon.

Trans-Asia ferries go to/from Maasin nightly except Tuesday.

Water Jet has eight fastcraft daily between Cebu City and Ormoc (P270, two hours).

Luzon Negros Navigation's passenger liners sail direct from Cebu City to Manila (P750, 20 to 22 hours), on Thursday morning and Saturday afternoon.

Sulpicio Lines has boats to Manila on Sunday and Friday mornings and Monday, Tuesday and Wednesday evenings. Book four days in advance and you'll get an economy berth for P599.

WG&A/SuperFerry has three passenger-liners weekly to Manila, and five from Manila to Cebu City.

Masbate Sulpicio Lines ferries go from Cebu City to Ormoc via Masbate on Monday evening. Trans-Asia Shipping Lines ferries go to Masbate town on Monday, Wednesday and Friday evenings.

Mindanao Cebu Ferries has boats from Cebu City to Cagayan de Oro (P217, eight hours) every night but Sunday, and in the other direction every night but Saturday.

Other Cebu Ferries boats from go from Cebu City to Nasipit (Butuan) on Tuesday, Thursday and Saturday evenings (P225, 10 hours) and from Nasipit to Cebu City on Monday, Wednesday and Friday evenings; to Ozamis (P218, 10 hours) on Monday, Wednesday, Friday and Saturday evenings and back again on Tuesday, Thursday, Saturday and Sunday evenings; and to Iligan (P217, 11 hours) on Monday, Wednesday and Saturday evenings and back again on Tuesday, Thursday and Sunday evenings.

Cokaliong Shipping liners go from Pier 1 to Surigao (via Dinagat), and to Dapitan, every evening but Sunday. Departures are from Pier 1 for Dapitan (via Dinagat) on Monday, Wednesday and Friday evenings.

George & Peter Lines go to Dapitan (via Dumaguete) every night, and direct on Monday, Wednesday and Friday nights. There are also boats from Cebu City to Zamboanga via Dapitan and Dumaguete on Monday night, and from Cebu City to Zamboanga via Dumaguete at noon Friday.

Negros Navigation passenger liners sail direct from Cebu City to Butuan's Nasipit port (P250, eight hours) on Wednesday night.

Sulpicio Lines sails from Cebu City to Surigao at noon Monday, and to Cagayan de Oro on Monday, Wednesday, Thursday and Friday nights. It has a weekly service between Cebu City and Dipolog, and leaves Cebu City for Ozamis on Saturday night. Sulpicio Lines ferries also go to Nasipit (P225, eight hours) on Monday, Wednesday and Saturday nights and on Thursday morning.

Every morning there's a SuperCat/Sea-Angels fastcraft from Cebu City to Dapitan (P510, four hours) via Dumaguete, and one back to Cebu City via Dumaguete and Tagbilaran. Delta Fast Ferry has a morning fastcraft from Dapitan to Cebu City via Dumaguete. Water Jet fastcraft go from Cebu City to Surigao (P470, 3½ hours) via Maasin (P270) in the morning.

Trans-Asia ferries go to Surigao every evening except Sunday; to Dipolog on Tuesday, Friday and Sunday nights; and to Cagayan de Oro daily. Trans-Asia sails to Ozamis on Sunday, Monday, Wednesday and Friday evenings; and to Cagayan de Oro via Tagbilaran on Monday at noon.

WG&A/SuperFerry boats go to Surigao on Tuesday night, and to Cagayan de Oro on Saturday night.

Negros Cokaliong Shipping liners go from Pier 1 to Dumaguete on Monday, Wednesday and Friday evenings, and on Sunday at noon. Delta Fast Ferry boats go direct to Dumaguete (P225, 3½ hours) and back, daily.

There's a Negros Navigation liner on Thursday night from Cebu City to Iloilo City, then on to Bacolod, and finally Puerto Princesa (P450, 48 hours). The return trip (Puerto Princesa-Bacolod-Iloilo City-Cebu City) heads off between 8 and 10 pm Saturday.

There are four daily SuperCat/SeaAngels fastcraft to Dumaguete (P290, 2½ hours) and four from Dumaguete to Cebu City. One of these boats in each direction goes via Tagbilaran (P210, 1½ hours) on Bohol. Every morning a Water Jet Shipping fastcraft sails to Dumaguete (P290, 2½ hours) and from Dumaguete to Cebu City.

Palawan A Negros Navigation liner sails once a week from Cebu City to Puerto Princesa (P450, 48 hours) via Iloilo City and Bacolod. See the Negros entry earlier for details.

Panay Cebu Ferries go to Iloilo City on Monday, Wednesday and Saturday evenings, and leave Iloilo City for Cebu City on Tuesday, Thursday and Sunday evenings. Cokaliong Shipping Lines has passenger liners from Pier 1 to Iloilo City (P230, 12 hours) on Tuesday, Thursday and Saturday evenings.

A Negros Navigation liner goes once a week from Cebu City to Iloilo City (P240) on its way to Puerto Princesa (P450, 48 hours). The return trip (Puerto Princesa–Bacolod–Iloilo City–Cebu City) heads off between 8 and 10 pm Saturday. Trans-Asia Shipping Lines has a ferry from Cebu City to Iloilo daily.

Samar Palacio Shipping has boats from Cebu City to Calbayog on Monday, Wednesday, Friday and Saturday nights. The boats leave Calbayog for Cebu City on Tuesday, Thursday, Saturday and Sunday nights.

Siquijor Every afternoon Delta fastcraft go from Cebu City to Larena (P300, three hours) via Dumaguete, while SuperCat/SeaAngels fastcraft sail to Larena (P390, two to three hours) via Tagbilaran and Dumaguete. For return trips, catch one of the regular Delta or SuperCat/SeaAngels fastcraft from Larena or Siquijor town to Dumaguete on Negros (see Getting There & Away entry under Boat for Siquijor).

Palacio Shipping has boats to Larena on Sunday, Tuesday and Thursday nights, and from Larena to Cebu City on Monday, Wednesday and Friday nights.

Bus The most popular destination outside of Cebu City is the popular southern dive-spot of Moalboal. The cushiest way to get to there and back is to catch the Fly the Bus, a three-times-weekly coach especially for foreign tourists. It starts from Cebu City's Pier 4 and drops you right at Panagsama Beach (P400, five hours). See Getting There & Away under Moalboal & Panagsama Beach, later.

If you're happy to travel south from Cebu City by public bus, go to the Cebu South bus station. It's a short taxi ride from downtown (around P25), and Basak–Colon, Urgello–Colon and Labangon–Colon–Pier jeepneys stop here. Buses from here do the following routes from Cebu City and back: Argao–Dalaguete–Alcoy (P20/30 regular/air-con); Bato (via Oslob and Barili); Carcar–Aloguinsan–Pinamungajan; Balamban–Tuburan. Direct buses go to Toledo (P26, 2¾ hours), Dalaguete, Alcoy, Damanjug, Boljon and Moalboal pretty much all day.

If you're after a public bus north, the Cebu North bus station has rather inconveniently shifted out to Mandaue, a P40 taxi ride from downtown. A Mabolo–Carbon, or Mandaue–Cebu City, jeepney will take you there, or bring you into town (P2.50). The station is on Wireless St, in the desolate Reclamation area of town. Although there are food stalls,

there's very little to do out here if you've got a long wait for a bus. Here you'll find buses to Hagnaya – the gateway town to Bantayan. They leave every hour or so, from 5.54 am to 6.55 pm. Buses to Maya, the gateway town for boats to Malapascua leave several times a day (P65, 3½ hours).

Getting Around

To/From the Airport There used to be a shuttle bus running between MCIA and the city centre (16km) but the contract ended, and that was that. The taxi drivers aren't complaining of course. They will tell you the 'fixed rate' into Cebu City is P150, P165 or P200 – it seesaws because it's completely made up.

Unfortunately, unless you're up to trudging all the way out of the airport to far-off tricycles or jeepneys, the best you can do is haggle a little over the 'fixed rate'. Find a few fellow travellers to share the fare while they're at hand.

That said, if Manila's taxi drivers have left you feeling angry at the world, try not to take it out on their Cebuano cousins. A gentler breed, cabbies here are less inclined to scare the hell out of you and more inclined to insist you employ them as city guides. Most drivers really will stick to the metered price for anything other than the airport or the pier.

As you step out of the airport arrival area, taxi drivers wave frantically from behind a barrier. They're not allowed to park outside the airport entrance, so establish a price (P165 is usual to Cebu City, P100 to P150 to a Mactan hotel or resort) and they'll bring their car to you. Don't worry if the car doesn't appear to be a genuine taxi – many airport taxis are not marked.

If you can make it through the throng of taxi drivers opposite the airport entrance, you can catch a tricycle from out on the main road. It'll take you to the bridge for P20, and from there you can grab one of the jeepneys pouring across to downtown Cebu City (around P5).

To/From the Pier At first, arriving at Cebu City pier seems startlingly similar to

Rough Riding

Cebu City-based bus company D'Rough Riders has had a few problems of late. The company made newspaper headlines in mid-1999 when it was discovered that D'Rough Riders buses – despite being quite new – were responsible for almost twice as many accidents as its rivals. Locals put this down to poor maintenance and reckless driving. The company has been told to lift its game or else, so if it's still operating in Cebu's northern regions by the time you read this, maybe its changed its ways.

Mic Looby

arriving at the airport – a throng of taxi drivers all desperately hoping you won't want them to use their meters. They'll oh-so-casually inform you that the 'standard' fare from the pier to central Cebu City is P150, or P155, or whatever they think they can get away with. But you only have to wander across to the other side of the road to find a cabbie who will quite happily switch on the meter for you. The *real* (ie, metered) rate into central Cebu City is P30 to P50.

Taxi Unless a big ship has just docked, or it's serious festival time, catching a taxi in Cebu City couldn't be easier. Flagfall is P20, and most drivers will automatically use the meter. Officially, the rate is P20 for the first 500m, and P1 for every 200m after that.

Around the uptown and downtown areas, P30 to P40 is a typical, fair fare. To reach fringe areas such as Lahug it's around P60 to P70. If you want to see all the sights, touring in a taxi for a day is a perfectly sensible way to do it – and it's definitely cheaper than hiring your own car (see the Car entry later in this section).

By the way, before you suspect your driver of taking the long way around, remember there's a huge number of one-way streets here, especially in the downtown area.

Jeepney Cebu City has no local buses, so jeepneys and taxis pretty much rule the road.

As in Manila, most jeepneys have a set route, and this is displayed in the front window and along the side. You'll pay P2 to P3 to travel the most common routes in the city.

Car Unlike in Manila, do-it-yourself driving here can be quite OK, but it's not cheap. Local car-hire companies generally charge around P1000 for 12 hours, with special deals for longer periods. Most rental companies also offer city tours, with driver supplied. The standard rate is P300 for the first two hours, P125 per hour after that.

Most hotels can arrange car hire for you, or you can contact Friends Rent-A-Car (☎ 032-340 5727, fax 340 5954, @ friends@ cebu.weblinq.com), which has a fleet of 1997 Nissan four-seater sedans; Avis Rent-A-Car (☎ 032-231 0941), on Archbishop Reyes Ave, uptown, and at MCIA (☎ 032-340 2486), which will rent you a Corolla Excel (P2400 for 24 hours); or Thrifty Car Rental at the airport (☎ 032-340 2486) or the Waterfront Hotel office (☎ 032-232 6888). Avis and Thrifty both offer weekly rental with one day free.

AROUND CEBU CITY
Mactan Island

If you're flying into Cebu City, nearby Mactan is actually where you'll land. Connected to Cebu City by the Mandaue-Mactan Bridge (with a twin bridge due for completion in 2000), this little island can certainly claim to have it all. Whether you *want* it all is another matter. There's an oil depot, a string of ritzy beach resorts, an export-processing zone, several guitar factories and, of course, an international airport. And it was here, on the Punta Engaño Peninsula, that the Portuguese explorer Ferdinand Magellan made the fatal mistake of underestimating the fighting spirit of Mactan's Chief Lapu-Lapu (see the boxed text 'Magellan's Last Stand').

Almost 500 years later, foreigners are still falling victim to Mactan, only these days it's their budgets that cop the beating.

One reader described it as 'a tourist hell-hole', another was disappointed to find that its beaches 'are nothing to write home

THE VISAYAS

THE VISAYAS

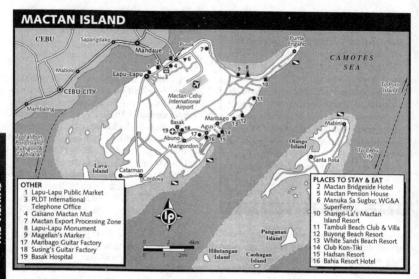

MACTAN ISLAND

OTHER
1 Lapu-Lapu Public Market
3 PLDT International
   Telephone Office
4 Gaisano Mactan Mall
7 Mactan Export Processing Zone
8 Lapu-Lapu Monument
9 Magellan's Marker
17 Maribago Guitar Factory
18 Susing's Guitar Factory
19 Basak Hospital

PLACES TO STAY & EAT
2 Mactan Bridgeside Hotel
5 Mactan Pension House
6 Manuka Sa Sugbu; WG&A
   SuperFerry
10 Shangri-La's Mactan
   Island Resort
11 Tambuli Beach Club & Villa
12 Buyong Beach Resort
13 White Sands Beach Resort
14 Club Kon-Tiki
15 Hadsan Resort
16 Bahia Resort Hotel

about'. Yes, most of Mactan's charm lies beneath the surface. About 30m beneath the surface, in gentle ocean currents, on reef ledges ideal for fish-feeding. Mactan is bejewelled with reefs, as is its little neighbour, Olango Island (see that section later). Alas,

great chunks of coral have been destroyed by dynamite fishing, and the coral-munching crown-of thorns starfish.

The good news is, dive centres and individuals have pooled resources to create the Dolphin Dive Club, dedicated to ridding

Magellan's Last Stand

A few sniggers must have gone around the royal palace when news reached Spain of Ferdinand Magellan's demise. It was 1521, and poor old Ferdinand had done the hard bit for his adopted country (he was Portuguese by birth). He'd sailed around the world. He'd quelled a mutiny. He'd landed in Samar and named and claimed the Philippines for Spain. And on Sugbu (modern-day Cebu), a vital trade centre, he'd carefully befriended all the scariest tribal chiefs – or so he thought. There was one chief, Lapu-Lapu of Mactan, who wasn't so easily impressed. So what did Ferdinand do? He ordered 60 of his most blood-thirsty soldiers to suit up, along with 1000 obedient Cebuano warriors, and in a huge flotilla he sailed to Mactan to have a word with this Lapu-Lapu fellow. In a rush of pure European blood, he even told the Cebuano warriors to sit back, relax, and learn how the civilised world dealt with troublesome natives. But Lapu-Lapu and his men defended their island with unimagined ferocity, and Ferdinand was soon back on his boat – fatally wounded by a spear to his head, a poisoned arrow to his leg and a mighty blow to his pride.

Mic Looby

Mactan's waters of all harmful elements. This group teams up with others (including the Philippine Navy) every third Sunday in September for a massive marine clean-up of Cebu's coast. These environmentalist saviours are fondly known as *scubasureros*.

For more information on **diving** around Mactan, contact Scotty's Dive Center (☎ 032-231 0288, fax 231 5075, ✉ scotty@ mozcom.com) at Shangri-La's Mactan Island Resort; or Seaquest Dive Center (fax 032-346 0592, ✉ seaquest@sequst.com) in Cebu City – its Web site is at www.se quest.com/seaquest. These dive companies make regular trips as far south as Cabilao, off nearby Bohol.

For a peek at a **guitar factory**, ask a tricycle driver to take you to Susing's, one of several such places in Abuno, the 'guitar town' in the centre of Mactan. There's an open-air workshop (closed Sunday), and over in the showroom you can have a play without too much hardsell from the staff. Susing's guitars range from the P1800 'cheapie' to the P10,000 'export quality'. Susing's also makes mandolins, ukuleles and the cute little *cocolele* – a native ukulele with a brightly polished coconut shell for a body. For around P1500, you too can be the proud owner of a cocolele.

Places to Stay & Eat There are two distinct sides to Mactan's accommodation options – east and west. There's nothing in between. The west is represented by the island's main metropolis of Lapu-Lapu City, a long, ugly stretch of road near the bridge to Cebu. Lapu-Lapu could be handy if you have an early morning flight, or if you're a diver and you're allergic to palm trees.

In Lapu-Lapu, on the thundering ML Quezon National Hwy, *Mactan Bridgeside Hotel* (☎ *032-340 8569*) is a pleasant enough place. As implied, it's right next to the bridge, so traffic noise is part of the package. Rooms are good and big, with timber floors, cable TV, air-con and bath for P700. There's a restaurant, and motorcycles can be rented for around P500 per day.

On the same side of the highway is *Mactan Pension House* (☎ *032-340 5524,*

✉ *mph@cebu.weblinq.com*). Tidy rooms with air-con, bath and cable TV start at P690. If you ask nicely, they'll throw in a karaoke machine. Check out time is a luxurious 6 pm.

Opposite the Mactan Pension House, Gaisano Mactan shopping mall has the usual *Jollibee* and *KFC* joints. Nearby is the thatch-roofed *Manukan Sa Sugbu* restaurant, specialising in fried chicken. The vast *Lapu-Lapu Public Market* is also worth a browse.

A dozen or so beach resorts have staked out Mactan's eastern coast. All have their own restaurants and diving facilities, and most provide free shuttle buses to and from the airport. It's not as easy as it looks on the map to browse the resorts along the eastern coast. The more expensive ones are walled in, with guards at the front gate, effectively cutting off the beach to casual strollers. For

THE VISAYAS

around P150, you can get a day pass to these high-security resorts.

In the cheap and cheerful category, **Bahia Resort Hotel** (☎ *0915 206 0406, ☎/fax 032-253 6597*) offers funny old rooms with bath, air-con, screened sunroom and loft for P1300. There's bedding for four to five people, making it the best budget deal on the island. Doubles are P1100. There's no beach here, but there is a private lagoon and a saltwater swimming pool. Meals are also great value, at a standard rate of P130.

A bit shabby but relatively good value, **Buyong Beach Resort** (☎ *032-492 0119*) has simple rooms with air-con and bath for P1200. Rooms without air-con are a Mactan bargain at P500.

Claiming a prime slice of sun and sand is **Tambuli Beach Club & Villa** (☎ *032-232 4811, fax 232 4913,* ❷ *tambuli@mozcom .com*), where the cost of exclusivity starts at around P2900. Considering the outrageous price, standard rooms here are nothing special, but there's a good palm-fringed swimming pool and wet bar.

One of the best and most grandiose options is **Shangri-La's Mactan Island Resort** (☎ *032-231 0288, fax 231 1688*), a vast oasis with *per-person* room-rates starting at P1998. Enticements include a 350m private beach cove, six-hole golf course, multilevel swimming pool, babysitting services, shopping arcade, and a complimentary shoeshine.

Other expensive beach-side resorts nearby have less memorable beaches. These include **Club Kon-Tiki**, **Hadsan Resort** and **White Sands Beach Resort**.

Getting There & Away Jeepneys run all day to Cebu City from Lapu-Lapu City (P10). The going rate by taxi to Cebu City is P150 from Lapu-Lapu City, P165 from the airport, and around P200 from the eastern beach resorts.

Be prepared for a slow crawl, as traffic is often heavy on and around the bridge. The traffic problem may ease a bit with the planned opening of a second bridge, just north of the old one.

Olango Island

In 1998 the Philippine government classified 610,607 hectares of coastal resources under an environmental protection program. Of these, several choice ecotourism spots were deemed National Integrated and Protected Areas (NIPAs). One of these NIPAs is Olango Island.

About 10km off the coast of Mactan, Olango **wildlife sanctuary** takes in almost 1000 hectares of sandflats, mudflats and mangroves on the Olango's southern shores. This is a vital refuelling depot for Chinese egrets *(Egretta eulophotes)* and other birds flying the east-Asian migratory route to Australia. The birds drop in twice a year – from August to November, and from February to May. The pick of the **birdwatching** months are said to be April and October.

The sanctuary is just as important as a nursery and breeding ground for fish. Or at least it would be if commercial fishing fleets, with their dynamite, cyanide and – more recently – chlorine, could be kept out once and for all. A lot of the reef on the western side of Olango has been blown to bits, but the lower part of the drop-off is still alive with coral and fish. The eastern side of the reef is even better, although strong currents make it dangerous for inexperienced divers.

Swagman Travel (☎ 032-254 1365, 412 5709) in Cebu City organises **kayak tours** of Olango for $US25 per person (minimum of three).

Accommodation on the island is minimal, with basic rooms available at the **Suba Community Center** (a P45 tricycle ride from the pier). It's about P200 per person, with meals provided by the centre.

Getting There & Away Most resorts on Mactan will organise a day trip for you, but if you want to put your time and money to better use, take the islander-run Olango Birds and Seascape Tour. It costs around P1500/US$50 per person for Filipinos/foreigners. This include meals, guides, side tours, binoculars, sanctuary entrance fees, and pick-up and drop-off at Mactan. Contact the Coastal Resource Management Project (☎ 032-232 1821, fax 232 1825) in Cebu City. Proceeds

VERONICA GARBUTT

Basilica Minore del Santo Niño, Cebu City, the Visayas.

MARK DAFFEY

Diniwid Beach, Boracay, the Visayas.

Participants in Kalibo's famous Ati-Atihan festival, the Visayas.

The stunning Chocolate Hills of Bohol, the Visayas.

go towards the upkeep of the sanctuary, and the development of livelihood alternatives for Olango fishing communities.

For less money and a little more hassle, you can take the boat that runs between Olango and Maribago (P7, 30 minutes) on Mactan. It leaves roughly every hour on the hour from 7 am to 6 pm.

Toledo

The port city of Toledo, due west of Cebu City, presents a cheap and quick way to travel between Cebu and Negros. Once home to one of Asia's copper-mining giants, and currently home to a massive coal and oil power plant, the city also produces sunsets that spill spectacularly over the mountains of Negros on the westerly horizon. Toledo's choice of food and accommodation is limited, but it's far from being the industrial nightmare you might expect. The local fish might beg to differ however – former resident Atlas Consolidated Mining & Development spent years pumping waste straight into the sea here. One of the by-products of copper, as local environmentalists are painfully aware, is cyanide.

The city's landscaped central square – aglow with coloured lights at night – is watched over by the **Toledo City Parish Church**, which in turn is watched over by a **giant monk**. This monk is San Juan de Sahagun, to whom the church was dedicated, according to its plaque, 'in blood and sweat by a whole people who pledged to God and to one another to finish it in 365 days'. The 365 days were those of 1978, and a loudspeaker in the church's tall belltower has been broadcasting services out across the city ever since.

North of Toledo is **Balamban**, a town that recently found fame as the site of a controversial Japanese–Philippines shipbreaking operation. The companies involved have been accused of allowing waste – including toxic paint and asbestos – to poison Balamban's soil, sea and residents.

Places to Stay & Eat *Aleu's Lodge* (☎ 032-322 5672), on Poloyapoy St, is a low-frills hotel above a general store in a quiet residential area. It has basic rooms with fan and common/private bath for P75/300,

Mt Manunggal

In 1957 President Ramon Magsaysay encountered a very sudden environmental problem when his presidential plane (spookily named *Pinatubo*) flew straight into Mt Manunggal, a 960m-high peak in the Central Cebu National Park, 1km from the town of Tabunan, near Balamban. Like most of Cebu's mountains, Mt Manunggal is sparse and relatively uninviting. Nonetheless, it's a popular climb for trekkers from 13 to 14 March, when loyal pilgrims mark the anniversary of the president's mysterious death by hiking to the crash site. For more information, drop by the Mayor's Office in Balamban or contact the Department of Environment & Natural Resources (DENR; Cebu City ☎ 032-346 9961).

Mic Looby

and rooms with air-con, private bath, cable TV and a very soft bed for P350. It is about 1.5km from the pier (P3 to P5 by tricycle).

A one-hour drive from Toledo proper, the stylish *Springpark Mountain Resort* (☎ 032-325 2044, 261 9511, fax 254 5296) is in the breezy cool of the nearby mountainous region of Cantabaco. Native-style cottages with bath start at around P1000, including all meals. Camping sites are also available. To reach the resort, ring ahead and have the staff collect you from the Toledo pier area.

In the centre of Toledo, there's no shortage of *bakeshops* and fruit stalls (watch for outrageous 'foreigner prices') next to the pier. This is also where you'll find *Goldda's Café*, serving a good *batchoy* special for P22. *Ran Ritch Café Bar & Restaurant*, one block inland from the bus station, is good for a late-night drink, and has OK Filipino food for around P30 to P40.

Getting There & Away There are four ferries daily from Toledo to San Carlos on Negros (30 minutes). There are also boats from the Toledo pier to San Carlos daily (P50/70 regular/air-con, 45 minutes to 1½ hours depending on the boat) at 7, 8, 9 and 10.15 am, and 1 and 4 pm.

THE VISAYAS

Buses run every hour or so daily between Cebu South bus station and the Toledo bus station (P26, 1¾ hours), near the pier. The first buses head off around 5 am, the last at around 4 pm. Jeepneys go from the Toledo City bus station to Balamban throughout the day.

NORTH OF CEBU CITY

Once free of Cebu City's industrial fringe, the island's northern coast is a generally impressive stretch, with many good beaches and mountain views along the road north of Sogod. The biggest metropolises are Danao, one of Cebu's bigger cities; and Bogo, which is on the verge of being officially recognised as a city.

Many buses now run up and down Cebu's northern coast from the Cebu North bus station in Mandaue. Companies include Cebu Auto Bus, TT Gemma Bus Liner, D'Rough Riders Express, and Phil-Cebu Bus Lines (PCBL). The most comfortable buses are operated by PCBL, which has distinctive yellow, air-con buses running daily from Cebu City to Daan Bantayan (P84, 3½ hours) – from where it's a short ride to Maya, and on to Malapascua – via Bogo and Bagay. PCBL buses depart from both Cebu City and Daan Bantayan about nine times daily (from about 4.30 am to 5.30 pm). With so many buses running, you can easily hop off along the way and wait for another bus to come along – these buses are rarely packed out, and waving one down is not a problem.

Liloan

About 15km north of Cebu City (P7, 30 minutes by regular bus), this coastal town has a big public market and the ramshackle Green Acres Horse Riding area. At the northern end of town is Pepito's Beach Cottages, providing thatched-roof seaside picnic shelters for rent (P25). There's another Liloan on the southern tip of Cebu (see Liloan & Sumilon later).

Danao

A thriving, seaside city it may be, but Danao is fairly rough around the edges. Rubbish-strewn beaches and abandoned industrial eyesores on either side of its central-pier area don't make for much of a welcome. Danao is best known for its gunsmithing industry, which employs around 10,000 people and supplies cheap weapons for security guards throughout the Philippines.

Buses running between Cebu City and the far north go via Danao (P10, 50 minutes). Pumpboats leave daily from the Danao City port for Poro town in the Camotes Islands. Pumpboats also run from here to Isabel, on Leyte.

Sogod

The gently curving coastline of Sogod is about 70km north of Cebu City. It's a quiet town with attractive **beaches** nearby. To the south, you'll find the Vima Beach Resort, which rents out picnic shelters (P25) along a pleasant, palm-shaded beach. Off the coast near Sogod, **Capitancillo** was once a pristine island rich in marine life, with a lighthouse the only sign of human contact. But in a frighteningly short time, dynamite fishing has robbed Capitancillo of its underwater charms. The exclusive Alegre Beach Resort (see Places to Stay & Eat later) still includes the island on its pricey dive-trip menu, but probably not for much longer.

Places to Stay & Eat About 5km north of Sogod is the resort that put the town on the international tourist map – *Alegre Beach Resort* (☎ 032-254 9800, fax 253 4345). Alegre is as high-brow as it is high-security. Turn up without a reservation at the big gates and the guards will want to know your name and your intentions. Filing you under 'room inquiry', a guard will escort you halfway across the lavish compound. Along the way, he'll ask what hotel you stayed at the night before – just to gauge exactly how poorly qualified you are to stay here. You'll then be handed over to another guard, for the final approach. At last, you'll get to walk down the aisle of the huge entrance hall, at the end of which is a disappointingly ordinary reception desk.

Rooms here start at US$264, and end somewhere in the upper stratosphere, at US$576. We'd tell you what one of the rooms or cottages are like, but we weren't allowed inside any. They were being cleaned. In the middle of the afternoon? Anyway, the grounds include a huge swimming pool, a library and billiard room, a putting green, and a tennis court. There's also *Pavilion Restaurant & Bar*, which sits atop the resort's very own white-sand beach. The restaurant serves sandwiches, but not just any sandwiches – grilled tuna on French bread with chilled ratatouille salad (P195). Even the butter is all the way from Normandy! Main meals are around P245.

Alegre's dive shop has many tours and dive options, and nonguests are allowed to arrange a diving trip. Diving here is more expensive than elsewhere in the Philippines. One dive at the resort's 'house reef' is US$30, with equipment rental US$20 per day.

The resort is a P20 tricycle ride from Sogod proper, but if you drop into the resort and don't have your own transport, you may be stranded. To get back to Sogod, or to the main road for buses farther north, you'll have to walk from the main gate to the main road (about 1km). From there, a passing tricycle should pick you up.

Cebu Club Pacific Beach Resort, Alegre's less expensive rival in Sogod, was closed for renovations at the time of writing. It may be up and running again by mid-2000.

Getting There & Away Buses pass through Sogod from Cebu City (P20, 1½–two hours) throughout the day.

Bogo

The road north from Sogod heads inland through lush mountains before returning to the sea to meet up with Bogo, one of the country's fastest-growing towns. A four-time winner of the national Clean & Green campaign, Bogo's heart is a central triangle of a plaza, surrounded by vibrant streets of shops and a huge, typically colourful church.

Nailon Beach Resort (☎ 032-253 1097), just to the east of Bogo proper, sits at the end of a prominent point and features a swimming pool and good rooms from

around P1200. Next door to the Nailon Beach Resort is the less-flashy *Hisoler Beach Resort*.

A regular/air-con bus from Cebu City to Bogo will cost you P45/66 and take about three hours. From Sogod to Bogo (one hour) it's P15/24.

Daan Bantayan

About 130km north of Cebu City, the drab town of Daan Bantayan is the quasi-capital of a quasi-island – this northernmost chunk is actually separated from Cebu by the Dayhogan tidal canal. The vegetation around Daan Bantayan is almost solid sugarcane, and the roads are constantly crumbling under the groaning weight of sugarcane trucks. In the village of Tapilon, about 5km from Daan Bantayan, pumpboats are available for trips out to nearby **Gato**. But be careful – this rich marine sanctuary is not only a breeding ground for sea snakes (from around February to September), it also has a resident fishery school employing armed guards to deter poachers. The island's feline-inspired title refers to its profile, which is a little like a sitting cat. You can also reach Gato by boat from Malapascua.

Places to Stay & Eat On the rocky coast east of Daan Bantayan, Ron and Fe Perry have painstakingly carved out a little piece of paradise they call *Virgin Beach Resort* (☎ 0918 773 0949). It has a private beach with a pier and picnic shelters, a large entertainment area with a bar, books, videos and computer games. A swimming pool and basketball court were under construction at the time of writing, as were several free-standing cottages. All room prices include *three* daily meals. The best rooms cost P1500 and come with a big, shared veranda, private cold-water bath, bedside lamps, air-con *and* fan, cable TV, and photos of past guests on the walls. Small doubles and dorm rooms with common bath cost P600 per person, which means, according to Ron, that your accommodation is free (if meals are priced at P200 each).

To get to the resort (which is officially in Malbago), you can ring ahead and have one of the resort's jeepneys collect you from

THE VISAYAS

Daan Bantayan. Alternatively, you can catch a Maya-bound bus and ask to be dropped at the Virgin Beach Resort waiting shed at Camaras, Bateria, just after the school. The blue-roofed shed is 1.5km from the resort.

Bantayan Island

Beautiful Bantayan Island, off the north-western coast of Cebu, has some good beaches on its southern coast. The island can also be used as a stepping stone to Negros. The wonderful little town of **Santa Fe**, on the island's south-eastern coast, is connected by ferry to Cebu. With perfect beaches and excellent, relaxed resorts, it attracts a small but steady stream of tourists.

About 10km from Santa Fe, **Bantayan town** is the island's largest (and ugliest) town. It has a lively port with ferries to and from Cadiz on Negros, but it lacks the pristine beaches of Santa Fe – not to mention the **Obtong Cave**, a small freshwater swimming hole about 10 minutes' walk from town (P20 entrance fee).

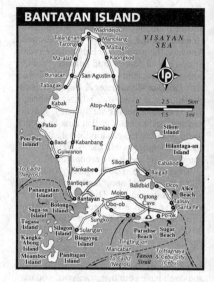

Places to Stay & Eat A short walk or tricycle ride north from the pier is the stark white **Santa Fe Beach Club** (☎ 032-255 0676), where swish air-con twin rooms cost P1000 to P1600, and cottages with fan and bath are P500 to P750. There's a good beach here but just about the only shade is provided by the Caltex oil tanks behind the main building. Good meals are available from P35 to around P120.

On the other side of Santa Fe, **Kota Beach Resort** (☎ 032-254 5661) is set among palm trees and offers rooms with fan for P610, and cottages with bath and fan/air-con for P840/1200. The air-con cottages are too plain for the price, but the **Ding Dong Bar & Restaurant** here makes up for it – great ocean views and excellent Filipino seafood cuisine for around P90. Right next door, the better-value **Budyong Beach Resort** has cottages with fan for P350 to P500 and air-con rooms for P900, all laid-out amid shady palms.

One of Bantayan's best kept secrets must surely be **Moby Dick's Beach Resort** (☎ 032-352 5269), on the road from Ban-

tayan town to Madridejos in the north (turn left at San Pedro Chapel). It's a fun seaside retreat with large cabins for P400 (P500 for full board), a pool, restaurant and free transport from Santa Fe.

Two eateries well worth trying in Santa Fe are **Yaga's Kitchenette**, for local cuisine; and **Moby Dick's** (known locally as Little Dick's), for imported Australian beef, great decor and lots of dick jokes.

Getting There & Away Bantayan is connected to destinations within Cebu and around the Visayas.

Air There is a now an airstrip on Bantayan operated by Pacific Airways.

Boat & Bus Look for PCBL's comfy yellow air-con buses at Cebu City's new Northern bus station. They leave for the northern port town of Hagnaya (P73, three hours) via Bogo at 5 and 6 am, and at 1.30 and 2.30 pm. From here, pay your P1 pier fee (and get a cute little souvenir ticket) and then hop on a Santa Fe boat (P55, one hour) – there are three a day each way, between 5.30 am and 8.30 pm.

Bantayan town has daily boats to Cadiz (P120, 3½ hours) on Negros. Palacio Shipping has boats from Cebu City to Santa Fe at 9 pm daily except Sunday and Monday. Boats to Cebu City leave Santa Fe at 9 pm daily, except on Monday and Tuesday.

Malapascua Island

For anyone who finds Boracay (see that section later in this chapter) too crowded, Malapascua is the perfect antidote. And as long as it continues to attract a quieter type of traveller, it will stay that way. This little island off Cebu's northern tip has everything the low-key sun-seeking traveller needs. Boats from the mainland drop you on the enticingly white **Bounty Beach**, which is lined with resorts to suit most budgets. The nearby main town (actually, *everything* on this compact island is nearby) of **Logon** is simple and friendly. It has some small eateries and general stores and is great to wander through on a stroll around the island. The island itself is often referred to by older locals as Logon.

There are no cars on the island, only a few bicycles and a network of walking tracks. These tracks wind past such attractions as the waterside town **cemetery**, with its sun-bleached graves (some of them are open, with skulls and bones on view), and the **lighthouse**, which provides views of the entire island (P20 to P30). Ask for the key to the lighthouse in the town of Guimbitayan (pronounced 'gim-bit-**ay**-an').

Snorkelling gear can be hired from several resorts for around P100 per day, and **dive trips** can be arranged through Malapascua Exotic Island Dive & Beach Resort. **Sea kayaks** can be hired from in front of Cocobana Resort for P100 per hour, and **beach volleyball** is also available. At the southernmost tip of the island, between the cemetery and Bounty Beach, a natural **lookout** provides a perfect spot for watching the island's brilliant sunsets.

Information The phones here are cellular only – and not all the resorts can afford such luxuries. The island's electricity is supplied by a diesel-powered generator. It operates from 5.30 to 11.30 pm (sometimes later)

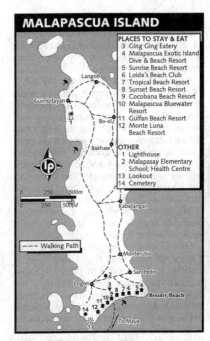

daily, although a bigger generator is expected to bring longer hours of power in the not-too-distant future. Some resorts, such as Cocobana, have their own generators.

Places to Stay & Eat The water supply on Malapascua is brackish, so most resort showers are rather salty. Mosquito nets are provided by many resorts, and you may well need them. In the low season (May to November) resort rates generally drop by 25% to 30%. The following rates are standard high season rates.

Starting at the western end of Bounty Beach, the low-key *Monte Luna Beach Resort* is nearest the sunset lookout. It has OK rooms with balcony and common bath for P350.

Next door, the little *Gulfan Beach Resort* has good, balconied cottages with private bath for around P400.

The big *Malapascua Bluewater Resort* (☎ 0918 773 4124) has spacious grounds, with rooms and cottages, all with balconies and private bath, from P500 to P800. Also on offer is free snorkelling gear (P50 for nonguests), 24-hour electricity supply, and a rather pricey restaurant.

Cocobana Beach Resort (☎ *0918 775 2942*), Malapascua's first resort, is a well-oiled machine run by long-time resident, Freddy. Balconied, beachfront cottages with private bath cost P850. Out the back, balconied cottages with common bath are good value at P300. The common shower-and toilet-blocks are shiny and new, and there's one for every two cottages. The Cocobana has a bar right on the beach, and a restaurant serving great mixed-fruit pancakes (P35). There's a sizeable collection of books in the restaurant, although you'll need to be able to read German.

Behind the Cocobana, *Ging Ging Eatery* not only does fine, cheap food, it also has a small number of great-value cottages and rooms on its menu. For the price of a hearty meal (P150), you can get comfy accommodation with common bath. Some of the best food on the island can be found here. Family-run and a lesson in simple efficiency, this open-air delight specialises in fish dishes (around P35), brewed coffee (P20), and generous fruit pancakes (P25). Order your meal during the day to avoid disappointment. Ging Ging and her young family appreciate it if diners don't stay here too late (after 10pm the kids start looking very sleepy).

Sunset Beach Resort has beachfront cottages for P400 to P500 with private bath and balcony. The *Tropical Beach Resort* has similar cottages for P400.

Loida's Beach Club has balconied cottages with private bath for P350 to P500. Spacious 2nd floor cottages have some lovely touches; they go for P600 and have sweet-water showers. Ideal for early risers, the rooms catch the full glory of the morning sun. Loida and her friendly staff will cook you a fish feast (P100 to P200) in the very good resort restaurant, or you can dine on the deck right by the water.

As the name suggests, *Sunrise Beach Resort* is well placed to bask in the Mala-

pascua dawn. Balconied cottages with private bath go for P400 to P500.

For a little more solitude, wander a little farther around the eastern corner of Bounty Beach to *Malapascua Exotic Island Dive & Beach Resort* (☎ *0918 774 0484*, ✉ *cebumibr@hotmail.com*). Its Web site is at www.malapascua.net. Cottages here are tidy and bright, with private bath and single or double beds (P500 to P600).

This resort is run by the friendly Cora and Dik de Boer, who have recently refurbished their dive shop – the only one on the island. Dive trips cost US$25 (introduction dives US$27), run all year round, and specialise in shark spotting (mostly thresher sharks). Dik is an enthusiastic ocean adventurer, and he can take you on diving and boating outings to brilliant spots including Chocolate and Manoc Manoc, where a well-preserved wreck lies. He'll also take you to some choice spots on Leyte, and can even drop you off or pick you up if you give him plenty of notice. There's a big menu at the resort, including banana pancakes (P50) and buttered lemon chicken (P120).

Also an easy stroll from Bounty Beach, *Sally's Eatery* is a basic, friendly place in Logon, serving Filipino food (P20 to P30).

Getting There & Away From Maya to Malapascua, it's P25/50 for the public/private banca. For around P300 you can get a boat to do a one-way trip at any time of the day. If the tide is low at Maya, the larger pumpboats can't dock, and must ferry passengers to and from shore using smaller craft.

To travel between Malapascua and Bantayan, you have to hire a pumpboat and pay 'special ride' rates of around P1500.

It's possible to do a diving or boating trip (eg, to Leyte) through the Malapascua Exotic Island Dive & Beach Resort (see Places to Stay & Eat earlier) and continue on your island-hopping way afterwards.

SOUTH OF CEBU CITY

The west and east coasts south of Cebu City tend to be mostly pebbly or rocky affairs, but there's plenty of diving and snorkelling to be had. Moalboal is an old favourite among travellers. This half of the island was flung open to travellers with the mid-1999 launch of Fly the Bus, a luxury coach service between Cebu City and Moalboal (see Getting There & Away under Moalboal & Panagsama Beach later).

Argao & Dalaguete

Spanish colonial-era buildings and limestone walls make Argao a little special, but it's the town's nearby **beaches** of Kawit, Mahawak, and Mahayahay that draw the crowds. Neighbouring Dalaguete is well known for its plaza and streets of flowering bushes. Its popular **Dalaguete Public Beach** has communal showers by the water and food and drink stalls.

Buses between Cebu City and Argao pass through the steel mill town of **Carcar**. Maybe you should hold your breath here – the resident steel company, AC Steel Corporation, has recently been accused of poisoning the air to the extent that the nearby residents' health has been affected.

Places to Stay Run by Irene and Gunther, the charming *Bamboo Paradise Beach Resort* in Argao has large, cosy rooms with bath, fan and excellent breakfast for P600. There's no beach here, but Dalaguete Beach is only a short tricycle ride away.

Getting There & Away Argao is about 65km from Cebu City, and plenty of ABC and Albines buses (some of them air-con) stop here (P25, 1½ hours) on the way between Cebu City and Bato, on Cebu's southern tip. Ask the bus driver to tell you when you've reached Argao – it's easy to miss it.

Lite Shipping boats go from Argao to Loon (Bohol) at 4 and 10 am Monday and Saturday and at 10 am Sunday.

Moalboal & Panagsama Beach

Diving, dining and drinking top the list of tourist activities on the beaches of Moalboal (hard to pronounce – try 'mo-all-bo-all'). About 90km from Cebu City, Moalboal proper is on the main road, with the lively tourist-haunt of Panagsama Beach a P25 tri-

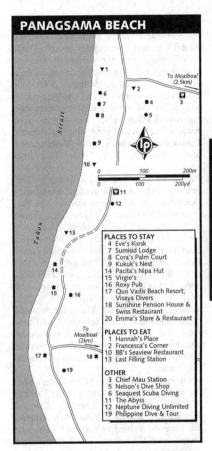

PANAGSAMA BEACH

To Moalboal (2.5km)

0   100   200m
0   100   200yd

PLACES TO STAY
4 Eve's Kiosk
7 Sumisid Lodge
8 Cora's Palm Court
9 Kukuk's Nest
14 Pacita's Nipa Hut
15 Virgie's
16 Roxy Pub
17 Quo Vadis Beach Resort; Visaya Divers
18 Sunshine Pension House & Swiss Restaurant
20 Emma's Store & Restaurant

PLACES TO EAT
1 Hannah's Place
2 Francesca's Corner
10 BB's Seaview Restaurant
13 Last Filling Station

OTHER
3 Chief Mau Station
5 Nelson's Dive Shop
6 Seaquest Scuba Diving
11 The Abyss
12 Neptune Diving Unlimited
19 Philippine Dive & Tour

To Moalboal (2km)

Tañon Strait

THE VISAYAS

cycle ride from town. There are always more than enough tricycles waiting to meet your bus.

While **mountain biking** is growing in popularity in these parts (ask at Roxy Pub and other local haunts), **diving** is still the No 1 passion. The average price of a dive with the resorts of Panagsama Beach is US$17 to US$22. The **snorkelling** here is good too, and most resorts rent out snorkel, mask and fins for around P100 per day.

An often-choppy 3km boat ride from Moalboal's Tongo Point diving spot, tiny **Pescador** offers some of Cebu's most spectacular diving. With generally excellent visibility and depths of around 50m, the island's waters are usually teeming with fish. Consequently, they're usually teeming with divers too – no dive trip around here is complete without a plunge at Pescador. Snorkelling is possible too; the best spot is said to be on the island's southern side. Nearby **Badian** also has some good snorkelling and diving, but it's better known for its exclusive resort (see Places to Stay following).

Places to Stay There's a wide range of accommodation on and around Moalboal's Panagsama Beach, from simple nipa huts through to luxurious air-con rooms. There's also some high-end accommodation offshore, on Badian, where the well-heeled traveller might like to stay at **Badian Island Beach Hotel** (☎ 032-253 6452, fax 253 3385, ❷ badiancebu@aol.com). This well-appointed resort offers luxury accommodation for P2000 per person (with a 50% discount for children). The price includes room, breakfast, glass-bottomed boat tour, food and drink discounts, watersports-gear hire, tennis and boat transfer. You can visit the resort's Web site at www.badian hotel.com.

On Panagsama Beach, at the lower end of the price scale, basic cottages for P150 to P250 can be had at **Emma's Store & Restaurant**, **Pacita's Nipa Hut**, **Virgie's** and the good-value **Eve's Kiosk** (fan/air-con rooms for P200/560 to P250/700).

Worthwhile mid-range places (around P350 to P450) include **Roxy Pub**, the newish cottages of **Quo Vadis Beach Resort & Visaya Divers**, the nearby **Sunshine Pension-House** (complete with swimming pool) and the more basic beachside **Kukuk's Nest** and **Cora's Palm Court**. **Sumisid Lodge** (☎ 0918 770 7986), next door, offers excellent rooms for P550 (doubles with fan) to P950 (with air-con) – with a hearty breakfast included in both prices.

Places to Eat & Drink Most places to stay have good restaurants, although there are plenty of other eateries worth a look.

Last Filling Station is famous for its breakfasts, while **BB's Seaview Restaurant** does fine, cheapish Filipino seafood.

There are plenty of pizza and pasta joints, including the new **Francesca's Corner** near Eve's Kiosk, and the fancy **Hannah's Place** nearby.

Lively drinking holes include **The Abyss**, **Chief Mau Station** and **Roxy Pub**. The Roxy has jam sessions every Saturday night.

Getting There & Away ABC or Albines buses leave throughout the day from Cebu North bus station to Moalboal (P40, three to four hours), but the most trouble-free, luxurious option is to take the Fly the Bus.

Run by Swagman Travel, Fly the Bus is a comfy but expensive shuttle service from Cebu City to Moalboal's Panagsama Beach (P400, four hours). At 8.15 am Tuesday, Thursday and Saturday, it goes from the Cebu City port (Pier 4), via the Swagman Travel office on Ramos St at 8.45 am and Kukuk's Nest Pension on Gorordo St at 9 am. On Tuesday, Thursday and Saturday, Fly the Bus goes from Moalboal to Cebu City, leaving from Panagsama Beach at 1 pm, with stops in Cebu City at Kukuk's Nest Pension at 4 pm, Swagman Travel at 4.30 pm and finally Cebu City's Pier 4 at 5 pm – in time to catch the last SuperCat/SeaAngels fastcraft to Tagbilaran (Bohol) at 6.30 pm. In Moalboal, you can book Fly the Bus tickets at most resorts on Panagsama Beach. In Cebu City, you can book at Kukuk's Nest Pension and Swagman Travel (☎ 032-254 1365, fax 254 1382).

To get from Moalboal to Bato (P27, 1½ hours) by ABC or Albines bus, just wait by the main road and be prepared for standing room only. Roxy Pub at Moalboal's Panagsama Beach can arrange six-seater minibuses to take you to Bato (P900 per vehicle) and several other spots around Cebu.

Samboan

On the western side of Cebu's south coast, Samboan has great views out across Tañon Strait from its impressive 19th century

Escala de Jacob stone staircase and watchtower above the town. Although less well-organised than Bais City across the strait on Negros, Samboan is a handy starting point for whale- and dolphin-watching trips. Boat hire can be arranged at the pier, or through the Samboan Coral Garden Resort.

The budget- and environment-friendly *Samboan Coral Garden Resort*, just out of town, has good-value doubles with bath, fan and balcony overlooking the water for P350. Don't miss a walking tour to the beautiful **waterfalls** nearby.

ABC and Albines buses go daily from Cebu City to Bato, via Moalboal and Samboan (three hours). Others go daily from Cebu City to Bato via Oslob. You can reach Samboan from Oslob by inland jeepney.

Bato

Bato, on Cebu's southern tip, is a pretty port town with regular boats making the crossing to Dumaguete's Tampi port on Negros. Solid old ferries sail to and from Bato (P27, 45 minutes) every 1½ hours or so, from 5.30 am to 5 pm daily.

By bus from Moalboal to Bato, it takes about 1½ hours (P27), but it can get very crowded. More expensive, but more comfortable, transport can be arranged by Roxy Pub (see Moalboal & Panagsama Beach, earlier), which has minibuses to take you to Bato (P900 per vehicle).

Liloan & Sumilon Island

Like it's nearby sister-town of Bato, Liloan is an attractive coastal town with boat connections to Negros. In the waters off nearby Liloan Point, manta rays are regular visitors between February and June. The town also offers easy access to the island of Sumilon, which is slowly recuperating from years of abuse. Despite its well-deserved title as the country's first marine reserve, the area was hammered for years by illegal fisherfolk. As long as the area's delicate revival continues, visitors are welcome.

In Santander, Liloan, you can stay at *Manureva Beach Resort* (☎ *0918 774 1410*), which specialises in diving, game fishing and island hopping. From here, the resort's

manager Jean Pierre can take you out to see **whales and dolphins** in Tañon Strait. Newly renovated rooms at Manureva come with bath, marble floors, TV and air-con for P800 to P1000.

Camotes Islands

Little more than an hour's boat ride from Cebu City, the Camotes are the most underrated islands in the Visayas. This group's two main islands, Poro and Pacijan, are connected by a mangrove-fringed land bridge that doubles the fun of exploring by motorcycle, the main mode of transport here. Hotels are very scarce. While there are several 'resorts', none of them seem to offer accommodation. Instead, they offer beaches or shelters for a small fee.

Fishing is a big part of life on the Camotes Islands, but it may not be for much longer. In mid-1999 it was discovered that chlorine is being used to stun and kill fish en masse. Previously known only in Mindanao, this practice is apparently spreading because fisherfolk believe chlorine is a safe alternative to cyanide or dynamite. It's not. Residents of Poro town have refused to buy the chlorinated fish and it's hoped the message will get through to the fishing industry.

Getting There & Away

Air An airstrip has been proposed for the Camotes Islands, but no details were available at the time of writing.

Boat Poro town is connected by boat to Cebu City and Danao on Cebu, and Ormoc and Isabel on Leyte. For information on services between Poro town and Cebu City, see Boat under Getting There & Away in the Cebu City section earlier. Several giant pumpboats operate between Poro town and Danao, north of Cebu City. Others serve Isabel on Leyte. Schedules and prices can vary from day to day, so ask for the latest information at the respective town piers. There's a SuperCat/SeaAngels booking office on the pier in Poro town.

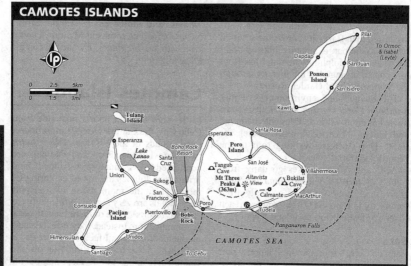

CAMOTES ISLANDS

Getting Around

Getting around the Camotes Islands is by motorcycle: most will have two, three, four or more passengers, plus the weekly shopping on board. Jeepneys are scarce. A motorcycle ride between the islands' main towns of Poro and San Francisco costs about P20.

PACIJAN ISLAND
San Francisco

Bigger and denser than Poro town, 'San Fran', as the locals call it, stands at one end of the long land-bridge and mangrove forest that runs all the way across to Poro Island. The main town on Pacijan Island, San Francisco welcomes travellers along this narrow causeway with a latticework gateway topped with a crucifix. Nearby is a giant basketball complex, a substantial **market**, and a pretty little town square. Motorcycles and their riders can be hired for trips around the island, or across to Poro Island, from around the town square. From San Francisco to Poro town, it's about P20.

Places to Stay & Eat

It's called *Multi-Cooperative Lodging House*, and as you may have guessed by the

name, it doesn't go in for heated towel-rails or rooftop jacuzzis. But it's next to the town square and it offers four clean, basic rooms with fan and common bath for a mere P75. For food, visitors must make do with the weekend market, general stores and bakeshops.

PORO ISLAND
Poro Town

The pretty little town of Poro is a pleasant place to wander. More compact and beachy than its sister town of San Francisco, Poro is lapped by a turquoise sea. Its curving main road takes in a basketball court built right on the water, and the marble-floored **Santo Niño de Poro Parish church**, overlooking a leafy town square. The church's high rafters are home to a lively congregation of birds.

Altavista View & Mt Three Peaks

About 5km from Poro town, Poro Island's interior peaks can be reached by a rough road up from the centre of town. This road takes you to the lookout area known as Altavista View. Hand over P5 to the young men manning the gate, and you can enter this enclosed area, which has a small treehouse, and a 'comfort room' (toilet) with views of neighbouring Pacijan Island to the west, and nearby Mt Three Peaks. The three fairly tiddly peaks making up Camotes' highest region are Elijan, Kaban-Kaban and Kantomaro.

A motorcycle ride up here from Poro town and back should cost P40 to P50.

Tangub Cave

About 1.5km west of Poro town, a sign on the main road, opposite Aika's Mini-Mart, announces 'Tangub Cave & Pagsa Monkeys – 3.5km'. If only it were that simple. The road to Tangub Cave takes several confusing twists and turns, and there are no more signs. The best thing to do is have a motorcycle rider take you to the cave, which is an attractive grotto surrounded by a bunch of very playful **monkeys**. The return ride should cost from P40 to P50 from Poro town, and a little more from San Francisco (on Pacijan Island).

Bukilat Cave

Beside a bumpy dirt road about 6km inland from Tudela, is the well-hidden Bukilat Cave. The road you want heads north from Tudela, then east, passing the Calmante Elementary School about 4km along. A sign for the cave pops up once you're almost there. There's a wooden waiting shed 500m past the sign and opposite, down a flight of concrete steps, is the cave. An entrance fee of P2 is payable at the shed, or at the shop nearby. A couple of round holes in the cave's ceiling let shafts of light play glittery games in the clear, shallow pools on the cave floor, then bounce around the walls. Swallows nest among the stalactites, and one inky-black corner of the cave is apparently the start of a long passage, which can be explored properly if you can rustle up a guide and some torches (flashlights). A motorcycle ride out to the cave and back from Poro town should cost P50 to P60.

Just east of Tudela, a 1km walking trail inland takes you to **Panganuron Falls**.

Boho Rock Resort

On the south-western tip of Poro Island, this 'resort' is an absolute gem of a swimming spot. You can see it from the Poro town pier, but to reach it by land you head about 2km west of Poro town, on the main road, until you reach the signposted turn-off at the big acacia tree. The sign says Boho Rock Resort is 200m from the main road – but it's a very long 200m, eventually bringing you to the loudly churning Camotes Electric Cooperative, and down to the right. Before you is a rocky islet that's been turned into an **aquatic playground**. If anything, the nearby power plant makes Boho Rock seem all the more stunning. Approached by land at least, it certainly ensures this magical spot qualifies as one of the world's best-disguised tourist attractions. At the top of the steep stairs, a regularly unstaffed toll booth asks visitors to pay P2/3 by day/night, and P10 for a 'mushroom cottage' (a thatched-roof shelter on the rock).

A motorcycle ride to the rock, from Poro town or San Francisco, should cost around P10.

Places to Stay & Eat

Unconfirmed reports suggest there's a **hotel** with rooms at about P500 a pop in the small town of Tudela, on the southern coast of Poro Island. But apart from camping out, or finding private board, that's about it on this island.

Food-wise, Poro's menu isn't huge either, but it's about the best you'll get on the Camotes. There are three general stores in Poro town; a mobile **burger bar**; a couple of **bakeshops** (including one that's open 24 hours!); and the tiny pier-side **Pantalon Café**, serving coffee and pastry (P10), and boiled eggs (P5). There's a small **market** behind the cafe.

Bohol

Poor old Bohol (pronounced 'bo-**hole**') has been accused by some of having only one attraction – the Chocolate Hills, in the centre of the island. Divers, nature-lovers and island-hoppers are bound to disagree. Some of the best examples of colonial Spanish churches, many of which are made from coral stone, can also be found here.

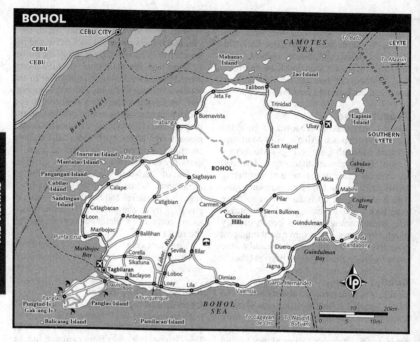

BOHOL

Bohol is known for its *ube* (yams), the bright purple sweet potatoes that give halo halo, the national dessert, its distinctive colour and flavour. Here, it's called *kinampay*.

Getting There & Away

Air There are daily flights from Manila to Tagbilaran airport and back again. Ubay's airport has flights to Tagbilaran.

Plans are afoot to shift the island's main airport from Tagbilaran to nearby Panglao Island. The new airport will be sited on the southern coast of Panglao, near Alona Beach. Part of the new Sikatuna Tourism Complex, it is expected to offer a tempting air-travel alternative to Cebu City.

Boat Tagbilaran is Bohol's main port. Other ports include Tubigon, Jagna, Ubay and Talibon. The three T's – Tagbilaran, Tubigon and Talibon – are well served by daily fastcraft and ferries from Cebu City.

See the Getting There & Away entry under Cebu City, earlier, for information on these services. Look under individual Getting There & Away entries in this section for information on boat travel between Bohol and other destinations in the Philippines.

If you're in Cebu City and short on time or patience, you should consider the popular two-day Bohol package deal offered by Aboitiz Express shipping lines and Super-Cat/SeaAngels fastcraft. Advertised as 'Skip Trips', the deals include a return fastcraft trip from Cebu City to Panglao or Tagbilaran, two days' accommodation at one of several local resorts, air-con bus transfer to and from the Chocolate Hills, and a cruise on the Loboc River. Breakfast is included in the overall price of P2300 per person. For more information, contact Aboitiz Express (☎ 032-231 9136, ✉ skiptrips.aboitizts@aboitiz.com.ph), or visit the Web site at www.esprint.com/~skiptrips.

TAGBILARAN

Unfortunately, what little there is to see in the port capital of Tagbilaran (pronounced 'tag-bill-**are**-an') is often obscured by a fog of exhaust fumes. But there is good accommodation here, and it's a popular base for day trips to the many great sights nearby. In the heart of town, have a look at the huge **Tagbilaran Cathedral**. It was built in 1767 and dedicated to St Joseph. Joseph must have had his back turned one day in 1798, when the cathedral burnt to the ground. It was rebuilt and enlarged in 1855, no doubt with a word to Joseph about not falling asleep on the job.

Orientation & Information

Carlos Garcia Ave is the main drag, but the M Clara St wharf is just as much a hive of activity in this busy port city.

The main post office is on JS Torralba St, next to the town hall.

There's a PT&T office on Carlos Garcia Ave, and a Philippine Long Distance Telephone (PLDT) office nearby on Noli Me Tangere St.

Email & Internet Access Internet cafes have sprouted like cyber-mushrooms in Tagbilaran, particularly around Divine Word College on C Galleres St. Met Internet must qualify as the world's cheapest Internet cafe – at the time of writing it was offering a promotional rate of P10 per hour from midnight to 6 am. If you can't beat the rush, go around the corner to Lesage St, where B&J Internet Café (P35 per hour) is open 24 hours, as is the nearby AC Goldchips Internet (P20 per hour). Then there's the 24-hour Internet Cathedral on MH del Pilar St, with rates of P35 per hour (P30 for students with ID card).

Medical Services Medical treatment is available at Provincial Hospital (☎ 038-411 3324), on Miguel Parras St, and at Ramiro Community Hospital (☎ 038-411 3515), at 63 C Gallares St.

Special Events

Tagbilaran is the headquarters of the giant Bohol Fiesta, which runs throughout May every year. For more information, call ☎ 038-411 2642. The town's own fiesta kicks off the proceedings on 1 May.

Places to Stay

Nisa Travelers Inn (☎ 038-411 3731), on Carlos Garcia Ave, is this town's backpacker haven. Despite the closed-down-looking entrance (make a U-turn left up the stairs), it's a friendly place with a lovely timber common balcony-area. The windowless singles with common bath (P140) are best avoided, but the doubles with fan for P160 are fine for the price. Rooms with air-con and bath are P500.

Directly opposite, *Charisma Lodge* (☎ 038-411 3094) isn't exactly charismatic, but it does have passable, clean singles with common bath for P150, doubles with fan and bath for P225 and doubles/twins with air-con for P375/395. Set to be in a similar price range, the as-yet-unfinished *Niza's Pension*, on Remolador St, should be worth checking out by the time you read this.

Similarly priced *Casa Juana*, on Carlos Garcia Ave, has nice polished floorboards throughout. But if all the rooms are as musty as the standard single/doubles (P250/325) and family room (P475) that we, err, smelled, then this place really only gets points for being central and cheap. It's attached to JJ's Dimsum Restaurant.

Closer to the water, *Sea Breeze Inn* (☎ 038-411 3599), on C Gallares St, does offer a little sea breeze in its harbourside rooms, but they're light on for any other luxuries. Rooms with fan and private bath are P200/300, singles/doubles with air-con are P400/550. This place is above the young groovers' nightspot, Club Zone (see Entertainment later).

One block along, at the start of Tagbilaran's main wharf, you can't miss the aquatic-green, optimistically named *Everglory Hotel* (☎ 038-411 4969), operated by one Captain Zosimo Arbasto. Not exactly glorious on the inside, it has small rooms with private bath for P350/400, and slightly bigger doubles with private bath and air-con for P550. If you can get a room looking out

THE VISAYAS

TAGBILARAN

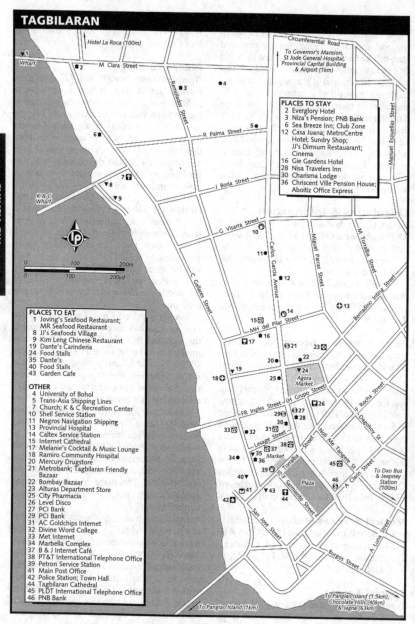

Hotel La Roca (100m)

Wharf

M Clara Street

Circumferential Road

To Governor's Mansion,
St Jude General Hospital,
Provincial Capital Building
& Airport (1km)

R Palma Street

J Borja Street

K & C
Wharf

G Visarra Street

PLACES TO STAY
2 Everglory Hotel
3 Niza's Pension; PNB Bank
6 Sea Breeze Inn; Club Zone
12 Casa Juana; MetroCentre
   Hotel; Sundry Shop;
   JJ's Dimsum Restauarant;
   Cinema
16 Gie Gardens Hotel
28 Nisa Travelers Inn
30 Charisma Lodge
36 Chriscent Ville Pension House;
   Aboitiz Office Express

MH del Pilar Street

Agora
Market

H Grupo Street

FR Ingles Street

Lesage Street

Market

Plaza

San Jose Street

Burgos Street

To Dao Bus
& Jeepney
Station
(100m)

To Panglao Island (1km)

To Panglao Island (1.5km),
Chocolate Hills (40km)
& Jagna (63km)

PLACES TO EAT
1 Joving's Seafood Restaurant;
   MR Seafood Restaurant
8 JJ's Seafoods Village
9 Kim Leng Chinese Restaurant
19 Dante's Carinderia
24 Food Stalls
35 Dante's
40 Food Stalls
43 Garden Cafe

OTHER
4 University of Bohol
5 Trans-Asia Shipping Lines
7 Church; K & C Recreation Center
10 Shell Service Station
11 Negros Navigation Shipping
13 Provincial Hospital
14 Caltex Service Station
15 Internet Cathedral
17 Melanie's Cocktail & Music Lounge
18 Ramiro Community Hospital
20 Mercury Drugstore
21 Metrobank; Tagbilaran Friendly
   Bazaar
22 Bombay Bazaar
23 Alturas Department Store
25 City Pharmacia
26 Level Disco
27 PCI Bank
29 PCI Bank
31 AC Goldchips Internet
32 Divine Word College
33 Met Internet
34 Marbella Complex
37 B & J Internet Café
38 PT&T International Telephone Office
39 Petron Service Station
41 Main Post Office
42 Police Station; Town Hall
44 Tagbilaran Cathedral
45 PLDT International Telephone Office
46 PNB Bank

THE VISAYAS

Renolidor Street

Carlos Garcia Avenue

C Gallares Street

Miguel Parras Street

M Torralba Street

Bernadino Inting Street

Manuel Espuellas Street

JS Torralba Street

Ir Rocha Street

Ir Dagohoy St

Noli Me Tangere Street

A Clarin Street

JF Sarmiento Street

A Luna Street

0   100   200m
0   100   200yd

over the wharf, this place is worth it – a fun spot to watch the world go by.

Just off Carlos Garcia Ave on MH del Pilar St, the large *Gie Gardens Hotel* (☎ *038-411 3182*) is plushly carpeted and has comfortable singles/doubles with air-con and bath for P490/590.

One of the more recent accommodation options is the four-storey *Chriscent Ville Pension House* (☎ *038-411 4029*), on C Gallares St. It offers clean, white-tiled standard rooms for P550/650, with air-con, private bath (with plenty of hot water), telephone and cable TV. Deluxe rooms (P750/850) have all this plus a bigger TV and a few extra square metres of space. The hotel has a restaurant, a coffee shop, an Aboitiz Express ticketing office, and a Christian bookshop.

Up at the northern end of town, *Hotel La Roca* (☎ *038-411 3179*), on Graham Ave, has comfy rooms with all the mod-cons, ranging from P600 to P850. There's a swimming pool as well.

But the newest top-end kid on the block is the swanky *MetroCentre Hotel* (☎ *038-411 2599, fax 411 5866,* ✉ *metroctr@ mozcom.com*), in the heart of town, next to Casa Juana on Carlos Garcia Ave. Aimed squarely at the executive dollar, small but perfect standard rooms cost P1000, and superior/deluxe rooms cost P1200/1400. Breakfast is included, as is a stylish private bath, state-of-the-art air-con, and a private safety-deposit box. There's also a 24-hour restaurant, a business centre with Internet access, and a great tropical fishtank behind the reception desk.

Places to Eat
Most hotels have reasonably priced restaurants, but you could also try *Garden Cafe*, on JS Torralba St, a popular spot next to Tagbilaran Cathedral. It has pizza and hot pot-style Filipino dishes for P30 to P40 per serve.

For a top feed at a low price, check out the eateries by the main wharf, just down from the Everglory Hotel. *Joving's Seafood Restaurant* and *MR Seafood Restaurant* both serve excellent-value Filipino-style seafood (P80 to P100), and both are perched on crazily twisted mangrove trunks. On balmy nights, with the sea breeze floating in, these places are the best in town.

Down near the town's other wharf (affectionately known as the K&C wharf), *JJ's Seafoods Village* and the virtually open-air *Kim Leng Chinese Restaurant* serve similar fare to the two restaurants at the main wharf, but specialise in catering to big crowds and group functions. JJ's Seafoods, a little more upmarket on the outside (but a fluorescent, plastic-chair kind of place on the inside), does a great tofu-and-fish cutlet in blackbean sauce (P140). And, as an appetiser, you can indulge in 'intestines' for only P75.

For snacks and cheap eats, there's a row of *food stalls* along Bernadino Inting St that do grilled meats and stay open till late. Hearty Filipino dishes are served straight from the pan at *Dante's* and *Dante's Carinderia*, both on C Galleres St. And finally, there's the *Sundry Shop*, below MetroCentre Hotel on Carlos Garcia Ave. It's one-half souvenir shop and one-half late-night grocery shop – a handy place if you suddenly get the urge for a chocolate bar and a hand-woven basket.

Entertainment
Launched in late 1998, *Club Zone*, right next to Sea Breeze Inn on C Gallares St, is a small, low-light, high-cool kind of nightspot, complete with groovy art and a well-stocked bar. It's open daily from around 6 or 7 pm, but Tagbilaran's young hipsters don't turn up till around 11 pm. Things usually die down around 2 am. Food is available most of the night, with steaks for P80, and sandwiches for P40 to P50. There's also a thirst-quenching deal on the iced tea – P25 for all you can drink.

Not far away, on MH del Pilar St, *Melanie's Cocktail & Music Lounge* is one of several karaoke bars (or KTV bars) that entertain drinkers and wannabe-crooners until the wee hours.

Getting There & Away
Air The airport is a short tricycle ride north of town. Asian Spirit flies from Manila (P2430) at 5.30 am daily.

Boat Offices of the super-efficient Super-Cat/SeaAngels fastcraft ferries are on the M Clara St wharf (☎ 038-235 4008) and the Dao bus station (☎ 038-53913). There's also a Water Jet fastcraft office (☎ 038-235 4849) at the wharf.

Cebu & Luzon The Tagbilaran–Cebu City route is serviced by several operators. See the Bohol entry under Boat in Cebu City's Getting There & Away section, earlier, for details.

Negros Navigation sails from Tagbilaran to Manila (P740, 25 hours) on Wednesday morning, and on Saturday afternoon.

Mindanao The most popular route to Mindanao is covered daily by SuperCat/SeaAngels fastcraft, which go from Tagbilaran to Dapitan (P400) via Dumaguete on Negros. The boat leaves Dapitan for Tagbilaran via Dumaguete at 11 am.

Cebu Ferries has boats from Tagbilaran to Cagayan de Oro at noon Saturday, and in the opposite direction at midnight Saturday. Negros Navigation sails from Tagbilaran to Surigao (P225, 11 hours) on Tuesday morning. There's a Trans-Asia ferry from Cebu City to Cagayan de Oro via Tagbilaran at noon Monday.

Negros There is a SuperCat/SeaAngels fastcraft from Tagbilaran to Dumaguete (P210, 1½ hours) and back every afternoon. There's also a SuperCat/SeaAngels fastcraft sailing from Cebu City to Dumaguete (P290) via Tagbilaran (P220) in the afternoon, and one in the other direction. A boat leaves Dumaguete for Cebu City via Tagbilaran each afternoon.

Siquijor Palacio Shipping has boats to Larena on Monday, Wednesday and Friday nights, and from Larena to Tagbilaran on Tuesday, Thursday and Sunday nights.

Bus Tagbilaran's new road-transport hub is the Dao (pronounced 'dah-oh') bus and jeepney station, on E Butalid St (at the end of C Marapao St), a P10 tricycle ride south of town.

Daily buses leave from the station for destinations including Loboc (P10, 24km), Loon (P12, 27km), Tubigon (P23, 53km), Jagna (P27, 63km), Carmen (P40, 92km), Talibon (P49, 114km) and Ubay (P53, 123km). For Panglao Island, buses cost P2.50 to Dauis (4km) and P11 to Panglao town (18km).

Car Hotels in Tagbilaran are happy to organise hire cars, particularly for trips to the Chocolate Hills. See Getting There & Away in the Chocolate Hills section later.

Getting Around
Tagbilaran airport is just north of town (P5 to P10 by tricycle).

Tagbilaran's taxis are a good, time-saving alternative to jeepneys. Many of the city's surrounding attractions are a short drive away on good roads, and most drivers go by their meters.

You can get from Tagbilaran to all the surrounding towns by jeepney (P5 to P10 for an average trip). For bus information, see that entry under Getting There & Away, earlier in the Tagbilaran section.

AROUND TAGBILARAN
Maribojoc
A pretty little town about 14km north of Tagbilaran, Maribojoc (pronounced 'maree-**boo**-hoc') has a particularly lively town fiesta each year around 24 November. Buses and jeepneys run all day between here and Tagbilaran (P6).

Loon & Cabilao Island
The **church** at Loon (pronounced 'low-on') was built in 1855 and features what is claimed to be the country's longest stone staircase, at 154 steps. The stairs lead you from the church to Napo, the town's former administrative centre. The town holds its annual fiesta in early September.

Like Balicasag and Pamilacan islands (see those sections later) to the south, the island of Cabilao in the waters off Loon is a startlingly rich **dive site**, with hammerhead sharks lurking at depths of around 30m. The island's prime spot is off the north-western point, near the lighthouse. See the Mactan

Island entry in the Around Cebu City section earlier in this chapter for information on dive trips to Cabilao Island.

Getting There & Away Loon is 27km from Tagbilaran (P12 by bus or jeepney), and Cabilao Island is a quick 10km pumpboat ride from Loon. From either Panglao or Mactan islands, it can take two to three hours.

Lite Shipping boats go from Argao to Loon on Monday and Saturday at 4 and 10 am and on Sunday at 10 am.

Antequera

Antequera (pronounced 'ahn-**tee**-care-a') is about 20km from Tagbilaran. The town has its annual fiesta in early October, but comes alive every Sunday, when **basket weavers** from nearby hills bring their beautiful woven creations to market. If you want to pick up one of Bohol's best handicraft items, you should aim get to Antequera by 7 or 8 am to avoid the rush. A cab to Antequera should cost around P100. A bus or jeepney will do it for around P12.

Just out of Antequera are **Mag-aso and Inambacan Falls**, as well as some of Bohol's best **caves**. Cave guides can be tracked down in Antequera itself, or in Tagbilaran.

Corella & Tarsier Visitors Centre

Corella (pronounced 'cor-**ell**-i-a') is an attractive, jungle-fringed town with a big garden of a central square. There's nothing in particular to see, but it's a good place to get lost. Fiesta fever hits Corella on the fourth Saturday of April.

The town is about 10km from Tagbilaran and jeepneys and buses head back and forth all day (P3 to P6, 20 minutes). You could also grab a cab (P70, 15 minutes).

Beyond the of town Corella, near the village of Sikatuna, in a barrio known as Canapnapan, is the Tarsier Visitors Centre. The tarsier *(Tarsius syrichta)* is the world's smallest primate. It has oversized, human-like hands and huge, imploring eyes. To be stared at by a tarsier is to be personally accused of destroying every precious thing on the planet. And the tarsier should know.

The tarsier, a saucer-eyed primate, is another endangered species of the Philippines.

The Tarsier Visitors Centre hopes to protect what's left of the tarsier population through captive breeding programs. The breeding areas are off-limits, but a small patch of forest beside the centre allows discrete ogling of several mature tarsiers. Peer hard into the foliage and you may just see a pair of eyes staring even harder back at you. The centre includes a model of its surroundings, as well as audio-visual displays. It also offers a 12.5km hiking trail which takes visitors through tarsier country and on to Loboc, to the south. A P20 donation grants you entry, but you might like to inquire about larger donations to the centre or to the affiliated Philippine Tarsier Foundation (☎ 038-411 5928).

To get here from Tagbilaran, a taxi will cost you around P80 (20 minutes). You can catch a bus or jeepney to Corella or Sikatuna (P10, 30 minutes), but tricycles from there to the centre can be scarce. You can also hike in from Loboc along the aforementioned trail.

Bool

At Bool (pronounced 'bo-oll'), about 3km east of Tagbilaran, you'll find a monument to a blood-compact mateship ritual known as *sanduguan* (literally, 'one blood'). This is where, in 1565, Spain's Miguel Lopez de Legaspi and native chief Rajah Sikatuna downed a cup of each other's blood in one of the first symbolic gestures of western-eastern accord in the Philippines. The blood compact, sealed on 16 March 1565, is seen as the first friendly treaty achieved between local and foreign powers in the Philippines.

Baclayon

About 6km from Tagbilaran (P3 to P5 by jeepney or bus), Baclayon was founded by a pair of Spanish Jesuit priests in 1595. **Baclayon Church**, one the country's oldest, was built a year later. Baclayon is also where they make the delicious little macaroon-like biscuits called *polboron* (around P13 in many shops in Tagbilaran). The town's fiesta is in early October, and boats go from here to nearby Pamilacan Island (you'll find that entry later in this section).

Alburquerque

Whenever Bugs Bunny got lost, it was because he took a wrong turn at Alburquerque. He probably wasn't referring to *this* Alburquerque. This small coastal town is well known for its magnificent **church** and belfry, built in 1886. There are also several **waterfalls** on the edge of town. Fiesta time is early May. Alburquerque is about 12km from Tagbilaran (P6 to P10 by jeepney or bus).

Loboc

The mighty Loboc River flows past the town of the same name, creating a thundering torrent for the popular **Tontonan Falls** and the Visayas' oldest hydro-electric plant. The town is also home to the huge 18th century **San Pedro Church**. In late May to June, Loboc hosts the Balibong Kingking Festival. For more information about this and other fiestas in Loboc, ring the local tourism authority on ☎ 038-411 2642.

Opened in early 1999, *Nuts Huts* (✉ *walterken@hotmail.com*) is a feisty river-resort just out of Loboc proper. Aimed at budget travellers with a taste for adventure, its Belgian managers promise plenty of mountain biking, hiking, river exploration and travel advice along with affordable accommodation (solid, duplex native-style huts for P150 to P550). There's also a hillside restaurant serving tasty budget meals.

The resort is about 3km past Loboc, coming from Tagbilaran. Take a jeepney or tricycle from Loboc and look for the big sign on the left marking the access road. You can also catch a pumpboat up the Loboc River to the resort from Loboc, which is about 24km from Tagbilaran (P8 to P12 by jeepney or bus, about P100 by taxi).

Bilar

About 40km east of Tagbilaran, Bilar is popular for its public swimming hole, known as **Logarita Spring**. Bilar's annual fiesta is held in mid-May. It's a P18 bus ride from Tagbilaran.

Near this town is **Rajah Sikatuna National Park** (also known as Datu Sikatuna National Park), which is popular with local hikers, but not with animal welfare groups. In 1999 caged Philippines macaques, a civet cat and several birds in the care of park staff died here amid claims of poor knowledge of wildlife and careless feeding.

JAGNA

Jagna (pronounced 'hahg-na') is a largish fishing village on Bohol's southern coast, about 63km east of Tagbilaran. *Garden Café*, behind the church in the centre of town, has rooms for around P300, and offers good food. Jagna's fiesta kicks off on 29 September.

About 12km west of Jagna, **Valencia** (pronounced 'val-en-**she**-a') is home to **Badian Spring**, a popular public bathing spot with a couple of pools. The second Saturday of January is fiesta day in Valencia.

Cebu Ferries has boats between Jagna and Cagayan de Oro on Mindanao at 8 pm Sunday and from Cagayan de Oro at noon Sunday, and between Jagna and Butuan (Nasipit port) at midnight Sunday. There's an Aboitiz Express and SuperCat/Sea-Angels booking office beside the Cruztelco telephone office. Buses travel daily between Tagbilaran and Jagna (P27, one hour) and many other neighbouring towns.

PANGLAO ISLAND

Two bridges connect Bohol to Panglao, an overnight success for diving-oriented beach resorts. From a virtually deserted beach in the early 1980s, Alona Beach has become a thriving tourism community just managing to keep commercialism at bay. Most places in Alona Beach rent out motorcycles for around P600 per day.

Fiesta time in Panglao town is in late August. In Dauis, it's in mid-August.

Things to See & Do

The refreshingly cold waters of **Hinagdanan Cave**, at Bingag, on the island's northern coast, would be worth a plunge if the bats here hadn't spent years pooping in

the water. The well-lit stalactites and stalagmites are a lot more appealing. Admission is officially free, but a P5 donation is the norm. **Diving** is the most popular tourist pursuit on Panglao. Apart from revelling in underwater paradises just south of Alona Beach (see the Balicasag Island and Pamilacan Island entries later), divers also use Panglao as a base from which to reach Cabilao (see the Loon & Cabilao Island entry earlier) to the north.

Places to Stay & Eat

There's no shortage of resorts along Alona Beach. The best on offer, with singles/doubles with fan at P150/200, is *Alonaville Beach Resort* (☎ 038-411 3254). It has good, rustic rooms with common bath for P250 and attractive little rooms and cottages (mostly twins) with fan for P500.

Alona Pyramid Resort has solid, standard rooms for P300. Unusual two-storey huts are P500. Next door is *Sea Quest*

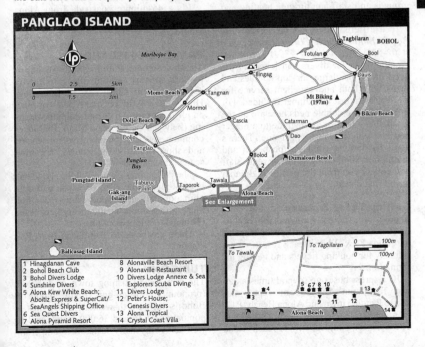

PANGLAO ISLAND

1	Hinagdanan Cave	8	Alonaville Beach Resort
2	Bohol Beach Club	9	Alonaville Restaurant
3	Bohol Divers Lodge	10	Divers Lodge Annexe & Sea Explorers Scuba Diving
4	Sunshine Divers	11	Divers Lodge
5	Alona Kew White Beach; Aboitiz Express & SuperCat/ SeaAngels Shipping Office	12	Peter's House; Genesis Divers
6	Sea Quest Divers	13	Alona Tropical
7	Alona Pyramid Resort	14	Crystal Coast Villa

THE VISAYAS

Divers. *Peter's House* is a divers' favourite, and has budget rooms from P400.

The quiet *Bohol Divers Lodge* has cottages with fan and bath from P600, and popular diving tours. *Divers Lodge* and *Sunshine Divers* nearby also have good dive tours.

At the quieter end of the beach, a really nice place to spend the night is *Alona Tropical* (☎ 0918 770 4709), which also has a deservedly popular restaurant. Cottages with fan and bath cost a rather high P800.

On the attractive, raised point at the eastern end of Alona Beach, *Crystal Coast Villa* has tidy rooms with air-con and bath from P800, and a swimming pool.

If you want to be surrounded by lots of greenery, try *Alona Kew White Beach* (☎ 0912 516 2904). It's a large, jungley compound offering cottages with fan and bath from P750 to P950 (depending on size), with air-con and bath from P1700 to P2000. There's a fine, big restaurant on the grounds and staff can arrange boating and diving excursions.

In a different area, on the beach near Bolod, *Bohol Beach Club* (Manila office ☎ 02-522 2301, fax 522 2304) is a quiet, swanky place for divers and lovers of the good life. It has large, air-con doubles and twins with bath and excellent service for US$75, breakfast and dinner included. For the money, the double beds here are on the small side – ask for an upgrade to a bigger bed and you'll probably get one. There's good snorkelling right on the beach and diving and snorkelling gear for rent. Staff will collect you from the pier in Tagbilaran if you ring ahead.

Getting There & Away

There's an Aboitiz Express and Super-Cat/SeaAngels booking office in front of the Alona Kew White Beach resort, which is handy for booking tickets and getting information.

JG Express buses go several times a day from Tagbilaran's Dao bus and jeepney station to Panglao town and Alona Beach (P11, 45 minutes). Just ask for the bus to Alona. The cheapest, simplest way to reach Alona

in a hurry is to hire a tricycle from anywhere in Tagbilaran (P100 to P150, 30 to 45 minutes).

There are often jeeps or minibuses hanging around after dropping off passengers in Alona. You can usually commandeer one of these for around P200 for a quick trip back to Tagbilaran.

BALICASAG ISLAND

About 6km south-west of Panglao, Balicasag is a magnificent **diving** spot. Low and flat, the island is ringed by a reef that drops away to impressive **submarine cliffs** as deep as 50m. Soft and hard corals can be found around the cliffs, as can trevally, barracuda, wrasse and the occasional whitetip shark. The reef has been declared a marine sanctuary.

Balicasag Island Dive Resort (Manilla ☎ 02-812 1984) has OK cottages with bath for around P2000, as well as a restaurant. It's run by the Philippine Tourism Authority (Tagbilaran ☎ 038-411 2192).

It's a 45-minute boat ride from Alona Beach to Balicasag's main drop-off spot, Duljio Point.

PAMILACAN ISLAND

The tiny island of Pamilacan (the name apparently means 'mating place of manta rays') is about 23km east of Balicasag. Highly rated by divers, the island was once an ideal spot for whale and dolphin watching (between October and May). But once-common species, including sperm whales and short-finned pilot whales, are now scarce, due to years of hunting.

The Philippines' World Wildlife Fund has been studying the state of whale and dolphin populations around Pamilacan. For more information, email the project team (@ cmu31@globe.com.ph).

There are boats to Pamilacan from Baclayon.

TUBIGON

The ramshackle fishing town of Tubigon (pronounced 'to-**bee**-gon'), in the middle of Bohol's lush north-western coast, has a population of around 36,000 people and is well served by daily fastcraft to and from

Cebu City. There's not a lot on offer here for travellers, although it is a handy access point for cutting across Bohol if you're in a hurry to see the Chocolate Hills. Fishing and farming are the mainstays of Tubigon, and its shores are mostly taken up by mangroves. In mid-May, the town celebrates its founding with a fiesta.

Places to Stay & Eat

A 15-minute walk or five-minute tricycle ride (P20) north from the central bus and market area of Tubigon is *Tinangnan Beach Resort & Lodging House*. It's a friendly, rudimentary, family-run place, with walls almost as thin as the mattresses. Rooms upstairs/downstairs are P250/200, and they come with fan, common bath and lots of mosquitoes. When the tide's in, this house on stilts is up to its knees in water, providing a pleasant lullaby if you can hear it over the TV and the howling dogs.

Getting There & Away

Boat Several boats make the trip between Tubigon and Cebu City daily. See the Bohol entry under Boat in Cebu City's Getting There & Away section, earlier in this chapter.

Bus Buses from Tubigon's market area (near the pier) pass through all day on the way to Tagbilaran (P31, 1½ hours) via towns such as Calape (P6, 15 minutes) and Loon (P16, 45 minutes). If you're heading straight for the Chocolate Hills from Tubigon, buses inland leave regularly for Carmen (P32, 1½ hours) until about 2 pm.

CALAPE & PANGANAN ISLAND

Calape (pronounced 'cal-**ah**-pay') is a lively little old coastal town about 12km from Tubigon (about 40km from Tagbilaran). It has several colonial buildings of note, including the **Municipal Building** and the towering **St Vincent Ferrer Parish**. It's hard to miss this graceful, twin-spired church, even if you're speeding by on a crowded bus. Built in the mid-1800s, it's filled with twittering birds when mass isn't in full swing. Calape's town fiesta, on 10 May is particularly fun-filled.

At the opposite end of Calape town (the northern end), a sign points the way to *Treasure Island Beach Resort* (☎ 0918 600 1388), a lonely place perched on the far end of Panganan Island. To get there, it's a long, bumpy 30-minute tricycle ride (P40) from Calape across Panganan's landbridge. The resort's facilities are basic and rather neglected, but if it's solitude you seek, this is it. There's a dorm room (P100 per person); a cluster of three cottages with private bath (P375); and one cottage down by the water (P475), with a rickety private balcony poking out over the crystalline sea. There's no restaurant as such, but food can be cooked for you on request.

Calape is a 15-minute bus or jeepney ride from Tubigon (P6). From Loon, it takes 45 minutes (P16).

CHOCOLATE HILLS

Opinion is divided over the deliciously named Chocolate Hills. One super-cynical reader has suggested they were 'planted by the Philippine government to get some tourism going on Negros'. Other travellers will tell you the hills are the most surreal natural wonder on Earth, and at sunrise on a clear morning, with the sound of the forest waking, we tend to agree with them.

Legend has it that these 1000 or so near-identical hills are the solidified teardrops of a lovelorn giant. Scientific explanations for this curious landscape are more mundane, with the boffins putting it down to volcanic activity on the ancient ocean-floor, submarine weathering, or both. In the dry season (December to May) the lawn-like vegetation roasts to a rich chocolate-brown. At any time of year, you can take great tours on the back of a motor bike (see Getting Around later) along exhilarating, winding roads to the main viewing sites, as well as to the lesser-known wonders such as the Eight Sisters Hillocks of the hills

The nearby town of Carmen is home to Fatima Hills. Pilgrims climb the steps up to the Our Lady of Fatima statue here every 13 May.

Places to Stay & Eat

The sole occupant of the utterly spectacular lookout area is the utterly disappointing *Chocolate Hills Complex*, a grotty place with tired old rooms with bath (P250) and a dorm (P75 per head) that even the lethargic staff seem embarrassed about. Of course the hills deserve better, but for the price – and the view – it's a crusty old bargain. New rooms were being built at the time of writing. The complex has a restaurant, two snakes and a poor little caged tarsier.

Getting There & Away

Bus Buses for Carmen (4km north of the Chocolate Hills) leave from the Tagbilaran bus depot near the Central Public Market hourly, on the hour (P40, two hours). St Jude Line buses make this bumpy trip, and they're often full to overflowing. A few air-con L-300 minibuses also hang around, with drivers offering to get you to the Chocolate Hills for P50 – the only problem is they'll wait there at the depot all day (and so might you) if no other passengers turn up.

From Carmen there are buses to and from Talibon (P20, two hours), Tubigon and Tagbilaran.

Car Most hotels in Tagbilaran (see the Tagbilaran section earlier) can organise a hire car to take you to and from the Chocolate Hills. The average price for a standard air-con sedan with driver for eight hours is P1300 to P1500. If you have the luxury of choosing when to go, try to get there as the sun is rising or setting.

Getting Around

At the Chocolate Hills drop-off point (on the main road, at the base of the Chocolate Hills Complex hill), there are usually a few motorcycle riders keen to whisk you up the steep hill to the complex for P5 (of course, you can also walk up the hill (20 to 30 minutes). The same bikers will take you to and from Carmen for P10.

TALIBON

Talibon (population 42,000), on Bohol's north coast, is the island's second-largest city after Tagbilaran. Its long pier has regular boats to and from Cebu, as well as to the reefy Jau (pronounced 'how') Island nearby. Talibon is also the name of a gracefully curved Visayan knife traditionally used for cutting up enemies, but these days used more for cutting up cane.

Places to Stay & Eat

On the main street, just before the pier, *Sea View Lodge* has simple little singles/doubles with fan and bath for P75/150, P400 for an air-con room.

Directly opposite is an excellent fresh-food *market* and, next to the FCRB bank, the friendly little *Costancia's Restaurant* does good main meals and great halo halo (P30).

Getting There & Away

VG Shipping Lines has five ships daily between Talibon and Cebu City (P75, three hours).

It's a four-hour bus ride from Tagbilaran to Tubigon (P40), with the Chocolate Hills almost exactly halfway (P20, two hours).

UBAY

At the opposite end of Bohol to Tagbilaran, remote Ubay is the island's largest metropolis after the capital, with a population of almost 50,000 people. Way off most travellers'

THE VISAYAS

maps, Ubay offers masses of uncharted tourism territory around nearby **Lapinin**.

J&N Lodge (☎ *0918 771 0681)*, opened in 1998, is a budget-priced place in the heart of town. Doubles with fan are P75 per person. Air-con doubles are P300 to P400.

Getting There & Away

Ubay's small 'feeder' airport has flights to Tagbilaran, and there are plans to expand airport services to other destinations.

Daily boats run to Maasin on Leyte (three hours), and there's a weekly ship from Ubay to Manila (26 hours).

Buses go daily between Ubay and Talibon, and Ubay and Jagna.

Negros

Wedged between the islands of Panay and Cebu, travellers too often treat Negros as a mere stepping stone. Surprisingly few stop to enjoy the laid-back charm of the southern university-city of Dumaguete and its surrounding beaches, or the time-capsule city of Silay on the north coast.

The island's rugged interior is home to the grumpy old volcanic giant Mt Kanlaon and several dormant relatives, while the startlingly remote south-west coast is classic Robinson Crusoe territory. The more accessible north-east coast boasts the precious Sagay Marine Reserve.

The Negrito are made up of several distinct ethnic groups, most of which are nomadic, and range across not only Negros, but also the nearby islands of Panay, Guimaras and Masbate. On Negros, the Bukidnon tribes traditionally live in the south-eastern interior, near the Twin Lakes. The Karolanos live in and around the town of Mabinay, as do the Ata. The Magahat inhabit a small southern-coastal region south of Sipalay. Hiligaynon and Ati people, both found in greater numbers on Panay and Guimaras, traditionally inhabit areas to the west and south-west of Negros' central mountain range. Apart from English, Visayan dialects dominate on Negros: Ilonggo (spoken by around 80%), Cebuano and Hiligaynon.

Since 1890 the island has been divided into two provinces – Negros Occidental to the west, with Bacolod its capital; and Negros Oriental to the east, with Dumaguete its capital. In both the major cities, and in many smaller cities and towns, historic buildings have been maintained in uncommonly good condition. Unfortunately, the same can't be said for much of the island's flora and fauna.

Negros, along with nearby Panay, has the dubious honour of having the country's highest number of endangered mammals – on average, 80% are nearing extinction. Meanwhile, Mt Kanlaon Nature Park, the island's most prominent wildlife reserve, is under threat from geothermal development. As if in retaliation, the double-cratered, 2465m-high volcano has been threatening to erupt in recent years and a 4km no-hiking zone has been imposed around it.

For more information on this and other environmental concerns on Negros, contact the local nongovernment organisation Broad Initiatives for Negros Development (BIND; ☎ 034-703 1013, fax 433 8315, ✉ bindbcd@bacolod.weblinq.com), Room 1, 2nd Floor, CGT Building, corner Luzuriaga and Locsin Sts, Bacolod City; or the Negros Forests & Ecological Foundation's breeding centre (see Things to See & Do in the Bacolod section, later).

Getting There & Away

Negros is a major destination in the Visayas, and is well connected to the rest of the Philippines by both sea and air. Because fares and schedules change with almost alarming regularity around here, it's always a good idea to do some checking of your own before you make your island-hopping plans.

Air Bacolod and Dumaguete airports are serviced by flights from Manila and Cebu City. There are also flights to Bacolod from Davao on Mindanao. See Getting There & Away in the Bacolod and Dumaguete sections later.

Boat Negros' busiest ports are Bacolod and Dumaguete, but smaller settlements on the

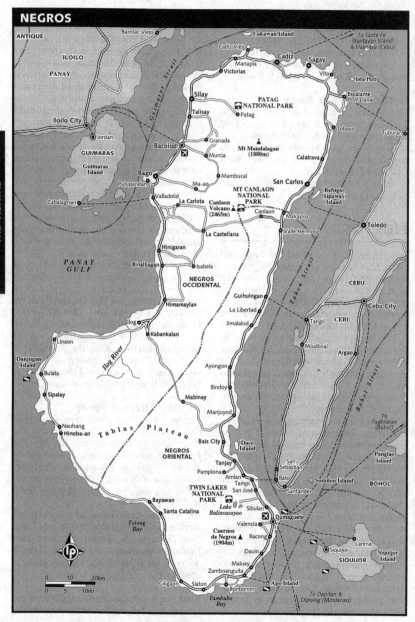

NEGROS

ANTIQUE

ILOILO

PANAY

Iloilo City

Jordan

GUIMARAS

Guimaras
Island

Cabalagnan

PANAY
GULF

Danjugan
Island

Bulata

Sipalay

Nauhang
Hinoba-an

Tablas Plateau

Linaon

Ilog River

NEGROS
ORIENTAL

Bayawan

Santa Catalina

Tolong
Bay

Giligaon

Tambubo
Bay

Barotac Viejo

Lakawan Island

Cadiz Viejo

Cadiz

Sagay

Vito

Manapla

To Sante Fe
(Bantayan Island)
& Hagnaya (Cebu)

Isla Puti

Victorias

Silay

Talisay

Patat

PATAG
NATIONAL PARK

Escalante
Port Danao

Toboso

Tuburan

Bacolod

Granada

Murcia

Mt Mandalagan
(1880m)

Calatrava

Bago

Ma-ao

Mambucal

San Carlos

Refugio
(Sipaway)
Island

Pulupandan

Valladolid

La Carlota

Canlaon
Volcano
(2465m)

MT CANLAON
NATIONAL
PARK

Canlaon

Makapso

Toledo

La Castellana

Valle Hermoso

Hinigaran

Binalbagan

Isabela

NEGROS
OCCIDENTAL

Himamaylan

Guihulngan

La Libertad

CEBU

Cebu City

Ilog

Kabankalan

Jimalalud

Tangil

CEBU

Moalboal

Argao

Ayongon

Bindoy

Bohol Strait

Manjuyod

Mabinay

Bais City

Daco Island

To
Tagbilaran
(Bohol)

Panglao
Island

Tanjay

San Sebastian

Pamplona

Amlan

Tampi

San José

Bato

Santander

Sumilon Island

BOHOL

TWIN LAKES
NATIONAL
PARK

Lake
Balinsasayao

Sibulan

Dumaguete

Valencia

Cuernos
de Negros
(1904m)

Bacong

Siquijor

Larena

Dauin

Maluay

Zamboanguita

SIQUIJOR

Siquijor
Island

Siaton

Bonbonon

Apo Island

To Dapitan &
Dipolog (Mindanao)

Guimaras
Strait

Tañon
Strait

0   10   20km
0   5   10mi

island are also accessible by boat. Major connections include ports on Bohol, Cebu, Luzon, Mindanao, Palawan, Panay and Siquijor. See individual destinations' Getting There & Away entries later in this section for information on boat services.

Getting Around

Along the north and east coasts it's 313km between Bacolod and Dumaguete, which are at opposite corners of the island. The coastal route (via San Carlos) takes seven hours, and it's wise to take an express bus if you want to avoid the many small village stops. The inland route (via Mabinay) is shorter and faster (5½ hours). Of course, hopping off anywhere along these routes is no problem.

BACOLOD

The earliest residents of Bacolod (pronounced 'back-**oll**-od') were from the nearby areas of Silay and Bago. From a small settlement of around 5000 people in 1770, it has become a vital centre of trade, and home to more than 300,000 people. This relatively young city became the capital of Negros Occidental in 1849. A bit of an acquired taste for most travellers, Bacolod does have some fine places of interest in its centre, and plenty of sights nearby.

Orientation

Jeepneys circle the central public plaza, which is surrounded by shops of all kinds, and guarded by the scary old San Sebastian Cathedral. The waiting sheds on either side of the plaza see more waiting than most – they're well-known haunts of Bacolod's prostitutes.

Near the airport, about 3km from downtown Bacolod, the late-to-bed Goldenfield Commercial Complex is four blocks of restaurants, hotels and nightspots.

Information

Tourist Offices There's an information office (☎ 034-435 1001) in the public plaza.

Post Bacolod's newly relocated post office is on Gatuslao St, near the intersection with Burgos St.

Email & Internet Access Next to the Sea Breeze Hotel on San Juan St, Chat World is open from 8 am to 9 pm Monday to Saturday (P50 per hour) and 10 am to 7 pm on Sunday (P45).

Around the corner, on Luzuriaga St, Dot@One is a self-confessed yuppie Internet cafe and bar. Its Internet rates are P50 per hour from 10 am to 7 pm, and P75 from 7 pm to 2 am. This is pure Internet chic, with terminals right at the bar, as well as on booth-style tables along the window.

The atmosphere is far more industrious at the large Capitol Institute of Technician's Internet Café, on Lacson St. This nononsense place charges the usual P50 per hour and is open from 9.30 am to 7 pm daily except Sunday.

In the Goldenfield Commercial Complex, Planet Internet (Weblink Bacolod) charges P50 per hour and is open from 9.30 am to midnight daily.

A couple of hotels also offer Internet access from their business centres (see Places to Stay – Mid-Range, later).

Things to See & Do

On Lacson St is a public plaza fronting the **Negros Museum** (☎/fax 034-433 4764), an impressive neoclassical 1930s building displaying artefacts from the region's sugar-growing industry, among other things. Dominating the main exhibition hall is the *Iron Dinosaur* steam train, which used to haul sugarcane. The museum is open from 9 am to 6 pm weekdays.

Nearby, on South Capitol Rd, is a remarkable living museum, the Negros Forests & Ecological Foundation Inc (NFEFI) **breeding centre** (☎/fax 034-433 9234, ✉ nfefi@moscom.com) – home to endangered animals endemic to Negros. With 97% of the island's original forest wiped out, this could well be one of the most precious pieces of land in the Philippines. Here you can meet Gerry, Sheila, Luis, Larry and Jane – Visayan spotted deer (also known as Prince Alfred deer); Visayan warty pigs *(buboy talunon)* – bizarre, long-snouted beasts; and leopard cats *(maral)*, which leap about like domestic kittens.

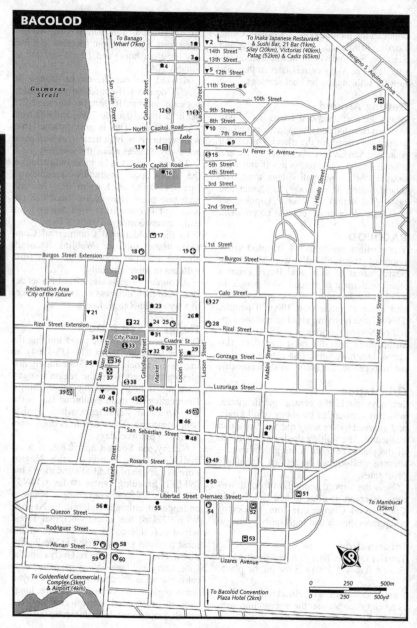

BACOLOD

To Banago
Wharf (7km)

Guimaras
Strait

Gatuslao Street

San Juan Street

Lacson Street

Benigno S Aquino Drive

To Inaka Japanese Restaurant
& Sushi Bar, 21 Bar (1km),
Silay (20km), Victorias (40km),
Patag (52km) & Cadiz (65km)

1
2
14th Street
13th Street
3
4
5   12th Street
11th Street   6
10th Street
7
12   9th Street
11   8th Street
North Capitol Road   Lake
10
13   14   7th Street
9
IV Ferrer Sr Avenue   8
15
16   5th Street
4th Street
3rd Street
2nd Street

Hilado Street

17
18   19   1st Street
Burgos Street Extension   Burgos Street

20
Galo Street
Reclamation Area
'City of the Future'
21   27
Rizal Street Extension   22
23
34   City Plaza   24 25 26   28   Rizal Street
33   31
35   36   32   30   29   Gonzaga Street
37   Market   Lacson Street
38   Luzuriaga Street
39   Locsin Street   Mabini Street
40 41   43   Lopez Jaena Street
42   44
45
46   47
San Sebastian Street   48
Rosario Street   49
50
Libertad Street (Hernaez Street)   51
56   55   54
Quezon Street   52
Rodriguez Street
Alunan Street   57   58   53   To Mambucal
59   60   Lizares Avenue   (35km)

To Goldenfield Commercial
Complex (3km)
& Airport (4km)

To Bacolod Convention
Plaza Hotel (2km)

0   250   500m
0   250   500yd

BACOLOD

PLACES TO STAY	40	Gaisano Food Plaza &	31	Negros Navigation
1 L'Fisher Hotel; L'Sea Dimsum &		Gaisano Department Store	33	Tourist Office
Noodle House; Calea Pastries			36	RCPI, PT&T International
4 Jacqueline's Pension Apartelle	**OTHER**			Telephone Offices
6 Pension Bacolod	3	Shirmano's Wine Cellar	37	Plaza Mart City Mall
23 Las Rocas Hotel	7	Ceres Liner Bus Station	38	Philippines National
26 Business Inn	8	Northern Bus Station		Bank (PNB)
29 Bascon Hotel	9	Negros Navigation; SuperCat/	39	Dot@One
30 Bacolod Pension Plaza;		SeaAngels Shipping	41	City Hall
McDonald's; Cinema	11	Philippines National	42	Bank of the Philippine
35 Sea Breeze Hotel; Air		Bank (PNB)		Islands (BPI)
Philippines; Chat World	12	Philippines National	43	Gaisano Mall
46 Halili Inn		Bank (PNB)	44	Equitable PCI Bank
47 Rosita's Hometel	14	Negros Museum	45	Capitol Institute of
48 Bacolod Executive Inn	15	Philippines National		Technician's Internet Cafe
56 Ester Pension		Bank (PNB)	49	Equitable PCI Bank
	16	Wildlife Breeding Centre	50	Morbai Maps & Charts
PLACES TO EAT	17	Main Post Office	51	Jeepneys to Mambucal
2 King Roy Lechon Manok	18	Caltex Service Station	52	Southern Bus Station
5 Vienna Kaffeehaus	19	CL Montelibano Memorial	53	Royal Express Bus Station
10 Cyber Heads Cafe & Bakery;		Regional Hospital	54	Caltex Service Station
Bank of the Philippine	20	Kama Kama Bar	55	Panaad Sports
Islands (BPI)	22	San Sebastian Cathedral		Stadium & Park
13 Food Stalls	24	Negros Navigation	57	Shell Service Station
21 Manokan Country	25	Shell Service Station	58	Caltex Service Station
32 Jollibee; Cinema	27	Equitable PCI Bank	59	Caltex Service Station
34 Reming's & Sons Restaurant	28	Caltex Service Station	60	Petron Service Station

Other creatures include sailfin lizards *(ibid)*, bleeding-heart pigeons, and a 3m-long python *(magkal)* that shares its enclosure with a succession of doomed chickens. Ironically, the chicken is the only species here that is *not* doomed.

Entry is P5/2 for adults/children, with donations gratefully accepted and urgently needed. It's open from 9 am to noon and from 2 to 4 pm weekdays. For more information, contact Gerry Ledesma or Dr Edgardo Delima at the centre. For the inspirational online story behind NFEFI, go to the Quantum Conservation Web site at www.quantum-conservation.org/NFEFI.html.

Special Events

On the weekend nearest 19 October, the city goes joyfully crazy with the annual MassKara (literally, 'many faces') Festival, which sees participants wearing – no, not eye makeup – elaborate, smiley face-masks, and dancing in the streets. The festival was launched in 1980 during one of Negros' worst economic slumps.

Held in April-May each year, the Panaad Festival (also known as Panaad sa Negros Festival), is a fantastic way to get to know Negros without leaving Bacolod. Originally a street festival, it's now held at Bacolod's Panaad Sports Stadium and Park, which has permanent displays of crafts, art and architecture from the province's 30 major towns and cities. While worth a look year-round, in April you can join in about a dozen individual minifiestas all going off at once.

Places to Stay – Budget

Pension Bacolod *(☎ 034-23883)*, on peaceful 11th St, offers good value for money: immaculate singles/doubles cost P95/145 with fan, or P155/200 with fan and bath; with air-con and bath it's P260/335. No wonder it's often fully booked.

On Gatuslao St, **Las Rocas Hotel** *(☎ 034-27011)* redefines 'basic' with its P183 single room. The bathroom is more like a tiled cupboard, and the window, with a view of a concrete wall, is sealed not with glass but with a metal grille. Doubles have less of a penitentiary feel, and go for P295. The hotel itself is dark and timber-panelled.

THE VISAYAS

The small, well-managed *Ester Pension* (☎ 034-23526), on Araneta St, has tiny rooms with fan and bath for P150/200, and with air-con and bath from P300. It's OK for the money.

Halili Inn (☎ 034-81548), on Locsin St, has a grim outlook over a large vacant lot, but its rooms are very cheap and quite inhabitable. Singles with fan and common bath are P100. Doubles with bath and air-con are P300, but they're windowless – for P100 less you get a double with window, bath and fan.

Staying at *Rosita's Hometel* (☎ 034-434 5136) is like stepping into a Philippines sitcom. The fun-loving cast includes giggly young Wilma, who runs the coffee shop and is keen to improve her English; Frieda, the coy hotel-manager; and 'Lefty John' – security guard and former boxer. Even the hotel's pink facade, which glows like a beacon on dreary Mabini St, looks to have been made for TV. Rooms are plain and clean, with good-value doubles with fan/air-con and bath for P300/400.

Places to Stay – Mid-Range

Jacqueline's Pension Apartelle (☎ 034-433 2638, fax 20754), up on 13th St, is a peculiarly designed old place, with a courtyard full of plastic plants, and a minigrocery at reception. The rooms here are OK, but don't go inspecting them too closely (we did, and found a used condom under the TV table). There are no toilet seats in the cheaper bathrooms, and the 'hot' water is lukewarm at best. Still, you can get air-con, cable TV, and a comfortable bed for P450. Twins/triples cost P550/650.

The friendly and centrally located *Bacolod Pension Plaza* (☎ 034-27076), on Cuadra St, has more than 60 quiet rooms with air-con and bath for P575 to P790.

Bascon Hotel (☎ 034-23141), on Gonzaga St, is neat, clean and has comfortable air-con singles/doubles at P550/650.

On San Juan St, the cavernous *Sea Breeze Hotel* (☎ 034-433 7994) is a good, centrally located old place with air-con, balconied rooms overlooking a forest of a courtyard. Surprisingly quiet singles/ doubles with air-con, private bath, telephone and cable TV are P670/750. Rumours about this place closing due to financial problems are, so far, nothing more than rumours. The rooms vary in standard, but most come with bedside lamps. There's not really any hot water. The food is good, and continental breakfast costs P48.

For much brighter, much newer rooms, you should try *Business Inn* (☎ 034-433 8877, fax 434 2114, @ businn@marapara .babysky.net.ph, 28 Lacson St). This immaculate place offers swish twins with private hot-water bath, soft lighting, air-con, telephone and cable TV for P690. Double-glazed windows make for blissfully silent nights. The hotel also gives you the chance to sleep your way to the top, with rooms including the 'junior executive' (P790), 'senior executive' (P890), 'presidential' (P990), and 'chairman' (P1190). There's even a managing director's room, but that's already taken by the hotel's managing director, Fatima Dela Rama. Apart from fine main meals (eg, pasta for P60 to P80), there's an excellent breakfast buffet (P135) from Wednesday to Sunday. The 'executive breakfast' (P160) is huge and meaty, the 'secretary's breakfast' (P70) is light and caffeine-free.

Another business-style hotel offering good-value accommodation is *Bacolod Executive Inn* (☎ 034-433 7401, fax 433 7442, @ executiv@lasaltech.com, 52 San Sebastian St). Comfy 'tourist' singles/doubles are P560/670, deluxe rooms are P670/780. Rooms have private hot-water bath, air-con and cable TV. This place has a business centre with Internet facilities, as does the Business Inn.

Places to Stay – Top End

Bacolod's most famous ritzy place to stay is *L'Fisher Hotel* (☎ 034-433 3730, 433 0951). On the corner of 14th and Lacson Sts, this classy giant with a massive foyer has deluxe singles/doubles for P1755/2195, super deluxe rooms for P2195/2630, and right on up to the royal suite for P7255. All rooms are plushly carpeted, with all the trappings you'd expect of a first-class hotel. The hotel's 24-hour Café Marinero looks out over an inviting swimming pool, and offers sumptuous buffet lunches for around P300.

At the other end of town, *Bacolod Convention Plaza Hotel (☎ 034-434 4551, fax 433 3757)*, on the corner of Magsaysay Ave and Lacson St, has spacious rooms well decked-out with air-con, cable TV and so on for upwards of P2000. It also has a swimming pool, tennis court, and the Four Seasons Chinese Restaurant.

Not far away, in the Goldenfield Commercial Complex, *Goldenfield Garden Hotel (☎ 034-433 3111, fax 433 1234)* looks like it was built to withstand a nuclear attack. Within its massive, sloping, concrete walls you'll find a huge foyer and large standard twin rooms for P1300. Rooms with double beds cost P1400, and deluxe rooms go for P1787. The hotel's Nihon Kitcho Japanese restaurant serves good sushi for around P250.

Places to Eat

Reming's & Sons Restaurant, near the city plaza, serves good Filipino fast-food, as does the popular *Gaisano Food Plaza* on Luzuriaga St, where Filipino and Chinese dishes for P20 to P30 are served till midnight, and live bands play most nights.

Barbecues and beers are the order of the day (and night) at the restaurants that make up the thriving *Manokan Country* eatery area, in the Reclamation Area. For similar fare up the other end of town, the busy *King Roy Lechon Manok* is a 24-hour, open-air, chicken-grilling feast-o-rama. It's opposite L'Fisher Hotel. There are also some excellent night food-stalls along Gatuslao St.

Next door to L'Fisher Hotel is *L'Sea Dimsum & Noodle House*, a very popular place offering fish tempura (P90) and generous noodle dishes. Vegetarians should know that most of the menu is meaty – even the *taosi* (a Chinese-style fermented soybean sauce, popular on spareribs and vegetables) eggplant is laced with pork. This restaurant has a takeaway booth on the street. In the same complex, *Calea Pastries* is a swanky cake shop selling slices of cake for P35, and 1-pint tubs of local ice cream for P75.

For the freshest-of-fresh bread, look for *Cyber Heads Cafe & Bakery*, on Lacson St opposite the Negros Museum and public plaza. This cafe doesn't have Internet computers – but it does have a bakery out the back, and if you head down the side of the building (on 7th St), you'll see a small window quietly advertising 'Hot Pandesal'. *Pandesals* are small, fluffy, savoury buns and these ones are sold hot out of the oven (P1 each). They're great with cheese and tomato, or whatever filling you can find. The bakery window is open from 5 to 8 am and from 3 to 5 pm daily.

Also on Lacson St, *Vienna Kaffeehaus* specialises in German dishes and big breakfasts (around P120). Its coffee is nothing special, but you do get two for the price of one (P30). And if you fancy a take-home drink, Shirmano's Wine Cellar, diagonally opposite the Vienna Kaffeehaus, has a good range of local and imported spirits and wines.

For excellent Japanese food, with plenty to please both meat-eaters and vegetarians, *Inaka Japanese Restaurant & Sushi Bar* is well worth the extra pesos. It's on the corner of 21st and Lacson Sts, up past L'Fisher Hotel. Mixed *misono* is P130, as are vegetable dishes. Sushi serves are P30 to P75, and a delicious shrimp curry with rice is P90. On Friday, the restaurant serves a huge seafood buffet for P325 per person.

Stand-out eateries in the Goldenfield Commercial Complex include *Carlo's Ristorante Italiano*, which does pizzas; the brightly lit *Seafood Market & Restaurant;* and the more relaxing *Hut Foods Native Restaurant*. Hut Foods is an open-air Filipino eatery that does good crispy shrimp for P70 and whole native chicken for P200.

Entertainment

The little *Kama Kama Bar* is a new place on Gatuslao St that has folk singers performing most nights. On the corner of 21st and Lacson St, opposite the wonderful Inaka Japanese Restaurant & Sushi Bar, is the understated *21 Bar* – perfect for an after-dinner drink.

A wander around the Goldenfield Commercial Complex in the south of town should turn up a few good forms of entertainment. Apart from the enormous *Quartermoon Castle* pub, there's the *Casino Filipino* (entry P100), several *pool halls* and a *ten-pin bowling centre*. The Goldenfield Commercial Complex is a P30 to P35 taxi ride from the centre of Bacolod.

Getting There & Away

Air Bacolod's airport has daily flights to and from Cebu City, Luzon and Mindanao. Airline offices at the airport include PAL (☎ 034-82685), Cebu Pacific (☎ 034-435 2690) and Air Philippines (☎ 034-433 9204).

Cebu Pacific flies from Cebu City to Bacolod (P1100, 30 minutes), and in the other direction, every morning. PAL flies to and from Cebu City and Bacolod on Monday, Tuesday, Friday and Saturday

Air Philippines flies from Manila to Bacolod once daily. Cebu Pacific flies from Manila to Bacolod (P2040, one hour) three times daily, with the three flights in the other direction. PAL also flies from Manila three times daily.

Cebu Pacific flies daily from Bacolod to Davao (P2900, 2½ hours) on Mindanao, via Cebu City. It has also has a daily Davao–Cebu City–Bacolod flight.

Boat Banago Wharf is about 7km north of central Bacolod – P10 by jeepney or P40 by cab. After the arrival of a ferry from Iloilo City on Panay, air-con shuttle buses will take you to the city plaza for P20.

The most popular route from Negros to Panay is the regular Bacolod–Iloilo City boat service, but you can also go via Guimaras from the town of Vallodolid, about 35km south of Bacolod.

Smooth and efficient SuperCat/Sea-Angels fastcraft ferries run ten times daily from Bacolod to Iloilo City (P195, 1½ hours) and back, between about 6 am and 5 pm. There's a SuperCat/SeaAngels information hotline in Bacolod (☎ 034-434 2350, 709 8971) and one in Iloilo City (☎ 033-336 8290, 336 1316). The SuperCat/SeaAngels office at Banago Wharf can be contacted on ☎ 034-441 0659. There's a Negros Navigation liner on Thursday evening from Cebu City to Iloilo City, then on to Bacolod, and finally Puerto Princesa (P450, 48 hours).

Bus & Jeepney The Royal Express Transport depot (☎ 034-433 0733) is on Lopez Jaena St. The Northern bus station and the Ceres bus station are a P2.50 trip from the city centre on a jeepney labelled 'Shopping'.

The shortest trip between Bacolod and Dumaguete (P100, five hours) is via Mabinay with Royal Express Transport buses. These air-con buses go from Bacolod to Dumaguete at 6 am and 1.30 pm daily, and at 10 am Monday, Wednesday and Friday. They leave Dumaguete for Bacolod at 6 am and 2 pm daily, and at 10 am Tuesday, Thursday and Saturday.

Ceres Liner buses take the longer route (P150, seven to eight hours) between Dumaguete and Bacolod, going via San Carlos. These buses leave daily, usually in the morning. It's also possible to hop off in San Carlos and catch a bus west across the mountainous interior (via Canlaon) to Bacolod (P75, four hours). Buses between San Carlos and Bacolod (P55, three hours), via Silay, go several times daily.

Ceres Liner buses also do a marathon trip between Dumaguete and Bacolod (P200, 12 hours) by going around the remote southern coast, via Sipalay and Hinoba-an.

Jeepneys run all day from Bacolod to surrounding towns, and to the nearby historic city of Silay (P5, 40 minutes).

Getting Around

A taxi from the airport to the city centre shouldn't cost more than P30. You can also catch a passing jeepney marked 'Libertad'. A taxi between downtown Bacolod and the Goldenfield Commercial Complex should cost P30 to P35.

PALAKA

Palaka, 30km south of Bacolod, is home to Game Fishing Ventures (☎ 034-433 9501, fax 433 9507, @ gamefish@bacolod.net), a fishing and recreational compound popular with families and business groups. On the main road, just south of the small city of

Bago, this place has a one-hectare lagoon filled with sea bass, bangus, eel and crabs. You can hire bamboo rafts and take to the water, or just drop a line in from the lagoon's surrounding shelters. There's also an excellent restaurant serving fish straight out of the lagoon. It's open from 8 am to 11 pm daily. Jeepneys and buses pass by here on the way to and from Bacolod (P6 to P10, 45 minutes). From the nearby town of Vallodolid, pumpboats sail regularly to Panay (via Guimaras).

LA CARLOTA

One of the six main cities in Negros Occidental, La Carlota lies about 45km south of Bacolod. With a particularly hyperactive population of around 57,000 people, the city is famous for fiestas. It's also well known among nature lovers for its lusciously ferny Guintubdan Nature Camp (see Places to Stay later), an alternative to Mambucal as a starting point for hikes into Mt Kanlaon Nature Park (see that section later).

La Carlota's annual **Kabankalan Sinulog** is a wild street-party held on the second Sunday in January. Dancers are daubed in black in honour of the island's Negrito people, and a feast is held in honour of the child Jesus. On 1 May, the city holds its annual **Pasalamat Festival**, a fun-filled, three-day thanksgiving ritual to honour the year's harvest and hard labour. A mardi-gras atmosphere and homegrown drumbeats build up to a closing ceremony with dazzling native costumes and huge parade-floats.

The city's centre is home to the stunning fortress-style 19th century **Church of Our Lady of Peace**, one of the country's best examples of Romanesque architecture. Another attraction is the La Carlota Sugar Central sugar mill. For the latest information about visiting the mill, contact the tourist information office (☎ 034-435 1001) in Bacolod.

Places to Stay & Eat

La Carlota itself is light on for accommodation. Basic huts and camping sites are available at **Guintubdan Nature Camp**, a 15km jeepney ride east of town. From here, excellent day-trips can be made into Mt Kanlaon Nature Park. Nearby, **Haguimit Hill Resort**, with its natural springs and no-frills cottages, is about 10km east of downtown La Carlota. Look for jeepneys bound for barangay Haguimit. Various **food stalls** can keep your stomach happy.

Getting There & Away

Jeepneys marked 'La Carlota' head off from Bacolod (P15, one hour) throughout the day. There are two popular jeepney-routes between Bacolod and La Carlota. One is via Bago (43km), the other via San Enrique (46km), a little farther south.

MT KANLOAN NATURE PARK & MAMBUCAL

With its dense forest and volcanic crowning-glory, the 25,000-hectare Mt Kanlaon Nature Park is particularly popular with hikers and birdwatchers. And as long as the volcano doesn't blow its top and developers can be kept out, it should stay that way. A 4km safety zone was imposed around the ominously rumbling volcano in 1998 and hikers are strongly advised to avoid the summit. The park's central highlands are rich in wildlife, including the perilously rare bleeding-heart pigeon and Philippine spotted deer. The central highlands are noted for several species of wild orchid.

Anything from day-hikes to week-long camping expeditions into the park can be arranged in Mambucal, just north of Mt Kanlaon. From Mambucal, the Wasay entrance station marks the start of the trail to Mt Kanlaon.

> ### La Carlota
>
> In September 1998, La Carlota made headlines when three young men were gunned down in a local mango orchard by security guards. The orchard was owned by the infamous Marcos crony and San Miguel beer magnate Eduardo 'Danding' Cojuangco. Take heed, and don't go pinching any mangoes in La Carlota.
>
> Mic Looby

THE VISAYAS

Places to Stay & Eat

Apart from camping in Mt Kanlaon Nature Park itself, there's adequate accommodation in Mambucal at the 24-hectare *Mambucal Resort*. Tent sites are available and basic rooms with bath cost P200 to P300. There's also a swimming pool and natural springs and waterfalls nearby. A *kiosk* sells basic meals.

Getting There & Away

Mambucal is about 35km from Bacolod, and buses make the trip daily (P15 to P20, one to two hours). You can also catch a Ceres Liner bus from the east-coast city of San Carlos along the steep road to the mountain town of Canlaon (P75, four hours) and continue to Mambucal by jeepney or motorcycle.

SILAY

The city of Silay, about 20km north of Bacolod, is a remarkable living museum. Long noted for its progressive local government and dedicated amateur historians, Silay has 31 ancestral homes, mostly built between 1880 and 1930. Two of the best are open to the public.

Silay tasted sweet success when sugarcane was planted by a French resident in the 1850s, and its pier swiftly became an international port of call. The 1898 Silay Revolution saw locals overpower their Spanish overlords and – for the first time – raise the Philippine flag as we know it today. Silay local Olympia Severino sewed her name into history by making the flag.

A golden age dawned in the early 1900s, when Silay became *the* place for European musicians and intellectuals to hang out. But its reputation as the 'Paris of Negros' wasn't to last. The waters around its pier were silting up, and Bacolod was building a bigger, better pier. In 1942 Japanese troops invaded Negros and occupied Silay, prompting the local Catholic Women's League to blacken the dome of the Church of San Diego, saving it from night bombing-raids.

SILAY

PLACES TO STAY & EAT

6	Coffee Shop
8	Baldevia Pension House; Iolo's Cafe
20	New City Cafe
25	Dunkin' Donuts

OTHER

1	Buses & Jeepneys to Barangay Hawaiian & Patag
2	Bernardino Jalandoni Ancestral House (The Pink House)
3	Petron Service Station
4	Market
5	Buses & Jeepneys to Victorias
7	Metrobank
9	Iglesia Ni Cristo Church
10	Akol Ancestral Home
11	Hofilena Ancestral Home
12	Jalandoni House
13	Green House Ancestral Home & Culture Centre
14	Police Station
15	Tourist Office; City Hall
16	Church of San Diego
17	Cine Silay Cinema
18	RCPI International Telephone Office
19	Philippines National Bank (PNB)
21	Silay Medical Clinic
22	Gamboa Ancestral Home
23	Civic Centre
24	Buses & Jeepneys to Bacolod
26	Caltex Service Station
27	Swimming Pool
28	Balay Negrense Museum

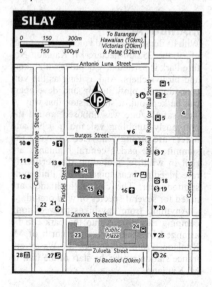

SILAY

To Barangay Hawaiian (10km), Victorias (20km) & Patag (32km)

Antonio Luna Street

Burgos Street

Zamora Street

Zulueta Street

To Bacolod (20km)

Public Plaza

Information
Staff at Silay's tourist office (☎ 034-495 0061) are very helpful. The office is on the 2nd floor of the City Hall.

Things to See & Do
Silay's past has been beautifully preserved in the form of two museums, both of which are former ancestral homes.

Built in 1908, **Bernardino Jalandoni Ancestral House** (☎ 034-495 5093), on Rizal St, is affectionately known as 'The Pink House'. Apart from the relatively new paint job, the building is said to be virtually unchanged from the days when it was home to the Jalandoni family. On display are antique law books, Japanese government banknotes from the days of occupation, an ornate four-poster bed, a 1907 Steinway piano, Chinese ceramics unearthed from around the area and many other intriguing objects. In the garden there's a kansilay tree, which lent its name to the city. The huge metal vat next to the tree was originally used to boil sugarcane juice to make *muscovado* ('poor man's sugar'). The house is open from 9 am to 5 pm daily except Monday. Entry is P10, and includes an optional guided tour.

On Cinco de Novembre St, you can't miss the **Balay Negrense Museum** (☎ 034-52263, ⓔ balay1898@hotmail.com). Also known as the Victor Gaston Ancestral Home, this spectacular house was built of balayong hardwood in 1901. Victor's father, Yves Leopold Germain Gaston, is credited with being the first to cultivate sugarcane commercially in the region. But it was the newly widowed Victor who built Balay Negrense, which has 12 identically proportioned bedrooms, and a massive living room designed to catch every passing breeze. Painstakingly restored, the house is furnished with antiques donated by locals. The ceilings are decorated with intricate woodcarvings by Chinese craftspeople, and many finely embroidered placemats are on display. In the carriageway there's an ancient four-cylinder motorcycle, along with an art gallery and gift shop. The museum is open from 10 am to 6 pm daily except Monday. Entry is P25, and includes an optional guided tour.

Designed by an Italian called Verasconi, the silver-domed **Church of San Diego** in the centre of town is topped by a crucifix that is lit at night, and was once included on international naval charts. During the 19th century it sat forlornly unfinished through years of bloody independence battles against Spanish and then US forces. On the fence around the church, several saintly statues stand guard.

Special Events
Silay has two week-long fiestas each year. The first is the charter anniversary, celebrating the birth of Silay as a city, on 12 June 1957. The second is a fiesta in honour of San Diego, who is said to watch over Silay. This fiesta kicks off on 5 November and includes a colourful street-dance competition.

Places to Stay & Eat
Unfortunately for travellers, nobody's thought to turn one of Silay's ancestral homes into an historic hotel yet. You'll have to make do with *Baldevia Pension House* (☎ 034-495 0272), on Rizal St. It's not exactly historic, but it has spotless, tiled rooms with views of the Church of San Diego dome. Standard/deluxe doubles and twins cost P450/500. All have private hot-water bath and air-con; deluxe rooms also have telephone and cable. More-spacious 'junior suites' (including a dining table) are P600. Attached to the hotel is the rather classy *Iolo's Cafe*. There's a *coffee shop* over the road, and *New City Cafe* on the main road near *Dunkin' Donuts*.

Getting There & Away
From Bacolod, jeepneys leave for Silay from Malaspina St, in the north of town (P5, 40 minutes). We never could establish where this was exactly, so it might be best to catch a taxi there (P25 to P30 from central Bacolod). These jeepneys also go past the Ceres bus station. In Silay, all buses and jeepneys heading north and south stop along Rizal St.

Getting Around
Walking around Silay is what it's all about – there's plenty of history to take in. If

you're feeling lazy, short trips around town by tricycle are no more than P2 to P3.

AROUND SILAY

The sugarcane capital of **barangay Hawaiian** is only a 15-minute ride by jeepney (P3) north of Silay, but you'll need written endorsement from the mayor before you visit the Hawaiian Philippine Sugar Company. The company apparently grew tired of looking after unannounced visitors. If you can get the required paperwork, **steam-train tours** of the company's sugarcane plantations are well worth the effort. Call the mayor's office (☎ 034-495 0061), or drop into the Silay City Hall – the mayor, and the tourism office (☎ 034-495 0061) are on the 2nd floor. You could also try contacting the Hawaiian Philippine Sugar Company (☎ 034-495 3200) directly. There's also historic sugarcane paraphernalia on display at the huge Victorias Milling Company (Vicmico) in the town of Victorias, north of Silay. Buses and jeepneys run regularly between Silay and Victorias (P8 to P10, 20 minutes).

Patag is a small village within **Patag National Park**, about 32km east of Silay (P15 by jeepney, one hour). Towards the end of WWII, the area was the scene of a bitter last stand by around 6000 Japanese soldiers and officials. Despite heavy air-and-land bombardment, starvation and high numbers of casualties, the Japanese stuck it out for more than five months before surrendering. Now a budding ecotourism area, Patag offers some great hikes from Patag village into the national park, with several **waterfalls** along the way. Overnight accommodation is limited to the *Patag Hospital* (beds for around P75). *Camping* is an attractive alternative, but you'll need to bring your own gear. To get to Patag, hop on a jeepney from the terminal at the north end of town.

NORTH-EAST COAST

This region takes in Cadiz, Sagay and Escalante, all of which have at least two buses passing through to Bacolod or Dumaguete daily. Regular jeepneys also connect these places.

Cadiz

About 65km from Bacolod, Cadiz is an important fishing port and exit point for all that Negros sugar. The city was given its present-day name in 1861 by the Spaniards, who thought the place looked a bit like the port of Cadiz back in their homeland. The city's annual Ati-Atihan Festival, in honour of patron saint Santo Niño, is held on the weekend nearest 26 January. Residents believe the holy infant protected the settlement from pirate attack.

Beside the Ceres bus station is *RL Apartelle*, offering small but OK rooms with common bath for P150 to P200.

There are daily pumpboats between Cadiz and Bantayan town (P120, 3½ hours) on Bantayan Island. Buses run from Bacolod to Cadiz (P30, 1½ hours), and from Dumaguete to Cadiz (P130, six to seven hours). There are also regular jeepneys to Sagay.

Sagay

Proclaimed a city in 1996, Sagay has wasted no time in becoming a dynamic regional hub. A combination of Old Sagay (on the coast) and New Sagay (on the National Hwy), the city has seen a frenzy of bridge building, roadworks and construction projects. Sagay City's Sinagayan Festival (in honour of St Joseph) takes place in mid- to late March.

Sagay Sugar Central and Lopez Sugar Central are the city's two **sugar mills**. To view the mills' locomotives, its best to contact the tourist information office (☎ 034-435 1001) in Bacolod.

The city is the proud guardian of the **Sagay Marine Reserve**, established in 1999 to protect one of the only areas on Negros still teeming with marine life. The sanctuary is centred on the good snorkelling spot of **Carbin Reef**, about 15km north-east of Old Sagay (one hour by pumpboat). Also here is **Maca Reef**, where flocks of migratory birds are a common sight. The nearby island of **Suyoc** can be reached on foot during low tide, when the island's giant crabs may also be wandering about. Unfortunately, recent unprecedented algal blooms have threatened the coral in the reserve. Fisherfolk and marine-reserve staff have reported a worry-ing drop in fish numbers since the outbreak.

At Pandanan Point, just outside Sagay, there's a good **beach** as well as *Pandanan Beach Resort*, where simple rooms go for around P300.

Construction of the Sagay City Develop-ment Port may well be finished by the time you read this, and boat services may be worth inquiring about. Jeepneys run regu-larly between Sagay and Cadiz, and Sagay and Escalante (30 minutes to an hour).

Escalante
Escalante, about 100km from Bacolod, was the scene of the massacre of 20 sugarcane workers by soldiers, during a long and bit-ter industrial dispute. The anniversary of the shooting (20 September) is remembered each year with street parades and speeches. A happier annual event is held on 30 May, when the town celebrates its patron, St Cruz, with a colourful street party.

The little **Isla Puti** (Enchanted Isle) is a 20-minute pumpboat ride from Escalante, and it has some attractive white-sand beaches.

Laida's Lodge, near the bus station in Es-calante, has no-frills rooms with common bath from P150.

Pumpboats go daily from Escalante's Port Danao to Tuburan on Cebu. Ceres Liner buses running between Dumaguete and Bacolod stop in Escalante. Escalante is on the bus route between Dumaguete (five to six hours) and Bacolod (2½ hours). For more information see Getting There & Away in the Bacolod section earlier.

SAN CARLOS
San Carlos is the booming port city on the east coast that connects Negros to Cebu. Fer-ries run daily between San Carlos and Toledo, on Cebu's west coast. This place isn't overflowing with charm, but it's fine for an overnight stay. There's a Metrobank and an Equitable PCI Bank on the main drag, which runs in a straight line from the pier.

The city is famed for its annual Pintaflo-res Festival, held on 5 November. This par-ticularly frenetic street festival harks back to the days when Filipinos would welcome foreign visitors by dancing en masse.

Refugio Island (also known as Sipaway Island), is a white-sand and coral outcrop about 4km off the coast of San Carlos. About 7km long and about 1.5km wide, the island has a couple of basic stores, a free public swimming pool, and some good **walking trails**. Regular pumpboats head for the island (P50 to P100, one hour) from near the main pier in San Carlos.

Places to Stay & Eat
Van's Lodging House, right next to the pier, has startlingly basic rooms with common bath for P75. You'd be more comfortable at *Coco Grove Hotel & Restaurant*, a few blocks in from the pier and about 500m from the Ceres bus station. The hotel is an airy old three-storey place with a fair bit of garden. You'll pay P100 for a dorm bed and common bath, P280/300 for singles/doubles with fan and private bath, and P500 for air-con, private bath and cable TV. The pricier rooms are quite spacious, with old timber floors and narrow balconies overlooking a leafy courtyard. A restaurant in the foyer does Filipino food and videoke.

Getting There & Away
Boats from San Carlos to Toledo (P50/70 regular/air-con, 45 minutes to 1½ hours de-pending on the boat) on Cebu sail three times daily.

There are daily buses from San Carlos' Ceres bus station (about 1km from the pier) to Dumaguete (P70, four hours), Bacolod via Silay (P55, three hours) and Bacolod via Canlaon (P75, four hours).

SOUTH-WEST COAST
Sipalay
About 200km from both Bacolod and Du-maguete, the remote town of Sipalay (pop-ulation 45,000) is surrounded by rugged **beaches** and scattered islets as beautiful as any of the country's better-known coastal areas. Boats can be hired from Sipalay for exploring the marine paradises of nearby **Maricalum Bay** and **Tinagong Dagat** (Hid-den Sea), and you'll find information about

Mine, All Mine

With the encouragement of the Mining Act of 1995, foreigners now occupy the area through gold and copper mining firms. Thus rich wildlife and tribal areas around Sipalay and nearby Hinoba-an have been mined with the blessing of successive governments. Canadian mining giant Philex Gold, the biggest primary gold producer in the Philippines, has operated an ever-expanding, open-pit mine here since 1996. As the company's unashamed corporate profile states: 'Philex Gold's vision is to become a substantial low-cost gold producer by capitalizing on the undeveloped potential of the Philippines.' You can visit Philex Gold's Web site at www.philexgold.com or send an email (paulak@philexgold.com). Such 'visions' have invoked heartfelt pleas against corporate mining by church leaders, indigenous people and environmental groups.

Mic Looby

the indigenous Magahat people at the town hall. Sipalay's annual Sacred Heart of Jesus Fiesta is held in late December.

Early settlers are thought to have come from what is now Iloilo City, on Panay. Sea trade has been vital to residents' survival ever since. The town's coastal vantage point saw it used as a strategic base by the Spanish, the Americans, and the Japanese.

Apart from a couple of basic guesthouses in town, there's **Arok Beach Resort**, a 7km walk or tricycle ride from the Ceres Liner bus station (or a P400 pumpboat ride from town). Smallish rooms with bath are P500, larger rooms are around P800.

Ceres Liner buses run between Sipalay and Bacolod (P80, 4–4½ hours) daily, and between Sipalay and Dumaguete (P120, seven to eight hours).

Danjugan

About the 3km west of the little coastal town of Bulata, the island of Danjugan (pronounced 'dan-**hoo**-gan') is within easy reach of Sipalay. A victim of dynamite fish-

ing, this virtually uninhabited 1.5km-long coral wonderland is now recovering nicely, thanks to NFEFI and the Danjugan Island Support Fund (under the auspices of UK-based the World Land Trust).

You can arrange a visit to Danjugan from nearby Bulata (30 minutes by pumpboat), but you should first contact NFEFI (Bacolod ☎/fax 034-433 9234, ✆ nfefi@moscom.com), or Coral Cay Conservation (✆ ccc@coralcay.demon.co.uk). You can visit the foundation's Web site at www.coralcay.demon.co.uk.

Bayawan

Gazing out over Tolong Bay on the remote southern end of Negros, Bayawan is about 100km from Dumaguete. Traditionally known as the rice bowl of Negros Oriental, the town is now more famous for its **Tawo-Tawo Festival**. The *tawo-tawo* is that lonely figure you may know better as a scarecrow, something Bayawan ricegrowers honour greatly. The tawo-tawo, along with other local legends such as the carabao, has been on the town's roll of honour since the festival was launched in 1987. Held every February, it fills the streets with fantastic, fully choreographed street-dances and parades.

Danjugan Island Triumph

One of the few small islands in the region that's managed to hold on to its rainforest, Danjugan came up for sale a few years ago and was bought by the environmental protection group World Land Trust, using donations. A research camp has since been established here for environmental groups and school students. Apart from reef dive sites and lagoons, Danjugan offers rugged, densely forested hills that reach a height of around 800m. It was here that Filipino researchers recently discovered the bare-backed fruit bat *Dobsonia chapmani* – formerly thought extinct – among the 10,000-or-so bats in the island's main colony. The World Land Trust has a Web site at www.worldlandtrust.org.

Mic Looby

In February 1999 the town wasn't feeling too festive as rice harvests were ruined by locust plagues. The problem was so bad, locals were being paid P15 per kilogram of locusts they brought to the municipal town hall.

Ceres Liner buses travel the surprisingly good road between Bayawan and Dumaguete (two hours) daily.

DUMAGUETE

The capital of Negros Oriental, Dumaguete (pronounced 'doo-ma-**get**-eh') is a leafy port city dominated by the large Silliman University campus, founded in 1901, and a wonderful waterfront stretch of hotels and restaurants on Rizal Blvd. Known as the 'City of Gentle People', Dumaguete's residents do indeed match the city's breezy, open and attractive feel. While other cities become ever more frantic and industrialised, Dumaguete's residents are busy pondering how best to trim their city's giant acacia trees.

Information

Money There are several banks in town, including the Philippine National Bank (PNB) on Silliman Ave, and the Equitable PCI Bank on the corner of Colon and Perdices Sts.

Post & Communications The main post office is on the corner of Santa Catalina and Pedro Teres Sts, near Rizal Park.

On Perdices St, you'll find a PT&T telephone office, and over the road next to Jollibee, an Islaphone telephone office.

Email & Internet Access A short walk from the pier, on Katada St, is Chatters Snack Bar & Internet Cafe. It's open 24 hours and charges P20 per hour for the Web, and P15 for a burger.

On Silliman Ave, near Home Quest Flats, Planetarium (P20 per hour) is open from 8.30 am to 11 pm.

If you've got a lot of emailing to do, head for Tavern Net on Ma Cristina St, a dimly lit place offering 'All You Can Surf – P150'. And if that's not enough incentive, it

also serves refillable iced teas for P25. Business hours are from 9 am to 10 pm.

Laundry The Brightwash Laundry is handily placed below the Home Quest Flats (see Places to Stay later).

Things to See & Do

A must-see in Dumaguete is Silliman University's **Anthropology Museum & Center for the Study of Philippine Living Culture**. The museum is in the central campus area, near the water at the eastern end of a big, grassy square (enter from Hibbard Ave, head past the Silliman Cafeteria, have a splash in the little Class of 1924 fountain, and stroll to the old building with the staircase at the front). A major development of this building is on the cards, but for now, it's open from 8 am to noon and from 2 to 5 pm Monday to Friday. Admission is P5. Displays include artefacts from Siquijor, as well as ancient Chinese bits-and-pieces dug up on a variety of Philippine islands.

Cockfighting, a cruel sport adored by millions, can be seen in all its chaotic glory at the **Dumaguete Cockpit**. The huge wooden stadium is next to the Ceres Liner bus station in the south of town, and fights usually happen all day Saturday.

Places to Stay

The cheapest places in town are around Silliman University (near the pier). On noisy Silliman Ave, *Jo's Lodging & Restaurant* has rock-bottom rooms with fan for P100. It's above a raucous fried chicken joint – but there's a very generous check-out time of 6 pm! Also on Silliman Ave, over Perdices St (the main drag), *Home Quest Flats* (☎ 035-225 3327) has windowless singles with fan and common bath for P176, and doubles for P283. Air-con singles/doubles (with common bath) are P292/395.

On the other side of Silliman University, *Opeña's Pension House & Restaurant* (☎ 035-225 0595, 27 Katada St) has rooms with fan for P385/440, and with air-con for P495/577.50. All have private bath and

THE VISAYAS

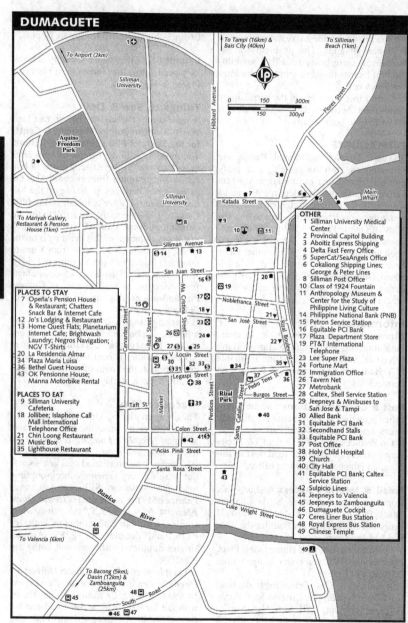

DUMAGUETE

To Airport (2km)

Silliman University

Aquino Freedom Park

Silliman University

To Mariyah Gallery, Restaurant & Pension House (1km)

Silliman Avenue

San Juan Street

Ma Cristina Street

Cervantes Street

Real Street

Taft St

Market

To Tampi (16km) & Bais City (40km)

To Silliman Beach (1km)

Hibbard Avenue

Flores Street

Katada Street

0   150   300m
0   150   300yd

Main Wharf

Noblefranca Street

San José Street

Rizal Boulevard

V Locsin Street

Legaspi Street

Rizal Park

Burgos Street

Pedro Teres St

Santa Catalina Street

Colon Street

Acias Pinili Street

Santa Rosa Street

Banica River

To Valencia (6km)

Luke Wright Street

To Bacong (5km), Dauin (12km) & Zamboanguita (25km)

South Road

OTHER
1 Silliman University Medical Center
2 Provincial Capitol Building
3 Aboitiz Express Shipping
4 Delta Fast Ferry Office
5 SuperCat/SeaAngels Office
6 Cokaliong Shipping Lines; George & Peter Lines
8 Silliman Post Office
10 Class of 1924 Fountain
11 Anthropology Museum & Center for the Study of Philippine Living Culture
14 Philippine National Bank (PNB)
15 Petron Service Station
16 Equitable PCI Bank
17 Plaza Department Store
19 PT&T International Telephone
23 Lee Super Plaza
24 Fortune Mart
25 Immigration Office
26 Tavern Net
27 Metrobank
28 Caltex, Shell Service Station
29 Jeepneys & Minibuses to San Jose & Tampi
30 Allied Bank
31 Equitable PCI Bank
32 Secondhand Stalls
33 Equitable PCI Bank
37 Post Office
38 Holy Child Hospital
39 Church
40 City Hall
41 Equitable PCI Bank; Caltex Service Station
42 Sulpicio Lines
44 Jeepneys to Valencia
45 Jeepneys to Zamboanguita
46 Dumaguete Cockpit
47 Ceres Liner Bus Station
48 Royal Express Bus Station
49 Chinese Temple

PLACES TO STAY
7 Opeña's Pension House & Restaurant; Chatters Snack Bar & Internet Cafe
12 Jo's Lodging & Restaurant
13 Home Quest Flats; Planetarium Internet Cafe; Brightwash Laundry; Negros Navigation; NGV T-Shirts
20 La Residencia Almar
34 Plaza Maria Luisa
36 Bethel Guest House
43 OK Pensionne House; Manna Motorbike Rental

PLACES TO EAT
9 Silliman University Cafeteria
18 Jollibee; Islaphone Call Mall International Telephone Office
21 Chin Loong Restaurant
22 Music Box
35 Lighthouse Restaurant

cable TV – and, apart from the screaming blue carpet, it's nice and quiet.

At the southern end of Perdices St, on Santa Rosa St, rooms at *OK Pensionne House* (☎ 035-225 5925) are indeed OK, as long as you can live without windows. Single rooms with fan are P275, and singles/doubles with air-con range from P385/440 to P550/770. The air-con rooms are set around an Arabian-style courtyard worthy of a Humphrey Bogart movie.

Overlooking the attractive Rizal Park, *Plaza Maria Luisa* (☎/fax 035-225 7994), on Legaspi St, is often full. It has singles/twins with private hot-water bath, air-con, telephone and cable TV for P450/650. A spacious 'royal suite' has all of the above plus balcony and minibar for P990. There are great views from the rooftop deck, which has a swimming pool. The pool is free to guests and open from 7 am to 8 pm. A good breakfast (P150) can be served on the rooftop, or at The Alley, a cafe on the 2nd floor.

On picturesque Rizal Blvd, the swish *Bethel Guest House* (☎ 035-225 2000, fax 225 1374, ✉ bethel@mozcom.com) is a six-storey place with spotless 'studios' (singles) and doubles with mod cons for P630.50 and P660. For great views of Dumaguete, see if you can get out onto the rooftop viewing deck.

A few blocks from Bethel Guest House, also on Rizal Blvd, is the freshly renovated *La Residencia Almar* (☎ 035-225 4724, fax 422 8466). Spanish-flavoured standard singles/doubles cost P800/1000, deluxe rooms are P900/1100, and a family room is P1500. Luxuries include air-con, private bath (complete with soft lighting), telephone and cable TV. The dearer rooms have balconies and great views of the water. Room prices include breakfast (from 7 to 10 am only) at the excellent hotel restaurant. The phone system is the only let-down. Local calls cost P5, and international calls aren't allowed unless you reverse the charges (call collect) – and even then the system is reluctant to connect you.

Places to Eat

You can get big servings of tasty Chinese and Filipino food at *Chin Loong Restau-*

rant, on the corner of San José St and Rizal Blvd; particularly recommended is the special dinner for P100, which includes bird's-nest soup. Half-serves are available and are a good idea if you want to sample a few different dishes. The restaurant has air-con in its main glassed-in section, as well as a covered outdoor-dining area, and a front bar on Rizal Blvd serving regular meals, takeaways and drinks.

One block down, *Music Box* does good Western food and is a popular, cheap eating-and-drinking hang-out. The nearby *Lighthouse Restaurant* is a fancy place serving good seafood. Within the Silliman University grounds, the big *Silliman University Cafeteria* is open to the public and serves tasty, cheap Filipino food. It fronts onto the University's attractive wide-open lawn area.

A wonderful dining experience can be had at *Mariyah Gallery, Restaurant & Pension House* (☎ 035-225 1687). Fine Filipino food (for around P200) is served in a beautiful garden, with art exhibitions and historical displays to peruse before and after. And if you just can't leave, tidy rooms with air-con are available for P575 per double. This tranquil cultural centre is in the west of town, on Larena Dr near Bogo Crossing (head west along Silliman Ave). Look for the large grassy compound with a sign indicating the Gallery Maria Cristina, as it's less often known. Business hours are from 9 am till late.

Shopping

The busy little NGV T-Shirts printing shop on Silliman Ave is always worth a look. T-shirts cost around P120, and there's an ever-changing range of Silliman University designs available – perfect for any silly man you might know. There's some good rummaging to be had at the second-hand stalls on Ma Cristina St.

Getting There & Away

Air PAL and Cebu Pacific fly regularly between Cebu City and Dumaguete. PAL has an office at Dumaguete airport (☎ 035-225 1352), just north of town. Pacific Airways offers charter flights to Siquijor.

Air Philippines flies daily from Manila to Dumaguete (one hour) and back again. There's an extra flight from Manila on Monday, Wednesday, Friday and Sunday afternoons.

Boat At the pier, you'll find the offices of the fastcraft operators SuperCat/SeaAngels (☎ 035-225 1540), Delta Fast Ferry (☎ 035-225 6358) and Water Jet (☎ 035-225 8299).

Cebu & Bohol Cokaliong Shipping, Delta Fast Ferries, SuperCat/SeaAngels and Water Jet Shipping all service the busy Cebu City–Dumaguete route. See Negros under Boat in Cebu City's Getting There & Away section for details. See Bohol, Mindanao and Siquijor in the same section for information on services from Cebu City that travel via Dumaguete.

There are boats from Dumaguete's port in Tampi (P10, 20 minutes from town by jeepney) to and from Bato (P27, 45 minutes) on Cebu every 1½ hours or so, from 5.30 am to 5 pm daily.

SuperCat/SeaAngels fastcraft sail once daily from Tagbilaran on Bohol to Dumaguete (P210, 1½ hours), and once in the opposite direction.

Luzon & Mindanao Delta Fast Ferry and SuperCat/SeaAngels both have daily fastcraft between Dumaguete and Dipolog (P185 to P210, one to two hours). WG&A/SuperFerry sails weekly between Dipolog and Manila via Dumaguete (P636, 34 hours). It's a 20-hour cruise between Manila and Dumaguete. Sulpicio Lines has a weekly boat doing the same run.

Siquijor Delta fastcraft travel between Dumaguete and Larena (P100, 45 minutes) eight times daily, and between Dumaguete and Siquijor town (P100, 45 minutes) four times daily. The services run from about 6 am to 7.30 pm.

SuperCat/SeaAngels fastcraft go direct from Dumaguete to Larena (P100, 45 minutes) in the evening, and from Larena to Dumaguete in the early morning. Palacio Shipping services the same route on Monday,

Wednesday and Friday, departing from Dumaguete in the afternoon, and from Larena in the morning. The leisurely MV *Catherine* (of Marjunnix Shipping Lines) sails from Dumaguete to Siquijor town (P40, 1½ hours) every afternoon, and in the other direction in the morning.

Bus & Jeepney The fastest bus connection between Bacolod and Dumaguete is via Mabinay (P100, five hours), with Royal Express Transport buses. In Dumaguete, the small Royal Express bus station (☎ 035-225 2234) is on South Rd, about 200m from the Ceres Liner depot, on the other side of the street.

Ceres Liner buses take the longer route between Dumaguete and Bacolod, going via San Carlos (P150, seven to eight hours). Ceres also does a marathon trip between the cities via Hinoba-an (P200, 12 hours). See Bus under Getting There & Away in the Bacolod section, earlier, for more information.

Buses and jeepneys leave from Real St for destinations north, such as San José, Bais and Tampi.

Jeepneys run all day between Dumaguete and the nearby town of Valencia (P4, 15 minutes). They leave Dumaguete from the unnamed road just south of the Banica River.

Getting Around

A tricycle into town from Dumaguete airport costs P10 to P20. There are tricycles everywhere, and motorcycles can be hired next to Chin Loong Restaurant on Rizal Blvd. Nearby, a free shuttle bus goes to El Dorado Beach Resort (see Dauin, later) at 11.30 am daily (20 minutes).

Manna Motorbike Rentals, next door to OK Pensionne House, rents out motorcycles for around P500 to P600 per day.

AROUND DUMAGUETE
Valencia

Head 6km south-east from Dumaguete along a tree-lined road and you'll find yourself at the foot of **Mt Talinis**. The mountain's twin peaks are also evocatively known as Cuernos de Negros (Horns of Negros). Valencia is a lovely town with a large, grassed central square. About 2km from the town centre, in a barrio called Terejo (pronounced 'ter-**eh**-ho') is **Banica Valley**, a richly forested area ideal for swimming, hiking and overnight stays.

Places to Stay & Eat Banica Valley Swimming Pool in barrio Terejo is a natural swimming hole that's been concreted and fenced in. Entry is P10, and the shop over the road has *rooms* upstairs for P200 (private bath, fan only). These rooms are OK if you can't get in at The Forest Camp, just around the corner.

The Forest Camp (☎ 035-225 2991, 0918 740 0527, **ⓔ** forestcamp@speed.com.ph) is on a choice stretch of river, with three landscaped pools and one natural, and Mt Talinis towering overhead. Entry here is P40/30 for adults/children. The stylish native-style huts can be rented for P1000, and food is available at a small kiosk. There's also a camping ground, a 4.5km nature-trail, and a life-affirming seven hour trek to the top of the mountain. Guides are available.

Getting There & Away Jeepneys run all day between Dumaguete and Valencia (P4, 15 minutes). In Dumaguete, jeepneys for Valencia wait for passengers at the unnamed road just south of the Banica River. You can hire a tricycle from Valencia to Banica Valley for about P10.

Twin Lakes
About 20km north-west of Dumaguete, the Twin Lakes area offers a good 15km hike from the main coastal road to two attractive crater lakes – Balinsasayao and Danao. Like the Mt Kanlaon Nature Park in the north, this unusually well-preserved forest area is under threat from power companies. In this case, a proposed hydro-electric power plant. It's also the traditional home of the indigenous Bukidnon people.

From Real St in Dumaguete, catch one of several daily buses and jeepneys heading north to the coastal town of San José (P8 to P10). Hop off about 2km before San José, or take a tricycle from the town to the start of the 15km hike to the lakes.

Bais City
About 40km north of Dumaguete, the squeaky-clean city of Bais (pronounced 'bah-iss') has managed to become both an industrial centre and a glorious ecotourism attraction.

Activities such as **snorkelling** and **island hopping** are popular around Bais, but **dolphin, whale and birdwatching** are the really special attractions here. March to September is usually the best time to spot sea mammals in Tañon Strait, which separates Negros and Cebu. Bais Bay is home to several mangrove-fringed islands making up the bird sanctuary, and the city's residents have built a network of raised walkways through the magnificent mangrove forests. For more information, contact the mayor's office (☎ 035-541 5161), in the centre of town.

Places to Stay & Eat Top of the range in Bais is *La Planta Hotel* (☎ 035-752 0307, fax 894 5725). In the middle of town, this landmark 24-room hotel has large, bright luxury twins and doubles with air-con, hot water, telephone and cable TV. Built around 1910, it's hard to believe the building was once the city's power plant. The hotel offers a four-day package deal including a double room, breakfast, a dolphin-watching and island-hopping trip and round-trip transfer between Dumaguete and Bais for P8500. Base room-prices are available on application. The hotel has an excellent coffee shop and restaurant.

The perfectly placed *Bahia de Bais Hotel* (☎ 0912 515 1899) is on nearby Dewey Islet, with gorgeous views of the bay. Comfortable rooms with bath and air-con are US$30 per double, and feature capiz windows.

Getting There & Away There are lots daily buses and jeepneys between Bais and Dumaguete (P15 to P20, one hour). In Dumaguete, many of these head off from Real St, going via other northern destinations such as San José and Tampi.

There's an Aboitiz Express and SuperCat/SeaAngels office (☎ 035-541 5002) in the centre of town.

THE VISAYAS

SOUTH-EAST COAST

A good road and plenty of buses make touring the south-east coast of Negros easy. The coast combines a string of small towns with mangrove forests, sugarcane crops and some worthwhile beaches. Accommodation options are limited, making day trips from Dumaguete a good idea.

Bacong

Bacong, about 5km from both Dumaguete and Valencia, has a wide, open central square that has a couple of statues, a soccer pitch and a tennis court. Beside the square, facing Bacong's long black-sand **beach**, is **St Augustine Church**. Built in 1849, it has a wonderfully weather-beaten bell tower, and a pipe organ in the main chapel.

At the village hall nearby, you can get information about the local **treehouses**, which overlook the beach and can be rented out (P400/600 for 12/24 hours). The official name is the Talisay Treehouse & Picnic Park. At the time of writing, the treehouses were under repair. Next to the treehouses is the **Negros Oriental Arts & Heritage Workshop**, which churns out all sorts of stoneware for export.

Dauin

The market town of Dauin has a nice 18th century **church**, and is the administrative guardian of the beautiful divers' haven of Apo (see that section later). About 1km south of Dauin is the Marine Reserve of Masaplod Norte.

Near the beach, *El Dorado Beach Resort* (☎ 035-225 7725, fax 225 4488) has rooms for P600 and cottages for around P700. It has a good restaurant and runs a free shuttle bus from Rizal Blvd in Dumaguete at 11 am daily.

If you're not using the El Dorado shuttle bus, Dauin can be a bad place to look for a lift – tricycle riders tend to see it as the end of the line, and buses and jeepneys are often too overloaded to stop on the way north to Dumaguete, or south to Zamboanguita and beyond. After an hour waiting for a ride south, we were asked by a bemused local: 'But why did you stop *here*?'

Apo Island

Rugged and volcanic, the little island of Apo is a superb **diving** spot with some gorgeous white-sand **beaches**. The island's marine life, from the high-tide mark to 500m off shore, makes up the **Apo Island Marine Reserve & Fish Sanctuary** (part of the Negros Oriental Marine Conservation Park). The sanctuary, on the south-eastern corner, is a vital marine breeding ground and a favourite among divers. Other dive sites include Mamsa Point, Rock Point, and Coconut Point.

Places to Stay & Eat A time-worn *cottage* is available for rent for around P100 on the island's south-eastern corner, beside the fish sanctuary. Basic meals can be arranged in the nearby town of Apo. For more information, ask at the mayor's office in Dauin.

On the other side of the island is *Kan Upe Cove Resort* (☎ 035-225 3299), with a restaurant and rustic cottages by the beach for around P500.

Getting There & Away Apo Island is about 25km south of Dumaguete. It can be reached directly by pumpboat from Dumaguete's Silliman Beach (1½–two hours), or from the towns of Dauin or Zamboanguita (30 to 45 minutes). Another excellent option is to take a day trip over from Siquijor (see Diving under Things to See & Do in the Siquijor section later).

Zamboanguita

At the town of Zamboanguita (pronounced 'zam-bwang-**ee**-ta'), you can stay at *Salawaki Beach Resort* (☎ 035-225 1319), about 2km from the centre of town, at the tip of a beautiful, crescent-shaped beach. This unpretentious resort is perfectly placed to catch the sunrise over Apo Island, and offers tours out to the island for around P700 per boat. The cottages (P600) weren't built to last forever, but they're solid enough and come with private cold-water bath, balcony, bedside lamp and a mosquito net (which you will probably need). The open-air restaurant serves delicious Filipino dishes for around P80.

From the main road in Zamboanguita, a tricycle to Salawaki will cost around P20. Most tricycles will stop about 200m before the resort, as the last stretch of road is soft and sandy.

Siquijor

Throughout the Philippines, Siquijor (pronounced 'see-kee-hor') has a reputation as a spooky place – its mountainous interior (around the village of San Antonio) being the traditional home of *mangkukulam* (healers). These days, Siquijor's healers can be found all over the island and their magic powers are mostly used to provide superb massage and herbal remedies.

But there's another form of magic on the island too. To witness it, choose a nice, still night in a dark corner of one of Siquijor's many gardens or forests. If you can find a native molave tree, all the better, because this kind of magic is at it's best around this precious hardwood tree. Now sit quietly and you may just see the stars begin to move around – they're fireflies. The ancestors of these fireflies apparently inspired the Spanish to call Siquijor 'Isla del Fuego' (Island of Fire).

Part coral and part limestone, Siquijor's limestone deposits lie around the coastal towns of Lazi and Maria, but only a relatively small chunk of this is viable for mining. But mined it is, much to the alarm of many local residents.

Siquijor has a fine range of resorts, all of which are small and friendly enough to make you feel special. Most have their own restaurants, or can at least arrange food given a little notice, and most also offer jeepney tours around the island, up to the caves, or to the many beaches and offshore spots for diving.

An excellent, sealed 72km coastal road rings this compact and picturesque island,

THE VISAYAS

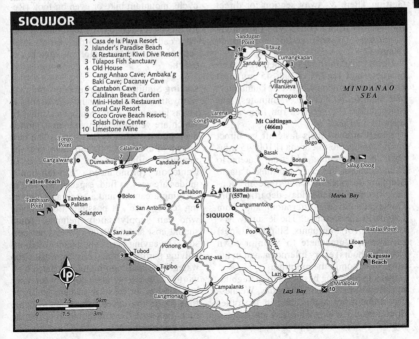

SIQUIJOR

1 Casa de la Playa Resort
2 Islander's Paradise Beach
   & Restaurant; Kiwi Dive Resort
3 Tulapos Fish Sanctuary
4 Old House
5 Cang Anhao Cave; Ambaka'g
   Baki Cave; Dacanay Cave
6 Cantabon Cave
7 Calalinan Beach Garden
   Mini-Hotel & Restaurant
8 Coral Cay Resort
9 Coco Grove Beach Resort;
   Splash Dive Center
10 Limestone Mine

MINDANAO SEA

Sandugan Point
Bitaug
Sandugan
Lumangkapan
Enrique Villanueva
Camogao
Libo
Larena
Congbagsa
Mt Cudtingan (466m)
Bogo
Salag Doog
Tongo Point
Calalinan
Cangalwang
Dumanhug
Candabay Sur
Siquijor
Basak
Bonga
Maria River
Maria
Paliton Beach
Cantabon
Mt Bandilaan (557m)
Maria Bay
Tambisan Point
Tambisan
Paliton
Solangon
Bolos
San Antonio
Cangumantong
SIQUIJOR
San Juan
Poo
Banlas Point
Ponong
Poo River
Liloan
Tubod
Cang-asa
Kagusua Beach
Tagibo
Lazi
Campalanas
Minalolan
Cangmonag
Lazi Bay

0   2.5   5km
0   1.5   3mi

making it an absolute joy to tour. Larena is its main port, Siquijor town its capital. The only telephone land-line on the island runs between Larena and Siquijor town, with most resorts hooked up by mobile phone.

The island's fiesta time is in May, when hardly a day goes by without a celebration.

Getting There & Away

Air Excellent boat connections have seen the demise of regular flights from Dumaguete or Cebu City to Siquijor's little airport, near Tambisan on the island's northwest corner. But wait! If you're desperate for a bird's-eye view, charter flights can be arranged through Pacific Airways (☎ 02-891 6252 in Manila).

Boat Delta Fast Ferries and SuperCat/SeaAngels have booking offices by the pier at Larena. Delta also has an office at the pier in nearby Siquijor town.

See Siquijor under Boat in Cebu City's Getting There & Away section for direct services from Cebu City to Larena, and for services from Cebu City to Larena via Tagbilaran (Bohol) and/or Dumaguete (Negros).

Delta fastcraft travel between Dumaguete and Larena (P100, 45 minutes) eight times daily, and between Dumaguete and Siquijor town (P100, 45 minutes) four times daily. The services run from about 6 am to 7.30 pm.

SuperCat/SeaAngels fastcraft go direct from Dumaguete to Larena (P100, 45 minutes) in the evening, and from Larena to Dumaguete in the early morning. Palacio Shipping services the same route on Monday, Wednesday and Friday, departing from Dumaguete in the afternoon, and from Larena in the morning. The leisurely MV *Catherine* (of Marjunnix Shipping Lines) sails from Dumaguete to Siquijor town (P40, 1½ hours) every afternoon, and in the other direction in the morning.

Palacio Shipping has boats from Tagbilaran (Bohol) to Larena on Monday, Wednesday and Friday nights, and in the other direction on Tuesday, Thursday and Sunday nights. It also has ships from Larena to Plaridel (near Oroquieta City on Mindanao) in the wee hours of Tuesday, Thursday and Saturday, and from Plaridel to Larena around noon Tuesday, Thursday and Sunday. There's one pumpboat boat a week from Lazi to Mindanao.

Getting Around

Jeepneys and tricycles are the main means of transport. A tricycle from Siquijor town to Larena costs P5 to P10 per person. See Things to See & Do following for details.

Things to See & Do

One of the best ways to experience Siquijor is by following its coastal road in one big, fascinating circle. By car, motorcycle or tricycle, the 72km round-trip takes a good day, allowing for leisurely stops along the way. Resorts generally charge P800 to P1200 per vehicle for guided day-trips around the island. Of course, if time isn't a problem, you can take it bit by bit, by tricycle, mountain bike or even on foot. (Resorts charge around P180 to P200 per day for bicycles, P380 to P500 for motorcycles.) The road passes through the island's main settlements, and some glorious stretches of beach.

Caving Siquijor's mysteries don't end with its mystic healers. The island's geography is just as intriguing. Limestone caves, many of which are yet to be fully explored, stretch deep into the island's dark heart. The best known of these is **Cantabon Cave**, near the mountain village of the same name. In Cantabon (pronounced 'can-**tah**-bon'), guides are easy to find, especially if you're carrying a camera and a torch and muttering 'cave, cave'. If possible, find a guide who can supply safety helmets. Tours should cost around P100 to P150 per person. The caving here is no picnic, often involving narrow, vertical climbs, waist-deep water, bats, and high humidity. But it's all worth it. Just remember not to wear your best clothes, or to swap camera lenses or film inside the caves, where microscopic fungi lurk with the sole ambition of ruining your prized Nikon.

Other great caves in this area include **Cang Anhao Cave, Ambaka'g Baki Cave**, and **Dacanay Cave**.

The best road to Cantabon from the main ring road heads up from Siquijor town from beside the Siquijor Central Elementary School, via the village of San Antonio (8km). A rougher route can be taken from San Juan, also via San Antonio (8km).

Diving Diving is popular year-round, and favourite spots include **Paliton Beach** (three submarine caves), **Salag-Doog Beach** (plenty of coral, and the odd mako shark), **Sandugan** and **Tongo** (colourful reefs). Nearby Apo Island (see that entry under South-East Coast in the Negros section earlier) opens up a whole new batch of diving options, and many divers include this on their Siquijor itinerary.

The biggest dive shop on Siquijor is Splash Dive Center (☎ 035-481 5007, fax 225 5490, ✉ splash@speed.com.ph), next to the Coco Grove Beach Resort, right on the sand looking out to the west. It's a sparkling new place with an ideal beginners' diving beach right on its doorstep (and an air-con classroom inside). Splash will take you on a beach dive for US$22, and a boat dive for US$25 (US$47 for two dives). It's US$17 to US$20 if you have your own equipment. By the time you read this, the impressive Coral Cay Resort (see Places to Stay under San Juan, later) should also have a dive shop up and running.

LARENA

The lively little port-town of Larena is Siquijor's main point of entry for travellers. The port area has many small stalls and eateries and there's always plenty of transport available to whisk you away to one of the island's many peaceful resorts.

There's a post office here (and in Siquijor town), and if you really must, you can send emails from the little computer office in Larena's main shopping street (ask for James).

Places to Stay & Eat

In Larena itself, you can stay at *Luisa & Son's Lodge*, opposite the pier, where no-frills singles/doubles with fan go for P200/250. The eatery here serves Filipino food for around P60. Having the pier and food stalls so close may be handy, but it can get very noisy and most travellers prefer the resorts out of town. On Roxas St, *Garden Orchid Bar* cooks up well-priced local food.

Three resorts share the beach of Sandugan, 6km north of Larena. A signposted turn-off from the main road points the way to all three. Follow this rough trail and it will branch off – to the right is Islander's Paradise Beach & Restaurant, and Kiwi Dive Resort – and to the left is *Casa de la Playa* (☎ 0918 740 0079), with lovingly built and lovingly decorated cottages. Named rather than numbered, and set among a thriving garden on a rise with wonderful ocean views, the cottages cost from P420 to P520 and include private bath, twin or double beds, and overhead fan. There are also cottages right on the beach.

Your gracious hosts, Terry and Emily, offer the usual snorkelling and cycling options, but that's where the comparisons with other beach resorts end. Casa de la Playa is a haven for the more contemplative traveller, with classes including painting and *hui chun gong* yoga (both P160). For P800, Terry will take you on her magical mystery tour of Siquijor. Afterwards, you can have a massage by a local healer (P150), while Freda the in-house chef prepares a local dish for you, made with vegetables straight from the garden (around P150). This place also has a big, round, open-air restaurant.

Islander's Paradise Beach & Restaurant (☎ 0918 775 2384, ✉ parabeech@ aol.com) is a welcoming, budget resort in a lovely spot. Run by Brian and Lucki, this long-established, simple paradise offers attractive, well-located beachside cottages with fan for a very reasonable P200 per night.

At *Kiwi Dive Resort* (☎ 0912 504 0596, ✉ kiwi@speed.com.ph), you'll be looked after well by Bruce and Marithes. They have a tidy, pretty little cottage (P350) with fan and private bath, on a rise above their private beach, and larger cottages on the water from P400 to P475.

SIQUIJOR TOWN

The laid-back capital of Siquijor is Siquijor town, about 8km from the main port town of Larena. Siquijor town has a lively old **market** selling excellent fresh fish. This market is soon to be shifted a few doors along to an uncharacteristically modern market complex. A short walk from the pier, the town's **coral-stone church** was built in 1783, and dedicated to St Francis of Assisi. You can climb the fortress-like bell tower, up a creaky spiral staircase, for a porthole glimpse of the town's surrounds. The bell tower wears a lovely boa around its neck – a climbing vine known as Santo Papa, which has an edible, orange-coloured fruit.

There are daily boats between Siquijor town and Dumaguete on Negros, and a Delta Fast Ferry office at the Siquijor town pier (see Boat under Getting There & Away, earlier in this section).

Places to Stay

Just 1km from Siquijor town, *Calalinan Beach Garden Mini-Hotel & Restaurant* (☎ *0912 515 0370*) has decent enough rooms (from P350 to P450) in an attractive beachside villa. All come with fan and private bath. The place is run by Nicolaas, a hefty Dutch bloke who dishes up equally hefty American breakfasts, beef curries (both P100) and homemade bread (P80). There's a basketball court nearby, as well as a couple of very bored caged monkeys.

PALITON BEACH

There's nowhere to stay on Paliton Beach, but it's one hell of a place to be stranded! About 1km from the main road (take the turn-off at the little church in Paliton village, near the island's western-most point) along a disintegrating dirt track, this beautifully stunning white-sand beach has several simple huts and the sun-bleached shell of a failed hotel. The water is clear as glass and there are also wonderful views out to Apo Island. Following the dirt track in, you first pass a small beach with about a dozen tall palm trees. You'll find the main beach a little farther on.

SAN JUAN

The little town of San Juan is blessed with its own **natural swimming pool**. The main road takes a scenic dog-leg around the pool, set in a landscaped enclosure known as Calipay's Spring Park. Entry is P5. Don't miss the nearby billboard extolling the wonders of Dr Wong's Medicinal Sulphur Soap.

About 500m past San Juan, heading southeast, you'll encounter the **San Juan Cemetery**. Creep through the central passageway between the graves (on the inland side of the road) and you'll quickly reach a dead-end – in more ways than one. Piled in a big concrete box, open to the elements, are assorted skulls and bones.

Places to Stay

Coral Cay Resort (☎ *0918 770 5578*) is right on a lovely stretch of beach at Solangon, about 3km from the town of San Juan. Run by David and Helen, Coral Cay is a resort with the lot. Right by the water, with a beach to itself, it offers jeepney tours around the island, dive tours, a swimming pool, a small thatched-roof open-air gym, mountain-bike rental (full-size, name-brand bikes P180 per day), paddleboats, kayaks, beach volleyball, table-tennis and pool, a small library, board games, and plenty of palm trees. Accommodation ranges from well-fitted-out rooms with overhead fan and private cold-water bath for P450 to P500, to balconied cottages with polished floorboards (P900 to P1000) and spacious superdeluxe air-con cottages with separate bedroom, a bar fridge and entertainment area (P1500). All have wall-mounted reading lamps. There's also a long, well-stocked bar and a restaurant serving some of the best food on the island – specialising in fresh fish (from P150), big breakfasts (P120), and Californian wines (P500 to P750).

Also about 3km from San Juan, in the opposite direction, is *Coco Grove Beach Resort* (☎ *0918 740 3707, fax 035-225 5490*). The island's longest-established resort, Coco Grove is in a stunning spot on the beach at Tubod. Behind a huge wall of local beachstone, there's a picture-perfect world of tropical gardens, pool, beach and cottages.

Cottages start at P700 and come with balcony, air-con and private cold-water bath. Bigger cottages with all of the above plus hot water are P800. For P1000, there's the lavish family deluxe. Outside the walled paradise, past the Splash Dive Center (see Diving under Things to See & Do earlier in this section), more-basic cottages (fan only) are good value at P500 – especially for divers.

Theoretically, entry to both Coral Cay and Coco Grove is P50 per person, 'consumable' – which means if you buy drinks or food, the P50 will be deducted from your bill.

LAZI
The quiet south-eastern town of Lazi (pronounced 'lah-si') is bisected by the island's only major river, the Poo (pronounced 'po-oh'). The town is home to the stylishly time-worn coral-stone **San Antonio de Padua Church**, built in 1857. Over the road is the oldest **convent** in the Philippines, a magnificent timber villa, creaky with age and eerily serene, with floorboards buffed to a high polish by years of soft footsteps. You're free to wander throughout, but donations are welcome – look for the 'Love Offering Box' in the entrance hall. Lazi's central market features a good, cheap eatery known as the *Foodhaus*.

Between the towns of Lazi and Maria, **Kagusua Beach** is reached via the pretty village of Minalolan. A good road leads from the village down to Kagusua, where steep concrete steps take you down to a string of beautiful, secluded coves.

MARIA
The **church** in the little town of Maria has a great belltower, and it houses one of the spookiest religious statues around. It's on the right as you face the altar. Locals won't say too much about this black-clad, evil-eyed figure, but they will tell you to watch for burrs on the hem of her dress – they turn up after she's been out wandering around at night … arrrrrghhhh!

SALAG-DOOG BEACH
Billed as the island's most picturesque beach, Salag-Doog is a natural marvel and a popular picnic spot. It has pristine white-sand coves and a rocky outcrop with a pagoda. Behind the pagoda, there's a long drop straight into the bright aqua waters below – just make sure it's not low tide when you take the plunge. The buildings here are a mixture of old and new, with several picnic shelters and barbecues for hire (P25). The *kiosk* is open weekends, when the place can get quite crowded. Little blue kingfishers *(ticarol)* flit about here.

The bumpy old road from Maria to Salag-Doog is about 2km long, and winds its way through a stand of molave trees, much loved by Siquijor's **fireflies**.

LIBO
The oldest house on Siquijor is right by the road near Libo, on the east coast. Home to some of the oldest people on Siquijor, it's an amazingly durable timber building, perched on high posts and gazing out to sea.

ENRIQUE VILLANUEVA
The sleepy town of Enrique Villanueva has a beautiful, sweeping **boulevard** skirting the beach and some magnificent old trees. Its church, new by Siquijor standards, is tiled with stone carted from Romblon Island.

Just north of the small town of Enrique Villanueva is the **Tulapos Fish Sanctuary** – follow the signposted turn-off left towards the beach from the main road (300m). Opened in 1986, the sanctuary covers 14 hectares of prime sandflat, beach, mangrove forest and reef. It supports 77 fisherfolk and has several **treehouses** perched high above the mangroves (presumably used to spot ocean-going trespassers). Visitors should check in at the guardhouse (or at least see if there's a guard on duty), and obey the sacred rules about not pinching shells, fish or anything else in the sanctuary. Swimming, snorkelling and diving is only allowed with the prior consent of the Department of Environment & Natural Resources (DENR). Contact its Special Concerns office in Manila on ☎ 02-926 8346.

THE VISAYAS

Panay

The large, triangular island of Panay has a number of decaying forts and watchtowers – relics from the days of the Moro pirates (see the 'More About Moors & Moros' boxed text in the Mindanao & Sulu chapter). There are also some interesting Spanish churches, especially on the south coast, which stretches from Iloilo City around the southern promontory at Anini-y to San José (Antique).

The amazing Ati-Atihan Festival, held in Kalibo in January, is the most famous fiesta of its kind in the Philippines. Much of Panay's festive spirit can be traced back to its indigenous tribal groups, namely the Ati and Ata. There are communities of both groups at the Kurong Ata Village, near Caticlan; at the Mt Tag-ao Reforestation Project south of Roxas; and at nearby Barotac Vejo. For information about anthropologically minded tours of these tribal areas, read about Panay Adventures in the Iloilo City Things to See & Do section later.

Church leaders recently urged several of the island's poorer towns to cancel their annual fiestas in the wake of the Asian financial crisis. But the townsfolk refused, and their fiestas proved to be even bigger, brighter and more morale-boosting than ever. On Panay, more than any other island, you can't keep a good fiesta down.

Getting There & Away

Air Apart from the main airport in Iloilo City, there's a string of domestic airports along Panay's north coast whisking people to and from Boracay. These are in the towns of Caticlan; Kalibo and Roxas. Iloilo City, Kalibo and Roxas are connected to Cebu City and Manila. Caticlan's airport serves flights to and from Manila and Busuanga on Palawan. Iloilo City is also connected to Davao on Mindanao. See the Iloilo City, Caticlan, Kalibo and Roxas sections later for more information on air transport.

About 15km north-east of Iloilo City, the Iloilo international airport project was approved in mid-1999, and is expected to be

---

Atis & Parties

One of the all-time favourite legends of the Philippines concerns a bunch of Malay *datus* (chiefs) of Borneo, who packed up their families and followers in AD 1250 and sailed for the greener pastures of Panay. Once there, the chiefs somehow convinced the aboriginal Ati tribe that the rich lowland area of Panay was a fair swap for a gold necklace and a hat. The generous Ati even agreed to get out of the newcomers' way by heading into the mountains, but not before holding a fantastic song and dance ritual to seal the deal. To this day, the Ati are to be found in Panay's mountain regions and their legendary party is re-enacted every year with the Ati-Atihan Festival in Kalibo, and several other towns.

Mic Looby

---

up and running by late 2000 or 2001. The site is between the towns of Cabatuan and Santa Barbara. Details about future international air routes here are sketchy, although the project has been bankrolled with plenty of *yen*, so you can expect direct flights from Japan to Panay.

Boat

Iloilo City and Kalibo (Dumaguit Port) have boat links with Cebu City. The Dumaguit, New Washington and Navitas ports (all near Kalibo) serve boats travelling to and from Manila. Caticlan and Roxas (Culasi port) are also connected to Manila by boat.

Fastcraft connect Iloilo City and Bacolod on Negros. Negros Navigation has boats from Iloilo to Cagayan de Oro, Davao, General Santos, Zamboanga, Cotabato, Ozamis and Iligan on Mindanao.

Bancas run between Roxas and Calumpang, Mandaon and Masbate, and connect Panay with Boracay, Odiongan and Santa Fe (on Tablas Island) and San Fernando (on Sibuyan Island).

See individual Getting There & Away entries for more information on transport to and from each destination.

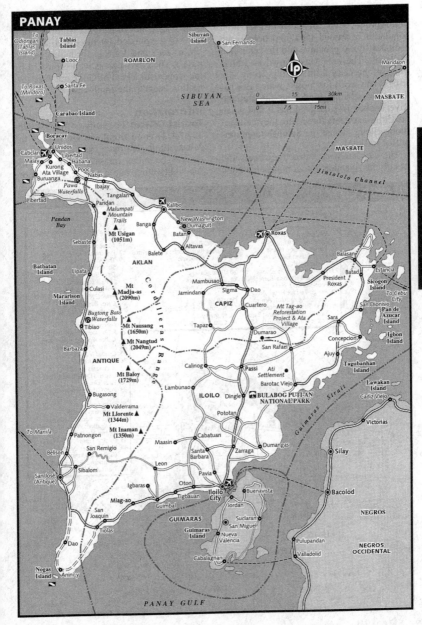

ILOILO CITY

Iloilo (pronounced 'ill-o-ill-o') City, with a population of around 350,000 people, is the capital of Iloilo province and the main hub of Panay. The area was known as Irong-Irong in the early 14th century. Irong is a Hiligaynon word for 'nose', which is what locals thought the land near the Batiano River looked like. Legend has it that when the Chinese traders turned up, they called it Illong-Illong, which the Spanish later simplified to Iloilo.

The city has wide, attractive streets and its curving riverside layout makes it a good place to explore, either on foot or with the help of a jeepney or two. 'Downtown' Iloilo City is surrounded by three old suburbs: Molo, Jaro and La Paz (pronounced 'la-pass'). The city's port is well-protected by the wonderful island of Guimaras (see that section later) to the south-east.

Information

Tourist Offices The tourist office (☎ 033-337 5411) is on Bonifacio Dr, next to the Museo Iloilo. It's open from 8 am to 5 pm daily. The maps on offer here are fine for sightseeing, but if you're doing more

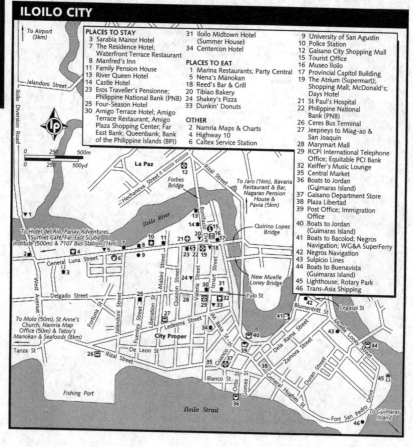

ILOILO CITY

PLACES TO STAY
3 Sarabia Manor Hotel
7 The Residence Hotel; Waterfront Terrace Restaurant
8 Manfred's Inn
11 Family Pension House
13 River Queen Hotel
14 Castle Hotel
23 Eros Traveller's Pensione; Philippine National Bank (PNB)
25 Four-Season Hotel
30 Amigo Terrace Hotel; Amigo Terrace Restaurant; Amigo Plaza Shopping Center; Far East Bank; Queenbank; Bank of the Philippine Islands (BPI)
31 Iloilo Midtown Hotel (Summer House)
34 Centercon Hotel

PLACES TO EAT
1 Marina Restaurants; Party Central
5 Nena's Manokan
18 Reed's Bar & Grill
20 Tibiao Bakery
24 Shakey's Pizza
33 Dunkin' Donuts

OTHER
2 Namria Maps & Charts
4 Highway 10
6 Caltex Service Station
9 University of San Agustin
10 Police Station
12 Gaisano City Shopping Mall
15 Tourist Office
16 Museo Iloilo
17 Provincial Capitol Building
19 The Atrium (Supermart); Shopping Mall; McDonald's; Days Hotel
21 St Paul's Hospital
22 Philippine National Bank (PNB)
26 Ceres Bus Terminal
27 Jeepneys to Miag-ao & San Joaquin
28 Marymart Mall
29 RCPI International Telephone Office; Equitable PCI Bank
32 Keiffer's Music Lounge
35 Central Market
36 Boats to Jordan (Guimaras Island)
37 Gaisano Department Store
38 Plaza Libertad
39 Post Office; Immigration Office
40 Boats to Jordan (Guimaras Island)
41 Boats to Bacolod; Negros Navigation; WG&A SuperFerry
42 Negros Navigation
43 Sulpicio Lines
44 Boats to Buenavista (Guimaras Island)
45 Lighthouse; Rotary Park
46 Trans-Asia Shipping

indepth exploring, try the offices of Morbai or Namria. Both specialise in topographical and nautical maps and charts. Morbai (☎ 033-338 1996) is on Tanza St. Namria is in the DA Building, on the corner of West Ave and General Luna St.

Money Many of Iloilo City's banks are huddled around the central area along Iznart St. Here you have all your regular banks, many with ATMs, plus the lesser-known Queenbank, which does cash advances on Visa cards.

Email & Internet Access Global Villagers, on the 3rd floor of the Gaisano City shopping mall, just over the river in La Paz. The Surfnet Café is opposite Hotel del Rio on MH del Pilar St (the western extension of General Luna St). There's another cyber-café inside The Atrium (Supermart) shopping mall, on General Luna St.

Some hotels, including Hotel del Rio, have business centres with Internet access.

Things to See & Do

The large **Museo Iloilo**, on Bonifacio Dr, has some fascinating permanent displays, including prehistoric relics of Panay, treasure plucked from sunken ships, and jewellery unearthed from Spanish burial sites. There's usually an interesting temporary exhibition of some sort also. It's open from 9 am to noon and from 1 to 5 pm daily. Entry is P10.

Just west of the city centre is the area known as **Molo**. Once a separate town, it's now more or less part of Iloilo City proper, but it retains its independence with a large central plaza. Overlooking the plaza is the wonderful **St Anne's Church**, a 19th century Gothic renaissance coral-stone structure with tall, twin spires and a domed roof. Molo is a P2.50 jeepney ride from downtown Iloilo.

North of Iloilo proper, over the Forbes Bridge (Bonifacio Dr) are the suburbs of **La Paz** and **Jaro**. Both are home to a number of ancestral houses and impressive churches. Jaro's plaza, in particular, is well worth a visit. Its Belfry Plaza, a P2.50 jeepney ride from downtown (look for jeepneys marked 'Jaro' or 'Jaro and Tiko'), is dominated by the

Belfry Tower, a lonely old figure standing high and handsome on the edge of the square.

Across the road is the huge **Jaro Metropolitan Cathedral**, the seat of the Catholic diocese in the western Visayas. Climb the cathedral's front steps and you'll come face to face with the Shrine to the Divine Infant and Nuestra Señora de la Candelaria, which is neon-lit at night. It must have been quite a sight in 1981 when Pope John Paul II addressed the people from this spot amid, as the plaque describes, 'an undreamed-of rejoicing'. An annual feast and fiesta (see Special Events later) is held here in honour of the church's patron saint, Señora de la Candelaria.

Day trips from Iloilo to other Panay attractions, as well as trips to Boracay and Guimaras, can be arranged through Panay Adventures (☎ 033-335 1171, 508 4230, fax 508 7480, ☏ panayad@iloilo.globalv.net), which is run by Daisy Yanson, an anthropology teacher at Iloilo's University of the Philippines, and a keen mountain-biker. Her young, enthusiastic team of guides and drivers can organise great tours to suit many tastes and budgets. They specialise in personalised trips for fans of mountain biking, hiking, caving, kayaking, diving, and what they call 'eco-cultural' tours of the Ati and Ata tribal areas. One of the quirkier jaunts arranged by this bunch was a tour of Panay's cemeteries. The company has its own L-300 vans, and an office at Iloilo airport, as well as at Hotel del Rio, on MH del Pilar St (see Places to Stay – Top End, later).

Despite the rich diving opportunities around Iloilo, the Far East Scuba Institute (☎/fax 033-509 2201, ☏ fesi@iloilo.net) is one of the very few diving outfits operating outside Boracay (it also has an office on Boracay – see Diving & Snorkelling under Activities in that section, later). From Iloilo, the dive shop specialises in trips to Guimaras and Nogas. And it's one of the few dive companies that advertises its rates in pesos, rather than US dollars. A single dive with full equipment and dive guide costs P750. If you've got your own wetsuit, mask, flippers and regulator, one dive is as little as P350 (including tank, weightbelt and dive guide). PADI open-water dive courses are P8000. Dive-boat hire (maximum 10 divers) is available, with prices negotiable, depending on the type of dives and dive spots. The dive centre is opposite the Hotel del Rio.

Special Events
Iloilo City is famous for its mardi gras-style **Dinagyang Festival**, held in the fourth week of January. Celebrating Santo Niño (Child Jesus) with outrageous costumes and dances, this three-day frenzy of imagination takes the form of a street party, capturing perfectly the fun-loving nature of the Illongo people – not to mention their stamina.

On 2 February every year the Jaro Metropolitan Cathedral hosts the **Nuestra Señora de la Candelaria** (Feast of Our Lady of Candles). As much a religious ritual as it is a good old-fashioned street-party, this event includes the blessing of all sorts of candles, and a spangly procession headed by the year's Jaro fiesta queen.

Also in February, on the third Sunday of the month, is the exciting **Paraw Regatta**, a race from Iloilo City over to Guimaras, in traditional sailing outriggers called *paraw*. Dating back to the 16th century, the race is a high-speed version of the trip supposedly taken by Panay's ancient Malay settlers on their journey to the island from Borneo.

Several outer suburbs and towns around Iloilo City proper hold annual **carabao races**. One such event is held in early May in Pavia, about 5km north of Iloilo City.

Places to Stay – Budget
For true budget accommodation, you can't go past *Centercon Hotel* (☎ 033-335 3431). Actually, you can very easily go past it – it's hidden down a narrow lane off JM Basa St (look for the lane entrance next to the Rose Pharmacy). Singles/doubles are P150/250 with fan and bath, P406/519 with air-con. Cable TV is P50 extra.

A couple of blocks north, past the Museo Iloilo on Bonifacio Dr, there's *Castle Hotel* (☎ 033-338 1021) and, about 200m on, *River Queen Hotel* (☎ 033-335 0176). Both have seen better days, and both have en-

trances far more impressive than their livable rooms with air-con (P433/522 at the Castle and P485/585 at the River Queen).

Around the corner, the popular *Family Pension House* (☎ 033-335 0070), on General Luna St, has clean, acceptable rooms with fan and bath for P225/300, and air-con doubles with bath and cable TV from P400.

Wander down the laneway on General Luna St, directly opposite St Paul's Hospital, and you'll find *Eros Traveller's Pensionne* (☎ 033-337 1359). A favourite with students, this casual establishment offers simple, tidy rooms with private bath and fan for P200/275 (P270/370 with air-con).

Places to Stay – Mid-Range
One of Iloilo's best is *Four-Season Hotel* (☎ 033-336 1070), on the corner of Fuentes and Delgado Sts. It looks far pricier than it is, with sparkling standard singles/doubles (with air-con, cable TV, phone and great hot showers) for P550/680. Deluxe rooms are P790/820. The swanky lobby also features a good restaurant. This place is owned by four friends fresh out of college who combined good business nous with some solid backing from their families.

On Yulo St (the eastern extension of Delgado St), the six-storey *Iloilo Midtown Hotel* (☎ 033-336 6688, fax 336 2288), also known as The Summer House, is centrally placed and good value for money. As long as you don't mind the live bands playing most nights over the road at Keiffer's Music Lounge (see Entertainment later), you should be happy with the rooms for P660/760. They come with new air-con units (which have a low, high *and* medium settings), excellent hot-and-cold showers, telephone and cable TV. There's also a coffee lounge in the lobby.

The Residence Hotel (☎ 033-335 2454), on General Luna St, is an interestingly designed place with balconied rooms overlooking the water for P870/950 and 'executive super saver' rooms without the view for P600/660. All come with hot water and cable TV. Its Waterfront Terrace Restaurant serves Filipino and Western lunch and dinner. Just down the street,

Manfred's Inn (☎ *033-335 0298, fax 336 5161)* is a modern mansion offering rooms with private bath, air-con and cable TV from P750 to P1100. It's opposite the University of San Agustin.

Nagarao Pension House (☎ *033-320 6290, fax 329 2139, 113 Seminario St, Jaro)* is in the northern suburb of Jaro, above the Bavaria Restaurant & Bar. It's a new place run by Helen and Martin, who also operate the Nagarao Island Resort, on the island of Nagarao off Guimaras (see Places to Stay & Eat under Guimaras, later). The Pension House has large, clean rooms at US$15 for one person, US$18/21 for two/three people. All rooms come with air-con and private bath. Most have cable TV. For a breezy view of the nearby Jaro Metropolitan Cathedral, you can climb up to the rooftop viewing deck.

Places to Stay – Top End

Hotel del Rio (☎ *033-335 1171)*, on MH Del Pilar St (the western extension of General Luna St), has comfortable singles/doubles for P950/1100. Larger, deluxe rooms are P1200/1400. The rooms have all the luxurious essentials such as hot water, air-con, telephone and cable TV. The hotel's Igma-an restaurant, beside the pool, does a yummy shrimp curry for P180. The hotel itself looks out over the nearby Iloilo River.

Sarabia Manor Hotel (☎ *033-335 1021, fax 337 9127,* **✉** *smx@iloilo.net)* is a large, well-run place on General Luna St. Plush twin rooms with bath, air-con and cable TV start at P1200. A nice touch is the local newspaper delivered to your door. The newly renovated hotel complex has a swimming pool (free for guests), casino, restaurant and disco.

Amigo Terrace Hotel (☎ *033-335 0908)*, on Iznart St, was the city's first modern, high-class hotel. Comfy rooms go for P1600/1800 and come with everything you'd expect for that price. Extensively revamped in 1998, this vast place has a disco, a coffee shop, a swimming pool, and the largest ballroom in the western Visayas. The Amigo Terrace Restaurant, on the ground floor, is a fancy place that dishes up

a tasty, boneless whole bangus for P180. It also has a Japanese dinner buffet on Saturday for P300 per person.

At first glance, you may not pick Iloilo's *Days Hotel* (☎ *033-337 3297, fax 336 8000)* as a first-class place to stay. It has a tiny reception desk outside the fast-food joints of The Atrium (Supermart) shopping mall, on General Luna St. But this is just an outpost. Head to the 4th floor of the shopping mall and you'll find a reception desk worthy of a hotel charging P2650 for its standard rooms. For great views down Bonifacio Dr, you'll pay P3200. Just so you know, the top room, or 'presidential suite', is P7300. All prices include continental breakfast, piping-hot water, huge beds, air-con, telephone and cable TV. At the time of writing, a promotional 50% discount applied if you stayed on a Saturday or Sunday. One reader said the Days Hotel staff deserve a special mention for going out of their way to find a less expensive hotel for him. You can visit its Web site, at www.dayshotel.com.ph.

Places to Eat

There's good Filipino food, and no cutlery in sight, at the prettily decorated *Nena's Manokan* restaurant, on General Luna St. But the most enduringly popular local-food restaurant is *Tatoy's Manokan & Seafoods*, about 8km west of town, past Molo. It's a P25 to P30 taxi ride, or P2.50 by Arevalo jeepney. It's on Arevalo Blvd, right by the water, in Arevalo.

Marina, just over the bridge on Iloilo Diversion Rd (the northern extension of West Ave), offers similarly authentic Filipino food with a strong seafood emphasis. Here you'll find several open-air restaurants laid out in a pleasant riverside compound, and your choices range from native-hut-style restaurants with live bands, to quieter dining right over the water. The menu includes a rich and tasty seafood in coconut chilli (P155) and *kare-kare* (rice with ox meat and vegetables in a thick broth) for P110. Great *buko* (coconut) shakes are P25, but of course there are also plenty of alcoholic drinks. To get here, walk from central

THE VISAYAS

Iloilo, or catch a Molo or Arevalo jeepney and hop off at the bridge (P2).

Reed's Bar & Grill, at the top of Iznart St opposite the Provincial Capitol Building, is a popular place for drinks and a hearty steak (around P120). It's open daily except Sunday.

The Atrium (Supermart) shopping mall, apart from housing McDonald's and other fast-food chains, is packed with busy little eateries and food courts, on several floors. And if you crave sweets, *Krystal Ice* here has some interesting varieties of halo halo (around P30).

At *Bavaria Restaurant & Bar*, in Jaro, Oliver the chef offers European specialities such as pork knuckles for P150. There's a wide range of European beers and spirits, and the bar stays open until midnight every night – after which, if you like, you can collapse in the Nagarao Pension House upstairs (see Places to Stay – Mid-Range, earlier).

For good baked munchies, try the big *Tibiao Bakery*, near the corner of Bonifacio Dr and General Luna St, opposite The Atrium (Supermart) shopping mall.

Entertainment

You don't need any help finding karaoke and videoke restaurants and music lounges in Iloilo, but finding other forms of entertainment can be difficult. *Keiffer's Music Lounge*, opposite the Iloilo Midtown Hotel is a fun place that tends to have more live bands and less videoke than most. *Highway 10*, on General Luna St, is a lively, open-air venue specialising in young bands and plenty of raucous drinking. At the time of writing, it's challenging its patrons to 'Party After 10'. Nothing to do with the hour of 10 pm, it refers to the 10 shooters they line up for you – if you can down all 10 and still party, you get a hangover … oh, and a Highway 10 T-shirt.

Staggering distance from Highway 10 is *Party Central*, in the Marina restaurant compound. This live music venue starts up after 8 pm and is all the rage with Iloilo's younger set. You can take it a bit easier at the serious drinking hole known as *Reed's Bar & Grill*, on Iznart St (see Places to Eat earlier).

Getting There & Away

There's a counter inside The Atrium (Supermart) shopping mall, on General Luna St, that may make life a lot easier for travellers. It's a combined ticket outlet for Air Philippines, Cebu Pacific, SuperCat/SeaAngels, Negros Navigation and WG&A/SuperFerry. It also has an official moneychanger. The counter is at the top of the first escalators.

Air Airline offices at Iloilo's Mandurriao airport (☎ 033-320 8048) include Cebu Pacific (☎ 033-320 6889), PAL (☎ 033-321 0260) and Air Philippines (☎ 033-320 8048).

PAL flies from Cebu City to Iloilo City four times a day on Monday, Tuesday, Friday and Saturday, with return flights the same days. Cebu Pacific flies from Cebu City to Iloilo City (P1300, 30 minutes) in the afternoon, with a return flight in the morning.

Air Philippines flies between Iloilo City and Manila (P1500, one hour) four times daily, from around 5 am to 6.30 pm. Cebu Pacific has about six daily services between Manila and Iloilo City (P1950), with an extra Manila-Iloilo flight on Monday, Wednesday, Friday and Sunday. PAL flies from Manila to Iloilo four times daily.

Cebu Pacific flies daily from Iloilo City to Davao (P3100, two hours) on Mindanao via Cebu City in the early morning. Davao–Iloilo City (via Cebu City) flights depart every afternoon.

Boat See the Panay entry under Boat in Cebu City's Getting There & Away section, earlier in this chapter, for information on boat services between Cebu City and Iloilo City. See Palawan in the same section for information on services to Puerto Princesa via Negros and Iloilo City.

Smooth and efficient SuperCat/SeaAngels fastcraft ferries run 10 times daily from Bacolod to Iloilo City (P195, 1½ hours) and back, between about 6 am and 5 pm. There's a SuperCat/SeaAngels information hotline in Iloilo City (☎ 033-336 8290, 336 1316) and one in Bacolod (☎ 034-434 2350, 709 8971).

There are plenty of daily ferries and pumpboats between Iloilo City and Guimaras' main ports of Buenavista and Jordan. See

Getting There & Away in the Guimaras section later for more information.

Bus Ceres Liner buses run between Iloilo City and Estancia, Roxas, and Pandan. The station is near the corner of Ledesma and Rizal Sts. Ceres buses no longer run all the way north to Kalibo and Caticlan – they terminate in Pandan, so you have to catch a jeepney from there. If you're bound for Boracay, you're better off catching a 7107 bus (P94, six hours), which goes all the way to Caticlan.

There are buses and jeepneys running all day every day to towns west of Iloilo; they may terminate in these places, or simply drop you off and keep going. Heading west from Iloilo, possible destinations include Tigbauan (22km), Guimbal (29km), Igbaras (38km), Miag-ao (40km), San Joaquin (53km), Tiolas (60km), Anini-y (80km), and San José (Antique; 96km).

Also running this route are L-300 minibuses, privately operated (and usually air-con) vehicles that, when full, head off along standard bus and jeepney routes for around the same price as the bus. Drivers tout for passengers – especially foreign passengers – at most of the main bus stations. For direct trips to Caticlan or Kalibo from Iloilo City (around P100), these are a cushy way to travel without blowing the budget.

Getting Around
To/From the Airport The airport is about 7km out and a taxi there costs about P100. Taxi drivers (and their meters) are quite reliable here.

Car Hire car companies in Iloilo include Lexus Transport Services (☎ 033-335 1171); Golden Buddleia Rentals (☎ 033-329 0887), at the Amigo Terrace Hotel; and Lopper's Car Rental (☎ 033-337 3788), at Manfred's Inn. For a late-model sedan, the going rate is about P530 for the first three hours and around P85 per hour after that, plus fuel. These rates apply only within the city limits. If you want to go to beyond Iloilo, you should inquire about the 'out-of-town' fixed rates (eg, Iloilo to San José in

Antique is around P1000 one way, plus fuel). Generally, it's about the same price to drive yourself as it is to have a driver – so save yourself a few traffic-related heart flutters and give a local driver a job.

Jeepney The ever-reliable jeepney offers a great way to explore Iloilo. For the standard P2.50 around-town rate, jeepneys marked 'La Paz', 'Jaro' and 'Tiko' will take you north of central Iloilo; 'Molo' and 'Arevalo' will take you west. Of course, they'll also bring you right back to where you started.

GUIMARAS
The brilliant little island of Guimaras (pronounced 'gim-**are**-ass' with a hard 'g') is far more than just a pleasant day trip from nearby Iloilo City. Recently made a province in its own right, Guimaras is renowned as an island playground and the home of the world's sweetest mangoes.

Big, blue tourist-friendly signs announce each attraction on the island and the scenic, winding roads have made Guimaras a hot favourite with mountain-bike riders (see Special Events later in this section). Island-hopping opportunities abound around Guimaras, with some of the best areas being around the lovely white-sand Alubihod Beach in Santa Ana Bay on the west coast; and around Nagarao, off the south-east coast.

San Miguel, the island's laidback capital, is not much more than a wide, main street. It has a PT&T telephone office, and a couple of no-nonsense foodhouses.

Things to See & Do
The time-ravaged **Navalas Church** is about 7km from Buenavista (pronounced 'bwen-a-vis-ta') on the northern end of the island, near a beachside boulevard of coconut trees. Built in the 17th century, the limestone church is fronted by some beautiful, big trees and a squat, roofless belltower which, like the church, appears to be held together by thick, creeping vines. The bell is in storage in the nearby parish convent. This site has endured several earthquakes, as well as heavy bombing during WWII, but the church facade, belltower, corner

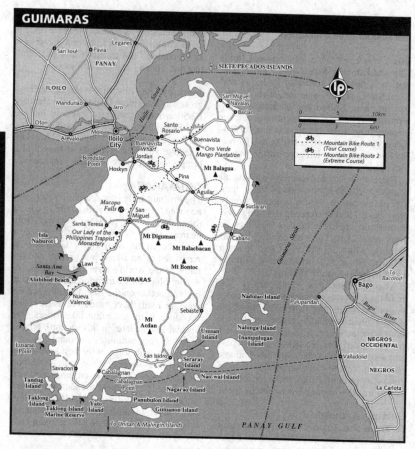

GUIMARAS

grottoes and a section of stone fence remain as testament to the strength of the original construction.

Head down the coconut boulevard from Navalas Church, towards the water, and you'll reach a villa known as **Roca Encantada** (Enchanted Rock). Perched on a rugged point between two attractive beaches, the house was built in 1910 and is the summer retreat of the wealthy Lopez family. This impressive place is a coastal landmark on the sea-route between Iloilo and Bacolod. From the beaches here you can often hire pumpboats to explore the

strange cluster of seven islands to the north, known as **Siete Pecados**, or the 'Islands of Seven Sins'.

To see the source of Guimaras' famous mangoes, try **Oro Verde mango plantation** (☎ 0912 520 0354), near Buenavista. A vast, mouth-watering stand of more than 50,000 trees (some more than 100 years old), the plantation is a very busy place come harvest time in April and May (see Special Events later). The soil in this area is reddish and acidic, which is just how mango trees like it. Contact the plantation directly to make an appointment for a visit.

Macopo Falls, just out of San Miguel (look for the hand-painted sign that says 'Farm Tourism'), offers hiking, swimming, great views, and cheap accommodation all in the one spot. Day-trippers pay P5 at the entrance booth at the car park, clamber down the steep hill trail with its carefully labelled trees, and plunge into the very welcome pool beneath the falls, which snake through pristine, rocky terrain high above. Halfway down the trail, you can picnic at thatched-roof shelters (P100 per day) or stay overnight at the four-room native-hut-style cottages with panoramic, shared-balcony views of the valley (P200 per double room). Blissfully quiet, the rooms have common bath – with the nearby falls providing a great shower (just don't pollute them with soap!). There are no stores or eateries here, so you should stock up on food in San Miguel.

Our Lady of the Philippines Trappist Monastery, on the main road south of San Miguel, looks to have landed a lucrative sponsorship deal with God. Looking more like a hotel for high-powered executive monks than a monastic retreat, this immaculate complex includes a turreted accommodation-and-seminar building, a modern church with blindingly well-polished tiles, and some prime farmland. A surprisingly humble store opposite the church sells monk-made sweets, cookies and preserves (a 320g jar of delicious *calamansi* – citrus – marmalade is P50) under the Trappist Monastic Products label. Even the bricks of the buildings here were made by the monks themselves.

To experience the underwater delights of Guimaras, contact the Far East Scuba Institute in Iloilo (☎/fax 033-509 2201, ✉ fesi@iloilo.net). This outfit offers an **island-hopping** and **snorkelling** package for P1140 per day, and a **dive trip** package for P3600 per day. Prices include transportation from Iloilo, food, and guide. Many of the resorts around Guimaras rent out snorkelling gear (around P100 per day), but the Far East Scuba Institute's Iloilo dive centre (☎/fax 033-509 2201, ✉ fesi@iloilo.net) is the closest place renting out diving gear.

Special Events

The Ang Pagtaltal Sa Guimaras draws big crowds to Jordan (pronounced 'haw-**daan**') every Good Friday (late March to April) to watch the re-enactment of Jesus Christ's crucifixion. Unlike the blood-spattering re-enactments in other parts of the country, the Guimaras presentation usually sees an amateur 'Christ' roped rather than nailed to his cross – and he's often helped up there with a few stiff drinks to overcome stage fright. After all, he has to bare (nearly) all to a sea of strangers armed with telescopic lenses. See also the boxed text 'Point Taken'. The Manggahan Sa Guimaras fiesta is held in late May. For more information about these fiestas, ring the local tourist authority on ☎ 033-503 0328.

The island's much admired mangoes are honoured every May (just after harvest time) with the Mango Festival. It's held on

Point Taken

In April 1999, the Philippines' most enduring *kristo* (symbolic Christ) decided he'd had enough of being nailed to a cross every Easter. For 11 consecutive years, Pampanga's (in Luzon) Heroshito Sangalang – a smoked-fish vendor by trade – had undergone this extreme form of Catholic Filipino *pamamanata* (holy devotion). The ritual, known as the Cenaculo, is often a painfully literal interpretation of Jesus Christ's crucifixion, death and resurrection.

First started in the 1950s by a local healer, crucifixion rituals have been condemned by the Catholic church, which has suddenly come over all squeamish after centuries of bloodthirsty reigns of terror.

But according to kristos like Sangalang, it's not the Church's tut-tutting that hurts, or even the 7cm alcohol-soaked nails driven through his freshly healed palms – it's the accusation that he does it for the money. He swears he has never earned a centavo for his suffering, unlike the touts who have recently been demanding 'viewing fees' from onlookers.

Mic Looby

the lawns in front of the Provincial Capitol Building in San Miguel.

The red soil that nourishes the island's mangoes also provides plenty of traction for its mountain-biking enthusiasts. Every February the island hosts the Guimaras International Mountain Bike Festival, a three-day event centred on a 45km rough road-circuit. For more information about the festival, contact Ed Leuenberger (☎ 033-244 0653) or Boysie Jamandre of the Iloilo Mountain Bike Association (☎ 033-200 645, fax 201 569). The association is based at the Castle Hotel in Iloilo. Of course, Guimaras is perfect for biking at any time of the year, and several resorts here rent out mountain bikes (around P300 per day).

Places to Stay & Eat

Colmenares Mountain Beach Resort (☎ 0918 761 6180), in Hoskyn, about 2km west of Jordan proper, has basic rooms with fan and bath for P150, and similar no-frills cottages for P200. There's no beach to speak of.

About 3km west of Buenavista, *Villa Encarnacion Mountain Resort* is a mountain playground for kids of all ages. It has a network of swimming pools and water slides in a large garden, with a treehouse, lily ponds, turtle pen, and small caves. It's a perfect place for a break if you're mountain biking or otherwise touring the island. Entry for day-visitors is P20/10 for adults/children), or you can linger overnight at the small cottages (fan only, common/private bath P200/300). There's a small store here selling snacks and drinks.

The *cottages* at the Macopo Falls (see Things to See & Do earlier), just outside San Miguel, make for peaceful, low-budget living.

Puerto del Mar resort (☎ 0918 761 4581) has an unusual approach by land (plus a P35 entry fee for nonguests). It's hidden behind a steep hill, next to Alubihod Beach. Follow the path around the hill, over a series of narrow land bridges, through a mangrove forest, past the heart-shaped pond, to Villa Corazon (*corazon* means 'heart'), the resort's main eating area. Beyond is a secret cove with a miniature beach, and nipa huts perched on steep hills on either side. The balconied huts go for P700/900 with private bath and fan/air-con. A couple of them have excellent, elevated views of the sea. From this sleepy spot you can hire pumpboats for trips around the many nearby islands and islets (around P200 per hour). The resort's over-the-top brochure deserves the last word here: 'Puerta del Mar is where you can feel the hand of the gentle tropical breeze as you lie trustingly in a hammock under the trees like a child.'

A short ride by pumpboat from Alubihod Beach is the thoroughly secluded *Baras Beach Resort* (☎ 0912 520 0820, ✉ barasbeach@iloilo.worldtelphil.com). Run by Peter, Mike and Baby, this place is incredibly quiet, except for the occasional wild party. Food – the best around, according to Peter – is excellent and well priced, with seafood a speciality. Breakfast is P140, lunch and dinner P175. On a hillside in a narrow cove, the resort's nine cottages have been positioned for optimum light, views and privacy, above a central white-sand beach. Each cottage is unusually spacious, with fan, private bath, and a highly seductive balcony. Prices are very reasonable at P650 (good for two) and P800 (two double beds). The beachside entertainment area includes a bar, pool tables, table tennis, and Clinton the monkey. The overly affectionate Clinton was named after Bill – watch he doesn't mistake you for Monica. You can rent snorkelling gear, power boats and sail boats (rowboat rental is free). Yachts are on hand for charter trips, but they're subject to availability and plenty of notice is needed.

The simplest way to get here is to arrange to be picked up by the resort's *Orion* pumpboat from Iloilo (P850 per boat, one hour). Otherwise, you can make your own way to Lawi, on the northern shore of Santa Ana Bay, or to nearby Alubihod Beach, and then hire a pumpboat around to the resort (P100 to P200 per boat, 20 to 30 minutes). Day-trippers are charged P50 to hang out.

Nagarao Island Resort (☎ 033-320 6290, fax 329 2139, ✉ nagarao@iloilo.net) has a small, Eden-esque island all to itself, with well-decked-out cottages costing a hefty US$60/96 per single/double. The island is off the south-east coast of Guimaras. A round-trip transfer from Iloilo (two hours one way) is US$30 for one person, US$25/20/15 for two/three/four people. These are per person rates. Banquet-like breakfasts are US$6, with lunch and dinner US$9 each. The island itself is yours to explore, and includes a freshwater swimming pool, a tennis court, jogging trails, an excavation site, 15 monkeys, two wild boar, and a forest of 'enchanted trees'. Day trips around nearby islands, or to Guimaras or Panay, range from US$30 to US$120. Check out its Web site at users.iloilo.net/nagarao.

San Miguel's foodhouses include *Tudavel's Eatery*, where a meal of *pancit* (noodles), fish and rice costs P30. A halo halo is a mere P10. Next door is *Salnor's Bakeshop*.

Getting There & Away

There are pumpboats and ferries all day every day (from around 5 am to around 6.30 pm) between Iloilo City and Guimaras. Pumpboats to Jordan (P5, 15 minutes) head off from Iloilo's Ortiz boat station, at the southern end of Ortiz St. Small ferries also operate between Iloilo and Jordan (P5, 30 minutes), leaving daily approximately every hour.

Pumpboats to Buenavista wharf (west of Buenavista town) leave from Iloilo's Parola boat station, on Muelle Loney St (P6, 20 minutes). *Parola* means 'lamp' – the boat station taking its name from the nearby shipping beacon.

Some resorts, such as the Baras Beach Resort (see Places to Stay earlier in this section), offer pick-up/drop-off services between Guimaras and Iloilo City for P850 to P1000 per boat. It's also easy to hire a pumpboat for a special ride over to Guimaras and back (around P150 one way). From Iloilo, ask at the boat stations. From Guimaras, ask at Jordan or Buenavista, or wherever there are pumpboats.

Pumpboats run daily between the west-coast Negros town of Valladolid and the southern Guimaras town of Cabalagnan.

Getting Around

Tricycles roam all over Guimaras, on sealed and unsealed roads, and cost around P100 per hour. This price easily includes waiting time at the various places of interest. Jeepneys are a common sight, mostly on the sealed road routes between the main towns. The average short-trip price is P4 to P5 (eg, Jordan to San Miguel costs P4). Pumpboats are also available for hire at port towns and many beaches. The average price per boat is about P200/800 per hour/day.

SOUTH-WEST COAST
Tigbauan

Only 22km from Iloilo City, the small town of Tigbauan (pronounced 'tig-**bow**-an') is an unassuming place centred on the **Tigbauan Church**, and a basketball court. The church, with its baroque facade, was the site of the country's first Jesuit school for boys, established in 1592.

At the eastern end of Tigbauan proper you'll find a sign pointing to *Coco Grove Beach Resort* (☎ 511 7909), where every cottage is named after a sea creature: Sea Urchin, Sea Horse, Sea Squirt and so on. With balconies, private bath, and in some cases grassy front yards, the cottages cost P400/600 with fan/air-con. Big, family cottages with fan are P700, and P1500 with air-con. There's Filipino food (around P60) served in the carefully tended garden.

Guimbal

Guimbal (pronounced '**gim**-bal' with a hard 'g') is 29km from Iloilo. It has one of the prettiest town plazas in the region, and on the western side of this plaza is the mighty sandstone landmark known as the **Guimbal Roman Catholic Church**. The church's facade was restored in 1999 and the interior features a simple, but quite beautiful, tiled aisle. Beyond the plaza, past the small Guimbal Baptist Church and down to the water, you'll find several incredibly solid, creeper-covered 17th century watchtowers squeezed in among the houses along the waterfront. Built by the Spanish, these towers, or *bantayan*, were very effective in keeping out marauding Moro (Muslim) pirates (see the

THE VISAYAS

'More About Moors & Moros' boxed text in the Mindanao & Sulu chapter).

Places to Stay & Eat *Shamrock Beach Resort (☎ 0912 520 0501)*, officially in the barrio of Nanga, is just west of Guimbal proper. Right on the water, it offers tidy, hotel-style fan rooms and cottages big enough for three to four people for P550. Similarly spacious air-con rooms and cottages start at P795. Check-out time is a rather ungenerous 10 am, but it's only enforced at peak times. 'Open huts' (picnic shelters) are available to rent for the day for P550. The resort's breezy, attractive Kildare Restaurant does *inihaw nga pusit* (grilled squid, good for two) for P88. Above the restaurant is the Shamrock Music Bar, open from 6 pm to 2 am nightly, and chess sets, darts and pool are also available.

About 1km west of the Shamrock is the vast *Bantayan Beach Resort (☎ 0973 200911)*. A popular and laidback place on the water, it has cottages at P750 (good for two people) and P1200 (good for six). Large rooms with balconies are P750 (good for two), P850 (good for six) and P1200 (good for 10!). Check-out time is a positively unfair 9 am but, as at the Shamrock, this is only enforced when the place is really busy. The canteen here serves excellent-value meals, such as chicken curry for P40. In the fishtank next to the canteen are a couple of young hammerhead sharks, and out in the carpark a row of cages house guinea pigs, parakeets and quails (known locally as *umbok*).

Nadsadjan Waterfall

Nadsadjan (pronounced 'nad-sad-han') Waterfall is a 15m-high torrent with a deep swimming hole at the base. To get there, take the inland road from Miag-ao.

A longer, but very scenic, route is to go via the rural town of **Igbaras** (pronounced '**igg**-bar-ass'), 10km to 12km inland from Guimbal. All up, Igbaras is 38km from Iloilo – take the signposted road at the western end of Guimbal. Jeepneys (P5) drop you at the dishevelled town plaza next to an old fort and – as always – a basketball court. From

here, the challenge is to make it to the falls. By whatever mode you can muster, take the street from the plaza towards the mountains, past Jocelyn Store, along a glorious, very rough road through a deep valley. You should cross the river three times, and pass through the rice-terrace village of **Igtalongon**, before finally arriving at the falls. Jeepneys do make the bumpy trip out to Igtalongon (and sometimes beyond), but you definitely shouldn't count on them.

Miag-ao

The attractive town of Miag-ao (pronounced 'mee-**ah**-gow') occupies a hill exactly 40km from Iloilo City. Taking pride of place at the top of this hill is the imposing **Miag-ao Church** (officially known as Santo Tomas de Villanueva), one of four Philippine churches to have made Unesco's world heritage list. Built between 1787 and 1797, the church was damaged by revolutionary fighting in 1898, fire in 1910 and earthquake in 1940. Seemingly indestructible, this prime example of Philippine rococo was restored to its former glory in 1962. Its bas-relief facade depicts St Christopher strolling through a tropical forest with baby Jesus.

At the eastern end of town, *Sea Breeze Beach Resort* has cottages with fan and private bath for P200 to P300. Cottages with air-con are P500. The black-sand beach here isn't much to look at, but there are picnic shelters available, along with chess sets. To get here, turn left off the main road at the ruins of an ancient bridge.

Nearer the Miag-ao Church, just to the west on the main road, is *Sulu Garden Restaurant*, serving good Filipino food for around P60.

San Joaquin

About 53km from Iloilo you'll come to San Joaquin (pronounced 'san-ho-kwin'), famous for its carabao fights, held every January. At the eastern end of town is the **Municipal Cemetery of San Joaquin**, with a creaky front gate, grand staircase and distinctive central burial-home with a domed roof of rusty corrugated iron. Through the porthole windows of this spooky structure you can see several memorial inscriptions (one of them topped with a skull and crossbones) and a colony of little bats clinging to the walls. It's just as well this building's gate is locked – its floor has a wall-to-wall carpet of bat crap and the aroma – even from the outside – could be enough to wake the dead. Behind the bat house, a huge bed of flowers thrives among multistorey graves.

Tiolas

The pretty little town of Tiolas (pronounced 't-yoll-ass'), 60km from Iloilo, is where the coast road forks. The main road – to San José (Antique) – heads inland through some spectacularly mountainous country, while a rough, mostly unsealed road follows the rugged coast to the remote town of Anini-y, on Panay's south-western tip.

Places To Stay & Eat On the road to San José (Antique), just north of Tiolas proper, is the inviting *Rest Along The River Restaurant*, serving Filipino cuisine for around P40 to P60. Along this stretch of road you'll also find *stalls* selling excellent, locally made peanut brittle for around P15. And about 10km from Tiolas on this same stretch, at the top of a steep hill, is the big, white *San Bernadino Mountain Resort & Restaurant*. It's known to the bus drivers as the '70km Hotel', because it's 70km from Iloilo. Basic, tidy rooms and bungalows with private bath go for P350. There's good Filipino food (around P50) and Western food (around P100) on offer, as well as a small swimming pool and wonderful views out over the nearby valley from the open-air dining room. Day trips from here to Anini-y and Nogas (see that section, later) are also available.

On the bumpy road to Anini-y, south of Tiolas, you'll find several beach resorts much-loved by Filipinos but rarely visited by foreigners.

Just south of Tiolas, *Basang Basa Beach Resort* is a friendly place with a row of cottages on a steep ridge above the water. Each cottage has a private bath and costs P500. There's no restaurant here, so you should bring your own food from Tiolas, or give the staff plenty of notice and they'll cook

for you. In Illongo, *basang basa* means 'very wet'.

About 2km farther south, *Tobog Beach Resort* (☎ 0912 887 0998) is a popular spot offering smallish cottages with private bath for P800, and larger cottages with private bath for P900. Entry to the resort to use the beach is P10. It's a bring-your-own-food arrangement here.

Right next door to Tobog is *Bogtong Bato Beach Resort*, where cottages with private bath go for P210 to P400. This place has steep steps down to an attractive, pebbly beach. Again, you'll have to provide your own food.

Farther south, about 17km from Anini-y, *Lawigan Beach Resort* (☎ 036-508 1837) is set on a picturesque, secluded corner of the coast. Well run and well patronised, it has cottages with private bath for P500, P550 and P650, depending on the size. There's basic food available from the canteen in the main building.

Scogliolandia Beach Resort (☎ 036-320 6321) is on a grassy, seaside slope about 15km from Anini-y, just around the rocky point from a large black-sand beach. It has picnic shelters by the water for P300 per day, and a large, two-storey hexagonal building with stylishly rustic, powder-blue rooms with new private bath for P800. On the top floor is an open-air dining area, where you can eat your own food or enjoy home-cooked meals (if you give the friendly staff a little time to prepare meals).

Anini-y & Nogas

There are two roads to Anini-y (pronounced 'ah-nee-nee') – one from Tiolas, the other from San José (Antique), but both are unsealed and the going can be pretty tough. About 80km from Iloilo, Anini-y is a lonely little place with some big attractions, as well as a handful of basic P150 *cottages*, and a couple of small *eateries*. The attractions include **hot springs**, in the town itself, and Nogas, with a marine sanctuary and one of Panay's best and most pristine coral reefs, just off shore. The Far East Scuba Institute dive centre in Iloilo City (☎/fax 036-509 2201, ✉ fesi@iloilo.net) offers snorkelling/diving packages for P1140/3600 per day to Nogas. Prices include transportation from Iloilo to Nogas, dive boat, food, and guide.

Boats to the island from Anini-y cost around P250 return.

These days, the island is uninhabited, but it was once a strategic US military outpost. On the southern side of Nogas, the island's reef juts into the Sulu Sea, forcing ships to give the island a very wide, very respectful, berth.

SAN JOSÉ (ANTIQUE)

On the west coast, about 96km from Iloilo, this largish port town suffers from an identity crisis. Being one of several places in the Philippines called San José (pronounced 'san-ho-say'), it is officially – but very rarely – known as San José de Buenavista. Most people will refer to it as San José Antique (Antique being the province of which it is the capital). Antique, by the way, is pronounced 'an-tee-kay'.

Information

On the street leading straight inland from the Provincial Capitol Building is a PT&T telephone office, a Metrobank and a PNB bank. Opposite the town's central plaza, there's an Equitable PCI Bank.

Places to Stay & Eat

About 200m from the pier (on the right when you're facing inland), accessible from

Evelio Javier

San José (Antique) is perhaps best known for being the home town of the late politician Evelio Javier. A supporter of Cory Aquino, Javier was gunned down here in February 1986, during the election campaign that saw Ferdinand Marcos ousted. Javier's assassination shocked the electorate and finally jolted the Catholic Church, the USA – and even some Marcos cronies – into finally admitting that Marcos was not a very nice man.

Mic Looby

the beach or by the road, is the rough and ready *Marina Lodge*. By road, head off the main street and walk down a private driveway. This place has shoddy but bearable rooms for P250 with fan and private bath.

At the pier there are a few small eateries, including the *Par-Q Store*. In town, you can try *Regina's Restaurant* near the plaza, and *Highway Haven* on the main road on the eastern side of town.

Getting There & Away

The town's pier serves MBRS Shipping's *VR Romblon*, which here sails from Manila to here every Wednesday, then to the Cuyo Islands on Friday. It then sails back here on Sunday, continuing to Manila the same day.

Ceres buses run daily, all day, between here and Iloilo City (P100, 2½ hours). Other buses travelling this route include Power Stars, Seventy Six and RM Buses.

TIBIAO

Near the town of Tibiao (pronounced 'tib-ee-ow'), north of San José, the mighty Tibiao River has plenty of white water and some excellent **kayaking** spots. There's no commercial accommodation in Tibiao, but the municipal tourism office in the centre of town can help you find a bed in a *private house*.

The **Bugtong Bato Falls** are a 6km walk from Tibiao. Head off from the main road near the municipal tourism office. There are 17 waterfalls all together, sprawled across a steep, 14km stretch of river. The first and second falls are the only safe swimming areas – falling rocks elsewhere make exploring too dangerous. The second waterfall is reached via a rope.

ROXAS (CAPIZ)

On the island's north coast, the city of Roxas (pronounced 'raw-hahs') is also known as Capiz, the province of which it is the capital. The hometown of the Commonwealth's first president, Manuel Roxas, the city has an attractive central district based around the Metropolitan Cathedral and belfry on Rizal St, on the banks of the Panay River. It makes a good alternative transport hub to the more crowded Kalibo, as it has two nearby ports, an airport, and buses to and from Iloilo City.

Information

There's a PNB branch with an ATM near the cathedral, on Magellan St, and a Metrobank two blocks away on Burgos St. Just over the bridge from the cathedral is a BPI branch. At the time of writing there was a PCI Bank and an Equitable Bank, but these banks have since merged, so check to see if both are still there.

There's a BayanTel international phone office on Arnaldo St, that also has an Internet service. There's an Islaphone international phone office at the Culasi Port gate.

Things To See & Do

Not yet rivalling nearby Kalibo's famous fiesta, Roxas' **Sinadya Fiesta** is pretty wild nonetheless. A colourful, four-day event held in early December, it culminates in the celebration of the Immaculate Conception of the Virgin Mary.

The **Ang Panublion** (Roxas City Museum) is on Arnaldo St, near the cathedral. Originally built as a water storage tank, this 1910 heritage building houses period furniture, local artefacts and a shell collection. It's open from 8.30 am to noon and from 2.30 to 6 pm Tuesday to Saturday.

Diagonally opposite the cathedral, the **Local Products Centre**, beside the river, has quite a range of souvenirs and artworks. Running along the belfry side of the cathedral, small eateries and religious-souvenir stores line a mall that's pleasantly treed and refreshingly free of cars and tricycles.

Baybay Beach, just north of downtown Roxas towards Culasi Port, is a long, brown-sand beach that is hugely popular with locals. It's lined with eateries and picnic shelters and even has lifeguard stations.

Places to Stay & Eat

The good-value *Halaran Plaza Hotel* (☎ 036-621 0649) is well placed beside the river, diagonally opposite City Hall. A 1970s-style timber villa, it has spacious rooms with fan and bath starting at P320. Air-con rooms are P570.

Roxas President's Inn (☎ 036-621 0208) is the city's classiest hotel, offering cosy, stylish singles with timber floor, bath, quiet air-con and cable TV for P950. Roomier twins/doubles are P1150/1300. Prices include breakfast at the fine restaurant, which specialises in local dishes (eg, sizzling squid for P120). The hotel is decorated with Filipino art and curios. It's on the corner of Rizal and Lopez Jaena Sts, around the corner from the Halaran Plaza Hotel.

Next to the Banica wharf, just to the east of central Roxas, you can stay at *View Deck Inn* (☎ 036-621 2698), which has plain fan rooms for P100 to P250. Fan rooms with cable TV are P300, and rooms with air-con, cable TV and hot showers are P400 to P500.

At Baybay Beach, a five-minute tricycle ride from the centre of Roxas, you can stay at *Marc's Beach Resort* (☎ 036-621 1103), which has rooms with bath and fan/air-con for P500/600. This place has huge grounds, and is right opposite the beach.

In Roxas proper, good fastfood-style Filipino meals are available at *Nesta's Food Center*, next door to the PNB branch on Magellans St. On the opposite side, a few doors away, is the popular local eatery known as *Lica's Food Haven*. A few blocks farther on, still on Magellanes St, is *Capiz Restaurant*, which specialises in native and seafood delicacies.

Getting There & Away

Air The Roxas City airport is a five-minute ride by tricycle (P5) north of central Roxas. PAL has an office at the airport (☎ 036-621 0244). Cebu Pacific's office is on Legaspi St (☎ 036-621 5092), which runs behind the cathedral.

Cebu Pacific flies Roxas–Manila (P1800, one hour) at 7.10 am daily, and Manila–Roxas at 5.30 am daily. PAL flies from Manila to Roxas at 5.45 am.

Mindanao Express also has flights from Cebu City to Roxas.

Boat There is a boat terminal on either side of Roxas, and an unofficial pumpboat-stop in town near the Panay Bridge. To the west, the large Culasi Port has boats going to

Manila. To the east of town, the little Banica wharf serves pumpboats to Masbate.

You'll find helpful staff at the Banica wharf coastguard office, and at the Philippine Port Authority (PPA) office (☎ 036-6211 2008) inside the Culasi Port terminal. Moreta Shipping lines has a Culasi Port office (☎ 036-621 0283), as do WG&A and Negros Navigation. In town, WG&A shares an office with Cebu Pacific on Legaspi St, Negros Navigation has a ticket outlet directly opposite (in the tailor shop), and the Moreta Shipping office is on Magellanes St (☎ 036-621 0283).

WG&A SuperFerry sails from Roxas' Culasi Port to Manila (P590, 17 hours) on Sunday, Tuesday and Thursday afternoons. It sails from Manila to Roxas on Wednesday and Saturday afternoons and on Monday evening. A Moreta Shipping ferry sails the same route (20 hours), leaving from Culasi Port at noon Tuesday, and from Manila on Sunday afternoon. A Negros Navigation ferry departs from Manila for Culasi Port at noon Friday, and leaves Roxas for Manila (via Kalibo's Dumaguit Port) on Saturday afternoon.

Roxas' Banica wharf services pumpboats to Masbate, with trips to Mandaon (P90, five hours) at 9 or 10 am Monday and Thursday, and to Calumpang (P80, four hours), at 9 or 10 am also on Monday and Thursday. Pumpboats sail from Mandaon to Banica wharf at 9 or 10 am Wednesday. On Saturday, the boat officially leaves at 9 or 10 am also – but it has been known to load up fast and head off as early as 7 am.

There's a regular, but unpredictable, pumpboat operating between Roxas and San Fernando on Sibuyan Island. It leaves once a week – *usually* on Friday – from the new Panay River bridge in the centre of Roxas. For the most reliable information about this trip, ring the PPA office (☎ 036-6211 2008) at the Culasi Port terminal.

Bus & Jeepney There are jeepneys and buses to Kalibo (P40 to P50, two hours) from the Alba station south of the river (P5 by tricycle from the cathedral). L-300 mini-vans also go to Kalibo from here (P70, 1½ hours). Ceres Liner buses for Iloilo City can be found nearby at the Ceres Liner station, opposite the Caltex service station.

KALIBO

Kalibo, the capital of Aklan Province, is thought to have been founded around AD 1250 by Malay settlers from Borneo. The town's residents have long been known for both their religious and festive zeal, which bursts forth each year in the form of the fantastic **Ati-Atihan Festival** in January – the nation's biggest and best mardi gras, which possibly dates back to the days of the Borneo settlers. A week-long street party raging from sun-up to sundown and peaking on the third Sunday of January, the festival offers prizes for the best costumes and dancers. And if this just isn't enough, similar festivals are held in January in the neighbouring towns of Batan (late January), Ibajay (late January), Makato (15 January) and Altavas (22 January).

Information

For international phone calls, the Kalibo Public Calling Office is on Burgos St. The i-Next Internet cafe (P90 per hour) is next door to the Air Philippines office on Roxas Ave.

Kalibo Rivers

A festive city it might be, but there's no celebrating the fact that Kalibo has allowed several of its provincial rivers to choke to death from domestic and industrial waste. The Aklan and Bulacan Rivers, which empty into the sea near Kalibo, are as close to biologically dead as rivers can get. Their course has been drastically altered, not by rains, but by unchecked gravel and sand quarrying, and many homes have been lost in the ensuing floods. Fisherfolk, environmental groups and a handful of politicians are desperately seeking solutions, but it may be too late.

Mic Looby

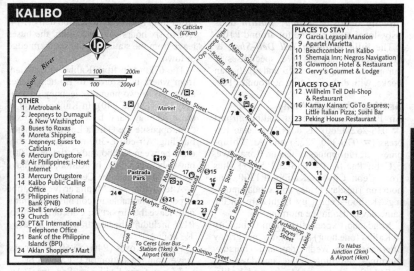

KALIBO

To Caticlan
(67km)

Spoc River

Soac River

0   100   200m
0   100   200yd

Oyo Torong Street

J. Magno Street

Roldan Street

Dr Gonzales Street

Market

C Laserna Street

S Martelino Street

Rizal Street

Jose Street

Pastrada Park

Martyrs Street

Pastrada Street

Luis Barrios Street

G Ramos Street

Acevedo Street

Roxas Avenue

Burgos Street

Veterans Avenue

Mabini Street

Archbishop
Reyes
Street

To Ceres Liner Bus
Station (1km) &
Airport (4km)

F Quimpo Street

To Nabas
Junction (2km)
& Airport (4km)

PLACES TO STAY
7 Garcia Legaspi Mansion
9 Apartel Marietta
10 Beachcomber Inn Kalibo
11 Shemaja Inn; Negros Navigation
18 Glowmoon Hotel & Restaurant
22 Gervy's Gourmet & Lodge

PLACES TO EAT
12 Willhelm Tell Deli-Shop
    & Restaurant
16 Kamay Kainan; GoTo Express;
    Little Italian Pizza; Sushi Bar
23 Peking House Restaurant

OTHER
1 Metrobank
2 Jeepneys to Dumaguit
   & New Washington
3 Buses to Roxas
4 Moreta Shipping
5 Jeepneys; Buses to
   Caticlan
6 Mercury Drugstore
8 Air Philippines; i-Next
   Internet
13 Mercury Drugstore
14 Kalibo Public Calling
    Office
15 Philippines National
    Bank (PNB)
17 Shell Service Station
19 Church
20 PT&T International
    Telephone Office
21 Bank of the Philippine
    Islands (BPI)
24 Aklan Shopper's Mart

THE VISAYAS

Places to Stay

To see the huge Ati-Atihan Festival from close up in Kalibo, you should book a hotel at least a month in advance.

Gervy's Gourmet & Lodge (☎ 036-262 4190), on quiet R Pastrada St, has simple, clean rooms with bath and fan for P125.

On S Martelino St, *Glowmoon Hotel & Restaurant* (☎ 036-868 5167) is a similar sort of place, although it has a wider range of rooms. Singles/doubles with fan and common bath are P250/350, or P500/800 with air-con.

On the town's main thoroughfare of Roxas Ave, the cheerful *Garcia Legaspi Mansion* (☎ 036-262 5588, 3rd Floor, 159 Roxas St) is one of the best budget deals in town. Doubles with fan and common/ private bath cost P350/650. Big air-con rooms start at P750. There's also a brightly decorated little coffee shop here. Also on Roxas Ave, *Apartel Marietta* has rooms with fan and bath starting at around P500, but it can get pretty noisy.

A few blocks away at the *Shemaja Inn* (☎ 036-268 6585), you get more floor space for your peso than at any other hotel in the Philippines. A tidy, spacious, twin or double

room with air-con, hot shower and cable TV comes with its own giant 'private receiving room' – complete with fiesta-style decorations. For all that, the price isn't too huge at P750.

Nearby, on Roldan St, the pricier *Beachcomber Inn Kalibo* (☎/fax 036-268 4765, ℯ bcombinn@kalibo.i-next.net) is a friendly, smoothly run establishment with marble-floored, air-con rooms with hot showers and cable TV for P950 to P1300.

Places to Eat

The ageing *Peking House Restaurant*, on Martyrs St, has fine Chinese food; the set menu for P65 is well worth it. *Glowmoon Hotel* (see Places to Stay earlier) also has a good, if not so cheap, restaurant.

There's a bit of everything on offer among the eateries on Archbishop Reyes St. *GoTo Express* has short-order Filipino and Western food for P40 to P60. Next door, *Little Italian Pizza* has pizzas for P100. And, under the same roof, *Sushi Bar* offers well-priced Japanese favourites for P60 to P90. You can eat your pizza or sushi in bamboo shelters outside, but watch you don't get speared on the way in

– the entrance is beside the dartboard area. Directly opposite, *Kamay Kainin* does tasty, local-style cuisine for around P100.

The little *Willhelm Tell Deli-Shop & Restaurant*, on Roxas Ave, specialises in European sausages and US and Australian steaks, with dishes starting at around P160.

Getting There & Away

Air PAL has an office at Kalibo airport (☎ 036-262 3260), as does Mindanao Express (☎ 036-340 7223) and Air Philippines. Air Philippines is also on Roxas Ave.

Cebu Pacific (☎ 036-262 5409) flies from Cebu City to Kalibo (P1300, one hour) on Tuesday, Friday and Sunday mornings. Kalibo–Cebu City flights are on the same days, also in the morning.

Mindanao Express flies from Cebu City to Kalibo (one hour) on Monday and Friday afternoons and Wednesday and Thursday mornings, returning on the same days.

PAL flies between Manila and Kalibo (P100) four times daily. Air Philippines does the same route twice daily. Cebu Pacific flies from Kalibo to Manila (P1800, one hour) and back twice daily.

Asian Spirit flies from Cebu City to Kalibo (P1500, one hour) and back, once a day.

Boat Boats go to Manila and/or Cebu from Kalibo's nearby ports at Navitas (P4 by tricycle), New Washington (P5 by jeepney) and Dumaguit (P6 by jeepney).

Negros Navigation has boats from Kalibo's Dumaguit Port to Cebu City (via Estancia) at noon Wednesday. It also sails from Dumaguit to Manila (P590, 17 hours) on Monday and Saturday evenings. Manila-Dumaguit services leave on Monday morning, Tuesday afternoon and at noon Friday.

Moreta Shipping has boats from Kalibo's port at Navitas to Manila (P470, 14 hours) on Tuesday afternoon, and from Manila to Navitas also on Tuesday afternoon. It also has a boat from New Washington to Manila (P470, 14 hours) at noon Saturday. This boat goes from Manila to New Washington at noon Thursday.

Bus & Jeepney There are Ceres Liner buses from Iloilo City to Kalibo daily (P74, five to six hours). From Kalibo, the buses leave from the station on the southern edge of town.

The 67km trip from Kalibo to Caticlan, from where boats cross to Boracay, takes about 1½ to two hours by jeepney or ordinary bus (P30 to P40). In Kalibo, some of these jeepneys and buses wait on Roxas Ave, opposite the Garcia Legaspi Mansion building. Air-con L-300 minivans also operate between Kalibo and Caticlan (P100), but only when full. In Kalibo, they have waiting sheds near the Ceres station.

After flights from Manila arrive at Kalibo airport, comfortable air-con buses and minivans leave the airport for Caticlan (P150, or P175 including the boat transfer to Boracay, 1½ hours).

Buses to Roxas (P40 to P50, two hours) leave from the station on C Laserna St.

To get from Kalibo to San José (Antique), you can catch the morning Lone Star bus from Nabas Junction (P10 by jeepney from Kalibo), or take the regular bus from Kalibo (P65).

CATICLAN

Outrigger boats cross from Caticlan to Boracay and there's also a small airport for the ever-popular flights from Manila. Apart from that, there's not much more to Caticlan.

Getting There & Away

Air Asian Spirit has four daily flights from Manila to Caticlan (P1550) – one in the morning, and three in the afternoon. There's a morning Caticlan-Manila flight, and two in the afternoon.

Golden Passage has a morning and afternoon flight to Caticlan from Manila (P2000) on Wednesday, Friday and Sunday. Pacific Airways (☎ 036-288 3162) has three Manila–Caticlan (P1650) flights daily, and offers a charter flight from Caticlan to Busuanga (P4500 per person, minimum of four).

Boat Caticlan's brand-new boat terminal has pumpboats going to and from Boracay every 20 to 30 minutes from 6 am to 6 pm (see Boat in the Boracay Getting There & Away section later for more details).

An MBRS passenger liner sails from Caticlan to Manila on Wednesday.

There's a pumpboat from Caticlan to Roxas (P200, five to seven hours) on Mindoro on Wednesday morning. Big pumpboats from Roxas to Caticlan leave on Monday and Friday mornings.

There's a pumpboat at 11 am from Santa Fe on Tablas Island to Caticlan, via Boracay (P80, two hours). It goes from Caticlan to Santa Fe (again, via Boracay) at 9.30 am.

Pumpboats also go from Odiongan on Tablas Island to Caticlan (P80, 1½ to two hours) on Thursday morning, and from Caticlan to Odiongan on Friday morning.

Bus & Jeepney There are several bus companies running between Iloilo City and Caticlan (P58 to P80 depending on the comfort factor), which is generally a six- to seven-hour trip. GM Lines (☎ 288 7030) buses go from Caticlan to Iloilo City twice daily. These buses don't come right to Caticlan pier, but it's only a short walk to the main road, where they wait for passengers.

Jeepneys and local buses from Caticlan to Kalibo (P30 to P40, 2 to 2½ hours) leave several times daily. L-300 minivans operate between Kalibo and Caticlan (P100). Several tour operators, including 7107, Boracay Star Express and Southwest, have air-con buses and minivans for the trip between Caticlan pier and Kalibo airport (P150), and farther afield to Iloilo and San José (Antique).

Boracay

Delicately poised between paradise and pandemonium, the internationally renowned island of Boracay is easily the best-known Philippine tourist spot. Often so crowded it's a wonder its famous White Beach is still above sea level, little Boracay remains a glorious playground for sun worshippers. The entire island is surrounded by dive spots.

Boracay is little more than a speck off the north-western tip of Panay, but its size certainly isn't in proportion to its fame. The

Boracay Clean-Up

Much has been written about Boracay's blink-of-an-eye tourism boom, with the most controversial issue of late being the quality of the waters around the island. To the relief of the island's tourism industry, the waters were recently given an official clean bill of health. For many locals, this was a timely warning. Now the Department of Tourism (DOT) oversees a weekly clean-up campaign by volunteer divers. Tourists' rubbish makes up most of the ocean debris here, but the onset of La Niña in 1999 has also brought the infamous crown of thorns starfish into the area to feed on Boracay's celebrated coral. DOT pays P1 for every one of these coral-munching menaces caught. For more information, contact the Boracay Foundation via its Web site at www.boracayisland.org. The foundation also publishes a regular newsletter (available at the Boracay Tourist Center).

Mic Looby

island is about 9km long, and only 1km wide at its narrow midriff. In just 15 minutes you can escape the heavily touristed White Beach on the east coast to the surprisingly quiet Bulabog Beach to the east. Wilder and windier, the east coast is a favourite for windsurfing. Also on the east coast, the Mt Luho View Deck (entry P20) offers magnificent views. Just climb the stairs near the main road near Lapuz-Lapuz.

White Beach, the main boat drop-off point from Caticlan on Panay, is where the action is. Here, lazing and browsing for food, drinks and souvenirs are the main activities. Electricity has well and truly arrived on Boracay, but a torch (flashlight) is still useful for night-time strolls on White Beach and elsewhere.

Orientation & Information

White Beach is the centre of Boracay's tourist area, and three 'boat stations' are stretched out across its sands. These can be hard to spot, being only patches of beach with waiting sheds set back. The beach is

THE VISAYAS

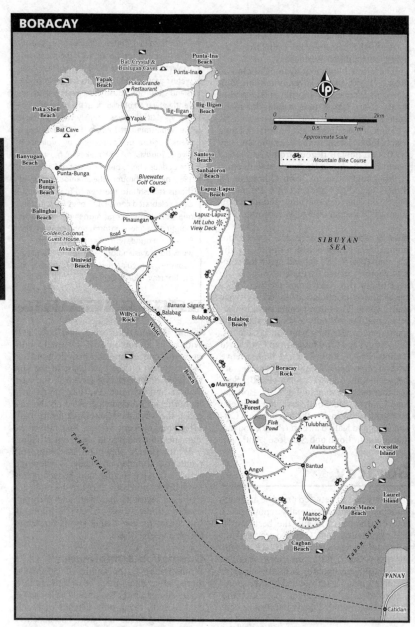

BORACAY

Bat, Crystal &
Buslugan Caves
Punta-Ina
Punta-Ina
Beach

Yapak
Beach

Puka Grande
Restaurant

Puka Shell
Beach

Ilig-Iligan

Ilig-Iligan
Beach

Bat Cave

Yapak

Banyugan
Beach

Santoyo
Beach

Punta-Bunga

Sanbaloron
Beach

Punta-
Bunga
Beach

Bluewater
Golf Course

Lapuz-Lapuz
Beach

Balinghai
Beach

Pinaungan

Lapuz-Lapuz
Mt Luho
View Deck

Golden Coconut
Guest House

Road 5

*SIBUYAN
SEA*

Mika's Place   Diniwid

Diniwid Beach

Willy's
Rock

Banana Sagang

Balabag

Bulabog

Bulabog
Beach

White

Boracay
Rock

Manggayad

Beach

Dead
Forest

Tablas Strait

Fish
Pond

Tulubhan

Malabunot

Crocodile
Island

Angol

Bantud

Laurel
Island

Manoc-
Manoc

Manoc-Manoc
Beach

Cagban
Beach

Tabon Strait

PANAY

Caticlan

0   1   2km
0   0.5   1mi
Approximate Scale

🚲 · · · · · Mountain Bike Course

dominated by a sandy pedestrian highway – the White Beach Path – where motorised vehicles are banned and it's almost compulsory to go barefoot.

Tourist Offices The Boracay Tourist Center, near the Alice in Wonderland Bar & Restaurant, is a hive of tourist-related activity. Attached to a large souvenir-and-convenience store, it has a noticeboard that's always worth perusing. The E-Z Map, published annually, is on sale here for P70. From behind a long row of desks, helpful staff offer the following: postal and telephone services; general Boracay info; money changing; and air, sea and land transport bookings. Most desks are open from 9 am to 7 pm daily.

Money The Allied Banks will change travellers cheques and cash, as will many resorts. The Boracay Tourist Center and the Swagman Travel office (near Villa Camilla) will give cash advances on major credit cards (with an 8% commission).

Post There's a postal counter at the Boracay Tourist Center, while the main post office is at the northern end of White Beach.

Telephone, Email & Internet Access
Several resorts have phone and fax facilities, but the rates are a lot higher than at the Boracay Tourist Center or the PT&T office near Charlh's Bar. There's also an international phone booth right on the sand, next to the Lapu-Lapu dive shop.

At the northern end of the beach near the main post office, the quiet little Station Internet has an international phone service as well as Internet access (P90 per hour). It's open from 8 am to 9.30 pm Monday to Saturday and from 1.30 to 8.30 pm on Sunday.

More central, the Computer Center, at the Boracay Imperial Beach Resort, charges P90 per hour. It's open from 10 am to 10 pm Monday to Saturday and from 1 to 10 pm on Sunday.

The Nigi Nigi Nu Noos resort has an Internet cafe charging a steep P150 per hour, but it does open early and close late – from 7.30 am to 11.30 pm daily.

Medical Services Readers unlucky enough to need medical attention here have strongly recommended the 24-hour Boracay Medical Centre (☎ 036-288 3147) over the Don Ciriaco Senares Tirol Sr Memorial Hospital (☎ 036-288 3041). Both are at White Beach.

Activities
The Boracay Tourist Center is a reliable organiser of daily activities. There's a board out the front listing what's on offer for the following day – you just add your name to the list of whatever takes your fancy.

Diving & Snorkelling You can easily arrange snorkelling and diving trips on Boracay. White Beach's many dive shops include: Calypso Diving School (☎ 036-288 3206, fax 288 3478), Far East Diving Institute (☎ 036-288 3223) and Scuba World (☎ 036-288 3310). The average dive with equipment is US$25.

Snorkelling gear costs about P200 per day to hire; diving trips cost around P750. The Boracay Tourist Center has a snorkelling tour from 10.30 am to 1.30 pm for P250 per head, including boat and gear.

Boating Half-day boat excursions (with food laid on) are about P500 to P600 (ask at just about any resort). The Boracay Tourist Center has pumpboat trips around the island (from 10.30 am to 4.30 pm) for P300 per head, barbecue lunch included. The centre also organises banana-boat rides (P150 per 15 minutes).

Tribal Adventures (☎ 036-288 3207), next to Aquarius Diving, has kayaks and all sorts of other craft for hire for P300 to P1250 per day. Its all-day boat and picnic tours are P500 per head.

Horse Riding Boracay Horse Riding Stables (☎ 036-288 3311) does great one-hour horse rides for P450. It has horses to suit your experience level, and rides head off from near the main road, north of the post office.

Massage If you're only up to a massage, try Fausto's Shiatsu (☎ 036-288 3305), near Boat Station 3 (P300 per hour).

THE VISAYAS

Parasailing Skyrider Parasail (@ borabe achboy@hotmail.com), next to the Bazzura Disco, has parasailing joyrides for P1800 per 10 minutes, and plenty of aquatic gear for hire. Mike, the English-born Hawaiian who runs this well-organised outfit, is the proud holder of the only parasailing operator's licence in the Philippines.

Places To Stay
Boracay accommodation rates are ruled by the high (or 'regular') season (1 December to 31 May) and the low (or 'lean') season (1 June to 30 November). Time your trip right and you'll get a P800 cottage for P400. Time it wrong, and you'll get a P400 cottage for P800. Many resorts pump their rates up by around 20% within the high season during the periods of 23 December to 3 January, Chinese New Year, and Easter. The rates quoted here apply to the standard high season.

The long, beautiful White Beach is a fun place to stroll, but if you're looking for accommodation it can became more of a trudge. Here's a tip: the cheaper, simpler places (under or around P500) are mostly south of the Boracay Tourist Center. If you chop the beach in half this way, and have a clear idea of your budget, you'll be soaking up the sun and the cocktails in no time.

And if it's all too much on White Beach, seek out the solitude of lovely Diniwid Beach's low-key resorts just to the north.

White Beach – South of Boracay Tourist Center Around Boat Station 3, there's the peaceful *Austrian Pension House & Sun-down Restaurant* (☎ 036-288 3406), where rooms with fan and bath cost P250 to P350. Then there's the glaring-white *Tin-Tin's Cottages* (☎ 036-288 3051), a popular place with singles/doubles for P300/500 (with fan and bath).

Close by is the stylish *Villa Camilla* (☎ 036-288 3354), which has great Spanish-style rooms with fan and bath for P600, or P1200 with air-con.

Next up, take the path leading away from the beach and you'll find *Moreno's Place*, where cheap cottages with bath are P300.

Next door is the hidden gem known as *Melinda's Garden* (☎ 036-288 3021). Run by the tireless Horst and Melinda, it has roomy, jungley cottages ranging from P400 to P750. Discounts are often possible, the staff are helpful and there's an excellent restaurant offering imported European wines. Close by is the friendly *Orchids Resort* (@ orchidslynn@hotmail.com), a great little place with cottages from around P700.

Back on White Beach Path, you can't miss the carefully landscaped *Mona Lisa White Sand* (☎ 036-288 3012), where exceptionally well-maintained nipa hut-style duplex cottages are very nice, if a little pricey, at P1200.

For better value, head down the next path leading off the beach (next to the Beach Life Bar) and look for *Michelle's Bungalows*, a tranquil courtyard of cottages priced at around P400 to P500.

Nearby is the little *Trafalgar Garden & Lodge* (☎ 036-288 3101), 'an oasis in the middle of the epicentre', according to one satisfied customer. The Trafalgar's friendly owners, Julia and Joel, offer a wide range of comfy rooms and cottages, from P150 to around P400. Their breakfasts also come highly recommended.

Also hidden behind the main beach strip in this area is the *Boracay Imperial Beach Resort*, which has its own Internet cafe (the Computer Center – see Telephone, Email & Internet Access earlier). Rooms here cost around P1500.

White Beach – North of Boracay Tourist Center Next to the Calypso Diving centre, *Greenyard* has good little cottages with bath and balcony for P300.

Nigi Nigi Nu Noos 'e' Nu Nu Noos (☎ 036-288 3101, fax 288 3112, @ nig inigi@pworld.net.ph) lives up to its fantastic name. Affectionately known as 'Nigi Nigi', this laidback upmarket place has towering nipa huts with generous balconies and marble-floored bathrooms (P1300/1600 with fan/air-con) all hidden in a lush, romantic garden of palms, ferns and figurines. The resort's Web site is at www.boracay-island.com.

Boracay Regency has ritzy rooms with the works for around P3000. Its equally ritzy rival nearby is *Boracay Peninsula*.

The fancy *Red Coconut Beach Resort (Manila ☎ 02-522 1405)* has nice-enough rooms with air-con for US$30 and, set back from the beach, outrageously luxurious rooms for US$60.

Just behind the Red Coconut's front building, the great-value *Seabird Resort Bar & Restaurant (☎ 036-288 3047)* has an excellent range of rooms, starting at P390 for doubles with fan and spotless common bath. Doubles/twins with hot shower are P750. The fancy *Crystal Sand Beach Resort (☎ 036-288 3149, fax 288 3087)* has hotel-style ground-floor rooms for P2800, and upstairs rooms with views from P3500. All come with air-con, hot showers, cable TV and telephone.

Galaxy Beach Resort is a big place with fairly roomy cottages with balcony and fan for P800, and swisher versions with air-con for P1700 to P1900. At the rear is *The Club Ten (☎ 036-288 3638)*, a luxurious, walled-in place with spacious unit-style accommodation starting at US$85.

The big *Ban's Beach Resort* has nipa hut-style cottages with balconies for P800.

On the main road, a short walk in from Boat Station 1, is *Jony's Place*. In a lovely yard, cottages here go for P700. A separate, three-storey building at the rear has spotless, tiled rooms with air-con for around P1000.

Willy's Beach Resort (☎ 036-288 3794, 288 3016, ✆ willys@boracay.i-next.net) is a multistorey place striving to bend the local development rules and add even more storeys. It offers package deals on its swish, air-con twin and double rooms – eg, P3300 for three days and two nights including airport transfer, daily breakfast, and dinner on the last night.

VIP Lingau has cottages starting at P600. Its restaurant has a set menu for P165.

Boracay Plaza Beach Resort (☎ 036-288 3702, ✆ bplaza@boracay.i-next.net) has tiled, fan rooms with balcony for P1500 (P2000 with air-con), and larger deluxe air-con rooms for P2350. The resort's nearby

Villa Regina annexe has roomy fan/air-con cottages in a high-walled compound for P1200/1800.

Waling-Waling Beach Hotel (☎ 036-288 5555, fax 288 4555, ✆ waling@boracay .webquest.com) has friendly staff and immaculate air-con rooms starting at P1400. *Pearl of the Pacific* is a huge place with luxury rooms from P3000. Equally upmarket are the neighbouring *Sea Winds*, *White House Resort* and *Chalet Tirol*.

At the far northern end, the finest stretch of White Beach has been staked out by *Friday's Boracay (☎ 036-288 6200, fax 288 6222, ✆ Fridays@boracay.webquest.com)*, a stunningly secluded gem of a resort. Of course, such location comes at a hefty price – cheerful, plush singles/doubles with air-con, balcony, cable TV, hot showers and telephone start at US$120/140. Red Coral Divers operates from here.

Next door, *Tete a Tete (☎ 036-288 6086)* is a simple, luxurious operation. It's a lovely, timber-floored house with open-plan kitchen and huge bedrooms available for rent as a whole (US$165 per day), or per room (US$55 to $65 per day). The services of an in-house cook are included in the price (the food is not).

Tucked into the far northern end of the beach, beside the rocky point dividing White Beach from little Diniwid Beach, is the futuristic complex known as *White Beach Terraces (☎ 036-288 4000)*. Ultra-modern unit-style twins and doubles with air-con, mini-bar, sound system and cable TV go for P3600.

Diniwid Beach If you take the concrete path around from the White Beach Terraces' restaurant (see North of Boracay Tourist Center under Places to Eat later), you get to Diniwid Beach (which is also accessible by tricycle from the main road back at White Beach). The path becomes a narrow ledge over the water before dropping you onto the sand. From there, it's a short stroll to *Mika's Place*, an unpretentious hideaway with simple nipa hut-style cottages with fan and bath for P300 and P500. In the main building, spacious rooms upstairs with large balcony are P1500. The little restaurant here offers homemade pizza (meaty, seafoody or vegetarian) for P150. Nearby, on the incredibly steep point above the northern end of the beach, *Golden Coconut Guest House* (☎ *036-288 6125*) has simple bamboo huts looking back across the beach for P500. These have a treehouse sort of feel to them, and are actually reached via a rickety bamboo ladder.

Bulabog Across Boracay's narrow middle from White Beach is the far-less-peopled Bulabog Beach. Here you'll find *Banana Sagang* (☎ *036-288 6121*, @ *banana@ boracay.i-next.net*), which offers nightly videos, Internet connection and basic rooms for P250.

Places to Eat

In this highly competitive market, even the over-the-top resorts are forced to keep their restaurant prices relatively low. Most places tempt customers with generous set-meals or buffets (from P120 to around P200 per person). Funny thing is, few places manage to offer truly outstanding food.

For breakfast and snacks, nearly every eatery here does good fruit-shakes, pancakes and set breakfasts, and *English Bakery* (with three outlets) is popular.

South of Boracay Tourist Center

Cocoloco Bar & Restaurant does a fine pizza for around P100. *Melinda's Garden*, nearby, specialises in European cuisine. Down the busy lane starting near the Queen's Beach Resort, savour cheap local flavours at the popular *Honey Bee Restaurant* and, opposite, *Lolit's*.

Back on the beach, past Mona Lisa White Sand, the big open-air *Casa Pilar* has nightly grills. Two doors along, *Dalisay Bar & Restaurant* is renowned for its P150 all-you-can-eat buffet.

The 24-hour *Diamond Garden Restaurant* does low price Filipino dishes.

North of Boracay Tourist Center

The 24-hour *Alice in Wonderland Bar & Restaurant* serves cheap Filipino dishes.

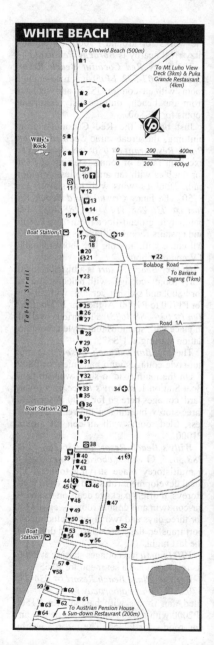

WHITE BEACH

WHITE BEACH

PLACES TO STAY

1 White Beach Terraces
2 Tete a Tete
3 Friday's Boracay; Red Coral Divers; Reynaldo's Bar & Restaurant
5 Waling-Waling Beach Hotel; Pearl of the Pacific; Sea Winds; White House Resort; Chalet Tirol
6 Willy's Beach Resort; VIP Lingau
7 Villa Regina (Boracay Plaza Annexe)
8 Boracay Plaza Beach Resort; Serena's Place Annexe
16 Jony's Place & Jony's Restaurant
20 Ban's Beach Resort; Zorba's Greek Restaurant
26 Galaxy Beach Resort
27 Crystal Sand Beach Resort; La Reserve Restaurant
28 Red Coconut Beach Resort; Seabird Resort Bar & Restaurant
35 Boracay Peninsula
37 Boracay Regency
40 Nigi Nigi Nu Noos 'e' Nu Nu Noos; Baracuda Bar; Victory Restaurant; Victory Divers
42 Greenyard; Calypso Diving School
47 Boracay Imperial Beach Resort; Computer Center
51 Michelle's Bungalows

52 Trafalgar Garden & Lodge
53 Mona Lisa White Sand; Beach Life Bar & Restaurant; Pizza da Baffo; Beach Life Diving Center
54 Queen's Beach Resort
60 Melinda's Garden
61 Orchids Resort
62 Moreno's Place
63 Villla Camilla; English Baker; Swagman Travel
64 Tin-Tin's Cottages

PLACES TO EAT

12 Plaza Café & Siam House
15 Daryn's Foods & Drinks; Jonah's Fruit Shake & Snack Bar; Beachcomer Bar
17 El Toro Restaurant; Sea Gaia Diving School
22 English Bakery & Tea Room
23 Neca Café; Scuba World Dive Shop; Jomar's Place
24 Rizzo Snack Bar; Fisheye Divers; Serina's Place
29 Real Coffee & Tea Cafe; Sea Lovers; Stables Boutique
32 Mango-Ray Restaurant & Laser Disc Cine Club; True Food Restauant; Lapu-Lapu Diving Center; Summer Palace
33 Restaurant Bar de Paris; Sea World Dive Center
43 Alice in Wonderland Bar & Restaurant
45 Diamond Garden Restaurant

48 Dalisay Bar & Restaurant
49 English Bakery; Boracay Scuba Diving School
50 Casa Pilar
56 Honey Bee Restaurant; Lolit's
58 Cocoloco Bar & Restaurant

OTHER

4 Boracay Horse Riding Stables
9 Main Post Office
10 Church
11 Station Internet
13 Moondog's Shooter Bar; Cocomangas
14 Far East Diving Institute
18 7107 Boracay Shuttle Office
19 Boracay Medical Center
21 Allied Bank; Landbank
25 Aquarius Diving; Tribal Adventures; Sand Castles; Gorio's Restaurant
30 Nautilus Diving
31 Skyrider Parasail; GP's Resort; Bazzura Disco
34 Don Ciriaco Senares Tirol Sr Memorial Hospital
36 DOT Tourist Office
38 PT&T International Telephone Office
39 Charlh's Bar
41 Allied Bank
44 Boracay Tourist Center
46 Police Station
55 Fausto's Shiatsu
57 Star Fire General Store
59 PAL

THE VISAYAS

The popular *Greenyard* has a fine all-you-can-eat Mongolian barbecue nightly for P175.

The *Victory Restaurant* (set back a little from the rest) is a pleasant place serving small helpings of Thai food, among other styles. *Nigi Nigi Nu Noos 'e' Nu Nu Noos*, next door, has a big range of food (four-course set-menu deal P190), and live jazz and blues most nights.

The large *Restaurant Bar de Paris* does a fine fish fillet in red curry for P190, as well as French-style dishes and pizza.

Near the Lapu-Lapu Diving Center, in a relaxed setting, *Mango-Ray Restaurant & Laser Disc Cine Club* does pasta and pizza for around P140. The equally laidback

Summer Palace, nearby, has OK, low-priced mains for around P100.

The cosy, cushiony *True Food Restaurant* is much-loved for its lamb rogan josh and great selection of vegetarian dishes (P80 to P180).

The best place to go for strong, fresh coffee and delicious food is *Real Coffee & Tea Cafe*, next to the footbridge and Stables Boutique. Run by the friendly mother-daughter team of Lee and Nadine, this cosy shack has the island's best-value omelettes and toast (around P65) and highly addictive chocolate brownies. The tasty vegetarian and vegan main meals are also a must. *Sea Lovers*, close by, does Filipino-style seafood for around P100.

Near Aquarius Diving, *Rizzo Snack Bar* and *Neca Café* both have tasty morsels for P65 to P100, as does the nearby *Gorio's Restaurant*, which specialises in crepes and coffee.

Crystal Sand Beach Resort restaurant has a generous, but overpriced, set-menu deal for P240. Nearby, the swanky *La Reserve Restaurant* has, among other rich pickings, Iranian caviar for P2400 per 100g.

Zorba's Greek Restaurant, near Ban's Beach Resort, is a big place struggling to draw the crowds. The menu, including vegetarian dishes, ranges from P110 to P170. Nearby, the well-established *El Toro Restaurant* certainly isn't cheap but it offers excellent, authentic paella for P230.

Jony's Restaurant has seating right on the sand next to Boat Station 1. Great position, but its Mexican food (around P140) is el crappo. If you're not at all hungry, you should order the hilariously tiny nachos (P50).

Nearby, *Moondog's Shooter Bar*, a lively nightspot, has good pizza for around P150.

Siam House is a comfy, well-priced place boasting a real Thai chef and some really good, spicy Thai curry set-meals for P150.

Daryn's Foods & Drinks serves a refreshing halo halo (P15), and the nearby *Jonah's Fruit Shake & Snack Bar* is a popular little place right on the sand.

The food at the exclusive *Friday's Boracay* is expensive and no better than elsewhere (salads start at P144, grilled seafood and meat P240), but it's a beautiful spot to drink or dine. Next door is the equally well-located *Reynaldo's Bar & Restaurant*. Hard up against the nearby rocky northern point of the beach is *White Beach Terraces* restaurant. Separate from the resort, it has a great view back down the beach. A good set menu is on offer here for P155.

For good seafood, *Puka Grande Restaurant* makes for an excellent dining excursion from White Beach. It's at the northern end of the island, near Yapak Beach.

Entertainment

White Beach is one very long liquor shelf. Most places have a happy 'hour' starting at 4 or 5 pm and finishing at 7, 8 or even 9 pm.

Bazzura Disco is big and lively, with some of the best dance music around. The little shack of *Charlh's Bar*, right on the sand, has good music, usually quite loud, usually quite late.

Moondog's Shooter Bar is a sprawling, tropical nightclub with plenty of drinking challenges and entertainment, including pool, chess and backgammon. Over the road, *Beachcomber Bar* can get just as lively after dark.

Getting There & Away

Large passenger-boats stopping here use the regular shuttle services to get passengers to and from the shore.

Air The swiftest way to Boracay from Manila is by air to Caticlan (see Getting There & Away in that section earlier) – but you won't be alone trying to book this flight during the high season. Good alternatives are the airports of Kalibo and Roxas, from where it's an easy two to four hours by road to Caticlan. See the Kalibo and Roxas Getting There & Away sections earlier for flight information.

Boat Pumpboats ferry passengers between Caticlan and Boracay (P16.50, 20 minutes) every 20 to 30 minutes from 6 am to 6 pm daily, stopping at one or more of the three boat stations on White Beach.

During the south-western monsoons from June to November, the sea on the White Beach side of Boracay can get too rough for outriggers. They then tie up on the east coast, at or near Bulabog, or at Manoc-Manoc. It's a P20 tricycle ride to White Beach.

A regular pumpboat goes at 11 am daily from Santa Fe on Tablas Island (in the Romblon islands) to Caticlan, via Boracay (P80, two hours). It goes from Caticlan to Santa Fe (again, via Boracay) at 9.30 am daily.

Getting Around

This compact island is perfect to explore on foot. Tricycles cost about P20 for short trips, mountain bikes can be hired for around P100 per day, and motorcycles and scooters for about P100 to P150 per hour.

Romblon

A great little grab-bag of islands, the Romblon Group hosts the Miss Gay Looc Festival (Tablas Island), produces world-class marble (Romblon Island), and nurtures forests of mind-bogglingly unique creatures (Sibuyan Island).

The small group of islands north of Panay stretches the name 'Romblon' a long way. Romblon is the name of the province comprising these islands, *and* the smaller of the three islands *and* the provincial capital city on that island.

Getting There & Away

Air connections are currently between Tugdan airport on Tablas Island and Manila. See the Tugdan section under Tablas Island, later, for flight information. There's also the soon-to-be-opened Azagra airport in San Fernando town on Sibuyan Island – check to see what flights are available.

San Agustin, Magdiwang (Sibuyan Island), Odiongan (Tablas Island) and Romblon town have boats links with Batangas on Luzon.

Cajidiocan (Sibuyan Island) is linked by boat to Mandaon in Masbate. Odiongan and

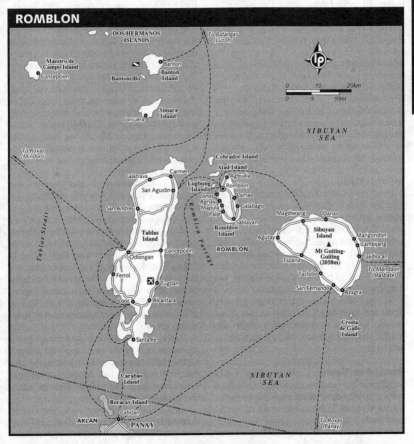

ROMBLON

DOS HERMANOS ISLANDS

To Batangas (Luzon)

Maestro de Campo Island
Concepcion

Banton
Banton Island
Bantoncillo

Corcuera
Simara Island

To Roxas (Mindoro)

SIBUYAN SEA

0   10   20km
0   5   10mi

Calatrava
Carmen
San Agustin
Cobrador Island
Alad Island
Agbudia
Lugbung Island
Romblon
Lonos
Lamao
Agnay
Calabago
Mapula
Paije
Sablayan
Romblon Island

Magdiwang
Danao

San Andres

Tablas Island

Odiongan
Concepcion
ROMBLON

Agutay
Sibuyan Island

Mt Guiting-Guiting (2058m)

Marigondon
Cambijang
Cajidiocan

Ferrol

Tugdan
Espana
To Mandaon (Masbate)

Looc
Alcantara

Taclobo
San Fernando
Azagra

Santa Fe

Cresta de Gallo Island

Carabao Island

SIBUYAN SEA

Boracay Island
Caticlan

AKLAN   PANAY

To Roxas (Panay)

Looc (Tablas Island) are connected to Roxas on Mindoro.

Looc, Odiongan, Romblon town and Santa Fe have sea links with Caticlan on Panay; Looc and Santa Fe also have connections to and from Boracay. There's an unreliable weekly pumpboat between Roxas (on Panay) and San Fernando.

See individual entries in this section for more information.

ROMBLON ISLAND

Romblon Island is most famous for its marble, which graces the floors of churches and homes all around the country. From the picturesque provincial capital of Romblon town, a ride around this compact island takes you past dusty marble quarries and workshops large and small, along a rough, exhilarating road haphazardly inlaid with marble offcuts. The road skirts the shore along the west coast, where there are several simple, idyllic beach resorts. On the eastern side of the island, the road heads inland through dense forest, mountain streams and rice-terraced valleys. A circuit of the island by motorcycle (see Getting Around, later) takes about two hours.

Information

Around the small triangular town plaza beside the dock in Romblon town, you'll find three international telephone offices (RomblonTel, BayanTel and PT&T). Also here is the post office, facing the water. One block inland, near the domed San Joseph's Cathedral, is the Romblon police station (☎ 078-2166). There's also a police post on the corner of the triangular plaza.

Several shops near the triangular town plaza are crammed with good-quality cane products, along with lots of homegrown marble items (mortars and pestles are a favourite).

Romblon Town

This beautiful, historic town is a delight to approach by sea. A deep port allows large ferries to dock right in the heart of town, surrounded by the lush, green hills of a well-protected cove. The capital of the province of the same name, this town boasts the 17th century **Fort San Andres**, **Fort Santiago** and the fantastically solid **San Joseph's Cathedral** and **belfry**. There are good views from the **Sabang** and **Apunan lighthouses**.

Fiesta time in Romblon town runs for a week, from 1 January.

Places to Stay & Eat

Romblon Town *Romblon Plaza Hotel* (☎ 078-2269) is the four-storey place one block from the pier. Recently refurbished, it has good standard rooms with fan and bath for P350, and larger rooms with super-efficient air-con – and a crucifix – for P550. The interior designers here had quite a fetish for man-made materials – the bedding is acrylic, the furniture is plastic and the many plants (including potted trees) are utterly fake. Small, shared balconies provide good views of a plaza, which is lined with real trees.

On nearby Quezon St, a sign announces the Felmar Pension House, but everyone knows this place as *Marble Hotel*. Well-furnished rooms with fan and bath go for P200. The reception area is not exactly obvious – just wander through the shop until you find someone.

Jak's Restaurant & Bar is near the water, on a side-street beside the triangular town plaza. This place is new and groovy, and offers a regularly updated menu of mainly Indian and Italian cuisine. The fish curry (P75) and the lasagne (P80) are excellent. The lighting is low, the service is friendly and there's a big CD collection. Behind Jak's, facing the triangular town plaza, *Romblon Shopping Center Eatery* has average Filipino fare for P25 to P30, but it's a good place to sit outside and watch the world go by.

Daily Bread Bakery – appropriately placed a few doors from the San Joseph Cathedral – has some of the best bread and biscuits in town. The *market*, in narrow side-streets near the triangular town plaza, has plenty of fresh produce.

Around Romblon Island There are several good beach resorts south of Romblon

THE VISAYAS

town, on the island's west coast. From town, the first of these is **Tiamban Beach Resort**, followed closely by **Palm Beach Resort**. Both places have OK cottages by the water for P250 to P500. Whitetip Divers offers drive trips for around US$25 from Babangtan Beach.

In San Pedro, about 10km south of Romblon town (about P100 by tricycle), are two of the island's best beach resorts: **Marble Cottages** and neighbouring **San Pedro Beach Resort**. Marble Cottages has lovely balconied bamboo cottages (P250) and more-substantial marble-floored ones (P350). The cottages, along with a small restaurant and a dive shop, are perched on a rocky headland with a very private beach. Food here includes Filipino dishes (P40) and pizza (P70). A standard dive is US$20, and an island-hopping day trip is P250 (minimum of two people). Mountain bikes and snorkel gear are also available for hire.

The quiet little **Pedro Beach Resort** is in a beautiful, grassy clearing beside a gorgeous little beach. Cottages, on a rise above the water, are spotless and marble-floored. They come with a balcony, bath and fan for P300. There's a small restaurant beside the beach.

Back on the main road, opposite the ridge road that leads to Marble Cottages and San Pedro Beach Resort, is a steep road leading to **Bird & Islands Mountain Resort**. Run by Raffy Molino, a retired Manila radio announcer, this place has magnificent views across the Romblon Passage. It also has a swimming pool, a restaurant, and standard balconied cottages with bath and fan for P250. Family cottages, with kitchen, are P500.

In Palje (pronounced 'pal-hey'), there's the 12-hectare **Palje Retreat Center** (☎ 078-2368). Its lush grounds are superbly landscaped, giving the impression that the place must be very expensive, but cute, rough-hewn timber cottages with balconies and fan are only P200, and there's a small restaurant serving meals for P100. Cottages for four people cost P400. The cottages overlook a shingle beach, good for swimming and snorkelling. Satanists and party animals should note the sign near the en-

trance – 'Smoking, drinking and any immoral act is strictly prohibited'. There's no sign for this place on the road, but you can't miss the owner's lavish villa on the hill above the resort. The short driveway to the resort is nearby, not far from the tree marked 'Genesis'.

On the mountainous eastern side of the island, about 10km south-east of Romblon town (30 minutes by motorcycle), is a well-hidden paradise, **Buena Suerte Resort** (☎ 078-2069). From the resort's sign, by the main road in the small village of Tambac, a rough road meanders for about 1km inland to this sloping, garden retreat set around a massive, marble-floored swimming pool. Roomy cottages to suit two to three people are P300, and there's a giant 12-person cottage for P500. A canteen beside the pool serves simple meals.

Getting There & Away

Daily pumpboats leave San Agustin on Tablas Island twice daily for Romblon town (P40, 45 minutes). There's one Romblon town–San Agustin service, in the afternoon. In Romblon town these boats come and go from *next* to the dock.

A daily pumpboat leaves Romblon town's dock in the early afternoon for Magdiwang (P75, two hours) on Sibuyan Island. Magdiwang–Romblon town boats go in the morning.

Big ferries (either Shipshape Ferry or Viva Lines) go from San Agustin to Romblon town (P65, 45 minutes) at 2 and 3 pm Sunday, Tuesday and Friday. From Romblon town to San Agustin, they go at 6 and 9 pm Monday, Wednesday and Saturday. There are also Romblon town–Magdiwang (two hours) trips at 6 pm Sunday, Tuesday and Friday, and Magdiwang–Romblon town trips at 10 am Monday, Wednesday and Saturday at 10 am.

Shipshape Shipping (Manila ☎ 02-723 7615) has boats from Batangas on Luzon to San Agustin (P250), Romblon town (P250) and Magdiwang (P275) on Monday, Thursday and Saturday evenings.

Viva Lines also plies the Batangas–San Agustin–Romblon town–Magdiwang route

THE VISAYAS

(P250, 21 hours) on Tuesday, Friday and Sunday, returning on Monday, Wednesday and Saturday. Boats departs San Agustin around 3 pm, and Romblon town at 9 pm.

An MBRS Lines boat sails direct from Romblon town to Caticlan on Wednesday at 12.30 am (ie, Tuesday night).

Getting Around

Tricycles can be hired from near the dock for short trips. A circuit of the island by tricycle is pretty much impossible on the steep, rocky road. You're much better off hiring a single motorcycle and rider for this trip (P300, around two hours). Just ask a tricycle rider, and they'll unbolt the bike from their side-car.

Pumpboats can be also be hired for day trips to the nearby islands of Lugbung, Alad and Cobradaor (P500 to P600 per boat).

TABLAS ISLAND

Tablas, the largest of the Romblon Group, is a three-hour boat ride from Mindoro's east coast. Its largest town is Odiongan.

Tablas Island is home to Romblon province's main airport, in the nondescript town of Tugdan. The airport is served by Asian Spirit and Pacific Airways (see Tugdan, later, for service information).

Apart from the big pumpboats that link Tablas Island to Mindoro and Panay, pumpboats and ferries operate daily between the east-coast town of San Agustin and Romblon town (P65, 45 minutes), on Romblon.

Looc

About 25km from Odiongan, Looc (pronounced 'lo-oc'), is a calm and quiet place – except when the week-long fiesta rolls around in late April. That's when the townsfolk kick up their heels in celebration of patron saint Joseph, host basketball and cockfighting tournaments, and go gaga over the **Looc Gay Federation's Fiesta** activities. The theme for this gay men's gala changes every year. In 1999 contestants represented a country of their choice and wore the appropriate national dress. Highlights included a swimsuit parade and a talent quest. An interisland event, the gay fiesta draws judges from the Philippines' film and TV world. The organisers told us that foreign tourists might just qualify as judges – so don't forget to pack your party frock. Other towns in Romblon province whose fiestas are more gay than most include Odiongan and San Andres, but Looc swears it's the original and the best.

Information The two-storey Looc tourist information centre is at the southern corner of the town plaza. Susan Noche, the helpful tourism coordinator here, can direct you to (among other things) the post office, which is about one block from the other side of the plaza. Staff here can organise motorcycle hire for you. The going rate is from P500 to P600 per day.

The ground floor of the Marduke Hotel building has a BayanTel international telephone office, and an Asian Spirit ticket-office.

Places to Stay *Morales Lodging Inn* is a cheap, eccentric hotel built amid the mangroves beside Looc pier. Run by the energetic Modesto Morales, it has eight simple rooms with common bath at P100 per person (P25 extra for a fan). There's a bar of sorts, a pool table, and plenty of tourist information. Mr Morales, apart from being one of Looc's volunteer tour guides, is in charge of the daily boat-trips to and from Boracay (see Looc's Getting There & Away later). The inn is a short walk from the southern corner of the town plaza, near the tourist information centre.

The rather grand *Marduke Hotel* is the large, white place peeking over its shorter neighbours beside the market and town plaza (behind the Koop Drug Store). Run by the Martinez family, it has five big rooms with shared balconies, bedside 'touch lamps', modern bathrooms and air-con for P400 for one person, P500/600 for two/three.

About 3km from Looc proper, *Roda Beach Resort* (☎ 0938 61424) is an excellent out-of-town alternative. Rooms above the restaurant in the main building are P250 with fan and bath, or P500 with air-con. Cottages nearby with fan and bath are P300.

Picnic shelters built over the water, and around trees, are P200 per day. Standard shelters on the attractive white-sand beach are P50 per day. The large restaurant does good fried fish for P55, and hamburgers for P20. A tricycle ride between the resort and the town (10 minutes) costs P30.

Places to Eat *Pacific Garden Restaurant*, facing the town plaza, is a friendly place offering a mix of Filipino, Chinese and Western food. Beef *tapa* (dried beef and raw onion), chop suey and cheeseburgers are all around P50 to P75. It also has a well-stocked bar. *Torilo's Restaurant*, closer to the market and Marduke Hotel, offers a similar menu.

Roberto's Bar is a night-time oasis two blocks of from the town plaza. It's on the same street as the Looc Foursquare Gospel Church. Open every day from early evening onwards, this place is one long, deep and green garden, furnished with rock-slab benches and tables, with an open-air bar at the far end. Drinks and snacks are available until late, the service is friendly and the atmosphere is very soothing.

Getting There & Away Looc's pier is beside the Morales Lodging Inn, near the southern corner of the town plaza.

Boat There are plenty of pumpboats between Looc (and nearby Santa Fe) to Mindoro and Panay.

To get to Boracay or Caticlan from Looc (P100, 1½ to two hours), you can take the 9.30 am daily pumpboats from the pier. Most of these boats continue to Caticlan, returning from Caticlan via Boracay in the early afternoon. Some of these boats are too big to moor at Boracay, and will drop you at nearby Caticlan. Others are based at resorts in Boracay and may not continue to Caticlan. Morales Lodging Inn (see Places to Stay, earlier) sponsors these trips, and you can pick up tickets and further information there.

Large ferry-type pumpboats leave Roxas (on Mindoro) for Looc (P85, 3 to 3½ hours) on Tuesday, Friday and Sunday mornings, and leave Looc for Roxas on Monday, Thursday and Saturday mornings.

Jeepney & Tricycle Jeepneys run up until about 4 or 5 pm from Looc to Odiongan (P18, one hour), Santa Fe (P25, 45 minutes), Tugdan (P15, 45 minutes) and San Agustin (P50, two hours). A tricycle on the rough old road between Looc and Santa Fe will probably cost no less than P150. Between Looc and Tugdan count on about P50.

Odiongan

The clean, green, port town of Odiongan (pronounced 'oh-**d'yong**-ahn') is known locally as the 'heartland of the archipelago'. It's somehow been calculated that the town is geographically slap-bang in the centre of the nation. Originally, this place was called 'Inodiongan', which literally means 'struck by an arrow' – the theory being that the community spent its early years fending off persistent attacks by pirates. These days, the peaceful town is a mix of brightly coloured houses and neatly trimmed hedges. Odiongan's fiesta is in early April.

Near the village of Tuburan, 7km from town, there's an impressive, multi-tiered *busay* (waterfall) known simply as **Busay**. You can get there by tricycle or single motorcycle for around P200 return (including waiting time). It's about a 500m walk up from the rough road.

Information You can get plenty of information on Odiongan – and life in general – from José Rizal Reyes (better known as 'Dodong') at the local office of the national Philippine Information Authority. The office is on the 2nd floor of the same building as the Traveller's Inn (see Places to Stay later).

There's a PNB bank on the corner of M Formilleza and JP Laurel Sts, a few blocks from the market. Opposite the bank is a PLDT international telephone office that is efficiently run and relatively cheap. There's an RCPI telephone office next to Shelborne Hotel.

Places to Stay The town's two hotels are both tucked inside buildings near the central market. On the 3rd floor of an anonymous building next door to the Golden Gift Convenient Store & Snack House is **Shelborne Hotel**. Its most impressive feature is the sky-blue vinyl lounge suite in the common area. If you can rouse anyone in the little information booth at the top of the stairs (on the right), you'll get a room here for P100 per person, with common bath, fan, and good views overlooking the market from the rooftop terrace.

A couple of blocks away, on ML Quezon St, **Traveller's Inn** is run by the friendly John, who has taken over the business from his father. A bed in the large, tidy, timber-floored dormitory is P70. It's P90 for a room with fan and common bath (via the family kitchen). There's also a common balcony overlooking the street. The inn is on the 2nd floor, above the Development Bank of the Philippines office – look for the little sign near the stairs at the side of the building.

Places to Eat About 100m from the Traveller's Inn, on the opposite side of the street, is the delightful **Kuyon Kuyon Restaurant**. Local dishes here includes a huge *sinigang na hipon* (tom-yum-style shrimp and vegetables in sour sauce, served in a clay pot) for P120, *daing na bangus* (marinated milkfish) for P70, and *pinasingawang gulay* (steamed vegies such as okra, *sitaw* – Chinese string beans, and *talong* – eggplant) for P40. Friendly service, soft lighting, bamboo decor and air-con make this an unusually delicious and relaxing dining experience … especially if there's no videoke happening (videoke hours are from 8 to 11 pm).

Getting There & Away Boats to and from Luzon, Mindoro and Panay serve Odiongan's pier, a P5 to P7 tricycle ride from town. Staff at the shipping office beside the pier gate are happy to provide information on boat schedules.

Boat Viva Shipping Lines' MV *Penafrancia IV* leaves Batangas on Luzon for Odiongan (P160) on Tuesday, Thursday and Saturday afternoons. The MV *Penafrancia III* leaves for Odiongan (P220), Romblon

town (P220) and Sibuyan Island (P230) on Monday, Thursday and Saturday evenings.

Shipshape Shipping (Manila ☎ 02-723 7615) sails from Batangas on Luzon to Odiongan (P180) on Wednesday, Friday and Sunday evenings; Montenegro Lines' MV *Don Francisco* does the same trip (P120) on Sunday and Wednesday evenings.

Pumpboats go from Odiongan to Caticlan (P80, 1½–two hours) on Thursday morning, and from Caticlan to Odiongan on Friday morning.

Large ferry-type pumpboats from Roxas on Mindoro to Odiongan (P85, three hours) leave at 10 or 11 am Tuesday, Friday and Sunday. Boats from Odiongan to Roxas depart at 10 or 11 am Thursday, Saturday and Monday.

Jeepney Jeepneys run up until about 3 pm from near the market, as well as from the pier, to and from towns north and south of Odiongan. The main destinations are Looc (P18, one hour) and Calatrava (P28, two hours).

Calatrava

There's nowhere to stay in little Calatrava (pronounced 'cal-ah-**trah**-vah'), but from here you can organise boat trips to **Tinagong Dagat** (Hidden Sea), a mysterious saltwater lake with an underground connection to the ocean. Nearby, **Lapos Lapos** (Through Through), is an intricate cave network carved by the sea. Several of the larger caves here remain unexplored. Along the way to Tinagong Dagat and Lapos Lapos you can take a dip at the **swimming holes** around Organ Rock. Pumpboats and guides can be organised in Calatrava for P500 to P600.

Calatrava is a two-hour jeepney ride from Odiongan (P28), or a one-hour jeepney ride from San Agustin (P18).

San Agustin

With a backdrop of high, rugged mountains and a deep, palm-fringed harbour, the serene town of San Agustin (pronounced 'san-ah-goos-tin') is a lovely place to miss a boat. It's almost a pity the place is well served by boats large and small.

There's a BayanTel international phone office on Moreno Blvd, next door to the general store and Fel-Nor Lodge.

Places to Stay *Kambaye Beach Resort* is the tallest place in town and has great views from its rooftop terrace. Simple fan rooms with bath are P100, more-spacious rooms with air-con P450. The staff are a fun-loving bunch and there's food available.

Around the corner, on the waterside Moreno Blvd, *Fel-Nor Lodge & Restaurant* has rooms for P100. There's a *general store* next door.

Getting There & Away Pumpboats to Romblon town (P40, 45 minutes) leave from *next to* San Agustin's long, concrete pier twice daily, in the early morning and early afternoon. A pumpboat goes to Sibuyan Island (P75, two hours) in the early afternoon.

Big ferries (either Shipshape or Viva Lines) go from San Agustin to Romblon town (P65, 45 minutes) on Tuesday, Friday and Sunday afternoons. They leave Romblon town for San Agustin at 6 and 9 pm Monday, Wednesday and Saturday.

Shipshape Shipping (Manila ☎ 02-723 7615) has boats from Batangas on Luzon to San Agustin (P250), Romblon town (P250) and Sibuyan Island (P275) at 6 pm Monday, Thursday and Saturday.

Jeepneys between Looc and San Agustin cost P50 (two hours).

Tugdan

There's little more to Tugdan than the airport, which can be contacted on ☎ 0912 388 5127. Asian Spirit has an office at the airport, as well as in the nearby town of Alcantara, in the GF Anviro Building beside the Rural Bank of Alcantara.

Asian Spirit's 19-seater aircraft fly from Manila to Tugdan airport (P1140, one hour) at 11.30 am Sunday, Monday, Wednesday, Friday and Saturday. There are flights from Tugdan to Manila on the same days at 12.50 pm. Pacific Airways flies from Manila to Tugdan (1½ hours) at 9 am Monday, Tuesday, Thursday and Saturday. Same-day flights from Tugdan to Manila are at 11 am.

Laoag International Airways has a flight from Manila to Romblon (P1140) on Monday and Thursday at 9.30 am.

Jeepneys meet all arriving flights, and head off to Looc (P15, 45 minutes), Santa Fe (P30, one hour), and San Agustin (P40, 1½ hours).

Santa Fe

About 23km from Looc, Santa Fe is a small, drab town with a main street running along the waterfront.

On the waterfront, you can stay at the *Mely Asis Restaurant/Lodging House*. It looks more suited to lodging cargo, but it has decent, basic rooms with fan and common bath for P100 per person. You can also try the cute, but tiny, *Payag-Payag Lodge* nearby.

The town's absolutely no-frills eateries include *Morillo's Snack Bar & Restaurant* and *Sylvia's Mini-Store and Restaurant*, both of which are on the waterfront. One block in from the water is *Asis Bakery*.

What would once have once a drab brown-sand beach along Santa Fe's waterfront is now a concrete wall. From this wall, you can clamber into a shuttle boat for the short trip (P10) out to a Caticlan-bound pumpboat. There's an ill-conceived pier on the edge of town used by only the smallest of boats. At high tide, the water here is barely 1m deep.

A regular pumpboat goes at 11 am daily from Santa Fe to Caticlan, via Boracay (P80 plus P10 shuttle boat service to/from the shore, two hours). It goes from Caticlan to Santa Fe (again, via Boracay) at 9.30 am.

Jeepneys operate up until about 4 pm between Santa Fe and Looc (P25). Tricycles can do the trip also (P150), but it's a tough ride.

SIBUYAN ISLAND

Wearing the massive Mt Guiting-Guiting (2058m) like a saw-toothed crown, Sibuyan Island (pronounced 'see-**boo**-yan') is blessed. While countless neighbours are being stripped bare, Sibuyan Island's natural resources are being protected and nurtured. Biologically, it's the Galapagos Islands of the region, having been cut off from all other land masses during the last Ice Age. In pristine isolation, five **unique mammal species** survive to this day – including the bizarre tube-nosed fruit bat. There's not a nation in Europe that can claim five endemic mammals, so it's fitting that the European Union has funded the protection of the island to the tune of P22 million.

Sibuyan Island is one of the recent success stories of the International Coastal Cleanup program (held annually in the third week of September). In 1999 thousands of Sibuyanos pitched in to collect a staggering 1.5 tonnes of waste – 40% of which was nonbiodegradable. The majority of it had washed ashore from other islands.

The entire island's main electricity supply cuts out from midnight to 4 am daily.

San Fernando

Home to the soon-to-be-opened (at the time of writing) Azagra airport, San Fernando has one of the island's three 'Residential Ranger Offices' just outside town, making it a good base for hikes into Mt Guiting-Guiting Natural Park.

A pumpboat goes from Roxas (on Panay) to San Fernando – *usually* on Friday – from the new Panay River bridge in the centre of Roxas. For the most reliable information about this trip, ring the PPA office (☎ 036-6211 2008) at the Culasi Port terminal in Roxas. In San Fernando, ask at the pier.

Jeepneys to and from Magdiwang take about two hours (P30).

Magdiwang & Mt Guiting-Guiting Natural Park

The gateway to Mt Guiting-Guiting National Park, Magdiwang (pronounced 'mag-**dee**-wang') is a friendly, no-frills port town. Its pier, 2km from the town, is lined with picture-perfect little houses on stilts, decorated with flowering pot-plants. Mangroves thrive in the clean, clear waters around the pier.

The town has three international telephone offices, but the nearest bank of any use to foreign tourists is in Romblon town, on Romblon Island.

About 8km from Magdiwang (heading east along the National Rd, then inland) is the sparkling new **Mt Guiting-Guiting Natural Park Visitors' Centre**. From here, you take the trail up to the 2058m-high mountain peak that stands before you. This is the only trail on the island that takes you to the summit. It's an eight-hour climb one way, so you definitely need two days if you plan to go the distance.

The standard **trek** involves a four- to five-hour walk to the base camp area of Mayos Peak, where you can pitch a tent, collect fresh water, and drop your heaviest gear. Then you can tip-toe across the knife-edge ridge to the rocky face of Mt Guiting-Guiting itself. From there, you 'kiss the wall' (as climbers like to say) all the way to the mossy, breathtaking summit, before returning to Mayos Peak for a well-earned sleep.

Tents are available free of charge from the visitors centre, which can also arrange guides (P300 per day) and porters (P250 per day) if required. If you plan to conquer the summit, you must bring your own climbing ropes and assorted gear.

About 12km from Magdiwang (4km past the turn-off to Mt Guiting-Guiting Natural Park Visitors' Centre) is the beautiful **Lambingan Falls** and swimming hole.

You can take a tricycle from Magdiwang to the visitors centre (P40, 20 minutes) and to the falls (P50, 30 minutes).

Places to Stay & Eat A godsend in a town with no hotels or restaurants is *Vicky's Place* (officially, but rarely, called the Corran Guesthouse). Officially a homestay, this large, family residence has been welcoming guests since 1975. Homely, timber-floored rooms upstairs are P150 per person, and come with fan and immaculate common bath. Vicky, the mastermind behind the whole smoothly run operation, cooks wonderful Filipino and Western meals on request. Vegetarians are happily catered for, and meat-lovers must try the homemade Filipino sausage. Alcoholic drinks and soft drinks are available, and there's also a laundry service.

From the pier, just ask a tricycle driver to take you to Vicky's Place (P5). It's on MH del Pilar St, just off the National Rd, opposite the school.

Getting There & Away Viva Shipping Lines' MV *Penafrañcia III* leaves Batangas on Luzon for Odiongan (P220), Romblon town (P220) and Magdiwang (P230) at 7 pm Monday, Thursday and Saturday.

Shipshape Shipping (☎ 02-723 7615 in Manila) has boats to San Agustin (P250), Romblon town (P250) and Magdiwang (P275) at 6 pm Monday, Thursday and Saturday.

There are Romblon town–Magdiwang ferry trips (two hours) on Tuesday, Friday and Sunday evenings, and two Magdiwang–Romblon town trips on Monday, Wednesday and Saturday.

Pumpboats go daily from Romblon town pier to Magdiwang (P75, two hours) in the afternoon, and leave Magdiwang for Romblon town in the morning.

Jeepneys operate from around 6 am between Magdiwang and Cajidiocan (P75, 1½ hours) and San Fernando (P30, two hours).

Cajidiocan

Cajidiocan (pronounced 'cah-ee-**d'yo**-can') is Sibuyan Island's access point for boats to and from Masbate. It's also a good base for trips into the Mt Guiting-Guiting Natural Park. From the 'Residential Ranger Station' just outside town, you can do a one-day trek to some excellent **caves** within the park.

The town's main street includes a Rural Bank and an RCPI international telephone office. Also on the main drag is *Atienza's Bakery*, and a *hotel* that should now be finished, making it the town's only commercial accommodation. Between the main drag and the pier is the little *Ian's Eatery*.

At 8 am Thursday, large pumpboats sail from the beach near the pier to Mandaon (P100, 4½ hours) on Masbate's east coast. They leave Mandaon at 9 am on Wednesday.

Coming from Magdiwang, you'll need to catch the 6 am jeepney (P20, 1½ hours) to make the boat in time.

Masbate

Broad, lumpy, hills dominate this most uncharacteristic of Philippine island-provinces. Grassy green and sparsely inhabited, the island is ideal for cattle grazing – which is what Masbate is best known for, apart from its annual rodeo (see Masbate Town later). This should be good news for travellers in search of a beach paradise far from the madding crowd. Masbate has some utterly stunning, unspoiled white-sand beaches (see Bagacay later).

A poor island-province even by Philippine standards, Masbate (pronounced 'mas-**bah**-tay') struggles to make the most of its marine and agricultural resources. Like many of the nation's smaller islands, it is always having its fish pinched by larger, better equipped fishing fleets from other islands. Masbate's fisherfolk have long made do with antiquated equipment, while also competing with farmers forced to live off the sea by chronic unemployment on the land. A shining light in all this is the provincial government's Fishery Development Program, aimed at improving Masbate's fishing industry through sustainable technology, conservation, tougher fishing laws and loans for local cooperatives.

Getting There & Away

Air Masbate isn't too well served by airlines. PAL, Air Philippines and Cebu Pacific have all overlooked the place, so it's up to the smaller operators. See Getting There & Away under Masbate Town, later, for more information.

Boat Sulpicio Lines ferries go from Cebu City to Ormoc via Masbate town on Monday night, and Trans-Asia ferries go from Cebu City to Masbate town on Monday, Wednesday and Friday evenings.

Regular morning pumpboats sail from the busy pumpboat area at Masbate town's pier to the nearby islands of Ticao and Burias (part of Masbate province) and from there you can continue by pumpboat to the south Luzon towns of Donsol and Bulan. Boats go to Bulan from San Jacinto on Ticao, and to Donsol from Claveria on Burias Island.

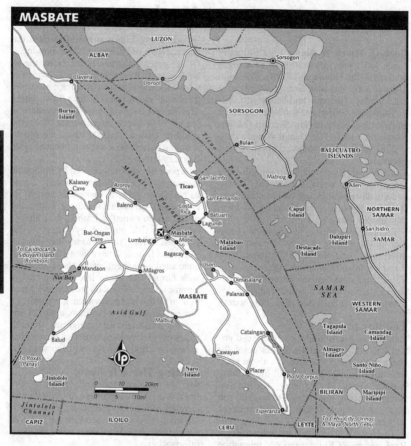

MASBATE

LUZON

ALBAY

Burias Passage

Claveria

Donsol

Sorsogon

SORSOGON

Bulan

Burias Island

Ticao Passage

BALICUATRO ISLANDS

San Jacinto

Ticao

Allen

Kalanay Cave

Aroroy

San Fernando

Capul Island

NORTHERN SAMAR

Baleno

Costa Rica

Batuan

Masbate Passage

Lagundi

San Isidro

SAMAR

Bat-Ongan Cave

Lumbang

Masbate

Mobo

Dalupiri Island

To Cajidiocan & Sibuyan Island (Romblon)

Bagacay

Matabao Island

Destacado Island

Mandaon

Milagros

Uson

Nin Bay

Dimasalang

SAMAR SEA

MASBATE

Palanas

WESTERN SAMAR

Asid Gulf

Malbug

Cataingan

Tagapula Island

Camandag Island

Balud

Cawayan

Almagro Island

To Roxas (Panay)

Placer

Santo Niño Island

Jintololo Island

Naro Island

Pio V Corpus

BILIRAN

Maripipi Island

0   10   20km

0   5   10mi

Jintololo Channel

Esperanza

To Cebu City, Ormoc & Maya (North Cebu)

CAPIZ

ILOILO

CEBU

LEYTE

THE VISAYAS

Large pumpboats sail from Mandaon pier to Roxas' Banica wharf (P90, five hours) at 9 or 10 am Wednesday. On Saturday, it officially leaves at 9 or 10 am also – but it has been known to load up fast and head off as early as 7 am – you should probably stay in Mandaon on Friday night, or at least turn up on the earliest bus or jeepney on Saturday morning. Boats leave Roxas for Mandaon at 9 or 10 am Monday and Thursday. These boat sails down the Panay River, through a forest of bamboo fishing-net poles, to reach Roxas' inland Banica wharf.

Large pumpboats sail from Cajidiocan on Sibuyan Island to Mandaon (P100, 4½ hours) on Thursday morning. Boats leave Mandaon for Cajidiocan on Wednesday morning.

MASBATE TOWN

Despite being sprawled around a large harbour, the town of Masbate is not overendowed with charm. It is, however, the capital of Masbate Province, and the venue for the rowdy **Rodeo Masbateño** (also known as the Rodeo Filipino, or Rodeo Pilipino). Usually held in April or May, this five-day event attracts cowpokes from all over the country and features men's and women's lassoing, barehand cattle wrestling and – the crowd favourite – bull riding. There's around P200,000 in prizes on offer, and it all happens at the Rodeo Arena, Minchs Annexe. For more information, call ☎ 056-333 2120.

The gem of a beach at Bagacay (see that section later), 14km south-east of Masbate town, makes Boracay seem like a waste of time. Don't miss it.

Information
On Quezon St, there's a PNB bank, opposite the Kawayan Bar & Restaurant, and a BayanTel international phone office near the Maxim Grocery Store. The post office is nearby also.

There's a police station beside the pier, below Quezon St. Call ☎ 166 in the event of an emergency.

Places to Stay
Most of Masbate town's accommodation is on Quezon St, running in an arc above the port area.

Offering the best value on Quezon St, **Masbate Lodge & Barber Shop** (☎ 056-333 2184) has large, spotlessly clean 2nd storey rooms with lovely polished floorboards. All rooms share a clean common bath and toilet, which has views out over the port area and harbour. Rooms with fan/air-con are P150, rooms with quiet, efficient air-con start at P350.

One block away, at **Ronnie's Inn**, you can get a dreary but OK air-con room with TV and bath for P550. The bathroom is an airless cupboard.

The relatively large **St Anthony Hotel** (☎ 056-333 2180) claims to be 'the best in the province'. Thankfully, this is only an idle threat. While the lobby is clean and bright and furnished with fishtanks and a lounge suite, the rooms don't continue the trend. Dark, box-like singles/twins with fan and bath are P250/300. Air-con versions are P380/450. The mattresses, even in the air-con rooms, are pancake thin.

Down on Tara St, which runs parallel to Quezon St in the nearby port area, is the large **Rancher's Hotel** (☎/fax 056-333 3931). Run by the friendly Mrs Chua, this place has views of the harbour, and plain, acceptable rooms with fan and common bath for P250. Spacious air-con singles/doubles with bath and TV are P500/700, and come with cooking facilities. A large, apartment-style set-up with separate bedroom, bath, lounge suite, TV, kitchen and narrow balcony facing the water is P800. The restaurant here serves good Filipino budget meals for P30.

Places to Eat
The Quezon St strip has plenty of cheap, lively eateries. At the far end, opposite the Shell service station and the bus station, **L & M Martinez Enterprises** is a street-side foodhouse serving local dishes for around P20 per serve. A few blocks towards the town centre, **D'San Restaurant** and **Elm's Snacks** do sit-down Filipino meals from P30 to P60.

A couple of blocks farther, opposite the PNB bank, **Kawayan Bar & Restaurant** is a new nightspot and eatery serving plenty of traditional beef and pork dishes for around P100. On either side of St Anthony Hotel, **Ronnie's Restaurant** and **JRF Sizzling Chicken** offer good local fare for P50 to P100.

Nearby Ibañez St, which runs off Quezon St (with **Maxim Grocery Store** on the corner), is a lively food street, especially at night. Stalls and small cafes offer freshly cooked chicken pieces, spring rolls and other snacks from P10 to P35. Among these eateries is the aqua-coloured **Xiamen Fresh Water & Restaurant**, where tasty mushrooms with shrimp balls cost P50, and spectacular sizzling beef costs P90. The fresh water is a sideline business – the restaurant delivers water to households not connected to town water.

For baked goods and groceries, there's the well-stocked, sit-down **La Concha Cakes & Bakes**, on Quezon St, opposite the church.

In the port area, near Rancher's Hotel on Tara St, cheap eateries include the Chinese-flavoured **Peking House**, towards the pier.

Entertainment

Masbate town shuffles off to bed pretty early, but a few places do stay up. *Kawayan Bar & Restaurant* is always good for a late-night drink, and *Ronnie's Inn* often has live bands.

Getting There & Away

Air Masbate town's airport is a P5 to P10 tricycle ride from Quezon St.

Asian Spirit flies from Manila to Masbate town (P1750, one hour) and back early each morning. Laoag International Airways has a flight from Manila to Masbate town (P1750) on Monday, Wednesday and Friday mornings and around noon Sunday.

Masbate Express (Corporate Air) flies from Manila to Masbate town (P1621, one hour) and back every morning. Masbate Express has an office (☎ 032-832 2316, 0917 925 1112) opposite Manila's domestic terminal on the 6th floor, Unit L, Ding Velayo Building and a desk at the Masbate town airport.

Boat The Masbate town pier is near the market, below Quezon St. There's a rustic WG&A ticket office (☎ 056-333 2211) near the pier, opposite the Shell service station. The thronging pumpboats here offer regular connections (usually around 9 or 10 am) to Costa Rica and Lagundi on Ticao, and Claveria on Burias Island. You can also hire these boats for 'special rides' (see Ticao & Burias Islands, later). You'll find information on other boat services under Boat in Masbate's introductory Getting There & Away section.

Bus & Jeepney Small minivans travel between Masbate town and Mandaon (P70, two hours), as do regular buses and jeepneys, which run from around 6 am to around 2 pm. In Masbate town, the minivans and many buses drop passengers at the Shell service station, at the end of Quezon St. Many more buses and jeepneys terminate next to the market in the pier area. From either spot, you can also catch jeepneys or buses to Cataingan (P50, two hours).

The scenic Masbate town–Mandaon route is sealed and smooth from Masbate town to the small town of Milagros, but from there to Mandaon it's unsealed and crumbly.

BAGACAY

About 14km from Masbate town, *Bituon Beach Resort* (☎ 056-333 2242), in Bagacay, is one of the Philippines' best-kept secrets. With a white-sand, coral-crumbed beach in a stunning, secluded cove, this place is an idyllic minivillage offering a wide range of accommodation. A long, sun-bleached row of small, tidy nipa hut-style rooms with bath and shared balcony are P350. Palm-shaded, concrete duplex cottages right on the sand come with bath, wall-mounted fan and small balcony for P500. More-lavish rooms next door have big balconies and air-con for P1500. The beachy, thatched-roof restaurant serves good Filipino and international breakfasts for P95 to P125, and main meals for not much more. The swimming pool here (entry P30/50 for children/adults) pales in significance to the turquoise waters of the beach, but it's a good place to dump the kids.

The resort is a P100 tricycle ride from Masbate town (30 to 45 minutes), 7km past the town of Mobo, at the end of an unpromising-looking dirt road.

TICAO & BURIAS ISLANDS

The islands of Ticao (pronounced 'tee-cow') and Burias (pronounced 'boo-ree-as') are wild and enticingly unexplored, with plenty of potential for free-form hiking. Good accommodation may be tricky to find on both islands and they may be best regarded as day-trip destinations from Masbate town.

For information about the unpredictable pumpboat schedules and prices for Ticao and Burias islands, ask at the security-guard booth at the Masbate town pier's gate.

Ticao Island

On Ticao's rugged west coast, **Costa Rica** is a lonely little fishing village with a long, brown-sand beach. Not exactly an island paradise, it at least makes for a good boat-trip – we saw **dolphins** and **flying fish** along the way.

Daily pumpboats go from the Masbate town pier to Costa Rica (P10, 45 minutes), Lagundi and several other villages and towns on Ticao. A hired 'special ride' pumpboat will cost P500 for the return trip.

Burias Island

In February 1999, in the town of **Claveria** on Burias, a **cave** of truly cathedral-like dimensions was uncovered by a visiting official. Thought to have been a prehistoric burial ground, the cave shows signs of relatively recent habitation in the form of scrawlings on the gravestones, as well as pieces of Ming Dynasty pottery. Known to locals for years, the cave has a well-hidden, narrow entrance. Negotiations are underway to have the cave officially recognised and protected. Guides may be found in sitio Macamote, barangay Boca Enganyo, just outside Claveria proper.

Farther out than Ticao, remote Burias is still a worthy day-trip destination if you start out early. Regular pumpboats from Masbate to Claveria (P75) take about three hours.

MANDAON

A knobbly, green hill provides an unusual backdrop to the port town of Mandaon (pronounced 'man-**dow**-on'), 64km from Masbate town. **Bat-Ongan Cave** is about half an hour by jeepney or bus, near the main road between Mandaon and Masbate town. Look for the high, rocky hill that seems so out of place it might have fallen out of the sky.

West of the goldmining town of Aroroy, about 40km by road from Mandaon, day trips can be made to the **Kalanay Cave**, which has yielded some interesting archaeological relics.

A particularly scenic connection if you can make it is the five-hour pumpboat trip between Mandaon and Roxas' Banica wharf, on Panay (see Masbate's introductory Getting There & Away section earlier). Boats in either direction go via several islands off Masbate, including the stunning, high-peaked island of **Cagmasoso**, about an hour's sailing from Mandaon.

Places to Stay & Eat

Right by the pier, *Mesa's Lodging House & Eatery* has small, tidy rooms upstairs (watch your head!) with fan, ancient common bath and a cosy little common lounge area for P75 per head. This simple, friendly place is run by Ernesto and Dorothea Mesa and their family. Rooms are above the eatery, which does good local dishes for P20 per serve.

Over the road, the less cosy *4-K's Restaurant & Lodging House* has large, plain rooms upstairs with fan and common bath for P150. It also pumps out loud videoke favourites most nights. Filipino food here is around P30.

A good bakery near the pier is *Mommy's Bread House*. *Lina's Store*, at the nearby bus station (via the market from the pier), is run by the friendly Lorna Manuel, who has fresh food available virtually 24 hours a day. She also has a two-way radio and can keep you posted on the boat, bus and jeepney situation. Opposite the square, you can while away the waiting time at the 4-K's Billiard Hall.

Getting There & Away

Ordinary (ie, non-air-con) buses and jeepneys run back and forth between Mandaon and Masbate (P40 to P50, two hours) up until about 1 or 2 pm. After that, you have to rely on 'air-con buses' (P70, two hours), which make their last runs around 3 or 4 pm. In Mandaon, the buses and jeepneys collect passengers at a square (locally known as 'the terminal') about 300m from the pier. Don't wait at the pier for these vehicles, they're often full by the time they pass by. Lorna Manuel, at Lina's Store (see Places to Stay & Eat earlier) is a great source of information on boats, buses and jeepneys.

Jeepneys tackling the particularly bad road to Aroroy (P50, around three hours) leave from the station. There are two per day, heading off at around 8 and 10 am.

CATAINGAN

Cataingan (pronounced 'kat-**ah**-ing-an') is 77km from Masbate town. Plenty of buses and jeepneys travel between Masbate town and Cataingan (P40 to P50, two hours), along a good, sealed road. There are a couple of *lodging houses* in Cataingan, and from here boats go to north Cebu (see the Masbate Getting There & Away section).

Samar

The island province of Samar still has many wild and beautiful places intact, and it remains relatively undeveloped for tourism. It has a narrow coastal plain, and a mountainous and heavily forested interior. Travelling to Samar by road, you cross the scenic San Juanico Strait by the 2km-long bridge linking it with the neighbouring province of Leyte. Try to do this in the daytime, so you can enjoy the great view of coastline and busy waterways. Flying to either Catarman or Calbayog, you'll see a mass of small offshore islands, wide river estuaries and millions of coconut palms.

Historically, Samar is interesting – ironically, it is in this province that both the first of the colonisers and the last of the liberators landed. Magellan first set foot in the Philippines in 1521, at the island of Homonhon in the south; and MacArthur's liberating troops landed at Guiuan, also in the south, to push the Japanese forces back in 1944.

As with so many places in the Philippines, copra is a major product here, and it's often quite a feat for drivers to dodge the ubiquitous piles of coconut meat drying along the narrow roadsides. Fishing and subsistence farming of rice, maize and root crops are the two other major economic activities. Samar also produces export-quality shell-craft, plus abaca and rattan products.

Waray is the language commonly spoken on Samar, and the traditional dance of welcome – the *kuratsa* – is, astonishingly, patterned after the courtship movements of chickens. Could this be why the DOT in Borongan includes *hinihigugma kita* ('I love you') on its list of useful Waray phrases for tourists?

Dangers & Annoyances

Samar's rugged terrain still provides refuge for antigovernment forces in the shape of small New People's Army (NPA) groups, and 'incidents' do occur. If you intend to travel in north-eastern Samar it's worth checking the security situation with the DOT before you go.

Getting There & Away

Air Asian Spirit flies from Manila to Calbayog (P1885) on Tuesday, Wednesday, Friday and Sunday mornings, returning the same days. Manila–Catarman flights (P1830) leave every morning except Monday and Friday; flights from Catarman leave on the same days.

Boat A boat leaves Calbayog for Cebu City (P275, 10 hours) on Tuesday, Thursday and Saturday evenings. There are Cebu City–Calbayog services on Monday, Wednesday, Friday and Saturday evenings.

There are daily boats from Allen to Matnog (P33, one hour) on Luzon, with six departures starting at 4 am. There may also be a boat between Matnog and San Isidro.

Bus There are regular departures to Tacloban on Leyte from Catarman (eight hours), Guiuan (eight hours) Calbayog (five hours), Borongan (five hours) and Catbalogan (three hours).

Philtranco and BLBT each have several daily services to Manila from Catarman, Calbayog and Catbalogan, and daily departures from Borongan and Guiuan (around P555/412 air-con/'1st class', 26 to 30 hours from all departure points).

Information

There are PNB branches in Catarman, Calbayog, Catbalogan, Borongan and Guiuan. They will only change US dollars. It is not yet possible to get cash advances on credit cards and there are no ATMs.

At the time of publication there was no public access to the Internet on Samar.

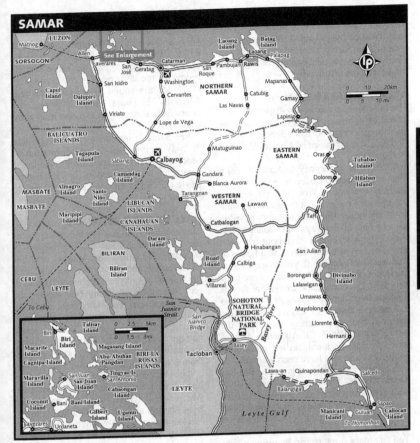

SAMAR

CATARMAN

A small and rather ramshackle town, Catarman is the point of air entry to northern Samar, and is a stopping-off point for trips along the north-east coast and into the centre of the island.

Places to Stay

If you are overnighting in Catarman try *Riverview Hotel*, where rooms are P350 to P600. Go for the air-con rooms; the others are musty, dark and cramped.

Diocesan Catholic Centre (DCC) has spartan but clean rooms with fan for P100

and you can order meals for P60 from the refectory.

As a last resort stay at *Joni's*, where the rooms for P70 to P600 are OK if you can get past the disgusting stairwell.

There are also two *lodgings* associated with the University of the Eastern Philippines (UEP), about 3km out of town and within walking distance from White Beach.

Getting There & Away

Asian Spirit, which flies between Catarman and Manila, has an office on Magsaysay St. The airport is 2km (P20 by tricycle) from town. Buses and jeepneys meet the boats at Allen and continue to Catarman. There are long-distance buses to and from Leyte and Luzon. See Samar's introductory Getting There & Away section, earlier, for flight and road-transport information.

AROUND CATARMAN

The following couple of day-trips were suggested by helpful Frumencio Lagrimas, the tourism officer for northern Samar. You can find him at the Provincial Capitol Building by the airport.

Take an early jeepney to Rawis/Laoang (one hour) then transfer to a jeepney to Catubig (one hour). From Catubig make a trip upriver by pumpboat to **Las Navas** (one hour) and return the same way. It's possible to go by boat all the way from Laoang to Las Navas, but it's about a three hour trip each way. The mayor in Las Navas will help you find *accommodation* if you want to stay overnight. **Pinipiskan Falls** is a three-hour hike from Las Navas, and from there there's a **jungle track** that continues to Matuguiano and takes a couple of days to walk. This beautiful and rugged area was part of the setting for the 1999 'Elf Authentic Adventure', an international skilled endurance competition, so you have been warned!

Alternatively you could go to the **Biri-Las Rosas Islands**. These undeveloped islands are a marine protected area and home to fishing communities. There is good **snorkelling** and **diving** at Biri, and occasionally good **surf**, but you'll need your own equipment. You can make a return trip by hiring a boat from Lavezares (P500 to P700 return, one hour each way). There is no commercial accommodation. If you're interested in exploring this area you may want to check with the DENR in Catarman. It may have more-current information than the DOT.

The road from Laoang along the north east coast is open as far as Lapiring. It is an undeveloped area of **surf beaches** and **rock formations** along the coast.

ALLEN

This is a small port town for boats to Luzon. If you need to stay overnight here try *Lau-*

reen's Lodging, right at the wharf, with a restaurant attached. It's clean, if basic and noisy, and is handy to the boats. Rooms cost P75 to P150. *Mary Ann Lodge*, by the jeepney stand in town, has the same sort of rooms for the same price.

All Manila-bound buses go via Allen. Allen is 1½ hours from Calbayog; 3½ hours from Catbalogan and one hour from Catarman.

See Samar's introductory Getting There & Away section, earlier, for information on boats to and from Luzon. Philtranco buses meet each boat and depart for Tacloban on Leyte (P211/157 air-con/'1st class', five to six hours).

BALCUARTRO ISLANDS

This group of islands is just below the northwestern point of Samar. The largest is **Dalupiri**, also called San Antonio, and has good beaches and clear water; but beware of the zillions of spiky sea-urchins and swim in reef shoes. Stay at *Flying Dog Resort*, the only commercial accommodation on the island. The setting is a beautiful landscaped garden right on the beach, but the pretty cottages for P500 to P1000 are under-maintained and tatty. There is electricity from 6 to 11 pm only, so rooms are fanless and can be hot if there is no breeze. You can hire a boat to the island of **Capul** to the west, which was a galleon staging post during Spanish days and has a ruined lighthouse.

Take a tricycle from Allen to San Isidro (P20/50 regular/hire), or get off north-bound buses in San Isidro. You may have to hire a boat to Dalupiri (P150, 15 minutes) if there are no other passengers. To return to San Isidro, stand on the beach and wave down a passing passenger boat (P20).

CALBAYOG

The pretty road from Allen to Calbayog hugs the coast, passing through villages and river estuaries framed with nipa palms, and has a backdrop of mountains. Calbayog has a busy and colourful wharf area that is full of painted cargo, fishing and passenger boats, and is walking distance from the town centre and hotels.

There is a good information brochure available from the City Information Office at City Hall. The one and, so far, only **museum** in Samar is located in the College of Christ the King and is open weekdays during school hours. It houses a collection of artefacts from around the province, as well as ancient ceramics, beads and coins.

Calbayog comes alive for the annual **fiesta** on 7 and 8 September, with parades, outdoor performances and re-enactments, cultural displays and huge street markets.

Nearby are the **waterfalls** of Bangon, Mawacat and Larik, the **Guinogo-an cave system**, and **Mapaso Hot Springs** (where, remarkably, small red crustaceans called *pokot* survive in the scalding water). All these attractions are between one and two hours' drive, plus between 15 and 40 minutes' walk, from the city.

Places to Stay & Eat
San Joaquin Inn and *Central Inn* offer rooms for P100 to P700. Neither is particularly appealing. The best hotel in town is *Eduardo's Tourist Hotel* (☎ 055-209 1558), where all rooms have air-con and TV and cost P500 to P1500. Each of these lodgings has a restaurant attached. There is a selection of *food stalls* at the bus station.

Getting There & Away
Asian Spirit flies to and from Manila four times a week.

There are many regular daily buses between Calbayog and Catarman via Allen (P40, four hours) and between Calbayog and Catbalogan (P30, two hours). Jeepneys ply the coastal road but it's faster to take a bus between the major towns.

CATBALOGAN
This is the provincial capital of western Samar, but has little to encourage a lengthy stay. It is the place to catch a bus over to the east coast, and you may need to overnight here.

Places to Stay & Eat
Fortune Hotel (☎ 055-251 2147) is in the noisy centre of town and has a good range

of rooms for P150 to P450. The attached restaurant has a varied and reasonable menu. For great sunset views stay at *Maqueda Bay Hotel* (☎ 055-251 2386). A few minutes by tricycle from the centre of town, its air-con rooms with bath range from P450 to P700. The restaurant has enormous windows looking directly onto the water.

Getting There & Away
Although Catbalogan is a port town, there are presently no passenger vessels operating.

There are daily buses between Calbayog and Catbalogan (P30, two hours). There are also jeepneys, but it's faster to take a bus. There are also daily bus services to Borongan (P60, three hours) on the east coast and to Tacloban (P50, three hours) on Leyte. Buray, about half an hour out of Catbalogan, is the junction for Borongan–Tacloban buses, so there are more services to the east coast from Buray than from Catbalogan.

BORONGAN
The road joining the east and west coasts rises over Samar's central range of mountains, passing through forested country before reaching the Pacific coast at Taft. There have been confirmed sightings of the **Philippine eagle** in the Taft Forest.

From here the road turns south towards Borongan. There is the possibility of good **surf** along the coast from Borongan to Umawas but it's fickle at best – December to May can be good, but surfers need to be prepared to wait for days or weeks for the right conditions. There are marlin and sailfish offshore and you can go **fishing** with locals if conditions are right.

Borongan town is the jumping-off point for the island of **Divinubo**, a pretty spot 10 minutes offshore, with a lighthouse built by Americans in 1906. It has been converted from gas power to electricity and is still in use, beaming out every 15 seconds. Divinubo has good snorkelling, caves and forested slopes.

Places to Stay
There are several basic lodgings in town. Of these, *Domsowir Hotel* is centrally located

on the river bridge. Rooms range from P125 to P755. For low-key and very stylish accommodation, stay at **Pirate's Cove**, near the port, where nipa cottages with a difference cost between P500 and P2600. Check out the mosaics and shell mirrors. There is a sea pool at low tide, good snorkelling and breezy pavilions out over the water. You can arrange day trips inland, fishing and boat-hire from here.

Getting There & Away
Regular buses run daily from Borongan to Catbalogan (P60, three hours) and Tacloban (P100, five hours) on Leyte via Buray. There are also buses to Manila (see Samar's introductory Getting There & Away section). Jeepneys make the journey to Guiuan (P40, 2½ hours) every hour until about 5 pm.

GUIUAN
This relaxed and easygoing township (pronounced 'ghee-won'), in a beautiful natural setting on the south-eastern tip of Samar, has a great range of historical attractions spanning the period of first colonisers to the days of the final liberators. Visit the 16th century **church** and fabulous carved Spanish doors and altar, which the rather mercenary Imelda Marcos was (luckily) prevented from buying in bulk up her already huge personal antique collection. Walk up to the **weather station** for wide, sweeping views across the Pacific Ocean and Leyte Gulf. Drive along the huge crumbling **WWII runway** and soak up the historical atmosphere. Go across the bay to the island of **Tubabao**, where a few traces remain of the period when White Russian emigres took refuge here after the end of WWII, under the protection of the International Refugee Organisation.

Places to Stay & Eat
Kevin's Pension and **Blue Star Lodging** are just passably clean, but what can you expect for P50 to P150? By far the best option in town is **Tanghay Lodge**, on the waterfront, 1km or so from the town centre. It has a swimming area in the bay and great sunset pavilions set out over the water. Rooms range from P140 to P780. There is good food here, as well as at **Sporks Restaurant**, in town. **DJ's Singalong**, about 2km away from Tanghay Lodge at the other end of the waterfront, is a great bar built on stilts out over the water and is open till late for beer and snacks.

Getting There & Away
Boat There's a nightly boat to Tacloban (P110 to P150, eight hours), leaving around 10 pm. This route has been unlucky in recent times, with one boat sinking and one burning up on the way.

Bus & Jeepney
Buses to Tacloban leave every night at around 8 pm but think twice about taking the coast and mountain road after dark. Regular jeepneys run to Borongan (P40, 2½ hours) and you can connect to daytime buses to Tacloban and Catbalogan from there.

The road north-west to Lawa-an via Basey is nominally open, but as yet no public transport runs from Guiuan to Basey, due to the bad condition of the track, especially after rain. There are plans to seal this section within the next two years and that will considerably improve access to Guiuan. It may be possible to hire a jeep to drive to Tacloban along this road, but it will cost you around P2500.

AROUND GUIUAN
The island of **Homonhon** is where Magellan first landed in the Philippines on 16 March 1521. Plans are underway to restore the historic marker and landing site. The island has blowholes, white-sand beaches and a freshwater cascade and creek. You can get a public banca from Guiuan (P20, two hours) during daylight hours and depending on the tide. Be prepared to overnight in the old *hospital building* if necessary.

Suluan, an hour beyond Homonhon, has a derelict lighthouse. The 500 steps up to it are good exercise and the reward is a fantastic view across the islands of Leyte Gulf and the Pacific Ocean. There are also coastal caves accessible at low tide. If you want to overnight on Suluan, the barangay captain will help you.

Also around Guiuan is **Sulangan Beach** for swimming, snorkelling and beachcombing for the beautiful **golden cowrie** shell. But be warned; these shells are protected by law, and are therefore illegal to collect. WWII historians will also want to see the remains of **Navy 3149 Base** at nearby Ngolos.

Kantican, also known as Pearl Island, has a pearl farm and clear water for swimming and snorkelling. Check with Rene Gallan, the Fisheries Office supervisor, if you want to go over there. He can be found near the Tanghay Lodge.

Balangiga

This small town, located between Basey and Guiuan, was scene of an infamous 'incident', on 28 September 1901, between the US garrison stationed here and local people. Filipinos attacked and killed most of the garrison, but a more terrible revenge was subsequently taken by the relieving US force, which was instructed to 'kill anyone capable of bearing arms', including all boys aged 10 years of age and over. The commanding officer was later court-martialled. There is an annual re-enactment and commemoration on that date.

Sohoton Natural Bridge National Park

This is Samar's premier natural attraction, a protected area of **caves** and **forest**, and home to at least six of Samar's endemic birds. Access is via Basey which, given the current state of the road linking Basey and Guiuan, is easiest to access from Tacloban on Leyte. It's worth checking to see if the road condition is passable when you visit. For further information see Sohoton Natural Bridge National Park in Around Tacloban in the Leyte section, later.

Leyte

The island of Leyte has a relatively narrow and fertile coastal strip that gives way to a rugged and mountainous interior. The staple crops are rice, maize and root vegetables with fishing, coconuts, abaca and tobacco providing cash income. Cattle are ranched in the hills of northern Leyte. Forestry is still a major industry, though it is now regulated more efficiently following the devastating Ormoc floods of 1991, which were caused largely by excessive deforestation above the city.

During the Japanese occupation, Leyte was the base of a formidable fighting force of Filipino guerilla units, led by local hero Ruperto Kangleon. Assurance of strong guerilla support was instrumental in MacArthur's choice to use Leyte for the liberation landings, and it remains a centre of WWII memorials and commemorative events. For travellers, Leyte offers pre-colonial, colonial and WWII historical interest; great natural beauty, with national parks and hiking trails; and exceptional diving in the waters off the southern coast.

There are several popular annual festivals on Leyte. The Pintados, or 'painted', festival in Tacloban on 29 June celebrates the traditional tattooing practiced here before the Spanish arrived; nowadays water-based paints are used for the festival's body decoration. In Abuyog, on the south coast, there are plans to revive the recently defunct Bugoyan festival on 19 August. *Bugoyan* means 'bee', an animal important in local legend, and performers and dancers wear fabulous bee costumes. In Calubian, the Lubi-Lubi Festival, which celebrates the town's namesake, the coconut, happens on 15 August.

Getting There & Away

Air PAL, Cebu Pacific and Air Philippines connect Tacloban with Manila. See Getting There & Away under Tacloban, later, for more information.

Boat Leyte has boat connections with Bohol Cebu, Luzon, Mindanao and Samar.

Bohol & Cebu There's a daily boat from Maasin to Ubay on Bohol (P100, three hours).

Most boat connections with Cebu are to Cebu City. A boat leaves Baybay for Cebu (P100 to P140, six hours) each night.

THE VISAYAS

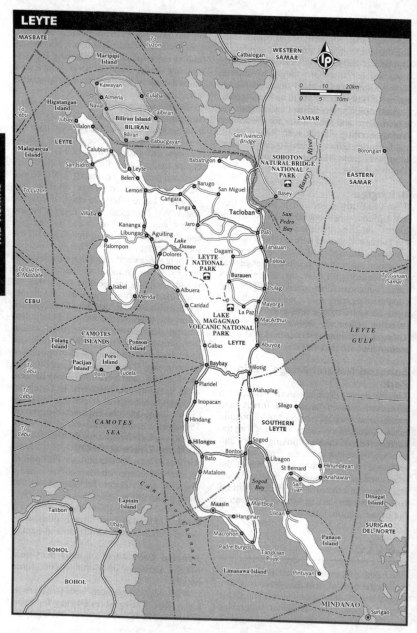

SuperCat/SeaAngels has a boat from Maasin to Cebu City (P330, two hours) each afternoon.

SuperCat/SeaAngels has four Ormoc–Cebu City (P360, two hours) services daily. Regular ferries run the same route (P100, five hours). WG&A leaves Wednesday, Friday and Sunday around midnight, Sulpicio Lines leaves late Sunday evening, and San Juan Ferries leaves each night.

Cebu Ferries MV *Manaoag* leaves Tacloban for Cebu on Tuesday and Thursday afternoons. WG&A's MV *Our Lady of Guadelupe* sails the Tacloban–Cebu City (P216 to P750) route on Tuesday and Friday afternoons, and Maypalad Lines leaves Wednesday, Friday and Sunday afternoons (P150). The journey from Tacloban to Cebu takes about 14 hours.

Luzon A boat leaves Baybay for Manila (P400 to P500, 24 hours) on Sunday. Sulpicio Lines leaves Ormoc for Manila (P578 to P816, 36 hours) on Tuesday afternoon, going via Masbate (P227 to P316).

Mindanao & Samar SuperCat/SeaAngels leaves Maasin for Surigao (P275, 1½ hours) daily. Regular boats leave Maasin for Surigao (five hours) every night. A boat leaves Baybay for Surigao via Maasin on Friday, and there's a morning ferry daily from Liloan to Surigao (five hours).

The daily boat from Tacloban to Guiuan takes about eight hours.

Bus There are bus services between Leyte and Biliran, Luzon, Mindanao and Samar.

Several daily buses run between Tacloban and Naval on Biliran, via Lemon (P70, three hours). You can also take an Ormoc to Tacloban bus and change at Lemon.

Philtranco has regular buses from Tacloban to Manila (P723 to P528, 26 hours), with several departures between 6.30 and 11.30 am, one departure around 4 pm, and another around 11.30 pm. Buses depart Ormoc for Manila (P600/817 regular/air-con, 26 hours) three times daily.

Philtranco runs from Tacloban and Ormoc to Davao (P470 to P355) on Min-danao, via Surigao, in the afternoon – departure times depend on the incoming bus arrival time.

There are regular bus services from Tacloban to Catbalogan (P70, three hours), Calbayog (4½ hours) and Borongan (P100, five hours).

All Manila-bound buses go via Samar.

TACLOBAN

This busy and compact town is the capital of Leyte, and hugs the southern edge of the beautiful San Juanico Strait. Activity centres on the bustling wharf area and market in the middle of town. Tacloban's most famous daughter is Imelda Romualdez Marcos, whose family home is at Tolosa, a little way south; the family's influence in the town is evident in street names and various public buildings.

Historically, Tacloban is better known as the place to which General MacArthur returned with US liberating forces on 20 October 1944 (actually, he landed at Palo, a few kilometres outside the city). This date is celebrated annually, and there are WWII memorials around the town, including moulded reliefs on outer walls of the Capitol Building that commemorate the landing.

Information

Tourist Office This is located in the Children's Park on Senator Enage St (☎ 053-321 2048, fax 325 5279, ✆ dotr8@mozcom.com) and is open weekdays. The staff are very helpful and knowledgeable. If you arrive on the weekend, the Leyte Normal University House (see Places to Stay later) usually has a good supply of DOT brochures.

Money The PNB bank is on the corner of Santo Niño and Justice Romualdez Sts and changes US dollars. The Equitable Bank on Rizal Avenue will advance cash against Visa cards. The PCI Bank on the corner of Salazar and Zamora Sts has an ATM that allows cash advances on MasterCard. Since we were there, these last two banks have been merged, so check to see what services are still offered, or if both branches are still operating.

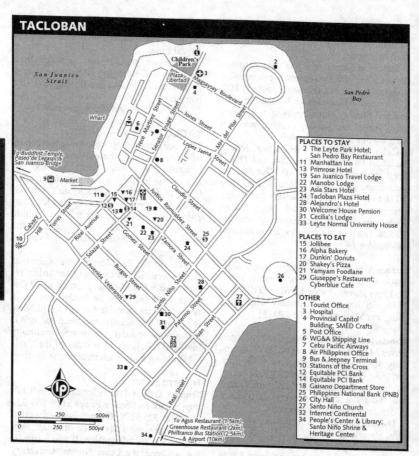

TACLOBAN

San Juanico Strait

Children's Park

Plaza Libertad

Magsaysay Boulevard

Jones Street

Lopez Jaena Street

Trece Martirez Street

Senator Enage Street

Mt del Pilar Street

San Pedro Bay

Wharf

To Buddhist Temple, Paseo de Legaspi & San Juanico Bridge

Market

Justice Romualdez Street

Claudio Street

Calvary Hill

Torres Street

Riza Avenue

Salazar Street

Gomez Street

Zamora Street

Santo Niño Street

Burgos Street

Avenida Veteranos

Paterno Street

Juan Street

Real Street

To Agus Restaurant (1.5km), Greenhouse Restaurant (2km), Philtranco Bus Station (2.5km), & Airport (10km)

0   250   500m
0   250   500yd

PLACES TO STAY
2   The Leyte Park Hotel; San Pedro Bay Restaurant
11   Manhattan Inn
13   Primrose Hotel
19   San Juanico Travel Lodge
22   Manobo Lodge
23   Asia Stars Hotel
24   Tacloban Plaza Hotel
30   Alejandro's Hotel
31   Welcome House Pension
32   Cecilia's Lodge
33   Leyte Normal University House

PLACES TO EAT
15   Jollibee
16   Alpha Bakery
17   Dunkin' Donuts
20   Shakey's Pizza
21   Yamyam Foodlane
29   Giuseppe's Restaurant; Cyberblue Cafe

OTHER
1   Tourist Office
3   Hospital
4   Provincial Capitol Building; SMED Crafts
5   Post Office
6   WG&A Shipping Line
7   Cebu Pacific Airways
8   Air Philippines Office
9   Bus & Jeepney Terminal
10   Stations of the Cross
12   Equitable PCI Bank
14   Equitable PCI Bank
18   Gaisano Department Store
25   Philippines National Bank (PNB)
26   City Hall
27   Santo Niño Church
32   Internet Continental
34   People's Center & Library; Santo Niño Shrine & Heritage Center

Email & Internet Access Internet cafes have hit Tacloban in a big way. They're mostly located along Avenida Veteranos and charge between P30 and P40 per hour depending on the time of day. Try Internet Continental at 225 Avenida Veteranos, open from 8 am to 10 pm daily; or Cyberblue Cafe, above Giuseppe's Restaurant, open from 9 am to 9 pm daily.

Things to See & Do
Take a sunrise climb along the **Stations of the Cross** to the top of Calvary Hill for wide views across the San Juanico Strait and some decent bird watching. Spare a thought for the people living in the huts at the top as they carry water up the steep steps. Visit the chaotic and colourful **market** early, as much of the fresh produce (including the gorgeous flowers) is gone by 7 am and the meaty section grows decidedly smelly. The latter is not for the faint-hearted.

A must is the **Santo Niño Shrine and Heritage Center**, an enormous palatial residence and opulent guesthouse built to Imelda Marcos' orders and *never* slept in! It houses an extraordinary collection of antiques and objets d'art from across the world, including personal gifts from Mao Tse Tung. There are some fabulous Russian icons, 18 of which were stolen in 1998 because of the lack of effective security. The centre is sadly under-curated, decaying almost before your eyes, but it's well worth the P200 entry fee for a guided tour. This fee covers up to six people. The centre is open from 8.30 to 11.30 am and from 1 to 4.30 pm daily. A museum at the University of the Divine Word closed when the university did in 1992, and it's hard to establish what happened to the collection, though it's still mentioned in some guides.

See the display of **WWII memorabilia** in the beautiful old part of Alejandro's Hotel and read the absorbing history of the building, used variously by Japanese troops, displaced Filipinos and liberating forces – while always being home to Alejandro's family.

The helpful leaflet *Do-it-yourself tour of Tacloban and Environs* from the tourist office includes most of these places and more, and describes an informative self-guided **walking tour** of points of interest in the city.

Places to Stay – Budget

There is a range of budget accommodation in town.

Manobo Lodge, on Zamora St, is tatty but spotlessly clean; it's also just off the main road and quieter than many places in town. Rooms range from P250 to P352 and a bathroom is shared between two rooms.

San Juanico Travel Lodge, on Justice Romualdez St, is fine for a basic lodge, with rooms at P150 to P350, but there are several surly male staff.

Cecilia's Lodge (☎ 053-321 2815), on Patermo St, is a rabbit-warren of rooms and doors. Rooms are charged per person and cost P120/190 with shared/private bath.

Best value for money is at *Leyte Normal University House*, a little beyond the town centre, which is spacious and airy and even has a grassy area outside. Rooms here range from P400 to P1050. All have air-con and bath, and there is a restaurant and tea room open during school hours on weekdays.

Places to Stay – Mid-Range

Manhattan Inn, on Rizal St next to the market and wharf, is getting a bit tired and needs some maintenance, but is still good value. All rooms have air-con, bath and TV, and singles/doubles cost around P500/650. Rates vary depending on whether you pay by cash or credit card. Its central location makes it very noisy though; all the other mid-range lodgings are quieter.

Tacloban Plaza Hotel (☎ 053-325 5850), on Justice Romualdez St, has been recently renovated and has good rooms, all with air-con, bath and TV for P530 to P1500.

The small *Welcome House Pension* (☎ 053-321 2739), at the end of Santo Niño St, is new and bright, with rooms with fan from P200, and rooms with air-con, bath and TV from P600.

Primrose Hotel is being renovated floor by floor, and the new rooms are fine. They cost from P300 with fan and bath to P700 with air-con, bath, TV and fridge.

Places to Stay – Top End

You still can't beat the *Leyte Park Hotel* (☎ 053-325 6000, fax 325 5587, *leypark@tac.weblinq.com*) for location, as it is right on the waterfront and has beautiful grounds. Rooms range from P2243 to P6727. Day use of the good-sized pool for nonguests costs P75. The Leyte Park offers nightly entertainment (also open to nonguests) which, depending on the day, may be a disco, ballroom dancing or sing-along. There is live music every evening in the open-air bar at the entrance to the hotel's grounds.

Opened in 1999, *Alejandro's* (☎ 053-321 7033, fax 523 7872), on Patermo St, is a fine hotel, built around the beautiful 1930s home of Alejandro Montejo. Rooms range from P950 to P1365.

Asia Stars Hotel (☎ 053-321 5388, fax 325 5889), on Zamora St, has big rooms and pleasant staff. Rates are from P600 to P1350.

Places to Eat

Seafood in Tacloban is good. For fish dishes, try *San Pedro Bay* restaurant at the

Leyte Park Hotel; and **Agus Restaurant**, 1km or so along the airport road. **Greenhouse Kitchen Inn**, about 500m beyond the Agus Restaurant, serves Filipino food with a welcome spicy touch.

Guiseppe's Restaurant, on Avenida Veteranos, serves great fresh pasta and pizza for those hanging out for an Italian fix. It has good salads and an extensive menu of other dishes too. Expect to pay around P200 per person. It is relaxed and unhassled.

Yamyam Foodlane has excellent Filipino fast-food, is clean and cool and has spotless – and functioning – Western-style toilets.

More traditionally, cruise the **lechon stalls** along Real St for slices of whole pigs on spits and barbequed chicken, or visit the **food stalls** around the market. Good bakeries are all over town; try **Alpha Bakery** on the corner of Rizal Ave and Zamora St, for example.

Shopping

Tacloban is famous for the quality of its abaca products, so check out the handicrafts at Small and Medium Enterprise Development (SMED), located in the old jail next to the Capitol Building.

The city's famously delicious cakes and sweetmeats are favourite *pasalubong* (souvenirs) for visiting Filipinos to take home. Try *binagol*, a sticky confection wrapped in banana leaves, and something else that's yummy, which comes baked in half a coconut shell. There are good shops selling these on Zamora St, near the waterfront.

Getting There & Away

Air The airport is about 12km south of town. A jeepney will cost P5, or hire a tricycle for P80.

PAL flies from Tacloban to Manila daily, and has an office at the airport. Cebu Pacific and Air Philippines also fly from Tacloban to Manila daily, and their offices are opposite each other on Senator Enage St.

Bus & Jeepney The Philtranco station is a couple of kilometres south of the city on the airport road. Long-distance buses leave from here north-bound to Manila and south-bound to Mindanao.

Regular daily buses and jeepneys from other parts of Leyte and Samar use the station by the market in the town centre. Example routes and fares include: Tacloban to San Isidro (P70, 3½ hours); to Ormoc (P62, 2½ hours); and to Maasin (P100, five hours).

AROUND TACLOBAN
Palo

This is the place to immerse yourself, if so inclined, in WWII history for half a day. The township of Palo, 12km from Tacloban, is the site of **Red Beach** where, on 20 October 1944, MacArthur fulfilled his vow to return and liberate the Philippines from the occupying Japanese forces (see the boxed text 'I Shall Return' in the Around Manila chapter).

At Red Beach itself, 1km or so from Palo town, there is the moving (though macho) **Leyte Landing Memorial** which, as you approach, gives a strong impression of figures walking out of the sea. Compare it with the photos of the actual event in the MacArthur Park Beach Resort (see Places to Stay, later). There's also a **rock garden** where many international tributes were set in stone to commemorate the 50th anniversary of the Leyte landing in 1994.

Visit Guinhangdan Hill, known then as **Hill 522**, the scene of fierce fighting. The beautiful 16th century **church** was turned into a hospital from October 1944 to March 1945. For those interested in a revisionist history of WWII in the Philippines, and in US involvement then and subsequently in the country, the beautifully written *America's Boy: The Marcoses and the Philippines* by James Hamilton-Paterson is an absorbing read.

Places to Stay The only place to stay at Palo is the government-run **MacArthur Beach Resort** (☎ 053-323 3015, fax 323 2877), just beyond the Red Beach monument. Its location is stunning and rooms range from P2226 to P2940; but there are usually 'promotion' rates that can halve the published rate, so be sure to ask. The resort facilities, including the swimming pool, can be used for P75 per person.

Getting There & Away Take a jeepney from the market in Tacloban for P10, or hire a tricycle for P100 per hour. Ask the driver to drop you off at Red Beach, on the Tacloban road about 1km before Palo township. Tricycles are available locally to travel the short distance between each site.

Sohoton Natural Bridge National Park

Although Sohoton Natural Bridge National Park is on Samar, it is easiest to access it from Tacloban, which is why it's included here. The park contains a series of **caves** under limestone outcrops. There are enormous sparkling stalactites and stalagmites, with **cascades** and **swimming holes** along the cave system. It's reached by boat, with forest and small villages on the riverbanks on either side. The forest in this area is home to at least six species of Samar's endemic birds, monkeys and other **wildlife**. Check conditions before you head off – after heavy rain the caves may be inaccessible.

Getting There & Away Take a jeepney or boat (both P10 per person, one hour) from the market in Tacloban across the San Juanico Strait to Basey.

In Basey call into the Community Environment & Natural Resources Office (CENRO) and ask for Francisco Corales or his assistants. They will organise transport and a guide. On the weekend they can be found around the market in Basey. (By the way, Basey is renowned for mat weaving, so you might want to check out the market if you've time.) From Basey to Sohoton takes 1½ hours by boat. The pumpboat will hold about five people, and rental will cost around P500. You pay a US$2 (or peso equivalent) park entry fee at Basey. Rent a kerosene lamp for P50 or take a good torch.

The tourism department in Tacloban recommends starting early (leave by 7 am). Take a packed lunch, and if you miss the last transport back in the late afternoon, you can stay at *Distrajo's Place* in Basey.

SOUTH OF TACLOBAN
Burauen

Burauen is 44km from Tacloban (P30, one hour by jeepney). It was the home of Justice Romualdez, Imelda's great-great-grandfather, a renowned composer of Filipino songs. The location of his house is being reclaimed as a historical site. The township also has a Japanese war cemetery. It is one of the starting points – the other is Ormoc – for the Leyte Mountain Trail.

Lake Mahagnao Volcanic National Park & the Leyte Mountain Trail

If you wish to visit this national park – site of former volcanic activity – or to hike the 40km mountain trail, you need first to visit the mayor in Burauen for information.

The trail takes in **rainforest**, **lakes** and **waterfalls** as it crosses the mountain range in the centre of Leyte. It finishes near Ormoc, at either Lake Danao National Park (see that section under Around Ormoc, later), or at the volcanically active Tongonan National Park. The DENR in Tacloban set up the trail, so you can get information and look at route maps there.

THE NORTH-WEST

Calubian and San Isidro are in the northwest of Leyte. **Calubian** is home to the Lubi-Lubi Festival, celebrating its namesake (the coconut) on 15 August each year. **San Isidro** is a small township on the coast with boat connections to Cebu. Each of these places has basic *lodgings* and can be reached by bus from Tacloban (3½ hours) and Ormoc (4½ hours).

ORMOC

This busy port town has a bustling wharf area – which is where all the bus and jeepney stations and shipping offices are located – and an attractive grassy promenade along the waterfront. Like much of Leyte, it has strong historical connections.

Ormoc is believed to be one of the early Malay settlements in the Philippines and its name probably comes from a spring called 'Ugmok', settled by Malays long before the

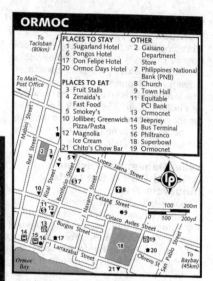

ORMOC

PLACES TO STAY	OTHER
1 Sugarland Hotel	2 Gaisano
6 Pongos Hotel	Department
17 Don Felipe Hotel	Store
20 Ormoc Days Hotel	7 Philippines National
	Bank (PNB)
PLACES TO EAT	8 Church
3 Fruit Stalls	9 Town Hall
4 Zenaida's	11 Equitable
Fast Food	PCI Bank
5 Smokey's	13 Ormocnet
10 Jollibee; Greenwich	14 Jeepney
Pizza/Pasta	15 Bus Terminal
12 Magnolia	16 Philtranco
Ice Cream	18 Superbowl
21 Chito's Chow Bar	19 Ormocnet

The Visayas

Spanish conquest. More recently, it was a centre of WWII activity, with some of the bloodiest battles on Philippine soil taking place over three days in 1944, between the allied US and Filipino forces, and the retreating Japanese. Yamashita's Gold, a quasi-mythical treasure-trove named after the Japanese commander and left behind by the fleeing Japanese, is believed by some to be hidden in the hills outside Ormoc (see the 'Gold-Diggers' boxed text in the Facts for the Visitor chapter).

The town has recovered well from the appalling effects of the typhoon of 5 November 1991, which brought down huge flash floods from the mountains behind the town. About 8000 people died and tens of thousands were made homeless. The flooding was exacerbated by logging operations that had left the hillsides bare of stabilising vegetation. Logging operations have since stopped.

Information

The PNB on Bonifacio St will change US dollars.

Ormocnet has public Internet access points on Bonifacio St, by the bus station and on San Pedro St, by the Ormoc Days Hotel. The offices are open from 8 am to 11 pm Monday to Saturday and charge P30 to P40 per hour, depending on the time of day.

Golf

The Leyte Golf & Country Club (☎ 053-255 0282, ✉ lgcc@gsilink.com) welcomes visitors. It is 7km outside Ormoc and there are overnight cottages and a swimming pool.

Places to Stay

Pongos Hotel (☎ 053-255 2540), on Bonifacio St, has a selection of rooms in its old and new buildings, ranging from an ordinary single with fan for P216 to a double with air-con for P600.

Don Felipe Hotel (☎ 053-255 2460, fax 255 4306) is comfortable and good value, with rooms with fan from P295 and air-con rooms from P400. It's on the waterfront and it's fun to watch the world go by from the hotel coffee shop.

A recent and lavish addition to Ormoc's accommodation is *Ormoc Days Hotel* (☎ 053-255 5003, fax 561 4065, ✉ dhorm@ormocnet.net.ph), on Obrero St, where rooms start at around P3000; there is often some sort of promotion that can halve prices, so ask at reception. Nonguests can use the pool for P100.

Places to Eat

The coffee shops in *Don Felipe Hotel* and *Ormoc Days Hotel* are good; expect to pay from P200 for interesting and tasty food. For cheaper meals, try *Zenaida's Fast Food* on Rizal St and *Chito's Chow Bar* on the waterfront. There are plenty of *bakeries* and *fruit stalls* in town.

Getting There & Away

There is a huge selection of vessels heading daily from Ormoc to Cebu. See Leyte's introductory Getting There & Away section earlier.

There are very regular buses to and from Tacloban (P62, 2½ hours) and to and from Maasin in the south of Leyte. You can also take buses north-west to Palompon and San Isidro on Leyte.

AROUND ORMOC

From the Ormoc waterfront you can see the Camotes Islands (see that section, earlier).

Tongonan

This is the site of geothermal activity that is being tapped as a power source. Formerly, there were hot springs here but the bathing pool has 'disappeared' in the last few years. You can visit the **power plant** by contacting the managing PNOC office (☎ 053-255 4662) in barangay San Isidro in Ormoc. Jeepneys run regularly from Ormoc to Tongonan (P20, one hour).

Lake Danao National Park

Lake Danao is a beautiful body of fresh water in the hills above Ormoc. You can swim and picnic for the day, or *camp* overnight. Regular jeepneys run from Ormoc (P20, one hour). It is also one starting point for the Leyte Mountain Trail; the other is in Burauen (for details of the trail see the entry under South of Tacloban, earlier in the Leyte section).

If you plan to start hiking from this end, contact the DENR field office at Lake Danao. Local guides can be hired from the small barangay at Lake Danao.

BAYBAY

The bumpy, dusty south-bound road from Ormoc to Maasin passes through Baybay. This small township has boat connections to Cebu, Manila and Surigao (see Leyte's introductory Getting There & Away entry, earlier), and some of the most aggressive and pushy tricycle drivers in the province.

Ellean's Lodge, 50m from the wharf on Bonifacio St, is in a nice old wooden house, but its room partitions don't quite reach the ceiling, so it's not too private and can be noisy. It costs P100 per person for a room with fan and share bath. There is one room with bath for P300.

Seven kilometres north of Baybay, the road passes the *Visayan State College of Agriculture* (VISCA), set on a large, rural block of land. There is a small guesthouse here with rooms (when available) from P200. Buses and jeepneys will drop you there.

MAASIN

This is another small and bustling port town, and is the provincial capital of southern Leyte. While the town itself holds no particular interest apart from its beautiful old **church**, built in 1700, there are attractions nearby for active travellers. Visit **Cagnituan Cave** and the **Guinsohoton Waterfall** with its swimming hole, a welcome cool-off after hiking the 6km in. Serious hikers may want to take the eight hours or so to climb up the town's mountainous backdrop to the '**roof of southern Leyte**', walking through **Patag Daku forest** to Yamog's Peak and camping overnight. It is a very beautiful but very steep hike up, and you will need a guide.

Information

The very knowledgeable Rio Cahambing, tourism officer with the provincial government, can help plan your visit to southern Leyte. Find him at the Provincial Planning Development Office (PPDO), in the Provincial Capitol Building (☎ 053-570 9017, fax 570 9018).

There is a PNB in town that changes US dollars.

Places to Stay & Eat

At the budget-end of the scale, try *Verano Pensionne*, a family house where small rooms cost P75 per person. There is also the basic and adequate *DW Pensionne*, where rooms range from P80 to P500.

More pleasant is *Maasin Country Lodge*, a few minutes' tricycle ride from the town centre, with rooms from P250 to good-value rooms with air-con and TV for P450. There is a restaurant here, with seating outdoors on the riverbank.

Another mid-range hotel is *Southern Comfort Pensionne*, in the centre of town, with air-con rooms from P500. It's quite noisy though.

Getting There & Away

Regular buses run to Maasin from Ormoc (P60, 3½ hours), and to Padre Burgos (P20, 45 minutes). There are also regular buses to Liloan (P80, four hours), the ferry port for Mindanao.

THE VISAYAS

Maasin has good sea connections to Mindanao (see Leyte's introductory Getting There & Away section, earlier).

SOUTHERN LEYTE

Southern Leyte is slated to become a major dive destination in the Philippines. There are dive sites in Sogod Bay and around Limasawa, with rich reefs and drop-offs. Wall and cave diving is possible at Lungsodaan in Padre Burgos. At Son-ok in Pintuyan, on the southernmost point of Leyte, local people are managing the area as a fish sanctuary and there has been a resulting increase in the population of *butanding* (whale sharks), dolphins and whales. Blue Depth Dive Center in Padre Burgos is presently the only commercial dive operator in the area and can be contacted via the DOT in Maasin (☎ 053-570 9017, fax 570 9018).

Padre Burgos

This township has good **beaches** with offshore **snorkelling** and **dive sites**, including Tangkaan Point, to the south of town. Blue Depth Dive Center, in town, charges around US$35 for two dives including equipment, and can also organise dive trips to the islands of Limasawa and Panaon. Stay at *Davliz Travel Lodge*, on a cliff above the beach, where cottages cost around P300 to P600 with air-con. There are also *lodges* in town.

Regular jeepneys run from Maasin to Padre Burgos (P20, 45 minutes) and from here you can get a boat to the islands of Limasawa and Panaon.

Panaon

This may become one of the great dive spots of the Philippines. The waters of Sogod Bay contain populations of **whale sharks** and **dolphins** and in the 15 years or so, since both dynamite and cyanide fishing practices have stopped. The corals and fish have made a remarkable recovery. Check out current **diving** possibilities in Padre Burgos (see that entry, earlier).

Limasawa

Limasawa is historically significant in the Philippines as the first place in which the Spanish celebrated mass, on 31 March 1521, thereby starting the Christianisation of the country. (The people of Magellanes in Mindanao claim the same distinction, incidentally.) A pumpboat makes the journey from Padre Burgos at noon daily (P20, one hour) and lands at barangay Magellanes. Here you need to contact the mayor and arrange to stay at the two-room *guesthouse* overnight. It costs P300 to P400. The site of the first mass and its commemorative marker is a half-hour hike away in barangay Triana, and a local person will probably offer to walk with you. The island also has beautiful beaches for **swimming**, **snorkelling** and **diving**. The daily boat to Padre Burgos leaves Limasawa around 6 am.

A warning: the boats do not run if the sea is rough, so be prepared to wait for calm weather.

Biliran Island

This small and quiet island province takes its name from borobiliran, an abundant native grass. Biliran became a province separate from Leyte in 1992, and a short bridge connects the two.

The island is about 32km long and 8km wide, and is packed with natural attractions such as waterfalls, hot and cold springs, and rice terraces. Offshore islands with white-sand beaches offer good snorkelling. You'll need to bring your own snorkel gear though, as the island is only geared towards very low-key tourism. It's a great place for nature lovers, but not for night-clubbers.

Biliran is green and lush and it can rain anytime, with the most rainfall in December and the least in April. This climate allows three rice-harvests annually, and some rice is exported. There is little else in the way of exports or industry though, and most people are subsistence farmers or fishers. They generally speak Cebuano on the west coast and Waray-Waray on the east. Literacy is high, at 92%, and many people speak English. This is a friendly, relaxing and clean place to spend a few days.

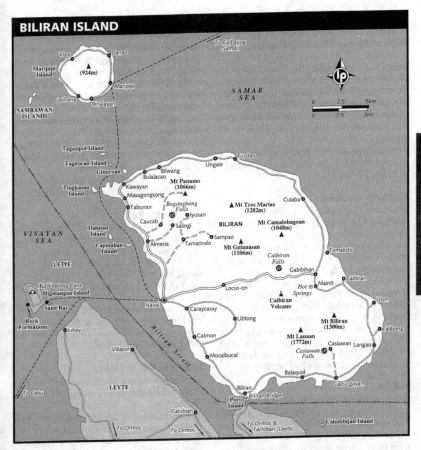

BILIRAN ISLAND

THE VISAYAS

Information

Tourist Offices Call in to see the helpful staff at the Provincial Tourism Council on the 2nd floor of the Capitol Building. Take a motorised tricycle there from Naval for P10.

Money You can change US dollars only, and only at the PNB in Naval. There are no credit card facilities.

Email & Internet Access As of early 2000 there was no Internet access on Biliran.

Telephone Biliran has no direct dialling. All calls go through the Biliran operator (☎ 053-541 9881), who will connect you if there is a relevant local number. You can call out from central public calling offices only, and this makes phoning and faxing expensive.

Getting There & Away

You can get to Biliran from Cebu, Leyte, Luzon and Samar.

Boat Boats to Cebu leave Naval on Tuesday, Thursday and Sunday (P160, 10 hours).

A boat is scheduled to leave Maripipi for Calbayog (P50, three hours) on Samar on Wednesday, but this can be erratic.

Bus Buses run regularly from Naval to Ormoc (P80, three hours) and Tacloban (P90, three hours). Nonstop air-con megataxis run between Naval and Tacloban (P100, two hours) roughly hourly until noon. There is a less frequent bus service from Caibiran to Tacloban.

Philtranco and PP Bus Company leave Naval early each morning for Manila (P650 to P700, 22 hours).

Getting Around

Buses and jeepneys make regular daily trips north to Kawayan (P12, 1½ hours), and south and east to Caibiran (P30, 1½ hours) via Biliran town. Motorised and pedal tricycles operate in the towns. The flat fee for short local trips is P3.

The round-island road is very bumpy, slow and dusty. Public transport does not run along the coast road between Kawayan and Caibiran, or along the cross-country road between Naval and Gabibihan. You can charter a multicab for these stretches for around P1000 to P1500 per day, or hire a motorcycle with driver for around P800 per day.

NAVAL

The provincial capital is a low-rise, easy-going harbour town. There are flowers everywhere. There's not much of interest in the town itself, but it's handy base for day trips to Higatangan and to the waterfalls to the east.

Places to Stay

Budget hotels in Naval are very cheap and fairly grotty. On Vicentillo St, *LM Lodge* redefines the word 'basic', with beds from P80 to P130, but the sheets are clean. Look for big grey gates with LM embossed on them; there's no other sign.

Brigida Inn, still sporting its old 'Bay View Lodge' sign, is on Castin St. It's cramped and dark, with OK dorm beds from P90 and poor-value air-con rooms for P450.

On Vicentillo St, *Rosevic Pension House* is marginally better, with a courtyard and outdoor sitting area. Small rooms range from P250 with fan and share bath to P500 for air-con and bath.

By far the best option is *Marvin's Place*. It's new, bright and clean, with big air-con rooms with bath for P600. There is a breezy balcony and garden overlooking the ocean. Take a pedal tricycle for P3 (give a bit more if you have heavy bags) or a motorised tricycle for P20 to barangay Atipolo, a couple of kilometres south of town.

None of these lodgings has a restaurant, but meals can be ordered at all of them.

Places to Eat

Most eating places are on Inocentes St, the main street leading from the market, jetty and terminal area. *Goldilocks* has a good selection of Filipino food. Next door, but with less choice, is *Armelan's*. During the day, *Geebees* does simple budget meals of meat or fish with rice, vegetables and soup for P29, and in the evenings it turns into a foodless sing-along bar. There are plenty of *eateries* and *BBQ places* at the terminal.

NORTH OF NAVAL

This pretty stretch of coast is the only part of the island that is easy to explore by public transport.

Two kilometres beyond Almeria is *Agta Beach Resort*, where dorm beds for P90 are spartan, but big air-con rooms with private bath for P450 are good value. It's on a stretch of beach with swimming at high tide only, and is busy with locals on the weekend. The resort is a good base for visiting **Dalutan**, an island with white sand and good snorkelling. Hire a banca for P25 and paddle yourself across in 30 minutes.

Walkers may want to visit **Bagongbong Falls**. These are a two-hour hike from Caucab, where the barangay captain will help you find a guide. You should pay the guide about P100.

The **rice terraces** of Sampao, Iyusan and Salangi are each about 5km off the main road and you'll need to walk in unless you charter a vehicle. They're pretty, but much smaller than those of northern Luzon.

At **Masagongsong cold spring**, the water has been tapped to fill a good sized pool. This is open daily for a P5 entry fee. Opposite the pool, on the main road, is the new *Villa Antonio*. This also has a spring-fed pool on a terrace overlooking the sea. Day use is P80 for nonguests and there are good air-con rooms for P700. Simple food can be ordered.

In Kawayan you can hire a banca for around P300 to take you to **Ginuroan**. The island has a steep and rocky foreshore but the offshore **coral gardens** are good.

You can walk around pretty and undeveloped island of **Maripipi Island** in less than a day, or hire a motorcycle for P100 per hour. There is a ruined pre-Spanish watchtower by the primary school in Maripipi township, and in several barangays women make **terracotta pottery**. Offshore, the uninhabited **Sambawan Islands** have white sand and good snorkelling. There is no commercial accommodation on Maripipi Island but the barangay captains will arrange *homestays*. You can charter a banca to Maripipi (P300 one way, 20 minutes) from Kawayan. There are also boats each morning from Naval to Maripipi Island (P30, 1½ hours), but these do not return until the following morning.

EAST & SOUTH OF NAVAL

Caibiran Falls is a steep 20-minute hike off the cross-island road. It is quite undeveloped and, if the water's not flowing too fast, there are two big **swimming holes** at its base. Nearby, **Caibiran Volcano** can be climbed in a steady 1½ hours. Check with the tourist office for directions to these as they are not signposted; you will need to charter a vehicle and guide.

Mainit hot spring is a series of small cascades with sitting pools, exposed on a riverbank beside rice fields. **Tomalistis Falls** pour from a cliff face and are only accessible by boat. They are reputed to pour the sweetest water in the world, and passing ships once used them to replenish their drinking water. To visit **Casiawan Falls** you need to drive 20 minutes on a track off the south coast road, and then walk for 10 minutes. The swimming hole there has recently been drained to make use of the water for farming.

WEST OF NAVAL

Due west of Naval is **Higatangan Island**. A shifting, white sandbar is good for **swimming** and **snorkelling**, and you can walk to the **Ka Ventong Cave**, with its reputed snake population. On the western side of the island, accessible by boat only, is a series of interesting **rock formations** with small sandy bays between them. Former President Marcos, along with fellow resistance members, reportedly took refuge on the island in WWII, and Marcos Hill is named in his memory.

The only accommodation is *Limpiado Beach Resort*, near the sand bar. Dorm beds/simple rooms cost P50/300. There are five boat-trips from Naval (P20, 45 minutes) daily, and the boats return the following morning. A one-way charter is around P500.

Mindanao & Sulu

The bulky island of Mindanao, comprising around 20 provinces, lies to the south of the Philippine Archipelago and has a landmass of almost 95,000 sq km. Its landscape is lush and varied, encompassing coastal plains and swamps, fertile volcanic plateaus and river valleys. A backbone of rugged forested mountains runs north to south and the Philippines' highest peak, Mt Apo, dominates the skyline of Davao City. There are numerous offshore islands.

Mindanao's two big river systems are the Agusan, which feeds wildlife-rich swampy plains to the east, and the Rio Grande de Mindanao – also known as the Pulangi – flowing from the centre southwards to Cotabato City. It was to the mouth of this river in 1475 that Mohammed Shariff Kabungsuan brought Islam to the Mindanao mainland.

To the south, the hundreds of islands of the Sulu Archipelago stretch towards Indonesia.

WARNING

While you can comfortably travel to much of the area without worry, certain areas of Mindanao and Sulu are risky. Depending on the area and the current situation, the risks range from possibly sticky to positively suicidal. Always check the local situation before you go.

The following places were trouble spots at the time of writing – for more details, see Dangers & Annoyances in the relevant sections of this chapter.

Filipinos consider Marawi on Lake Lanao to be dodgy for travel. Road travel to Zamboanga City from other parts of Mindanao isn't advisable generally, but the road between Dipolog and Zamboanga is definitely out. It is also unwise to travel by road north of Cotabato.

Basilan remains a crisis area, and as we went to press only Isabela and Lamitan were open to foreigners. Unless the situation has changed dramatically, travel on the rest of the island is not on.

HIGHLIGHTS

- Catching sunset and sunrise on Lake Sebu, the heartland of the T'boli people
- Snorkelling the coral gardens at Talikud Island
- Immersing yourself in history at Fort Pilar, Zamboanga and in Dapitan, José Rizal's waterfront home-in-exile
- Seeing Camiguin's variety of rainforests, reefs, volcanoes, waterfalls, hot and cold springs
- Making sense of how peoples settled around the Philippines, thanks to the ancient *balangays* (outriggers) at Butuan

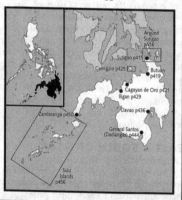

In the Sulu Archipelago, only Bongao Island in the Tawi-Tawi Group was considered safe for travel at the time of publication.

Mindanao

Christianity is the major religion in Mindanao, though there are more Muslims in the province than elsewhere in the Philippines. Predominantly Muslim areas include Marawi City and the area around Lake

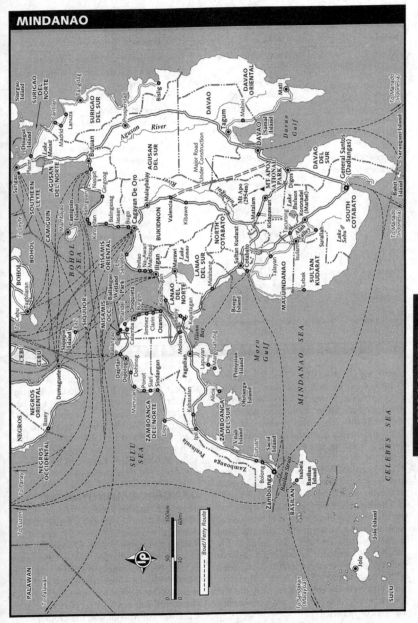

MINDANAO

MINDANAO & SULU

Crafts of the Indigenous Peoples of Mindanao

People	Area	Products
Tausug	Sulu Archipelago	*kris* daggers, *gabbang* xylophone, and *tanggungo* and *kulintang* gongs
Sama	Sulu Archipelago	weavings and carvings
Yakan	Basilan Island	weavings in bright colours and geometric designs
Subanon	Zamboanga provinces	pottery and basketware
Maranao & Ilanun	Lanao del Norte & Lanao del Sur	weaving and brassware
Maguindanao	Pulangi River	brassware
Higanon & Talandig	Bukidnon	cast iron implements and weapons.
Manobo	Agusan River Valley	weaving
Ata	Around Davao	*bangkakaw* (a hollowed drum)
Bagobo	Davao province	*agong* (a gamelan-like musical ensemble)
T'boli	Lake Sebu	*t'nalak* cloth weaving, betel-nut boxes
B'laan	Lake Buluan	betel-nut boxes
Mandaya & Mansaka	Davao Oriental & Agusan provinces	carvings and music
Sangir	Around Davao	traditional songs, stylised dances

Source: Dr Heidi K Gloria, Indigenous Peoples of Mindanao, in *Mindanao – a portrait*. Bookmark, 1999.

Lanao, and Cotabato City. There is a sizeable Muslim minority in Zamboanga City. Mindanao remains home to many indigenous people and it's still possible to have encounters with different cultures on their own terms and on their ancestral land. Rather than taking a 'tribal people tour' – and there are plenty of those – wander around, say, the T'boli heartland of Lake Sebu on market day and be as much of an observer or participant in the day as you choose.

Mindanao's economy rests largely on agriculture, and there are vast plantations of pineapples, bananas, maize, coconuts and citrus fruits. There are also large cattle ranches. While there is legislation in force to prevent the excessive logging operations of the past, forestry is still both an industry and an environmental issue. Outside the cities, most local people are subsistence farmers or fishers.

For a detailed photographic journey through Mindanao in all its geographic, historic and cultural variety, you can't do better than read *Mindanao – a portrait*. It's a beautiful coffee-table book of photos and essays published in 1999. It's much too heavy and expensive to carry around, but some tourist offices have it in their library for visitors to browse through.

DANGERS & ANNOYANCES

There are tangible tensions between Christians and Muslims in some areas of Mindanao, as a reading of reports in almost any daily newspaper in the Philippines will show. Since the signing of the 1996 peace accord between the government and the Moro National Liberation Front (MNLF), much of this tension has subsided, although the accord was not fully supported by either Christians or Muslims on the ground.

The more radical Moro Islamic Liberation Front (MILF) is still actively engaged in armed opposition to the government, and in places there remain small but active cells of the communist New People's Army (NPA). These religious and political differences may impact on travellers in some destinations and, where necessary, warnings are given in the relevant sections of this chapter.

GETTING THERE & AWAY

You can get to Mindanao from Bohol, Cebu, Leyte, Luzon, Negros, Palawan, Panay and Siquijor in the Philippines, and from Indonesia, Malaysia and Singapore. Specific travel information is given under the relevant destination elsewhere in this chapter.

Transportation schedules and prices should be taken as guidelines only. While this is true for all the Philippines, Mindanao's size and the varieties of its public transport mean it has suffered particularly during the South-East Asian economic crisis, with cuts to many air services and fuel price-hikes restricting some of the boat and bus services. There are regular transport strikes, and security issues intermittently effect some transport routes.

The island's provinces are still reeling from the aftereffects of the closure and subsequent restructuring of Philippine Airlines (PAL). National competitor airlines such as Air Philippines and Cebu Pacific, and local carriers like Mindanao Express, leapt in to fill the gaps and often overserviced some destinations, while completely ignoring others.

Thus you find all airlines servicing Cagayan de Oro from Manila several times daily, for example, with good competitive prices, sometimes as low as P1900 return during mid-week promotions, but flights to big, busy industrial Iligan City are nonexistent. On the other hand, one small airline services the whole of the Sulu Archipelago from Zamboanga, three times a week only, on a 14-seater plane and is therefore able to charge P2000 one way for the hour's flight! Shop around for flights and ask for the cheapest deals: it's often much cheaper, for example, to fly to Manila in the quiet late afternoon than in the busy early morning.

Long distance bus fares are subject to fluctuating fuel prices. It's better to travel air-con on, say, the endless Manila–Davao run (around P1200, 48 hours) as the bus stops less frequently and the drivers are more likely to stay alert (even if you're not sitting beside them and nervously poking them every time their heads nod).

Boat routes seem to change less frequently than do their schedules and prices. It's probably safe to assume (though not guaranteed) that you will be able to get from, say, Cebu to Surigao (P180, 11 hours on the old Cokoliong Lines vessel; P600, 3½ hours by SuperCat) although the days, timings and prices of the route might change. Do travel by bigger, newer, faster boats where possible. Sea safety issues are being addressed, but change is slow on the older boats and filling in your name and nationality on a passenger list in case of an accident or sinking is hardly the most reassuring way to start a journey.

Air

There are flights from Manila to Butuan, Cagayan de Oro, Davao, Dipolog, General Santos and Zamboanga, from Cebu to Davao and General Santos, and from Panay to Davao.

Bouraq Airlines flies from Davao to Manado in Indonesia and Malaysia Airlines flies from Sandakan in Malaysia to Zamboanga. Silk Air flies from Singapore to Davao via Cebu City.

Boat

There are boats from Manila to Camiguin, Cagayan de Oro, Cotabato, Dapitan, Davao, General Santos, Iligan, Nasipit (Butuan), Ozamis, Surigao and Zamboanga.

On Bohol there are boats from Tagbilaran to Cagayan de Oro and Surigao, and from Jagna to Cagayan de Oro and Nasipit (Butuan). Boats run from Cebu City to Cagayan de Oro, Dapitan, Iligan, Nasipit (Butuan), Surigao and Ozamis. There is also a boat from Maasin on Leyte to Surigao.

On Negros, there are boats from Bacolod to Nasipit (Butuan), and from Dumaguete to Cagayan de Oro, Dapitan, Ozamis and Surigao.

Boats also run from Iloilo on Panay to Cagayan de Oro, Cotabato, Nasipit (Butuan) and Ozamis, from Palawan to Cagayan de Oro and Nasipit (Butuan) and from Lazi on Siquijor to Iligan.

To Indonesia and Malaysia, there are boats from Davao and General Santos to Manado in Indonesia and boats from Zamboanga to Sandakan in Malaysia.

Bus

Buses run from Manila to Davao via Surigao. Manila-Davao buses also go via Calbayog and Catbalogan on Samar and via Tacloban on Leyte.

SURIGAO

Surigao is capital of the province of Surigao del Norte, entry point to northern Mindanao. It is a crowded, busy and dusty city, with not much to hold a traveller's interest, but you may need to overnight here and cash up with pesos before heading off island-hopping.

If you are in Surigao for a couple of days, things to see close to the city include **Silop Cave**, 7km away, with its 12 entrances leading to a big central chamber. **Day-asin**, a floating village, is 5km away from the city and **Mati**, to the south, is where the Mamanwas people have created a 'village' to showcase their culture. There are good beaches around the city.

Information

The Surigao City Tourist Office (✆ surigao@surigao.philcom.com.ph) is opposite the city hall, at the corner of the children's park. For information about travel elsewhere in the region, the provincial Department of Tourism (DOT) is located by the city grandstand on Rizal St.

The Equitable PCI Bank on San Nicolas St will advance cash against Visa cards. The Philippine National Bank (PNB), for changing US dollars, is on Rizal St. There are no facilities for changing money on the offshore islands, so make sure you take enough.

There are several Internet cafes in town. Computronics (P35 per hour), below Leomondee's Hotel, on Borromeo St, and Cyberstop (P35 per hour), on Magallanes St, are both central.

Places to Stay & Eat

Of the budget hotels in town try *The Dexter Pensionne*, on San Nicolas St, where basic rooms start at P150. Next door is the *Garcia Hotel* with much the same rates. These two are pretty noisy.

The *Tavern Hotel and Restaurant* (✆ 086-231 7300, fax 231 7301) also has cheap rooms from P150 in its old wing near the kitchen, which is a bit smelly. There are brighter, cleaner rooms costing up to P700 in the new wing. The newish *Leomondee's Hotel* (✆ 086-232 7334) on Borromeo St has rooms from P200 to P1000; ask for a room at the back, off the noisy main road.

The best hotel in Surigao is the new *Gateway Hotel* (✆ 086-826 1283, fax 826 1285), about 3km from the wharf and along the airport road. Good-value big, bright rooms at P680 have air-con, bath and cable TV.

The Gateway has a good *restaurant* where you can expect to pay around P200 for a meal; the Tavern Hotel has a pleasant light *restaurant* overlooking the sea. The *Cherry Blossom* restaurant on San Nicolas St has been around for a while and is popular in the evenings, though it looks a bit tired from the outside. There are some Filipino fast food places on the streets around the city plaza, including the popular *Alesandra's Chicken House*, and masses of *barbecue stalls* along the wharf. Fruit stalls are opposite the cinemas on San Nicolas St.

Shopping

Lovely Souvenirs on Rizal St has a good selection of Filipino basketwork and other crafts. Eduhome Supermarket next to the PNB is a decent supermarket.

Getting There & Away

Boat Negros Navigation has boats leaving for Manila at noon Monday (P885 to P1850, 40 hours); WG&A leaves at 6 pm Wednesday (P766 to P3000), Cebu Lines

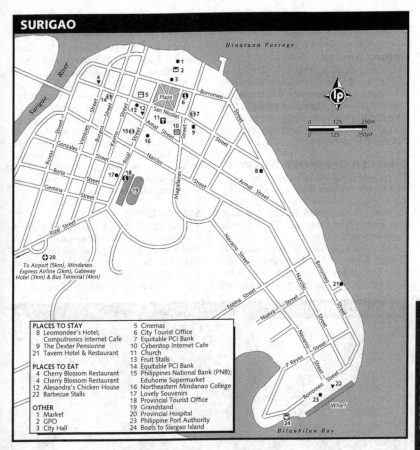

SURIGAO

Hinatuan Passage

Surigao River

Plaza

San Nicolas

Bilanbilan Bay

To Airport (5km), Mindanao
Express Airline (2km), Gateway
Hotel (3km) & Bus Terminal (4km)

Wharf

0   125   250m
0   125   250yd

PLACES TO STAY		5	Cinemas
8	Leomondee's Hotel;	6	City Tourist Office
	Computronics Internet Cafe	7	Equitable PCI Bank
9	The Dexter Pensione	10	Cyberstop Internet Cafe
21	Tavern Hotel & Restaurant	11	Church
		13	Fruit Stalls
PLACES TO EAT		14	Equitable PCI Bank
4	Cherry Blossom Restaurant	15	Philippines National Bank (PNB);
4	Cherry Blossom Restaurant		Eduhome Supermarket
12	Alesandra's Chicken House	16	Northeastern Mindanao College
22	Barbecue Stalls	17	Lovely Souvenirs
		18	Provincial Tourist Office
OTHER		19	Grandstand
1	Market	20	Provincial Hospital
2	GPO	23	Philippine Port Authority
3	City Hall	24	Boats to Siargao Island

MINDANAO & SULU

leaves Thursday and Sulpicio Lines leaves Thursday (P790 to P1900).

For boat details from Manila, see the Boat entry under Getting There & Away in the Manila chapter.

Negros Navigation has boats leaving at 11 pm Tuesday, arriving in Tagbilaran on Bohol at 8 am Wednesday.

SuperCat has boats leaving at 1 pm daily for Cebu via Maasin (P600, 3½ hours); Cokoliong Lines has trips leaving at 7.15 pm Wednesday, Friday and Sunday, arriving at 6 am the following morning (P180 to P220); and Sulpicio Lines also has boats

that run daily (P182 to P700, 10 hours). SuperCat leaves for Maasin at 1 pm daily (P275, 1½ hours).

For boats to Negros, ask at the Port Authority about possible boats to Dumaguete. Boats also run regularly to the offshore islands of Dinagat and Siargao. Sulpicio Lines may run a weekly boat to Davao (P418 to P1480). Check schedules wherever possible.

Bus Very regular buses run daily to Butuan (P40, two hours) and Cagayan de Oro (P125, six hours), along the west coast, to

Davao (P195, eight hours) in the south and to Tandag (P109) in the east.

Getting Around

From the wharf, public utility vehicles (PUVs) and tricycles run along Borromeo St towards the bus terminal, which is about 5km out of town towards the airport. These cost P2.50 anywhere along this route. A special trip by tricycle will cost between P20 and P40, depending on distance.

SMALLER OFFSHORE ISLANDS

There is a group of islands offshore and within easy day-tour reach of Surigao City. These seem to have erratic accommodation facilities, so check with the city tourist office on the current situation if you want to stay overnight.

The islands include Hikdop Island, 45 minutes away by a public *banca* (pumpboat) that leaves at around 10 am. It has good beaches and the beautiful **Buenavista**

Cave. Nonoc Island was formerly a nickel mine and the vegetation is sparse, but it is at one end of an extraordinary 391m footbridge that links it with Sibale Island. There is a shade-house in the middle of the bridge to rest on the walk across! Nonoc is 30 minutes away from Surigao by pump boat.

Tiny and uninhabited Raza Island is locally known for simultaneously having high tide on one side of the island and low tide on the other. Bayanagan Island is reached through mangrove swamps, and was the site of an early scientific expedition in 1887; many marine species collected here at the time remain unclassified.

SIARGAO

The relaxed island of Siargao is a haven after dusty and crowded Surigao. It is well known on the surfing trail for the 'Cloud Nine' surf break. The Siargao Cup surfing competition is held in late September or early October every year. Surfing can be

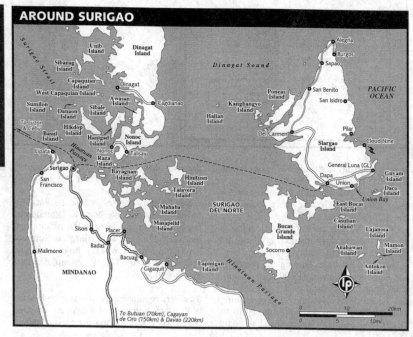

AROUND SURIGAO

The Cloud Nine surf break is world famous.

good from April to October and great on the north-west coast during the north-east monsoon, but like many places in the Philippines, surf can't be guaranteed. Surfers call the country the 'Ficklepines' and fickle the surf can be, so be prepared to wait for the right conditions.

Siargao has plenty of natural attractions for nonsurfers too, with beaches and rock pools, extensive mangrove swamps, inland forest, and waterfalls, and offshore islands. This is not the island for people seeking an active nightlife, but there are enough places for a quiet drink or two and people to talk and explore with.

The port is in the main township of Dapa. On arrival you'll probably want to head straight over towards General Luna (known locally as GL) and the east coast, where the low-key beach resorts are located.

General Luna
General Luna (or GL) is a small township on the south-east coast. Eat at *Maridyl's Eatery* on the main street or at *The Pub* near the school; the owner of the latter has produced a good information pamphlet on the tourist attractions of the island.

Some of the earliest established resorts on Siargao are to the south of the township, and most have loyal return visitors every year. Nearest to the township going south is *Maite's Beach Resort*, which is undergoing renovations and building practical concrete – rather than pretty wooden – cottages. P300 per person gets you basic accommodation and all meals daily.

Jade Star and the newer *N and M Resort* come next and are next door to each other, with simple bamboo cottages and gardens on the beach. They both charge between P150 and P200 for rooms and meals are around P75 each. The food at Jade Star is highly recommended by a regular guest.

The *BRC Beach Resort*, a little further along, has a big grassy garden leading to the beach and very simple rooms for P50 per person or P350, including all meals.

A couple of kilometres further along the coast is the low-key but very beautiful, stylish and private five-star *Pansukian Tropical Resort*. Weary travellers in need of a treat can buy sheer luxury from US$150 per person per day, all meals included.

Cloud Nine
This surf break is about 6km north of GL. The newer resorts and surf camps here are mostly run by seriously laid-back expat Australians. Stay at *Cloud 9 Resort* with its cottages on the beach (P400 to P800) facing the surf break and indoor/outdoor restaurant and pool table. (This is where drivers will drop you if you just ask for 'Cloud Nine', so say if you want to go somewhere else.) Further along is the *Green Room Resort*, and next door to that is the *Jungle Reef Resort* (P150 to P500).

All resorts have big bamboo pavilions for hanging-out over the water, and in front of Cloud 9 Resort there is a long public walkway out over the reef which is good for rock-pool watching at low tide. Eat at any of the resorts or walk up the beach to *Snag Miguel's Beach Club Restaurant* (no that isn't a spelling mistake) for good fresh Western and Filipino food in a prime sunset setting. All the resorts can help organise day tours and boat trips, and they prefer to use the boats and skills of local people as guides when possible.

Elsewhere on Siargao

Visit *barangay* (small village or neighbourhood) Pilar, largely built on stilts over mangrove flats; take a boat around to the mangrove swamps of Del Carmen and look for crocodiles (but don't hold your breath!); take a motorcycle around the island and up to Burgos on the north-east coast to a small resort built by Richard, a craftsman who also makes surfboards finished in bamboo.

Offshore Islands

Visit the tiny white-sand-and-palm hummock of **Guyam** (a classic Robinson Crusoe desert island); the bigger **Dako**, with its beautiful beach, snorkelling and diving; and **Bucas Grande** with the Sohoton Lagoon hidden from the sea.

Getting There & Away

Siargao is serviced by at least three fast boats a day from Surigao (P100, 1½ hours), leaving between about 7 am and 10 am. The companies are Fortune Jet, Askha Queen and New Frontiers Express and all their offices are opposite the main entry to the wharf on Borromeo St in Surigao. Check times at the wharf though, as schedules can change or boats may be out of service. The same boats return to Surigao daily. There are also slower boats running; check at the wharf for current details.

Getting Around

Jeepneys run from Dapa to GL (P10, one hour). Alternatively you can hire a motorcycle and driver to take you there (P100, 25 minutes). The going rate for motorcycle hire is around P300 for half a day to P800 for the day depending on your destination. These motorcycles can seat large families at one hit and are known locally as *habal-habal*, a choice phrase for copulating pigs. Having ridden groin-to-groin with the driver and a complete stranger, plus several bags, this writer understands the associations of intimacy.

DINAGAT

This large island is accessible by daily boat from Surigao, and is home to several fishing communities. There doesn't appear to be a set boat schedule, so check at the wharf. There are rumours of one small resort on the west coast, but details are sketchy.

BUTUAN

If you're interested in history, don't let Butuan's chaotic appearance put you off spending at least a day here. The city has been a major port to a greater or lesser degree since at least the 4th century AD.

Butuan is widely recognised as the earliest known place of settlement and sea trade in the Philippines. In 1976 the oldest boat in the Philippines – a carefully crafted *balangay* (sea-going outrigger) was discovered here that has been carbon-dated to AD 320. This find, along with finds of extensive wooden coffins of tribal peoples who practised skull deformation, has made Butuan a centre of archaeological and ethnographical importance. Visit the **museum**, a kilometre or so from the town centre, with its small but excellent collection. It is open from 9 am to noon and from 1 to 4.30 pm Monday to Saturday, and stands in a quiet garden of lily ponds; take a picnic and enjoy the surroundings.

Towards the airport, at barangay Libertad, is the **balangay discovery site**, open from 8.30 am to 4.30 pm Monday to Saturday, where the remains of the several boats discovered are on display, along with coffin burials. Confusing spellings these, but the word 'barangay' in fact derives from 'balangay', as the boats were big enough (around 15m long and 2.5m wide) to move whole communities of settlers in one journey. A tricycle will take you to the discovery site for P100 per hour, which should be enough time to look around.

There is also a **Diocesan Ecclesiastical Museum** at the cathedral convent, commemorating missionary work in the region. Butuan, like Limasawa in Samar, claims the honour of the first mass held by Magellan on Philippines soil at nearby **Magallanes**; a memorial marks the spot.

Orientation & Information

Several key streets have changed their names recently but shop signs carry the old

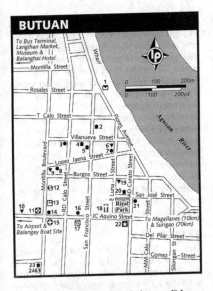

BUTUAN

PLACES TO STAY
2   Imperial Hotel
4   Emerald Villa Hotel
5   Hensonly Plaza Inn
20 Almont Hotel
23 Embassy Hotel

PLACES TO EAT
6   New Mansion House
9   Shakey's Pizza
10 Jollibee
19 New Narra Restaurant

OTHER
1   GPO
3   PAL Agent
7   WG&A Shipping Lines Agent
8   Negros Navigation Agent
11 Otis Department Store
12 Bank of the Philippine Islands (BPI)
13 Cinemas
14 Crown Thrift Market
15 MJ Santos Hospital
16 Urios College
17 Urios Gym; Cybercafe
18 St Joseph Cathedral
21 Greenwich Supermarket
22 Police Station
24 Philippines National Bank (PNB)

street names. Concepcion St is now E Luna St; Juan Luna St is now AD Curato St; Zamora St is now JC Aquino St.

There is a PNB for changing US dollars and the Bank of the Philippine Islands (BPI) will advance cash against your MasterCard.

There are several Internet cafes. Most central is the Cybercafe, underneath the Urios College Gym on JC Aquino St.

Places to Stay & Eat

There is a huge range of accommodation in Butuan to suit all budgets. Good value is the *Hensonly Plaza Inn* (☎ 085-342 5866, fax 225 2040) on San Francisco St. It's old and tatty but spotlessly clean and rooms range from P100 with fan and shared bath, to P250 for a single with fan and bath and P450 with air-con and bath.

The *Imperial Hotel* (☎ 085-341 5309) is also cheap, with rooms with fan and share bath for P120 and air-con rooms with bath for P330. It's OK – what more can you expect for the price? – but take a room with bath, as the shared bathrooms are pretty smelly and grubby.

In the mid-range, the *Embassy Hotel* (☎ 085-342 5883) is not bad but on a noisy road. Air-con rooms with bath cost between P300 and P600, and there's a restaurant and videoke bar attached.

Better value is the *Emerald Villa Hotel* (☎ 085-225 2141, fax 342 5378), where all rooms have air-con, bath and TV and start at P350. The attached restaurant looks fine.

There are a couple of top end hotels at mid-range prices. The *Almont Hotel* in town is a fine place, with rooms from P750 to P1850. Better still is the *Balanghai Hotel* (☎ 085-342 3064, fax 342 3067, ✉ blhotel@mozcom.com), beside the museum, with a good-sized, clean swimming pool and overlooking restaurant. Rooms all have air-con, bath and TV, and prices range from P750 to P2500 for the Presidential Suite. The hotel offers an interesting (but pricey) range of day-tour options, including to the region's marsh and forest habitats.

For good Filipino food try the *New Narra Restaurant* on E Luna St, around the corner from Rizal Park. The *New Mansion House* serves good seafood.

Getting There & Away

Air PAL flies at 10.30 am daily from Manila to Butuan and back. The PAL office (☎ 085-341 5257) is at the airport and there is a ticket agent in town on Villanueva St, opposite the Veterans Bank.

Boat Butuan's main port area is at Nasipit, about 10km west out of town. Jeepneys run between Nasipit and Butuan (30 minutes).

WG&A has boats leaving at 5 pm Wednesday and Saturday for Manila (36 hours). Negros Navigation boats leave at 11 am Thursday, arriving at 5 pm Friday. For details about boats from Manila, see the Boat entry under Getting There & Away in the Manila chapter.

Cebu Ferries has boats leaving at 3 pm Sunday for Bohol on Jagna, arriving at 9 pm.

For Cebu, Negros Navigation has trips leaving at 11 am Thursday, arriving at 7 pm in Cebu City, while WG&A has boats going at 7 pm Monday, Wednesday and Friday, arriving 5 am the following day.

Negros Navigation has boats going to Negros via Iloilo on Panay leaving at 11 am Thursday, arriving in Bacolod at noon Friday.

Negros Navigation has boats going via Cebu to Palawan at 11 am Thursday, arriving at 8 am Saturday.

Bus There are regular departures from Butuan to Surigao (P56, 2½ hours), Cagayan de Oro (P70, four hours) and Davao (P120, six hours). These times and prices are for ordinary services; the less frequent air-conditioned buses run direct and are much faster.

Getting Around

The airport is 10km out of town. A jeepney ride costs P5 and a taxi will cost around P70.

The bus terminal is about a kilometre from the city centre. Jeepney and tricycle rides cost P2.50; a special ride by tricycle will cost P100 per hour.

AROUND BUTUAN

Inland and a little south from Butuan is the floodplain of the Agusan River and the Agusan marshes. There are villages of houses floating on bamboo poles and tree trunks around the township of Bunawan, and the swamps around Talacogon are a prime habitat for bird life. The forested area north of the Agusan River remains the habitat of the tarsier, the tiniest primate in the world.

It is difficult to get accurate information about transport in this area, but if you want to go exploring your best bet is to contact the Department of Environment & Natural Resources (DENR) in Butuan and ask for their suggestions. Alternatively, the Balanghai Hotel in Butuan runs expensive day tours to this region, but may be able to suggest a local guide to help you. Philguides Maps series includes Agusan del Norte and Agusan del Sur maps, which cover these areas. They are available at National Book Store outlets.

BALINGOAN

This is a blink-and-you'll-miss-it township about two-thirds of the way from Butuan, heading south towards Cagayan de Oro. With the 1999 cancellation of the Fast Ferry service from Cagayan de Oro to Camiguin Island, this is the only port serving Camiguin Island by ferry (see the Getting There & Away entry for Camiguin later). There are extremely basic lodgings at the wharf above the eatery. Regular bus and jeepney services run between Cagayan de Oro and Balingoan (P35, 1½ hours).

CAGAYAN DE ORO

You know you're approaching a comparatively large and wealthy city by the number of new car yards on the northern access road from Butuan, and the vast Limketkai and Gaisano shopping malls on the edge of the city centre.

The 'Oro' part of Cagayan's name comes from the Spanish discovery of gold in the river here. Today, much of its economic activity centres on the vegetable gold of the Del Monte pineapple processing plant a few kilometres north of town, and the company's plantations in the hills above Cagayan.

It is also a university town, and the Xavier University maintains a **Folk Museum** at its campus on Corrales Avenue. The museum is open from 8.30 to 11.30 am and from 2.30 to 5 pm Tuesday to Friday, and from 8.30 to

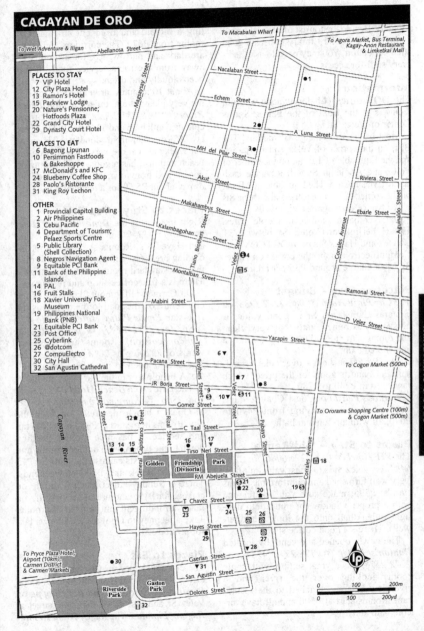

CAGAYAN DE ORO

To Macabalan Wharf

To Wet Adventure & Iligan

To Agora Market, Bus Terminal, Kagay-Anon Restaurant & Limketkai Mall

Abellanosa Street

Nacalaban Street

Echem Street

PLACES TO STAY
- 7 VIP Hotel
- 12 City Plaza Hotel
- 13 Ramon's Hotel
- 15 Parkview Lodge
- 20 Nature's Pensionne; Hotfoods Plaza
- 22 Grand City Hotel
- 29 Dynasty Court Hotel

PLACES TO EAT
- 6 Bagong Lipunan
- 10 Persimmon Fastfoods & Bakeshoppe
- 17 McDonald's and KFC
- 24 Blueberry Coffee Shop
- 28 Paolo's Ristorante
- 31 King Roy Lechon

OTHER
- 1 Provincial Capitol Building
- 2 Air Philippines
- 3 Cebu Pacific
- 4 Department of Tourism; Pelaez Sports Centre
- 5 Public Library (Shell Collection)
- 8 Negros Navigation Agent
- 9 Equitable PCI Bank
- 11 Bank of the Philippine Islands
- 14 PAL
- 16 Fruit Stalls
- 18 Xavier University Folk Museum
- 19 Philippines National Bank (PNB)
- 21 Equitable PCI Bank
- 23 Post Office
- 25 Cyberlink
- 26 @dotcom
- 27 CompuElectro
- 30 City Hall
- 32 San Agustin Cathedral

A. Luna Street

MH del Pilar Street

Riviera Street

Akut Street

Aguinaldo Street

Makahambus Street

Ebarle Street

Kalambagohan Street

Corrales Avenue

Velez Street

Tiano Brothers Street

Montalban Street

Ramonal Street

Mabini Street

D Velez Street

Yacapin Street

Pacana Street

6

To Cogon Market (500m)

JR Borja Street

7

8

To Ororama Shopping Centre (100m) & Cogon Market (500m)

Gomez Street

9

10 11

Burgos Street

General Capistrano Street

Rizal Street

C Taal Street

12

Pabayo Street

13 14 15

16

17

Tirso Neri Street

Golden

Friendship (Divisoria)

Park

18

RM Abejuela Street

21

22 20

19

Corrales Avenue

T Chavez Street

23

24

25 26

27

Hayes Street

29

28

To Pryce Plaza Hotel, Airport (10km), Carmen District & Carmen Markets

Gaerlan Street

31

30

San Agustin Street

Riverside Park

Gaston Park

Dolores Street

32

Cagayan River

0   100   200m
0   100   200yd

MINDANAO & SULU

11.30 am Saturday. It's closed Sunday and Monday. Beside the tourist office and sports complex, the Public Library houses a good **shell collection**. You may need to ask the library staff for access.

Information

The DOT office (✉ dot10@cdo.weblinq .com) is at the front of the Pelaez Sports Center on Velez St.

Most banks will change US dollars. The BPI, on the corner of Velez and Borja Sts, and the Equitable PCI Bank on the corner of Velez and Abejeula St will advance cash against MasterCard. The Equitable PCI Bank on the corner of Tiano Brothers and Borja Sts will advance cash against Visa cards.

Cagayan has a number of Internet cafes. Try Cyberlink on Velez St between T Chavez and Hayes Sts or @DOTCOM and CompuElectro around the corner on Hayes St. Most charge around P35 per hour.

Places to Stay – Budget

The *City Plaza Hotel* (✆ 088-2272 3788) on General Capistrano St is good value, if noisy. It's extremely tatty but very clean and rooms start at P120 for a single with fan and shared bath.

The *Parkview Lodge* overlooks Friendship Park and is good for the price, which ranges from P240 to P780.

Nature's Pensionne, on T Chavez St has good sized rooms ranging from P470 to P670, all with air-con and bath.

Places to Stay – Mid-Range

The *VIP Hotel* (✆ 088-2272 6080, fax 2272 6441) on Velez St is the best value in town. Very well furnished and comfortable rooms start at P595; make sure you ask for one with a proper window (opening onto daylight rather than onto the inner building-well). There's a good coffee shop.

The newly opened and centrally located *Ramon's Hotel* (✆ 088-2272 4738, fax 2272 2578) has a great setting, with some rooms looking over the river and a riverview balcony attached to the restaurant. Rooms start at P500 and all have air-con, bath and TV.

The *Grand City Hotel* on Velez St is getting a bit old and tired but still has OK rooms from P670. The corridors and lobby are dark and narrow; ask for a room well away from the room-service food lift that beeps loudly and often.

About 10 minutes' drive north of town is the very pleasant and quiet *Coconut Beach Resort* (✆ 088-855 2702), with fine air-con cottages with bath and TV from P680. There is a 20% discount from Monday to Thursday, but weekends can be very busy. It's on the beach and also has a good-sized swimming pool. A taxi from town will cost around P80, or pay about P5.50 for a jeepney ride.

Places to Stay – Top End

Right in town is the *Dynasty Court Hotel* (✆ 088-857 1250), on the corner of Tiano and Hayes Sts. Rooms start at P1150, including breakfast and lunch, but be warned that the standard rooms have no windows. There is a fine coffee shop and restaurant.

On Carmen Hill, about 3km west of the city centre on the road to the airport is the five-star *Pryce Plaza Hotel* (✆ 088-858 4536, fax 2272 6687, ✉ prycepht@cdo .philcom.com.ph). Rooms here cost upwards of P2200 plus 20% tax and service. The pool is open to nonguests for a P100 fee. A band plays in the bar every night.

The *Lauremar Beach Hotel* (✆/fax 088-858 7506, ✉ lauremar@mozcom.com) is in Opol, a beachside area 7km from the city. Rooms here start at P950 plus 20% tax and service. It has nice grounds leading down to the beach, with outdoor dining and a pool. Nonguests can use the pool for P75 during the week and P100 at weekends. There is Sunday buffet lunch with all you can eat for P195 and use of the pool if you fancy an indulgent and relaxed afternoon. Take a jeepney to Opol for P5.50, or a taxi for around P80.

Places to Eat

There is good food in Cagayan to suit all tastes. Filipino food is served in town at the *Persimmon Fastfoods and Bakeshoppe* on Velez St and just down the same street at *Bagong Lipunan*. The *Kagay-Anon Restau-*

rant, a little out of town at the Limketkai Mall, is popular with locals but not cheap. *King Roy Lechon*, behind the Dynasty Court Hotel on Gaerlan St, is popular.

Vegetarians rejoice! Head straight for the *Blueberry Coffee Shop* on the corner of Velez and T Chavez Sts where, among fresh and tasty goodies including salads, you can get tofu burgers and spaghetti with a good tofu-tomato sauce, along with cappuccino, juice and great cake. Beware of the sugar-free apple pie – it is SUGAR-free but is sweetened with lashings of Nutrasweet synthetic sweetener.

Paolo's Ristorante, on the corner of Velez and Gaerlan Sts, does simple pizza and pasta and the bar is popular with a young crowd. You can eat outside or in the air-con room.

The Site Bar, opposite the Dynasty Court Hotel, does some food and is a popular watering hole in the evenings.

The balcony of *Ramon's Hotel* is a good shady place to breakfast looking over the river; there's also live music every night.

Getting There & Away

Air There are daily flights to Cagayan de Oro from Manila with Cebu Pacific (at 5.10, 9.30 and 11.40 am), PAL (at 5 and 10 am and 1.10 pm) and Air Philippines (at 5.45 and 10.15 am).

Mindanao Express (☎ 088-857 5530) has flights to Cebu, Davao and Zamboanga.

Boat Macabalan Wharf is 5km from the city centre. You can get there by jeepney; a taxi will cost about P40.

WG&A has boats leaving for Manila at 10 pm Tuesday, Friday and Saturday (P930 to P2400, 48 hours), while Negros Navigation boats leave Sunday and Wednesday evening. For boat details from Manila, see the Boat entry under Getting There & Away in the Manila chapter.

Cebu Ferries has trips to Jagna (P135 to P613, five hours) and Tagbilaran (P170 to P840, seven hours) on Bohol, leaving at noon Saturday.

There is boat to Cebu City at 8 pm daily (P220 to P1100). Boats to Dumaguete on Negros leave at 10 pm Tuesday and Friday (P175 to P1100, six hours). Negros Navigation has boats leaving for Iloilo on Panay Wednesday and Sunday and going to Palawan via Bacolod at 7 pm Wednesday, arriving at 10 am Saturday.

Bus There are regular bus services northbound to Butuan (P70, four hours) and Surigao (P136, seven hours). Buses leave several times a day for Davao. South-bound buses go to Iligan (P50, 1½ hours). The bus terminal is by the Agora fruit and vegetable wholesale market, a couple of kilometres out of town.

Getting Around

The airport is 10km west of town, and it will cost you around P100 to get there by taxi. Jeepneys also meet the planes.

Jeepneys and tricycles travel around town and to nearby destinations from the terminal. A trip in town costs a set P2.50. Tricycles can be hired for around P100 per hour. These operate around town and are metered. There is an automatic P20 flag fall.

AROUND CAGAYAN

The **Malasag eco-village**, about 20 minutes out of town to the north, showcases the ecology and ethnic cultures of northern Mindanao. Set in acres of botanical garden with a small wildlife collection of butterflies, birds and deer, it is a theme park of sorts, featuring tribal houses (with tribal people engaged in 'authentic' activities), a museum and an education centre. You can stay here camping or in cottages and there's a swimming pool and good – though not particularly cheap – restaurant. Entry is P20 and it costs P50 to use the pool. To get here, take a jeepney to Cugman and get off at Malasag, then take a motorcycle up the hill to the eco-village. A taxi will cost about P150 one way.

Depending on the state of the river, there's the possibility of different grades of **white-water rafting** on the stretches of river beyond the airport. Call the river guide on ☎ 088-856 4639 or ✆ rupertd14@hotmail .com.

MINDANAO & SULU

Del Monte offers free tours of the company's enormous **pineapple processing factory** at Bugo, about 15km north of Cagayan, between 8 am and 1 pm Saturday. You need to call the public relations person (☎ 088-855 4312, ext 2591 or 2592) a day or so in advance to book. The pineapple plantations, all 95 sq km of them, are about 35km north and east of Cagayan, on the Bukidnon plateau at Camp Phillips. There are pineapples as far as the eye can see (an extraordinary sight) and some really weird-shaped harvesting equipment. Jeepneys run to Camp Phillips (P10, one hour) but the plantations lie behind the complex, so it's best to hire someone on site there to drive you on a looping back road through the plantations to the Del Monte Clubhouse and Golf Course about 5km away. You can then pick up a bus to Malaybalay or back to Cagayan from the main road there. A special return trip by taxi will cost around P500. It was to the Del Monte plantation airfield that MacArthur fled after the battle of Corregidor in 1942.

The **Makahambus Cave** is about 14km out of Cagayan beyond the airport. The cave marks the spot of a violent encounter between (victorious) local people and US forces in the 19th century; there's a small shrine and beyond the cave chamber a viewing deck over the Cagayan River. Take

a torch (flashlight). From here you can walk down 150 steps to the gorge and see large ferns; depending on the depth and force of the river, you may be able to cool off in plunge pools. To get there take a jeepney marked Dansolihon/Talakag. A return taxi ride will cost between P200 and P300.

MALAYBALAY

This small city is the capital of Bukidnon province. It is in the mountains above Cagayan de Oro and can be cool at night. For three days in early September Malaybalay is the setting for the annual **Kaamulan Festival**, a celebration of unity between the tribal people living in the area. Seven tribal groups are represented and activities include dance, song, storytelling, local food and wine, and ritual enactments. The festival is held in the pretty Pines View Park.

Thanks to Gail Cockburn of Ontario for the following information:

For great hikes in one of the only untouched forests in the area go to the Impalutao reforestation centre (it also has natural growth forests) about 40 minutes north of Malaybalay (between Kisolon and Malaybalay). Waterfalls and rivers throughout the reserve offer a cool place to swim and get away from people. Take a bus from Cagayan to Malaybalay but ask the conductor to let you know where to get down. Locally it is known as Gantugan – you

People Picking Precious Pineapples

A gigantic, surreal, Heath-Robinsonish machine makes its interminable way up and down endless grey-green rows of spiky plants. It has two long, low arms extending sideways on each of which, seated invisibly under big bright umbrellas, are about ten pickers. They bend to slice away the pineapples – which grow at ground level – then reach behind their backs to put them on a conveyor belt that snakes along the extending arms and transfers the fruit to a huge bin at the centre of the machine. When the bin is full, the fruit is transferred to trucks that leave in a heavily guarded convoy to rumble slowly down the mountain to the processing plant.

Rumour has it that Del Monte's security guards are licensed to kill – such is the threat of pineapple thieves, and the plantation's importance to the Filipino economy. Pineapple chunks will never seem the same again.

Virginia Jealous

may have to ask people on the bus for help if the conductor is not from the area ...

Just north of Valencia (south of Malaybalay) off the highway is the Monastery of the Transfiguration. Even for nonreligious types this is a gorgeous drive into the hills, which are planted with coffee by the monks. On Sunday at 8 am there is an English service with a lovely boys' choir and you can buy the coffee and peanuts grown by the monks. You will need a motorcycle or a friend to take you as there is no public transport.

Driving up to Malaybalay from Cagayan you'll see in the distance the impressive 3000m Mt Kitanglad, one of the highest mountains in the Philippines and still a habitat of the Philippine eagle. There is apparently good bird watching at Lalawan Dalwagan, at the base of the mountain 6km from the highway.

Places to Stay

Unfortunately during our attempted visit 200 local farmers, engaged in a land rights dispute, were lying across the only road in to Malaybalay, refusing access to all travellers, and intending to be there for several

days. So these recommendations come from reliable sources and the tourism department's most current list of accommodation.

Savers Plaza Lodging Inn has budget rooms from P150 to P275. *Haus Malibu* (☎/fax 088-841 2714), on Bonifacio Dr, has a range of rooms from P160 to P700. At the top of the scale is the *Pine Hills Hotel* (☎ 088-841 3211), on the highway, which offers rooms from P972 to P1920. It has good food, as does the *Zion Ranch* on the plaza.

Getting There & Away

Malaybalay is on the Cagayan to Davao and Cotabato run, and buses run regularly every day. The journey normally takes about two hours.

Camiguin

The pear-shaped volcanic island of Camiguin lies off Mindanao's north-west coast. While it's small enough to become

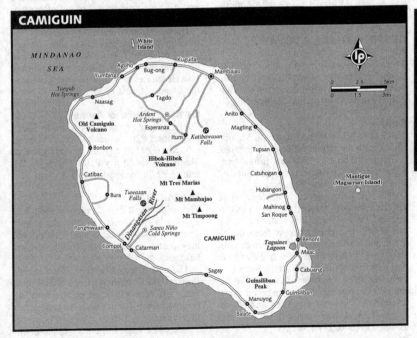

familiar within just a few days, the landscape is lush and varied, with active volcanoes, pockets of forest, clear waterfalls, hot and cold springs, and an alternately black-and white-sand coastline. Diving around the island's best sites can be arranged in Agoho.

Mention the name Camiguin to just about any Filipino and they'll say 'Ah! Lanzones!', as Camiguin is widely recognised for having the sweetest *lanzones* in the archipelago. The annual **Lanzones Festival** takes place around the third week of October, when you can join in with everyone else and make an unashamed glutton of yourself on these truly delicious fruit.

Camiguin is a relaxed place to stay, and non-American travellers especially will enjoy being greeted with 'Hi friend!' instead of 'Joe!' or 'Hey, kano!'. Many of the 70,000 islanders are fishing folk, though tourism is becoming increasingly important to the economy. You'll find that tourism so far is pretty low-key and based around the island's natural attractions; no wild nightlife here, and no-one seems to want it.

GETTING THERE & AWAY
Air
There are currently no air connections to Camiguin. The nearest airport is at Cagayan de Oro; for flight information see the Getting There & Away section for that city.

Boat
There may be a boat on Sunday to Manila. Check with the tourist office in Mambajao.

There are boat connections from Mambajao to Cebu City leaving at 8 pm Sunday. The journey takes about six hours.

The Fast Ferry service from Cagayan de Oro to Camiguin stopped operating in December 1999. Check if it's started again, but if not, you need to cross from Balingoan, about 80km north of Cagayan de Oro, to Benoni. At least three boats make this run and they run about hourly from 6 am to 4 pm. Tickets cost between P20 and P30 for the hour's crossing. Buses run about every 15 minutes between Cagayan and Balingoan (P35, 1½ hours) and Butuan and Balingoan (P40, 2½ hours).

GETTING AROUND
The road around the island is 64km long, so it's possible to make the circuit in a few hours if you have to. There are jeepneys, but they are few and far between, unless they are meeting the boats, and you may have to wait quite a while for the next one, especially along the west coast between Mambajao and Catarman. For ease of travel and access to places that jeepneys don't go, think about hiring a motorcycle (P500) or multicab that can comfortably seat about six people (P800) to take you around for a day.

BENONI
Benoni has an artificial lagoon to the south of its wharf. This is a fish-breeding area and you can stay at *J and A's Fishpen* (☎ *088-387 4008*). There are some rooms out over the water, but the rubbish tip seems to be encroaching on the walkway here and it's quite smelly. There is also a restaurant here and it's nice to eat perched out over other parts of the fishpens.

Between Benoni and Mambajao you'll see Mantigue – sometimes called Magsaysay – Island offshore. A few fishing families live here and there's still good coral. From the Islet Beach Resort at Mahinog a return trip to the island will cost P350.

Getting There & Away
Public jeepney or multicab rides to Mambajao costs P20. A special ride to Mambajao costs P150; to the resorts north of Mambajao you'll pay P200. There is a flat rate of P2.50 for local rides.

MAMBAJAO
This is the capital of Camiguin, about half an hour's ride from the port at Benoni. There are a few places to stay here, but you may prefer to stay closer to the northern beaches.

There is a tourist office on the second floor of the Provincial Capitol Building. The staff here has a list of homestay accommodation if you prefer to stay with a local family.

You can change US dollars at the PNB.

Places to Stay & Eat

Budget accommodation can be found at *Tia's Pension* (☎ 088-387 0103), where very simple rooms in the family home cost P100. *Tia's Beach Cottages* (☎ 088-387 1045) are just out of town in a sizeable but low-key setting. Cottages cost P300. It's a popular venue for local seminars and the food is great.

In town the *Casa Grande* (☎ 088-387 2075) has four rooms, costing P800, in a high and airy old house with lots of polished wood floors. Its attached *restaurant* has a varied menu.

Just out of town is one of the top resorts in Camiguin, the *Bahay Bakasyunan* (☎/fax 088-387 1057), where rooms are P1500 plus tax. It's fine but is too new to have much character. Nonguests can use the pool for P75.

AROUND MAMBAJAO

Hibok-Hibok Volcano last erupted in 1951. About half a kilometre off the main road is the Philippine Institute of Volcanology & Seismology (PHILVOLCS) station, which monitors the volcano's activity. A hired motorcycle or multicab will take you there to see the equipment and memorabilia of past eruptions. It's possible to climb the volcano, but be warned that it's a steep climb and you should be reasonably fit. Most resorts have a list of local guides who will take you up the trail; aim to leave around daybreak if you want to get up and down in a day.

Less energetic is the trip to **Katibawasan Falls**. This is a beautiful clear stream of water dropping about 70m to a plunge pool. You can swim here but the changing rooms and picnic tables have seen better days. Entry to the falls is P10. A special trip by jeepney or multicab from Mambajao will cost about P250 return; from the resorts around Agoho it's about P350 return.

Nearby are the **Ardent Hot Springs**. These are HOT hot springs – about 40ºC – so head out late afternoon when the air temperature has cooled down a bit. The springs and their nicely landscaped grounds are open from 6 am to 10 pm daily, but the big pool is emptied for cleaning on Wednesday and takes the best part of the day to refill.

Entry is P20. There is a good *restaurant* here, and attractive *dorms and cottages* from P150 to P1000; guests can swim all night after closing time. Ardent Hot Spring gets very busy at the weekends.

About a kilometre from the springs, going towards the highway, the new *Abu Nature Camp* is a pleasant collection of cottages in a pocket of forest.

AROUND THE ISLAND
Kuguita, Bug-ong, Agoho & Yumbing

These are the most developed of the northern beaches. Coming from Mambajao, you first reach Kuguita, where there is the *Turtles Nest Beach resort* (☎ 088-387 9056). It's a bit dilapidated and loses its beach completely at high tide, but there's good coral about 100m offshore and nonguests can access it from the resort. You should probably at least buy a drink at the bar if you do!

At Bug-ong, *Jasmine by the Sea* (☎ 088-387 9015) continues to be excellent value. Good roomy cottages with balconies are available from P400 to P500 (P250, P350 off-season). There are mountain bikes for hire for P100 per day, and both the Western and Filipino food is very good, with home-made sugar-free breads and salads. Next door is *Morning Glory Cottages* (☎ 088-387 9017), where rooms directly on the waterfront cost P400, P250 just behind. There is no restaurant, but you can cook for yourself or order food from the staff.

At Agoho, the *Caves Resort* (☎ 088-387 9040) has OK rooms from P100 to P700 and a big and airy restaurant and bar on the waterfront. It's also the base for Genesis Diving (☎ 088-387 9063, ℮ genesisc@skyinet.net), presently the only dive base on the island. A single dive, including equipment and boat ride will cost around US$30; it will organise charter dives to any location.

The *Camiguin Seaside Resort* (☎ 088-387 9031) has lots of roomy cottages for P400 and a big restaurant area, and is popular with group travellers. Opposite here, check out the small restaurant *Sagittarius Serve Food*; if it's open it comes highly recommended. Between Bug-ong and Agoho is *Paradiso Restaurant*, with a good menu featuring fish and fresh pasta; expect to pay around P150 for a main dish.

In Yumbing there are three mid- to top-range lodgings. *Secret Cove (☎ 088-387 9084)* has very new, very blue rooms for P500 to P600 (and two unhappy looking monkeys on chains in the garden). *Para's Resort (☎ 088-387 9008, ✉ paras@oronet .com.ph)* has rooms from P1275 plus tax, a good restaurant and a pool overlooking the water. Nonguests can use the pool for P50. Just up the road is *Camiguin Beach Club (☎ 088-387 9028, ✉ pcrbank@skyinet.net)*, which also has a good-sized pool open to nonguests. Rooms range from P800 to P1250 for an air-con room with share bath that sleeps four to six.

All these resorts give easy access to tiny **White Island**, a pure, white-sandbar a few hundred metres offshore. A return trip should cost around P200, but will cost considerably more from the more expensive resorts.

Tangub Hot Spring

This is a completely undeveloped spring that wells hot under the sea bed, a few metres offshore at Tangub, just beyond barangay Naasag. At low tide it's HOT; at high tide you'd never know it was there. It's fun to sit in the water at lowish tide as cold sea water and hot spring water mix.

Bonbon

Just before Bonbon you pass the Old Camiguin Volcano, the slopes of which have been turned into a steep and beautiful **Stations of the Cross**. There are great views from the top. Between the hillside and Bonbon you'll see an enormous white cross floating on a pontoon in the bay; this marks the spot of the **Sunken Graveyard**, which slipped into the sea following the earthquake of 1871. The same earthquake destroyed the **17th century Spanish church** in Bonbon; its quiet ruins still stand, with grazing cattle and a makeshift altar inside.

Catarman

About 10km further along the island road from Bonbon is Catarman. At the vice-mayor's office in the Municipal Hall there's a small display of **antique ceramics**; the office is closed from noon to 1 pm and weekends. You can stay in Catarman at *SRJ Balhon's Lodging* for P100 to P700, but there's only a small pebbly beach and it's quite noisy due to the attached open-air restaurant.

Near to Catarman is the undervisited and unspoiled **Tuasan Falls**. The road to it is impassable after rain, but if it has been dry a jeepney or multicab can take you to the start of the path. From there it's about a 15-minute hike to the falls, walking twice through the river (this is also not possible after heavy rain as the river is too high). The falls thunder into a plunge pool which may be too rough to plunge into; but it's nice to see the tree ferns and rainforest created by the spray. This area is slated for tourism development along the lines of horse rides and overnight camping; check how that's progressing with the tourism office if you're interested.

Also near Catarman is the **Santo Niño Cold Spring**, a terrific huge pool, 40m long, filled by the spring. And cold it is! Entry to the springs costs P10, and it's open from 8 am to noon and from 1 to 5 pm. It's closed for cleaning between 8 and 10 am on Monday.

Guinsiliban

This is an alternative port to Benoni, and some ships from Cagayan de Oro dock here. At time of writing the port was closed and undergoing extensive rebuilding, and all shipping was going through Benoni except for the Sunday boat from Mambajao to Cebu. Behind the elementary school by the wharf is the remains of an **old Spanish tower**, used to watch out for possible Moro invaders from the mainland. A pretty shrine is maintained here.

ILIGAN

The first impression of Iligan as you arrive by road is of industrial plants, with the road passing endless cement factories and food-processing factories. The harnessing of water from Lake Lanao, in the hills above the city, to provide hydroelectricity has allowed for major development, and the city is busy.

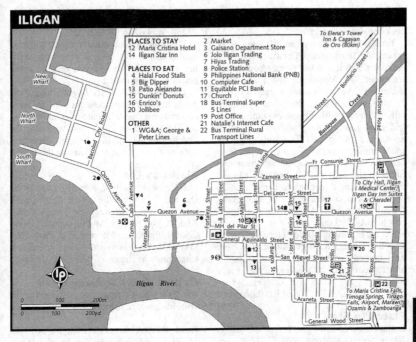

ILIGAN

PLACES TO STAY
12 Maria Cristina Hotel
14 Iligan Star Inn

PLACES TO EAT
4 Halal Food Stalls
5 Big Dipper
13 Patio Alejandra
15 Dunkin' Donuts
16 Enrico's
20 Jollibee

OTHER
1 WG&A; George & Peter Lines

2 Market
3 Gaisano Department Store
6 Jolo Iligan Trading
7 Hiyas Trading
8 Police Station
9 Philippines National Bank (PNB)
10 Computer Cafe
11 Equitable PCI Bank
17 Church
18 Bus Terminal Super 5 Lines
19 Post Office
21 Natalie's Internet Cafe
22 Bus Terminal Rural Transport Lines

Along with the provision of hydroelectricity there are also, inevitably, plenty of waterfalls, and the city prefers to market itself to tourists as 'City of Magnificent Waterfalls'. Late September is **Ang Sinulog fiesta** time, when the streets into town are lined with fantastic bamboo and nipa arches to honour San Miguel, the city's patron saint. The main day of celebrations is 29 September, when the *sinulog*, a fight-dance, and miracle plays are performed, and girls dressed in traditional costume go from house to house singing in local dialects.

Information
Tourist Offices The DOT (☎ 063-221 3426, fax 517 602) is in the ABC Building just below City Hall. It is closed on the weekend.

Money There is a PNB to change US dollars and the Equitable PCI Bank will advance cash on Visa cards.

Email & Internet Access There are several Internet cafes in Iligan. Try the Computer Cafe on MH del Pilar St beside the Equitable PCI Bank, or Natalie's Internet Cafe on Agoncillo St.

Shopping This is a good place to look for Muslim crafts, especially if you are not going up to the market at Marawi. Both Jolo Iligan Trading on Quezon St and Hiyas Trading on Fortaleza St have a good selection of weavings, traditional motif batiks and brassware.

Things to See & Do
The still-magnificent **Maria Cristina Falls** have been dammed above and below the waterfall itself and sometimes the water is cut off to regulate flow downstream. You can walk out over a road bridge midway between the upper and lower levels for good views up and downstream. A taxi ride from Iligan to this government-secured road costs about P70, or you can take a jeepney

MINDANAO & SULU

to Agus Bridge and ask directions to walk the kilometre or so in.

Tinago Falls is more beautiful and more accessible than Maria Cristina; the falls thunder down into a big plunge pool (there are about 300 steps down to it!), and there is a nice pocket of rainforest created by the constant spray. Above the privately owned falls is a resort with a good swimming pool and a not good minizoo with, among other animals, a full-grown lion and a tiger in small concrete pens. It's pretty bizarre to hear the lion's roar echo through the gorge. Entry to the falls is P30, and you can get there by taking a jeepney to Burun (P5, 30 minutes) and connecting with another up the hill to the falls. A taxi from Iligan will cost about P100 one way.

On the highway, a little before the Tinago turn-off, **Timoga Springs** cold springs have been tapped to fill several swimming pools, all of which have attached facilities. Entry to most of the pools is P20. Jeepneys go there for P5; a taxi will cost P100 one way.

Places to Stay

In the centre of town you'll find the budget *Iligan Star Inn* (☎ 063-221 5272). Rooms range from P200 with fan and share bath to P500 for an air-con room with bath. The cheaper rooms are pretty grotty and the common bathrooms stink; the others are OK.

Close by is the *Maria Cristina Hotel* (☎ 063-221 3352, fax 221 3940), where rooms range from P560 to P950. For a long time this was the best hotel in Iligan but it now needs some maintenance.

A better standard of comfort and cleanliness can be found at *Elena's Tower* (☎/fax 063-221 5995), just off the main drag, where very pink rooms go for between P690 and P1730.

The *Iligan Day Inn* (☎ 063-221 3855, fax 221 3491) has seen better days; its restaurant is closed and it looks a bit tired, but the rooms are OK for P590 to P1280.

The best place in town, as suggested by the price, is *Cheradel Suites* (☎ 063-223 8118, fax 221 4926), five minutes east of town on La Salle Road. It's a very comfortable place with private pool and about 10

tasteful rooms with great bathrooms from P1200. It is often booked out.

The tourism department keeps a list of quality homestays, several with pools, starting at around P700, if you're after more personal accommodation.

The *Tinago Residence Inn* at Tinago Falls has pretty rooms and cottages – lots of bamboo and nipa – all with balconies, air-con and private bath from P980. You will hear the lion roaring on and off all night. There is a good restaurant here overlooking the falls.

Places to Eat

Eat Chinese food at the *Big Dipper* on Quezon St, around the corner from a good line of *halal food stalls* on Tomas Cabili Ave, if you're sick of the sight of pork. Good Filipino food is served at *Patio Alejandra* and at *Enrico's*, one of the oldest restaurants in Iligan.

Getting There & Away

Air The nearest airport is at Cagayan de Oro, from where Iligan is 1½ hours by road.

Boat WG&A has services leaving at 10 pm Monday and Saturday for Manila (from P1000, three days) and 7 pm Tuesday, Thursday, Friday and Sunday for Cebu City (P220, 11 hours).

George & Peter Lines has boats leaving at noon Sunday for Lazi on Siquijor (five hours).

Bus There are very regular services north to Cagayan de Oro (P50, 1½ hours) and south to Pagadian. Ozamis is 1½ hours away (P35). There are two bus terminals on Roxas Avenue serving the same destinations, one for Super 5 Lines and its associates and one for Rural Transit.

Getting Around

The flat fare around town by jeepney is P2.50. No tricycles are allowed in the city centre, but there are plenty of taxis.

MARAWI & LAKE LANAO

Marawi is the centre of Muslim culture in the Philippines. The Islamic City of Marawi, as it is properly known, is about an hour's drive south of Iligan and it's like driving into another world. At the border of Lanao del Sur the churches disappear and the spires of mosques appear on the skyline, women wear headscarves and there are signs in Arabic.

The city sits prettily in a bowl of hills and on the shore of Lake Lanao. Places to visit include the **Aga Khan Museum** (open from 9 am to noon and 1 to 4 pm daily) on the campus of the Marawi State University (MSU); the **market** for fabrics and brassware crafted in the township of Tugaya across the lake; **Dayawan weaving village** outside the city proper; and the ceremonial wooden **Torongan** buildings.

Warning

Having whetted your appetite for cultural diversity, here comes the bad news. It's not too strong to say that most Filipinos you'll come across, both in Iligan and Marawi, are paranoid about travel in this area, as Marawi has long been a crisis area, even though trouble only flares up occasionally. It is not forbidden to visit the city unaccompanied, but the local tourism offices and hotels strongly advise against it. Women travelling alone may feel particularly uncomfortable. Your four options are:

• to check the current situation in Iligan before going up and then decide whether or not to go;
• to hire a car and driver (ask the tourism department in Iligan for help with this – many drivers are too scared to make the trip) and make a day trip, calling in at the tourism office in Marawi to pick up a local city guide;
• to ignore all advice, take a jeepney up, and see what happens;
• don't go.

Information

The tourist office is located in the City Hall and is closed on Friday and Saturday. It may be open on Sunday.

Places to Stay

The only hotel in Marawi is the *Marawi Resort Hotel* (☎/fax 063-520 981). It is on the MSU campus and has huge grounds, lots of trees, a pool and restaurant and a good view of the lake. Cottages with balconies cost from P850 to P1000. The bathrooms leave a lot to be desired.

Getting There & Away

Jeepneys and buses run regularly to/from Iligan. A return trip by taxi (if you can find a driver to take you), with a couple of hours waiting time, will cost between P800 and P1000.

OZAMIS

While Ozamis is not the provincial capital of Misamis Occidental, it has a capital city feel to it and is bigger and busier than the capital Oroquieta. It has a busy port area and compact central commercial area, but apart from that there's little here to hold a traveller's interest.

Places to Stay & Eat

There are several lodgings in Ozamis. In the budget range try *The Country Lodge* on Ledesma St Extension. It's simple and a bit tatty but clean as a whistle, and rooms range from P120 to P240 for fan and bath and P250 to P350 with air-con and bath.

The *Soriano Pension* on Mabini St Extension has rooms with fan and bath for P150 to P180, P250 to P350 with air-con and bath. It's fine for the price, and very clean, but rooms are around a central space with loud TV and are quite noisy. It's owned by a nice family.

In the mid-range, try the *Palace Hotel* (☎ 088-521 0573, fax 521 3240). It's new and has good rooms with air-con, bath and TV for P450 to P950.

Best in town is the *Royal Garden Hotel* (☎ 088-521 2888, fax 521 0008) with rooms from P750. There is a good restaurant and Filipino fast-food outlet attached.

Getting There & Away

Boat All the shipping agents are located at the wharf. Ferries run constantly between Kolambugan (an hour's drive south of Iligan) to Ozamis and all buses use this service. The cost of the boat ride (P8.50, 25 minutes) is in addition to the bus fare and is collected on board the ferry.

MINDANAO & SULU

Boats leave Sunday, Monday and Tuesday for Manila and take about 48 hours. Cebu Ferries and Trans-Asia Lines has boats leaving daily except Monday for Cebu City (12 hours). There is a boat on Sunday to Dumaguete on Negros (five hours) and one on Tuesday for Iloilo on Panay (five hours).

Bus Buses run every 15 minutes to/from Iligan (P35, 1½ hours), Pagadian, Dipolog, Oroquieta (P25, 1½ hours). All buses go from an integrated transport terminal that is a P10 ride by tricycle from the port.

OROQUIETA

Oroquieta is a sleepy riverside town and seems an unlikely setting for the provincial capital of Misamis Occidental. The market comes alive in the late afternoons, when the fishing fleet has delivered the day's catch.

Places to Stay

Sheena's Hotel (☎ *088-531 1158)* on Barrientos St has plenty of character. It's a rambling old house with garden and restaurant but is on a very noisy stretch of road. Rooms with fan start at P200 and those with air-con and bath start at P675.

Two hundred metres further along Barrientos St is the new *Casa Kristina Hotel* (☎/fax *088-531 1272),* where bright rooms start at P660. The hotel has direct river frontage and a good restaurant with a balcony over the water.

Getting There & Away

All buses from Ozamis to Dipolog (and vice versa) go via Oroquieta (P25, one hour). Get off the bus at the petrol station in town on the way through, rather than at the bus terminal on the outskirts.

Getting Around

There is a flat rate of P2.50 anywhere in town by public transport. A special ride by tricycle to Sheena's or Casa Kristina costs P10.

BALIANGAO WETLAND PARK

This small but great spot is way off the beaten track, with mangrove-lined river estuaries to explore, good snorkelling off-

shore beside the marine protected area, and white-sand beaches a short boat ride away. The only noise you'll hear is birdsong and the occasional fishing boat.

Excuse the acronyms, but this is a community-based sustainable tourism (CBST) initiative, in which several local barangays are being supported by nongovernment organisations (NGOs) and the DENR in a very low-key development. This consists of four simple bamboo and nipa cottages and a meeting and eating shelter, all powered by solar energy (not a radio or television in sight), with septic tanks for sewage, and rainwater collection for drinking and quick showers. If you like your creature comforts, you may wish to just make a day trip and overnighters should be prepared for lots of mosquitoes (nets are provided in the cottages).

Cottages that sleep six cost P300 or P75 per head and it costs P50 per meal. A boat to go snorkelling (bring your own equipment) costs P150 for half a day; a 30-minute tour upriver costs P150; a boat ride to Sunrise Beach for swimming costs P200 for half a day. Staff live on-site but they need to make a trip to town to get provisions for visitors, so it's best to ring a day or so ahead, especially as the cottages can occasionally be full of students on field trips. Contact the NGO PIPULI in Ozamis on ☎ 088-521 1928, or fax 521 1992. On weekends call ☎ 0918-490 2476.

Getting There & Away

Get a bus from Dipolog (P30, 1½ hours) or Oroquieta (P25, one hour) to Calamba. Here, it's easiest to take a special trip by tricycle to the park which, with a couple of hours waiting time, will cost about P150 return. Tell the driver to head towards Baliangao and as he may not know where you want to go watch the kilometre markers carefully; just after the '4km to Baliangao' marker a track goes right with a faded signpost to the park. It's about two bumpy kilometres down this track and it is impassable to vehicles when wet. At the end of the track walk a delightful 400m or so along a series of boardwalk bridges through mangrove forest to the park buildings.

Marawi, in Mindanao, is the centre of Islamic culture in the Philippines.

Muslim dancers, Marawi, Mindanao.

Mosque, Zamboanga.

Badjao (sea gypsy) houses, Davao, Mindanao.

Weaver at work, Mindanao.

Stilt house, Zamboanga, Mindanao.

Fish farm, Davao, Mindanao.

Breaking Down Barriers – CBST

Several innovative nongovernment organisations (NGOs) and people's organisations (POs) in the Philippines have started working with local communities on small-scale CBST projects. These often involve homestay accommodation in fishing or agricultural communities, or in protected areas, and allow travellers the opportunity to interact with local people in a more equitable and interesting way than simply responding to the 'Hey Joe, are you married?' norm.

Maybe you'll go fishing with your host and then help cook the catch; or hike to collect weaving fibres; or snorkel in a marine sanctuary, while your hosts get on with an environmental monitoring survey. Maybe you'll just sit quietly watching as different lives go on around you in their usual fashion.

This is not tourism for the seeker of five-star comfort or wild nightlife, but it's a great chance to briefly feel like an insider rather than an outsider in someone else's culture and country. And it's good to know that your money is staying within (and benefiting) the local community.

ASSET (✉ asset@pacific.net.ph) is the umbrella organisation for NGOs with CBST projects in Camiguin Island, Baliangao, Davao del Sur and Sarangani in Mindanao; in Metro Manila and Ifugao in Luzon; and in Palawan, Cebu, Bohol, and Marinduque provinces.

Virginia Jealous

DIPOLOG

Dipolog is the capital of Zamboanga del Norte, and has a busy town centre just off the waterfront. If you're in an energetic mood you can climb the many, many steps of the **Stations of the Cross** to Linabo Park. At 486m above sea level, this lookout gives a good view of Dipolog and its neighbouring city of Dapitan. **Sicayab Beach** is a fine grey-sand beach about 4km from town, and further out is the **Pamansalan Oisca Forest Park and Waterfall**.

Information

The DOT has an office in the City Hall on Rizal St.

The PNB will change US dollars.

There are plenty of Internet cafes in town. Try Cyberspot, on Ramos St just off General Luna St, or the Goodwill Internet Cafe on General Luna, near the Top Plaza Hotel.

Places to Stay & Eat

There is a range of accommodation in town. Budget travellers could try the **Ramillo Pension** (☎ 065-212 3536) on Bonifacio St, where rooms range from P100 to P350. It's fine for the price. Similar in standard is the **Hotel Arocha** (☎/fax 065-212 3197) with

rooms from P200 to P784. The budget rooms are fine, but the more expensive rooms are not good value when compared with other hotels in town.

The **CL Inn** (☎ 065-212 3216) on Rizal St is central but quite noisy and a bit tatty; its budget rooms (P400) are fine but the more expensive ones (P800) aren't. It has an OK but gloomy restaurant serving Filipino fast food.

Good value is the **Hotel Camila** (☎/fax 065-212 3008), a few hundred metres along General Luna St, heading out of town. Well-furnished and comfortable rooms with air-con, bath and cable TV start at P500, but make sure you have a room on the opposite side from the church: early mass is broadcast over loudspeakers from 4.30 to 5.15 am every day. A **Sunburst Chicken Restaurant** is attached.

At the top end of accommodation is the **Top Plaza Hotel** (☎ 065-212 5777, fax 212 5788, ✉ topplaza@mozcom.com) with rooms from P825 to P1540. The hotel has a good restaurant and the **Top Diner** fast-food place attached.

In the Festival Shopping Arcade in the fruit and vegetable market look out for **Pizza Deli**, which has a 'real' pizza oven and lots of tourist information on the walls. *Micki's* on Rizal St is bright and clean and serves chicken, burgers and spaghetti-style dishes.

Getting There & Away
Air PAL flies from Manila to Dipolog at 6 am Tuesday, Thursday, Saturday and Sunday, and at 9.20 am Friday.

Boat Dipolog's Palauan Port is technically in the nearby city of Dapitan, though geographically it's halfway between the two. Details of boats are in the Dapitan section of this chapter.

Bus Regular buses link Dipolog with Ozamis via Oroquieta (P75, 3½ hours). They drop off right in town on General Luna St. Southbound buses to Zamboanga (P200 air-con, P180 non air-con, eight to 10 hours) leave from the Satellite bus terminal on the southern edge of town, next to the post office.

Warning There are regular 'incidents' on the road between Dipolog and Zamboanga. These range from hold-ups and robberies to lethal bus bombings. Think twice before going south by road. For alternative routes and means of transport to Zamboanga see Getting There & Away in the Zamboanga section of this chapter.

Getting Around
The airport is about 3km out of town and a tricycle will cost about P20.

Flat fare in town for tricycles is P2. RBS Minivans have a stand on General Luna St opposite the high school; you can charter an air-con van for P250 an hour or P1800 per day (negotiable).

AROUND DIPOLOG
There is a pretty and safe stretch of coast south of Dipolog, pleasant for day tours. Off the highway, about an hour from Dipolog (though it'll take closer to two hours by public transport), is the **Villaester/ Villavalle Mountain Resort** at Carupe. It's a family-run property in the foothills of the mountains, where a spring has been tapped to fill a fair-sized pool. The surrounding

scenery and vegetation is lush and damp (take a mosquito coil) and the 6km dirt road in, through small villages, gives a good glimpse of rural life off the beaten track. Entry is P15, and the pool is closed for cleaning on Thursday. There are very basic *cottages* for P500; bring sleeping mats and mosquito nets. You can order food from the owners. To get there take a multicab from Dipolog to Villa Ramos (P12, 45 minutes) and then a van or extended motorcycle (P15) to Carupe, 6km off the highway. A special trip by RBS Minivan will cost around P250 an hour. The road will probably be impassable after heavy rain.

Another 8km down the highway on the coast at Punta Blanca is **Crystal Beach Resort**, where a spring fills a clear 20m pool and there is a small beach and day cottages for hire; bring your own food. Pool use costs P30 and you can overnight in a simple and breezy *cottage* right over the water for P300. Catch a multicab or bus from Satellite terminal in Dipolog (P20, one hour) and get off at the entrance to the small resort.

DAPITAN
This really is a clean, green and peaceful city on the edge of a wide and clean bay; you may choose to stay here rather than in Dipolog if you're spending a few days in the area.

Dapitan's most famous temporary resident was the national hero José Rizal, who lived in exile here from 1892 until shortly before his death in 1896. During that time he designed the town's waterworks, fashioned a **grass relief map** of Mindanao that can still be seen opposite the **old church** in the town plaza, practised as a doctor and natural scientist and taught school to local boys. The **Rizal Museum** is at Talisay, just over the bridge in Dapitan where Rizal lived. The main building houses a collection of Rizal memorabilia and in the grounds are beautifully crafted, life-size, bamboo and nipa replicas of the house, clinic, school and chicken house where Rizal lived. There is a good stand of natural forest in the grounds, with boardwalks and paths along the water.

The museum is a fine memorial to a fine man and is open daily. Rizal's **landing site** is marked by a memorial on the waterfront.

Aliguay Island, a white-sand island with good coral, is a 45-minute banca ride from Dapitan.

Places to Stay & Eat
There are several places along Sunset Blvd to stay, overlooking the bay. *Aplaya Vida Pension* consists of simple air-con rooms for P450 in a nice old wooden house. Across the road there is a seafood restaurant attached to the pension.

Close by, *Casa Patricia* rents rooms with fan and share bath for P300, though the house is a bit dark and dreary.

Dapitan City Resort Hotel (☎/fax 065-213 6542) has full water frontage and all rooms have balconies. Room rates start at P1200. There is a pool which nonguests can use for P75, and a nice-looking restaurant.

You can eat at *Corazon de Dapitan*, where very good Filipino dishes and cakes (try the fantastic *bibingka*) are served on the ground floor of a beautiful, old two-storey building on the corner of the plaza in town. There's a clean, flushing, Western-style loo that even has a seat!

Absolute top of the range for accommodation is the *Dakak Park Beach Resort* (☎/fax 065-212 5932, ✆ dakak@pacific .net.ph), on Dakak Bay, about 15 minutes from Dapitan by road or 40 minutes by boat. The resort offers a private beach, golf course, horse riding, water sports and diving and nice rooms and cottages. Its standard is indicated by the room rates, which range from P8000 to P12,000. Guests are transferred to the resort by hotel transport, but other visitors need to ride an extended motorcycle (P100 return, depending on waiting time) from Dapitan. Nonguests can have day use of the resort beach – but not the swimming pools – for P200.

Getting There & Away
Minivan From Dipolog catch an RBS minivan (P8, 30 minutes) from the RBS stand on General Luna St, opposite the high school.

Boat Palauan Port is halfway between Dipolog and Dapitan, about 2km off the highway. Ask the RBS minivan to drop you at the turn-off, and then take a tricycle (P5) to the port. The tricycles wait interminably for a total of eight – yes eight! – passengers, so you might want to pay for an extra couple of places so that you can get going.

Cebu To Manila, WG&A has boats leaving at midnight Sunday, while Sulpicio Lines trips leave at 9 am Monday. The journey takes between 29 and 36 hours.

SuperCat has boats leaving at 5 pm daily for Cebu City via Dumaguete (P365, four hours), while Delta Fast Ferries services leave at 10.45 am daily (P580, five hours).

SuperCat also has boats going to Negros at 5 pm daily (two hours).

DAVAO
Sprawling at the foot of Mt Apo, Davao is the fastest-growing city in Mindanao. While predominantly Christian, it has an interesting and eclectic mix of Muslim, Chinese and tribal influences. The latter is showcased during the second week of August each year, during the Kadayawan sa Dabaw Festival, with costumed street parades, dances and performances, along with fantastic displays of fruit and flowers.

Davao also has a long-standing Japanese history associated with early abaca-processing warehouses in the area and, less happily, with WWII, when the thriving Japanese community dispersed. There are still strong ties between the mother country and 'little Japan', as Davao is also known.

Outside the city, export quantities of pineapples, bananas and citrus are produced and plantations can be visited. For the natural history enthusiast, there are walking tracks around nearby Mt Apo and there's a breeding program for the endangered Philippine eagle at nearby Eagle Camp. The offshore islands of Samal and Talikud offer clear water, good corals and wreck-diving.

Orientation
A couple of key streets have changed names but are still confusingly referred to by both

DAVAO

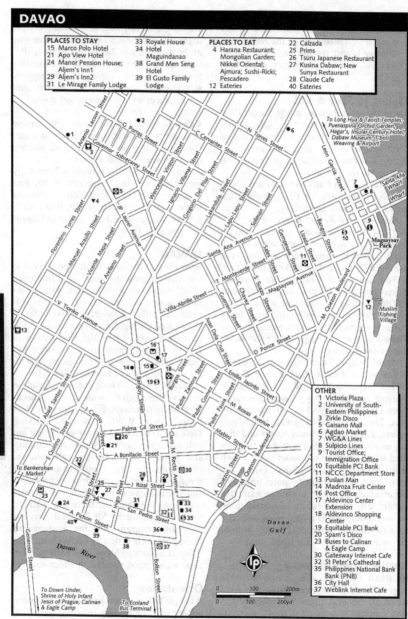

PLACES TO STAY
15 Marco Polo Hotel
21 Apo View Hotel
24 Manor Pension House;
   Aljem's Inn1
29 Aljem's Inn2
31 Le Mirage Family Lodge
33 Royale House
34 Hotel
   Maguindanao
38 Grand Men Seng
   Hotel
39 El Gusto Family
   Lodge

PLACES TO EAT
4 Harana Restaurant;
   Mongolian Garden;
   Nikkei Oriental;
   Ajmura; Sushi-Ricki;
   Pescadero
12 Eateries
22 Calzada
25 Prims
26 Tsuru Japanese Restaurant
27 Kusina Dabaw; New
   Sunya Restaurant
28 Claude Cafe
40 Eateries

OTHER
1 Victoria Plaza
2 University of South-
   Eastern Philippines
3 Zirkle Disco
5 Gaisano Mall
6 Agdao Market
7 WG&A Lines
8 Sulpicio Lines
9 Tourist Office;
   Immigration Office
10 Equitable PCI Bank
11 NCCC Department Store
13 Puslan Man
14 Madroza Fruit Center
16 Post Office
17 Aldevinco Center
   Extension
18 Aldevinco Shopping
   Center
19 Equitable PCI Bank
20 Spam's Disco
23 Buses to Calinan
   & Eagle Camp
30 Gateway Internet Cafe
32 St Peter's Cathedral
35 Philippines National Bank
   Bank (PNB)
36 City Hall
37 Weblink Internet Cafe

FROM DU ROYAUME DE SIAM, BY SIMON DE LA LOUBÈRE

Mindanao, home to many fruit plantations, is also famous for its Davao durians.

old and new names. These are F Inigo St (formerly Anda St) and Pelayo St (formerly Legaspi St).

Information

Tourist Offices The regional DOT office (☎ 082-221 6955, ✉ dotr11@mozcom .com) is at Magsaysay Park. It's open from 8 am to noon and from 1 to 4.30 pm Monday to Friday. The City Tourism Office is in City Hall opposite San Pedro Cathedral.

Money The PNB opposite the cathedral will change US dollars. The Equitable PCI banks on Monteverde St near Santa Aña Wharf, and on Claro M Recto heading towards the Aldevinco Center will advance cash against Visa cards.

Consulates The Indonesian Consulate (☎ 082-229 2930, fax 297 0139) is at Ecoland Dr in the Ecoland Subdivision near the southern bus station.

Email & Internet Access There are many Internet cafes in town. Try Gatesway Cafe, off Claro M Recto St near the Hotel Maguindanao, or the Weblink Cafe on A Pichon St behind city hall. There is also an Internet cafe in the Aldevinco Center Extension beside the post office.

Things to See & Do

You can easily fill a pleasant half-day in the north of the city towards the airport. Coming from the city, take a jeepney in the direction of Sasa and get off at the **Long Hua Temple** on Cabaguio St, two to three kilometres from the city centre. It's an easy landmark, a huge Chinese Buddhist temple with beautiful wooden floors and carved walls and doors. It's open from 7.30 am to 4.30 pm; walk also behind the main temple to see the smaller altar behind. Walking back towards the city for a couple of hundred metres, you'll see a sign on a small side street on the right to the **Taoist Temple**, with its fantastic red pagoda. Ring a bell on the gate if you want to go inside. Back on the main road, walk another 500m or so south and turn left into Bolcan St. At the end is the **Puentaspina Orchid Garden**. It's more of an orderly nursery than a garden, but it has some great specimens on show, including the gorgeous *waling-waling*, endemic to Mindanao. It's open every day and entry is free.

Continue north by jeepney or taxi to the **Dabaw Museum**, next to the Insular Century

MINDANAO & SULU

Hotel. It has a good collection of local historical interest and a selection of tribal weavings and artefacts from most of the Mindanao tribes. It's open from 9 am to 5 pm Monday to Saturday and entry is P20. Walk through the grounds of the Insular Century to the **T'boli Weaving Centre**, to the left of the hotel jetty. There is a small collection of weavings and T'boli handicrafts and, if you're lucky (or if any of the sales staff deign to notice you), you'll see weavers working complicated textiles on backstrap looms.

West of Davao, in the hillside barangay of Matina, is the **Shrine of the Holy Infant Jesus of Prague**. From here there's a good view of Davao Gulf and the city. Take a jeepney from Bankerohan Market to Matina and then a tricycle to the shrine. A taxi there will cost about P50.

Places to Stay – Budget
Le Mirage Family Lodge (☎ 082-226 3811), on San Pedro St, is fine for a central lodging. Its rooms are tatty and noisy, but it's clean and secure. Rooms range from P140 with fan and share bath to P400 with air-con and bath.

Sunny Point Lodge (☎ 082-221 0155, fax 244 0562) and *El Gusto Family Lodge* (☎ 082-227 3662) are close to each other on A Pichon St and offer much the same standard, with rooms from P150 to P600. El Gusto has a central courtyard though, which makes it lighter and brighter.

Places to Stay – Mid-Range
The *Manor Pension House* (☎ 082-221 2511), just off A Pichon St, has been newly renovated and the rooms are good value for P525 and P630, including breakfast.

Next door is *Aljem's Inn 1* (☎ 082-221 3060, fax 221 3059), which is a little cheaper at P500 but older and darker. The newer *Aljem's Inn 2*, on J Rizal St, offers reasonable rooms at P560 to P750.

The *Royale House* (☎ 082-227 3630, fax 221 8106), near the cathedral, on Claro Recto St, has rooms which are expensive and ordinary for P590 to P850, unless the regular 50% promotion is happening. This makes them good value!

Hotel Maguindanao (☎ 082-222 2894, fax 221 8121, @ hmsales@mozcom.com), opposite the cathedral is an older, good-quality hotel with comfortable rooms from P745.

Places to Stay – Top End
Best value of these is the *Grand Men Seng Hotel* (☎ 082-221 9040, fax 221 2431, @ grand@menseng.com.ph), on A Pichon St, with first class rooms, a lively lobby and coffee shop and good-sized pool. Rooms start at P1850 plus tax and service. Nonguests can use the pleasant pool and surrounds for P100.

The *Apo View Hotel* (☎ 082-221 6430, fax 221 0748, @ apoview@interasia.com .ph) has rooms from P2800, but at time of writing its pool had been out of service for some months.

A new arrival in town is the *Marco Polo* (☎ 082-221 0888, fax 225 0111, @ davao@marcopolohotels.com) on Claro M Recto St, opposite the Aldevinco Center, with first class rooms and prices to match, starting at P4800 plus tax and service. Nonguests can use the 25m lap pool for P150.

The superbly landscaped *Insular Century Hotel* (☎ 082-234 3050, fax 235 0915) is about 8km out of town on the way to the airport. It has extensive grounds, a swimming pool and a private beach with water sports, diving facilities and a jetty. Rooms usually start at P3000, but ask about promotions that can drop rates by 30%.

Places to Eat
Kusina Dabaw and *New Sunya Restaurant* on San Pedro St serve good Filipino fast food and are always busy. Around the corner on Pelayo St is *Tsuru*, a restaurant where you can expect to pay around P200 or more for an authentic Japanese meal. A little further up Pelayo St is the cheap and cheerful *Prims*, a lively barbecue place that does good fish, has lots of tables and a band at night.

Calzada on Duterte St is the local hardrock cafe. There are good cakes and cappuccino at the *Gatesway cafe* on Claro Recto St. The *eateries* around Santa Aña

Wharf and the Muslim Fishing Village have, as you'd expect, a strong emphasis on fish; they're lively – especially in the early evening – and cheap.

Claude Cafe, on Rizal St, is a French restaurant with an extensive menu and good food. You'll pay P200 plus for a meal here. On F Torres St, off Laurel St, is a line of international restaurants if you want to browse before eating. The *Harana Restaurant* has Filipino food and barbecue; next door is the long-established *Mongolian Garden*; a little further along on the left is *Nikkei Oriental* (selling Chinese food despite the name) and then *Ajmura* and *Sushi Riki* Japanese restaurants, followed by *Pescadero* for seafood.

Entertainment

Most of the top end hotels offer live music nightly and ballroom dancing at least once a week (try the seventh floor of the *Hotel Maguindanao* if you want to trip the light fantastic), with discos usually on Friday.

Folk Music can be heard at the *Puslan Man Bar* on F Torres St, between Mabini St and Camus St.

Dance at *Zirkle Disco*, open every night, behind Victoria Plaza on JP Laurel Ave or at *Spam's* on Palma Gil St. These are the twenty-somethings' scenes. There's also dancing at *Calzada* restaurant.

If you need a dose of Western company and food, there are a couple of recommended expat bars. *Hagar's*, a block before the Insular Century Hotel (coming from the direction of the city), is famous for European sausages, salamis and cheese. There's good bar food, a restaurant upstairs and live music on Friday. Also try the *Downunder Bar*, across Generoso Bridge, for UK-style fish and chips. It's a good place to watch international sporting events on cable TV.

Shopping

If you're looking for handicrafts shop around at the Aldevinco Mall (also known as the Aldevinco Shopping Center). It's a rabbit warren of stalls with fabric, batik, weavings, carvings and so on. Bargain and look carefully before you buy; some stuff is of very poor quality. The stallholders are very keen to change your US dollars or Japanese yen. The T'boli Weaving Center at the Insular Century Hotel has some beautiful (and pricey) artefacts and fabric, but with nonexistent service.

The New City Commercial Center (NCCC) and Gaisano Mall are the big department stores in town.

Locals tell you that once you eat Davao durian you'll always come back to the city, and when it's in season there are plenty of stalls selling this strange and delicious fruit. You may have to work at acquiring the taste for it. It's in season from September to December, and when it's out of season they say durian ice cream has the same effect!

Getting There & Away

Air From Manila, PAL flies to Davao at 5.10 and 11 am daily. There's another flight to Davao at 2.50 pm daily except Wednesday. Air Philippines has daily flights from Manila to Davao at 5 am and 3 pm, while Cebu Pacific flies at 5 and 10 am and 1.20 and 3.20 pm daily.

Cebu Pacific and PAL (☎ 082-221 5641) fly several times a day to Davao from Cebu.

Mindanao Express (☎ 082-235 0621, @ dvocai@weblinq.com) flies to and from Cagayan de Oro but the schedule changes frequently.

The current Brunei, Indonesia, Malaysia, Philippines East Asian Group Area (BIMP-EAGA) initiatives have made travel to and from Indonesia theoretically simpler. Presently Bouraq Airlines (☎ 082-233 0016) flies to Manado from Davao and vice versa on Tuesday and Thursday.

Silk Air (☎ 082-221 6430) flies to Davao from Singapore via Cebu on Wednesday and Sunday.

Boat Big interisland boats use the terminal at Sasa, 8km north of town. This is also where boats to Paradise Island Beach Resort on Samal Island leave from, by the Caltex tanks. Jeepneys run here, or take a taxi for around P70.

Other boats to Samal and Talikud islands go from Santa Aña Wharf in town.

WG&A has vessels leaving for Manila via Iloilo on Panay at midnight Monday and 11 pm Friday. There are also trips via Zamboanga leaving at 10 pm Monday. Negros Navigation has boats going via General Santos, Zamboanga, Iloilo on Panay and Bacolod on Negros, leaving at noon Thursday, arriving at 10 am Sunday.

To Cebu City, Sulpicio Lines has boats going via General Santos leaving at 8 pm Sunday, and via Surigao leaving at 7 pm Wednesday.

WG&A has boats going to Zamboanga 10 pm Monday, and Negros Navigation has boats to General Santos and Zamboanga leaving at noon Thursday.

There is a scheduled boat from Davao to Indonesia via General Santos every Friday from Sasa Pier, but details are sketchy; check with the city tourism officer at city hall.

Bus Buses run between Davao and Cagayan de Oro, Butuan and Surigao (around P200, eight to 10 hours to each destination), south to General Santos (P85, 3½ hours) and west to Cotabato City.

All these services run several times daily and all long-distance bus transportation is based at the Ecoland terminal 2km south of Davao City centre. Manila-bound buses also leave from here. Keep your eyes open at the terminal; several bombs, thought to have been placed by disgruntled former bus line employees, exploded here during late 1999 and early 2000.

Buses to Eagle Camp at Calinan leave from a small terminal on the corner of San Pedro St and Quirino St.

Getting Around

To/From the Airport The airport is 12km north of the city. A taxi to the city will cost around P70. From the city, jeepneys in the direction of Sasa go towards the airport; you'll then need to take a tricycle to the terminal.

Bus The terminal for long-distance buses is at Ecoland, 2km south of the city centre. A taxi will cost about P50, a jeepney about P5.

AROUND DAVAO
Samal Island

Samal is a sizeable island lying off Davao. Pearls are again being cultivated on a small scale near the site of a once-lucrative pearl farm near Kaputian, but most island communities rely on fishing for their livelihoods. There are a few resorts and settlements along the west coast, along which a rugged road runs. Extended motorcycles will take you around.

The island makes an easy day trip from Davao, with Paradise Island Beach Resort (entry fee P30) a comfortable budget base. For those in need of pampering, the five-star Pearl Farm Beach Resort is a luxurious alternative and a day trip from the Insular Century Hotel, including boat transfers, use of the resort's facilities and a superb buffet lunch will cost P1000. There's snorkelling and diving around the island – including two Japanese wrecks just off Pearl Farm beach – but you need to take local advice on the best and safest places to go, as Samal is on a busy shipping channel and there are some strong currents.

Places to Stay *Paradise Island Beach Resort* offers overnight cottages from P500; be warned it can get very busy and noisy at weekends. There's a good, reasonably priced restaurant.

The *Pearl Farm Beach Resort* (☎ 088-221 9970, fax 221 7729, ❷ pearldav@weblinq.com) has, as you'd expect from a five-star resort, tasteful and comfortable accommodation set in lush grounds, with private beaches and swimming pools, and diving and other water sports facilities. Room rates start at US$135, but ask about promotional specials.

Further south is the newish *Samal Island Casino Resort*. Rooms are reasonable, starting at P800, but the restaurant is relatively expensive. It is a favourite venue for seminars and group meetings.

Getting There & Away Pump boats go regularly to Paradise Island Beach Resort from the big Caltex tanks near Sasa Pier (P5, 10 minutes). The other resorts organise transfers for their guests from Santa Aña Wharf in the city.

Talikud Island

This is the little island off the south-west point of Samal. It is much less developed than Samal and has some spectacular coral gardens off its west coast that have regenerated well since dynamite and cyanide fishing stopped about 10 years ago.

Places to Stay Budget travellers will enjoy *Isla Reta* on the east coast of the island. Simple bamboo cottages cost P400 and P500, and you can get equally simple food (or bring your own and the staff will cook it for a small fee). There are extensive grounds and beaches to explore, and a fish sanctuary for snorkelling just offshore.

Travellers chasing luxury should stay just north of Isla Reta at the exquisite and private *Pacific Little Secret (☎/fax 082-227 8216)*. It sleeps a maximum four people in two beautiful breezy houses decorated with ethnic art. There is a gazebo on the edge of the water, and secluded sitting areas and verandas. Rates are US$100 per person, per day, for a minimum of two people. This includes speedboat transfers to and from Davao, all meals, and use of a pump boat and boat driver on call.

Getting There & Away Boats run to Talikud five times a day from Santa Aña Wharf (P20, one hour). The first boat usually leaves at around 7 am. The tiny township and jetty at Santa Cruz is a couple of hundred metres from Isla Reta, though most boats will drop off at the resort.

Eagle Camp

A must for nature lovers, Eagle Camp at Malagos, 36km from Davao, is the headquarters of the Philippine Eagle Foundation, which is dedicated to conserving these fantastic and endangered birds with the wild punk hair-dos. Here you can see the results of the captive breeding program – there have been several successes – along with other rare and endemic species of birds and animals such as Philippine deer and the wonderfully-

The *haribon* (Philippine eagle) is a truly magnificent bird, and sadly, very rare.

named Philippine warty pigs. The camp is set in a pocket of native forest, and there are enough wild birds flitting around to keep the most avid bird-watcher happy. There is an informative video about eagles in the wild and the threats they are facing.

The camp is open from 8 am to 5 pm daily, and volunteer guides are around at weekends to answer questions. Entry is P25 and donation boxes are strategically placed around the grounds to help further the foundation's work. It gets *very* busy though, and if watching animals among hordes of noisy groups isn't your thing, you should plan to get there at opening time to beat the crowds.

A couple of kilometres before the camp as you drive up from Calinan you pass the **Malagos Garden Resort**, which is open for day use and has a swimming pool and garden with orchids; stop and cool off on the way back. Again, weekends can be very busy.

Getting There & Away Take a bus to Calinan (P15, 45 minutes) from the bus terminal on the corner of San Pedro St and Quirino St in Davao. Buses leave every 20 minutes. In Calinan, take a jeepney or tricycle (P5, 10 minutes) to Eagle Camp at Malagos. A special ride up to the camp from Calinan will cost around P50.

Mt Apo

At 2954m Mt Apo is the highest mountain in the Philippines and, most mornings, is clearly visible towering above Davao from unexpected points around the city. There are recommended climbing routes up the mountain, but these are not mere strolls – you need to be pretty fit to tackle them. The trek takes in forest, waterfalls, volcanic craters, the possibility of Philippine eagles in the wild along with other animals and birds, and exotic plants such as orchids and carnivorous pitcher plants. Travellers not wanting to make the full climb can still camp at the start of the trail and walk in the foothills.

Current information on the state of the trail, guide hire, security issues and so on can be found at the regional tourism department in Davao, but for better and more local information contact the Kidapawan Tourism Council (☎ 064-238 1831) in Kidapawan. A good brochure is available from both these offices detailing transport to the region, recommended routes, guide and porter fees and recommended equipment.

This is the minimum three-day suggested schedule for trekking, starting from Kidapawan.

Day One Morning registration and briefing at Kidapawan Tourism Council at the Museum Building on Laurel St. The registration fee is P20 for locals, P50 for 'foreign' trekkers. Then take a jeepney to Ilomavis and Lake Agko. Arrange porters and overnight at Lake Agko.

Day Two Early start to hike to Lake Venado. Packed lunch on the way. Arrive Lake Venado mid-afternoon and camp.

Day Three Pre-dawn trek to the summit (leave camp at 3 am!). Reach summit by 6 am; eat snacks and spend a couple of hours. Back at Lake Venado by 9.30 am for late breakfast. Start hiking back by 10.30 am to Lake Agko; lunch on the way; arrive back at camp at 5.30 pm and take jeepney back to Kidapawan.

There is an alternative route in and out via Kapatangan.

Getting There & Away From Davao, take a bus from the Ecoland bus terminal to Kidapawan. Buses leave every 30 minutes (P45 to P63, two hours).

From Cotabato, take a bus from Magallanes St terminal to Kidapawan. Buses leave every 30 minutes (P54 to P72, three hours).

To jump-off points for the trek, take a jeepney from Kidapawan bus terminal to Ilomavis, 17km away (P12, one hour, or special trip P500).

DAVAO DEL NORTE

This province lies between Davao City and the Compostela Valley, and is little developed for tourism. Using Tagum as a base, you can visit the Santo Tomas Penal colony 40km north-west; this unlikely sounding tourist attraction consists of a plantation worked by the prisoners and an outlet for their carvings and other handicrafts. You can also visit the Tadeco banana and abaca plantations at Panabo, 25km east of the city, and the Hijo banana, cacao, coconut and guava plantation 10km away. The latter has a *guesthouse*. There are several lodgings in Tagum, the best of which is probably the *Molave Hotel* on Osmena St.

COMPOSTELA VALLEY

This area, to the north of Davao City, split from Davao del Norte and became a separate province in 1998. It is little visited and

MINDANAO & SULU

little developed, and more adventurous travellers may wish to explore, using Maragusan township, 76km north-east of Tagum, as a base. There is a community of indigenous Mansaka people here and the wildlife-rich Bagong Silang Cold Spring area where tarsiers (locally called *amagu*) and *maral* (wild cat) can still sometimes be seen. In Mainit National Park, near the provincial capital of Nabunturan, two rivers, fed by one hot and one cold spring, meet in a large swimming area believed to have curative powers because of its high sulphur content. Stay at the *Agwacan Inland Resort* in Maragusan for P350 to P800.

GENERAL SANTOS (DADIANGAS)

Formerly Dadiangas, the city was renamed in 1965 in honour of General Paulino Santos who, with accompanying Visayans and people from Luzon, established a settlement here in 1939. Prior to this time, the area was inhabited mostly by Maguindanao Muslims and B'laan tribespeople. The city's history is showcased in two small museums: At the Notre Dame Dadiangas College (NDDC) is a **museum of memorabilia** about General Santos (the person); and at the Mindanao State University (MSU) campus near the airport is a **museum of Muslim and tribal culture**. Both of these are open during school hours. The annual cultural event, the **Kalilangan Festival**, takes place from 22-27 February.

A fast-growing city, General Santos is the centre of a big tuna fishing and canning industry (seven of the 12 canneries in the Philippines are based here), and is surrounded by asparagus farms and cattle ranches. The tuna in all its glory is celebrated annually in the **Tuna Festival** from 1-5 September when, among other things, there is – we kid you not – a competition for best-dressed tuna, a parade of fishing floats and a sashimi night. The **fishing boats unload** and sell their catch at the fishing port near Makar Wharf from about 5 am to 9 am and it's fun to watch.

About 8km out of town on the road to Koronadal (Marbel) is the Lagare Springfield Resort and the Olaer Spring Resort. **Cold springs** have been tapped into small falls and big pools, and there are day-use facilities from P10 to P30. Weekends are very busy and it's probably wise to steer clear of the inevitable parties of men drinking beer.

Information

Tourist Offices The very helpful tourist office (☎ 083-554 3097, fax 552 8385, ✉ gemgsc@mozcom.com) is located in the Department of Trade & Industry on the National Hwy.

Money The PNB is by the city hall to change US dollars. There's an Equitable PCI Bank next to the Sydney Hotel and it advances cash on MasterCard. Another Equitable PCI Bank is on Irenco Santiago Ave and will advance cash on Visa cards.

Email & Internet Access Nenita's Internet Cafe is small and doesn't get too busy. There are other Internet cafes near the church on Osmena St.

Diving

Tuna City Scuba Center (☎ 083-554 5681, fax 301 0887, ✉ dicegensan@gslink.net) on Quirino Ave organises dive trips around Sarangani Bay and is hoping to start dive trips out to the islands of Balut, Sarangani and tiny Ulanbani in the south.

Places to Stay – Budget

South Sea Lodge II (☎ 083-552 5146, ✉ anchor@gslink.net), on the corner of Magsaysay and Salazar Sts, has good, clean rooms with fan from P240. P590 or more gets you air-con and bath.

Vince's Pension House (☎ 083-553 5983), on Magsaysay St, is tatty but clean and there are lots of luminous flashing sacred heart pictures on the walls. These can be reassuring or very disturbing, depending on your frame of mind. Rooms start at P220.

The *Matutum Hotel* (☎ 083-552 4901) on Acharon Blvd is OK, with rooms from P200, but it's noisy and the bathrooms need some serious maintenance.

MINDANAO & SULU

GENERAL SANTOS (DADIANGAS)

To Lagare Springfield
Resort, Olaer Spring
Resort, Cambridge
Farm Hotel &
Koronadal (Marbel)

To Davao
(120km)

National Highway

To Fish Market,
Makar Wharf and Airport

Silway River

Jose P Laurel Avenue

Quezon Avenue

Claro M Recto Street

Balimbing Street

Roxas Avenue

Sampaguita Street

Roxas Avenue

Champaca Street

Camia Street

Ireneo Santiago Boulevard

Quirino Avenue

Sergio Osmena Street

To Gaisano Mall,
Fiesta sa Barrio,
Ni-moshi-be
& Davao

Atis St

Pioneer Ave

Magsaysay Avenue

Papaya St

Salazar St

Saging St

Pedro Acharon Boulevard

Market

To Makar Wharf,
MSU & Airport

Magsaysay Park

Sarangani Bay

0   125   250m
0   125   250yd

PLACES TO STAY
1 Tierra Verde 1
2 T'boli Hotel
5 East Asia Royale Hotel
20 Sydney Hotel
22 Vince's Pension House
23 South Sea Lodge II
25 Hotel Sansu & Wok
'n' Chow Restaurant
26 Matutum Hotel

PLACES TO EAT
17 NR Lechon House
21 Billabong Café

OTHER
3 Doctor's Hospital
4 Dept of Trade and Industry;
Tourist Office

6 St Elizabeth Hospital
7 NDDC
Museum
8 Mindanao State
University (MSU)
9 Nenita's Internet Cafe
10 Bula-ong Terminal
11 Police Station
12 City Hall
13 Philippines National
Bank (PNB)
14 Post Office
15 Internet Cafe
16 Tuna City Scuba Center
18 Church
19 Equitable PCI Bank
24 Equitable PCI Bank
27 PAL & Air
Philippines

Places to Stay – Mid-Range

There are some good mid-range hotels in General Santos. Best of these is the *T'boli Hotel* (☎ 083-552 3042) on the National Hwy. Good-sized, quiet rooms with private sitting rooms go for P450 to P750. There is a restaurant.

Next door the *Tierra Verde 1* (☎ 083-552 4500) has reasonable, clean and simple rooms from P483 to P788. It has an outdoor bar and decent-sized swimming pool, which nonguests can use for P50.

Hotel Sansu (☎ 083-552 7219, fax 552 7221) is certainly central but it's also very noisy. Rooms here start at P350.

An extraordinary place, the *Cambridge Farm Hotel* (☎ 083-553 6310, fax 554 5614) gets full marks for originality and eccentricity. The rooms – which range from P400 for singles to P1000 – are cluttered with knick-knacks and each is individually furnished. The bathrooms are a treat; there is a garden bar and restaurant,

a good-sized pool (day use is P25) and – not so great – a mini-zoo. There is also a truly remarkable collection – which must be the largest in the Philippines – of Princess Diana memorabilia, filling a huge room! The hotel is about 10 minutes out of town on the road to Koronadal. Taxis to/from town cost about P50, and about P150 from the airport.

Places to Stay – Top End

The recently opened *East Asia Royale Hotel* (☎ 083-553 4119, fax 553 4129, ✆ royale@gslink.net) is a first-class business hotel with the sort of comfortable rooms you'd expect, but no pool. Room rates start at P1500 plus service and tax.

In the centre of town is the *Sydney Hotel* (☎ 083-552 5479, fax 552 5478). Very pleasant rooms start at P1184 but rooms overlooking the park and traffic circle are VERY noisy; ask for somewhere quiet.

MINDANAO & SULU

Places to Eat

The *NR Lechon House* on Quirino St does good barbecue. Near the Gaisano Mall is *Fiesta sa Barrio*, a seafood place specialising in Filipino fish dishes. In the same area is the *Ni-moshi-be*, a good Japanese restaurant. The *Billabong Café* beside the Sydney Hotel, bakes good sugar-free 'Australian' bread and serves Filipino food.

Getting There & Away

Air PAL flies from Manila to General Santos at 6.30 am daily. Air Philippines also has flights from Manila at 7 am, returning daily (via Cebu).

Mindanao Express (☎ 083-301 3295) flies to Zamboanga on Monday and Wednesday.

Boat Negros Navigation has boats bound for Manila via Iloilo on Panay and Bacolod on Negros, leaving at noon Thursday.

Sulpicio Lines boats leave for Cebu City late Sunday evening.

EPA Shipping Line has boats leaving Monday and Thursday for Bitung (Manado). Schedules change, so check with the shipping line; its office is inside the port compound at Makar. The journey costs P1800 one way and takes about 36 hours. Officially, there is no problem with foreigners making this trip, but you may wish to check with the tourism office first. You will need to finalise any Indonesian visa requirements with the consulate in Davao before leaving.

Bus There are regular bus services between General Santos and Davao (P85, 3½ hours), Cagayan de Oro (eight to 10 hours), Koronadal (Marbel; one hour) and Butuan (eight to 10 hours). The bus terminal for all services is at Bula-ong, on the western edge of town.

Getting Around

The passenger airport has relocated to an area beyond Makar Wharf. A taxi to town will cost about P100.

Boat Makar Wharf is 4km from town. A taxi will cost about P50 and a tricycle P20. The shorter road there can be very busy and slow, but there is an alternative route along the National Hwy. This is a distance of about 10km and will cost about P60.

Jeepney, Tricycle & Taxi There is a flat fare around town by jeepney and tricycle of P3. There are plenty of taxis and the flag fall is P20. The integrated bus and jeepney terminal is at Bula-ong on the western edge of town, about 1km from the town centre.

AROUND GENERAL SANTOS

There are white-sand beaches and areas of good snorkelling and diving around Maasim and Glan on the edge of **Sarangani Bay**. Take an L300 minibus from Bula-ong terminal to either town (P35, one hour).

Further south are **Sarangani Island**, **Balut Island** and **Ulanbani Island**, presently undeveloped but apparently with good dive spots. The Tropicana Express boat (☎ 083-552 7628) leaves Makar Wharf in General Santos on Monday, Wednesday, Friday and Sunday for Balut and Sarangani (P200 one way, three to four hours). There is no commercial accommodation at the time of writing, though it is planned. Contact Tuna City Scuba Center (see General Santos section earlier) for further information.

It's possible to climb **Mt Matutum** in either two or three days, camping at the top. There are also day hikes in this area. If you're interested in doing this, check with the Sarangani Bay Area Outdoor Club (☎ 083-522 3861) in General Santos. To get to Mt Matutum, take a jeepney or motorcycle to Polomolok and then take another up to Lemblisong in the foothills.

LAKE SEBU

Beautiful Lake Sebu, ancestral home of the T'boli people, sits at an elevation of about 300m in a bowl of hills and forests. Enjoy the cool evenings at this altitude, where suddenly the thick woven T'boli clothes make sense. The annual **Lem-Lunay Festival** takes place in the second week of November and is a celebration of T'boli culture, culminating with horse fights – the sport of royalty in local culture – when two stallions fight over a mare in heat. (It's neither as bloody nor as fatal as cockfighting.)

Try to visit in time for the **Saturday market**, when tribespeople come in from the surrounding communities. Visit the recently opened **T'boli Museum**, on the road to Punta Isla. It's open from 7 am to 5 pm daily for a P5 entry fee and has a small but good collection. A weaver is usually there, dyeing abaca with vegetable dyes and weaving the dyed fibre on a backstrap loom. Take a **boat trip** on Lake Sebu, **bird-watch**, and hike to either (or both) **Seven Falls** and **Traankini Falls**. A motorcycle will take you to within about a half-hour walk of each.

Dangers & Annoyances

Lake Sebu has been the scene of some security alerts in past years. There have been no major problems since 1996, but it's wise to check the current situation with the tourist offices in General Santos, Koronadal (Marbel) or Cotabato before setting off.

Places to Stay & Eat

Punta Isla is a pretty resort on the lakeside, with a restaurant specialising in fresh-cooked tilapia fish caught from the lake, and great views. It has good cottages for P300 and dorm beds for P75. During the day, music booms from every day-use cottage, which detracts somewhat from the peaceful outlook.

On the same road, and offering facilities for about the same price, are *Estares Resort* and *Artacoo Resort*. Both are nicely located on the lake, but have less attractive cottages than Punta Isla. Weekends are very busy.

A kilometre or so further along the main lakeside road is *Gono Lembong Lodge*, managed by the local tourism department. Rooms are P300 and dorm beds P60; the view is good but the grounds aren't attractive.

The *Lakeview Tourist Lodge*, near the jeepney terminal, has one very basic double room for P100, with a small souvenir shop attached.

All the resorts have *restaurants* and there are *eateries* at the terminal.

Shopping

Lake Sebu is a good place to buy T'boli handicrafts – brassware and beads particularly – and weavings. Try Mindanao Etnika about halfway along the lake road, and browse in the many roadside souvenir stalls.

Getting There & Away

Bus, Jeepney & Minivan Koronadal (Marbel) is the junction for trips to Lake Sebu. Get there by bus from Cotabato or General Santos (P33, one hour).

Buses drop off in Koronadal on General Santos Dr at their respective terminals; from there make your way to the L300 minivan terminals near the junction of General Santos Dr and Alunan Ave. You can take an L300 minivan (P10, 45 minutes) or a jeepney to Surallah. At the terminal in Surallah take a jeepney (P18, 45 minutes) or hire a motorcycle (P100, 30 minutes) to Lake Sebu.

In spite of the vehicle changes, there's lots of traffic on this road and the trip should take little time.

Getting Around

Motorcycles are the public transport in Lake Sebu. Rides to the local resorts cost between P5 and P10 depending on distance. You can negotiate special-trip rates of between P75 and P100 per hour.

SURALLAH

You pass through Surallah on your way to Lake Sebu from Koronadal (see Getting There & Away in the Lake Sebu section). If you need to overnight go to *VIP Trading* on Camia St, just opposite the L300 terminus, and take a simple room there with the Lagamayo family for P200 to P250. If you want to make any special trips by jeep, they can put you in touch with the Fernandez family, who may be willing to hire out their private car and driver.

KORONADAL (MARBEL)

While Koronadal has been the official name of the provincial capital of South Cotabato since 1947, many people still refer to it as Marbel – a B'laan word meaning 'murky waters' – and that is the word you will see on most public transport vehicles heading there. Historically, it's linked to the animist B'laan people and Maguindanao Muslims, though now the population is predominantly Christian. The small **museum** in the Gymnasium and Cultural Centre on Alunan Ave showcases primarily T'boli culture (and devotes much wall- and shelf-space to the museum's benefactors). Koronadal is the jump-off point for trips to Lake Sebu.

Information

There's a tourist office in the Vice-Mayor's department in the City Hall.

The PNB opposite the Ramona Plaza Hotel will change US dollars.

For email, Weblink is opposite the Cultural Centre on Alunan Ave. The server is long-distance though, which makes it a comparatively expensive P75 per hour.

Places to Stay & Eat

In the budget range, stay at *Alabado's Home* on the corner of Alunan Ave and Rizal St. It's on the main road and pretty noisy, but cheaper rooms are fine value at P175 for fan and bath. Small and dismal air-con rooms at P450 for a double with bath are not such good value.

Mid-range accommodation is good at the *Ramona Plaza Hotel* (☎ 083-228 3284, fax 228 3151) on General Santos Dr, with room rates starting at P550 for air-con, bath and cable TV.

The best hotel in town is the *Marvella Plaza* (☎/fax 083-228 2063), also on General Santos Dr. Room rates range from P650 to P1150; rooms are OK but in need of some maintenance. A swimming pool is under construction.

The Ramona Plaza and Marvella Plaza both have good *coffee shops* attached.

Getting There & Away

There are regular bus services from General Santos (P33, one hour) and from Cotabato (three hours). Make a connection here for Lake Sebu via Surallah.

COTABATO

This city of Maguindanao people lies on the Rio Grande de Mindanao, often called the Pulangi River. 'Maguindanao' is a compilation of the local words for kin, country and

lake, so literally they are 'people of the lake country', from the floodplains around this great river.

Islam is the oldest religion here, introduced in 1475, with Christianity a comparatively recent arrival, brought in by Jesuits in 1871. Cotabato City does not hold a great deal of interest for travellers, though the **Araw ng Kutabato Festival** in mid-June, with its mammoth dance parades, is a cultural highlight. In December the **Shariff Kabungsuan Festival** commemorates the arrival of Islam in the region and involves river parades of decorated boats.

Around the city itself, head up **Piedro Colina Hill** for good views of the city and coast and note the American-designed **old Provincial Capitol** building. At the foot of the hill lies **Kutawato Cave** which is, bizarrely, right in the middle of a busy road intersection; inside are salt-water pools, an underground river and bats. The **Cotabato City Hall** has an interesting facade of mostly Muslim influence.

A couple of kilometres out of town is the **Regional Autonomous Government Centre** which houses a museum and is the seat of government for the Autonomous Region of Muslim Mindanao.

Information

The tourist office (☎ 064-421 7804, fax 421 8969) is located in the old Provincial Capitol Building on Piedro Colina Hill.

The PNB will change US dollars.

Infotech on S Pendatun Ave provides Internet access for P30 per hour and is open from 8 am until 8 pm.

Dangers & Annoyances

This area is the political heartland of Muslims in the Philippines. While the city has been generally secure since the signing of the 1996 peace accord between the MNLF and the government, there are occasional skirmishes and bombings on the roads in and out of the city and in the hinterland. The roads to and from Koronadal and Davao are generally secure, but it is unwise to travel by road north of Cotabato.

MINDANAO & SULU

The Tasaday

In 1971 a mysterious Filipino and Harvard-educated amateur anthropologist reported to the world that he'd found a previously unknown tribe, trapped in the Stone Age in the rugged heartland of Mindanao's South Cotabato province. Manuel Elizalde told dumbfounded scientists that he'd heard about the tribe – called the Tasaday – through a local hunter, and later located them by helicopter.

Anthropologists the world over went crazy, as photos were published showing the Tasaday wearing crude loincloths and clutching crude tools. The find was hailed as one of the most important anthropological events of the 20th century.

Experts flew in to study the Tasaday and, through interpreters from nearby tribes, pieced together a tale that told of a people isolated from all outside influences for around 2000 years.

Short in stature and numbering only 27, the Tasaday were apparently cave-dwellers who foraged for the most basic food to survive.

But it all fell to pieces in 1986, after years of manipulation and cover-ups during the Marcos martial law years. A persistent Mindanao journalist discovered that the Manobo people who traditionally live near the caves were pawns in a giant, government-backed land-grabbing game.

It turned out that the people didn't live in the caves at all, and that before Elizalde turned up, they had lived in huts and farmed the nearby land. With promises of cash and protection from attacks by rival communities, Elizalde had bribed the people into posing as semi-naked primitives and selling off their land to timber contractors. In the process, he'd left much bitterness among local tribespeople, not to mention the scientific community – including National Geographic, which had swallowed the hoax whole in a 1971 article entitled First Glimpse of a Stone Age Tribe.

When Elizalde fled the country in 1983 (taking with him a small fortune in treasury funds), it became blatantly obvious he was just another Marcos crony – albeit an imaginative one. To this day, the tribespeople at the centre of the controversy are fighting to regain the land they lost.

Virginia Jealous

Places to Stay & Eat

In the centre of town the *El Corazon Hotel* on Makakua St is OK, with fan rooms with bath from P290 and air-con rooms with bath and TV from P510.

Newer and brighter, but a bit noisy, is *City Plaza Hotel (☎ 064-421 9148),* also on Makakua St, where rooms range from P281 to P720.

Hotel Castro (☎ 064-421 7523, fax 421 6404), on Sinsuat St, has small rooms from P550 to P810 but friendly staff and a small, quiet coffee shop. There is a good Filipino fast-food restaurant on the ground floor and there are fruit stalls opposite.

The best hotel in town – well, a couple of kilometres out of town next to the Regional Autonomous Government Centre on Governor Gutierrez Blvd – is the *Estosan Garden Hotel (☎ 064-421 6777, fax 421 5488),* where rooms start at P1440. There is a pool which nonguests can use for P100 and a pleasant coffee shop.

Mami King, on Don Rufino Alonzo St, has tasty Filipino fast food with a good bakery attached.

Getting There & Away

Air Air Philippines (☎ 064-421 1767) and PAL (☎ 064-421 2086) fly daily to/from Manila.

Mindanao Express (☎ 064-421 3788) flies Monday, Tuesday, Wednesday, Thursday and Friday to Zamboanga.

Boat Note that there are two wharf areas in Cotabato. Boats to Pagadian go from the wharf right in the centre of town. Inter-island boats, and boats to Zamboanga, leave from Polloc Pier, 24km away. A jeepney there costs P15.

Negros Navigation has boats going to

Manila via Zamboanga and Iloilo on Panay at 11 am Monday (53 hours).

Boats to Zamboanga leave several times a week. Negros Navigation has boats leaving at 11 am Monday (nine hours).

Boats to Pagadian (P110, five to six hours) leave around 7 pm nightly, depending on the tide.

A boat leaves for General Santos at 7.30 am Saturday (12 hours).

Bus & Minivan Regular buses run daily between Davao and Cotabato (P150 aircon, five hours). There are no direct buses from General Santos and Koronadal. You have to take a bus to Tacurong (P12, 45 minutes) and then an L300 minivan to Cotabato (P60, 1½ hours).

Getting Around

To/From the Airport The airport is about 10km south of town. A jeepney going to Awang will take you there for P5, or a taxi will cost around P100.

ZAMBOANGA

There are three possible derivations of Zamboanga's name. It may come from the 16th century Malay word *jambangan*, meaning 'land of flowers', or from *samboangan*, a 'docking point' identified in an early Spanish map. Its origin may also lie in *sabuan*, the wooden pole used by local tribespeople to navigate their *vintas* – shallow draft sailboats – over the coastal flats. Take your pick!

Zamboanga has been a trading post for centuries and this, together with its closeness to the island of Borneo, has given the area an interesting and eclectic mix of inhabitants and cultures. Islam is strong here, as is Christianity, while animist beliefs and practices are still subscribed to by many of the people of the Sulu Archipelago. The most commonly spoken language is Chavacano, a heavily Spanish-influenced language. Spanish speakers will find themselves understanding most of what they hear.

The city's main festival is from 10-12 October, the Fiesta de Nuestra Senora Virgen del Pilar. It is a Christian festival, but is also a great opportunity for street parties,

Taluksangay mosque, Zamboanga

parades, dances, markets and food fairs enjoyed by all the community. And there's a big regatta as part of the fiesta that brings vintas with traditional brilliantly coloured angular cloth sails out on the water.

The city takes more energy and patience to be in than many other Filipino cities. There are groups of lounging, aggressive youths on street corners and in the plaza, which may be intimidating for women travelling alone, and lots of persistent and demanding beggars, many of whom are distressingly disabled. Zamboanga is the headquarters of Southcom, the Philippine Army's Southern Command post, and the military and police presence is noticeable.

Information

Tourist Offices The tourist office (☎ 062-991 0218, ✉ dotr9@jetlink.com.ph) is next to the Lantaka Hotel on Valderoza St. There is a small but good library of books about the Philippines here that travellers are welcome to browse through, including the wonderful 1999 publication *Mindanao – a portrait*.

Money PNB on the plaza will change US dollars.

Email & Internet Access There are many Internet cafes in town. Near the town centre try RMH Internet, open daily, on Almonte St. If you're staying near the airport, use Tigris Net at the top of Mayor Jaldon St. It's closed on Sunday and – unusually for Internet cafes – doesn't allow browsing of sex sites. It's quite a relief to just do your email without catching glimpses of enormous willies waving on the next screen.

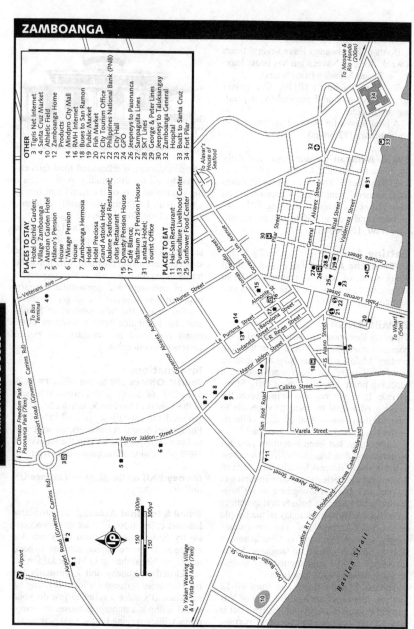

ZAMBOANGA

PLACES TO STAY
1 Hotel Orchid Garden; Village Zamboanga
2 Marcian Garden Hotel
5 Atilano's Pension House
6 L'Mirage Pension House
7 Zamboanga Hermosa Hotel
8 Hotel Preciosa
9 Grand Astoria Hotel; Abalone Seafood Restaurant; Lotus Restaurant
15 Dynasty Pension House
17 Café Blanca; Platinum 21 Pension House
31 Lantaka Hotel; Tourist Office

PLACES TO EAT
11 Hai-San Restaurant
13 Puericulture Livelihood Center
25 Sunflower Food Center

OTHER
3 Tigris Net Internet
4 Santa Cruz Market
10 Athletic Field
12 Zamboanga Home Products
14 Mindpro City Mall
16 RMH Internet
18 Buses to San Ramon
19 Public Market
20 Fish Market
21 City Tourism Office
22 Philippines National Bank (PNB)
23 City Hall
24 GPO
26 Jeepneys to Pasonanca
27 Sampaguita Lines
28 SKT Lines
29 George & Peter Lines
30 Jeepneys to Taluksangay
32 Zamboanga General Hospital
33 Boats to Santa Cruz
34 Fort Pilar

Dangers & Annoyances

Zamboanga has a reputation among Filipinos from other areas of being a place of kidnaps and robberies and Muslim insurgency, a reputation that is fostered by the national media.

Don't confuse the city with the rest of the province though. At time of writing (late 1999) the city, and the area covered by the Around Zamboanga section later, were secure enough to travel freely in and around, though you should probably check out current travel conditions with the DOT on your arrival.

The hinterland is definitely out of bounds to all but the most adventurous (or foolhardy) traveller. Kidnappings of both locals and foreigners do occur, there are regular shooting incidents between government forces and NPA and MILF groups, and buses are bombed on the road. Road travel to Zamboanga from other parts of Mindanao is not advisable; not all buses are bombed or robbed of course, but the number that are is significant enough to be an issue. It's safer to arrive by boat or plane.

Fort Pilar

Spend an hour or two at Fort Pilar. It's a solid and squat building, partially and sympathetically restored, and its chequered history reads like this: founded by the Spaniards in 1635; attacked by the Dutch in 1646; deserted in 1663; reconstructed in 1666; rebuilt in 1719; stormed by 3000 Moros in 1720; cannonaded by the British in 1798; abandoned by the Spaniards in 1898; occupied by the US in 1899; seized by the Japanese in 1942 and, finally, claimed by the Philippines in 1946.

Inside is a **museum**, open from 9 am to noon and from 2 to 5 pm daily except Saturday, with two impressive galleries. One is a **marine exhibit** where you can learn everything you wanted to know (and much, much more) about marine ecosystems and animals. The information may be a bit dry and dusty for lay people, but there are some good displays. Across the inner courtyard of the fort is a terrific **ethnographic gallery** concentrating on the boat-dwelling Sama Dilaut (otherwise known as the Badjao, or

More About Moors & Moros

The Muslims in Mindanao, Sulu and Palawan are known collectively as Moro, a word that derives from the Spanish word 'Moor'. The Moors were the Muslim conquerors of Spain, who ruled for 700 years from AD 711 , and for the Spaniards the word had negative connotations of savagery and barbarity. In the Philippines, among non-Muslims, it can still be used as a derogatory term and it's probably best not to use it.

The word is gradually being reclaimed by supporters of Muslim autonomy and independence – such as the Moro National Liberation Front (MNLF) and the Moro Islamic Liberation Front (MILF) – and is now used to self-describe the so-called warriors of Islam.

Virginia Jealous

sea gypsies) of the Sulu Archipelago. Walk around the **ramparts** for 360-degree views of Zamboanga City and the busy ocean. On the fort's outer wall is an altar and shrine to the Virgin of Pilar and masses of candle sellers providing the individual 'bunches' of thin, coloured candles that are burned at the shrine.

Rio Hondo

East of Fort Pilar is the Muslim stilt village of Rio Hondo; its mosque is a clear landmark visible from the ramparts of the fort. The village is built out over the edge of the water, and the houses are joined by foot bridges. You can wander around Rio Hondo, but prepare to be the focus of attention. It's a good idea to be appropriately dressed for a visit to this Islamic community.

The Waterfront

Spend late afternoon on the **terrace of the Lantaka Hotel**, watching the action on the water and the sunset. Unobtrusive hawkers lay beautiful shells and pearls on the sea wall of the hotel to tempt guests, but be sure you know what you can legally take out of the Philippines – and to your destination – if you want to buy marine products.

MINDANAO & SULU

Beyond the hotel are the chaotic and colourful **markets**. Keep walking and you come to **Justice RT Lim Blvd** just beyond the main port area. It's busy at sunset with families walking, kids swimming, people fishing and boating, and food stalls and hawkers. This is where vinta regattas take place during fiesta.

Places to Stay – Budget
Atilano's Pension House (☎ 062-991 0783), on a quiet side road off Mayor Jaldon St, is a rambling series of buildings with sections of grass and garden. It's fine for the price, which ranges from P180 for a fan room and shared bath to P380 for aircon and bath.

L'Mirage Pension House (☎ 062-991 3962), also on Mayor Jaldon St, is simple, clean and good value, with rooms ranging from P220 to P400. Ventilation slats between rooms mean you'll hear your neighbours though.

Right in the centre of town, *Dynasty Pension House* (☎ 062-991 4579), on Almonte St, offers good budget rooms at P250 for fan and bath, but the air-con rooms for P600 are grubby and small; look at one of the mid-range hotels if this is your price range.

Places to Stay – Mid-Range
Near the city centre, *Hotel Preciosa* (☎ 062-991 2020, fax 993 0055) on Mayor Jaldon St, with lazy catfish drifting in the atrium pool, has good-sized and clean, if dull, rooms for P680 to P1000.

The *Zamboanga Hermosa Hotel* (☎ 062-991 2040), on Mayor Jaldon St, has rooms which are OK, but a bit small and stark for P650 and P750.

Newest of the mid-range hotels, the *Grand Astoria Hotel* (☎ 062-991 2510, fax 991 2533), on Mayor Jaldon St, is good value – and always busy – with neat rooms ranging in price from P650 to P2500.

Platinum 21 Pension House (☎ 062-991 2514, fax 991 2709), on Barcelona St, is a bit old and tatty in comparison with the other hotels in this price range, charging P620 to P700 for rooms.

Places to Stay – Top End
The *Marcian Garden Hotel* (☎ 062-991 2519, fax 991 1874), near the airport, has a nice garden and pool area, and rooms are big and good value for P860 to P920. But it's really noisy, being on the main road, with all rooms overlooking the function centre and, at time of writing, a construction site behind.

Nearby is the *Hotel Orchid Garden* (☎ 062-991 0031, fax 991 0035), an international-standard business hotel with good facilities including a big pool but not much character. Rooms start at P2400.

Best of the lot is the ageing but characterfull *Lantaka Hotel* (☎ 062-991 2033, fax 991 1626) on the waterfront. It has big rooms with balconies, a nice garden and pool, and great views everywhere you look. Rooms officially start at P1150, but ask about any current promotional offers. If you can afford it, stay here. If you can't afford it, at least treat yourself to a drink on the terrace at sunset.

Places to Eat
Zamboanga is packed with eating places. For extremely cheap and tasty Filipino food, eat at the food stalls of the *Puericulture Livelihood Center* on La Purisma St. There's a great selection with lots of fresh fish and vegetable dishes. Near city hall on the plaza is the *Sunflower Food Center*, which serves good Filipino fast food and great desserts. For outdoor eating Filipino-style, in a decent beer garden with live music, go to *Village Zamboanga*, next to the Hotel Orchid Garden on the airport road.

Good cheap Chinese food is served at *Lotus Restaurant* next to the Grand Astoria Hotel and in the hotel itself is the *Abalone Seafood Restaurant*. Other good seafood restaurants include *Alavar's House of Seafood*, a long-established restaurant recently relocated to Toribio St, and *La Vista del Mar*, about 7km out of town near the Yakan weaving village, with good sea views as its name suggests. On San José St in town, *Hai-San* serves Japanese-style seafood.

The *Lantaka Hotel* does good Sunday all-you-can-eat buffet lunches in the terrace dining hall overlooking the harbour.

Shopping

The market on the waterfront has cheap clothing and batik from Malaysia and Indonesia. On the corner of San José and Mayor Jaldon Sts is the Zamboanga Home Products store, which sells lots of rather ordinary souvenirs and some interesting and good-quality carvings, basketwork and woven fabrics. A good shopping mall in the town centre is the Mindpro City Mall. At David's Salon inside you get a terrific neck-and-shoulder massage when you get your hair washed, cut and dried for P110. Don't expect a high-fashion result for such a bargain price!

Getting There & Away

Air PAL flies from Manila to Zamboanga at the ungodly hour of 4.50 am daily, and there is another flight at 2.10 pm daily except Friday and Sunday. Other flights are Cebu Pacific at 6 am daily, and Air Philippines at 10.15 am.

Air Philippines flies to and from Cebu on Monday, Wednesday, Friday and Saturday.

Air Philippines flies to and from Davao on Tuesday, Thursday and Saturday.

Mindanao Express (☎ 062-991 9813) flies to/from Cotabato on Monday, Tuesday, Wednesday, Thursday and Friday, to/from Cagayan de Oro on Wednesday and Friday and to/from General Santos on Monday and Wednesday. This schedule changes regularly, so check before you plan to fly.

Malaysia Airlines flies Monday and Friday to Sandakan in Borneo. This route opened in late 1999 and may be subject to change.

Boat WG&A has boats leaving for Manila direct at 8 pm Thursday, via Cotabato and Iloilo on Panay at 5 am Thursday, and via Bacolod on Negros at 10 pm Sunday. Depending on the route, journey time is around 48 hours.

Negros Navigation boats leave for Manila at noon Thursday, going via Iloilo on Panay and Bacolod on Negros, and at 11 am Monday via Iloilo. The trip takes about 53 hours. Sulpicio Lines boats leave for Manila via Iloilo at 3 pm Saturday.

George & Peter Lines leaves for Cebu City via Dumaguete on Negros at 6 pm Wednesday, and to Cebu via Dapitan on Mindanao and Dumaguete 6 pm Saturday.

WG&A has boats leaving at 10 pm Tuesday for Davao and for Cotabato at 5 am Thursday. Smaller boats also run daily to Cotabato.

There is a daily service to Pagadian at 1 pm taking four hours and Sulpicio Lines has boats leaving for General Santos at 5 pm Thursday.

Aleson Lines has boats leaving Zamboanga for Sandakan in Malaysian Borneo at 2 pm Monday and at 4 pm Wednesday (P500, 17 hours).

Sampaguita Lines (☎ 062-993 1591) boats leave for Sandakan at noon Monday and Thursday (P500 to P1500, 17 hours).

Bus If you must travel by road, buses to Zamboanga run several times daily until late morning from Dipolog (P200 air-con, eight hours) and Iligan (12 hours). But it really is not advisable to travel to Zamboanga by road (see Warning earlier in this section).

Getting Around

To/From the Airport The airport is 2km from the centre of Zamboanga. Walk out of the arrivals hall and catch a public tricycle for P5, or take a special trip for P20. Taxis will cost around P50. From town you can take a jeepney marked 'Canelar–Airport' for P3.

Tricycle, Jeepney & Bus Flat fare around town is P3 by tricycle and jeepney. Special trips by tricycle will cost around P100 per hour. If for some reason you're determined to travel north by bus, the terminal is near the Santa Cruz market on the outskirts of town.

AROUND ZAMBOANGA
Pasonanca Park & Climaco Freedom Park

These public park areas are in the foothills of a nearby range, and offer opportunities for walking, getting a sense of green and space, and hearing birdsong. In Pasonanca Park there are three big landscaped public swimming pools, an amphitheatre where conventions are held, and a permanent campsite, where squads of cadets train. Just opposite this site is a pretty and well-equipped treehouse, which you can ask the Mayor's office for permission to stay in, but be prepared to be on very public display if you do.

Climaco Freedom Park, named in honour of Mayor Climaco who was murdered by unknown assailants in the 1970s, is beside Pasonanca Park and has the Abong-Abong River running through it. It is the site of the former mayor's well-tended grave. There is a steep walk up a Stations of the Cross hillside, and good views out across the city and ocean.

Jeepneys to Pasonanca, which is 7km from the city, run from Campaner St off the plaza. Be prepared for a fair bit of hiking once you get there, as public transport is erratic inside the park. It's easier – but more expensive of course – to hire a tricycle for a couple of hours.

Yakan Weaving Village & San Ramon Penal Farm

Also 7km out of Zamboanga, but heading west, is the Yakan Weaving Village. Village is the wrong term really; it's no more than a collection of six or seven stalls selling some good Yakan weavings, a little brassware and lots of very ordinary Indonesian and Malaysian mass-produced batiks. Yakan are the indigenous people of nearby Basilan Island, and their woven designs are characterised by bright colours and geometric designs. You can find wall hangings, table runners and place mats here, and there is a backstrap loom set up on which a weaver works, except at Friday prayer times. The Village is open daily.

Heading in the same direction, about 20km out of the city, is San Ramon Penal Farm. There used to be an outlet at the prison gates selling handcrafts made by prisoners, but this no longer exists. Still, it's nice to get out of the city and see some countryside. The road is secure up to San Ramon.

Taluksangay

This is a Muslim settlement about 20km north-east of Zamboanga City. Like Rio Hondo in town, it's built partially out over the water and a mosque dominates the skyline. The same sort of unwritten rules for visitors apply here; wear appropriate clothing and ask if you want to take photos. Taluksangay is on the organised day-tour route from Zamboanga, so local people are used to visitors and can be quite forceful in asking for money. Jeepneys for Taluksangay leave from Pilar St in town.

Santa Cruz & Sacol Islands

Great Santa Cruz Island is just 15 minutes off the Zamboanga waterfront, and is home to small fishing communities. Visitors go to see the pinkish beach, so coloured from coral washing ashore. You can swim here, but it's on a busy shipping channel and currents are strong. Boats for the island leave from the waterfront between the Lantaka Hotel and Fort Pilar; a return trip will cost about P300 in a pumpboat seating four people.

Little Santa Cruz Island is a military base that is occasionally open to the public as a public relations exercise. Sacol Island is not generally visited by tourists and is undeveloped except for fishing villages. There are security concerns about active NPA and MILF groups in the island's hills.

Basilan

The island-province of Basilan is only 30 minutes by fast boat away from Zamboanga. It is mostly mountainous, and settlement is around the coastal strip. The island is home to the Yakan people, some of whose animist beliefs and practices survived their conversion to Islam in the 14th century. They were gradually forced inland as other settlers colonised the coast, and are now subsistence farmers, cultivating rice, corn and cassava in the uplands. Yakan are accomplished weavers (you can visit the Yakan Weaving Village outside Zamboanga; see Around Zamboanga in this chapter), producing brilliant coloured fabrics in intricate geometric designs. They celebrate elaborate festivals and ceremonies, the biggest of which is the Lami-Lamihan festival, a mass of colourful parades, dances and horse races, held in Lamitan in mid-April.

DANGERS & ANNOYANCES

Basilan remains a crisis area. In late 1999, only Isabela and Lamitan were open to foreigners, and travellers should be prepared for grillings by the police and military if they intend to stay overnight. It would be foolish to go elsewhere on the island as there are regular shootings, kidnappings and skirmishes between government forces and their opponents in the hills.

ISABELA

This is the capital of Basilan. The **old mosque** and **stilt houses** at Kaun Purna are visible as the boat docks. Behind the modern cathedral is a display centre and sales outlet for **Yakan crafts**. In the plaza is a **relief map** of Basilan worked on the forecourt. A **co-operative plantation** can be visited just out of town. Isabela makes an easy half-day tour from Zamboanga.

Places to Stay

If you do decide to overnight, stay at *The New Basilan Hotel* on JS Alano St. Rooms cost from P100 to P350.

LAMITAN

This township, on the coast east of Isabela, has a busy daily **market**. Thursday and Saturday or Sunday (check with the tourist office in Zamboanga, which is generally busier) are the best days to go, when a mix of Yakan people from the hills, Badjao people from the coast, Chinese merchants, and Visayan settlers come together to trade and barter. There is also a small **museum and information centre**, with displays about the annual **Lami-Lamihan Festival**. Lamitan makes an easy day tour from Zamboanga.

Places to Stay

The *Traveller's Inn* and *Neva Hotel* have simple lodgings from P100 to P300.

GETTING THERE & AWAY
Boat

Boats from Zamboanga to Isabela leave from the wharf behind the Lantaka Hotel. Basilan Lines and AS Express fast boats leave regularly from 7.30 am and take 30 minutes. Basilan Lines and Aleson Lines slow boats also make the run at 7 am and 1 pm, returning at 10 am and 4 pm. The journey takes 1½ hours.

Boats to Lamitan leave from the same wharf. Alano Shipping Lines runs at 7 am and 1 pm, returning at 8 am and 3.30 pm. Journey time is 1½ hours.

GETTING AROUND

It would be unwise to travel by land from Isabela to Lamitan. Take the daily boat from/to Zamboanga.

Sulu Islands

The 500 or so islands of the Sulu Archipelago stretch some 300km from Basilan to Borneo, separating the Sulu and Celebes seas. The archipelago is divided into two provinces: Sulu with its capital of Jolo (pronounced 'ho-lo'), and Tawi-Tawi, with Bongao as its capital. It is further subdivided into the Jolo Group, Tawi-Tawi Group and Sibutu Group of islands. The isolated Cagayan de Tawi-Tawi Group lies off the coast of Borneo, mid-way between Palawan and the Sulu Archipelago. These are still dangerous waters for sailors, less because of the elements than because of pirates and smugglers. Smaller passenger vessels as well as cargo boats are regularly plundered in these seas.

About 94% of the archipelago's population is Muslim, and this area is part of the Autonomous Region of Muslim Mindanao (ARMM). The people of Sulu were the first in the Philippines to be converted to Islam in the 14th century. It remained a stronghold of Islam during the Spanish era and, in the early 20th century it was the scene of pitched battles between US forces and the tough local Tausug people. Later, during WWII, local people joined with the US

MINDANAO & SULU

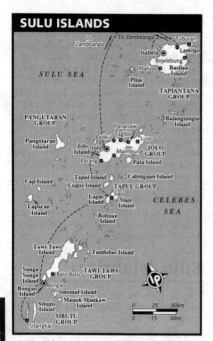

SULU ISLANDS

liberating forces against occupying Japanese troops. During 1974 the MNLF, opposed to the imposition of martial law, fought fiercely against government forces in and around Jolo. The town was destroyed and hostilities continue, to a greater or lesser degree, throughout the region.

Culturally the region is dominated by the Tausugs, or 'people of the current'. In and around Tawi-Tawi, the Samal people live in stilt houses by the coast. Terminology for the people of the region can be confusing. Samal is a generic term covering four distinct groups of people, sharing the Sama language, who inhabit the islands south of the Jolo Group. These are the Sama Talon, Sama Gimba, Sama Laut and Sama Pala-u peoples. The Sama Laut, meaning 'sea Sama' and often referred to in English as 'sea gypsies', are generally referred to as Badjao, though they themselves do not use this term. However 'Badjaw', from which Badjao is derived, is a word used along the coast in north Borneo to describe communities of tribal sea Dyaks.

There are still communities of Badjao living on boats in the southern part of the archipelago, but many now live on permanent sites, either in stilt houses or on their boats at moorings. For a good glimpse into the lives of these people, read H Arlo Nimmo's *Songs of Salanda*, a book of short stories about the writer's two years living in the Sulu Archipelago during the 1960s. Probably not much has changed in the intervening years for those Badjao who have chosen to retain a traditional lifestyle. Although most Badjao are Muslim, animist beliefs and practices are still observed. Sitangkai, in the Sibutu Group, is known as the Venice of the Philippines, as many Badjao floating communities have settled there.

DANGERS & ANNOYANCES

Travellers should be wary of roaming freely around the Sulu Archipelago, and should take seriously any current travel advice from the DOT in Zamboanga. As we went to press, the only area secure enough to be recommended for travel was Bongao Island in the Tawi-Tawi Group. Throughout the region, particularly inland, MILF, NPA and government forces are still engaged in hostilities. Travelling by boat can still be hazardous, and travellers should use bigger, faster boats where possible.

GETTING THERE & AWAY

All scheduled access to the Sulu Archipelago is from Zamboanga.

Air

Mindanao Express (☎ 062-991 9813) flies Monday, Tuesday and Thursday to and from Bongao (P2000, one hour). The plane is a 14-seater and is always heavily overbooked, so plan your trip in advance. The schedule changes frequently.

Boat

SKT Lines and Sampaguita Lines (☎ 062-993 1591) are two of the bigger companies running vessels to the Sulu Archipelago. Both run a similar schedule.

Sampaguita Lines has boats leaving at 7 pm Sunday and Tuesday for Jolo (P110 to P300), Bongao (P260 to P600), Siasi (P157 to P350) and Sitangkai (P310 to P800), and at 8 pm Monday and Thursday for Jolo and Bongao only.

TAWI-TAWI GROUP

Bongao, the capital of Tawi-Tawi province, derives its name from the Tausug word *bangaw*, meaning heron. Today Bongao's wildlife is less famous for herons than for monkeys in great numbers on **Mt Bongao**, a sheer mountainous outcrop behind the township. There's an hour's hiking trail to the summit at 314m, with a **royal Muslim burial site** at the top (dress appropriately if you want to visit this) and good views across the

island chain. This sacred mountain is site of a festival celebrated by Muslims and Christians alike in the second week of October. There is a small museum in the **old Spanish fort** near Bongao. Local people were instrumental in helping American forces to land and liberate the area from the Japanese in WWII, and here Westerners are called 'Milikan', a local distortion of 'American'.

Places to Stay

There are several simple lodgings in Bongao. Near the harbour the *Southern Hotel* has rooms for P350. Two kilometres out of town is *Kasulutan Beach Resort*; rooms are P350. Three kilometres from town on the way to the airport is the *Beachside Inn and Restaurant*, with rooms again at P350.

Palawan

This long sliver of an island province deserves its exotic 'last frontier' aura. Stretching from the Mindoro Strait down to the tip of Borneo, it's a magnificent submerged mountain range of unrivalled ruggedness. You could spend a lifetime discovering new islands, beaches and reefs, particularly in the northern regions around El Nido and Busuanga Island. As other parts of the Philippines are done to death, the danger is that Palawan will also start to suffer from too much attention. But a passionate local environmental movement and strong eco-tourism ethics may help Palawan buck the trend and get as much out of tourism as tourism gets out of it.

Getting There & Away

Air Palawan's main airport is in Puerto Princesa, but Palawan also has a whole bunch of small airports in the north, with regular flights to/from Manila and Puerto Princesa. On Busuanga Island, there's an airport in the southern town of Coron and the YKR airport to the north near San José. On the Palawan mainland, there's the Lio airport north of El Nido, and another airport at Sandoval, about 20km south-east of El Nido.

Cebu There are no flights between Cebu and Palawan – a great pity for travellers. PAL dropped its Cebu City–Puerto Princesa route in 1998. There are faint whispers of another airline (most likely Air Philippines) picking up this route.

Luzon PAL has a flight from Manila to Puerto Princesa at 11.50 am daily, while Air Philippines flies there at 10 am daily.

From Manila to Sandoval, Seair flies at 7 am daily (or just about daily). This is officially a charter flight, with bookings organised in Manila through Asia Travel (☎ 02-752 0307, fax 894 5725), or Noah's Century (☎ 02-810 2623). For Manila-Coron town flights you should contact Seair

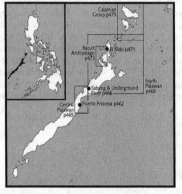

HIGHLIGHTS

- Wreck diving, beach hopping, hiking and generally getting physical in the pristine waters and jungles of Palawan

at their office at the domestic airport in Manila (☎ 02-891 8709).

A Soriano Aviation offers charter flights from Manila to El Nido at 7.30 am and 3.30 am daily for US$141/230 one way/return. In the reverse direction, flights leave El Nido at 9.30 am and 5 pm. When booking, you need to give four days' notice from Manila and one day's notice from El Nido (in El Nido, you can book at the Ten Knots travel office, also known as the White House).

Golden Passage has charter flights to El Nido at 11.30 am Friday and Sunday (P4485) continuing to Puerto Princesa. Flights back to Manila leave Puerto Princesa at 1 pm and El Nido at 3 pm. There are rumours that this may become a daily flight. There is also a flight to Puerto Princesa via Busuanga at 7.30 am Monday, returning the same day. From Manila to El Nido, there's also a daily charter flight available with Corporate Air (☎ 02-832 2316 or 0917 925 1112).

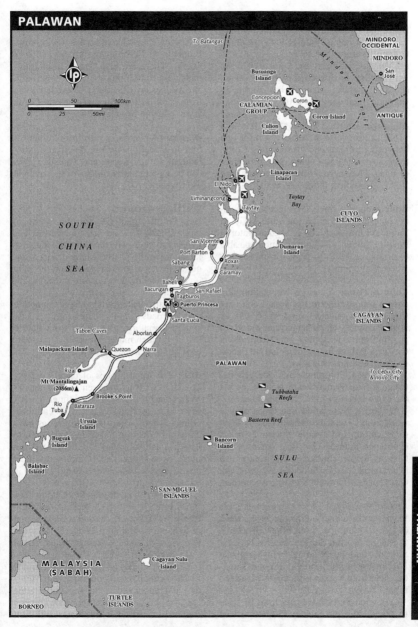

PALAWAN

For the diving resort of Coron on Busuanga Island in the Calamian Group, Asian Spirit has a flight at 9.45 am daily. Golden Passage flies to Busuanga at 7.30 am Monday, Thursday and Sunday (P2000). Air Ads flies to Busuanga daily at 7.30 am (P2000). Pacific Airways has flights to Coron at 8 am daily (P1650).

Mindoro Pacific Airways (☎ 036-288 3162) can organise a charter flight for you between Caticlan and Busuanga's Coron town airport (P4500 per person, minimum of four). They need a few days' notice, and flights are subject to aircraft availability.

Boat Shipping lines serving Palawan include Negros Navigation and WG&A. Sulpicio Lines is chiefly a cargo operator in Puerto Princesa, although you might be able to arrange a berth to/from Luzon or elsewhere with them.

Cebu & Panay A Negros Navigation ship does a weekly Puerto Princesa–Cebu City trip (via Bacolod and Iloilo City) (P450, 48 hours), usually leaving between 8 and 10 pm Saturday. This boat goes from Cebu City (via Iloilo City and Bacolod) to Puerto Princesa at 8 pm Thursday.

Milagrosa Shipping sails weekly between Puerto Princesa and Iloilo City via the Cuyo Islands (P330, 28 hours).

A Negros Navigation liner goes once a week from Cebu City to Iloilo City, then on to Bacolod, and finally Puerto Princesa (P450, 48 hours). This boat leaves Cebu City at 8 pm Thursday. The return trip (Puerto Princesa–Bacolod–Iloilo City–Cebu City) heads off around 8 to 10 pm Saturday.

Luzon A WG&A/SuperFerry liner sails from Manila to Puerto Princesa once a week (P550, 24 hours), at 5 pm Friday. It returns to Manila at 9 am Sunday. Negros Navigation also has boats going from Manila to Puerto Princesa (18 hours) at noon Thursday, and from Puerto Princesa to Manila at 6 pm Friday.

Asuncion Ferry has boats from El Nido to Manila at 2 pm Sunday (30 hours); and

from Manila to El Nido at 7 pm Wednesday. For bookings, phone ☎ 02-711 3743.

Several ships also sail twice weekly from Batangas to Coron town (around P300, 18 hours). There are also ferries from Liminangcong to Manila (via Coron town) at 6 am Wednesday (25 hours). These ferries go from Manila to Liminangcong (via Coron town) at 2 pm Monday.

Mindoro A pumpboat sails from Mindoro's San José to Concepcion, on Busuanga Island, at 4 am Tuesday and Thursday. This can be a particularly rough voyage, even in mild weather.

Getting Around
Heavy-duty roadtrips are the norm in Palawan, and these are made by jeepney/bus hybrids (overgrown jeepneys with the seats facing forward). On these long-distance juggernauts, it's a good idea to sit on the right – you'll swallow less dust from the oncoming traffic.

Palawan's waters tend to be far smoother than its roads (and its waters aren't exactly smooth), making trips north from Puerto Princesa much more enjoyable if taken by boat rather than bus or jeepney.

Boat Two rival groups of resorts operate regular boat trips between Sabang and El Nido (via Port Barton) four times a week each. For simplicity's sake, we'll call them Group A and Group B. Both groups have daily air-con minibuses between Puerto Princesa and Sabang (P250, two hours), but these aren't necessarily timed to meet boats, so you may have to spend a night in Sabang.

Group A has its headquarters at the Trattoria Inn (☎ 048-433 4985) in Puerto Princesa. Ticket offices are at Sabang pier in Sabang, Swissippini Lodge & Resort in Port Barton, and El Nido Boutique & Art Café in El Nido.

Group A's boats go Sabang–Port Barton–El Nido (P850, eight hours) at 7 am Thursday and Sunday. The Sabang–Port Barton leg takes 2½ hours and costs P350. The Port Barton-El Nido takes five hours and costs

Plenty More Fish in the Sea?

A third of all Filipinos live on the coast, with a diet that's 30% fish. That's almost double the global average. But as the human population rises and the fish population falls, increasingly extreme measures are taken to feed hungry mouths. The Japanese-inspired fishing technique known as *muro-ami* (dive net) is a particularly brutal example of such extremes. Muro-ami, or *kayakas*, as it's sometimes known in the Philippines, involves smashing up reefs to force fish out from under the coral. As many as 300 swimmers, often underpaid children, may be harnessed to a waiting net loaded down with 'scarelines' that are dragged across the ocean floor. Plastic streamers or coconut leaves are attached to these lines at 1m intervals to create the illusion of a wall, which slowly closes in on the fish. Cruel, dangerous, exploitative, nonselective and terribly desperate, this form of fishing is banned in the Philippines and carries a penalty of up to P5000 or six months jail, but it continues around many islands including Palawan and Mindanao.

Mic Looby

P500. Boats go El Nido–Port Barton–Sabang at 7 am Wednesday and Saturday.

Group B is based at the Sabang Beach Resort (☎ 048-434 3762) in Sabang. Ticket offices are at the Sabang Beach Resort office in Puerto Princesa, and at Lucing's Restaurant in El Nido.

Group B's boats go Sabang–Port Barton–El Nido (P850, seven hours) at 7.30 am Monday and Wednesday. The Sabang–Port Barton leg takes two hours and costs P500. The Port Barton-El Nido leg takes fours hours and costs P500. Boats go El Nido–Port Barton–Sabang at 8 am Tuesday and Thursday.

PUERTO PRINCESA

The carefree capital of Palawan (population 130,000) is generally regarded as little more than a step-off point for excursions elsewhere on the island. Often overlooked as an attraction in its own right, underrated, it has some mighty fine hotels and excellent restaurants.

Orientation

Puerto Princesa is really an overgrown country town, with the main street of Rizal Ave its long, straight spine. Rizal Ave runs from the pier through the city centre, past the market and main bus and jeepney terminal, and past the front doorstep of the airport.

Maps Luckily, Puerto Princesa has a straightforward layout, as there are no maps of the place. For good 1:250,000 scale maps and nautical charts of Palawan, try the Morbai Maps & Charts office (☎ 048-433 6678). It's on Rizal Ave, on the 2nd floor of the Olorga Building (entrance at rear).

Information

Tourist Offices The staff are helpful at the city tourist office (☎ 048-433 2983) at the airport. There's also a provincial tourist office in the Provincial Capitol Building on Rizal Ave.

Money There are several big banks with ATMs along Rizal Ave, as well as moneychangers. The DBP bank has an ATM accepting Visa credit cards, as does the nearby Equitable PCI Bank. The Go Palawan travel agent next door to the Trattoria Inn & Restaurant and Swiss Bistro Garden (see the later Places to Stay entry) gives cash advances on major credit cards (with a hefty 10% commission).

Post & Telephone The main post office is just off Rizal Ave on Burgos St.

A number of telephone offices can be found along Rizal Ave.

Email & Internet Access Near the market, the fast-expanding Kawing Internet (P90 per hour) is open from 9 am to 7 pm daily. The Hexagon Cafe (P90 per hour), near the post office, offers similar rates and

PALAWAN

PUERTO PRINCESA

PLACES TO STAY
4   Puerto Pension
14 Trattoria Inn & Restaurant;
    Swiss Bistro Garden; Go
    Palawan Travel Agent
21 Casa Linda Inn & Restaurant
22 Badjao Inn; Negros
    Navigation Office
40 Duchess Pension House

PLACES TO EAT
16 Ka Lui Restaurant;
    Island Divers
19 Café Kamarikutan & Galeri
25 Filipino Kamayan Folkhouse
    & Restaurant
27 Jollibee
30 Pho Vietnamese Restaurant;
    Bruno's Delicatessan
38 Vegetarian House

39 Backpackers Cafe,
    Bookshop & Inn

OTHER
1   Provincial Hospital
2   Jeepney Terminal
3   Buses, Minibuses; Jeepneys
    to North, South Palawan
5   Milagrosa Shipping Lines
6   Petron Service Station
7   Kawing Internet Café;
    WG&A SuperFerry
8   Philippines National Bank (PNB)
9   Jeepneys to Iwahig
10 Equitable PCI Bank
11 RCPI International Telephone
    Office
12 Allied Bank; Metrobank; Bank
    of the Philippine Islands (BPI)
13 Equitable PCI Bank

15 WG&A SuperFerry
17 City Tourist Office; Palawan
    Treasures & Gift Shop
18 PAL
20 Air Philippines
23 Provincial Tourist Office;
    Provincial Capitol Building
24 Culture Shack
26 NCCC Supermarket &
    Department Store
28 DBP Bank
29 Museum
31 Air Philippines; Police Station
32 Post Office
33 Morbai Maps & Charts Office
34 Piltel International Telephone
    Office
35 Hexagon Internet Cafe
36 Sulpicio Lines Office
37 Cathedral

services. The Trattoria Inn & Restaurant and Swiss Bistro Garden has an in-house Internet service (P100 per hour), as do several other resorts and hotels around town.

Special Events
First held in April 1999, the Kamarikutan Pagdiwata Arts Festival is all set to become a regular event on the nation's cultural calendar. It features the work of traditional and contemporary Filipino artists through exhibits, performances and workshops in various Puerto Princesa venues. For more info, contact festival organisers on ☎ 048-433 5182, fax 433 9088 or ✆ kamarikutan@ yahoo.com.

PALAWAN

Places to Stay

The *Duchess Pension House* (☎ 048-433 2873, 107 Valencia St) has tiny singles/doubles with common bath for P120/220, and more livable doubles with fan and bath for P300.

Diagonally opposite the Duchess is the *Backpackers Cafe, Bookshop & Inn*. A friendly, relaxed hang-out, it has basic rooms for P150/220 and a dorm (or four-bed room) for P100 per head. This place also does good pancakes (P40), delicious bargain curries (P50) and a generous *tom yam* seafood soup (P90). Mountain bikes can be hired for P100 per day and the big range of second-hand books cover seven languages. Happy hour (25% off drinks) is from 4 to 5 pm Monday to Friday, and there's plenty of in-depth info about things to see and do in Palawan.

The *Trattoria Inn & Restaurant* and *Swiss Bistro Garden* (☎ 048-433 2719, fax 433 8171, ✉ trattori@pal-onl.com, 353 Rizal Ave) is a very popular place with Germans. Rooms with fan and common bath start at P320/P350. The common bath is fairly mucky and uninviting. Singles with 'semi-private' bath (shared with another room), air-con and cable TV are P650. A private bath will cost you P750. Check out its Web site at www.palawan.net/trattori/palawan.htm.

Just over the road is the *Badjao Inn* (☎ 048-433 2380). Nice place, shame about the facade. It looks much better from the inside, where big, good-value rooms with fan and spotless bath are P400 (with air-con they cost P650 to P750). There's also a nice courtyard.

Behind the Badjao Inn, down little Trinidad Rd, is the serene *Casa Linda Inn & Restaurant* (☎ 048-433 2606, ✉ casalind@mozcom.com), with its manicured garden courtyard and pergola. The rooms are a tasteful mix of hotel-style luxury and nipa hut-style character. Rooms with fan are P350/450, or P650/750 with air-con. A shoes-off-at-the-door rule insures blissful silence and gleaming floorboards.

The *Puerto Pension* (☎ 048-433 2969, fax 433 4148, ✉ ppension@pal-onl.com), well placed on Malvar St between the pier and the main bus/jeepney terminal, has rooms with fan and 'semi-private' bath for P220/360 (with private bath its P380/490) and air-con rooms for P590/700. The rooms come with wide balconies furnished with wooden tables and chairs. This place was built from indigenous materials and has the best views in town from its little rooftop restaurant/bar. Even if not staying here, it's worth the climb to the top for a drink or bite to eat. Filipino-style mains such as *calamares* (squid) are P100, a Spanish omelette is P60. Only the blaring TV spoils the effect.

Places to Eat

For breakfast or a light lunch, the *Café Kamarikutan & Galeri*, just past the airport on Rizal Ave, serves an incredible range of coffees – all in a huge, airy bamboo mansion with an enormous oasis of a garden.

Great fresh-fruit pancakes (along with an ever-changing lunch and dinner menu) are available at the *Backpackers Cafe, Bookshop & Inn* (see the earlier Places to Stay entry). The rooftop restaurant/bar at the *Puerto Pension* serves breakfast with great views for around P80.

On the corner of Burgos and Manalo Sts, *Vegetarian House* is a rarity of a restaurant in the meat-mad Philippines. But don't expect hippy decor or organic muffins here. In simple, spotlessly white air-con surrounds, you're offered a big range of tasty mock-meat dishes (with gluten used as a meat substitute). A generous serve of vegetable spring rolls is P30, 'shrimp' and stir-fried vegetables are P60, 'beefsteak' with fries is P70 and 'turkey leg' with rice is P50.

Near *Jollibee* is the traditional *Filipino Kamayan Folkhouse & Restaurant*, set on a large, leafy plot complete with a tree-house dining area.

A few blocks along, out the back of the Trattoria Inn, is the lively *Swiss Bistro & Garden* – a great place if you're craving hearty Western meat dishes or pizza. If not, try the brilliant *Ka Lui Restaurant* nearby, serving sophisticated Filipino set meals, including a succulent (no, really) seaweed appetiser. The giant P275 set meal should be enough for two people.

PALAWAN

There are three *Pho Vietnamese Restaurants* in town, the most authentic being about 2km past the airport on Rizal Ave Extension.

Getting There & Away

Air PAL's office (☎ 048-433 4575) is at the airport. Air Philippines is on Rizal Ave (☎ 048-433 7003). Pacific Airways' office (☎ 048-433 4872) is at the airport. Pacific Airways offers charter flights in three-seater planes from Puerto Princesa to Sandoval (P1800), El Nido (P1800), Cuyo (P2300), Culion (P2300) and Coron town (P2300).

Boat The Negros Navigation office, just off Rizal Ave (on Roxas St), usually has a monthly and/or weekly schedule posted on a board out the front.

The office of Sulpicio Lines (☎ 048-433 2641) is nearby on Rizal Ave, and the Milagrosa Shipping Lines office is to the left of the pier gate (on the outside of the enclosure).

For boat trips between Sabang, Port Barton and El Nido, see the Getting Around entry for Palawan, at the beginning of the chapter.

Bus & Jeepney Malvar St, near the market, is crammed with buses, jeepneys and minivans (three terminals in all). For buses and jeepneys to the popular northern destinations of Port Barton, Taytay and El Nido, it's a good idea to turn up early and book a seat. Considering the gruelling trip ahead, you should then go and pass the time with a stiff drink at the rooftop restaurant/bar of the nearby Puerto Pension.

Oversized jeepneys go from Malvar St to El Nido (via Roxas and Taytay) at 4 pm daily (P300, 12 hours). This is a particularly torturous journey, and the winches on the front of these jeepneys aren't just for looks. In mid-1999, jeepneys doing this run were being towed over the worst sections by bulldozers.

If you'd prefer to get to El Nido in gentler stages, take a bus or jeepney at around 7 am or 3 pm from Puerto Princesa to Taytay (P150, around 7½ hours) and stay overnight. A more leisurely way to reach El Nido is to take the jeepney to Port Barton at around 7 am (P100, five hours), and from there take a boat (see the Boat entry in the Getting Around section at the beginning of the chapter).

Buses and jeepneys from Puerto Princesa to Roxas leave from the Malvar St terminals from 6 am to around 9 am daily, and a bus goes at around 1 pm (P100, four hours). Roxas-Puerto Princesa buses and jeepneys leave from the large bus terminal in the middle of town from around 6 am to 9 am daily.

From Puerto Princesa to Sabang, jeepneys (P50 to P70, 2½ to 3 hours) and buses (P150, 2½) go several times a day from the Malvar St terminals. Air-con minibuses go from the Trattoria Inn in Puerto Princesa to Sabang at 7.30 am daily (P250 to P300, two hours), and from Sabang to Puerto Princesa at 3.30 pm.

Minivans head off two or three times daily from the Malvar St terminal to the southern towns of Quezon (P100), Brooke's Point (P150) and Rio Tuba (P200).

Getting Around

Tricycle feeding frenzies are the norm in Puerto Princesa, especially around the market and bus terminals, the pier, and the strolling tourist. Unless you're happy to pay extra for being a Kano (a Westerner), insist on the official tricycle fare rate of P3 for every 2km.

For motorcycles, try Hidalgo Motorbike Hire (☎ 048-433 7721), which has bikes for P500 per day that can be hired through various hotels, including Puerto Pension.

Mountain bikes can be hired from the Backpackers Cafe, Bookshop & Inn for P100 per day (see the earlier Places to Stay entry).

AROUND PUERTO PRINCESA

From crocodile farms to underground rivers, there's a great range of attractions within an easy day trip of Puerto Princesa. For more extended excursions into areas less travelled, you can take the long roads into the far-flung reaches south of the capital.

The low-key town of Port Barton, on the west coast of Palawan.

Church in El Nido, Palawan.

Big Lagoon, Miniloc Island, Palawan.

Malapacao Island, Palawan.

Towering Miniloc Island offers crystal-clear swimming holes.

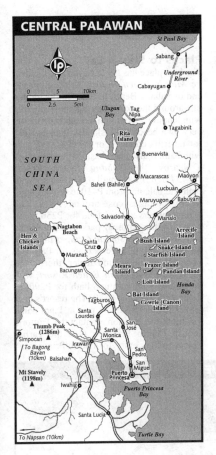

CENTRAL PALAWAN

South China Sea

St Paul Bay
Sabang
Underground River
Cabayugan
Ulugan Bay
Tag Nipa
Tagabinit
Rita Island
Buenavista
Macarascas
Maoyon
Baheli (Bahile)
Lucbuan
Maruyugon
Babuyan
Manalo
Salvacion
Nagtabon Beach
Arrecife Island
Bush Island
Snake Island
Santa Cruz
Starfish Island
Maranat
Meara Island
Frazer Island
Pandan Island
Bacungan
Loli Island
Honda Bay
Bat Island
Tagburos
Cowrie (Canon) Island
Santa Lourdes
Thumb Peak (1286m)
San José
Santa Monica
Simpocan
Irawan
San Pedro
To Bagong Bayan (10km)
Balsahan
San Miguel
Mt Stavely (1198m)
Iwahig
Puerto Princesa
Puerto Princesa Bay
Santa Lucia
Turtle Bay
To Napsan (10km)

Hen & Chicken Islands

0   5   10km
0 2.5 5mi

Irawan

Recently flattened (at the time of writing) by a vicious storm, the **Crocodile Farming Institute** in Irawan has rebuilt itself and re-opened for business.

This place is a breeding centre for the Philippines' two endangered crocs – the estuarine crocodile and the Philippine crocodile. It's open from 1 to 4 pm Monday to Friday and from 9 am to 5 pm Saturday. Guided tours are provided every hour on the hour. Entry is free. To get there from Puerto Princesa, catch a south-bound jeepney or bus to Irawan (P7, 30 minutes), or grab a tricycle (P80).

Iwahig

Far more pleasant than its sounds, the **Iwahig Penal Colony** was set up in 1905 and is claimed to be the biggest institution of its kind anywhere in the world. Effectively a model prison, this place chains newly arrived prisoners for a few months before allowing them to roam relatively free and mix with an integrated community of convicts and their families. **Handicrafts** produced here include knives and basketry.

Jeepneys marked 'Iwahig' leave throughout the morning from Manalo St in Puerto Princesa, returning to town around 1 pm.

Honda Bay

On the way out to Sabang, Honda Bay is dotted with small islands ideal for snorkelling and island hopping. Perfect for day trips, the islands include the dazzling, aptly named **Snake Island**, a winding strip

The endangered Philippine crocodile can be found in all its glory at the Crocodile Farming Institute in Irawan.

PALAWAN

of white sand that changes shape with the tides. Snorkelling gear and boats can be hired at Santa Lourdes Pier, just north of the town of Tagburos (P12 by bus from Puerto Princesa).

SABANG & UNDERGROUND RIVER

Sabang is a beautiful little beach settlement on the edge of the **St Paul Subterranean National Park**, home to an underground river that empties into the sea and can be explored by boat.

From the beach in Sabang you can either take a boat to the mouth of the river for P400 or walk there over the **monkey trail** through the beautiful jungle of the national park – it takes about two hours. Of the river itself, you'll only get to see about 2km of its 8km total, because most of the river is off-limits for research purposes.

If you're not on a package tour, you should pick up a national park permit at the information office next to the pier (P150, payable at the Underground River itself).

Day-trippers take note: the bumpy trip to/from Puerto Princesa and the sheer beauty of Sabang the and national park area may have you wishing you'd brought your luggage from Puerto Princesa after all.

Places to Stay & Eat

The best place has got to be the simply idyllic **Mary's Beach Resort**. At the opposite end of Sabang Beach to the pier, it's hidden just around the point, has a giant shady tree with hammocks right on the sand and has its very own beach (and island!). It costs P200 for no-frills cottages, or P300 for cottages with bath. It also has a basic little restaurant.

Nearby, the **Sabang Beach Resort** (☎ 434 3762) has small, OK cottages with bath and balcony from P450 to P500. Large, family cottages cost around P800. The restaurant serves local food for P250.

Within the national park itself, you can stay at the **ranger station cottages** for P100, or in one of the ranger's tents for P50. Beyond the Underground River, there's the reclusive **Panaguman Beach Resort**, with big rooms with common bath for P290, or deluxe cottages for P480. The resort's boat leaves from the Sabang pier at 1 pm daily. For more information, contact the Trattoria Inn in Puerto Princesa (see the earlier Places to Stay entry for Puerto Princesa).

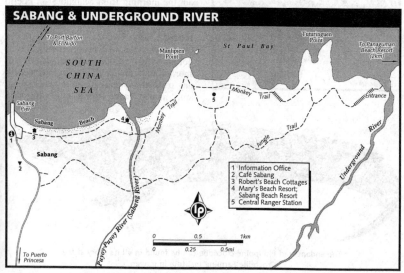

SABANG & UNDERGROUND RIVER

To Port Barton & El Nido

Tuturinguen Point

To Panaguman Beach Resort (2km)

Manlipien Point

St Paul Bay

SOUTH CHINA SEA

Sabang Pier

Monkey Trail

Entrance

Sabang   Beach

4

5

Sabang

Monkey Trail

Jungle Trail

Underground River

1   Information Office
2   Café Sabang
3   Robert's Beach Cottages
4   Mary's Beach Resort;
     Sabang Beach Resort
5   Central Ranger Station

Puyoy-Puyoy River (Sabang River)

To Puerto Princesa

0   0.5   1km
0   0.25   0.5mi

Good food in a nice setting can be found at *Café Sabang*, on the main road into Sabang, about 500m from the beach.

Getting There & Away
It's a pretty nasty old road out to Sabang (P250 to P300, 2 to 2½ hours) – even by air-con minibus – but it's well worth it. The Trattoria Inn in Puerto Princesa operates air-con minibuses to Sabang at 7.30 am, and from Sabang at 3.30 pm daily.

There are also jeepneys between Puerto Princesa and Sabang (P50 for locals, P70 for foreign tourists). In Puerto Princesa, they leave from the Malvar St terminal.

Boats go from Sabang to El Nido (via Port Barton) on Monday, Wednesday, Thursday and Sunday (P850, 7½ to 8 hours). Boats from El Nido to Sabang (via Port Barton) go on Tuesday, Wednesday, Thursday and Saturday. For more information see the Boat entry under Getting Around for Palawan, at the beginning of the chapter.

South Palawan

In contrast to the north, Palawan's southern region has little to offer the traveller. **Quezon**, about 100km from Puerto Princesa, is the nearest major town to the archaeologically interesting **Tabon Caves**. This massive network of caves has recently yielded remnants of prehistory in the form of crude burial grounds. The caves are a half-hour boat ride from Quezon.

Places to Stay
Near Quezon, the best place to stay in this area is *Theo's Cottages* on Malapackun Island. Rooms here go for around P300 and newly built cottages with a deck view near a great waterfall are also available for around the same price.

Getting There & Away
Daily buses travel between Puerto Princesa and Quezon (P65, three hours). Air-con minivans head off two or three times daily from Puerto Princesa's Malvar St depot to

Quezon (P100), Brooke's Point (P150) and Rio Tuba (P200).

North Palawan

ROXAS
The uninspiring town of Roxas (pronounced 'raw-hahs') is 135km from Puerto Princesa, along a chewed-up road that the government swears will be fully concreted come 2001. Roxas specialises in roadside cafes for the steady stream of buses and jeepneys stumbling to and from Puerto Princesa. To tourists, Roxas is best known as the coastal gateway to a cluster of comely deserted islands, along with Coco-Loco, home to the Coco-Loco Island Resort.

Getting There & Away
Boat The only regular boat between Puerto Princesa and Roxas belongs to the Coco-Loco Island Resort. It goes from Coco-Loco Island at around 7 am daily (P100, one hour), and from Puerto Princesa at around 9 am.

Bus & Jeepney Plenty of buses and jeepneys cool their wheels in Roxas on their way north or south, but if you're planning to catch a ride in one of these vehicles, be prepared for a tight squeeze – they're nearly always packed.

Buses and jeepneys from Puerto Princesa to Roxas leave from the Malvar St terminal from 6 am to around 9 am daily, and a bus goes at around 1 pm (P100, four hours). Roxas-Puerto Princesa buses and jeepneys leave from the large bus terminal in the middle of town from around 6 am to 9 am daily.

A couple of jeepneys go from Roxas to Port Barton between 6 and 9 am daily (P50, two hours). From Port Barton to Roxas, jeepneys also head off between 6 and 9 am daily.

PORT BARTON
On the west coast, the refreshingly quiet town of Port Barton is a low-key tourist haunt. The town itself is on an attractive beach well accustomed to spectacular sunsets, but better beaches can be found on the islands scattered throughout the sheltered bay. Just outside the

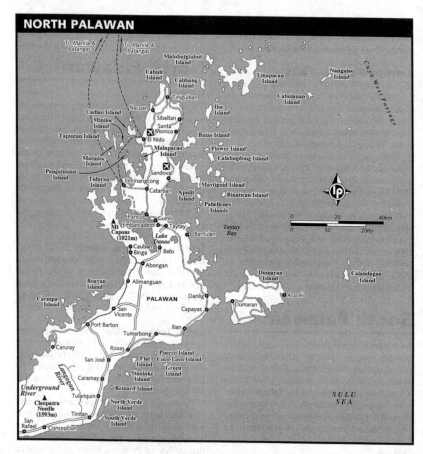

NORTH PALAWAN

To Manila &
Batangas

To Manila &
Batangas

Malubutglubut
Island

Cabuli
Island

Calibang
Island

Linapacan
Island

Nangalao
Island

Tiniguiban

Cabulauan
Island

Cuyo West Passage

Nacpan

Iloc
Island

Cadlao Island

Sibaltan

Miniloc
Island

Santa
Monica

Tapiutan Island

El Nido

Batas Island

Malapacao
Island

Flower Island

Matinloc
Island

Calabugdong Island

Pangalusian
Island

Sandoval

Tuluran
Island

Liminangcong

Maytiguid Island

Catarban

Apulit
Island

Binatican Island

Pabellones
Islands

Pancol

Guinlo

Mt
Capoas
(1021m)

Embarcadero

Taytay

Taytay
Bay

Bantulan

Lake
Danao

Cauban
Binga

Bato

Abongan

Boayan
Island

Alimanguan

Dumaran
Island

Calandagan
Island

Cacnipa
Island

San
Vicente

PALAWAN

Danlig

Dumaran

Araceli

Capayas

Port Barton

Ilian

Tumarbong

Caruray

Roxas

Puerco Island

San José

Flat
Island

Coco-Loco Island

Caramay

Stanlake
Island

Green
Island

Langogan
River

Reinard Island

Underground
River

Tulariquin

North Verde
Island

Cleopatra
Needle
(1593m)

Tinitan

South Verde
Island

San
Rafael

Concepcion

SULU
SEA

0   20   40km

0   10   20mi

bay is Cacnipa Island, home to the Coconut Garden Island Resort (see the following Places to Stay & Eat entry).

Places to Stay & Eat

Port Barton has several beachside cottage places to stay. The swishest of these is the central *Swissippini Lodge & Resort*, with big A-frame balconied huts in a giant garden setting for P600 (by the water) and P400 (set back a little from the water). Swissippini accepts major credit cards, changes money and travellers cheques and organises boat trips to/from Sabang and El Nido.

A few doors along is *Elsa's Beach Cottages*, with good little huts for P300 (P400 for a triple), and the *El Busero Inn*, with simpler cottages for P300 and tawdry rooms for P150. All cottages have private bath.

Over the creek at the north end of town is the new *El Dorado Sunset Cottages*. The front ones go for P300, the back ones for P275. All have private bath. El Dorado's management only accepts guests planning to stay for two nights or more.

All places mentioned here have restaurants and bars attached, but the wonderful fish curry (P65) at the *Filipiniana Restau-*

rant, opposite Elsa's Beach Cottages, would put the fanciest of resorts to shame.

The *Coconut Garden Island Resort* is on a lovely white sand beach on Cacnipa Island, about 15km from Port Barton by boat. Attractive A-frame cottages with balcony and common bath are P370. Cottages with bath cost from P500 to P530 It also has a lodging house with singles/doubles for P220/340, and two-person tents for P240. There are good discounts for long stays (three days or more). The resort's menu includes good Western and Filipino food, including vegetarian dishes. Excellent island-hopping jaunts are offered from P480 per boat, and snorkelling and jungle walks are also popular. A 'special ride' from Port Barton to Cacnipa Island costs P450 per boat.

Getting There & Away

Boat There are eight pumpboat trips a week between Sabang and El Nido and these all go via Port Barton. But take note: unless you've made prior arrangements, or they have passengers or cargo to drop off, these boats won't necessarily *stop* at Port Barton. Fares between El Nido and Port Barton are P500 (4 to 5 hours). Fares between Sabang and Port Barton cost from P350 to P500 (2 to 2½ hours). Every day except Friday, these pumpboats pass Port Barton either heading south to Sabang or north to El Nido (with boats heading in both directions on Wednesday and Thursday).

For more information, see the Getting Around entry for Boat under Palawan, at the beginning of the chapter and/or contact the Swissippini Lodge & Resort in Port Barton.

Between Port Barton and nearby Cacnipa Island (Coconut Garden Island Resort), there's a shuttle service most days (P100, 30 minutes). A chartered special ride should cost about P500 per boat.

Bus & Jeepney A jeepney runs from Port Barton to Puerto Princesa between 7 and 8 am daily (P100, five hours). It heads off from the waiting shed at the beach end of Ballesteros St, and cruises through town picking up passengers. From Puerto Princesa's Malvar

St terminal, a jeepney heads for Port Barton at around 7 am daily.

A couple of jeepneys go from Roxas to Port Barton between 6 and 9 am daily (P50, two hours). From Port Barton to Roxas, jeepneys also head off between 6 and 9 am daily.

TAYTAY

Taytay is a quiet coastal town dominated by a broad, flat **fort** – a solitary reminder of the town's glory days as the capital of Palawan. Built in 1667 by the Spanish, the fort encloses an attractive **public garden**. The town's population is around 50,000 people. Fiesta time is early May, when the town honours its patron, the Miraculous Lady of Santa Monica.

For an excellent day trip, take the 30-minute jeepney ride from Taytay proper to **Lake Danao**, a picturesque freshwater lake surrounded by some good forest hiking trails.

Places to Stay & Eat

Pem's Pension & Restaurant backs onto the water and has a garden courtyard, complete with a feasting table and views of the nearby fort. Narrow, prison-style singles with common bath are P75. Small, solid cottages for two with fan and bath cost from P250 to P300 (P150 for singles). Larger cottages are P500 to P600. The restaurant does basic Western-style breakfasts for P40 and standard western and Filipino mains for around P60.

In the middle of town, *Publico's International Guest House* has basic rooms around a courtyard for P60/150 a single/double with fan, and P200 with fan and bath.

The *Casa Rosa Restaurant* offers the best food in town, all served in a large pergola perched on the hill above the town. Delicious Western and Filipino dishes cost around P150. The restaurant is easy to spot from town, and is a short walk up from Taytay's main street.

Getting There & Away

Boat For boats to/from El Nido, Liminangcong and other east coast towns, you must

PALAWAN

use the pier at Embarcadero, a scenic 8km tricycle ride east of Taytay (P80, 15 minutes). The quiet little inland pier has a small eatery. Boats to/from Coron town in the Calamian Group moor in the bay at Taytay.

Pumpboats go from the Embarcadero pier to Liminangcong between 9 am and noon daily (P100, 1½ to 2 hours). Boats from Liminangcong to the Embarcadero pier also leave between 9 am and noon daily. Like many boat rides in this region, this is a beautiful trip. If the season's right (early to mid-year), you may sail through great trails of pink and purple jellyfish.

Irregular pumpboats between Taytay (Embarcadero pier) and El Nido may leave any time from around 7 am to noon (P200, 3½ to 4 hours). Special ride pumpboats can be arranged from the Embarcadero pier or El Nido for P2500 per boat.

Large pumpboats from Taytay to Coron town (often via Linapacan Island), head off between 7 and 8 am Monday and Friday (P450, eight hours). These boats go from Coron town to Taytay between 7 and 8 am Wednesday and Saturday.

Bus & Jeepney There are two jeepneys from Taytay to El Nido at 7 am and 8 am daily (P150, 2½ to 3 hours). From El Nido, one or two jeepneys go via Taytay on their way to Puerto Princesa, leaving El Nido at 7 or 8 am.

Despite valiant attempts, no bus or jeepney has ever managed to maintain a regular link between Taytay and Liminangcong. You'd be much better off catching a boat (see the previous Boat entry for details).

APULIT ISLAND
Less than 2km long, the very private paradise of Apulit Island is home to the exclusive Club Noah Isabelle. The resort organises pumpboat and kayak tours of the island's many natural wonders, including Puerto del Sol Beach and several caves and swimming holes.

Places to Stay & Eat
Club Noah Isabelle (☎ 02-752 0307, fax 894 5725) has a fine restaurant and a stunning row of cottages built directly over the

water. The cottages, equipped with both air-con and ceiling fans, cost US$165. Package deals for divers are available on request.

Getting There & Away
Club Noah Isabelle has a regular shuttle service between Sandoval airport and Apulit Island (P60, 1 to 1½ hours). The resort can also organise a boat for you between Taytay and Apulit Island (one hour).

You can also get to the island from El Nido, via Sibultan (see the following entry for Flower Island).

FLOWER ISLAND
The peaceful, utterly beautiful Flower Island houses the *Flower Island Beach Resort*, where somewhat overpriced cottages with bath are available for P2500. Don't come here expecting high-end resort attractions – there's no electricity and diving and water sports enthusiasts generally have to bring their own equipment.

The best way to get to Flower Island is from El Nido. Jeepneys go daily from El Nido to Sibultan on a surprisingly good road (P50 to P60, 1½ hours). Boat hire from Sibultan to nearby Flower Island is P500 to P600 per boat.

Pumpboats can also be hired from Taytay for the scenic 2½ to 3 hour trip to Flower Island (P1000 per boat).

LIMINANGCONG
A ramshackle fishing village with a jaunty charm, Liminangcong's not a bad place to get stuck on your way between Puerto Princesa and the northern extremes of Palawan.

Places to Stay & Eat
On the main street near the main pier, *Kaver's Inn*, a big old colonial place, is probably your best bet. It has ageing, timber-floored rooms with tidy common bath, no fan, and balcony for P250. There's a battered but browse-worthy bunch of books in the family room/reception area.

The best place in town for dinner is the dock-side *Puerto Paraiso Inn & Restaurant*. Not much to look at from the main street, it leads through to an open-air platform overlooking the harbour. Cheap and hearty meals include fried fish and rice (P50), vegetable curry (P70) and pork dishes (P70). Rooms are OK and come with common bath for P150/200 a single/double.

Getting There & Away
Liminangcong's harbour is crammed with four piers. The main pier (for boats to Manila, Batangas etc) is next to the Petron service station.

Pumpboats go daily from here to El Nido and Taytay.

EL NIDO
In the north-west reaches of Palawan, a beautiful bay jealously guards El Nido. This increasingly popular little town is hemmed in by jagged cliffs and a lovely beach. It's not easy to get to, but most travellers find it's well worth the effort. A boat trip to the offshore islands of the **Bacuit Archipelago** is an absolute must.

The Bacuit Archipelago is a spectacular hiding place for several classy island resorts – some of which have entire islands to themselves.

Towering **Miniloc Island**, south-west of El Nido, is a favourite among snorkelling day-trippers, with its Small Lagoon and Big Lagoon – crystal clear saltwater swimming holes on the north coast.

Matinloc Island has the amazing **Secret Beach**, completely hidden from the outside of the island. It also has the quite bizarre **Matinloc Shrine** – a revolving statue of Mary. Other sights within a couple of hours boat ride from El Nido include the snorkelling havens of little **Simisu Island** and **Cathedral Cave**, the rocky sightseeing beauty of **Snake Island**, and the mysterious **Cudugman Cave**, with its narrow entrance guarded by human bones.

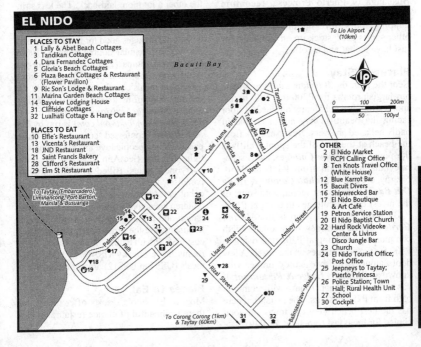

EL NIDO

PLACES TO STAY
1 Lally & Abet Beach Cottages
3 Tandikan Cottage
4 Dara Fernandez Cottages
5 Gloria's Beach Cottages
6 Plaza Beach Cottages & Restaurant (Flower Pavilion)
9 Ric Son's Lodge & Restaurant
11 Marina Garden Beach Cottages
14 Bayview Lodging House
31 Cliffside Cottages
32 Lualhati Cottage & Hang Out Bar

PLACES TO EAT
10 Elfie's Restaurant
13 Vicenta's Restaurant
18 JND Restaurant
21 Saint Francis Bakery
28 Clifford's Restaurant
29 Elm St Restaurant

OTHER
2 El Nido Market
7 RCPI Calling Office
8 Ten Knots Travel Office (White House)
12 Blue Karrot Bar
15 Bacuit Divers
16 Shipwrecked Bar
17 El Nido Boutique & Art Café
19 Petron Service Station
20 El Nido Baptist Church
22 Hard Rock Videoke Center & Livirus Disco Jungle Bar
23 Church
24 El Nido Tourist Office; Post Office
25 Jeepneys to Taytay; Puerto Princesa
26 Police Station; Town Hall; Rural Health Unit
27 School
30 Cockpit

Bacuit Bay

To Lio Airport (10km)

To Taytay (Embarcadero), Liminancong, Port Barton, Manila & Busuanga

To Corong Corong (1km) & Taytay (60km)

Tambon Street
Tabangka Street
Pakita St
Calle Hama Street
Calle Real Street
Abdulla Street
Amboy Street
Balinnasayaw Road
Palmera St
Path
Lisang Street
Rizal Street

0   100   200m
0   50   100yd

PALAWAN

Back on dry land, **mountain climbing** is becoming more popular around El Nido's impressively vertical landscape. For organised trips, drop by the Elm St Restaurant.

Information

Power in El Nido officially cuts out at midnight (and unofficially at any other time).

The RCPI Calling Office on Tabangka St is open long hours from 8 am to noon, from 1 to 5 pm and from 6 to 9 pm Monday to Friday.

There are no banks here, but there are several moneychangers (dealing mainly in US dollars), including the friendly El Nido Boutique & Art Café near the pier.

Things to See & Do

The El Nido Boutique & Art Café, run by the energetic Judith and Tani, has everything you'll need for making the most of the area. From here, you can design your own diving and snorkelling trips, book boats to Busuanga or Puerto Princesa, reconfirm flights, add your name to upcoming island-hopping tours, hire mountain bikes and other sports gear, stock up on souvenirs, or just have a chat and a coffee.

Places to Stay

Near the pier, the **Bayview Lodging House** has largish rooms for P200 to P400. It also sports a big, broad balcony on the 2nd floor facing the beautiful bay and a couple of badly behaved showers. Next, set back from the beach at the foot of the spooky cliffs is the popular **Cliffside Cottages**, with separate huts with bath from P350 to P450. Nearby, the quiet **Lualhati Cottage & Hang Out Bar** is a well kept secret, with some of the nicest budget cottages in town at P150.

Back on the beach strip is the **Marina Garden Beach Cottages**, with cottages with common bath starting at P200 and rising to P500 for fancier cottages on the beach. A few doors along is the two storey timber villa known as **Ric Son's Lodge & Restaurant**. It has airless but cheap rooms with common bath from P250 upstairs. The restaurant here has the best beach views in town – a good choice for breakfast (omelette for P40).

Clumped together you have **Gloria's Beach Cottages** (shady, balconied cottages with bath for P400, and a bigger four person cottage with bath for P630), **Dara Fernandez Cottages** (from P400 to P500 per cottage with bath) and **Tandikan Cottage** (P500 with bath).

The nearby **Plaza Beach Cottages & Restaurant (Flower Pavilion)** has fairly irksome old rooms with common bath for P200 and is best avoided.

At the far end of town from the pier is the **Lally & Abet Cottages**, with roomy, balconied bungalows with bath from P700 to P800, and rooms with shared bath right by the water for P350.

In Corong Corong, a P5 tricycle ride south of El Nido, beachside cottages are offered by the peaceful **Dolarog Beach Resort** and the new El Nido **Buena Suenta Beach Cottages**.

The magical Malapacao Island has two resorts – one famously, fiercely New Age and the other a lot more laid-back. The less stringent of the two, **Marina del Nido** (☎ 02-831 0597, fax 831 9816) resort has spacious beachfront cottages good for five to eight people (P2500), regular double rooms (P1000), four-person rooms (P2000) and a four-bed dorm with common bath (P300 per person). Lavish set meals cost from P250 to P300. On the other side of the island, The wonderfully located **Malapacao Island Retreat** (fax 433 4829, ✉ leeann@pal-onl.com) is run by Lee Ann, the self-confessed 'crazy lady of Malapacao'. Many people love this place, but it's a tight ship that Lee Ann runs and it's not to everyone's tastes. Billed as a 'nonsmokers paradise', the resort has strict rules about alcohol consumption, and guests with young children are actively discouraged. Yoga, meditation and a mind-boggling array of beauty treatments are the order of the day. Cottages cost US$70 with bath, US$65 without. Dorm rooms are a cheeky US$45 to US$55 and meals (US$7 to US$12) are *not* included.

Places to Eat

Most of El Nido's resorts offer meals, but there's a handful of choice restaurants here as well.

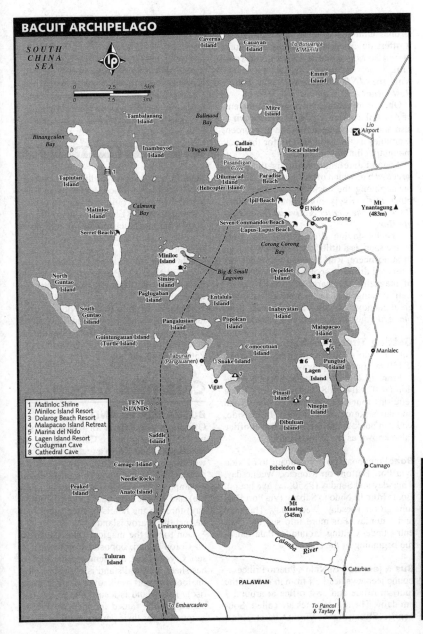

BACUIT ARCHIPELAGO

SOUTH
CHINA
SEA

0   2.5   5km
0   1.5   3ml

To Busuanga
& Manila

Caverna
Island

Cauayan
Island

Emmit
Island

Lio
Airport

Mitre
Island

Tambalanang
Island

Balinaod
Bay

Binangculan
Bay

Inambuyod
Island

Ubugun Bay

Cadlao
Island

Bocal Island

Tapiutan
Island

1

Matinloc
Island

Calmung
Bay

Pasandigan
Cove

Dilumacad
Island
(Helicopter Island)

Paradise
Beach

Ipil Beach

El Nido

Mt
Ynantagung ▲
(483m)

Secret Beach

Seven Commandos Beach
Lapus-Lapus Beach

Corong Corong

Miniloc
Island

2

Corong Corong
Bay

North
Guntao
Island

Simisu
Island

Big & Small
Lagoons

Depeldet
Island

3

Paglugaban
Island

Entalula
Island

South
Guntao
Island

Pangalusian
Island

Popolcan
Island

Inabuyatan
Island

Malapacao
Island

4
5

Manlalec

Guintunguaan Island
(Turtle Island)

Comocutuan
Island

Tabunan
(Pangauanen)

Snake Island

6

Pungtud
Island

7

Lagen
Island

Vigan

Pinasil
Island

8

1 Matinloc Shrine
2 Miniloc Island Resort
3 Dolarog Beach Resort
4 Malapacao Island Retreat
5 Marina del Nido
6 Lagen Island Resort
7 Cudugman Cave
8 Cathedral Cave

TENT
ISLANDS

Ninepin
Island

Dibuluan
Island

Saddle
Island

Camago Island

Bebeledon

Camago

Needle Rocks

Peaked
Island

Anato Island

Mt
Maateg
(345m)

Liminangcong

Cataba
River

Catarban

Tuluran
Island

PALAWAN

To Embarcadero

To Pancol
& Taytay

PALAWAN

One of the best is *Vicenta's Restaurant*, an unassuming place that's consistently full. It offers quick, tasty, big meals for around P60. Also very good is *Clifford's Restaurant*, which specialises in seafood, along with the *JND Restaurant*, and *Elfie's Restaurant*.

Open from around November to the end of April, the friendly *Elm St Restaurant* is also one of the best eateries. Set in a garden, it doubles as the headquarters for the local mountain climbing club.

A good late-night haunt is the *Shipwrecked* bar, which offers good seafood and pizza among the cocktails and beers. Another fairly lively nightspot is the *Hard Rock Videoke Center & Livirus Disco Jungle Bar*.

The fun-loving *Blue Karrot Bar*, right on the sand, is a little beach shack with a lot of atmosphere. Run by Rose and Rudi, it's a relaxed drinking spot with a good supply of magazines, guitars, and board games. Late closing and early opening, it offers great hangover-easing shakes for P25. Simple, generous main meals cost around P60.

Getting There & Away

Air El Nido's Lio airport is north of town (P150 by tricycle one way).

From El Nido to Manila, Soriano Aviation (☎ 02-804 0408) has a charter service requiring four days' notice from Manila and one day's notice from El Nido. In El Nido, you can book at the Ten Knots travel office (also known as the White House).

Boat Pumpboats go from Sabang to El Nido (via Port Barton) on Monday, Wednesday, Thursday and Sunday (P850, 7½ to 8 hours). Boats from El Nido to Sabang (via Port Barton) go on Tuesday, Wednesday, Thursday and Saturday. For more info see the Boat entry, under Getting Around for Palawan, at the beginning of the chapter.

Bus & jeepney El Nido's Puerto Princesa-bound jeepneys head off from in front of the tourism office and post office at around 7 am daily. The regular ones are called 'Souvenir', 'Sweetie' and 'Virgin Chaser'. It's a

The Tagbanua

Living in the northern reaches of Palawan, the elusive Tagbanua are a deeply animist people who have retained much of their ancient clothing, customs and language, despite the ever-growing presence of mainstream communities nearby. Tagbanua tribes of Busuanga Island are renowned for their pottery skills.

Mic Looby

good idea to book a seat the night before – ask at the tourist office. A new jeepney terminal has been built in nearby Corong Corong to serve El Nido, but so far nobody's taking much notice of it. Corong Corong is 1km south of El Nido (P5 by tricycle).

For more information on jeepneys between El Nido and Puerto Princesa, see the earlier Getting There & Away entry for Puerto Princesa.

Jeepneys go daily from El Nido to Sibultan on a surprisingly good road (P50 to P60, 1½ hours). Boat hire from Sibultan to nearby islands such as Flower Island costs P500 to P600 per boat.

Calamian Group

BUSUANGA ISLAND

Offering a wonderland for wreck divers as well as snorkellers, **Coron town** on Busuanga Island is also a great base for sun-worshipping explorers (the town itself has no beach). The best-value thing to do is hire a pumpboat (around P700, limit eight people) and snorkelling gear (about P100 per day) through the hotels or dive shops, and inspect the nearby islands.

Don't miss the magical **Lake Cayangan** on Coron Island, opposite Coron town itself. Crystal clear, this semi-freshwater lake has sheer rock walls and is only accessible on foot (a short walk over a steep rocky rise). This island is also home to the **Tagbanua people**, famed for their elusiveness as much as for their pottery skills.

PALAWAN

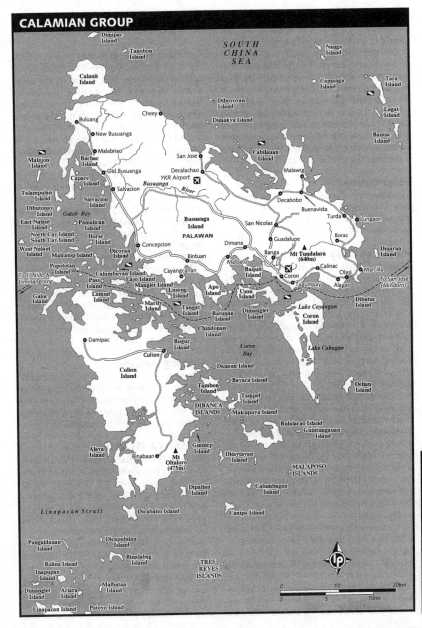

Another activity often included in a pumpboat day trip is a soak in the **hot spring** just out of Coron town.

Diving – and wreck diving in particular – is the other great pastime in this area. For information about extended trips (five days or more), contact Tartaruga Diving at @ gulerheinz@hotmail.com, through the Bayside Lodge & Restaurant in Coron town. This impressive outfit uses restored fishing boats for its trips, which explore Busuanga from November to April and Tubbataha from May to June.

Information

The Swagman Travel office just up from the pier now offers email facilities, as well as the usual moneychanging and telephone services.

Places to Stay & Eat

A short tricycle ride (about P5) from the Coron town wharf will bring you to the market area, the centre of Coron town, half of which is perched on bamboo stilts. Places to stay here include: the *Bayside Lodge & Restaurant* (starting with dorm rooms for P150 per head, up to big rooms with a view and bath for P600), the *Bayview Lodge* with a similar deal and the *Sea Breeze Lodge* (singles from P100 to P150, doubles for P200).

A 20-minute walk onwards, up the sloping main road past the Swagman Travel office (or grab a tricycle for about P10), is the *Kokosnuss Garden Resort & Restaurant* – one of the best places, if you don't mind the relative isolation. Cottages and nipa hut-style rooms in this large garden compound range from P400 (with possibly the fanciest common bath in South-East Asia) to P800 (for big rooms complete with bathroom murals).

Another very good place just out of town is the waterside *Krystal Lodge*, where double rooms over the water go for P300. A friendly, family run place, it also serves up great pancakes.

All places to stay have their own *restaurants*, and while the food won't exactly entrance your taste buds, the tastiest dishes are served at the Bayview Lodge (which does a great pizza).

Getting There & Away

Air Ads, Pacific Airways and Asian Spirit all serve the little YKR airport on the north side of Busuanga Island (about a one-hour bumpy jeepney ride from Coron town). There are flights three times a week to and from Manila (P2000), Boracay (P1260) and Puerto Princesa (P2000). There's an Air Ads office in Coron town, next door to the Bayside Lodge & Restaurant.

MBRS Lines has a big passenger/car ferry doing the Manila–Coron–Liminangcong–Coron–Manila trip each week. Leaving at noon Monday from Pier 8 in Manila, it hits Coron town around 8 am Tuesday and costs P250 for a standard ticket to Liminangcong (eight hours). The same boat returns at 1.30 pm Wednesday for the run back to Manila.

Viva Lines has solid little wooden ferries sailing between Batangas and Coron town. They leave Coron at noon Monday and Friday and cost P330 and the trip takes 17 hours – up to 22 hours if the ship's heavily laden. From Batangas, they leave around 6 pm Sunday and Thursday.

Getting Around

If you're game, you can hire 125cc Suzuki motorcycles from the Blue Heaven Hang-Out Bar on the road to the Kokosnuss Garden Resort & Restaurant. The usual charge is P500 per day, without petrol.

DIMAKYA ISLAND

North of central Busuanga Island, the glorious little Dimakya Island is a pocket-size tropical playground. It has a long, white-sand beach, plenty of reef and a Japanese WWII wreck just offshore, and wildlife on view via several hiking trails. Equally idyllic islands are within easy reach of Dimakya, and boat trips can be organised through the island's resort, Club Paradise. The resort also specialises in safari tours to **Calauit Island**, the rather surreal home of around 500 imported African animals. If you want to organise your own visit to Caluit Island, you'll need permission from the Conservation & Resources Management Foundation (☎ 02-705 001).

Places to Stay & Eat

Club Paradise (☎ 02-893 8280, fax 894 5725) has standard cottages and rooms with fan and bath for US$100/130 a single/double, and marble-bathroomed air-con quarters for US$110/140. These prices include three daily meals at the large, local food restaurant. Also on offer is a swimming pool, tennis court, library and heaps of water sports equipment.

Getting There & Away

Club Paradise organises transfer trips from Busuanga Island's YKR airport to Dimakya Island by jeepney and boat (one hour). The cost of this trip is included in the price of your room.

SANGAT ISLAND

If you're after a place to stay, *Sangat Island Reserve (call the Manila Swagman Travel office ☎ 02-523 854, fax 522-3663, ☻ sangat@epic.net)*, on Sangat Island, is part of a chain of 'bioresorts' and offers quite stylish beachside cottages with bath and balcony starting at US$60 per person, or US$95 per person with four diving trips (diving gear hire costs US$7 per dive). Prices include boat transfer to and from Coron town, and meals.

Language

Pilipino (also known as Tagalog) is one of two official languages of the Philippines. The other is English and, along with Pilipino, it's used for most business, government and legal transactions.

Tagalog ranks as the principal regional language out of around 100 languages or dialects spoken in the Philippines. It belongs to the Malayo-Polynesian language family whose members extend from Madagascar to Tonga.

In 1937 Tagalog was declared the official national language, a choice based on the fact that, as the dialect spoken in Manila, it was already understood and spoken by most Filipinos. Historically, it was also the language used by the leaders of the Philippine revolution against Spanish rule, since most were from Tagalog-speaking regions. After debate over the elevated status of Tagalog it was decided to call the official national language Pilipino, with the view to making the new name (and language) more acceptable to Filipinos from non-Tagalog regions.

Most Filipinos can speak and understand both Pilipino and English, so foreign travellers will find that getting around isn't difficult, even beyond the cities.

Pronunciation

English speakers should have little trouble with Pilipino pronunciation. Words are generally pronounced as they are written and vowels and consonants have a consistent pronunciation.

Vowels

a	as in 'far'
e	as in 'get'
i	as the 'ee' in 'beef'
o	as in 'more'
u	as in 'June'

When several vowels occur in a sequence, each vowel is pronounced separately, eg, *panauhin* (visitor) is pronounced 'pana-uhin'.

Some Pilipino vowels are pronounced with what is called a glottal stop. This is done by making the sound of the vowel, then abruptly stopping it, as the 'tt' in the Cockney pronunciation of 'bottle'. Glottal stops often occur on a word-final vowel.

Diphthongs

There are a few diphthongs (combinations of vowel sounds) in Pilipino:

ay	as the 'uy' in 'buy'
aw	as the 'ou' in 'mount'
ey	as the 'ay' in 'ray'
iw	produced by making the sound 'ee' and continuing it to 'oo'
oy	as the 'oi' in 'noise'
uy	produced by making the sound 'oo' and continuing it to 'ee'

Consonants

Most Pilipino consonants are pronounced in the same way as their English counterparts, with the exception of the following:

g	always hard, as in 'good'; never as in 'gentle'
h	as in 'haste'; always aspirated, never silent
ng	as in 'sing'; can occur at the beginning of a word, eg, *ngayon* (now)
r	rolled to produce a faint trill
s	as in 'sun', never as in 'his'

Word Stress

Word stress is marked by the acute accent sign (') over the vowel on which the stress falls, eg *masayá* (happy). If stress falls on a word-final vowel which has a circumflex accent (^), the vowel is pronounced with a glottal stop, eg *masamâ* (bad).

Greetings & Civilities

Pilipino has polite and informal modes of address. It's better to use the polite form for adults you don't know well. When you use the formal mode with friends or younger adults, you'll more than likely get the comment: 'Don't use *hô/pô* with me. I'm not that old yet'. Where both the polite and informal are given in this guide, they are marked 'pol' and 'inf' respectively.

Use the title *mamà* for a man who is a stranger or *ale* for a woman. You may also use *misis/mis* (Mrs/Miss) for adult female strangers. Use *sir* for a professional man or *ma'am* for a professional woman. The more friendly and familiar term *páre* (for a man) or *brad* (for a younger adult, if you are yourself one) may also be used for a man who is a stranger, eg, *Iskyús lang, páre* (Excuse me, my friend).

Good morning.	*Magandáng umaga hô.* (pol) *Magandáng umaga.* (inf)
Good morning. (response)	*Magandáng umaga naman hô.*
Good afternoon.	*Magandáng hapon hô.*
Good evening.	*Magandáng gabí hô.*
Hello.	*Kumusta hô.*
Goodbye.	*Paalam na hô.*
Bye.	*Sige na muna.* (inf)
Yes.	*Ohô/Opò.*
No.	*Hindi hô.*
Excuse me.	*Mawaláng-galang na nga hô.*
Sorry.	*Iskyus/Sori hô.*
Thank you (very much).	*(Maráming) salámat hô.*
You're welcome.	*Waláa hong anuman.* (lit: 'it's nothing')
What's your name?	*Anóng pangalan ninyó?*
My name is ...	*Akó si ...*
May I take your photo?	*Maári ko ba kayóng kunan ng litrato?*

Language Difficulties

Do you speak English?	*Marunong ba kayóng mag-Ingglés?*
Does anyone here speak English?	*Meron hô bang marunong mag-Ingglés dito?*

Body Language

Most Filipinos signify 'Yes' by raising the eyebrows or lifting the head upwards slightly. They also do this when they greet friends.

You can hiss to gain attention, for example, when calling a waiter in a restaurant. When you want to pay the bill, make the figure of a rectangle in the air with your index finger and thumb.

It's considered impolite to pass between people conversing or facing one another. If you must do so, the Filipino polite way is to extend an arm or two arms with the hands clasped and pointing downwards either without saying anything or murmuring *iskyús*.

Touching, especially women, is not taken well by Filipinos. You'll notice that a Filipino man will extend his hand to shake yours but a Filipino woman will not readily do so. When being introduced to a couple or greeting them, you shake hands with the man and smile with a nod of the head to the woman.

Do you understand?	*Náiintindihán ba ninyó?*
I understand.	*Náiintindihán ko hô.*
I don't understand.	*Hindî ko hô náiintindihán.*
Please write it down.	*Pakisulat niyó ngâ yón.*
How do you say ...?	*Papáno hô ba sabíhin ...?*
What does ... mean?	*Ano hô ang ibig sabíhin ng ...?*

Getting Around

Most of the signs in airports and stations are in English, so you won't encounter any problems getting around.

Where is the ...?	*Násaán hô ang ...?*
bus station	*terminál ng bus*
train station	*istasyón ng tren*
road to ...	*daán papuntáng ...*
nearest LRT station	*ang pinakamalapit na istasyón ng LRT*
Metro station	*ang istasyón ng Metro Tren*

What time does the ... leave/arrive?	*Anóng oras hô áalís/ dárating ang ...?*
plane	*eropláno*
boat	*bapór*
bus	*bus*
train	*tren*

Where can I buy a ticket?	*Saán hô maaring bumilí ng tiket?*

I'd like a ... ticket.	*... tiket nga hô.*
one-way	*isáng one-way*
return	*isáng round trip*
1st class	*1st class*
2nd class	*2nd class*

How do we get to ...?	*Papano hô namin marárating ang ...?*
Is it far from here?	*Malayò hô ba dito?*
Is it near here?	*Malapit hô ba dito?*
Can we walk there?	*Puwede hô bang lakarin?*
Can you show me (on the map)?	*Puwede hô ba niyóng ipakita sa mapa?*

What ... is this?	*Anó hô bang ... itó?*
street	*kalye*
city	*siyudád*
village	*baryo*
province	*probinsya*
town	*bayan*

Go straight ahead.	*Tulóy-tulóy lang hô.*
Turn ...	*Liko hô ...*
to the right	*kanan hô/lang* (pol/inf)
to the left	*kaliwâ hô/lang* (pol/inf)
at the next corner	*sa súsunod na kánto*
at the traffic lights	*sa ílaw*
behind ...	*sa likód ng ...*
in front of ...	*sa haráp ng ...*
opposite	*katapát ng*
north	*norte/hilagà*
south	*sud/timog*
east	*silangan*
west	*kanluran*

When you want to get off a regular bus, you say *Para!* (Stop!) loudly. There are designated bus stops, but you can get off anywhere you like, depending on the mood of the driver and the traffic situation.

Where is the bus stop?	*Násaán hô ang hintúan ng bus?*
Which bus goes to ...?	*Alíng bus hô ang papuntá sa ...?*
Does this bus go to ...?	*Papuntá hô ba itóng bus na itó sa ...?*
I want to get off at ...	*Bábabâ hô ako sa ...*

What station is this?	
Ano hóng istasyón itó?	
What's the next station?	
Anó hô ba ang susunód na istasyón?	
Does this train stop at ...?	
Humíhintô hô ba ang tren na itó sa ...?	
The train is delayed/cancelled.	
Náhulí/Nákanselá hô ang tren.	
How long will it be delayed?	
Gaano katagál hô mahúhulí?	

Is this taxi free?	*Bakánte hô bang taksing itó?*
Please take me to ...	*Dalhín nga niyó akó sa ...*
Stop here!	*Para na hô dito!*
Where does the boat leave from?	*Mulá hô saán áalís ang barkó?*
How long does the trip take?	*Gaano hô katagál ang biyahe?*
Is that seat taken?	*May nakaupô na hô ba diyán?*
Where can I rent a car?	*Saán hô maáring umupa ng awto?*
Where can I hire a bicycle?	*Saán hô puwedeng umarkilá ng bisikleta.*

Accommodation

I'm looking for a ...	*Nagháhanáp hô akó ng ...*
campground	*kampingan*
guesthouse	*bahay para sa mgáturista*
hotel	*otél*
motel	*motél*
youth hostel	*youth hostel*

What's the address?
Ano hô ang adrés?
Could you write the address, please?
Pakisulat niyó ngâ ang adrés.
I'd like to book a room, please.
Gústo ko hong magreserba ng kuwarto.
Do you have any rooms available?
May bakante hô ba kayó?

How much is it for ...?	*Magkano hô para sa ...?*
one night	*isáng gabí*
a week	*isáng linggó*
two people	*dalawáng táo*

Does it include breakfast?
Kasama na hô ba doón ang almusál?
Do you have a room with two beds?
May kuwarto hô ba kayó na may dalawáng kama?
Do you have a room with a double bed?
May kuwárto hô ba kayó may kamang pangdalawahan?

I'd like ...	*Gústo ko hô ...*
a single room	*ng pángisahan na kuwarto*
to share a dorm	*na makísunong sa isáng malaking kuwarto*

May I see it?	*Maarì ko hô bang tignán?*
Where is the bathroom?	*Násaán hô ba ang banyo?*
It's fine. I'll take it.	*Sige hô. Kukunin ko.*

air-conditioning	*erkon*
bathroom	*banyo*
bottle of water	*bote ng tubig*
clean	*malinis*
key	*susì*
mosquito coil	*katól*
shower	*dutsa*
soap	*sabón*
toilet	*kubéta/CR/toilet*
toilet paper	*tisyu*
towel	*tuwalya*
water (cold/hot)	*(malamíg/mainit na) túbig*

Signs

Mainit/Maginaw	Hot/Cold
Pasukán	Entrance
Lábasan	Exit
Bawal Pumasok	No Entry
Bawal Manigarílyo	No Smoking
Bukás/Sará	Open/Closed
Bawal	Prohibited
CR	Toilets

Around Town

Where is a ...?	*Saán hô may ...?*
bank	*bangko*
consulate	*konsulado*
embassy	*embahada*
market	*palengke*
museum	*museo*
police station	*istasyón ng pulís*
post office	*pos opis*
public telephone	*teléponó*
public toilet	*comfort room/CR/ pálikuran*
town square	*plasa*

I want to change ...	*Gústo ko hong magpapalít ng ...*
cash/money	*pera*
travellers cheques	*travellers check*

aerogram	*aerogram*
air mail	*ermeyl*
envelope	*sobre*
letter	*sulat*
stamps	*sélyo*

I want to call ...	*Gústo ko hóng tawagan ...*
Where can I use email?	*Saán hô kayâ akó makakagamit ng email?*
I need to check my email.	*Kailangan ko hóng tignán ang email ko.*
I want to send a fax.	*Gústo ko hóng magpadalá ng fax.*
What time does it open/close?	*Anóng oras hô itó nagbúbukás/ nagsásará?*

Shopping

general store	*tindahan*
bookshop	*tindahan ng libró*
chemist/pharmacy	*botika/parmasya*
market	*palengke*

Where can I buy ...?	*Saán ako makakabili ng ...?*
I'd like to buy ...	*Gústo ko hóng bumili ng ...*
I don't like it.	*Ayoko nitó.*
Can I look at it?	*Maarì bang tignán?*
I'm just looking.	*Tumítingín hô lang akó.*
How much is this?	*Magkano hô itó?*
Do you accept credit cards?	*Tumátanggáp ba kayó ng credit card?*
I think it's too expensive.	*Ang mahál-mahál namán.*
Can you lower the price?	*May tawad hô ba iyán?*

big	*malakí*
small	*maliít*
more	*mas marami*
a little bit	*katitíng*
many	*marami*
too much/many	*masyadong marami*
enough	*sapát*

Health

Where is the ...?	*Násaán hô ang ...?*
doctor	*doktór*
hospital	*ospitál*
chemist	*botíka*
dentist	*dentista*

I'm sick.	*May sakít hô akó.*
My friend is sick.	*May sakit hô ang kasama ko.*
I need a doctor who speaks English.	*Kailángan ko hô ng doktór na marúnong mag-Ingglés.*
I feel nauseous.	*Naalibádbarán/ Nasúsuká hô ako.*
I have a headache.	*Masakít hô ang ulo ko.*
I have a stomach-ache.	*Masakít hô ang tiyán ko.*

Could I see a female doctor?	*Puwéde hong magpatingín sa babáeng doktór?*
I'm pregnant.	*Buntís hô akó.*

I'm ...	*May ... ako*
diabetic	*diabitis*
asthmatic	*hikà*
anaemic	*anemya*

I'm allergic to ...	*Allergic ako sa ...*
antibiotics	*antibiyotiká*
penicillin	*penisilín*

antiseptic	*antiseptiko*
aspirin	*aspirina*
bandage	*benda*
Band-aids	*koritas*
condoms	*kondom*
painkillers	*gamót na pang-pakalma ng kirót*
sanitary napkins	*tampon*
soap	*sabón*
sunblock	*sunblock*
tampons	*tampon*
toilet paper	*tisyu/papél sa kubeta*

Time, Dates & Numbers

The Pilipino counterparts of 'am' and 'pm' are *n.u.* for *ng umaga* (in the morning), *n.t.* for *ng tanghalì* (at noon), *n.h.* for *ng hapon* (in the afternoon) and *n.g.* for *ng gabí* (in the evening/at night)

What time is it?	*Anong óras na?*
It's (five) am.	*Alas (singko) n.u.*
It's (seven) pm.	*Alas (siyete) n.g.*

'Half past' is expressed by the word *imédya*, eg, It's half past (six), *Alas (seis) imédya.*

Monday	*Lunes*
Tuesday	*Martes*
Wednesday	*Miyérkolés*
Thursday	*Huwebes*
Friday	*Biyernes*
Saturday	*Sábado*
Sunday	*Linggó*

January	*Enero*
February	*Pebrero*

March	Marso
April	Abríl
May	Mayo
June	Hunyo
July	Hulyo
August	Agosto
September	Setyembre
October	Oktubre
November	Nobyembre
December	Disyembre

morning	umaga
afternoon	hápon
night	gabí
now	ngayón
today	ngayón araw
this morning	ngayón umága
this afternoon	ngayón hapon
tonight	ngayón gabí
tomorrow	bukas
this week	ngayóng linggó
this month	ngayóng buwán
yesterday	kahapon

There are two sets of numbers: the native Pilipino and the Spanish, written the Pilipino way. Spanish numbers are used for times, dates and prices which have both the high and low denomination or are above 10 pesos. English numbers are also widely used to express prices. For example the price 'P1.50' is *uno singkuwenta* or *one fifty*, but 'P1.00' is simply *piso* in Pilipino.

	Spanish	Tagalog
1	uno	isá
2	dos	dalawá
3	tres	tatló
4	kuwatro	apát
5	singko	limá
6	seis	ánim
7	siyete	pitó
8	otso	waló
9	nuwebe	siyám
10	diyes	sampû
11	onse	labíng-isá
12	dose	labíndalawá
13	tróse	labíntatló
14	katórse	labíng-ápat
15	kínse	labínlimá
16	disiseis	labíng-ánim
17	disisiyete	labímpitó

Emergencies

Help!	Saklolo!
Watch out!	Ingat!
Call the/a ...!	Tumawag ka ng...!
the police	pulís
a doctor	doktór
an ambulance	ambulansiya
I've been raped!	Ginahasà akó!
I've been robbed!	Ninakawan akó!
Thief!	Magnanakáw!
Fire!	Sunog!
Go away!	Umalís ka!
Where are the toilets?	Násaán hô ang CR?

18	disiotso	labíng-waló
19	disinuwebe	labínsiyám
20	beynte	dalawampû
21	beynte uno	dalawampu't isá
30	treynta	tatlumpû
40	kuwarenta	ápatnapû
50	singkuwenta	limampû
60	sisenta	ánimnapû
70	sitenta	pitumpû
80	otsénta	walumpû
90	nobenta	siyamnapû
100	siyento	sandaán
1000	isang mil	isáng libo/sanlíbo

one million	
isang milyon	isang angaw

1st	úna
2nd	ikalawá
3rd	ikatló

FOOD & DRINKS

breakfast	almusal/agahan
lunch	tanghalian
dinner	hapunan
snack	meryenda

I'm a vegetarian.	Gulay lamang ang kinákain ko.
I don't eat meat.	Hindî akó kumákain ng karné.
Please bring ...	Pakidalá nga hô ...
Is service included in the bill?	Kasama ba ang serbisyo sa kuwenta?

fork	*tinidór*
glass	*baso*
knife	*kutsilyo*
plate	*plato*
spoon	*kutsara*
serviette/napkin	*sirbilyeta*

Main Dishes

Names of dishes often describe the way they are cooked, so it's worth remembering that *adobo* is stewed in vinegar and garlic, *sinigang* is sour soup, *ginataan* means cooked in coconut milk, *kiliwan* is raw seafood, *pangat* includes sauteed tomatoes and *inihaw* is grilled meat or fish. The word for 'spicy' is *maangháng*.

adobo – often called the national dish; salty stewed chicken or pork, marinated in vinegar and garlic
adobong pusit – cuttlefish in vinegar and coconut milk soup
arroz caldo – Spanish-style thick rice soup with chicken, garlic, ginger and onions
aso – dog; eaten with relish (or just plain) by northern Luzon's hilltribes
baboy – pork
balut – boiled chicken egg containing a partially formed embryo
bangus – milkfish; lightly grilled, stuffed and baked
calamares – squid
carne – beef
crispy pata – crispy fried and seasoned pig skin
gulay – vegetables
lechon – spit-roast baby pig with liver sauce
lumpia – spring rolls filled with meat or vegetables
mami – noodle soup; similar to *mee* in Malaysia or Indonesia
manok – chicken
menudo – stew with vegetables, liver or pork
pancit – thick or thin noodle dish
pochero – mix of beef, spicy sausage and vegetables
pusit – cuttlefish
tocino – pork dish made with saltpetre (also used in the recipe for homemade gunpowder)

Basics

bread	*tinapay*
butter	*mantikilya*
cheese	*keso*
coconut milk	*gatâ*
cooking oil	*langís panluto*
eggs	*itlóg*
flour	*arina*
honey	*pulút-pukyutan*
milk (fresh)	*(sariwang) gatas*
yoghurt	*yoghurt*

Meat & Poultry

beef	*karnéng-baka*
chicken	*manók*
duck	*pato*
goatmeat	*karnéng-kambing*
ham	*hamón*
meat	*kárné*
pork	*karneng-baboy*
turkey	*pabo*
venison	*karnéng-usa*

Seafood

clams	*tulyá*
crabs	*alimángo* (large, with dark, thick shell) *alimasag* (spotted, thin shelled) *talangkâ* (small)
lobster	*uláng*
mussels	*tahóng*
oysters	*talabá*
sea crabs	*alimásag*
shrimp	*hípon*

Vegetables

vegetables	*gulay*
beans	*bataw*
bean sprouts	*toge*
bitter melon	*ampaláyá*
cassava/manioc	*kamóteng káhoy*
Chinese string beans	*sítaw*
eggplant	*talóng*
lima beans	*patáni*
mild radish-type vegetable	*singkamás*
onions	*sibuyas*
peppers (capsicum)	*sili*

ramie leaves	salúyot
spinach-like vegetable	kangkóng
squash	kalabasa
sweet potatoes	kamote
onion	sibuyas
tomatoes	kamatis

Fruit

fruit	prutas
avocado	abokado
banana	saging
cantaloupe	milón
custard apple	atis
lime	dayap
mandarin	dalanghita
mango	manggá
orange	dalandan
papaya/pawpaw	papaya
pineapple	pinyá
pomelo	suhà
Spanish plum	sinigwélas
star apple	kaimíto
watermelon	pakwán

(*kalamansi* is a small citrus fruit used for juice)

Spices & Condiments

garlic	bawang
ginger	lúya
pepper	pamintá
saffron	kasubhâ
salt	asin
small hot chilli peppers	labuyo
soy sauce	toyò
sugar	asukal
vinegar	sukà

Drinks

water	tubig
boiled water	pinakuluáng tubig
cold water	malamíg na tubig
hot water	mainit na tubig
mineral water	mineral water
(cup of) tea	(isang tásang) tsaá
ginger tea	salabat
cocoa	tsokolate
coffee	kape
avocado drink	abokádo dyus
lemonade	limonáda
mango drink	mango dyus
with/without ice	may/waláng yelo
with/without milk	may/walang gátas
with/without sugar	may/walang asúkal

Glossary

arnis de mano – a pre-Hispanic style of stick-fighting

bagyo – typhoon
bahala na – you could almost call this the 'national philosophy'. Christianising colonists once translated this as 'without god', but bahala na actually expresses a kind of confidence despite everything. It's somewhere between an Australian 'no worries' and Kurt Vonnegut's 'so it goes', but less individualistic than either: all things shall pass and in the meantime life is to be lived – preferably in the company of one's friends and – most importantly – family.
balangay – artfully crafted sea-going outrigger
balikbayan – an overseas Filipino
balisong – fan or butterfly knife
banca (or *bangca*) – a pumpboat, usually powered by a cannibalised Toyota engine
barangay – small village or neighbourhood, the basic division of the Filipino social unit
barong – local formal attire, the 'national dress'
barrio – Spanish: district or neighbourhood
butanding – whale shark

calesa – horse-drawn carriage
carabao – water buffalo

fronton – *jai alai* court

guybano – soursop

haribon – the Philippine eagle

jai alai – a fast-paced ball game, and one of the most popular sports in the Philippines
jeepney – a brightly painted ex-army jeep fitted with benches, adorned with everything but the kitchen sink and crammed with passengers

kundiman – a mournful mode of words and music; one of the most-loved musical idioms in the country

lahar – rain-induced landslide of volcanic debris; in other words, volcanic mud

mestizos – Filipinos of mixed descent
Moro – Spanish colonial term for Muslim Filipinos, now worn with some pride

narra – a yellow-flowering tree, the Philippine national tree
nipa – a type of palm tree, doubtless the most recognised tree in the country

pasyon – Christ's passion, re-enacted every Easter
Pilipino – the aspiring 'national language'; created out of Tagalog, with some alterations
piña – fabric woven from pineapple fibres
Pinoy – term Filipinos call themselves
poblacion – town centre

roro – car ferry

sabit-sabit – small fishing boat
sabong – cockfighting
santo – religious statue
sari-sari – convenience store

Tagalog – the dominant dialect of Manila and parts of Luzon; it's being pushed as the national language, called Pilipino
tinikling – the Philippine national folk dance
tricycle – Philippine rickshaw (pedal-powered in Manila, motorised elsewhere)

zona caliente – red-light district

ACRONYMS
CBST – Community-Based Sustainable Tourism
DENR – Department of Environment & Natural Resources
DOH – Department of Health

DOT – Department of Tourism
MILF – Moro Islamic Liberation Front
MNLF – Moro National Liberation Front
NPA – New People's Army

PHILVOLCS – Philippine Institute of Volcanology & Seismology
PNP – Philippine National Police
VFA – Visiting Forces Agreement

Acknowledgments

THANKS

Many thanks to the travellers who used the previous edition and wrote to us with helpful hints, useful advice and interesting anecdotes:

AM Bunker, A Priem, A Proctor, A Robinson, Abby Antonio, Adam Preece, Adrienne Cerefice, Ahrni G Planco, Aileen Lainez, Alan Brown, Alan Colville, Alan Stepney, Alan Whitlock, Alana Krider, Alexander Winter, Alfafara L Catalino, Alfred Espedido, Alistair Lathe, Allan Rimmington, Allen Reilly, Amy Siak, Andrea Tan, Andreas Mattheiss, Andreas Pavlis, Andrew Borlace, Andrew Fuller, Andrew Holten, Andrew Purdy, Andrew Simpson, Annabel Ferrer, Anne Kristiansen, Anne Place, Annette & Karen Brunner, Anson Yu, Anthony Tosti, Antony Van Zalk, Archie Mallare, Arno Schroor, Arthur Keefe, Aurelia & John Rogers, Bart van den Broek, Becky Eisses, Bee Brink, Ben Mallorca, Ben Petts, Ben Rasmussen, Bertil Hagnell, Betty Sheets, Bill & Lorna Collings, Bo Jonsson, Bob Blackham, Bob Denny, Boris Lelong, Brad Harsch, Bradford Tiffany, Brendan Luyt, Brian & Mette Jakobsen, Brian Dudden, Brian Wolf, Bridget & David Trump, Britta Jensen, Bruce & Marithes Mattingley, Bruce Cornfoot, Bryant Vallejo.

C Donaghy, Carl Pickin, Carlo B, Carmencita & Rudi Winger, Carol Chua, Carol Valdez, Casey Wong, Cassandra Klayh, Cath Parkinson, Cathy Alvarez, Charles Poynton, Charles R Marks, Cheiko Ishikawa, Chris Anderson, Chris Bisbee, Chris Morey, Christine Bader, Christine Kruyfhooft, Christoph Kalthoff, Christopher McDaniel, Christopher N Gimenez, Chuck Collins, Cindi Lundy, Claire Benedicto, Clare Lucas, Claudio Milletti, Clem Parry, Clifford Martin, Clive Walker, Clyde Shoebridge, Colin Sweeney, Conrad D Wenham, Cora & Dik de Boer, Cristina Gunn, Cynthia Pyle, DE Brock, D Kusabs, Daisy Flores, Dale Franco Betonio, Dale Harshman, Dan Carmi, Dan Coultas, Dan Hoban, Dan Lloyd, Dan Neisner, Dan Schlichtmann, Dan Unger, Daniel & Karina Arsenault, Daniel Delorto, Danielle Wieggers, Danny Hahn, Danny Nicolas, Darina Farrell, Dave Vicars, David Beales, David Coombes, David Douglas, David Han, David Martin, David Thompson, David Yu, Davy & Joisy King, Del Vanhook, Diana H Youell, Didier Lhulillier, Dimple Doherty, Dina Priess, Dirk Verschueren, Don MacAdam, Don Reyna, Don Welch, Doreen B Samolde, Dory Blobner, Doug Reynolds, Doug Stevens, Dr B Abtmaier, Dr Irmgard Ehlers, Dr Pablo Ortega Gallo, Dr Thom Kleiss, Drei Tan, Eden Williams, Edik Dolotina, Edith Rebulado, Edmund Carew, Edward McCrossan, Edward Stanton, Eliane Cavalcante de Almeida, Elisabeth Hansen, Eliza Diana Iliescu, Ellen Stuiver, Emma Langstaff, Emma Lobban, Emma M Malabanan, Emma Ryan, Emma Woodard, Enmi Sung, Eric F Canzier, Eroka O'Connor, Eve Mora.

Francesca Araneta, Francis Burkett, Frank L Veroy, Frank Schrolkamp, Frank Toelle, Frank Verhagen, Frederic Dominioni, Frederic Schneider, Frits & Ceci Hillenaar, Frits Groenewegen, Fumiko Hattori, Gail Cockburn, Gail Rollason, Gary Fondren, Gary M Grady, Gavin Fahey, Geert Creffier, Geir Naess, Gemma Bigby, Geoff Breach, Geordie McConnell, George Boraman, George Campbell, George Rady, Gerardine Laffan, Gerome Garcia, Gio Bacareza, Glenn Davidson, Glenn Hartell, Goran Nordin, Graeme Wilkie, Greg Sweetnam, Greory Chesser, Guido Schrijvers, Gunter Bernert, H Bekker, Harold Gary, Harry Boin, Heda Beechey, Helen Black, Helen Keraudren, Helen Lowy, Helen Stanton, Helga Boom, Helmut Gartenhaub, Henrik Josephsen, HH Saffery, Howard Digby, Huy B Passage, Ian Lloyd, Ian Owen, Ian Stevens, Ingrid Heiss, Inna Costantini, Ino Laurensse, Isabelle Rochard, Iwakami Katsuhiko.

J Al Staszel, JD Spector, J Hagelgans, JR Bennewitz, J Slikker, Jack Gallagher, Jacqueline Dimeen, Jacqueline Stanton, Jacqueline Woodand, James Halsema, James Parsons, James Schones, James Vol Hartwell, Jamie Lee, Jan Etteridge, Jan van Zadelhoff, Jane Griffiths, Jane Kruuk, Jason Carmichael, Jason Vorderstrasse, Jay Caisip, Jay Walder, Jean Pierre Marsac, Jeannine Laurens, Jean-Pierre Franck, Jeff Haire, Jeffrey Parrott, Jeremy Bright, Jessie Tan, Jillian Spencer, Jim Louie, Joanna Badura, Jody Aboitiz, Joel Fagsao, Joel Matsuda, Joerg Ausfrlt, Joey Montalvo, Johan D Timp, John & Gaye Dopper, John Anderson, John Baley, John D Sanchez, John Francis, John Funk, John J Bromley, John Orford, John P Sevilla, John

Telford, Joke Koppen, Jon Robinson, Jonathan Miller, Jonathon P Lang, Jorg Ausfelt, José Lord, Joseph Kennedy, Joseph Murphy, Joshua Inman, Joyce van Dijk, Julia & Joel Tiejada, Julian Chan, Julie A Gaw, Julie Ashcroft, Julie Bancilhon, Julien Bodart, Juliet Porritt, Justin Brock, Justin Mog, Justin Tooth, K Edward Moore, K O'Neill, Kannan Amaresh, Karen Vidler, Karsten & Rikke M Petersen, Karsten Bohm, Keith A Crandall, Kelly Theil, Ken Sloane, Kerem Cosar, Kevin Braend, Kevin Scott, Khoo Hsu Jenn, Klaudia Krammer, Krzysztof Kurdowicz.

Lachlan Burnet, Larry L Hobbs, Lars von Lampe, Laszlo Wagreer, Lauraine Brin, Laurie McMahon, Lawrence Reif, Laz Solang, Lee Kokpiew, Leonora Rosaia, Liam Toner, Lilibeth Jalapadan, Livvy Tee, Lolita Adaro, Lone Oesterlund Jensen, Lorcan Bolster, Lorna Herradurra, Louie Hechanova, Louis Rubigny, Louise & JoJo Solacito, Lucinda Cawley, Lucy Colton, Lucy Fuchs, Luke Hendricks, Lyndsey Cal, MD Burke, MH Tiba, ML Oliveros, M Meijer, M Pierre Benoit, Malcolm MacKellar, Marc Jensen, Marcel Schrijvers, Margit Kastner, Marileth Barrios, Marin Aldrich, Marisa Goudie, Mark A Schneider, Mark Bush, Mark Kanning, Mark Vawdrey, Mark Whiffin, Marnie Dolera, Marshall Hughes, Martine Broeders, Martiua Asclierl, Mary Ann Weber, Mary Hapalla-Mangaoang, Matt Chabot, Matthew & Brigitte Awty, Matthew North, Max Beeson, McNamara Family, Meg Gonzales, Melanie Cabalza, Meynardo Luna, Michael Bennett, Michael Bolton, Michael Duday, Michael Fox, Michael Kohn, Michael Lehman, Michael Lu, Michael Narciso, Michael Ramos, Michael Stephenson, Michelle Cohen-Peak, Michelle Fernandez, Miguel Zulueta, Mike Elliott, Mike Lu, Mike Shen, Mira Indorf, Moira Sambey, Mr & Mrs Gray, Mylene Manlogon, N Denoga, Neil Agustin, Neil Ring, Nicholas Tousley, Nick Benbow, Nicole Mazza, Niki Knight, Nikki Singh, Noel Yuseco, Norman Faner.

Odette Tabobo, Ophir Glezer, Ophir Michaeli, Ori Dvir, Ozelle Tellie Clement-Tarrosa, P Screach, Pam Hendriks, Patrick Brunner, Patrick Uy, Paul & Sheila Doherty, Paul de Vries, Paul Rhodes, Paul

Tetrault, Paula Buur, Peter Boers, Peter Capostosto, Peter Chong, Peter Freeman, Peter Harvey, Peter Pontikis, PF & LD Stonehouse, Phil Barnes, Phillip Croft, Pieter Zegwaart, Prof Dr Manfred Malzahn, RJ Gnanalolan, R Smits, RW Le Sueur, R Wallis, Radka Langhammerova, Rae Stevenson, Ralph Alejandrino, Ralph Bird, Ralph Pauly, Rammal Valenzuela, Raoul Craemer, Ray Hossinger, Reca Fucsok, Restituto R Ramos, Rhoderic Davies, Rich Vaughn, Richard Carter, Richard Stokes, Rick Vaughn, Rik de Lange, Rim Woodward, Rob de Groot, Rob Erickson, Robert Brown, Robert Diamond, Robert Johnson, Robert Wilkinson, Robin McCorkle, Roland Flageollet, Roland Tuando, Ron Gaul, Ron Griffin, Ron van Mastrigt, Ron Walker, Ronald Mariano, Ross Cashmore, Ross Thompson, Roy White, Rudolf Paul Maierhofer, Rupert Kelly, Rupert Thompson, Russell & Lilian Stapleton, Rusty Cartmill, Ruth Simon.

Sabine Duewel, Sandrine Presles, Sarah Gaitanos, Sarah Stokoe, Scott Bennett, Scott Hildebrand, Scott True, Scotty Fox, Searle Loughman, Shaheed Ali, Shane Howe, Sietse Fritsma, Silke Kerwick, Stan Wilson, Stefan Backes, Stephen Clay, Stephen Donaldson, Stephen Malone, Stephen Porras, Steve Darnien, Steve Davies, Steve Golik, Steve Gonsalves, Steve Jackson, Steve Kinsman, Steve Starlight, Steven Parsa, Stu Wilson, Stuart McLean, Sue Holdham, Sue Roff, Sue Smith, Susanna Chow, Susanne Thanheiser, Suzie Wong, Tanja Haller, Tas Bognar, Ted Reader, Tere Lauron, Terry Jellicoe, Terry Kempis, Tess Salvador, Thomas Abtmeier, Thomas Hodges, Thomas Jansson, Tiki Sonderhoff, Tim Poate, Tim Watt, Tina Cortez, Toby Martin, Tom Dyson, Tom Rafetto, Tomasz Czyzewski, Tony Brunschwiler, Tony Cummins, Toto Cinco, Trevor Taylor, Troy Hale, Tuesday Gutierrez.

Ulrich Fischer, Vic Miranda, Victor Benson, Victor van Straten, W Chua, WE Anderson, Walter Witt, Wayne Gee, Weng Dumlao, Will Markle, William Burgin, Winnie Law, Winston White, Wong Bacareza, Yenda Carson, Yiu-yin Ho, Ziga Ogrizek.

LONELY PLANET

Guides by Region

Lonely Planet is known worldwide for publishing practical, reliable and no-nonsense travel information in our guides and on our Web site. The Lonely Planet list covers just about every accessible part of the world. Currently there are 15 series: travel guides, Shoestring guides, Condensed guides, Phrasebooks, Read This First, Healthy Travel, Walking guides, Cycling guides, Pisces Diving & Snorkeling guides, City Maps, Travel Atlases, Out to Eat, World Food, Journeys travel literature and Pictorials.

AFRICA Africa on a shoestring • Africa – the South • Arabic (Egyptian) phrasebook • Arabic (Moroccan) phrasebook • Cairo • Cape Town • Cape Town city map • Central Africa • East Africa • Egypt • Egypt travel atlas • Ethiopian (Amharic) phrasebook • The Gambia & Senegal • Healthy Travel Africa • Kenya • Kenya travel atlas • Malawi, Mozambique & Zambia • Morocco • North Africa • Read This First Africa • South Africa, Lesotho & Swaziland • South Africa, Lesotho & Swaziland travel atlas • Swahili phrasebook • Tanzania, Zanzibar & Pemba • Trekking in East Africa • Tunisia • West Africa • Zimbabwe, Botswana & Namibia • Zimbabwe, Botswana & Nambia Travel Atlas • World Food Morocco
Travel Literature: The Rainbird: A Central African Journey • Songs to an African Sunset: A Zimbabwean Story • Mali Blues: Traveling to an African Beat

AUSTRALIA & THE PACIFIC Auckland • Australia • Australian phrasebook • Bushwalking in Australia • Bushwalking in Papua New Guinea • Fiji • Fijian phrasebook • Healthy Travel Australia, NZ and the Pacific • Islands of Australia's Great Barrier Reef • Melbourne • Melbourne city map • Micronesia • New Caledonia • New South Wales & the ACT • New Zealand • Northern Territory • Outback Australia • Out to Eat – Melbourne • Out to Eat – Sydney • Papua New Guinea • Pidgin phrasebook • Queensland • Rarotonga & the Cook Islands • Samoa • Solomon Islands • South Australia • South Pacific • South Pacific Languages phrasebook • Sydney • Sydney city map • Sydney Condensed • Tahiti & French Polynesia • Tasmania • Tonga • Tramping in New Zealand • Vanuatu • Victoria • Western Australia
Travel Literature: Islands in the Clouds • Kiwi Tracks: A New Zealand Journey • Sean & David's Long Drive

CENTRAL AMERICA & THE CARIBBEAN Bahamas, Turks & Caicos • Bermuda • Central America on a shoestring • Costa Rica • Cuba • Dominican Republic & Haiti • Eastern Caribbean • Guatemala, Belize & Yucatán: La Ruta Maya • Jamaica • Mexico • Mexico City • Panama • Puerto Rico • Read This First Central & South America • World Food Mexico
Travel Literature: Green Dreams: Travels in Central America

EUROPE Amsterdam • Amsterdam city map • Andalucía • Austria • Baltic States phrasebook • Barcelona • Berlin • Berlin city map • Britain • British phrasebook • Brussels, Bruges & Antwerp • Budapest city map • Canary Islands • Central Europe • Central Europe phrasebook • Corfu & Ionians • Corsica • Crete • Crete Condensed • Croatia • Cyprus • Czech & Slovak Republics • Denmark • Dublin • Eastern Europe • Eastern Europe phrasebook • Edinburgh • Estonia, Latvia & Lithuania • Europe on a shoestring • Finland • Florence • France • French phrasebook • Germany • German phrasebook • Greece • Greek Islands • Greek phrasebook • Hungary • Iceland, Greenland & the Faroe Islands • Ireland • Italian phrasebook • Italy • Krakow • Lisbon • The Loire • London • London city map • London Condensed • Mediterranean Europe • Mediterranean Europe phrasebook • Munich • Norway • Paris • Paris city map • Paris Condensed • Poland • Portugal • Portugese phrasebook • Portugal travel atlas • Prague • Prague city map • Provence & the Côte d'Azur • Read This First Europe • Romania & Moldova • Rome • Russia, Ukraine & Belarus • Russian phrasebook • Scandinavian & Baltic Europe • Scandinavian Europe phrasebook • Scotland • Slovenia • Spain • Spanish phrasebook • St Petersburg • Sweden • Switzerland • Trekking in Spain • Tuscany • Ukrainian phrasebook • Venice • Vienna • Walking in Britain • Walking in Ireland • Walking in Italy • Walking in Spain • Walking in Switzerland • Western Europe • Western Europe phrasebook • World Food Ireland • World Food Italy • World Food Spain
Travel Literature: The Olive Grove: Travels in Greece

INDIAN SUBCONTINENT Bangladesh • Bengali phrasebook • Bhutan • Delhi • Goa • Hindi & Urdu phrasebook • India • India & Bangladesh travel atlas • Indian Himalaya • Karakoram Highway • Kerala • Mumbai (Bombay) • Nepal • Nepali phrasebook • Pakistan • Rajasthan • Read This First: Asia & India • South India • Sri Lanka • Sri Lanka phrasebook • Tibet • Tibetan phrasebook • Trekking in the Indian Himalaya • Trekking in the Karakoram & Hindukush • Trekking in the Nepal Himalaya
Travel Literature: In Rajasthan • Shopping for Buddhas • The Age Of Kali

LONELY PLANET

Mail Order

onely Planet products are distributed worldwide. They are also available by mail order from Lonely Planet, so if you have difficulty finding a title please write to us. North and South American residents should write to 150 Linden St, Oakland CA 94607, USA; European and African residents should write to 10a Spring Place, London, NW5 3BH, UK; and residents of other countries to PO Box 617, Hawthorn, Victoria 3122, Australia.

ISLANDS OF THE INDIAN OCEAN Madagascar & Comoros • Maldives • Mauritius, Réunion & Seychelles

MIDDLE EAST & CENTRAL ASIA Bahrain, Kuwait & Qatar • Central Asia • Central Asia phrasebook • Dubai • Hebrew phrasebook • Iran • Israel & the Palestinian Territories • Israel & the Palestinian Territories travel atlas • Istanbul • Istanbul City Map • Istanbul to Cairo on a shoestring • Jerusalem • Jerusalem City Map • Jordan • Jordan, Syria & Lebanon travel atlas • Lebanon • Middle East • Oman & the United Arab Emirates • Syria • Turkey • Turkey travel atlas • Turkish phrasebook • World Food Turkey • Yemen
Travel Literature: The Gates of Damascus • Kingdom of the Film Stars: Journey into Jordan • Black on Black: Iran Revisited

NORTH AMERICA Alaska • Backpacking in Alaska • Baja California • California & Nevada • California Condensed • Canada • Chicago • Chicago city map • Deep South • Florida • Hawaii • Honolulu • Las Vegas • Los Angeles • Miami • New England • New Orleans • New York City • New York city map • New York Condensed • New York, New Jersey & Pennsylvania • Oahu • Pacific Northwest USA • Puerto Rico • Rocky Mountain • San Francisco • San Francisco city map • Seattle • Southwest USA • Texas • USA • USA phrasebook • Vancouver • Washington, DC & the Capital Region • Washington DC city map
Travel Literature: Drive Thru America

NORTH-EAST ASIA Beijing • Cantonese phrasebook • China • Hong Kong • Hong Kong city map • Hong Kong, Macau & Guangzhou • Japan • Japanese phrasebook • Japanese audio pack • Korea • Korean phrasebook • Kyoto • Mandarin phrasebook • Mongolia • Mongolian phrasebook • Seoul • South-West China • Taiwan • Tokyo
Travel Literature: Lost Japan • In Xanadu

SOUTH AMERICA Argentina, Uruguay & Paraguay • Bolivia • Brazil • Brazilian phrasebook • Buenos Aires • Chile & Easter Island • Chile & Easter Island travel atlas • Colombia • Ecuador & the Galapagos Islands • Healthy Travel Central & South America • Latin American Spanish phrasebook • Peru • Quechua phrasebook • Rio de Janeiro • Rio de Janeiro city map • South America on a shoestring • Trekking in the Patagonian Andes • Venezuela
Travel Literature: Full Circle: A South American Journey

SOUTH-EAST ASIA Bali & Lombok • Bangkok • Bangkok city map • Burmese phrasebook • Cambodia • Hanoi • Healthy Travel Asia & India • Hill Tribes phrasebook • Ho Chi Minh City • Indonesia • Indonesia's Eastern Islands • Indonesian phrasebook • Indonesian audio pack • Jakarta • Java • Laos • Lao phrasebook • Laos travel atlas • Malay phrasebook • Malaysia, Singapore & Brunei • Myanmar (Burma) • Philippines • Pilipino (Tagalog) phrasebook • Read This First Asia & India • Singapore • South-East Asia on a shoestring • South-East Asia phrasebook • Thailand • Thailand's Islands & Beaches • Thailand travel atlas • Thai phrasebook • Thai audio pack • Vietnam • Vietnamese phrasebook • Vietnam travel atlas • World Food Thailand • World Food Vietnam

ALSO AVAILABLE: Antarctica • The Arctic • Brief Encounters: Stories of Love, Sex & Travel • Chasing Rickshaws • Lonely Planet Unpacked • Not the Only Planet: Travel Stories from Science Fiction • Sacred India • Travel with Children • Traveller's Tales

LONELY PLANET

You already know that Lonely Planet produces more than this one guidebook, but you might not be aware of the other products we have on this region. Here is a selection of titles that you may want to check out as well:

the Lonely Planet Philippines video
ISBN 1 90097 935 7
US$19.95 • UK£12.99

Pilipino (Tagalog) phrasebook
ISBN 0 86442 432 9
US$5.95 • UK£3.99 • 40FF

Read This First: Asia & India
ISBN 1 86450 049 2
US$14.99 • UK£8.99 • 99FF

Healthy Travel Asia & India
ISBN 1 86450 051 4
US$5.95 • UK£3.99 • 39FF

Available wherever books are sold

Index

Text

Bold indicates maps.

Bold indicates maps.

Boxed Text

MAP LEGEND

CITY ROUTES

Freeway	Freeway	====	Unsealed Road
Highway	Primary Road	—	One Way Street
Road	Secondary Road		Pedestrian Street
Street	Street	⊓⊓⊓⊓⊓	Stepped Street
Lane	Lane	)= =	Tunnel
	On/Off Ramp		Footbridge

HYDROGRAPHY

	River, Creek	◉ ◉	Dry Lake; Salt Lake
	Canal	◉ →	Spring; Rapids
◯	Lake	◉ ⊰	Waterfalls

REGIONAL ROUTES

	Tollway, Freeway
	Primary Road
	Secondary Road
	Minor Road

TRANSPORT ROUTES & STATIONS

⊢⊣⊶⊢	Train
⊹ ⊹ ⊹ ⊹	Underground Train
⊸Ⓜ⊸	Metro
	Tramway
⊢⊣⊶⊢	Cable Car, Chairlift

BOUNDARIES

	International
	State
— — —	Disputed
▬▬	Fortified Wall

- - -⊡ ◙	Ferry, Transport
- - - - -	Walking Trail
• • • • •	Walking Tour
	Path
	Pier or Jetty

AREA FEATURES

	Building		Market		Beach		Campus
	Park, Gardens		Sports Ground	+ + +	Cemetery		Plaza

POPULATION SYMBOLS

✪ CAPITAL	National Capital	● CITY	City	● Village	Village
◉ CAPITAL	State Capital	● Town	Town		Urban Area

MAP SYMBOLS

♠	Place to Stay	▼	Place to Eat	●	Point of Interest

✚ ✕	Airfield, Airport	⊠ ⚲	Dive Site, Surf Beach	⌒	Mountain Range	⊞	Stately Home
⑨	Bank	▢ ✛	Embassy, Hospital	⊡	National Park	⊠	Swimming Pool
▣	Bus Terminal	✾ ⚑	Garden, Golf Course	◉	Petrol Station	☎	Telephone
⚓ ≍	Cave, Shipwreck	▣	Internet Cafe	✚	Police Station	⬛	Temple
✚ ✚	Cathedral, Church	▥	Library, Museum	✉	Post Office	❶	Tourist Information
▣	Cinema	☀ ※	Lighthouse, Lookout	◚	Pub or Bar	▲ ▲	Volcano, Mountain
⚙	Cycling	⚑ ⚱	Monument, Fountain	✪	Shopping Centre	▦	Zoo

Note: not all symbols displayed above appear in this book

LONELY PLANET OFFICES

Australia
PO Box 617, Hawthorn, Victoria 3122
☎ 03 9819 1877 fax 03 9819 6459
email: talk2us@lonelyplanet.com.au

USA
150 Linden St, Oakland, CA 94607
☎ 510 893 8555 TOLL FREE: 800 275 5555
fax 510 893 8572
email: info@lonelyplanet.com

UK
10a Spring Place, London NW5 3BH
☎ 020 7428 4800 fax 020 7428 4828
email: go@lonelyplanet.co.uk

France
1 rue du Dahomey, 75011 Paris
☎ 01 55 25 33 00 fax 01 55 25 33 01
email: bip@lonelyplanet.fr
www.lonelyplanet.fr

World Wide Web: www.lonelyplanet.com *or* AOL keyword: lp
Lonely Planet Images: lpi@lonelyplanet.com.au